JEFF C. DAVIS, JR., Ph.D., University of California, Berkeley, is Associate Professor of Chemistry at the University of South Florida. Dr. Davis previously taught at The University of Texas, is a Director of a National Science Foundation In-Service Institute in Chemistry, has participated in several NSF Institutes and writing projects, and is a former Chairman of the Central Texas Section of the American Chemical Society. Dr. Davis' research interests and publications are in the field of nuclear magnetic resonance and infrared spectroscopy.

ADVANCED PHYSICAL CHEMISTRY

Molecules, Structure, and Spectra

JEFF C. DAVIS, JR.

UNIVERSITY OF SOUTH FLORIDA

THE RONALD PRESS COMPANY · NEW YORK

To
Sylvia

Preface

This textbook is designed for courses in advanced physical chemistry Its purpose is to introduce students in all chemical specializations to the basic ideas and methods of quantum mechanics and statistical mechanics, with particular emphasis on the application of these theories to the investigation of molecular structure.

Many students have had little or no grounding in these modern topics, so that the initial emphasis, after an introductory discussion of classical physical chemistry and physics, is placed on the basic postulates and techniques of quantum mechanics and statistics. A number of simple molecular examples are discussed which utilize these methods and provide a connection with the more familiar conclusions from classical treatments. The results of this introductory treatment are used to explore in some detail a number of important spectroscopic and physical methods that throw light on the details of molecular structure and properties. It is felt that spectroscopy and its relation to molecular structure provides the most direct link between the student's research experience and physical chemical theory and thus it is discussed at sufficient length to uncover not only the basic principles involved but also the details of various kinds of spectra and the nature of different phenomena that can be explored by these methods.

This material is for the advanced undergraduate and graduate levels, and the order of presentation is such that very elementary or more detailed discussions can be omitted when desirable for a particular need.

The first two chapters introduce the student to some of the important physical concepts and experiments that lead to modern quantum mechanics and that are the basis for discussing many models and problems. These chapters will serve as review for many. It is hoped that they will provide a particularly convenient summary and reference source. Supplementary discussions and information are collected also in the Appendix. The chapters on statistics and quantum mechanics are presented in an elementary form and will prepare the student for more thorough courses or reading in these subjects. The chapters on specific spectroscopic methods demonstrate the theoretical foundations of these techniques. The theoretical treatment is sufficient to bridge the gap to the more detailed monographs on spectroscopic theory.   The treatment is suitably detailed for individual study as well as for course work.   The problems are designed to supplement the text toward this end.   Discussions have been provided in the introductory sections with the aim of making the path as clearly marked as possible for the student in establishing fundamental concepts and methods.   Although the discussion penetrates in some depth several spectroscopic methods, the text is not intended to be a comprehensive treatise on molecular structure and spectroscopy.   The basic concepts involved in the use of group theory and normal coordinate analysis in molecular calculations are introduced, for example, but detailed discussions are left to specialized works in this area.

It is hoped that a healthy skepticism will be aroused regarding the results obtained from approximate methods of calculation, often the source of considerable argument and interpretation.

Every researcher is indebted to many teachers and colleagues who have in some way shaped his outlook on his chosen profession and its relation to the rest of human endeavor.   I would like to express my gratitude to those former teachers who inspired and nurtured a deep interest in physical chemistry and its relation to all of science, Drs. Millard G. Seeley, Leon Blitzer, Lathrop E. Roberts, Kenneth S. Pitzer, and George C. Pimentel.   These men are a tribute to the joys of research and teaching.

I would also like to acknowledge the helpful comments and suggestions of many students and colleagues, particularly Dr. James E. Boggs and Dr. Ralph J. Thompson.   The art work is the joint effort of Mr. Luis Santoya, Mrs. Pauline West, and myself, and acknowledgment is made for contributions from other sources.   The valuable contributions of Mr. Tony Cantu and Mr. Shep Burton and the patient efforts of Mrs. Margie Stancil, Mrs. Fran Hamilton, Mrs. Sandra Turnbo, Mrs. Sandra Stanley, and the author's wife, Sylvia, are also gratefully appreciated.

JEFF C. DAVIS, JR.

Tampa, Florida
September, 1965

Contents

APPENDIX

ADVANCED
PHYSICAL CHEMISTRY

1

Chemistry and Theory

1.1 THE SCOPE OF PHYSICAL CHEMISTRY

Over half a century ago, when physical chemistry was just beginning to develop under the guidance of such pioneers as Ostwald, Helmholtz, Gibbs, Nernst, and G. N. Lewis, this branch of inquiry was limited largely to investigations of the mechanical, electrical, optical, and thermal properties of matter, all of which seemed to have little bearing on the chemical behavior of substances. The following decades, however, disclosed the truly fundamental nature of physical chemical theory and saw a revolution in the basic structure of the natural sciences that is accelerating and expanding even today.

Early in this century G. N. Lewis and his school brought to light the power of thermodynamics in predicting thermal and equilibrium properties of chemical and physical systems. At the same time the revolution in physics brought about by the discovery of the electrical nature of atomic and molecular structure and the resulting formulation of the quantum theory by Planck, Einstein, and Bohr threw new light on the interactions that govern both chemical and physical behavior. The more exact quantum mechanics devised shortly thereafter by Schrödinger, Heisenberg, and Dirac was applied quickly to atomic and molecular systems with amazing success. Paralleling the theoretical development in physics and chemistry has been the development of many new physical methods such as the numerous spectroscopic techniques which have now become as commonplace to the chemist as measurements of melting points, refractive indices, and densities were a few years ago.

In the broad realm that is modern chemical science it is certainly true that physical chemistry is not a separate and specialized discipline, but rather is the cornerstone and foundation of physical phenomena and theory upon which all chemical problems are based. Inorganic and organic chemists are no longer concerned only with the synthesis of new

3

substances of unknown structure and unsuspected properties, as was their habit a brief century ago. Today synthesis is directed toward predictable ends, properties are correlated and explained by theory, and physical methods are employed to seek out and verify new facts. The analytical chemist turns to equilibrium and solution theory to broaden his utilization of classical chemical methods of analysis and to electromagnetic theory and quantum mechanics for ingenious instrumental methods. It is essentially an understatement to say that the influence of thermodynamics and kinetics, quantum mechanics, solid state and semiconductor theory, and spectroscopy on the maturing of biochemistry has been spectacular.

Introductory courses in physical chemistry often are limited largely to the study of the states of matter, thermodynamics, electrochemistry (with emphasis on thermodynamics), and chemical kinetics. These subjects are studied not only because of the mathematical proficiency required for more theoretical subjects, but also because of the historical importance and contemporary use of these basic areas. It would be difficult, however, to formulate a clear understanding of the nature of atomic and molecular structure, chemical reactivity, and the significance of spectroscopic techniques, thermodynamic measurements, and a score of other fundamental physical phenomena without an additional acquaintance with quantum mechanics, statistical mechanics, and related subjects often not investigated in an introductory course. It is the purpose of this text to explore such topics as these and to provide a background for the use and interpretation of modern physical chemical techniques in chemical problems.

1.2 MEASUREMENT AND THEORY IN THERMODYNAMICS

All of science is concerned with the discovery, classification, and measurement of phenomena. But man has inevitably taken the step beyond these functions and inquired into the causes for what he observes. There are two reasons for this inquiry. One is obviously the curiosity of man and his desire to understand ultimate reality in so far as this is possible. The second reason for this search is that the construction of a logical, consistent, conceptual pattern from observation leads naturally to the logical prediction of additional phenomena which may well not have been formerly suspected. The measurement of such predicted behavior in turn serves to substantiate or vitiate the original premises. This is the essence of the scientific method, which is fundamental to the philosophy and development of all the sciences. The construction of consistent, verified theory not only makes possible a more detailed and more knowledgeable understanding of the way in which the universe operates, but hopefully brings us closer and closer into contact with an understanding of the significance of the existence of this universe and man's place in it.

One of the most significant theoretical formulations in man's search for understanding has been quantum mechanics, a highly abstract system which describes nature in strange and unfamiliar terms. Students more at ease with the physical world about them than with the internal consistency of mathematics often are greatly disturbed by the atomic and molecular world described by quantum mechanics. Nevertheless, we put considerable faith in this theory because its observable predictions are verified by experiment. For this reason it may be worthwhile to examine briefly the nature of measurements and theory in science and the role they play.

Not all theories are similar in detail, but they all have the common characteristic that they begin with one or more fundamental axioms from which all conclusions must follow logically. The starting propositions must be consistent with observation, and the theory remains significant only so long as the conclusions drawn from the theory are also consistent with measurement. Despite this fundamental structure, however, the theories which have played a role in the development of science have differed greatly in the viewpoint and scope with which the fundamental axioms have been formulated. In particular, the theories of importance in chemical science tend to fall into one of two general categories. The first of these is the so-called macroscopic viewpoint in which observable phenomena of bulk matter serve as the basis of the formulation. The most familiar macroscopic theory in physical chemistry is thermodynamics. The second viewpoint is that taken in the microscopic approach where one formulates the theory on the assumed existence of unseen atoms and molecules and their properties from which the behavior of large collections of these molecules is deduced. The kinetic theory of gases and quantum mechanics are examples of this approach.

The macroscopic approach, as represented by thermodynamics, has definite advantages but also limitations. Thermodynamics, it will be recalled, is based on three axioms, the familiar first, second, and third laws of thermodynamics. These laws are statements of certain observations which have been made of nature and the way it behaves. In particular, the first law is a statement of the conservation of energy and voices our consistent experience that we can account for gains and losses of various kinds of energy in different parts of the universe without recourse to actually creating or eliminating energy. Although generally formulated in different terms, the second law is essentially a statement of the fact that energy in the form recognized as heat is always observed to flow spontaneously from a region of higher temperature to one of lower temperature and never in the opposite direction. To cause energy to flow from the lower temperature to the higher has always been observed to require the expenditure of work. The third law is a recognition of the fact that all experimental measurements are consistent with the assumption that a thermodynamic function known as the entropy becomes zero for a perfectly ordered crystalline solid at zero degrees Kelvin. From these laws follow a multitude of relationships between measurable quantities such as pressure, volume, temperature, and concentration.

Thermodynamic theory relies on the definition of certain quantities such as heat, work, and temperature which can be measured by defined operations, and on certain defined mathematical functions such as enthalpy and entropy. The laws of thermodynamics, its basic axioms, are statements of how these quantities have always been observed to behave in nature. The logical structure, based on mathematics, then produces new relationships between these measurable quantities and mathematical functions which allow us to make predictions regarding the thermal, mechanical, electrical, and chemical properties of systems. There is no need here to emphasize the extremely valuable and important information regarding chemical and physical equilibria, the energy changes accompanying processes, and similar quantities fundamental to practical science that are the result of thermodynamics.

The primary advantage of such a macroscopic theory is that its validity rests solely on the continued experience that nature does indeed appear to act always as stated in the three laws on which the theory is based. It is for this reason that thermodynamic theory has been effective, while numerous atomic and molecular theories have risen and fallen in turn. Since we make no assumptions about molecules and atoms in thermodynamics, the theory is not shaken as our view of these unseen particles changes. Except for unfamiliarity with mathematical methods or the tedium of calculations, one can feel quite at home with thermodynamics because it deals almost exclusively with quantities that we observe and measure continually in the world about us.

1.3 ATOMIC AND MOLECULAR THEORIES

Although the strength of macroscopic theories lies in their direct reliance only on observable phenomena, herein also lies their weakness. Although we continually relate thermodynamic results to our ideas about atoms and molecules, the theory does not tell us anything directly about the underlying structure of matter. It only concerns itself with the over-all bulk properties. For this reason the history of chemistry is also the history of atomic-molecular theories which have sought to explain bulk behavior in terms of atomic behavior. Obviously, when such predictions are not substantiated by experiment, the microscopic theory must be modified or discarded.

The earliest microscopic theory of importance in physical chemistry was the familiar kinetic-molecular theory of gases. By the early nineteenth century the pressure-volume-temperature properties of gases were well known and the evidence was accumulating for the belief that matter was not continuous, but consisted instead of small, indivisible particles called atoms and combinations of these atoms called molecules. On the assumption that such particles exist, the kinetic theory of gases attempts to predict the bulk properties of a gas by determining what these particles will do if they obey the laws of physics as observed for bodies of macroscopic size. It is found, of course, that such particles give the gas as a whole the fluid properties that are observed experimentally, and this was a great boost for the atomic-molecular viewpoint.

It is important to note at this stage that although their existence was assumed, and their regulation by the ordinary laws of physics was also assumed, no experiments were forthcoming that observed these atoms and molecules directly. Our belief in their existence is based on the fact that microscopic theories predict what observable phenomena will result from the motions and interactions of the postulated particles. The closer we approach a direct observation of an atom, the more devious and indirect are the means of making the observation. Eventually the assumption that these atoms and molecules are governed by the laws of classical physics was shown to be unsubstantiated, and new theories, namely quantum mechanics and the theory of relativity, were constructed.

So long as the laws of classical physics, which are observed to apply to macroscopic bodies of dimensions and motions comparable to our everyday experience, were applied to the unseen atoms, the microscopic theory of atomic and molecular behavior caused little concern. Even though we could not see atoms, we were assured by the success of the theory that they behaved like the things we observed around us. But at present the only successful theory consistent with our observations predicts behavior on the atomic level that is quite contrary to our expectations from what we observe on a macroscopic scale. This certainly does not discredit the theory, however, because it must always be remembered that we cannot see things on an atomic level directly, and thus far the microscopic theory has predicted physical and chemical behavior with remarkable success. We should not be disturbed that on the atomic level things behave differently from what we might have expected, but should instead turn to the successful theory in order to understand better what does occur.

There is little doubt that quantum mechanics as presently constituted will undergo many changes in the future in order that all phenomena can be successfully accounted for. We shall not despair that our present view of the atom may change, for we recognize that this picture is more inclusive than our earlier ideas and represents a means of organizing our thoughts into productive avenues.   At the same time we must realize that any model or picture of things we cannot see directly is bound to be limited by our mental images and mathematical methods to such an extent that it cannot be said with certainty to represent ultimate reality.

Our present course will be to examine the basic formulation of quantum mechanics and to apply it to the question of molecular structure.   We will turn our attention particularly to spectroscopic methods, as these provide a direct and extremely practical connection between theory and experiment.

2

The Development of Physics

2.1 THE ORIGINS OF NEWTON'S MECHANICS

In order best to understand the form in which quantum mechanics and statistics have been constructed, it is worthwhile to survey briefly the course by which physics developed in the years preceding the twentieth century and to note the formulations that were of greatest generality and usefulness. Interest in subjects physical dates back to antiquity, and a number of fundamental mathematical, astronomical, and physical relations had been discovered by the time of the Greeks. Perhaps one of the earliest quantitative accomplishments was the study of hydrostatics by Archimedes. Despite these early interests in physical science, however, the tremendous influence on thought and action exerted by the medieval combination of Aristotelian philosophy and Christian theology was such that physics as a science did not begin to emerge until the sixteenth century, and then only under trying circumstances.

The beginnings of physics were intimately tied up in astronomical theory and observation. In order to conform to the Christian view that the earth is the center of the universe, it had been necessary to construct a very complicated pattern for the motions of the stars and planets around the earth, based largely on the model suggested by Ptolemy in the first century. In the sixteenth century the astronomer Copernicus argued that there were many observational and logical difficulties with Ptolemaic theory which could be eliminated if the view were taken that the planets, including the earth, moved around the sun. His published views had a profound influence on at least three important figures in the following century. In Denmark a thorough observational astronomer, Tycho Brahe, completed in the latter half of the century a highly accurate catalog of the motions of the stars and planets. His observations were made largely for the purpose of reconciling experiment with his own geocentric model for the universe. A one-time assistant of his, however, had read and was convinced by Copernicus' treatise and with Tycho Brahe's accurate data set about to find in detail a model based on the heliocentric view which could accurately match observation. This man was Johann Kepler, mathematician at Prague. Kepler found that the Ptolemaic model, although roughly in agreement with observation, differed from the latter by as much as eight minutes of arc, a difference which might not seem to be particularly significant. Kepler was not able to reconcile the heliocentric view with the data until he gave up attempts to maintain uniform circular motion of the planets. Trying other possibilities he found that non-uniform motion in elliptical orbits was able to fit the data very precisely. In short, Kepler's findings are summarized in his three laws of planetary motion:

1. The planets move around the sun in orbits which are ellipses, with the sun at one focus.
2. The radius vector (from sun to planet) sweeps over equal areas in equal times.
3. The squares of the periods of revolution of the planets around the sun are proportional to the cubes of the mean radii of their respective orbits.

Kepler also considered the question of why the planets move at all. He arrived at the idea of an attraction between two material bodies, but did not develop his ideas further. Nevertheless, a quantitative theory in complete agreement with observation had been established, and the dawn of physics was breaking.

A contemporary of Kepler was Galileo Galilei, professor of mathematics at the University of Pisa and also at Padua. Galileo, originally headed for a medical career, was a brilliant combination of experimentalist and theoretician. Perhaps his most important asset was his refusal to accept the unsubstantiated writings of Aristotle and others regarding physical phenomena, which were the product of imagination and not of experiment. Galileo was one of the first to take advantage of the newly discovered optics of the telescope, and he made many important observations. He was firmly convinced by the Copernican model of planetary motion, and this conviction was the cause of considerable trouble between Galileo and the church. Of most interest here is Galileo's study of the motions of bodies. From his observations of the motions of falling masses Galileo came to the conclusion that two bodies released from the same height would fall to the earth with equal velocities if it were not for air resistance. In addition, he deduced the formulas of uniformly accelerated motion and elaborated on several kinds of projectile motion.

The successful application of models and mathematical formulas to the motions of heavenly and earthly bodies by Kepler and Galileo was only the beginning. It remained for the genius of an English mathematician,

Sir Isaac Newton, to synthesize these findings into the basic laws of physics which govern the motions of all things. Newton was born less than a year after the death of Galileo, and although from a farming family his mechanical and mathematical abilities sent him to Cambridge, where as a student he discovered the binomial theorem, developed the methods of infinite series, and discovered the principles of the differential calculus. Newton's early interest in gravitation resulted in a theory which was not published for some years because a prediction regarding the moon's motion around the earth was incompatible with the current knowledge concerning the earth's circumference. A later re-evaluation of this distance was found by Newton to fit perfectly in his calculations, and in 1687 there appeared the first edition of his *Principia* under the sponsorship of the Royal Society.

Newton had attacked the problem of finding a law of attraction between two bodies which would explain both Kepler's and Galileo's equations. He found that a gravitational attraction varying as the inverse square of the distance between the bodies was perfectly consistent. He formulated the science of mechanics on the basis of three laws of motion, which, as in thermodynamic theory, were assumed to be true and to represent observed nature. These laws are essentially definitions of mathematical quantities which are convenient to use in handling problems of motion:

1. A body will remain at rest or move with a uniform velocity unless acted upon by a force.
2. The net force acting on a body is equal to the time rate of change of momentum of the body.
3. For every force there is an equal and opposite reaction.

The familiar treatments of static and dynamic mechanics are based primarily on these three laws. They serve as a basis for handling mathematical quantities and making predictions about velocities, acceleration, rotational motions, trajectories, and related phenomena. The concept of energy originally arose from considerations of such problems, and different kinds of energy are defined by equations involving measurable quantities such as mass, velocity, and distance. It might also be observed that there are a number of valuable such quantities in physics which are perhaps less familiar to the uninitiated. The concepts of mass and velocity, for example, are generally familiar ones and are directly interpretable in terms of what we can see and measure for a moving body. A more fundamentally useful quantity in physics, however, is momentum, which is defined as the product of the mass and velocity of a body,

$$\mathbf{p} = m\mathbf{v}.$$

The basic importance of this quantity is expressed by the fact that Newton's second law is easily formulated in terms of this function,

$$\mathbf{F} = \frac{d\mathbf{p}}{dt} = \frac{d(m\mathbf{v})}{dt} = m\frac{d\mathbf{v}}{dt} = m\mathbf{a}, \tag{2-1}$$

and problems in motion are often most directly attacked from the viewpoint of the law of conservation of momentum. It will be recalled that quantities analogous to mass, velocity, momentum, etc., have been defined for motion involving angular changes. Thus such functions as moment of inertia, angular velocity, and angular momentum serve as fundamental quantities in studying the rotational motions of bodies.

2.2   THE GENERALIZED FORMULATIONS OF LAGRANGE AND HAMILTON

The century that followed Newton was an active one. Mechanical problems were attacked with newly developed mathematical techniques by a number of investigators. Optical phenomena were discovered and studied. The realm of electrical and magnetic interactions was approached by eager experimentalists. As the catalog of phenomena grew, so did the number of interactions that could be solved mathematically in the tradition of Newton's *Principia*. The accumulation of such varied experiences led slowly to the generalization of Newton's ideas into a more encompassing view of forces, energies, and motion. Analogous to the law of gravitation was to be postulated a similar law of electrostatic attraction, and analogous to gravitational potential energy was to be postulated an electrostatic potential energy. The beauty of physics lay in its ability to unify these views into similar equations and arguments.

The familiar mechanical problems considered in elementary physics are generally simple ones involving small numbers of particles and a limited number of interactions and forces. Thus, in studying the trajectory of a missile fired from a gun, one can analyze the motion by separating the net force acting on the particle into the component in the vertical direction and the component in the horizontal direction, the motions in the two directions being solved independently except for limiting conditions which relate the two (such as the cessation of motion when the projectile strikes the earth). Similarly, the collision of two bodies can conveniently be handled by resolving the momenta of the bodies into components along two or three rectangular coordinates and applying the law of conservation of momentum separately to each problem. An example of this procedure is illustrated in Fig. 2–1.

Unfortunately, the handling of problems in this way becomes more and more complex as the number of particles and interactions increases. The more generalizations that can be realized to unify these interactions and motions, the less complicated the problem will be. One generalization that was discovered in the early stages of physics is the relation between potential-energy functions of various kinds (gravitational, electrostatic, etc.) and the forces acting on bodies. It is common to regard a body with a finite mass as having around it a gravitational field, or a body with an electric charge as having around it an electric field. If another body with a finite mass is placed at some point in space, it will have a potential energy by virtue of the gravitational force exerted upon it by the first body (or as is sometimes stated, by virtue of the gravitational field at the

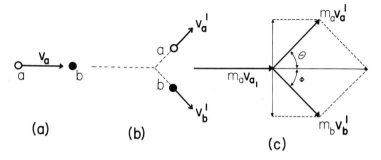

Fig. 2–1. Conservation of momentum: motion of particles (a) before and (b) after collision; (c) resolution of momenta into x and y components. According to the law of conservation of momentum, for the x components $m_a v_a = m_a v'_a \cos \theta + m_b v'_b \cos \phi$, and for the y components $m_a v'_a \sin \theta = m_b v'_b \sin \phi$.

point at which the second body is placed). Similarly, a second charge placed at some point in space will have a potential energy by virtue of the electrostatic force exerted upon it by the first charge (or, again, by virtue of the existence of an electric field at the point in space at which the second charge was placed).

In many problems of interest the potential-energy function is dependent only on position in space, but not explicitly on time. Such a system is said to be conservative, and it can be shown that for conservative systems the force at any point is equal to the negative of the gradient of the potential function at that point,[1]

$$\mathbf{F} = -\operatorname{grad} V = -\nabla V = -\left(\mathbf{i}\, \frac{\partial V}{\partial x} + \mathbf{j}\, \frac{\partial V}{\partial y} + \mathbf{k}\, \frac{\partial V}{\partial z} \right), \quad (2\text{–}2)$$

or, in terms of components of force along the three rectangular coordinates,

$$F_x = -\frac{\partial V}{\partial x}, \qquad F_y = -\frac{\partial V}{\partial y}, \qquad F_z = -\frac{\partial V}{\partial z}. \quad (2\text{–}3)$$

[1] Appendix A reviews vector relations.

It can be shown that, for any pair of coordinates and components of force in a conservative system,

$$\frac{\partial F_x}{\partial y} = \frac{\partial F_y}{\partial x}$$

or, more generally,

$$\text{curl } \mathbf{F} = \nabla \times \mathbf{F} = 0.$$

From the relation between force and potential, Eq. (2–3), and Eq. (2–1) one can rewrite Newton's second law in the form

$$\frac{d(mv_x)}{dt} = -\frac{\partial V}{\partial x},$$

with similar expressions for the y and z components. Also, if the kinetic energy is written in terms of velocity components, one obtains

$$T = \frac{m}{2}\left(v_x{}^2 + v_y{}^2 + v_z{}^2\right),$$

and since $\partial T/\partial v_x = mv_x$, Newton's second law can be cast into the form

$$\frac{d}{dt}\left(\frac{\partial T}{\partial v_x}\right) + \frac{\partial V}{\partial x} = 0.$$

The French mathematician Lagrange noted that it was convenient to define a function $L = T - V$, now called the Lagrangian function. Since the kinetic energy depends on the velocity components and potential energy on position coordinates, it follows that L is a function of six variables, three coordinates and three velocity components. In addition, it follows, since T is a function only of velocities and V a function only of coordinates, that $\partial L/\partial v_x = \partial T/\partial v_x$, $-\partial L/\partial x = \partial V/\partial x$, etc. Hence the equations of motion are

$$\frac{d}{dt}\left(\frac{\partial L}{\partial v_x}\right) - \frac{\partial L}{\partial x} = 0$$

and similar equations for y and z.

The importance of Lagrange's equations of motion lies in the fact that they hold not only in rectangular coordinates but in any set of coordinates that may be convenient to use so long as T and V are expressed in terms of that set. If, for example, one is considering a situation in which an electric field arises from a point charge, the symmetry of the field around the charge makes it more convenient to study the problem in spherical polar coordinates rather than rectangular coordinates. In this case V is a function of r only and does not depend on the angles. Thus much simpler relations result than would be encountered in rectangular coordinates. If T and V are expressed, then, in terms of spherical polar coordinates, Lagrange's equations are valid in the coordinates r, θ, and ϕ.

If generalized coordinates are designated $q_1, \ldots, q_n$, and the time derivatives of the coordinates are denoted by the symbols $\dot{q}_1, \ldots, \dot{q}_n$, the equations of motion in generalized coordinates are

$$\frac{d}{dt}\left(\frac{\partial L}{\partial \dot{q}_i}\right) - \frac{\partial L}{\partial q_i} = 0.$$

In general, for n particles in a system there will be $3n$ coordinates which must be specified and $3n$ time derivatives, and hence there will be $3n$ such

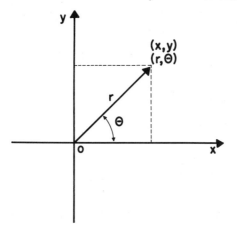

Fig. 2–2. Description of the location of a point in rectangular x, y coordinates and in polar r, θ coordinates.

equations of motion. The proof of the generality of Lagrange's equations in any coordinate system will not be given here.

A simple example of how Lagrange's equations can be used is afforded by the case of two-dimensional motion in a plane in which the potential-energy function is a function only of the distance r from a given point (Fig. 2–2). This would be a model for the relative motion of two atoms in a molecule, for example, with one atom held at the origin, or similarly for the motion of an electron around the nucleus, which is held at the origin. For simplicity, motion is confined to a plane in both examples. In this case polar coordinates are the most convenient to handle;[2] it would be difficult to discuss the motion using rectangular coordinates.

Writing L as a function of r, θ, $\dot{r}$, and $\dot{\theta}$, we have

$$\frac{d}{dt}\left(\frac{\partial L}{\partial \dot{r}}\right) - \frac{\partial L}{\partial r} = 0,$$

$$\frac{d}{dt}\left(\frac{\partial L}{\partial \dot{\theta}}\right) - \frac{\partial L}{\partial \theta} = 0.$$

[2] Appendix B.

The velocity component of a particle along the radius is $\dot{r}$; that along the tangent to a circle about the origin is $r\dot{\theta}$, so that $v^2 = \dot{r}^2 + r^2\dot{\theta}^2$ and

$$L = T - V = \frac{m}{2}(\dot{r}^2 + r^2\dot{\theta}^2) - V(r). \tag{2-4}$$

Differentiating, one obtains

$$\frac{\partial L}{\partial \dot{r}} = m\dot{r},$$

$$\frac{\partial L}{\partial \dot{\theta}} = mr^2\dot{\theta},$$

$$\frac{\partial L}{\partial r} = mr\dot{\theta}^2 - \frac{\partial V}{\partial r},$$

$$\frac{\partial L}{\partial \theta} = 0,$$

so that Lagrange's equations are

$$\frac{d}{dt}(m\dot{r}) - mr\dot{\theta}^2 + \frac{dV}{dr} = 0, \tag{2-5}$$

$$\frac{d}{dt}(mr^2\dot{\theta}) = 0. \tag{2-6}$$

The second of these can be integrated immediately to

$$mr^2\dot{\theta} = \text{constant},$$

which is simply a statement that the angular momentum is constant according to the usual definition of angular momentum. It should be pointed out that one can define a generalized momentum associated with a generalized coordinate by the expression

$$p_i = \frac{\partial L}{\partial \dot{q}_i}. \tag{2-7}$$

Linear and angular momentum are therefore only special cases of generalized momenta associated with generalized coordinates.

Equation (2–5) can be rearranged to

$$m\frac{d^2r}{dt^2} = mr\dot{\theta}^2 - \frac{dV}{dr},$$

which, upon substitution of the angular momentum $p_\theta = mr^2\dot{\theta}$ becomes

$$m\frac{d^2r}{dt^2} = \frac{p_\theta^2}{mr^3} - \frac{dV}{dr} = -\frac{d}{dr}\left(V + \frac{p_\theta^2}{2mr^2}\right),$$

in which r and θ have now been separated and the equation has assumed the form of a one-dimensional problem along r with a potential $V + p_\theta^2/2mr^2$. The second term can be looked on as a sort of fictitious potential energy coming from the centrifugal force. Insertion of a particular form for $V(r)$ allows solution for the detailed motions. For example the gravitational potential-energy function $V = -Gmm'/r$ results in finite elliptical orbits with the attractive center (the origin) at one focus, and in open hyperbolic orbits. An electrostatic potential, $V = qq'/r$, yields a similar result since the dependence on r is similar.

The generalized momentum associated with a coordinate, as introduced in Eq. (2–7), bears further scrutiny. In rectangular coordinates it is seen that since V is a function of coordinates only, and not of velocities,

$$p_x = \frac{\partial L}{\partial \dot{x}} = \frac{\partial T}{\partial \dot{x}} = m\dot{x}.$$

Note also that the kinetic energy can be expressed in terms of momenta rather than velocities. Since $\dot{x} = p/m$, we have

$$T(p_x,\ p_y,\ p_z) = \frac{1}{2m}(p_x{}^2 + p_y{}^2 + p_z{}^2),$$

$$\frac{\partial T}{\partial p_x} = \frac{p_x}{m} = \frac{m\dot{x}}{m} = \dot{x}, \tag{2–8}$$

with similar relations for the derivatives of T with respect to p_y and p_z. Relations of this structure led Hamilton to suggest another useful function, now called the Hamiltonian function, which is defined in generalized coordinates as

$$H = \sum_i p_i \dot{q}_i - L. \tag{2–9}$$

Although defined in terms of the Lagrangian function, it can be shown that an equivalent definition of the Hamiltonian function is

$$H = T + V; \tag{2–10}$$

i.e., the Hamiltonian function is the total energy of the system. From this relation (and Newton's second law) it can be seen that

$$\frac{\partial H}{\partial q_i} = \frac{\partial T}{\partial q_i} + \frac{\partial V}{\partial q_i} = \frac{\partial V}{\partial q_i} = -\frac{dp_i}{dt} = -\dot{p}_i \tag{2–11}$$

and also from (2–8)

$$\frac{\partial H}{\partial p_i} = \frac{\partial T}{\partial p_i} = \frac{p_i}{m_i} = \dot{q}_i. \tag{2–12}$$

These two important relations are known as Hamilton's equations. They bring to light direct relationships between the total energy of the system, the coordinates, their associated momenta, and their time derivatives. For a system of n particles there will be $3n$ such pairs of equations, and their solution leads directly to important equations of motion.

As an example of the application of Hamilton's equations, let us consider again the case of the system in which V is a function only of r, the distance from a point. From (2–7) and (2–4) we calculate that

$$p_r = \frac{\partial L}{\partial \dot{r}} = m\dot{r},$$

$$p_\theta = \frac{\partial L}{\partial \dot{\theta}} = mr^2\dot{\theta},$$

where p_r is the ordinary linear momentum along r, and p_θ is the familiar angular momentum. The definition of the Hamiltonian function, Eq. (2–9), gives

$$H = (m\dot{r})\dot{r} + (mr^2\dot{\theta})\dot{\theta} - L$$

$$= m(\dot{r}^2 + r^2\dot{\theta}^2) - \frac{m}{2}(\dot{r}^2 + r^2\dot{\theta}^2) + V(r)$$

$$= \frac{m}{2}(\dot{r}^2 + r^2\dot{\theta}^2) + V(r).$$

Note that this result could have been obtained directly from the equivalent definition of H, Eq. (2–10), by substitution of T and V. Since $\dot{r} = p_r/m$ and $\dot{\theta} = p_\theta/mr^2$, the Hamiltonian function becomes

$$H = \frac{1}{2m}\left(p_r{}^2 + \frac{1}{r^2}p_\theta{}^2\right) + V(r).$$

Hamilton's equations, (2–11) and (2–12), are then

$$\frac{\partial H}{\partial p_r} = \frac{p_r}{m} = \frac{dr}{dt} = \dot{r}$$

$$\frac{\partial H}{\partial p_\theta} = \frac{p_\theta}{mr^2} = \frac{d\theta}{dt} = \dot{\theta}$$

$$-\frac{\partial H}{\partial r} = \frac{p_\theta{}^2}{mr^3} - \frac{dV(r)}{dr} = \frac{dp_r}{dt} = \dot{p}_r \qquad (2\text{–}13)$$

$$-\frac{\partial H}{\partial \theta} = 0 = \frac{dp_\theta}{dt} = \dot{p}_\theta. \qquad (2\text{–}14)$$

The first two results are already known as the definitions of linear and angular momentum. The third shows that the time rate of change of radial momentum equals the external force, $-\partial V/\partial r$, in the r direction plus the centrifugal force $p_\theta{}^2/mr^3$. The last equation shows that the time rate of change of angular momentum is zero, a result arising because there are no torques.

In addition to these general conclusions one can calculate the detailed motions of the particles involved upon substitution of a function for $V(r)$. An example will serve to illustrate this point. Let us consider two masses, one fixed at the origin, the other a distance r from the origin. Let us further assume that the motion of the second mass relative to the first is governed by the Hooke's law potential $V(r) = \frac{1}{2}k(r - r_e)^2$ where r_e is the equilibrium separation of the two masses. This is, of course, the familiar mechanical analogy of two masses separated by a spring, often used to describe the vibrational motions of a molecule. Since V depends only on r, this model corresponds to the situation we have been discussing, so that Eqs. (2–13) and (2–14) apply. To simplify the problem further, let us assume that the system has no rotational motion, i.e., $p_\theta = 0$. Hence substitution of the Hooke's law potential into (2–13) with $p_\theta = 0$ gives us

$$\frac{dp_r}{dt} = -\frac{dV(r)}{dr} = -k(r - r_e),$$

and since $p_r = m\dot{r}$, this becomes

$$\frac{d(m\dot{r})}{dt} = -k(r - r_e),$$

or

$$m\frac{d^2r}{dt^2} + k(r - r_e) = 0.$$

This is a differential equation which, on application of boundary conditions, can be integrated, to yield the solution

$$r - r_e = c_1 \sin\left[\sqrt{\frac{k}{m}}\, t + c_2\right] = c_1 \sin(2\pi\nu t + c_2)$$

where c_1 and c_2 are the constants of integration. This is an equation which describes simple harmonic oscillatory motion along r with frequency $\nu = (1/2\pi)\sqrt{k/m}$.

Or consider a more trivial case. If there is no potential energy of interaction between the two bodies, then $V(r) = 0$. If there is no rotational motion, $p_\theta = 0$ and (2–13) becomes

$$\frac{dp_r}{dt} = 0,$$

which states simply that if the second body is not in motion to begin with, then it will remain motionless. If it has an initial momentum along r, then this momentum will remain constant—an expected result since there are no forces. If $V(r) = 0$, but p_θ is not zero, then from (2–13)

$$\frac{dp_r}{dt} = \frac{p_\theta^2}{mr^3}$$

which describes the change in radial momentum due to the rotational motion of the body, i.e., the effect of the centrifugal force of rotation.

Although the application of Hamilton's equations may seem to be an unnecessary abstraction of more familiar momentum and energy quantities, it becomes apparent that even for reasonably complex systems it is not too difficult to write expressions for kinetic and potential energy in a convenient coordinate system. Therefore one can write the Hamiltonian function in terms of these coordinates and momenta and solve the Hamilton equations for a number of fundamental relations describing the motions of the system. It can be seen that momentum is a fundamental quantity in describing physical systems.

The choice of a suitable coordinate system is governed largely by the symmetry of the potential-energy function and constraints which may apply to the system. It is convenient to make V depend on as few variables as possible and in as simple a manner as possible. Once a particular coordinate system has been selected and V written as a function of these coordinates, it may be necessary to transcribe the kinetic energy from more familiar rectangular coordinate terms to the coordinates of interest.

2.3 PHASE SPACE

We have seen that in its most generalized formulations physics deals primarily with coordinates and momenta in describing the states and motions of a system. In particular, for a system of n particles it is necessary to specify $3n$ position coordinates and $3n$ momentum components along these coordinates, making a total of $6n$ quantities that must be specified in order to define the system completely and predict its future motions. In simple problems involving one or two particles we are able to draw graphs of the positions of particles in a three-dimensional coordinate system and can indicate momenta and momentum components by means of vectors on these diagrams. However, following the changes of a system with time in this manner is difficult, and if a few more particles are added to the system, it becomes impossible to visualize the states and the motions.

A more convenient, and in the long run more useful, means of visualizing the states and motions of a system is phase space. Phase space is simply a multidimensional space made up for n particles of $6n$ variables, these variables being the $3n$ coordinates and the $3n$ momenta. In other words, to describe the behavior of a single particle in phase space we would need a six-dimensional space defined by three coordinate and three momentum axes. Although this six-dimensional space is impossible to draw or illustrate in detail, it serves a very useful purpose since we can at least formulate in our minds its existence and its properties; we note, first of all, that one property is that our single particle is represented by a single point in this six-dimensional space. Whereas in ordinary space we needed to show the position in terms of three coordinates and to indicate its motion in terms of vectors, in phase space all these variables are coordinates and hence a single point in phase space gives both position and motion information. The history of the motion of our particle then is followed simply by following a point in phase space, and we observe that this is particularly simple if we use the Hamiltonian formulation of mechanics since this generalized form is completely in terms of the total energy and its changes with momenta, position, and time. For a system of n particles we would have one point in a $6n$-dimensional phase space, and we can follow the history of this system of particles by the motion of the point in phase space. It is found that a number of generalities are observed from the phase-space viewpoint that are obscure otherwise.

In considering Hamilton's equations one important property we find for conservative systems is that the motion will take place with constant energy. This is seen by taking the time derivative of H, which is the total energy:

$$\frac{dH}{dt} = \frac{\partial H}{\partial q_1}\frac{dq_1}{dt} + \frac{\partial H}{\partial q_2}\frac{dq_2}{dt} + \cdots + \frac{\partial H}{\partial p_1}\frac{dp_1}{dt} + \frac{\partial H}{\partial p_2}\frac{dp_2}{dt} + \cdots$$
$$= \frac{\partial H}{\partial q_1}\frac{\partial H}{\partial p_1} + \frac{\partial H}{\partial q_2}\frac{\partial H}{\partial p_2} + \cdots + \frac{\partial H}{\partial p_1}\left(-\frac{\partial H}{\partial q_1}\right) + \frac{\partial H}{\partial p_2}\left(-\frac{\partial H}{\partial q_2}\right) + \cdots$$
$$= 0.$$

Thus the motion of a point in phase space will be such that it moves on a constant-energy surface. Other quantities which can be found to be constant, such as angular momentum, define additional surfaces in phase space, and the requirement that all be constant restricts the motion of the point to the intersections between these constant-energy, constant-angular-momentum, etc., surfaces.

Purely periodic motions are particularly adaptable to phase-space consideration since there are a number of restrictions that reduce the effective dimensionality of the phase space. As a simple example consider the motion of a harmonic oscillator. Linear harmonic oscillation has a two-dimensional phase space for a single oscillating particle (Fig. 2–3); therefore the constant-energy surface is simply a line. The energy of a harmonic oscillator is given by

$$E = \tfrac{1}{2}mv^2 + 2\pi^2 m v^2 q^2,$$

where v is the frequency of oscillation and q is the displacement from equilibrium $(r - r_e)$. The Hamiltonian function is

$$H = \frac{p^2}{2m} + 2\pi^2 m v^2 q^2.$$

Setting this equal to a constant, E, the equation of a line of constant energy becomes on rearrangement the equation of an ellipse having semiaxes $\sqrt{2mE}$ and $\sqrt{E/2\pi^2 m\nu^2}$:

$$\frac{p^2}{(\sqrt{2mE})^2} + \frac{q^2}{(\sqrt{E/2\pi^2 m\nu^2})^2} = 1.$$

For a given energy, the path of an oscillator in phase space will be around such an ellipse.

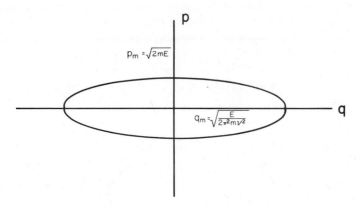

Fig. 2–3. Representation of a constant-energy path of a linear harmonic oscillator in phase space.

2.4 EQUIPARTITION OF ENERGY AND THE CALCULATION OF HEAT CAPACITIES

The separate and independent quantities which need to be known to specify completely the position and configuration of a body are called its *degrees of freedom*. A monatomic molecule can exhibit only translational motion, and hence three coordinates are necessary to specify its position. A diatomic molecule can be viewed in terms of the translation of its center of mass, in which case there are again required three coordinates to describe the position of the center of mass and hence three degrees of freedom of translation. In addition, a diatomic molecule can undergo rotations, and investigation shows that an analysis of this motion requires two additional coordinates to specify the orientation of the molecule, axes which are mutually perpendicular to each other and to the line joining the atoms of the molecule (Fig. 2–4a). Thus, because of its rotational motions a diatomic molecule has two additional degrees of freedom corresponding to the two additional coordinates which must be specified to describe its position and orientation.

Most elementary physical chemistry texts derive from the kinetic-molecular theory of gases an equation giving the average kinetic energy of a molecule undergoing translational motion. The relation is $\bar{T} = \frac{3}{2}kT$, where $\bar{T}$ is the average kinetic energy, and $k = R/N$ is the Boltzmann constant. It will be recalled that usually it is assumed that the average values of the squares of the three velocity components along cartesian axes are equal because of the completely random nature of the motions over a period of time, and so we might additionally surmise that the motions along these three coordinates might contribute equally to the total average kinetic energy of the molecule. If this were the case, then

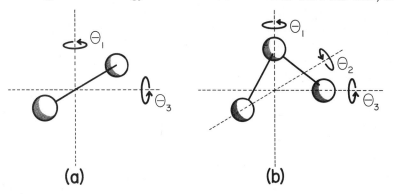

Fig. 2–4. The coordinates necessary to describe the rotational motions of (a) diatomic and (b) non-linear polyatomic molecules.

the average kinetic energy contributed per degree of freedom would be one-third the total, or

$$\bar{T}_1 = \frac{1}{2}kT.$$

On the basis of this reasoning we might consider whether or not other degrees of freedom, such as rotational degrees of freedom, might not also contribute to the total energy, and if they might not also each contribute $\frac{1}{2}kT$ to the total. Investigation indicates that they do.

The *principle of the equipartition of energy* states that each degree of freedom for a molecule contributes $\frac{1}{2}kT$ to the total energy. Thus in the diatomic molecule, which can rotate as well as translate, there are a total of five degrees of freedom, and hence the total energy of the molecule will be $\frac{5}{2}kT$. A non-linear polyatomic molecule requires three coordinates to specify its rotational orientation (Fig. 2–4b), and hence a polyatomic molecule has six degrees of freedom (three translational and three rotational), so that according to the equipartition principle its total energy will be $3kT$. From the relation between the Boltzmann constant and the molar gas constant it is obvious that for one mole of molecules the energy of a monatomic gas would be $\frac{3}{2}RT$, that of a diatomic gas would be $\frac{5}{2}RT$, and that of a polyatomic gas $3RT$.

It might appear that in order to determine the number of degrees of freedom it is necessary only to determine the number of coordinates needed to describe all the possible motions of the molecule. Since the equipartition principle is concerned with energy contributions, however, it is necessary to define the degrees of freedom somewhat differently for this particular purpose. Investigation shows that, as far as the equipartition principle is valid, those variables (coordinate or momentum) which contribute a quadratic (square) term in the analytical equations for the energy serve as degrees of freedom. In translational motion the only energy is kinetic energy (we have assumed no forces and hence no potential energy), and the kinetic energy can be expressed in terms involving the momentum components squared. In either case three such quadratic terms are required. Therefore, there are three degrees of freedom of translation, as we have already deduced.

In the terms for energy of rotation we again have only kinetic energy, and for each axis of rotation the energy term is of the form

$$\epsilon_r = \frac{p_\theta^2}{2I},$$

where p_θ is the angular momentum about the axis of rotation and I is the moment of inertia about the same axis. Thus each axis of rotation contributes as one degree of freedom to the total energy since each involves only one quadratic component.

An important case that differs from these is the case of the linear harmonic oscillator mentioned in the previous sections. In generalized coordinates the energy of a harmonic oscillator is given by

$$\epsilon_v = \frac{p^2}{2m} + \tfrac{1}{2}kq^2, \tag{2--15}$$

where the first term, involving the momentum, is the vibrational kinetic energy and the second term, involving position, is the vibrational potential energy. (The k in this equation is not the Boltzmann constant, but the so-called force constant of the vibration.) Thus for a single vibrational mode there are *two* quadratic variables involved and hence two degrees of freedom. Thus one mode of vibration contributes $2 \times \tfrac{1}{2}kT = kT$ to the total energy.

The diatomic molecule is capable of vibrating as well as translating and rotating. There is only one mode of vibration possible, motion along the line joining the atoms. Thus the vibrational mode contributes kT to the total energy making the latter for the diatomic molecule $\tfrac{7}{2}kT$ for translation, rotation, and vibration. In general, for non-linear polyatomic molecules containing N atoms the vibrational motions can be analyzed in no less than $3N - 6$ vibrational modes, so that there will be a vibrational contribution of $(3N - 6)kT$ to the total energy. A non-linear triatomic molecule will have 3 modes of vibrational motion and therefore a vibrational contribution of $3kT$ per molecule or $3RT$ per mole to the total energy. The total energy in this case would then be $6RT$ per mole.

On the basis of the equipartition principle we are thus able to predict the total energy in terms of contributions by the various motions of the molecule. It might be mentioned that, although we have used very qualitative arguments for the equipartition principle, the results as we have given them follow directly from the Maxwell-Boltzmann distribution law.

TABLE 2–1.   Molal Heat Capacities of Gases at 288°K*

Gas	$\gamma = \dfrac{C_p}{C_v}$	$\dfrac{C_p}{R}$	$\dfrac{C_p - C_v}{R}$	Gas	$\gamma = \dfrac{C_p}{C_v}$	$\dfrac{C_p}{R}$	$\dfrac{C_p - C_v}{R}$
A	1.668	2.52	1.00	CO_2	1.304	4.41	1.03
Ne	1.66	2.52	1.00	N_2O	1.303	4.44	1.03
Xe	1.66	2.52	1.00	NH_3	1.31	4.49	1.06
Hg	1.67	2.52	1.00	CH_2	1.31	4.27	1.01
H_2	1.410	3.44	1.00	H_2S	1.32	4.35	1.05
N_2	1.404	3.50	1.00	SO_2	1.29	4.89	1.10
O_2	1.401	3.52	1.00	CN	1.26	5.36	1.09
CO	1.404	3.50	1.00	C_2H_2	1.26	5.02	1.03
NO	1.400	3.52	1.00	C_2H_4	1.255	5.08	1.03
HCl	1.41	3.56	1.00	C_2H_6	1.22	5.84	1.05
Cl_2	1.355	4.10	1.08				

* National Academy of Sciences, *International Critical Tables of Numerical Data*, vol. 5, McGraw-Hill Book Co., New York, 1929.

A thermodynamic quantity which we should be able to obtain easily from the application of the equipartition principle is the heat capacity of a gas. We have found in this discussion the energies of monatomic, diatomic, and polyatomic molecules as a function of temperature; i.e., all the results are in terms of kT or RT. Since the heat capacity at constant volume is $(\partial E/\partial T)_v$ it follows immediately that for a monatomic gas C_v is $\frac{3}{2}R$ or about 3 cal mole^{-1} deg^{-1}. For a diatomic gas C_v should be $\frac{7}{2}R$ or about 7 cal mole^{-1} deg^{-1}, while a non-linear triatomic molecule we would expect to have a C_v of $6R$ or about 12 cal mole^{-1} deg^{-1}. From statistical arguments we have predicted values for a thermodynamic quantity which, without the equipartition rule could be obtained only by experimental measurement.

We hasten to compare our predictions with experiment and find (Table 2–1) that for monatomic gases the agreement is very good. For more complicated molecules, however, we meet difficulty. It will be noticed, for example, that the heat capacity of the diatomic molecules listed are close to 5 cal mole^{-1} deg^{-1}. Immediately the question arises as to why it is too low. A convenient explanation is that at normal temperatures the vibrational motion does not contribute to the heat capacity, and thus we observe a value lower than that expected by R, or 2 cal. Unfortunately, our theory has not given us any reason to expect this deficiency. A similar situation is found for triatomic molecules. We note that the actual heat capacity appears to be that which we would predict if we had ignored vibrational contributions. As if it were not enough of a difficulty that our predictions are too high, we find (Table 2–2) that if the diatomic and triatomic gases are elevated to much higher temperatures, the heat capacities begin to rise and eventually begin to approach at several

TABLE 2–2. Heat Capacities at 1 Atm.*

Temperature (°C)	O_2, N_2, CO		CO_2		H_2O		CH_4	
	γ	C_P	γ	C_P	γ	C_P	γ	C_P
0	1.402	6.97	1.310	8.68			1.307	8.55
100	1.399	6.98	1.281	9.17	1.324	8.71	1.232	10.60
200	1.396	7.00	1.263	9.60	1.31$_0$	8.63	1.188	12.57
400	1.391	7.08	1.235	10.47	1.30$_1$	8.65	1.139	16.25
600	1.383	7.17	1.217	11.14	1.29$_0$	8.88	1.113	19.57
800	1.375	7.29	1.204	11.71	1.27$_3$	9.29		
1000	1.365	7.44	1.195	12.16	1.25$_2$	9.89		
1400	1.342	7.80	1.184	12.81	1.20$_6$	11.66		
2000	1.303	8.54	1.171	13.60	1.15$_5$	14.94		

* National Academy of Sciences, *International Critical Tables of Numerical Data*, vol. 5, McGraw-Hill Book Co., New York, 1929.

thousand degrees the values we have predicted. But again, our theory has no explanation for this variation.

The heat capacity of solids also is open to investigation by this method. A very simple view of atomic solids is that the atoms are undergoing oscillations about their equilibrium positions, and that these oscillations can be analyzed in terms of three component harmonic oscillations along three rectangular coordinates. We have already seen that for a single mode of vibration there is a contribution of kT to the total energy and so for three such vibrations there should be a total energy of $3kT$ per atom or $3RT$ per gram atom. The heat capacity C_v of an atomic solid should be about 6 cal deg^{-1}. The fact that many solids do have heat capacities close to this value was expressed many years ago in the law of Dulong and Petit. At the same time, there are many solids that have a somewhat lower heat capacity than this, and the heat capacities of all solids are observed to fall as the temperature is lowered, approaching zero at the absolute zero of temperature (Fig. 2–5). Our theory is inadequate to explain these phenomena.

Perhaps this discussion has been somewhat unfair in its criticism of the equipartition principle since the principle was highly successful in the solution of a large number of physical problems. Our main interest, however, has been to see where the difficulties in classical theory lie, and we will choose not to elaborate on the further use of these ideas in classical theory except in a few useful cases. Although the classical application of the equipartition of energy is not correct except in certain cases,

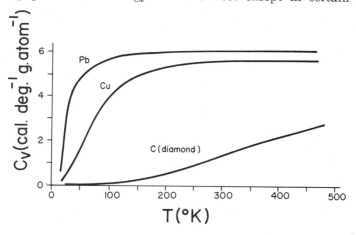

Fig. 2–5. The heat capacities of several solids as a function of temperature.

we shall see later that in an altered form it is still applicable to many situations and serves a continually useful purpose in statistical energy calculations.

2.5   THE PROBLEM OF BLACKBODY RADIATION

The nineteenth century not only saw the successful application of physical laws to the atomic-molecular concept and the beginning of statistical methods in molecular problems, but was an era of ferment and activity on every front. The science of thermodynamics was established during this century, and by 1850 a number of precise experiments had established the wave theory of light almost beyond doubt. Perhaps the most notable successes were in the fields of electricity and magnetism, beginning with the remarkable experiments by Faraday in the first half of the century and culminating in Maxwell's brilliant electromagnetic theories, which unified electrical, magnetic, and optical phenomena.

The electromagnetic view of radiation—optical, x-ray, and radio waves alike—is that energy is transmitted through space in the form of electric and magnetic field waves, i.e., electric and magnetic fields oscillating in a periodic manner in directions perpendicular to the direction of propagation of the beam of radiation (Fig. 2–6). If one were to stand at a fixed point in space, the propagation of a beam of light past that point would be observed as electric and magnetic fields oscillating in time. Alternatively, if one were to remain with a constant electric and/or magnetic field strength, one would travel through space in the

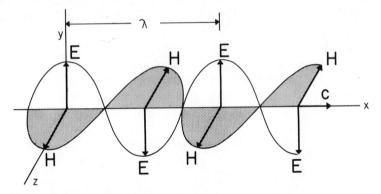

Fig. 2–6. Classical electromagnetic picture of a plane wave of light progressing in the x direction with velocity c.

direction of the beam. The interactions of radiation with matter usually lead to gains or losses of energy by the matter, so that if the law of conservation of energy is valid, energy must exist in the radiation field as well as in matter. Thus it can be shown by electromagnetic theory that energy is distributed throughout a radiation field with a certain density dependent on the electric and magnetic field strengths associated with the radiation. In addition, the interactions of radiation with matter indicate that electromagnetic fields are capable of changing the momenta of bodies.

The oscillatory behavior of the electric and magnetic fields can be expressed by relations[3] such as

$$E_y = A \sin 2\pi \left(\frac{x}{\lambda} - \nu t \right) \tag{2-16}$$

and

$$H_z = \sqrt{\frac{\epsilon}{\mu}} A \sin 2\pi \left(\frac{x}{\lambda} - \nu t \right) \tag{2-17}$$

[3] Some of the basic relations of electricity and magnetism are reviewed in Appendix F.

for a beam progressing in the x direction. E_y and H_z are the electric and magnetic field strengths at point x, λ the wavelength, and ν the frequency of the oscillation. The last two are related to the velocity of the light in free space by

$$\lambda\nu = c.$$

ϵ and μ are the dielectric constant and the permeability of the medium. Equations (2–16) and (2–17) are explicitly for a plane wave.

Utilizing different means of generation and detection, man has been able to study a wide range of the electromagnetic spectrum all the way from the low-frequency radiation of the audio- and radio-frequency region through the microwave, infrared, visible, and ultraviolet regions to the extremely high frequencies of x-rays and γ-rays.

One is able to derive from electromagnetic theory equations for the energy density in a radiation field, for the energy passing through a unit area perpendicular to the beam (the intensity), the momentum carried, the pressure exerted by radiation when absorbed by matter, and similar quantities.[4]

Another consequence of electromagnetic theory is that an accelerating charge must radiate energy. The consequences of this phenomenon are that charges undergoing curvilinear or oscillatory motion will radiate energy and therefore lose energy unless it is replenished from some source. The oscillating charge is of particular interest since it can be considered a source of radiation caused by thermal motions of atoms and molecules in a solid and also can be used to explain the production of radio waves by an antenna.

The electromagnetic theory of Maxwell as developed by Lorentz, Hertz, and others was successful in explaining many phenomena and successfully predicted many others. The development of radio techniques at the turn of the century can properly be ascribed to the predictions of this theory. However, there were also several points of difficulty that began to emerge at the end of the last century. For one thing, although the mathematics did not really require it, the wave basis of electromagnetic radiation led to a search for some medium to support the oscillating electric and magnetic fields. This medium, called the *aether*, was an integral part of classical physics before the famous experiment of Michelson and Morley, whose measurements of the velocity of light in different directions relative to the earth's motion through space disagreed with the predictions that had been made and set the stage for Einstein's formulation of the theory of relativity.

[4] If the pressure exerted on matter appears trivial, note that the sun's radiation has a perceptible effect on the orbits of large, lightweight satellites traveling around the earth, causes the diffuse tails of comets always to point away from the sun, and is being given serious consideration as a means of propelling space vehicles.

Another area in which the theory ran into difficulty was in the consideration of thermal, or blackbody, radiation emitted by a heated solid. In an equilibrium situation, radiation can be treated by classical thermodynamics just as any other energy, and such an equilibrium situation can be constructed experimentally. It is well known that when a solid is heated, it begins to glow, and that the higher the temperature, the less red and more white the light becomes. The spectral distribution of this thermal radiation is found to be continuous. If the radiation is produced in a completely enclosed cavity, so that no radiation can leave or enter, then the radiation will come to equilibrium with the walls of the cavity. Experimentally, this can be done by means of a furnace, heated electrically on the outside, with only a tiny opening to the interior to observe the radiation inside. The radiation obtained in this way is known as blackbody radiation. Because of the requirements of equilibrium the blackbody producing the radiation must be a perfect absorber and emitter of radiation. Actually many solids that do not seem to be in an equilibrium situation, such as a heated tungsten filament, approach blackbody spectral distributions closely. The spectral distribution of a blackbody as measured experimentally is shown in Fig. 2–7.

Two relations can be inferred from thermodynamic arguments which are found to agree with experiment, but they will not be derived here. The first is the Stefan-Boltzmann law, which states that the total emissive power of a blackbody (i.e., the total amount of energy radiated per square centimeter of surface per second) is proportional to the fourth power of the absolute temperature:

$$W = \sigma T^4.$$

This relation was found by Boltzmann by applying the equations of the Carnot cycle to an engine in which the radiation played the part of the working substance. The energy density and radiation pressure discussed above are important quantities in this derivation.

The second important relation found by thermodynamics, known as the Wien displacement law, states that the monochromatic energy density in an isothermal enclosure and the monochromatic emissive power of a blackbody when taken at corresponding wavelengths are both directly proportional to the fifth power of the absolute temperature. From this fact it can be shown that the wavelength at which the emissive power is a maximum is related to the temperature by

$$\lambda_{max} T = \text{constant.}$$

These relations are found by studying the behavior of an adiabatic expansion of a system in equilibrium with radiation. The numerical value of σ in the Stefan-Boltzmann law is about 5.70×10^{-5} erg cm^{-2} sec^{-1} deg^{-4} and the constant in the λ_{max} equation is 0.289 cm deg.

Both these relations are derived on a purely thermodynamic basis, and hence it is not surprising that they agree perfectly with observation. However, they are incomplete because they do not predict the complete

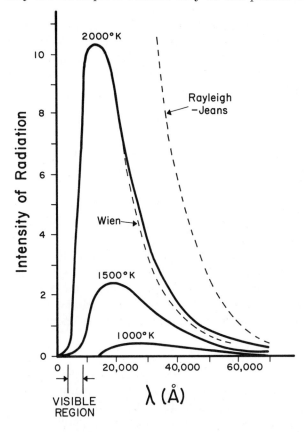

Fig. 2–7. The spectral distribution of a blackbody at several temperatures. The behavior of the Wien and Rayleigh-Jeans equations is shown also. The Planck equation fits the experimental curves exactly.

spectral distribution itself. We must turn to more detailed models for this information.

The equipartition principle was applied to this problem by Rayleigh and Jeans. They suggested that in the cavity producing the blackbody radiation this radiation not only is in equilibrium with the walls of the solid but can be analyzed in terms of standing waves of electric and magnetic fields in the enclosure. They calculated the number of modes of free vibrations in the aether in an enclosure of a given volume and, by assuming that each mode of vibration contributes kT to the total energy, calculated the energy density.

The situation with electromagnetic radiation in an enclosure is somewhat similar to the standing waves set up in an organ pipe. In both cases there are expected to be a great many possible modes of vibration, corresponding to fundamental vibrations and many overtones. Although we will not derive the equations here, Rayleigh and Jeans showed that for electromagnetic radiation in an enclosure the number of modes of vibration of the system of waves, per unit volume in the enclosure, in the wavelength range λ to $\lambda + d\lambda$ is

$$dn = \frac{8\pi \, d\lambda}{\lambda^4}. \tag{2-18}$$

The number of modes of vibration times kT should then be the amount of energy per unit volume in this wavelength range:

$$\rho_\lambda \, d\lambda = 8\pi kT\lambda^{-4} \, d\lambda,$$

where $\rho_\lambda \, d\lambda$ is the amount of radiant energy per unit volume in the range between λ and $\lambda + d\lambda$.

The Rayleigh-Jeans formula agrees with experiment at long wavelengths, but it predicts that at short wavelengths the energy density should increase rapidly to infinity, which it definitely does not (Fig. 2–7).

By a somewhat different process Wien arrived at a formula, based on his ideas about the process of absorption and emission, which had the form

$$\rho_\lambda = c_1\lambda^{-5}e^{-c_2/\lambda T},$$

c_1 and c_2 being constants to be evaluated from the experimental data. This relation was successful in the low-wavelength region below the maximum in the spectral distribution, but failed at higher wavelengths (Fig. 2–7). Thus, using accepted views of the equipartition principle and electromagnetic theory it was not possible to construct an equation which properly described the dependence of radiation energy density on wavelength.

2.6 PLANCK'S QUANTUM HYPOTHESIS

The unsatisfactory state of affairs between theory and observation was attacked in 1900 by the German physicist Max Planck,[5] who set out to find a mathematical expression which would reproduce the measured spectral distribution of a blackbody. Planck, guided by electro-

---

[5] Planck, *Ann. Physik,* **4,** 553 (1901).

magnetic theory, felt that the key to the problem lay in the nature of the oscillations in the solid that gave rise to the radiation in the first place. In our heated enclosure there should be electrical oscillators of all frequencies, and the number of oscillators at any given frequency and with a given energy should determine the energy in the radiation field at that frequency. He felt that an electric oscillator could affect only radiation at the same frequency. The problem was to find the average energy of an oscillator at a given temperature. Classical theory had predicted that the average energy would be equal to kT but Planck rejected the equipartition principle in this case since it obviously gave erroneous results.

We have seen that the total energy of a harmonic oscillator involves a kinetic-energy term and a potential-energy term (Eq. 2–15). Elementary theory also gives for the frequency of vibration

$$\nu = \frac{1}{2\pi} \sqrt{\frac{k}{m}}.$$

Statistical arguments give an expression for the number of oscillators, dN, that have their values of q and p lying in any given range of magnitude dq and dp in thermal equilibrium. This equation is similar to the Maxwell distribution. It is

$$dN = NCe^{-\epsilon/kT} \, dq \, dp, \quad (2\text{–}19)$$

where ϵ is the energy of a single oscillator.

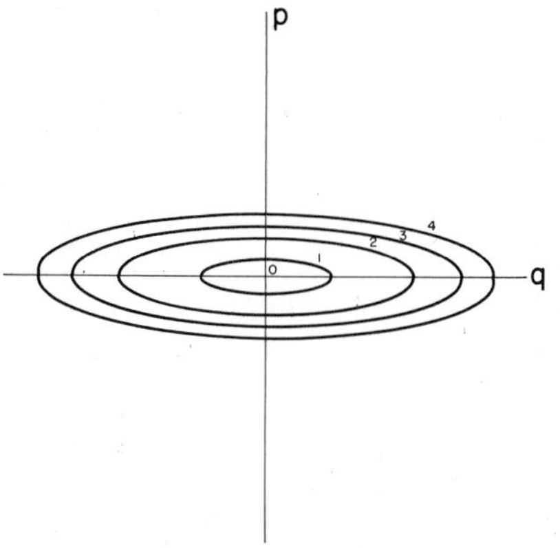

Fig. 2–8. Constant-energy ellipses for a linear harmonic oscillator in phase space with rings of equal areas.

It is convenient to discuss the motions of a harmonic oscillator in phase space (Sec. 2.3). We have seen that in this situation there will be only two dimensions in phase space, and the energy will remain constant in the absence of disturbing forces. In addition we have seen that a path of constant energy in phase space is an ellipse for the harmonic oscillator. If, therefore, we consider the element of area between two ellipses corresponding to ϵ and $\epsilon + d\epsilon$ we shall be considering an increment in energy rather than in coordinate and momentum, and we are primarily interested in energy (Fig. 2–8).

The entire area inside an ellipse of constant energy in phase space is easily seen from the geometry to be

$$A = \pi p_m q_m,$$

where p_m and q_m are the semiaxes of the ellipse. These, of course, can be found immediately from Eq. (2–15) since at $q = 0$, $p = p_m$, while at $p = 0$, $q = q_m$, so that

$$p_m = \sqrt{2m\epsilon}, \qquad q_m = \sqrt{\frac{2\epsilon}{k}}$$

and

$$A = 2\pi\epsilon \sqrt{\frac{m}{k}} = \frac{\epsilon}{\nu}.$$

The area of a ring corresponding to the increment $d\epsilon$ is therefore

$$dA = \frac{d\epsilon}{\nu}.$$

Since $dA = dp\, dq$, and letting $C_1 = C/\nu$, we obtain from Eq. (2–19)

$$dN = NC_1 e^{-\epsilon/kT}\, d\epsilon, \qquad (2\text{–}20)$$

which is the number of oscillators out of the total number N that have energy between ϵ and $\epsilon + d\epsilon$ when in thermal equilibrium at the temperature T.

The total energy E of all N oscillators is the sum of the individual energies of the oscillators, and E/N is the average energy per oscillator. The equipartition principle simply assumed that this procedure was not necessary since it would automatically be kT. Planck, however, discarded this assumption and instead made a startling innovation.

Classically there was no reason why one could not assume any value for ϵ from zero to infinity. The whole of physics was based on the ability to transfer energy from one system to another in any amount, so that the energy of a system could vary continuously through all ranges. Planck, however, assumed that the energy of an oscillator cannot vary continuously, but must take on one of the discrete set of values 0, $h\nu$, $2h\nu$, . . . , $nh\nu$, . . . , where n is an integer, h is a constant, and ν is the frequency of the oscillator. This assumption has a drastic effect on the calculated average energy of the system.

In terms of phase space this assumption amounts to dividing the space into a series of elliptical rings such that the area of each ring is equal to a constant h and each ellipse on the inner boundary of a ring is one representing an energy

$$\epsilon = nh\nu = A\nu, \qquad (2\text{–}21)$$

the total area inside an elliptical ring outside ellipse number n being $A = nh$. This corresponds to Planck's hypothesis since the range of energy represented by points between the boundaries of one ring is

$$\Delta\epsilon = \nu\, \Delta A = h\nu.$$

The number of oscillators represented by points in ring number n is the integral of dN in Eq. (2–20) over the range $\Delta\epsilon$ within the ring,

$$N_n = NC_1 \int_{\Delta\epsilon} e^{-\epsilon/kT} \, d\epsilon,$$

and if h and $\Delta\epsilon$ are small, we can treat the exponential as a constant equal to its value at a point on the inner boundary of the ring, so that

$$N_n = NC_1 e^{-\epsilon/kT} \int_{\Delta\epsilon} d\epsilon = NC_1 e^{-\epsilon/kT} \Delta\epsilon = N_0 e^{-nh\nu/kT},$$

where we have replaced $NC_1 \Delta\epsilon$ by N_0 and ϵ by its equivalent from Eq. (2–21). N_0 can be seen to represent the number of oscillators in the inner ring (which is simply an elliptical area) $n = 0$.

The summation which will obtain the total number of oscillators is seen then to be

$$\begin{aligned} N &= N_0 + N_1 + \cdots + N_n + \cdots \\ &= N_0(1 + e^{-h\nu/kT} + \cdots + e^{-nh\nu/kT} + \cdots). \end{aligned}$$

Since the series $1 + x + x^2 + \cdots$ has the sum $1/(1 - x)$, N becomes

$$N = \frac{N_0}{1 - e^{-h\nu/kT}}.$$

To find the total energy of the oscillators we must know the contribution by the oscillators in each ring in phase space. This is simply the number of oscillators in the ring times the energy of an oscillator in the ring, and since h and $\Delta\epsilon$ have been assumed small, the energy of any oscillator in the ring is the energy of the inner boundary ellipse $= nh\nu$. Therefore

$$\begin{aligned} E &= (N_0 \times 0) + (N_0 e^{-h\nu/kT} \times h\nu) + \cdots + (N_0 e^{-nh\nu/kT} \times nh\nu) + \cdots \\ &= N_0 h\nu e^{-h\nu/kT}(1 + \cdots + n e^{-(n-1)h\nu/kT} + \cdots). \end{aligned}$$

This series is of the form $1 + 2x + 3x^2 + \cdots = 1/(1 - x)^2$, so that

$$E = \frac{N_0 h\nu e^{-h\nu/kT}}{(1 - e^{-h\nu/kT})^2}.$$

The average energy of an oscillator is therefore

$$\bar{\epsilon} = \frac{E}{N} = \frac{h\nu e^{-h\nu/kT}}{1 - e^{-h\nu/kT}} = \frac{h\nu}{e^{h\nu/kT} - 1}. \tag{2–22}$$

We might note that this result follows in a similar manner from the Maxwell-Boltzmann law by assuming that the states which are integral multiples of $h\nu$ are the only ones possible and summing the finite states rather than integrating over a continuous range of energies. Note also that in the limit of a long wavelength (low frequency) the average energy obtained by Planck approaches kT as in the classical partition principle.

The energy density of the radiation can be found readily by multiplying the number of modes of vibration per unit volume in the radiation field previously determined in Eq. (2–18) by Eq. (2–22) instead of kT, to obtain

$$\rho_\lambda \, d\lambda = \frac{8\pi \, d\lambda}{\lambda^4} \frac{h\nu}{e^{h\nu/kT} - 1},$$

which on substitution of $\nu = c/\lambda$ results in Planck's distribution formula,

$$\rho_\lambda \, d\lambda = \frac{8\pi ch}{\lambda^5} \frac{1}{e^{ch/\lambda kT} - 1} \, d\lambda. \tag{2–23}$$

The Planck distribution formula can be expressed also in terms of an energy density of radiation that has a frequency lying between ν and $\nu + d\nu$. This energy density is identical with that in (2–23) but is formulated in terms of frequency rather than wavelength, i.e., $\rho_\lambda \, d\lambda = \rho_\nu \, d\nu$. Since $\lambda\nu = c$, a constant, it follows that $\lambda \, d\nu + \nu \, d\lambda = 0$. If we neglect signs and assume both $d\nu$ and $d\lambda$ to be positive quantities, we have

$$d\lambda = \frac{\lambda}{\nu} \, d\nu.$$

Substituting $\rho_\nu \, d\nu$ for $\rho_\lambda \, d\lambda$, $d\nu \, \lambda/\nu$ for $d\lambda$, and c/ν for λ, (2–23) becomes

$$\rho_\nu \, d\nu = \frac{8\pi h\nu^3}{c^3} \left(\frac{1}{e^{h\nu/kT} - 1} \right) d\nu. \tag{2–24}$$

These results agree exactly with measurement. It can be shown that in the limit of small wavelength Eq. (2–23) has the form of Wien's equation, while for long wavelengths it agrees with the Rayleigh-Jeans formula. In addition, Planck's equation for the spectral distribution of blackbody radiation gives the Stefan-Boltzmann relation and Wien's displacement law, so that it is consistent with the thermodynamic requirements. It can also be used to derive expressions for the constants in these relations plus such quantities as radiation pressure.

The constant h, now known as Planck's constant, was evaluated from the experimental data to be about 6×10^{-27} erg sec. It has since been found to occur in connection with many atomic and molecular phenomena, and a variety of accurate methods for its determination have given as a reliable value $h = 6.6256 \times 10^{-27}$ erg sec.

The most important aspect of Planck's theory is that he was led, not by a logical extension of current physical theory, but rather by the necessity to agree with observation, to the assumption that the energy of the oscillators in a solid cannot vary continuously, but can only assume certain definite energies which are a function of the frequency of the oscillation. In addition, then, energy cannot be absorbed or emitted continuously, but only in definite amounts likewise equal to multiples of $h\nu$. It was assumed that an oscillator remains in a state of constant energy (a stationary state) until such energy has been absorbed or emitted. This unit of energy was called by Planck a quantum of energy. The quantum concept was a drastic revision of man's thinking about matter and energy.

2.7 THE PHOTOELECTRIC EFFECT

A phenomenon familiar to most persons from its practical applications is the emission of electrons from the surface of a metal when the metal is irradiated with light. The emission is sufficiently great in the case of some metals that a significant current of electrons is produced. We will not go into the details of how measurements of these effects are made but will point out some of the important relationships which have been found.

The electron current and the energy of the electrons emitted depend on several factors. One of these is the intensity of the bombarding radiation. It is found experimentally that as the intensity of light falling on the metal surface increases, the electron current increases (that is, the number of electrons leaving the surface per second increases), but the maximum energy of the emitted electrons is not affected. We should expect, since we have a collection of electrons, that the energies of the electrons are actually distributed over some range of energies; and this is observed. However, so long as the spectral distribution of the radiation is not changed, the maximum energy observed is not affected by a change in the intensity of the radiation.

A second relationship of interest is the fact that the energies of the electrons are a function of the frequency of the radiation; more exactly, the maximum energy of the electrons is a linear function of the frequency of the radiation, and electrons cease to be emitted below a certain frequency ν_0. It is of considerable interest to find that the frequency below which no electrons are emitted is characteristic of the metal, but the slope of the energy vs. frequency line is independent of the substance studied (Fig. 2–9). Thus it is possible to express this behavior by a linear equation of the form

$$\tfrac{1}{2}mv_m{}^2 = h(\nu - \nu_0) = h\nu - h\nu_0 = h\nu - \omega_0$$

where v_m is the maximum velocity observed for the electrons, ω_0 is called the work function of the metal, and h is found to be the same numerical constant as the h introduced by Planck in his theory of blackbody radiation.

Classical electromagnetic theory is powerless to explain this behavior. One would expect, for example, that since a radiation field contains energy, radiation of increased intensity and therefore increased energy would increase the energy of the emitted electrons. In addition, there is no reason why the maximum energy should be a linear function of frequency. It is also difficult to see how the energy of a radiation field could be concentrated in a small enough space to affect one electron as observed. An explanation was given by Einstein[6] in 1905 that had startling conclusions similar to Planck's. Einstein reasoned that not only is energy absorbed from radiation by a solid in discrete quanta of energy, but it is transmitted via the radiation in such quanta. Einstein called these quanta of radiation "photons," and on the basis of Planck's work and the requirements of the photoelectric effect stated that the

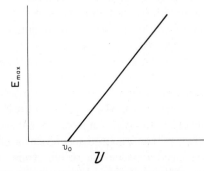

Fig. 2–9. Dependence of the maximum energies observed for photoelectrons on the frequency of the incident radiation.

energy of a photon of radiation is proportional to the frequency of the radiation:

$$\epsilon = h\nu.$$

On this basis Einstein explained the photoelectric effect in the following manner. There are electrons in a metal which can be removed if they gain sufficient energy. Radiation provides energy in the form of quanta, each of which has energy $h\nu$. If the energy of these photons is not enough to remove the electrons, there will be no electron current. As the frequency of the radiation is increased, however, the quanta have greater energies, and eventually a frequency is reached at which the energy of a photon is great enough to eject an electron. This quantity is represented by the work function and depends on the particular metal. Since the energy of the photons is proportional to frequency, the energies of the electrons emitted by successively higher-frequency radiation should also be proportional to frequency. In addition, a beam of greater intensity will have more photons and hence will be able to eject more electrons,

[6] Einstein, *Ann. Physik*, **17**, 132 (1905).

but since the energy of the photons depends only on frequency, the number of photons will have no effect on the energies of the electrons, but only on the number of electrons. Thus the maximum energy of an ejected photoelectron is equal to the energy of the absorbed photon less the work function (the amount of energy required to eject the electron), while the electron current depends on the number of photons absorbed or the intensity of the beam.

It should be apparent that a number of conceptual difficulties have arisen. When Planck made his assertion that the energies of a set of oscillators are restricted to certain fixed states, he was imposing an unfamiliar condition on what had hitherto been considered a continuous variable. The postulate by Einstein that energy is transmitted by light quanta, or photons, rather than continuously brings up even more problems. If light is corpuscular in this way, what is the significance of the frequency or wavelength concepts? And how can we use such quantities as frequency to calculate the energy of these quanta? Finally, how can one explain such phenomena as interference fringes, which require wave behavior, if radiation is corpuscular?

These problems raise many interesting philosophical questions, and it is hoped that subsequently we shall be able to make clearer the meaning of these conflicts. Perhaps we can indicate part of the difficulty by observing that the theoretical framework which we erect to explain a phenomenon depends on many factors. The nature of the experiments themselves may tend to accent some aspects of nature to the exclusion of others. Also, our mathematical equations usually are based in part on models that rely on familiar conceptual quantities that we experience in everyday existence, such as the motions of bodies and the behavior of water waves on the surface of a pond. Even if the model was not conceived first, the appearance of equations in certain forms leads us to think in terms of these familiar models. The extension of these concepts into a submicroscopic region which we cannot actually observe directly is dangerous unless we are careful not to be bound by literal pictures at all times. We will elaborate on these questions again.

2.8 ATOMIC SPECTRA AND BOHR'S THEORY OF THE ATOM

We have seen that when a solid is elevated to high temperatures, a continuous spectrum of radiation is emitted. In addition, the spectral distribution does not tell us anything about the chemical nature of the solid since it depends only on temperature, and not on the particular solid. However, there are a number of other phenomena involving the emission and absorption of radiation that are of considerably more chemical interest.

As early as 1750 Melvill noticed that when different gases were placed in a flame, different colors of light were emitted. In addition he found that if the emitted radiation were passed through a prism, there was not obtained the familiar continuous spectrum of color, but instead there were spots of colors with gaps of darkness between them. He further found that the locations of the spots in the spectrum were characteristic of the substances being "excited" by the flame. More precise optical techniques involving focusing the beam of radiation and passing it through slits showed that these spots are actually very narrow lines occurring at characteristic frequencies or wavelengths in the spectrum (Fig. 2–10).

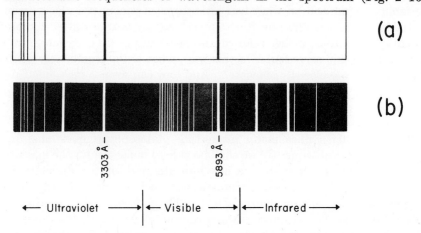

Fig. 2–10.   (a) Absorption and (b) emission spectra of sodium vapor.

It soon became possible to identify the presence of elements by the presence of certain lines in the emission spectrum, as by the closely spaced doublet of yellow lines occurring at 5890 Å in the sodium spectrum. By 1860 Kirchhoff and Bunsen had discovered two new elements, rubidium and cesium, by the presence of spectral lines which were unreported for the known elements, and the following decades saw repeated such discoveries several times.

Another kind of discontinuous line spectrum was also discovered. It was observed that on detailed examination the continuous spectrum obtained from sunlight actually contained a set of dark lines (Fig. 2–10). Fraunhofer was able to show that if sodium vapor is placed in the path of a beam of continuous radiation, dark lines appear in the continuous spectrum at the frequencies expected for the emission spectrum of sodium. Apparently, then, the relatively cool atmospheres around the sun and other stars are able to absorb some of the continuous radiation coming from the hotter interior, to produce the dark-line spectra. In this way the species present in the sun's atmosphere could be detected.

As spectral techniques became more refined and more and more data were accumulated, attempts were made to find regularities in the emission and absorption spectra of the elements. Although striking regularities and similarities appeared to be present in many spectra, it was not until 1885 that Balmer found a mathematical expression which would accurately express the observed wavelengths in the prominent emission spectrum of hydrogen in the visible region (Fig. 2–11). The formula Balmer constructed to follow the wavelengths of four lines measured by Ångström is

$$\lambda = b\left(\frac{n^2}{n^2 - 2^2}\right),$$

where b is a constant determined empirically, and n an integer. Not only did the equation fit the lines then known, but it also accurately

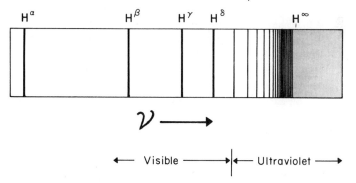

Fig. 2–11. The Balmer series of lines of the emission spectrum of hydrogen atoms.

predicted the positions of many additional lines that were subsequently found to agree very closely with the equation. The particular spectral lines following Balmer's equation are now familiarly known as the Balmer series of hydrogen.

Balmer also predicted that there might be other series of lines corresponding to the replacement of 2^2 in his equation by other numbers, 1^2, 3^2, 4^2, etc. It was indeed found there were several other series of lines in the hydrogen spectrum occurring in the infrared and ultraviolet regions which could be accurately described by a modification of Balmer's equation made by Rydberg, the equation being of the form

$$\bar{\nu} = \frac{1}{\lambda} = R_H\left(\frac{1}{n_1{}^2} - \frac{1}{n_2{}^2}\right),$$

where n_1 and n_2 are both integers, the former being held constant for a given series of lines. R_H, the Rydberg constant, can be determined experimentally. The reciprocal of the wavelength, $\bar{\nu}$, is a frequency measure in units of cm^{-1}, which is convenient to use in spectroscopic measurements. Studies by Rydberg and others disclosed a number of such relationships for spectra of other atoms and were successful in accounting for and predicting many spectral features. An understanding of the cause of line spectra was to wait, however, on further developments in atomic theory.

Toward the end of the 1890's Thomson discovered the electron, and within a few years the charge and mass of this elementary particle had been determined, as well as those of the positively charged proton. Finally, just before the first World War, experiments by Geiger and Marsden[7] and an analysis by Rutherford[8] produced strong evidence that the structure of atoms was basically a small positively charged nucleus about which negative electrons moved, these electrons being at immense distances from the nucleus (10^{-8} cm) in comparison with the sizes of the particles themselves (10^{-13} cm).

This model, although consistent with experimental evidence, faced grave difficulties with electromagnetic theory. The latter requires that an electric charge undergoing acceleration, such as the electrons in curvilinear paths around a nucleus are undergoing, must lose energy by radiating it away. As energy is lost, the electron will then spiral closer and closer to the nucleus, eventually collapsing completely with a continuous emission of radiation during this process. The theory indicated that the lifetime of an atom should be only 10^{-8} sec. Not only does the apparent finite lifetime of atoms preclude these predictions, but the precise line structure of atomic spectra also is in disagreement with the prediction of continuous radiation.

An answer was suggested in 1913 by Bohr,[9] who made what we would now consider a natural extension of the ideas forwarded by Planck and Einstein concerning radiation and the energy of stationary states. Bohr made three assumptions to bring the known facts into line:

1. The electron in a hydrogen atom revolves around the nucleus in a circular orbit. While in this orbit the energy of the system is constant (a stationary state). The electron will remain in this stationary state unless energy of exactly the correct amount is absorbed or emitted.

2. The orbits in which the electron can revolve are limited to those of such diameter that the angular momentum of the electron is an integral multiple of $h/2\pi \ (= \hbar)$.

3. Radiation is emitted or absorbed in the form of quanta of radiation such that the energy of the photon is exactly equal to the difference in the energies

[7] Geiger and Marsden, *Phil. Mag.*, **25**, 605 (1913).
[8] Rutherford, *Phil. Mag.*, **21**, 669 (1911).
[9] Bohr, *Phil. Mag.*, **26**, 1 (1913).

of the two stationary states between which the transition has occurred, and also is related to the frequency of the radiation by the equation

$$\epsilon = h\nu = E_2 - E_1, \tag{2-25}$$

where h is the constant of Planck and Einstein.

From these postulates it is possible to solve for the energies of the possible stationary states and for the frequencies of the radiation that can be absorbed or emitted. Assuming the charge on the nucleus to be Z times the unit electronic charge, and assuming the electron to be revolving in an orbit of radius a around the nucleus, Coulomb's law gives the attractive force between the nucleus and electron to be

$$F = \frac{Ze^2}{a^2}.$$

In order that the motion of the electron remain circular with constant radius a this force must be exactly balanced by the centrifugal force on the rotating electron:

$$F = ma\omega^2,$$

where ω is the angular velocity, so that

$$ma\omega^2 = \frac{Ze^2}{a^2}. \tag{2-26}$$

Bohr's second postulate requires that the angular momentum of this electron be an integral multiple of $h/2\pi$:

$$p_\theta = ma^2\omega = \frac{nh}{2\pi}, \quad n = 1, 2, 3, \ldots \tag{2-27}$$

Combining Eqs. (2–26) and (2–27) to eliminate ω yields

$$a = \frac{n^2h^2}{4\pi^2me^2Z}.$$

The potential energy of the electron, by virtue of its position a distance a from the positively charged nucleus, is

$$V = -\frac{Ze^2}{a}, \tag{2-28}$$

and its kinetic energy, by virtue of its rotational motion, is

$$T = \tfrac{1}{2}mv^2 = \tfrac{1}{2}ma^2\omega^2 = \tfrac{1}{2}\frac{Ze^2}{a},$$

so that the total energy is given by

$$E_n = T + V = -\tfrac{1}{2}\frac{Ze^2}{a} = -\frac{2\pi^2me^4Z^2}{h^2n^2}.$$

We again have a situation in which only certain stationary states are possible, and investigation of this relation shows that the most stable state is that with the smallest value of n, $n = 1$, this being the state of lowest (in this case most negative) energy. It can be verified that by Bohr's third postulate the difference in energy between two stationary states gives, for the frequency of the radiation absorbed, the same equation as (2–25), the Rydberg constant having the form

$$R = \frac{2\pi^2 m e^4}{ch^3}.$$

Insertion of the values of m, c, e, and h into this equation gives the same numerical value for R as spectral measurements. An additional interesting calculation gives, for the radius a of the most stable state ($n = 1$), $a = .527$ Å, which agrees well with estimates of atomic radii from kinetic theory.

The energy states predicted by Bohr's theory for hydrogen are shown in Fig. 2–12 with the transitions corresponding to some of the observed spectral series indicated. Since the initial and final energies in each transition are stationary states, then the energy of the quanta of light absorbed or emitted must be of definite frequencies; and therefore distinct line spectra are observed, rather than continuous radiation. By our usual definition of electrostatic energy, as in Eq. (2–23), the zero of energy is taken when the charges are separated an infinite distance, so that the more stable conditions when the charges approach one another are of lower (more negative) energy. By this convention, any energy is possible above zero, but this corresponds to separate protons and electrons, with their own kinetic energies of motion, and not to a stable atom.

The most important feature of Bohr's theory is the postulate of stationary energy states which are quantized. Again, it was possible to agree with observation only by assuming that energy is not absorbed continuously but in quantized amounts, and that the system itself can exist only in certain stationary energy states.

Bohr's formulation of atomic structure can be extended somewhat as was done by Sommerfeld[10] and Wilson.[11] It is not necessary to specify circular orbits. Instead, the quantization rule takes the general form

$$\oint p_i \, dq_i = nh,$$

where p_i is the generalized momentum associated with the generalized coordinate q_i and the integral is taken over one complete cycle of the

[10] Sommerfeld, *Ann. Physik*, **51**, 1 (1916).
[11] Wilson, *Phil. Mag.*, **29**, 795 (1915).

motion.   This extension allows elliptical as well as circular orbits and introduces in its final results the quantization of the component of angular momentum along a given direction as well as the quantization of the total angular momentum and quantization of the energy.   The details

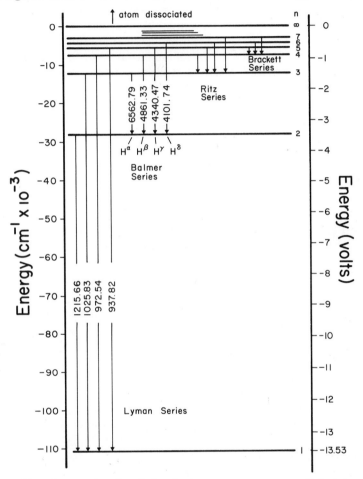

Fig. 2–12. Energy levels of the hydrogen atom as predicted by Bohr's theory, with some of the transitions observed in the hydrogen atom spectrum. Energy is measured as zero at infinite separation of the electron and proton. All positive energies are allowed and form a continuum of states. These correspond to the possible kinetic energies of the free electron and proton.

of this method applied to the hydrogen atom are given in several of the references cited at the end of this chapter.

The Bohr-Sommerfeld picture of atomic structure was satisfactory for only a short time.   It was able to predict the spectra of hydrogen and hydrogen-like ions (ions with only one electron) but failed to reproduce the spectra of more complex systems, and even failed to account for fine structure observed in the hydrogen-like spectra. It was, however, the turning point in our concepts of atomic and molecular systems. No longer did it seem possible to doubt that stationary states remain undisturbed until energy in the form of quanta of exactly the correct energy enter or leave the system. As we shall see, quantum phenomena are primarily of concern on the atomic-molecular scale and eventually become indistinguishable experimentally on a larger scale from the results predicted by classical physics.

2.9 MATTER WAVES

The simultaneous wavelike and corpuscular nature of light appeared to be here to stay in the 1920's. In making comparisons between the nature of light and matter, de Broglie suggested that we might well expect such dual character for material particles as well as for electromagnetic radiation.

If light is assumed to consist of photons, the momentum of a photon would be its mass times its velocity or, since $E = h\nu = mc^2$, simply mc or $h\nu/c$, which is also equal to h/λ. Why, de Broglie argued, cannot a mass of momentum p also have associated with it a wave of wavelength h/λ? This suggestion found verification in the experiments of Davisson and Germer,[12] who showed that a beam of electrons can be diffracted by a crystal in exactly the same way that electromagnetic x-rays are diffracted (Fig. 2–13). Their work showed that the wavelength associated with electrons of known energy agreed with de Broglie's prediction. Thus matter as well as radiation exhibits both corpuscular and wavelike characteristics.

The eventual explanation of this behavior has been in terms of probability arguments. That is, the wavelike nature is a mathematical explanation forced upon us by the results of certain experiments and in reality represents the fact that we cannot describe the system exactly, but can only find the most probable values of different quantities in terms of how many times a certain value will be measured if many measurements are made. In those experiments in which we can use a corpuscular explanation certain quantities such as position can be specified precisely, but in those experiments described by wavelike equations we have lost the ability to specify these quantities exactly. A diffracted electron beam, in other words, is consistent with the idea that we cannot predict exactly where an electron will be found after passing through the crystal, but from the diffraction pattern we can predict the probability

[12] Davisson and Germer, *Phys. Rev.*, **30**, 705 (1927).

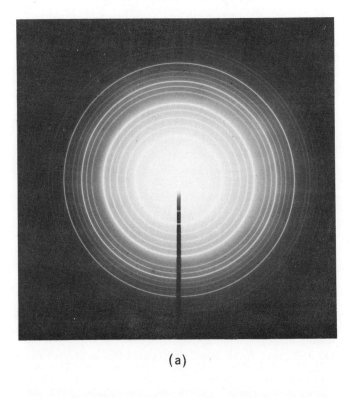

(a)

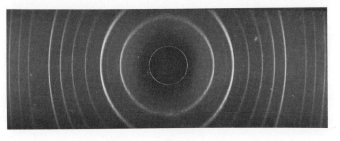

(b)

Fig. 2–13. Comparison of x-ray and electron diffraction: (a) electrons diffracted (Thomson type) by thallous chloride; (b) x-ray diffracted (Debye-Scherrer type) by thallous chloride. Wavelength of electrons .055 Å, of x-rays 1.54 Å. (From Goble and Baker, *Elements of Modern Physics*, Ronald Press Co., 1962, p. 240, courtesy of Ernest F. Fullam, Inc.)

that it will be found at a certain point. We shall see that for many atomic and molecular phenomena there is much information that cannot be obtained exactly, even by precise measurement, and we must resort to probability language to describe the system.

SUPPLEMENTARY REFERENCES

Introductory

HOLTON, G., and D. H. D. ROLLER, *Foundations of Modern Physical Science*, Addison-Wesley Publishing Co., Reading, Mass., 1958.

CHRISTIANSEN, G. S., and P. H. GARRETT, *Structure and Change*, W. H. Freeman and Co., San Francisco, 1960.

    Both the above texts give excellent accounts of the historical and logical development of concepts and methods in physics and chemistry. Highly recommended.

Intermediate

BORN, M., *Atomic Physics*, 6th ed., Blackie and Son, Ltd., Glasgow, 1958. A lucid survey of modern physics.

GOBLE, A. T., and D. K. BAKER, *Elements of Modern Physics*, Ronald Press Co., New York, 1962. Contains excellent discussion of momentum, angular momentum, and electrical and magnetic phenomena.

RICHTMYER, F. K., and E. H. KENNARD, *Introduction to Modern Physics*, 4th ed., McGraw-Hill Book Co., New York, 1947. Contains fairly detailed descriptions of the early experiments and theoretical problems that led to quantum mechanics. Although more recent editions are available, the volume cited is more detailed in the areas pertinent to this chapter.

PAULING, L., and E. B. WILSON, *Introduction to Quantum Mechanics*, McGraw-Hill Book Co., New York, 1935. A classic work on quantum mechanics with introductory chapters on classical physics and early quantum theory.

SLATER, J. C., *Introduction to Chemical Physics*, McGraw-Hill Book Co., New York, 1929. This text reviews many areas of common interest in physics and chemistry.

Advanced

GOLDSTEIN, H., *Classical Mechanics*, Addison-Wesley Publishing Co., Reading, Mass., 1950. An oft-quoted text on mechanics.

SLATER, J. C., and N. H. FRANK, *Introduction to Theoretical Physics*, McGraw-Hill Book Co., New York, 1939. A unified account of mechanics, electricity and magnetism, and quantum mechanics.

PROBLEMS

2–1. Verify that Planck's radiation formula is consistent with Wien's displacement law and with the Stefan-Boltzmann relation.

2–2. Compare for a blackbody at 3000°K the ratio of its spectral emittance at 10,000 Å (infrared) to its emittance at 5000 Å (visible). How will this ratio change with increasing temperature?

2–3. If λ_{max} for sunlight is 4650 Å, what is the sun's approximate surface temperature? The star Antares has a surface temperature around 2500°K. What is its λ_{max}, and how will its color compare with that of the sun?

2–4. Electrons are not ejected from tungsten metal by light with a wavelength more than 2700 Å. What is the maximum kinetic energy of electrons ejected by light of wavelength equal to 1700 Å?

2–5. Calculate the value of the Rydberg constant for hydrogen as predicted from Bohr's theory. How does it compare with the experimental constant obtained spectroscopically?

2–6. Show that when an excited hydrogen gas atom goes from the state with $n = 1000$ to $n = 999$, the frequency of the light radiated is approximately the same as the frequency of the orbital motion of the electron as expected classically.

2–7. Verify that (2–22) approaches kT as ν becomes small.

2–8. Show that the kinetic energy in any circular Coulomb orbit is equal in magnitude, but opposite in sign, to the total energy. What, then, is the relationship between the kinetic energy and the potential energy?

2–9. Show the velocity of the electron in the lowest Bohr orbit is $2\pi e^2/h$ and express this as a fraction of the velocity of light (v/c is known as the fine-structure constant and appears in many other problems).

2–10. Solve, in the same manner as used for the H atom, the problem of a satellite rotating about the earth. A typical period of rotation is about 90 minutes. Are quantum effects important here?

2–11. Calculate the wave number difference between the H Balmer series lines for ordinary hydrogen and for deuterium. This is the means by which the hydrogen isotopes were first detected. Also, calculate the difference in terms of wavelengths. Note this difference as contrasted with the separation of the lines in the series.

2–12. Calculate the radius and energy of the electron in the first Bohr orbit of Li^{++}, and compare these values with those for hydrogen.

2–13. What is the wavelength associated with an electron that has been accelerated through a potential of 100 v? 100,000 v?

2–14. What is the wavelength of a proton of energy 100,000 ev?

3

The Principles of Quantum Mechanics

3.1 THE STRUCTURE OF QUANTUM MECHANICS

In the preceding chapter we outlined some of the important formulations upon which classical physics was based. We saw that in a number of important problems involving phenomena on the atomic and molecular scale classical physics was unable to describe observed behavior adequately. Such difficulties were particularly apparent in situations in which energy in the form of electromagnetic radiation was absorbed or emitted by atoms and molecules. The only means of reconciling theory with experiment was to break away from the fundamental postulates of classical physics and reformulate them so as to be consistent with all processes.

The first steps in this revolution were taken by Planck, Einstein, and Bohr, who introduced the revolutionary idea that atomic systems remained in stationary states of constant energy and that only a selected number of such stationary states were possible. In addition, an atom remained in a particular stationary state until exactly the correct amount of energy in the form of a quantum of radiation was absorbed or ejected by the atom. The energy of this quantum of radiation was required to be exactly the amount necessary to change the energy of the system from that of the initial stationary state to that of the final stationary state. Quanta of any other energy could not be absorbed or released. In addition, it was postulated that the energy of this photon was directly related to the frequency of the radiation by the Planck constant.

These early formulations were limited in scope primarily because they tacked on to classical physics certain limitations, which were required to explain particular phenomena. They did not involve, however, a complete reformulation of the basis of physics, and thus could not themselves completely cope with other effects. Bohr's theory of atomic structure, even as expanded by Sommerfeld, could not account for more complex atomic systems than hydrogen and hydrogen-like ions and was helpless in explaining molecular stability. The real breakthrough in this development came in the 1920's, when physics was completely reformulated beginning with the basic postulates; this was the birth of quantum mechanics.

Just as thermodynamics and classical mechanics are based on a small set of "true" postulates which are assumed to describe accurately the behavior of the universe or parts thereof, a number of defined functions, and a logical mathematical development of relations between them, so also is quantum mechanics a postulatory system which is assumed to be valid so long as it can satisfactorily explain natural events and does not make contradictory predictions. The original construction of quantum mechanics required much insight into the significance of deviations from classical physics and the mathematical nature of the assumptions that were made to "doctor up" the classical ideas. Such problems as the wave-particle duality that had appeared both for electromagnetic radiation and for atomic particles suggested certain approaches based on the types of equations common to each viewpoint. The mathematical foundations of classical mechanics and electromagnetic theory were searched for generalities and analogies which could help in the sought-for structure. As a result of these methods the formulations of quantum mechanics which evolved depend strongly on the long-established formulations of classical physics, but, as we shall see, depart from them in several fundamental ways.

Typical of the situation with postulatory disciplines, there is more than one formulation of quantum mechanics. Each is based on slightly different assumptions and differs in its mathematical techniques. Each serves a usefulness that varies with the systems under study. The two most familiar systems of quantum mechanics are those first erected by Schrödinger[1] and Heisenberg.[2] The former is strongly dependent on analogies with the equations of wave motion and is handled largely with the familiar techniques of partial differential equations. Heisenberg's system is based on the mathematical properties of matrices and develops its results by means of matrix algebra. There are many similarities between them, of course, and the terminology of quantum mechanics today is actually a mixture of the language and techniques of both viewpoints as well as others. Because matrix methods are generally less familiar to the average chemistry student, we shall be concerned with quantum mechanics in the form originated by Schrödinger.

[1] Schrödinger, *Ann. Physik*, **79**, 361, 489, 734; **80**, 437; **81**, 109 (1926).
[2] Heisenberg, *Z. Physik*, **33**, 879 (1925); Born, Heisenberg, and Jordan, *Z. Physik*, **35**, 557 (1926).

We will begin, then, by considering a convenient set of basic postulates and techniques and will then investigate the interesting results that are obtained when they are applied to atomic and molecular systems.

3.2 THE STATE FUNCTION AND ITS SIGNIFICANCE

The first postulate which we will introduce is an immediate departure from the spirit of classical physics. Let us first state the postulate and then elaborate on its significance.

Postulate Ia. *The state of a system is described as fully as possible by a function* $\Psi(q_1, q_2, \ldots, t)$ *which is a function of the coordinates and time. This function, called the state function or wave function, must be well-behaved, i.e., single-valued, finite, and continuous.*

In classical physics we were content to describe a system by simply listing all the coordinates involved and specifying all the velocities or

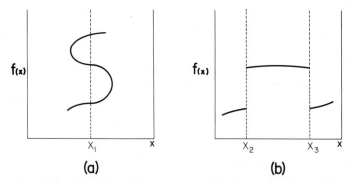

(a)   **(b)**

Fig. 3–1. Examples of poorly-behaved functions: (a) a multivalued function which has three solutions for $x = x_1$. (b) A function which is discontinuous at $x = x_2$ and $x = x_3$.

momenta so that we could accurately predict at some future time exactly what the coordinates and velocities would be under the influence of a given set of forces. In quantum mechanics, however, we are going to endeavor to construct a single mathematical function which contains inherently all the information it is possible to know about a system.

The way in which information about a system can be obtained from such a state function is the subject of the additional basic postulates, but we can observe briefly why the particular requirements mentioned in the first postulate must be met. If a function is to specify the state of a system, it would be of little use if it were not single-valued, for there would then be an ambiguity as to which value of the function should be considered the correct value (Fig. 3–1a). In addition, the function must be continuous for the same sort of reasoning—it would be impossible to relate the function to physical reality if the function were discontinuous at different values of the variables (Fig. 3–1b). Finally, since the numerical value of the function for given values of the coordinates and time is somehow to have some physical significance, the function must not become infinite. This latter requirement, as stated in Postulate I, is actually more restrictive than necessary, as will be mentioned shortly.

Although the first postulate has said that there is a function that describes the state of a system, we have not yet specified either how one obtains this function or how it provides information about a system. The latter is disclosed by the remainder of the postulate.

Postulate Ib. *The nature of the state function $\Psi(q_1, q_2, \ldots, t)$ is such that the product $\Psi^*\Psi\, dq_1\, dq_2 \cdots$ is the probability that the system represented by the wave function Ψ have at the time t the configuration represented by a point in the volume element $dq_1\, dq_2 \cdots$ of configuration space, that is, that q_1 lie between q_1 and $q_1 + dq_1$, etc.*

In this statement Ψ^* is the complex conjugate of Ψ and is obtained from the latter by replacing i by $-i$ [where i is the imaginary $(-1)^{1/2}$] wherever it occurs in Ψ. If Ψ is a real function, then $\Psi^*\Psi$ is just Ψ^2. According to the postulate, if one obtains the product $\Psi^*\Psi$ and then substitutes particular values for the variable coordinates $q_1, q_2, \ldots$, then the number that is obtained gives the probability that in this system the coordinates can actually lie in the range between these assigned values and an infinitesimally larger value.

Immediately we see why in the first half of Postulate I the statement was made that the wave function describes the system *as completely as possible*. In quantum mechanics it is recognized as a fundamental fact of nature that in many cases, primarily in atomic and molecular phenomena, it is not possible to locate all particles exactly and know and predict all their future motions exactly in the classical sense. Instead, it is possible only to specify the probability that a certain course of action will occur.

In the last chapter we found that a number of experiments involving matter and radiation could be most readily explained by assuming the traditional wave nature of radiation and the particulate nature of matter. That is, the results of these experiments could best be described by means of the equations formulated originally from these points of view. In other areas, though, exactly the opposite behavior appeared to be in evidence; e.g., the photon explanation of the photoelectric effect and the diffraction of electrons by crystals to form wavelike diffraction patterns.

Note that it is the mathematical form applying to the situation that suggests whether we are dealing with particles or waves. This inference is based on the earlier fact that equations of each type were the kind obtained in the original formulations of particulate systems and of the wave motions seen in vibrating strings, etc. It is perhaps unfortunate that we feel the need to continue this process of analogy from the original source to the secondary phenomena by means of the form of the equations involved. Nevertheless, science has certainly made great strides in this manner. At this stage, however, it is necessary to exercise greater caution since we are extending our ideas from large-scale observable quantities to the realm of the only indirectly observable world of the atom and subatomic particles.

The significance of this wave-particle dilemma was suggested by Born and Heisenberg to lie in our inability to observe atomic systems directly. In experiments involving the motions or structures of atoms and molecules we make observations of quantities which are affected one way or another by interaction with the atomic systems of interest, and from the way in which the interaction affects the observing "tool" we make inferences about the atomic systems themselves. Heisenberg pointed out that in probing an atomic system with some tool such as electromagnetic radiation or high-energy particles we not only interact with the atomic system, but also disturb it in such a way that it is left in a state different from the state before the experiment took place. The result of this disturbance is that we are no longer able to specify exactly all there is to know about the system. Depending on the particular tool used in the experiment and the nature of the interaction, we may be able to determine some dynamical variable such as the momentum of a particle very exactly, but in doing so we have disturbed the system so that we can no longer specify exactly where the particle is located or where it will be in the future. In turn, an experiment may be such that an electron can be located with great precision, but in disturbing it to measure its position we change its original motion and hence have again lost a certain amount of information.

The nature of this mutual exclusiveness of certain kinds of information is easily illustrated by a simple hypothetical experiment, which, if not strictly valid in every respect, still shows the nature and magnitude of the effects we are describing. Consider a microscope used to observe very small particles and their motions. The resolving power of a microscope sets a limitation on the smallest distance that can be distinguished and hence limits the preciseness of locating the position of a particle in the microscopic field. This resolving power depends on the wavelength of the radiation used to illuminate the particles in the field according to the equation (Fig. 3–2)

$$\Delta x = \frac{\lambda}{2 \sin \epsilon}, \tag{3-1}$$

where Δx is the uncertainty in the position measurement, i.e., the resolving power of the lens, and ϵ is the angle of aperture. It can be seen that as the wavelength of the radiation decreases the resolving power of the lens increases, so that we should begin to be able to position atomic and subatomic particles precisely if we use extremely high-frequency radiation such as ultraviolet, x-rays, and γ-radiation. A complication, however, arises.

Since light carries momentum, it is able to exert a force on interaction with material bodies. This is most easily visualized when we consider light as consisting of photons each with energy $\epsilon = h\nu$ and momentum

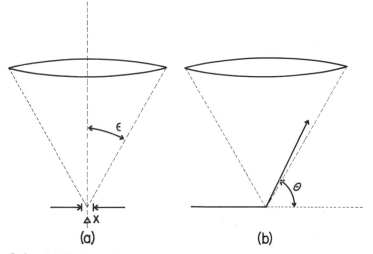

Fig. 3–2. (a) Relation between angle of aperture of a lens and the resolution possible. (b) The scattering of a photon by an electron initially located at the focal point of the lens.

$p = h\nu/c = h/\lambda$. As the wavelength of the radiation decreases, the energy of the photons and their momenta increase. In its simplest conception we can regard the interaction of radiation with an atomic-sized particle as the collision of a photon with momentum h/λ with a particle of mass m. We thus have a problem in the conservation of momentum such as we discussed in Sec. 2.2. Such an interaction was observed experimentally by Compton, who showed that the loss in momentum of the photon on collision with a particle can be detected by means of the lower frequency of the scattered light and corresponds to the gain in momentum of the particle as predicted by the law of conservation of momentum.

In terms of our hypothetical experiment, in order to observe the particle in the range Δx the photon, coming say from the x direction, must be deflected into the aperture of the lens in order to be observed. Conservation of momentum requires that if the particle is initially at rest, the momentum after collision is

$$p_x = \frac{h}{\lambda} - \frac{h}{\lambda'} \cos \theta,$$

where λ is the original wavelength of the radiation and λ' the wavelength after collision, and θ is the angle through which the photon is scattered. It can be shown that, unless the electron is moving extremely rapidly, the loss of energy by the photon is small, so that, very nearly, $\lambda = \lambda'$, in which case we can write

$$p_x = \frac{h}{\lambda} (1 - \cos \theta).$$

In order to observe the scattered photon, the angle θ must be in the range $\theta = 90° \pm \epsilon$, but we cannot further tell what actual value θ has for a given collision when we observe the photon after it has come through the microscope. All we can say is that θ must have been somewhere between these limits imposed by the aperture of the lens, and the momentum of the electron must as a result be somewhere in the range

$$\frac{h}{\lambda} (1 - \sin \epsilon) \leqslant p_x \leqslant \frac{h}{\lambda} (1 + \sin \epsilon).$$

In other words, there is an uncertainty in the momentum of the electron amounting to

$$\Delta p_x = \frac{2h}{\lambda} \sin \epsilon. \tag{3-2}$$

It is of interest to calculate the product of the uncertainty in position of the particle from Eq. (3–1) by the uncertainty in its momentum from Eq. (3–2). The result is

$$\Delta x \, \Delta p_x = h.$$

Calculations of other sorts of uncertainties in various canonically conjugate quantities, such as position and momentum, energy and time, etc., lead to results of the same order, and the generality of this relation has been formulated in the statement known widely as the Heisenberg uncertainty principle. It is seen that as the uncertainty in the measurement of one quantity is decreased, the uncertainty in specifying the other increases. In our hypothetical experiment, the particle can be more precisely located by decreasing the wavelength of the radiation used, thus utilizing the maximum resolving power of the lens; but this radiation is of increasingly high energy, so that when it interacts with the particle, it changes the motion of the latter drastically and thus increases the uncertainty in the momentum of the particle. One could avoid the latter by using low-frequency radiation, but then the resolving power of the lens would be considerably less, so that a large uncertainty in the position of the particle would result.

Different experiments emphasize the ability to determine one of two such quantities more precisely at the expense of information about the second. As an example, consider the experiment in which Davisson and Germer observed diffraction patterns for electrons reflected from crystals. The technique by which the initial beam of electrons was produced, acceleration by an electric field, allowed reasonably precise knowledge about the energies of the electrons and hence about their momenta. The resulting diffraction pattern (Fig. 3–3) was in turn a

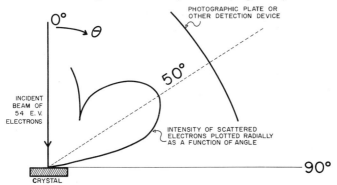

Fig. 3–3. The scattering of electrons from the surface of a crystal. Aside from a strong beam reflected back in the direction of the incident electron beam a strong flux of electrons is observed with a maximum intensity at an angle of 50°.

result of the fact that the positions of the electrons after being reflected from the crystal could not be predicted precisely. The over-all pattern of light and dark bands is the result of the impact of many electrons. Let us instead consider only one such electron. At the beginning of the experiment we may assume that the momentum of this electron is known quite precisely, and the reflection from the crystal should not change this knowledge. Can we predict, however, where the electron will impinge on a photographic plate after the reflection? The light parts of the diffraction pattern are obviously those regions in which many electrons reached the screen, while the dark regions are those in which few or no electrons reached the screen. We can do no more than predict that our single electron will probably reach the screen in one of the light regions and probably not in a dark region. This is the extent to which we can specify the position of the electron, and no more.

It is generally true that experiments of this sort, which emphasize the inability to specify the position of an atomic particle, are those experiments whose results are most easily expressed in terms of wavelike equations. We might note in connection with the light and dark regions of a diffraction pattern that the intensity of a light wave is proportional to the *square* of the amplitude of the wave. This is analogous to the manner in which we have defined the state function in quantum mechanics, so that its square gives the probability distribution. In our diffraction-pattern experiment we have already interpreted the intensity of the pattern as representing the probability of finding an electron in that location. This similarity arises because of the similarity of the equations and functions and was one of the analogies that aided in formulating a working structure for quantum mechanics.

It will be recalled that the probability of a given value of a variable is simply the fraction of measurements of the variable which yield that particular value, out of a large number of measurements. The maximum possible probability is unity, i.e., complete certainty. In considering a system described by a state function $\Psi(q_1, q_2, \ldots, t)$, if we include all possible configurations, letting every variable range over every possible value in the limits to which the system is confined, then we should have complete certainty of specifying all the possible configurations of the system, so that

$$\int \cdots \int\int \Psi^*(q_1, q_2, \ldots, t)\Psi(q_1, q_2, \ldots, t) \, dq_1 \, dq_2 \, dq_3 \cdots = 1$$

or introducing the symbol $d\tau$ for a volume element $dq_1 \, dq_2 \cdots$,

$$\int \Psi^*\Psi \, d\tau = 1, \tag{3–3}$$

where the integral is taken over all space available to the system.

In obtaining wave functions it will be seen that arbitrary constants often appear in the solution. These constants can often be evaluated by imposing the condition of Eq. (3–3), and when the constants have been determined from this integration so that the wave function obeys the equation, then the wave function is said to be *normalized*.

Finally, we might observe that since it is $\Psi^*\Psi$ and not Ψ that gives the probability of a configuration, it is not necessary that Ψ be finite, but rather that $\Psi^*\Psi$ be finite.

3.3 OPERATORS AND THE DETERMINATION OF DYNAMICAL VARIABLES

We have seen that one way in which the state function specifies the state of a system is that the square of the function is the probability that a given configuration will be measured. If the state function is really going to specify a great deal about systems, however, it must be able to tell us something about the motions of the system as well as its configuration. It should, in fact, tell us something about the results that would be obtained in the measurement of any dynamical variable. The way in which it is able to do this is specified by the second postulate.

Postulate II. *For every dynamical variable there must be assigned a mathematical operator. The physical properties of a dynamical variable can be deduced from the mathematical properties of the operator assigned to the variable. In particular, the possible results of an exact experimental measurement of a dynamical variable G are the eigenvalues g of the corresponding operator ĝ operating on the state function.*

Before continuing on, let us be sure we have clarified exactly what is meant by some of these terms. The concept of a mathematical operator is not really a new one, although the reader may not be used to thinking of mathematical operations divorced from the functions on which they are operating in a typical algebraic or differential equation.

Consider the equation

$$\frac{d^2f(x)}{dx^2} + 3f(x) = 0.$$

In such an equation one is usually concerned with solving the equation for some function $f(x)$ that satisfies the equation, i.e., that is consistent with the requirements specified by the equation. Just what does the equation specify? It says that if one performs the operation of taking the second derivative of a function with respect to x and adds the resulting quantity to the result of multiplying the function by 3, then the sum of these will be zero.

Both the operation of taking the second derivative with respect to x and the operation of multiplying by 3 are operations that require only following certain rules which define the operation and which are in no way dependent on the particular function involved. The *results* of the operations depend on the particular function on which the operations are performed, but the procedure of taking the derivative or performing the multiplication is defined for each operation in a completely general way. For many purposes it is convenient to consider the properties of the operators themselves and their interrelations independently of any particular functions to be operated upon.

In this light we could consider the preceding equation to be

$$\left(\frac{d^2}{dx^2} + 3\right)f(x) = 0$$

where we now recognize that operation on $f(x)$ by the operator in parenthesis will result in the value zero. The operator is a sum of two separate operators, one the operation of taking the second derivative, the other multiplication by 3. From this example we can infer as a general property of operators that if the operator $\hat{c}$ is the sum of two operators $\hat{a}$ and $\hat{b}$

$$\hat{c}f(x) = (\hat{a} + \hat{b})f(x) = \hat{a}f(x) + \hat{b}f(x).$$

It is possible to deduce many such operator equations independently of functions, although in many cases a quick verification of such a relation can be found by carrying out the operations on suitable convenient functions.

Of importance is the product of two operators $\hat{a}$ and $\hat{b}$. Consider the case where $\hat{a}$ is the operation of multiplication by x and $\hat{b}$ is the operation of taking the derivative with respect to x. The product $\hat{a}\hat{b}$ is specifically the following:

$$\hat{a}\hat{b}f(x) = \hat{a}[\hat{b}f(x)] = \hat{a}g(x) = h(x) = x\frac{df(x)}{dx}.$$

In other words, in an operator product one first carries out the operation indicated by the operator nearer the function to be operated on. Then after this operation has been performed, the second operator operates on what remains. The extension to a product of three or more operators should be obvious.

Operator products provide an excellent example of the difference between operator algebra and more familiar algebraic relations. Since an operator product $\hat{a}\hat{b}$ requires a specific sequence of operations, it is by no means assured that the reverse product $\hat{b}\hat{a}$ will be the same operator and will give the same results when operating on a function. Our example is of this type. Taking a simple function for ease of calculation, let $f(x) = x^2$. Then for $\hat{a}\hat{b}f(x)$,

$$x\frac{d(x^2)}{dx} = x \cdot 2x = 2x^2$$

but the operator product $\hat{b}\hat{a}$ operating on $f(x)$ is

$$\frac{d(x \cdot x^2)}{dx} = \frac{dx^3}{dx} = 3x^2,$$

which is clearly different. In more general terms,

$$\hat{a}\hat{b}f(x) = x\frac{df(x)}{dx},$$

$$\hat{b}\hat{a}f(x) = \frac{d[xf(x)]}{dx} = x\frac{df(x)}{dx} + f(x).$$

From this particular case it can be seen that

$$\hat{a}\hat{b}f(x) - \hat{b}\hat{a}f(x) = -1f(x)$$

or, in the terms of the operators only,

$$(\hat{a}\hat{b} - \hat{b}\hat{a}) = -1.$$

The quantity in parenthesis is called the *commutator* of the two operators $\hat{a}$ and $\hat{b}$. It will be different, of course, for different pairs of operators. In the particular case where the commutator of two operators is zero it is said that the two operators *commute*.

Not all operators have the property that

$$\hat{a}[f(x) + g(x)] = \hat{a}f(x) + \hat{a}g(x),$$

but if an operator does behave in this manner, it is said to be a *linear* operator. In quantum mechanics we deal with linear operators.

There is a particular class of operators which also are of interest in quantum mechanics. These are operators which are *Hermitian*, i.e., which obey the relation

$$\int \phi^*(\hat{a}\psi) \, d\tau = \int \psi(\hat{a}^*\phi^*) \, d\tau,$$

where ϕ and ψ are two functions being operated upon by the Hermitian operator $\hat{a}$. Operators of use in quantum mechanics are those that are linear and Hermitian and that obey certain commutation rules, which we will specify shortly.

In observing the relations between operators, and between operators and the functions upon which they operate, a number of interesting generalities can be made. There is one particular situation which is of considerable interest to us in connection with quantum mechanics. In some cases it is found that when an operator $\hat{a}$ operates on a function $f(x)$, the result is that the function $f(x)$ is reproduced and is now multiplied by a constant number a,

$$\hat{a}f(x) = af(x).$$

Those functions which show this behavior with the operator $\hat{a}$ are said to be *eigenfunctions* of the operator $\hat{a}$, and the constant multipliers, a, are called the *eigenvalues* of the operator $\hat{a}$. As an example of this behavior, consider

$$\frac{d}{dx} e^{kx} = k e^{kx}.$$

In this case the entire class of functions e^{kx}, with k being any value, are eigenfunctions of the operator d/dx, the corresponding eigenvalues being the k's. Also,

$$-\frac{d^2}{dx^2} \sin x = \sin x$$

so that sin x is an eigenfunction of the operator $-d^2/dx^2$ with the eigenvalue 1. It should be apparent that the whole class of functions sin nx are also eigenfunctions of this same operator. Numerous additional examples could be cited, but this should be sufficient to illustrate the meaning of these terms.

It will be recalled that in Postulate I we have already specified that the only functions of interest are those which are continuous. The Hermitian operators have a particular significance in quantum mechanics because their eigenvalues for well-behaved eigenfunctions are always real.

We are now in a position to return to Postulate II and explore its significance. First we note that we assume that there is some mathematical operator associated with every dynamical variable, such as momentum, position, and angular momentum. Secondly we observe that if it is possible to measure one of these variables exactly, we can determine from quantum mechanics what the results of this measurement will be simply by operating on the state function Ψ with the operator corresponding to the variable of interest. If the variable can be known exactly, then the state function will be an eigenfunction of that operator, and the eigenvalue obtained will be numerically equal to what would be measured for the variable for a system in the state represented by Ψ. We see here why Hermitian operators are important since the values of dynamical variables must be represented by real numbers. The actual procedure of carrying out the necessary operations and obtaining the eigenvalues will be clearer later when some particular cases are treated.

Aside from stating that there are operators corresponding to dynamical variables, and that they are linear and Hermitian, we have not really stated how they are obtained. The following definition imposes a condition which allows one to construct them by mathematical procedures.

Definition. *The operators $\hat{a}$ and $\hat{b}$ associated with two canonically conjugate dynamical variables A and B must satisfy the equation*

$$(\hat{a}\hat{b} - \hat{b}\hat{a}) = \frac{ih}{2\pi} = i\hbar.$$

Two variables are said to be canonically conjugate if they obey Hamilton's equations, i.e., if

$$\frac{\partial H}{\partial A} = -\dot{B}, \qquad \frac{\partial H}{\partial B} = \dot{A}.$$

This restriction allows calculation of different operators from other operators, but we will not explore the details of finding operators for different variables; instead, we will list in Table 3–1 several important dynamical variables and the operators that can be used to represent them in quantum mechanics.

The operations corresponding to coordinates such as the generalized coordinate q_i or the rectangular coordinate x, etc., simply amount to multiplication of the function being operated on by the value of that coordinate. The operations corresponding to momenta, energy, etc., are more complicated. The momentum operator involves taking the derivative of the function operated on with respect to the conjugate

TABLE 3–1.　Quantum-Mechanical Operators

Dynamical Variable	Operator	Operation
x	$\hat{x}$	x (multiplication by x)
q_i (generalized coordinate)	$\hat{q}_i$	q_i (multiplication by q_i)
q_i^2	$\hat{q}_i^2$	q_i (multiplication by q_i^2)
p_i	$\hat{p}_i$	$-i\hbar \dfrac{\partial}{\partial q_i}$
p_i^2	$\hat{p}_i^2$	$-\hbar^2 \dfrac{\partial^2}{\partial q_i^2}$
$q_i p_i$	$\hat{q}_i \hat{p}_i$	$q_i \left(-i\hbar \dfrac{\partial}{\partial q_i} \right)$
$p_i q_i$	$\hat{p}_i \hat{q}_i$	$\left(-i\hbar \dfrac{\partial}{\partial q_i} \right) q_i$
t (time)	$\hat{t}$	t (multiplication by t)
E (energy)	$\hat{E}$	$i\hbar \dfrac{\partial}{\partial t}$
H (Hamiltonian function for single particle in one-dimension q_i)	$\mathcal{3C}$	$-\dfrac{\hbar^2}{2m} \dfrac{d^2}{dq_i^2} + V(q_i)$
H (Hamiltonian function for single particle in three dimensions)	$\mathcal{3C}$	$-\dfrac{\hbar^2}{2m} \nabla^2 + V(q_1, q_2, q_3)$
H (Hamiltonian function for general case of n particles)	$\mathcal{3C}$	$\left(-\dfrac{\hbar^2}{2} \sum_{j=1}^{n} \dfrac{1}{m_j} \nabla_j^2 \right) + V(q_1, \ldots, q_{3n})$

coordinate. The momentum-squared operator involves taking the second derivative. Note that the latter is not just the first derivative squared; it is the operator product, which means carrying out two successive operations of taking a derivative.

More complicated operators such as the Hamiltonian operator are constructed by substituting in the original Hamiltonian function quantum-mechanical operators for the corresponding classical variables. Thus the kinetic energy in one direction is the momentum squared over $2m$, so that in the Hamiltonian operator this term has the operation corresponding to momentum squared, which is taking the second derivative with respect to x. Since the Hamiltonian function classically corresponds to the total energy of the system, we might suspect that the Hamiltonian operator plays an important part in the basic formulation of quantum mechanics, and we shall see that it does.

Several forms of the Hamiltonian operator are given in Table 3–1 for cases of differing complexity. When one advances from a one-dimensional problem (say along the x axis) to a three-dimensional one, then there are three second derivatives, and this particular operator corresponds to the Laplacian operator ∇^2 discussed in Appendix A. For each particle in the system such a Laplacian term is required. Finally, it is the Laplacian operator that is fundamental in the Hamiltonian operator, so that for any coordinate system one needs only to find the explicit form of ∇^2 in that coordinate system to write out the Hamiltonian operator in detail.

According to Postulate II, we can determine the values that would be obtained from experiment for the exact measurement of a dynamical variable by operating on Ψ and noting the value of the eigenvalue obtained. However, we have already seen numerous cases in which an exact value of a variable cannot be measured. Instead, different measurements give different results, although some may be found to be more probable than others over a large number of measurements. In the same way it is found that the wave function is not an eigenfunction of every operator of interest, and if eigenvalues cannot be obtained, then we do not have exact knowledge about the corresponding variables. The significance of this situation is revealed in the next postulate.

Postulate III. *When a great many measurements of any dynamical variable G are made on an assembly of systems whose state function is Ψ, the average value found, $\langle G \rangle$ or $\bar{G}$, will be given by*

$$\langle G \rangle \equiv \bar{G} = \frac{\int \Psi^* \hat{g} \Psi \, d\tau}{\int \Psi^* \Psi \, d\tau}, \qquad (3\text{--}4)$$

where $\hat{g}$ is the operator corresponding to the dynamical variable G, and the integration is over all configurations accessible to the system. Two notations are given for the average value of G. Because $\langle G \rangle$ represents the probable result of an experimental measurement, it is often called the *expectation value* of G.

Even though we may not obtain eigenvalues when operating on the state function with the operator $\hat{g}$, we are still able to determine the average value of G by the integrations described by Eq. (3–4). This equation is closely analogous to ordinary statistical equations involving probability distributions and average values. We might note that in statistics the standard deviation σ from the mean of the measured values of a variable, which essentially corresponds to the uncertainty in the value of that variable, is given by

$$\sigma^2 = \langle G^2 \rangle - \langle G \rangle^2.$$

If σ is zero, this corresponds to all measured values of G having the same value, so that this variable is known exactly. If by Eq. (3–4) we find that the average value of G^2 is equal to the square of the average value of G, then we also find that Ψ is an eigenfunction of $\hat{g}$, so that G is known exactly. This is illustrated graphically in Fig. 3–4. The calculation of eigenvalues and average values will be illustrated for specific cases in the following

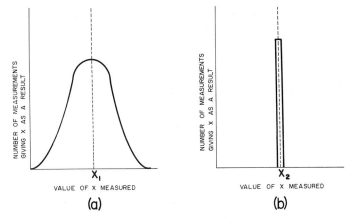

Fig. 3–4. (a) Distribution of measurements of an inexactly measurable quantity over a range of values, with the average of all the measurements equal to x_1. (b) Distribution of measurements for an exactly known quantity. All measurements give the same value $x = x_2$.

chapter, and it will be seen that the Heisenberg uncertainty principle will be uncovered naturally by a consideration of σ for canonically conjugate variables, such as position and momentum.

If the wave functions used are normalized, then the denominator of Eq. (3–4) is unity, so that only the numerator need be evaluated.

3.4 THE SCHRÖDINGER EQUATION

We see that in the state function Ψ we have an extremely powerful quantity. It gives the probability of a given distribution of values of the coordinates, the exact values of those dynamical variables which can be measured exactly, and the average values of those dynamical variables which give a different experimental result with each attempt at measurement. We have assumed that such a state function is available for every system, and we have indicated the nature and source of the operators corresponding to dynamical variables. We have still to see how this state function is obtained for a given system.

Postulate IV. *The state functions* Ψ *satisfy the equation*

$$\mathfrak{IC}\Psi = \hat{E}\Psi, \tag{3-5}$$

where $\mathfrak{IC}$ *is the Hamiltonian operator for the system and* $\hat{E}$ *is the energy operator.*

This equation, known as the Schrödinger equation including time, is the fundamental equation of quantum mechanics. In order to make the structure of the Schrödinger equation clearer, consider the case of the motion of a single particle in one dimension. In this case the Hamiltonian operator will involve only the second derivative in one coordinate, and the Schrödinger equation will be

$$- \frac{\hbar^2}{2m} \frac{\partial^2 \Psi(x, t)}{\partial x^2} + V(x)\Psi(x, t) = i\hbar \frac{\partial \Psi(x, t)}{\partial t}, \tag{3-6}$$

where $V(x)$ depends on the particular gravitational, electrostatic, magnetic, or other interactions that are present. In order to determine the state function for the system, it is necessary to solve this differential equation for Ψ.

If a single particle moves in three-dimensional space under the influence of an unspecified potential energy, then the Schrödinger equation in rectangular coordinates will be

$$- \frac{\hbar^2}{2m} \left(\frac{\partial^2 \Psi}{\partial x^2} + \frac{\partial^2 \Psi}{\partial y^2} + \frac{\partial^2 \Psi}{\partial z^2} \right) + V(x, y, z)\Psi = i\hbar \frac{\partial \Psi}{\partial t},$$

while in spherical polar coordinates, since ∇^2 has a form different from that in rectangular coordinates, the equivalent equation would be

$$- \frac{\hbar^2}{2mr^2} \left[\frac{\partial}{\partial r} \left(r^2 \frac{\partial \Psi}{\partial r} \right) + \frac{1}{\sin \theta} \frac{\partial}{\partial \theta} \left(\sin \theta \frac{\partial \Psi}{\partial \theta} \right) + \frac{1}{\sin^2 \theta} \left(\frac{\partial^2 \Psi}{\partial \phi^2} \right) \right]$$
$$+ V(r, \theta, \phi)\Psi = i\hbar \frac{\partial \Psi}{\partial t},$$

where Ψ is now a function of r, θ, ϕ, and t.

If the system contains two particles with masses m_1 and m_2 which are under the influence of a potential energy V, then the Schrödinger equation is

$$\left(- \frac{\hbar^2}{2m_1} \nabla_1^2 - \frac{\hbar^2}{2m_2} \nabla_2^2 + V \right) \Psi = i\hbar \frac{\partial \Psi}{\partial t}$$

where the form of the ∇^2 terms and of V will be determined by the coordinate system used. The extension to more complicated systems should be obvious. The Hamiltonian operator contains a ∇^2 term for each particle in the system, and all interactions that may lead to a potential energy term are included in V. The exact analytical form of the terms will depend on the particular coordinate system used.

The solution of a differential equation such as one of the preceding is not necessarily easy. In many, if not most, physical systems of interest an exact solution of the Schrödinger equation is impossible, and approximation methods must be used. Even the simple one-dimensional Eq. (3–6) is inconvenient with both position and time dependence. Fortunately there is a possible simplification.

In discussing the general formulations of classical mechanics we saw that particularly simple relations were obtained for conservative systems, i.e., systems in which the potential energy is a function of position coordinates but does not depend explicitly on time. In this particular case it is possible to separate the Schrödinger equation into two separate space- and time-dependent parts. In generalized coordinates let us assume that the wave function can be expressed as the product of two functions, one of which depends only on the coordinates and the other only on time,

$$\Psi(q_1, q_2, \ldots, t) = \psi(q_1, q_2, \ldots)\phi(t).$$

Introducing this expression into the general Schrödinger equation (3–5) and dividing by $\Psi = \psi\phi$ yields

$$\frac{1}{\psi}\left(-\frac{\hbar^2}{2}\sum_{j=1}^{n}\frac{1}{m_j}\nabla_j^2\psi + V\psi\right) = i\hbar\frac{1}{\phi}\frac{d\phi}{dt}, \qquad (3\text{–}7)$$

where the summation includes terms for each of the n particles in the system. Since the left side of this equation is a function of coordinates only, and the right side a function of time only, both sides must be equal to the same constant quantity, which is a function of neither coordinates nor time. By calling this constant E, Eq. (3–7) can be written as two separate equations,

$$\frac{d\phi}{dt} = -\frac{i}{\hbar}E\phi$$

and

$$-\frac{\hbar^2}{2}\sum_{j=1}^{n}\frac{i}{m_j}\nabla_j^2\psi + V\psi = E\psi. \qquad (3\text{–}8)$$

The first of these can be integrated easily to give

$$\phi(t) = e^{-(i/\hbar)Et},$$

while the second has essentially the same form as the time-dependent Schrödinger equation except that the time dependence has been removed.

Instead of involving a time derivative, a time-independent wave function ψ is now multiplied by a constant E.   This result leads to an important corollary.

Corollary. *If the state function Ψ is an eigenfunction of the Hamiltonian operator $\mathcal{3C}$ with the eigenvalue E, then Ψ satisfies the equation*

$$\mathcal{3C}\Psi = E\Psi,$$

where E, the eigenvalue, is the energy of the state represented by the corresponding eigenfunction Ψ.   In such a case the state function is of the form

$$\Psi(q_1, q_2, \ldots, t) = \psi(q_1, q_2, \ldots)\phi(t), \tag{3-9}$$

where ψ is a solution of the equation

$$\mathcal{3C}\psi = E\psi. \tag{3-10}$$

This last equation is identical with Eq. (3–8) and is known as the Schrödinger amplitude equation.   It is the relation of most concern to us because many problems of interest deal with conservative systems.   In such situations we need to consider only a space-dependent wave function, ψ, since the total state function can easily be obtained by Eq. (3–4).   Of most interest is the fact that this time-independent wave function is an eigenfunction of the Hamiltonian operator, and in addition the energy of the state is also time-independent.   Such a *constant-energy state*, called a *stationary state*, is of great importance in atomic and molecular systems as we have already begun to infer.

In Postulate IV and its corollary there have been no restrictions on the solutions that will be obtained, either the variety of state functions which might be solutions or their possible energies.   There is only the restriction, aside from being a solution of the Schrödinger equation, that the wave functions be well-behaved.   One of the interesting results of quantum mechanics is that in most physical situations involving atomic and molecular motions, the requirement of well-behaved state functions essentially selects from an infinity of possible solutions only a certain set of allowable state functions with a corresponding set of stationary state energies.   Thus Planck's quantized oscillators and Bohr's stationary electronic states are a natural result from the basic postulates we have set forth in this chapter.

The idea of stationary states is not unique to quantum mechanics. We have seen that in the absence of disturbing forces a point in phase space follows a path of constant energy.   The interesting development in quantum mechanics is that only certain specified stationary states are possible, out of the continuous spectrum of energy states that would be possible classically for a given system.

3.5 FURTHER PROPERTIES OF EIGENFUNCTIONS AND OPERATORS

Before we investigate some important examples of physical systems that can be treated easily by quantum mechanics, it is worthwhile to elaborate a little further on some of the most important properties of functions and operators, since these have some bearing on the way in which suitable wave functions can be constructed and handled.

If two functions $\phi_i(x)$ and $\phi_j(x)$ have the property that

$$\int_{x_1}^{x_2} \phi_i^* \phi_j \, dx = 0 \tag{3-11}$$

between the limits x_1 and x_2, then the functions are said to be *orthogonal in the interval* x_1 to x_2. If for a set of functions every pair of functions is orthogonal in an interval, this is said to be an *orthogonal set* in that interval. We have already mentioned the property of normality. In general, if every function in a set of functions is normalized between the limits x_1 and x_2, the set is said to be *normalized* in the interval. These two properties can be expressed in the single equation

$$\int_{x_1}^{x_2} \phi_i^* \phi_j \, d\tau = \delta_{ij},$$

where δ_{ij} is the Kronecker delta which has the value zero when $i \neq j$ and the value unity when $i = j$. A set of functions obeying this equation is said to be *orthonormal* in the interval.

Orthonormal functions are of considerable utility in quantum mechanics. It can be shown that *all well-behaved functions can be expanded in a series of orthogonal functions in some suitable interval*

$$\psi = c_1\phi_1 + c_2\phi_2 + \cdots, \tag{3-12}$$

where the c's are constants. A familiar expansion of this sort is the Fourier series. It is possible to approximate any function within specified limits by a series of sine and cosine terms. A square-wave function, for example, can be reproduced by the series

$$\phi(x) = a_0 + a_1 \sin x + b_1 \cos x + a_2 \sin 2x + \cdots$$

in the interval 0 to π.

An infinite number of terms would be required for an exact reproduction of the function, but an arbitrary number of terms will reproduce the desired function to any required degree of accuracy as can be seen in Fig. 3-5. The entire collection of terms required to reproduce the desired function completely is called a *complete set*.

The evaluation of the constants in Eq. (3-12) can be carried out from the desired function and the orthogonal set. The way in which this is accomplished can be seen by multiplying both sides of Eq. (3-12) by ϕ_n^*, where ϕ_n is a member of the orthonormal set, and integrating, so that

$$\int \phi_n{}^*\psi \, d\tau = \int c_1 \phi_n{}^*\phi_1 \, d\tau + \int c_2 \phi_n{}^*\phi_2 \, d\tau + \cdots.$$

But since all members of the set are orthogonal to one another, all the terms on the right side of this equation are zero except one; and if all the functions of the set are also normalized, this term is

$$\int c_n \phi_n{}^*\phi_n \, d\tau = c_n.$$

Therefore,

$$c_n = \int \phi_n{}^*\psi \, d\tau.$$

Another important fact relating functions and operators is that *the eigenfunctions of a Hermitian operator are orthogonal in the interval corresponding to the complete range of variables so long as the eigenfunctions*

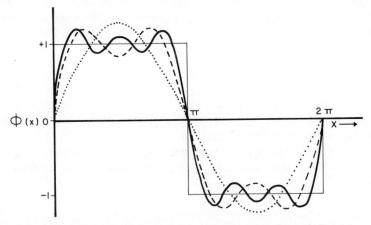

Fig. 3–5. Approximation of a square wave by a series of sine terms. The curves shown are for Fourier terms up to and including terms in $\sin x$, $\sin 3x$, and $\sin 5x$. (After Pauling and Wilson, *Introduction to Quantum Mechanics,* McGraw-Hill Book Co. 1935, p. 153; used by permission.)

have different eigenvalues. This can be shown as follows: Let g_1 and g_2 be the eigenvalues of the operator $\hat{g}$ corresponding to the eigenfunctions ψ_1 and ψ_2, i.e.,

$$\hat{g}\psi_1 = g_1\psi_1, \qquad \hat{g}\psi_2 = g_2\psi_2.$$

It follows that since $\hat{g}$ is Hermitian,

$$\int \psi_1{}^*\hat{g}\psi_2 \, d\tau = \int \psi_2 \hat{g}^*\psi_1{}^* \, d\tau = g_1 \int \psi_2\psi_1{}^* \, d\tau$$

($g = g^*$ since the eigenvalues of Hermitian operators are real), while at the same time it is true that

$$\int \psi_1{}^*\hat{g}\psi_2 \, d\tau = g_2 \int \psi_1{}^*\psi_2 \, d\tau.$$

Thus

$$g_1 \int \psi_2 \psi_1{}^* \, d\tau = g_2 \int \psi_1{}^* \psi_2 \, d\tau,$$

or

$$(g_2 - g_1) \int \psi_1{}^* \psi_2 \, d\tau = 0;$$

and if $g_1 \neq g_2$, then

$$\int \psi_1{}^* \psi_2 \, d\tau = 0,$$

as stated. Although this argument is not valid when the eigenvalues are equal, it is always possible to construct a set of orthogonal functions from the eigenfunctions, and these orthogonal functions will also be eigenfunctions. If g is the common eigenvalue of ψ_1 and ψ_2, then

$$\hat{g}\psi_1 = g\psi_1, \qquad \hat{g}\psi_2 = g\psi_2,$$

and in general

$$\int \psi_1{}^* \psi_2 \, d\tau = b \neq 0;$$

but if we construct a function $\psi'_2 = \psi_2 - b\psi_1$, it is seen that

$$\int \psi_1{}^* \psi'_2 \, d\tau = \int \psi_1{}^* \psi_2 \, d\tau - b \int \psi_1{}^* \psi_1 \, d\tau = b - b = 0,$$

so that ψ'_2 is orthogonal to ψ_1. In addition,

$$\hat{g}\psi'_2 = \hat{g}\psi_2 - \hat{g}b\psi_1 = g(\psi_2 - b\psi_1),$$

so that ψ'_2 is also an eigenfunction of $\hat{g}$.

It is of interest to see the significance of states represented by the combination of two or more eigenfunctions of the same operator. It will be recalled from Postulate II that if one obtains an eigenvalue when operating on a state function, that eigenvalue is the observed value of the dynamical variable represented by the operator. In the case of a state function that is the sum of two state eigenfunctions with different eigenvalues, the constructed function is a solution of the Schrödinger equation, but is not an eigenfunction of the Hamiltonian operator. However, since the functions making up the sum are eigenfunctions of the operator, it can be shown that there is a particular significance to the coefficients of the eigenfunctions in the sum. The relation of interest is known as the principle of the superposition of states (Postulate V).

Postulate V. *If ψ_1 and ψ_2 are eigenfunctions of the operator $\hat{g}$ corresponding to the variable G with eigenvalues g_1 and g_2, then the state represented by $\psi = c_1\psi_1 + c_2\psi_2$ is the state in which the probability of observing the value of G to be g_1 is $c_1 c_1{}^*$ and the probability of observing the value g_2 for G is $c_2 c_2{}^*$.* This postulate is illustrated in Fig. 3–6.

It will not be proved here, but it can be shown that *if two operators $\hat{a}$ and $\hat{b}$ commute, there exists a set of functions which are simultaneously eigenfunctions of both operators.* This also holds for more than two operators, and it can be shown also that the converse holds; *if there exists a complete set of orthogonal functions which are eigenfunctions of two operators $\hat{a}$ and $\hat{b}$, then $\hat{a}$ and $\hat{b}$ commute.* We have already seen that eigenvalues represent real, exact measurements of dynamical variables. If two operators commute, then it is possible to have states of the system in which both variables have definite values, and vice versa.

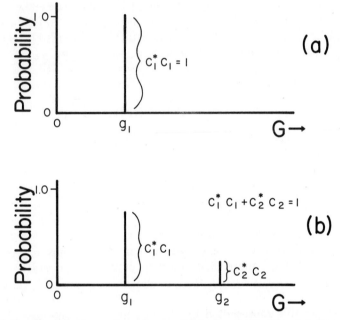

Fig. 3–6. Expectation values for a physical quantity G. (a) The system is described by the function $\psi = c_1\phi_1$, and the probability that a value g_1 will be measured for G is unity, or complete certainty. (b) The system is described by the function $\psi = c_1\phi_1 + c_2\phi_2$. The probability that g_1 will be measured is $c_1c_1^*$, and the probability that g_2 will be measured is $c_2c_2^*$. The sum of these two probabilities is unity.

These properties of operators and functions, while somewhat abstract at this stage, are included here since they are of value in constructing suitable wave functions, as will be seen in specific cases later.

3.6 SYMMETRY OPERATORS

The simple multiplicative and differential operators considered in the previous sections are not the only kind of operators of use in quantum mechanics. An especially important class is that of symmetry operators. The symmetries of nature are familiar to us in such diverse places as the exquisite symmetry of a snowflake, the regular arrangement of ions in a crystal lattice, and the behavior of curves representing various mathematical functions.   The presence of symmetry in a system implies some degree of order and hence suggests that some simplification of the mathematical description of the system might result if these symmetry properties can be taken into account.

The symmetry of a molecule, a crystal lattice, or a mathematical function is described in terms of *symmetry elements* such as a reflection plane or an axis of rotation.   The five basic types of symmetry elements are listed in Table 3–2.   Associated with each symmetry element is a corresponding *symmetry operation*, which brings about a transformation with respect to the element.   The symmetry operations corresponding to the basic symmetry elements are given also in Table 3–2.

TABLE 3–2.   Symmetry Elements and Operators

Symmetry Elements		Symmetry Operations
Symbol	Description	
E	Identity	No change
σ	Plane of symmetry	Reflection through the plane*
i	Center of symmetry	Inversion through the center
C_n	Axis of symmetry	Rotation about the axis by $360/n$ degrees
S_n	Rotation-reflection axis of symmetry	Rotation about the axis by $360/n$ degrees, followed by reflection through the plane perpendicular to the axis

* If the major symmetry axis is assumed to be in the vertical direction, a plane of symmetry containing this axis is said to be a vertical plane and is given the symbol σ_v. A symmetry plane perpendicular to the vertical axis is a horizontal plane σ_h. One which is diagonal is given the symbol σ_d

There are many molecules in which various symmetry elements are seen easily.   The symmetry elements of water, ethylene, and benzene are illustrated in Fig. 3–7.   It can be seen that performing each symmetry operation, such as rotation of the molecule by 180° or reflection in a plane through the molecule, places the molecule in a configuration which cannot be distinguished from its original configuration unless the individual atoms are labeled in some way.   These examples should be studied carefully to be sure the various types of symmetry elements and operations are understood.

The result of a symmetry operation can be expressed mathematically. If we consider a function $f(x, y, z)$, operation on that function by a symmetry operator is likely to change the nature of the function.   For example, a rotation of 180° about the z axis is equivalent to replacing x in $f(x, y, z)$ by $-x$ and y by $-y$ with z remaining unchanged.   Thus

$$\hat{C}_{2_z} f(x, y, z) = f(-x, -y, z).$$

Similarly,

$$\hat{\sigma}_{xy}f(x, y, z) = f(x, y, -z),$$
$$\hat{i}f(x, y, z) = f(-x, -y, -z),$$
$$\hat{S}_{2_z}f(x, y, z) = f(-x, -y, -z),$$

and so on.

Symmetry operators conform to an operator algebra just as the other operators we have discussed. The multiplication of symmetry operators

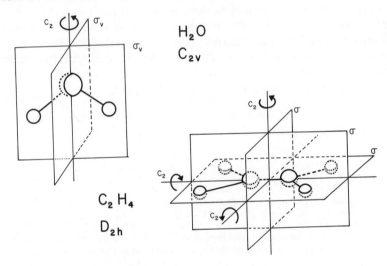

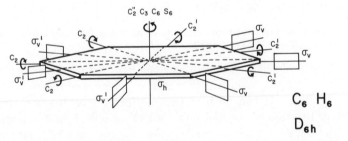

Fig. 3–7. Symmetry elements of H_2O, C_2H_4, and C_6H_6 and the point groups to which these molecules belong.

corresponds to successive operations. In performing such a set of operations, the convention is maintained that the symmetry elements remain fixed in space regardless of any rotations, reflections, or inversions which a molecule may undergo. Investigation shows that successive operations result in a configuration which can also be obtained by some other single symmetry operation. In the case of H_2O, for example, it is seen that the reflection $\hat{\sigma}'_v$ followed by the reflection $\hat{\sigma}_v$ results in a configuration which is exactly equivalent to that obtained by the single rotation $\hat{C}_2$. Thus,

$$\hat{\sigma}_v \hat{\sigma}'_v = \hat{C}_2,$$

and it can be verified in addition that

$$\hat{C}_2 \hat{\sigma}_v = \hat{\sigma}'_v,$$
$$\hat{C}_2 \hat{\sigma}'_v = \hat{\sigma}_v,$$
$$\hat{E} \hat{C}_2 = \hat{C}_2,$$

and so on.

An additional property of symmetric systems is illustrated by the H_2O molecule. If all possible combinations of symmetry operators correspond- ing to the symmetry elements of H_2O are investigated, it is found that the product of two symmetry operators always results in an operator which also corresponds to one of these elements. This was just seen above, for example, and can be verified for other operations. A given molecule (or wave function, or similar representation of a system) is described by a certain set of symmetry elements, and it is found that all possible products of the symmetry operators for those elements are also symmetry operators of the set. Such a set of symmetry elements is called a *point group*. Some of the important point groups are listed in Table 3–3. Included in the list are the symmetry elements comprising each group. The symbols for the point groups are in boldface to be distinguished from the sym- metry elements. By designating the point group of a molecule, a great deal of symmetry information is conveyed immediately.

The symmetry elements of a point group obey a number of mathematical relations which are of considerable utility in quantum mechanics and many other areas of chemical and physical theory. We will not elaborate on the mathematics and applications of group theory here, but almost any extensive exploration of molecular systems invariably leads to the use of symmetry properties. The student of quantum mechanics and spectros- copy will find the structure of group theory beautiful and its utility exciting.

The fundamental problem in quantum mechanics is solution of the Schrödinger equation, that is, finding the possible eigenfunctions of the Hamiltonian operator for the system. It is these eigenfunctions that con- tain information about the possible states of the system.

In the preceding section it was stated that a very important property of operators is that if two operators commute, then there exists a set of functions that are eigenfunctions of both operators. Symmetry operators play an important role in this respect. The Hamiltonian operator con- structed for a system displays some kind of symmetry. Hence it will commute with one or more symmetry operators, and these symmetry operators can be used to sort out suitable eigenfunctions. This is often a

TABLE 3–3. The Major Point Groups

Point Group	Symmetry Elements	Examples
C_1	E	CH_3—CHClBr, N_2H_4, CHFClBr
C_2	E, C_2	H_2O_2, HClC=C=CHCl
$C_i \equiv S_2$	E, i ($\equiv S_2$)	CH_3—CHCl—CHCl—CH_3 (trans.)
$C_{1v} = C_{1h}$	E, σ	NOCl
C_{2v}	E, C_2, $2\sigma_v$	H_2O, CH_2Cl_2, H_2CO, H_2C=CCl_2
C_{3v}	E, C_3, $3\sigma_v$	NH_3, $HCCl_3$, H_3CCl
C_{4v}	E, C_4, C_2 (coincident with C_4), $4\sigma_v$	Non-planar $(PtCl_4)^{-}$
$C_{\infty v}$	E, C_∞, $\infty\sigma_v$	HCN, OCS, CN, HC≡CCl
C_{2h}	E, C_2, σ_h, i	ClHC=CHCl (trans.)
$D_{2d} \equiv V_d$	E, $3C_2$ (mutually perpendicular), S_4 (coincident with one of the C_2), $2\sigma_d$ (through the S_4 axis)	H_2C=C=CH_2
$D_{3d} \equiv S_{6v}$	E, C_3, $3C_2$ (perpendicular to the C_3 axis), S_6 (coincident with the C_3 axis), i, $3\sigma_d$	C_6H_{12} (cyclohexane), C_2H_6 (staggered)
$D_{4d} \equiv S_{8v}$	E, C_4, $4C_2$ (perpendicular to C_4), S_8 coincident with C_4, C_2 (coincident with C_4), $4\sigma_d$	S_8 (puckered octagon)
$D_{2h} \equiv V_h$	E, $3C_2$ (mutually perpendicular), 3σ (mutually perpendicular), i	H_2C=CH_2, N_2O_4 (planar)
D_{3h}	E, C_3, $3C_2$ (perpendicular to the C_3 axis), $3\sigma_v$, σ_h	BCl_3, C_2H_6 (eclipsed)
D_{4h}	E, C_4, $4C_2$ (perpendicular to the C_4 axis), $4\sigma_v$, $4\sigma_h$, C_2 and S_4 (both coincident with C_4), i	C_4H_8 (cyclobutane), $(PtCl_4)^{-}$
D_{6h}	E, C_6, $6C_2$ (perpendicular to the C_6 axis), $6\sigma_v$, σ_h, C_2 and C_3 and S_6 (all coincident with C_6 axis), i	C_6H_6 (benzene), C_6Cl_6
$D_{\infty h}$	E, C_∞, C_2 (perpendicular to the C_∞ axis), $\infty\sigma_v$, σ_h, i	H_2, CO_2, HC≡CH, C_3O_2
T_d	E, $3C_2$ (mutually perpendicular), $4C_3$, 6σ, $3S_4$ (coincident with the C_2 axes)	CH_4, P_4, ·C$(CH_3)_4$ (sym.)
O_h	E, $3C_4$ (mutually perpendicular), $4C_3$, $3S_4$ and $3C_2$ (coincident with the C_4 axes), $6C_2$, 9σ, $4S_6$ (coincident with the C_3), i	$(PtCl_6)^{-}$, SF_6, $[Co(NH_3)_6]^{3+}$

simpler process than attempting to solve the Schrödinger equation directly. The mathematics of group theory is utilized in this process.

In addition to simplifying the problem of finding the eigenfunctions for a system, symmetry considerations often aid in other mathematical manipulations, such as the evaluation of integrals involving wave functions and operators. Consider as an example the integral

$$\int_{-\infty}^{\infty} f(x)\, dx.$$

If, on inverting the coordinates through the origin $(x \to -x)$, the function remains unchanged, i.e., if $f(-x) = f(x)$, then the integral may have a non-zero value.   If, on the other hand, $f(-x) = -f(x)$, then the integral will be zero because the integration over the negative values of x up to the origin will be equal and opposite in sign to the integration over positive values of x.

A function which does not change sign on inversion of all the coordinates through the origin is said to be *symmetric* to inversion or is said to be an *even* function.   One for which the sign of the function changes is *antisymmetric* to inversion or an *odd* function.   These functions are also said to have *even and odd parity*, respectively.

Often an integral may contain the product of several functions.   In determining the expectation value of x, for example, an integral of the form

$$\int_{-\infty}^{\infty} f(x)xf(x)\ dx$$

might be employed.   If $f(x)$ is an even function, the product $f(x)xf(x)$ would be odd since x is odd.   Thus the integral would vanish.   On the other hand the integral

$$\int_{-\infty}^{\infty} f(x)x^2f(x)\ dx$$

would not vanish since x^2 also is even.   In general, the product of two even functions is even, the product of two odd functions is even, and the product of an even and an odd function is odd.

The most general case will require consideration of more than one coordinate.   In spherical polar coordinates, inversion through the origin equivalent to $x \to -x,\ y \to -y,\ z \to -z$ is $r \to r,\ \theta \to \pi - \theta,\ \phi \to \pi + \phi$. Consideration of the symmetry of integrals can be a helpful time-saver in calculations if many of the integrals of interest can be shown to vanish because of symmetry without having to carry through the detailed steps of integration.   Numerous examples of this procedure will be illustrated in later sections.

3.7   NOTATION

Several different mathematical formalisms have been employed in formulating the axiomatic structure and the operators of quantum mechanics. The use of differential operators is perhaps the most familiar to students in chemistry, but other approaches have proved to be equally useful and often more comprehensive.   It has been mentioned that operators can be defined in terms of matrices, a formally defined array of numbers or elements.   The behavior of matrices is described by matrix algebra, and it is found that matrix operators can be constructed in such a way that, when employed in a manner consistent with the rules of matrix algebra, their behavior is analogous to that of the differential operators we have used here as examples. One can compute the commutators of matrix operators, eigenfunctions and eigenvalues, and similar quantities. The matrix formulation of quantum mechanics has proved to be a powerful tool for the solution of physical problems.

The several formalisms which have been developed for quantum mechanics have resulted in a variety of different notations and symbols. Some of these conventions have found their way from one system to another and have enjoyed general use in the literature. Because they are frequently used and also are an aid in simplifying mathematical statements, we will note here some items of notation that will be employed in later sections.

A frequently used integral in quantum mechanics is the so-called overlap or non-orthogonality integral. Such an integral involves the product of a wave function and its complex conjugate as in Eq. (3–3), or more generally two different functions as in the integral (3–11). The most general form of the overlap integral and the shorthand notation often used is

$$\int \psi_m^* \psi_n \, d\tau \equiv \langle \psi_m^* | \psi_n \rangle \equiv \langle m | n \rangle.$$

It can be seen that the shorter notation not only eliminates the cumbersome integral sign but also permits using only indices to designate the functions involved. Since several such indices may be necessary to specify a particular wavefunction completely, the use of these indices in the form of subscripts and superscripts becomes unwieldy. In this shorthand notation only the necessary indices themselves need be listed.

A second important type of integral involves an operator as well as two functions. The numerator of Eq. (3–4) is an example of such an integral. As in the case of the overlap integral, there are integrals of this form that include two different functions. The general integral and some of its shorthand forms are

$$\int \psi_m^* g \psi_n \, d\tau \equiv \langle \psi_m^* | g | \psi_n \rangle \equiv \langle m | g | n \rangle \equiv g_{mn}.$$

This type of integral is often called a matrix element for reasons that will be discussed later.

With this notation in mind, some of the important equations of this chapter can be rewritten. The normalization condition (3–3) becomes

$$\langle i | i \rangle = 1,$$

and the average-value equation (3–4) becomes

$$\langle G_i \rangle = \frac{\langle i | g | i \rangle}{\langle i | i \rangle}.$$

The orthonormality conditions can be written

$$\langle i | j \rangle = \delta_{ij},$$

where $\delta_{ij} = 0$ when $i \neq j$, and $\delta_{ij} = 1$ when $i = j$.

Similar simplification of the writing of other equations in which integrals of these types appear can be carried out when desirable.

3.8 SUMMARY

The general approach of quantum mechanics to a physical problem is somewhat different from that of classical physics, although the tradition and techniques of the latter have strongly influenced the formal structure of the more recent theory. In classical physics one does not try to construct a single mathematical function that will describe the system completely. Instead, all the necessary coordinates and momenta of a system are specified, and the interactions accounted for, from which the configuration and the motions of the system at any later time can be calculated. If the number of degrees of freedom involved becomes too large, it may be necessary to resort to statistical methods in order to make the mathematics reasonably simple. In principle, at least, every move of every particle is exactly predictable.

In quantum mechanics the view is different. First of all, a single function is constructed to describe the system. This function is found, in principle, by a simple method. All one does is construct the Hamiltonian operator for the system by including ∇^2 terms for every particle and including in the potential energy term every interaction involved. The Schrödinger equation is then solved for functions which are satisfactory solutions. Characteristically, only a certain set of state functions with definite stationary state energies are well-behaved solutions.

Although the state functions obtained in this way describe the system as completely as possible, we find that there are many things about atomic- and molecular-sized systems that cannot be known with exact certainty. However, from the state functions one can determine the probability of different distributions in space, the exact values of some dynamical variables, and the average values of those variables that cannot be determined exactly. The inability of a state function to predict certain variables exactly is consistent with experiments which also fail to determine these variables precisely. Thus, quantum mechanics is consistent with observation where the application of classical methods leads to serious inconsistencies.

The whole validity of quantum mechanics rests, of course, on its consistency with nature. The tremendous successes of the last thirty years give us no reason to doubt that quantum mechanics is much closer to "truth" in the atomic realm than the methods and assumptions of classical physics. There is also little doubt that quantum mechanics as we now know it will be modified and perhaps completely supplanted by a more general scheme that accounts for microscopic, relativistic, and macroscopic phenomena. At this time, however, the tool which is at our disposal and the tool which has so far been completely valid for most systems of interest is quantum or wave mechanics. We will now turn to some physical and chemical systems and try to show that this is so.

SUPPLEMENTARY REFERENCES

BORN, M., *Atomic Physics*, 6th ed., Blackie and Sons, Ltd., Glasgow, 1956.

HEISENBERG, W., *Physical Foundations of Quantum Mechanics*, Dover Publications, New York, 1930.

RICHTMEYER, F. K., and E. H. KENNARD, *Introduction to Modern Physics*, 4th ed., McGraw-Hill Book Co., New York, 1947.

These three texts discuss the relation between physical phenomena and the mathematical formulation of quantum mechanics.

SHERWIN, C. W., *Introduction to Quantum Mechanics*, Holt, Rinehart & Winston, New York, 1959. A lucid and unusual discussion of how quantum mechanics can be formulated and how stationary state solutions are obtained. The mathematical treatment emphasizes numerical and graphical methods which may be useful for students who have less acquaintance with more abstract mathematics. Many of the topics in future chapters are discussed in this text.

EYRING, H., J. WALTER, and G. E. KIMBALL, *Quantum Chemistry*, John Wiley & Sons, New York, 1944.

GLASSTONE, S., *Theoretical Chemistry*, D. Van Nostrand, Princeton, 1945.

PAULING, L., and E. B. WILSON, *Introduction to Quantum Mechanics*, McGraw-Hill Book Co., New York, 1935.

Three generally useful and readable discussions of quantum mechanics which are useful in most of the areas discussed in this text.

MATTHEWS, P. T., *Introduction to Quantum Mechanics*, McGraw-Hill Book Co., New York, 1963. A short text which emphasizes the operator approach and discusses the Dirac method.

PITZER, K. S., *Quantum Chemistry*, Prentice-Hall, Englewood Cliffs, N.J., 1953. A lucid and far-ranging discussion covering many areas of current interest. An excellent reference on many topics, although rather concise for a beginning.

FANO, V., and L. FANO, *Basic Physics of Atoms and Molecules*, John Wiley & Sons, New York, 1959. A more advanced and sophisticated account of the foundations of quantum mechanics.

PROBLEMS

3-1. The binding energy (ionization potential) of an electron in a hydrogen atom is 13.5 ev. We could consider the hydrogen atom as a system in which an electron has an unknown energy, but we know that if its momentum becomes $\pm (2mE)^{1/2}$, where E is the binding energy of the electron, the atom will lose its electron and cease to exist. Thus we could say that in a hydrogen atom $\Delta p = 2(2mE)^{1/2}$. If $\Delta p \, \Delta x = h$, then what would be the approximate "size" of a hydrogen atom? What would be the size of a molecule in which the binding energy of an electron is 5 ev?

3–2. Assuming an electron with momentum p in a hydrogen atom to have a wave of wavelength $\lambda = h/p$ associated with it, and assuming that the circular orbits of this electron must be such that the de Broglie wave is continuous around the orbit, calculate the energies of the possible electronic orbits and compare with the Bohr theory.

3–3. A beam of silver atoms is produced by collimating atoms that vaporize from silver in a furnace at 1200°C. If the beam travels 1 m to a screen, what is the size of the smallest spot that this beam could produce on the screen?

3–4. Would a hydrogen atom at 300°K moving with kinetic energy $\frac{3}{2}kT$ be diffracted by a crystal?

3–5. If a microscope cannot resolve distances much smaller than a wavelength, what energy would be required for electrons in an electron microscope to give a theoretical resolution of 1 Å?

3–6. Show that the operators a (a constant) and d^2/dx^2 commute.

3–7. Find the commutator of the operators x^2 and d/dx.

3–8. Show that $\cos 4x$ is an eigenfunction of the operator d^2/dx^2 and find the corresponding eigenvalue.

3–9. Show that e^{kx} is an eigenfunction of the operator d/dx. What is the eigenvalue?

3–10. Show that $\sin kx \sin my \sin nz$ is an eigenfunction of the Laplacian operator, and find the eigenvalue.

3–11. What would be an eigenfunction of the operator $-i\, d/dx$?

3–12. Show that $xe^{-x^2/2}$ is an eigenfunction of the operator $-d^2/dx^2 + x^2$.

3–13. The classical Hamiltonian function for a system of particles is given by

$$H = \tfrac{1}{2} \sum_{i=1}^{3n} \left[\frac{p_i^2}{m_i} + V(q_i) \right].$$

Derive the quantum-mechanical Hamiltonian operator $\mathcal{H}$ for this system by substituting the appropriate operators in the classical expression.

3–14. The Laplacian operator ∇^2 in cartesian coordinates is very simply

$$\frac{\partial^2}{\partial x^2} + \frac{\partial^2}{\partial y^2} + \frac{\partial^2}{\partial z^2}.$$

Derive the form of the Laplacian in spherical coordinates from the relations

$$x = r \sin\theta \cos\phi, \qquad r = (x^2 + y^2 + z^2)^{1/2},$$
$$y = r \sin\theta \sin\phi, \qquad \theta = \cos^{-1}(z/r),$$
$$z = r \cos\theta, \qquad \phi = \tan^{-1}(y/x).$$

(*Hint:* $\dfrac{\partial}{\partial x} = \dfrac{\partial}{\partial \theta}\dfrac{\partial \theta}{\partial x} + \dfrac{\partial}{\partial \phi}\dfrac{\partial \phi}{\partial x} + \dfrac{\partial}{\partial r}\dfrac{\partial r}{\partial x}$, and similarly for y and z.)

3–15. Show that the operator for a coordinate of position and the operator for momentum along that coordinate obey the rule for the commutator of conjugate quantum-mechanical operators.

3–16. Verify that quantum-mechanical coordinate operators commute with one another, that momentum operators commute with one another, and that momentum operators commute with coordinate operators which are not conjugate.

3–17. Write down the Schrödinger equation for the helium atom.

3–18. Consider a situation in which there are four particles of masses m_1, m_2, m_3, and m_4, the first two have negative charges equal to $-e$ and the remaining two have charges of $+e$. Write the complete Hamiltonian operator which would be used in the Schrödinger equation to find the state function for this system. Use any kind of coordinate system you think is most convenient, but be consistent.

3–19. Derive the angular momentum operator $\hat{\mathbf{M}}$ of a system of n point masses whose position and momentum coordinates are r_1, r_2, . . . , r_n and p_1, p_2, . . . , p_n, respectively. The classical angular momentum vector $\mathbf{M}$ is given by $\mathbf{M} = \Sigma_i \mathbf{r}_i \times \mathbf{p}_i$.

3–20. Show that in the region $-l \leqslant x \leqslant l$, the functions

$$\psi_0 = \frac{1}{\sqrt{2l}}, \quad \psi_n = \frac{1}{\sqrt{l}}\cos\frac{n\pi}{l}x, \quad \phi_n = \frac{1}{\sqrt{l}}\sin\frac{n\pi}{l}x$$

form an orthonormal set.

3–21. When the probability of having a particular value of the variable x is given by a probability function $p(x)$, then the average value $\langle g(x) \rangle$ of some function of x, $g(x)$, is given by $\langle g(x) \rangle = \int g(x)p(x)\,dx$, with the integral taken over the appropriate limits. Calculate $\langle f(x) \rangle$, $\langle f^2(x) \rangle$, and σ, where

$$f(x) = -b \text{ for } 0 \leqslant x < \frac{a}{2},$$

$$f(x) = +b \text{ for } \frac{a}{2} < x \leqslant a,$$

when the probability distribution function $p(x)$ is

$$p(x) = \text{constant for } 0 \leqslant x \leqslant a,$$

and also for the case when

$$p(x) = k\left(\sin\frac{2\pi x}{a}\right)^2.$$

In each case normalize $p(x)$.

3–22. If for $0 \leqslant x \leqslant a$ a normalized wave function is

$$\Psi(x, t) = A \sin\frac{\pi x}{a} e^{-iE_0 t/\hbar},$$

where E_0 and A are real constants,
  a. find A;
  b. calculate the expectation value of x;
  c. calculate $\langle x^2 \rangle$;
  d. calculate the expectation value of the energy;
  e. calculate the expectation value of the square of the energy.

3–23. Show that

$$\hat{S}_{2_z} f(x, y, z) = \hat{i} f(x, y, z),$$
$$\hat{S}_{4_z} f(x, y, z) = f(-y, x, -z),$$
$$\hat{C}_{6_z} f(x, y, z) = f\left(\tfrac{1}{2} x + \frac{\sqrt{3}}{2} y, \; -\frac{\sqrt{3}}{2} x + \tfrac{1}{2} y, \; z\right),$$

$$(\hat{C}_n)^n = \hat{E},$$
$$\hat{\sigma}^2 = \hat{E},$$
$$\hat{i} = \hat{S}_2,$$
$$\hat{S}_n = \hat{C}_n \hat{\sigma}_h = \hat{\sigma}_h \hat{C}_n.$$

3–24. For the particular case $f = 2x^2 + y^2 + z^2$, show that

$$\hat{C}_{2_y} f = \hat{C}_{2_z} f = \hat{C}_{2_x} f = \hat{i} f = \hat{\sigma}_{xy} f = f,$$
$$\hat{C}_{4_x} f = f,$$
$$\hat{C}_{4_y} f = x^2 + y^2 + 2z^2.$$

3–25. Which of the following pairs of operators commute?

$$\hat{C}_{4_z} \text{ and } \hat{\sigma}_{xy},$$
$$\hat{C}_{2_z} \text{ and } \hat{i},$$
$$\frac{d}{dx} \text{ and } \hat{C}_{2_z},$$
$$\frac{d}{dx} \text{ and } \hat{C}_{2_x}.$$

3–26. Show for the C_{2v} point group (H_2O) that

$$\hat{E}\hat{C}_2 = \hat{C}_2, \qquad \hat{C}_2 \hat{\sigma}_v = \hat{\sigma}'_v,$$
$$\hat{C}_2 \hat{\sigma}'_v = \hat{\sigma}_v, \qquad \hat{\sigma}_v \hat{\sigma}'_v = \hat{C}_2,$$
$$\hat{C}_2 \hat{C}_2 = \hat{E}, \qquad \hat{\sigma}_v \hat{\sigma}_v = \hat{E},$$
$$\hat{\sigma}'_v \hat{\sigma}'_v = \hat{E},$$
$$\hat{\sigma}'_v (\hat{C}_2 \hat{\sigma}_v) = \hat{\sigma}'_v (\hat{\sigma}'_v) = \hat{E},$$
$$(\hat{\sigma}'_v \hat{C}_2) \hat{\sigma}_v = (\hat{\sigma}_v) \hat{\sigma}_v = \hat{E}.$$

3–27. Verify the point groups assigned to the molecules given as examples in Table 3–3.

3–28. Show that the commutator of x^n and $\partial/\partial x$ is nx^{n-1}.

3–29. Find the commutator of $\partial/\partial x$ and $\partial^n/\partial x^n$.

3–30. Verify that

$$\left(\frac{\partial}{\partial x} + x\right)\left(\frac{\partial}{\partial x} - x\right) = \frac{\partial^2}{\partial x^2} - x^2 - 1$$

and

$$\left(\frac{\partial}{\partial x} - x\right)\left(\frac{\partial}{\partial x} + x\right) = \frac{\partial^2}{\partial x^2} - x^2 + 1.$$

3–31. Determine which of the following operators are linear:

a. $\dfrac{d}{dx}$;

b. x;

c. $\exp$;

d. $\sqrt{}$;

e. $(\ )^2$;

f. $\sqrt[3]{}$.

4

Simple Quantum-Mechanical Systems

4.1 CONSERVATIVE SYSTEMS

The basic postulates of quantum mechanics are best illustrated by a few simple examples, which also will be of interest later in considering atomic and molecular problems. We will limit our considerations initially to conservative systems, i.e., systems in which the potential energy is explicitly a function only of the coordinates of the system and is independent of time (except, of course, insofar as the coordinates may vary with time). In this case, according to the corollary of Postulate IV, it is possible to consider the simpler time-independent Schrödinger equation

$$\mathcal{H}\psi(q_i) = E\psi(q_i),$$

where E is the eigenvalue of the Hamiltonian operator corresponding to the eigenfunction ψ and is the energy of the system in the state represented by ψ. The wave function of the coordinates of the system and the time variation of the system, according to the corollary of Postulate IV, is given by

$$\Psi(q_i,\ t) = \psi(q_i)e^{-iEt/\hbar}.$$

4.2 THE FREE PARTICLE

According to Newton's postulates of classical physics, a body will remain at rest or move with constant velocity in a given direction until acted upon by a force. According to Eq. (2–2), the absence of any forces implies a potential energy that is constant throughout space. For convenience' sake let us take for the case of the "free" particle $V(x,\ y,\ z) = 0$ throughout all space.

Under these conditions, then, the Schrödinger equation becomes for a single particle

$$-\frac{\hbar^2}{2m}\left[\frac{\partial^2\psi(x,\,y,\,z)}{\partial x^2}+\frac{\partial^2\psi(x,\,y,\,z)}{\partial y^2}+\frac{\partial^2\psi(x,\,y,\,z)}{\partial z^2}\right]=E\psi(x,\,y,\,z),$$

since $V(x,\,y,\,z)=0$ over all values of the coordinates. This can be rearranged to

$$\frac{\partial^2\psi(x,\,y,\,z)}{\partial x^2}+\frac{\partial^2\psi(x,\,y,\,z)}{\partial y^2}+\frac{\partial^2\psi(x,\,y,\,z)}{\partial z^2}+\frac{2mE\psi(x,\,y,\,z)}{\hbar^2}=0.$$

$$(4\text{--}1)$$

This equation cannot be solved directly because of its dependence on three variables, but a simplification is possible. Let us make the assumption that the wave function $\psi(x,\,y,\,z)$ can be expressed as the product of three wave functions $X(x)$, $Y(y)$, and $Z(z)$, each of which depends on only one of the variables:

$$\psi(x,\,y,\,z)=X(x)\cdot Y(y)\cdot Z(z). \qquad (4\text{--}2)$$

Substitution of this identity into Eq. (4–1) followed by division of both sides of the equation by $\psi(x,\,y,\,z)=X(x)\,Y(y)\,Z(z)$ leads to

$$\frac{1}{X(x)}\frac{d^2X(x)}{dx^2}+\frac{1}{Y(y)}\frac{d^2Y(y)}{dy^2}+\frac{1}{Z(z)}\frac{d^2Z(z)}{dz^2}+\frac{2mE}{\hbar^2}=0, \qquad (4\text{--}3)$$

in which we note that each of the three derivatives involves only one of the three variables, x, y, or z. Hence these no longer need to be written as partial derivatives. In addition, the sum of the four terms equals a constant (0) regardless of the particular values of x, y, and z. This can be so only if each of the differential terms is independently equal to a constant. In other words, if a change is made in x, the terms in y and z do not change since they are independent of x; and since the sum of the terms must equal 0 at all times, the term involving x must itself remain constant while x varies. Similarly, the remaining terms must be constant during variations in y and z. This convenient fact leads to the separation of Eq. (4–3) into three separate equations,

$$\frac{1}{X(x)}\frac{d^2X(x)}{dx^2}+\frac{2mE_x}{\hbar^2}=0, \qquad (4\text{--}4)$$

$$\frac{1}{Y(y)}\frac{d^2Y(y)}{dy^2}+\frac{2mE_y}{\hbar^2}=0, \qquad (4\text{--}5)$$

$$\frac{1}{Z(z)}\frac{d^2Z(z)}{dz^2}+\frac{2mE_z}{\hbar^2}=0, \qquad (4\text{--}6)$$

where comparison with Eq. (4–3) shows that

$$E_x+E_y+E_z=E.$$

This simplification process, known as separation of variables, is purely a mathematical operation. In this fortunate case the task of separation was very simple. In other cases we shall find similarly that a simple assumption such as that of Eq. (4–2) leads to a separation into equations which can be handled individually with less difficulty. In many other situations, however, this particular assumption may not be sufficient for a complete separation of variables; and indeed in many problems of interest such a separation cannot be effected at all, and other techniques of solution must be used.

Our problem now is to solve an equation of the type of Eq. (4–4) for each of the variables. This particular differential equation is of a well-known form and has as a possible solution

$$X(x) = N_x e^{ix(2mE_x)^{1/2}/\hbar}, \tag{4–7}$$

where N_x is a constant which can be determined by applying the normalization conditions of Eq. (3–3). This normalization unfortunately is difficult in this case because the limits of integration of the variable are infinite. We will return to a consideration of this normalization process shortly.

The fact that Eq. (4–7) is a solution of Eq. (4–4) can be verified by substituting the former into the latter. Equation (4–4) is the equation of motion for a particle moving only in the x direction. If we first investigate the wave function (4–7) in the light of Postulate I, we observe that in order that the wave function be well-behaved and remain finite as $x \rightarrow \infty$, the exponential $(2mE_x)^{1/2}$ must be real, so that E_x must be 0 or positive. There are no other restrictions, and thus we can state that the energy of the system can assume any value from 0 to $+ \infty$. Since we have set $V(x) = 0$, the energy of the system is equal to the kinetic energy of motion of the particle, and we have therefore determined that the particle can be at rest or moving with any positive kinetic energy, a result already familiar from classical physics.

If we had assumed some constant potential energy, $V(x) = V_0$, instead of $V(x) = 0$, then the solution of the Schrödinger equation would have had the form

$$X(x) = N_x e^{ix[2m(E_x-V_0)]^{1/2}/\hbar}, \tag{4–8}$$

and in order for $X(x)$ to be well-behaved, it would be necessary for $E_x \geqslant V_0$, which again reflects the classical expectation that the kinetic energy of a particle which is not moving is zero so that its total energy $E_x = V_0$, while, if it is moving, its kinetic energy is $E_x - V_0$, and this can have any value from 0 to infinity.

Let us now apply Postulate Ib to this system. According to this postulate the probability of finding the particle at some point x is given by

$$X(x)^*X(x)\,dx = N_x^*N_x e^{i\alpha x}e^{-i\alpha x}\,dx = N_x^*N_x\,dx,$$

where the abbreviation $\alpha = (2mE_x)^{1/2}/\hbar$ has been made. Since $N_x^*N_x$ is constant, and not dependent on x, we predict that all positions x are equally probable. We have put no restraints of any kind on the particle ($V = 0$ everywhere), so this result is also expected classically.

Further insight into the motion of the particle and into the methods of quantum mechanics can be obtained if we consider some of the physical quantities that are useful in describing motion. If, for example, we consider the momentum of the particle in the x direction, p_x, we expect from Postulate III that the average value of a series of measurements of p_x is given by

$$\langle p_x \rangle = \frac{N_x^*N_x \int_{-\infty}^{\infty} e^{-i\alpha x}(-i\hbar\,\partial/\partial x)e^{i\alpha x}\,dx}{N_x^*N_x \int_{-\infty}^{\infty} e^{-i\alpha x}e^{i\alpha x}\,dx} = (2mE_x)^{1/2}.$$

Again this result is familiar from classical physics, since $p_x = mv_x = [2m(\tfrac{1}{2})mv_x^2]^{1/2} = (2mE_x)^{1/2}$. We also find

$$\langle p_x^2 \rangle = \frac{N_x^*N_x \int_{-\infty}^{\infty} e^{-i\alpha x}(-\hbar^2\,\partial^2/\partial x^2)e^{i\alpha x}\,dx}{N_x^*N_x \int_{-\infty}^{\infty} e^{-i\alpha x}e^{i\alpha x}\,dx} = 2mE_x = \langle p_x \rangle^2,$$

which, according to the discussion following Postulate III, means that $X(x)$ is actually an eigenfunction of the momentum operator with the eigenvalue $(2mE_x)^{1/2}$. Since momentum is a vector quantity, the positive value of p_x shows that Eq. (4–7) describes the motion of a particle in the $+x$ direction only as we have already inferred. A second equally satisfactory solution of Eq. (4–4) is

$$X(x) = N_x e^{-i\alpha x}, \tag{4–9}$$

from which it can similarly be shown that $\langle p_x \rangle = -(2mE_x)^{1/2}$, describing motion in the $-x$ direction.

Since the wave function $X(x)$ is an eigenfunction of the momentum operator, the momentum is known exactly, so that the uncertainty in momentum is $\Delta p_x = 0$. This is consistent with our finding that all positions, x, are equally probable, since the latter implies that the uncertainty in finding the particle is $\Delta x = \infty$, as required by the uncertainty principle.

A more general solution of the Schrödinger equation for the free particle would be a linear combination of (4–7) and (4–9):

$$X(x) = Ae^{i\alpha x} + Be^{-i\alpha x}, \tag{4–10}$$

where A and B are the normalization constants. We will not discuss this solution in detail, as the principles involved are the same. Since this function obviously describes motion in both the $+x$ and $-x$ directions, and both directions should be equally probable, we expect that $A = B$. In addition it can be shown that $\langle p_x \rangle = 0$ while $\langle p_x{}^2 \rangle = 2mE_x$, which would be expected also for equal motions in both directions (recall that p_x is a vector quantity).

Obviously the solutions of Eqs. (4–5) and (4–6) in the coordinates y and z will be similar to the solutions (4–8), (4–9), and (4–10), and in order that the wave functions be well-behaved, the only limitations on E_y and E_z will be that they be zero or positive.

Although direct normalization of these solutions is complicated by the infinite limits of integration, it is instructive to approach the problem from a slightly different point of view. Instead of considering only one particle, let us consider a stream of particles moving in the $+x$ direction with momentum p_x containing ρ particles per unit length along the beam. The normalization of (4–8) then requires

$$\int_{-\infty}^{\infty} X(x){}^*X(x)\,dx = \rho l,$$

where $(2mE_x)^{1/2}l/\hbar \gg 2\pi$. The result of this integration is

$$|N_x|^2 = \rho,$$

where $|N_x|^2 = N_x{}^*N_x$ is the absolute value of the normalization constant squared. In other words, $|N_x|^2$ is the density of particles moving in the $+x$ direction. Application of this method to Eq. (4–10) gives

$$|A|^2 + |B|^2 = \rho,$$

$|A|^2$ being the density of particles moving in the $+x$ direction and $|B|^2$ the density moving in the $-x$ direction. With no restraints one would expect

$$|A|^2 = |B|^2.$$

4.3 POTENTIAL BARRIERS

Consider now a slightly more complicated case, illustrated in Fig. 4–1, where the potential energy has a constant value, say $V(x) = 0$, from $x = -\infty$ up to a point $x = 0$ where it assumes the higher constant value $V(x) = V_0$ for $x = 0$ to $+\infty$. We will describe motion only in one dimension to keep clear the essentials of the problem.

For this one-dimensional problem the Schrödinger equation becomes

$$\frac{d^2\psi(x)}{dx^2} + \frac{2m}{\hbar^2}[E_x - V(x)]\psi(x) = 0. \qquad (4\text{–}11)$$

In the region $x \leqslant 0$ the situation corresponds to that of the preceding section:

$$\psi(x) = Ae^{i\alpha x} + Be^{-i\alpha x},$$

where the first term describes particles moving in the $+x$ direction (toward the barrier) while the second describes particles moving in the $-x$ direction.

In the region $x \geqslant 0$ the laws of classical physics tell us that a particle must have an energy $E_x > V_0$; otherwise it could not be in this region. It is in this sense that the discontinuity in the potential energy at $x = 0$ is a barrier. Particles in the $x < 0$ region moving toward this barrier with some energy E_x (and therefore with kinetic energy E_x since in this region $V(x) = 0$) could continue to travel in the $+x$ direction beyond $x = 0$ if $E_x > V_0$. If $E_x = V_0$, then all kinetic energy of the particle would be converted to potential energy at $x = 0$ and the particle would come to rest; while if $E_x > V_0$, then the particle would continue in the $+x$ direction with kinetic energy $E_x - V_0$. A particle reaching the

Fig. 4–1.   A simple potential barrier.

barrier with $E_x < V_0$ would be reflected back in the $-x$ direction with the same kinetic energy as before. On this basis we would not expect any particles to be moving in either direction in the region $x > 0$ with energy $E_x < V_0$. The results of the quantum-mechanical calculation, however, are quite different.

In the region $x \geqslant 0$ the solution of the Schrödinger equation would be

$$\psi(x) = Ce^{\beta x} + De^{-\beta x}, \qquad (4\text{--}12)$$

where we have written $\beta = [2m(V_0 - E_x)]^{1/2}/\hbar$.

In considering the system as a whole, we recall that the wave function must be well-behaved, and in particular we note that continuity requires that at $x = 0$ the wave functions of Eqs.(4–10) and (4–12) must be equal:

$$\psi(0) = A + B = C + D.$$

From the Schrödinger equation (4–11) we observe also that at a point of discontinuity in $V(x)$ such as that at $x = 0$, the first derivative of $\psi(x)$ must be continuous. This requirement leads to

$$\frac{d\psi(0)}{dx} = i\alpha(A - B) = \beta(C - D),$$

and simultaneous solution of these two continuity relations gives

$$A = C \frac{i\alpha + \beta}{2i\alpha} + D \frac{i\alpha - \beta}{2i\alpha}, \qquad (4\text{-}13)$$

$$B = C \frac{i\alpha - \beta}{2i\alpha} + D \frac{i\alpha + \beta}{2i\alpha}. \qquad (4\text{-}14)$$

We saw in the previous section that we can consider the absolute values of the squares of the normalization constants to be proportional to the density of particles moving in a given direction in the appropriate region of space. Let us now interpret (4-13) and (4-14) in this light.

If we consider the case in which the kinetic energies of the particles are greater than the potential energy barrier ($E_x > V_0$), then classically we expect that all the particles moving in the $+x$ direction in the region $x < 0$ would continue to move into the region $x > 0$. If all the particles were initially coming from the $-x$ direction, then after a period of time there would still be no particles moving toward the $-x$ direction since all the particles would continue on past the barrier at $x = 0$ without being reflected back.

If particles are not coming from the $+x$ direction, then $D = 0$ and from (4-13) and (4-14) we find that

$$\frac{B}{A} = \frac{i\alpha - \beta}{i\alpha + \beta} = \frac{(E_x)^{1/2} - (E_x - V_0)^{1/2}}{(E_x)^{1/2} + (E_x - V_0)^{1/2}},$$

or

$$\frac{|B|^2}{|A|^2} = \frac{2E_x - V_0 - 2[E_x(E_x - V_0)]^{1/2}}{2E_x - V_0 + 2[E_x(E_x - V_0)]^{1/2}}.$$

For the situation where $V_0/E_x \ll 1$, the binomial theorem reduces this to

$$\frac{|B|^2}{|A|^2} = \tfrac{1}{16} \left(\frac{V_0}{E_x} \right)^2.$$

Since $B \neq 0$, this means that a fraction of the particles reaching the barrier will be reflected back to the $-x$ direction even though $E_x > V_0$, an entirely unexpected result. With E_x twice V_0, the fraction reflected is about 2 per cent.

An even more unusual situation results if we look at the case in which $V_0 > E_x$, a situation which classically would allow no particles in the region $x > 0$. In the quantum-mechanical solution we see that $C = 0$ to prevent the exponential βx from going to infinity with increasing x. Also, from (4-13) and (4-14) we now have

$$\frac{B}{A} = \frac{i\alpha + \beta}{i\alpha - \beta},$$

and since β is real,

$$|i\alpha + \beta| = |i\alpha - \beta| = (\alpha^2 + \beta^2)^{1/2},$$

from which

$$\frac{|A|^2}{|B|^2} = 1.$$

Again, this is the classical prediction that all particles are reflected at the barrier. But note also that from (4–13)

$$(i\alpha - \beta)D = 2i\alpha A$$

and

$$|D|^2 = \frac{4\alpha^2}{\alpha^2 + \beta^2}\,|A|^2.$$

In other words, unless V_0 is infinite, D is not zero and there is a finite probability of finding a particle in a region where classically it does not have enough energy to be.

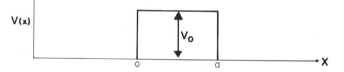

Fig. 4–2. A single finite potential barrier.

A similar and only slightly more complicated situation also is of interest. The potential barrier of height V_0 may extend only for a limited distance, say from $x = 0$ to $x = a$ as in Fig. 4–2.   In the three regions of constant potential energy we would obtain as solutions of the Schrödinger equation

$$\begin{aligned}
\psi(x) &= Ae^{i\alpha x} + Be^{-i\alpha x}, & x &\leqslant 0, \\
\psi(x) &= Ce^{\beta x} + De^{-\beta x}, & 0 &\leqslant x \leqslant a, & (4\text{–}15) \\
\psi(x) &= Ee^{i\alpha x} + Fe^{-i\alpha x}, & a &\leqslant x. & (4\text{–}16)
\end{aligned}$$

If the particles are coming only from the left, then $F = 0$.

A number of relationships can be found among the various normalization constants, but applying the continuity conditions at $x = a$ is of particular interest.   Setting the functions (4–15) and (4–16) equal at $x = a$, and similarly for the first derivatives, we obtain

$$\psi(a) = Ce^{\beta a} + De^{-\beta a} = Ee^{i\alpha a},$$
$$\frac{d\psi(a)}{dx} = \beta(Ce^{\beta a} - De^{-\beta a}) = i\alpha Ee^{i\alpha a},$$

from which

$$C = E\,\frac{\beta + i\alpha}{2\beta}\,e^{(i\alpha-\beta)a},$$
$$D = E\,\frac{\beta - i\alpha}{2\beta}\,e^{(i\alpha+\beta)a}.$$

Substitution of these into (4–13), which represents the continuity of $\psi(x)$ at $x = 0$, gives

$$A = E \left[\frac{\beta^2 + 2i\alpha\beta - \alpha^2}{4i\alpha\beta} e^{(i\alpha - \beta)a} + \frac{\alpha^2 + 2i\alpha\beta - \beta^2}{4i\alpha\beta} e^{-(i\alpha + \beta)a} \right]$$

$$= \frac{Ee^{i\alpha a}}{4i\alpha\beta} [4i\alpha\beta \cosh \beta a + 2(\alpha^2 - \beta^2) \sinh \beta a],$$

or

$$|A|^2 = |E|^2 \left[\cosh \beta a + \frac{(\alpha^2 - \beta^2)^2}{4\alpha^2\beta^2} \sinh \beta a \right], \tag{4–17}$$

where cosh and sinh are the hyperbolic cosine and hyperbolic sine, respectively.

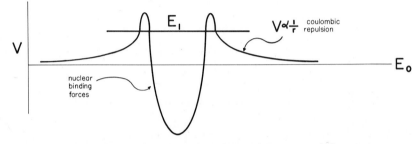

Fig. 4–3. Schematic representation of a nuclear potential-energy curve.

From (4–17) we see that there is actually a finite probability that a fraction of the particles impinging on the barrier at $x = 0$ will penetrate the classically impenetrable region and emerge into the right-hand region. The fraction so transmitted, or the probability of penetration, is simply

$$P = \frac{|E|^2}{|A|^2},$$

which simplifies, when $\beta a \gg 1$, to

$$P \simeq 16E_x(V_0 - E_x)V_0^{-2}e^{-2\beta a} \simeq 4e^{-2\beta a}. \tag{4–18}$$

This penetration of potential barriers is of considerable importance in many chemical and physical phenomena and is often referred to as quantum-mechanical *tunneling*. The emission of alpha particles from radioactive nuclei has been explained on this basis, for example. The approximate potential energy of an alpha particle near a nucleus is illustrated in Fig. 4–3.

An alpha particle may exist inside the nucleus with an energy E_1 that is greater than the energy E_0 at complete separation from the nucleus, but is insufficient to raise it over the barrier. Tunneling, however, permits escape of the alpha particle, and this theory has been used successfully to explain the Geiger-Nuttal relations between nuclear half-life and alpha particle kinetic energies.

Other important processes involving electron transfer such as oxidation-reduction processes, electrode reactions, and emission from metals also operate by the tunneling mechanism. In these cases the small mass of the electron increases the probability of transmission (4–18). For more massive particles such as complex atoms the tunneling mechanism is important where potential barriers are relatively low or the width of the barrier is small. Important examples are molecular inversion and internal rotation. These will be discussed in greater detail in future chapters.

4.4 THE PARTICLE IN A BOX

Another potential-barrier problem of considerable interest is that in which a particle is confined to a region of space by virtue of two potential

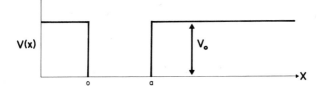

Fig. 4–4. A square potential well.

barriers. A simple one-dimensional case is illustrated in Fig. 4–4, where the potential energy is zero for $x = 0$ to $x = a$, but is V_0, elsewhere.

This type of problem is most easily attacked if it is assumed that V_0 is infinite, so that the Schrödinger equation can be satisfied only if $\psi(x) = 0$ at all points outside the region where $V(x) = 0$. This is the problem of a particle in an infinite-walled box:

$$-\frac{\hbar^2}{2m}\frac{d^2\psi(x)}{dx^2} = E_x\psi(x),\qquad(4\text{--}19)$$

which is identical in form with Eq. (4–4), the general solution of which we know to be

$$\psi(x) = Ae^{i\alpha x} + Be^{-i\alpha x}.$$

Another perfectly valid solution of (4–19) is

$$\psi(x) = A'\sin \alpha x + B'\cos \alpha x,\qquad(4\text{--}20)$$

which can be verified by substitution in (4–19) and by the mathematical identity $e^{icx} = i \sin cx + \cos cx$. Although at first sight this solution appears to be the same as in the motion of a free particle, we must note that in this case there are additional restraints that must be placed on (4–20) in order that it be a well-behaved function. In the region where $V = \infty$ the wave function vanishes. Therefore, $\psi(x)$ must go to zero at $x = 0$ and at $x = a$. At $x = 0$ the requirement $\psi(x) = 0$ requires that $B' = 0$. At $x = a$, in order that $\psi(a) = 0$, either it is necessary for A' to be zero, which is trivial because it would result in $\psi(x) = 0$ everywhere, or else $\sin \alpha a$ must be zero. The latter requirement is fulfilled if αa is equal to π or an integral multiple of π. In other words,

$$\alpha = \frac{n\pi}{a}, \tag{4–21}$$

where n can have any integral value 1, 2, 3, ... The value $n = 0$ would again be trivial since it would make $\psi(x) = 0$ at all points, implying the absence of any particle in the box. We thus find that for the infinite-walled potential well

$$\psi_n(x) = A' \sin \frac{n\pi x}{a}, \tag{4–22}$$

and from (4–21) rearrangement gives

$$E_n = \frac{n^2 h^2}{8ma^2}, \tag{4–23}$$

where the subscript n is used to denote that a particular value of the energy of the system, E_n, will be obtained corresponding to each possible value of n, which in this case can be any integer.

The results of this problem, then, are quite different from those in the free-particle case. In particular, we see that only certain "quantized" energies are possible for the particle in the potential well, and corresponding to each particular energy state (with a particular value of n) there corresponds a wave function (involving the same value of n) that describes the system. The number n is commonly called a *quantum number* since it is a convenient index for identifying states and calculating their energies. This interesting quantization of energy is a consequence of the mathematical boundary conditions at $x = 0$ and $x = a$ which were present in this case but not in the example of the free particle. In the potential-barrier problems an infinity of solutions can be found which satisfy the continuity conditions at the barrier, but in the potential-well situation the boundary conditions are satisfied by only a limited number of functions out of all those which might satisfy one of the conditions but not the other.

Several of the lower energy states and their corresponding wave functions are shown in Fig. 4–5.   Also shown are the values of $|\psi|^2$ from which the probability distribution of the particle in the box can be discerned.   Note that, unlike the classical expectation that all values of x should be equally probable for a particle bouncing back and forth

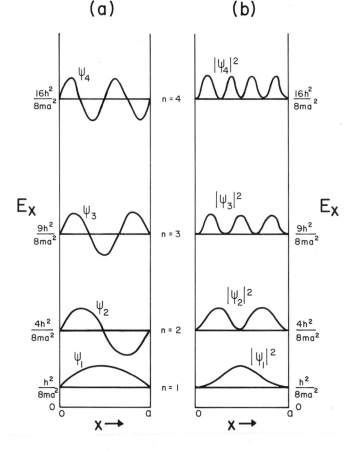

Fig. 4–5.   Energy levels for the particle in an infinite-walled potential well. (a) The wave functions corresponding to each state are superimposed on the corresponding energy levels.   (b) The probability distributions for each state are superimposed on the corresponding energy levels.

between the potential walls, quantum mechanics predicts certain regions to be more probable than others, and at some values of x the probability is actually zero.   Mathematically these results are identical with the analysis of the vibrations of a string with its ends fixed, in which case we obtain the fundamental and harmonic vibrations, which are similar to Fig. 4–5.

The normalization constant A' is found easily in this case, for then

$$\int_0^a A'^2 \sin^2 \frac{n\pi x}{a} \, dx = 1 = A'^2 \frac{a}{2},$$

or

$$A' = \left(\frac{2}{a}\right)^{1/2},$$

so that

$$\psi(x) = \left(\frac{2}{a}\right)^{1/2} \sin \frac{n\pi x}{a}.$$

With this wave function we can now calculate expectation values of physically measurable quantities such as position:

$$\langle x \rangle = \frac{2}{a} \int_0^a x \sin^2 \frac{n\pi x}{a} \, dx = \frac{a}{2},$$

$$\langle x^2 \rangle = \frac{2}{a} \int_0^a x^2 \sin^2 \frac{n\pi x}{a} \, dx = \frac{a^2}{3} \left(1 - \frac{3}{2n^2\pi^2}\right),$$

and momentum

$$\langle p_x \rangle = \frac{2}{a} \int_0^a \sin \frac{n\pi x}{a} \left(\frac{\hbar}{i} \frac{d}{dx}\right) \sin \frac{n\pi x}{a} \, dx = 0,$$

$$\langle p_x^2 \rangle = \frac{2}{a} \int_0^a \sin \frac{n\pi x}{a} \left(-\hbar^2 \frac{d^2}{dx^2}\right) \sin \frac{n\pi x}{a} = 2mE_x,$$

all of which correspond to the classical results for a particle moving back and forth with constant velocity. Note that the denominator of Eq. (3–4) was not included in these calculations since the wave function had already been normalized.

There are a number of interesting points about this simple problem which we might discuss briefly. Note, for example, that the separation of the energy levels depends on several parameters, notably the mass of the particle and the dimensions of the potential well. As either becomes very small, the energy difference between successive levels becomes greater, but as the particle becomes more massive or the dimensions of the box become greater, then the separation between the levels diminishes. It is for this reason that we do not observe quantization of the motion of baseballs and other macroscopic bodies and, as we shall see, the dimensions of ordinary laboratory containers make this quantization essentially unimportant even for molecules in a gas.

Observe also that there is no energy state corresponding to a particle at rest with zero kinetic energy. The lowest state, with $n = 1$, has an energy $h^2/8ma^2$. This energy, the zero-point energy, is consistent with the uncertainty principle. We know the particle is located somewhere in the region $0 \leqslant x \leqslant a$ so that the uncertainty in x is equal to a, which being a finite quantity requires that there also be an uncertainty in the momentum of the particle. In fact, using the statistical standard deviation as a measure of Δx and Δp as suggested in Sec. 3.3, it is seen from the definition of σ and the expectation values just calculated that

$$\sigma_x^2 = \frac{a^2}{3}\left(1 - \frac{3}{2n^2\pi^2}\right) - \frac{a^2}{4},$$

$$\sigma_x = \frac{a(n^2\pi^2 - 6)^{1/2}}{2(3)^{1/2}n\pi},$$

$$\sigma_p^2 = \frac{n^2\hbar^2\pi^2}{a^2},$$

$$\sigma_p = \frac{n\pi\hbar}{a},$$

and

$$\sigma_x\sigma_p = \frac{(n^2\pi^2 - 6)^{1/2}\hbar}{2(3)^{1/2}} \geqslant \frac{\hbar}{2}.$$

Finally, we might also observe that as n becomes very large, the quantum-mechanical situation goes to the classical result as a limit. The nodes and crests in the wave functions of Fig. 4–5 increase as n increases, so that for large values of n all regions in the box are essentially of equal probability. This is also seen in the equation for $\langle x^2 \rangle$, which for large n approaches

$$\langle x^2 \rangle = \frac{a^2}{3},$$

the classical result. This approach of highly excited states to the classical prediction is generally found in quantum mechanics and is known as the Bohr correspondence principle.

The particle-in-a-box problem is easily extended to three dimensions. Consider, for example, a region where $V = 0$ for $0 \leqslant x \leqslant a$, $0 \leqslant y \leqslant b$, and $0 \leqslant z \leqslant c$, and $V = \infty$ everywhere else. In this potential well the Schrödinger equation is

$$-\frac{\hbar^2}{2m}\left[\frac{\partial^2\psi(x,\,y,\,z)}{\partial x^2} + \frac{\partial^2\psi(x,\,y,\,z)}{\partial y^2} + \frac{\partial^2\psi(x,\,y,\,z)}{\partial z^2}\right] = E\psi(x,\,y,\,z)$$

but we have already seen that this equation, which is identical with Eq. (4–1), can be separated by assuming that $\psi(x,\,y,\,z) = X(x)Y(y)Z(z)$ into three equations of the form

$$-\frac{\hbar^2}{2m}\frac{d^2X(x)}{dx^2} = E_xX(x),$$

each of which is a one-dimensional particle-in-a-box problem. Thus the solution of the three-dimensional problem is

$$\psi(x,\ y,\ z) = \left(\frac{2}{a}\right)^{1/2} \left(\frac{2}{b}\right)^{1/2} \left(\frac{2}{c}\right)^{1/2} \sin\frac{n_x\pi x}{a} \sin\frac{n_y\pi y}{b} \sin\frac{n_z\pi z}{c}$$

and

$$E = \frac{h^2}{8m}\left(\frac{n_x{}^2}{a^2} + \frac{n_y{}^2}{b^2} + \frac{n_z{}^2}{c^2}\right), \tag{4-24}$$

where n_x, n_y, and n_z can each have independently any integral value except zero.

The spacing of the possible energy states in the three-dimensional case is obviously more complicated than the simple geometric progression in the one-dimensional problem. The spacing depends primarily on the relative dimensions of the box, the simplest case being that of a cube when $a = b = c$. Here (4–24) reduces to

$$E = \frac{h^2}{8ma^2}\ (n_x{}^2 + n_y{}^2 + n_z{}^2).$$

The state of lowest energy is that for which $n_x = n_y = n_z = 1$:

$$E_{(111)} = \frac{3h^2}{8ma^2}.$$

The subscript notation indicates the values of n_x, n_y, and n_z, respectively. The next highest state is that with one of the quantum numbers equal to 2 while the remaining two quantum numbers are each 1. We see, however, that three different such states will give us the same energy, namely

$$E_{(211)} = E_{(121)} = E_{(112)} = \frac{6h^2}{8ma^2}.$$

The existence of several states with the same energy is called *degeneracy*. In this case the energy level with $E = 6h^2/8ma^2$ is said to be *threefold degenerate*, there being three states with this energy. The level with $E = 3h^2/8ma^2$ is non-degenerate since there is only one state with this energy. The degree of degeneracy of a given energy level is often called the *quantum weight*, or *statistical weight*, of the level and given the symbol g. Several of the lower energy levels of a particle in a cubic potential well are shown in Fig. 4–6 along with their statistical weights and an indication of the states corresponding to each energy. The high degree of degeneracy of many of these levels is due to the symmetry of the physical situation. In a box with unequal sides there would be much less likelihood of degeneracies.

An infinite-walled potential well is only a convenient limiting case. In more likely physical situations this potential rise would be finite, in which case the results would be slightly different.   If V_0 in Fig. 4–4 were finite, our problem would again become similar to that in our previous potential-barrier situations.   In the three regions of interest the solutions of the Schrödinger equation would be

$$\psi(x) = Ae^{\beta x} + Be^{-\beta x}, \qquad x \leqslant 0$$
$$\psi(x) = Ce^{i\alpha x} + De^{-i\alpha x}, \qquad 0 \leqslant x \leqslant a$$
$$\psi(x) = Ee^{\beta x} + Fe^{-\beta x}, \qquad a \leqslant x$$

where it is necessary to make E and B equal to zero in order that $\psi(x)$ remain finite.   The boundary conditions that $\psi(x)$ and $d\psi(x)/dx$ must

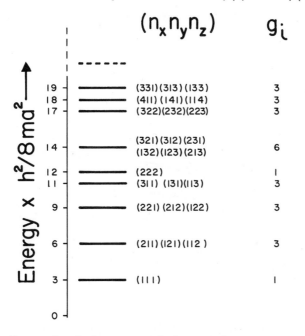

Fig. 4–6. Energy levels for a particle in an infinite cubic potential well. The quantum numbers identifying the states and the degeneracies are given for each level.

be continuous at $x = 0$ and $x = a$ can then be applied and relations found between the various parameters.   We will not study the complete solution in detail, but will note the results, which are qualitatively similar to the infinite-walled potential.   The first difference we note is that the possible energy levels are somewhat lower in energy than if V_0 were infinite, and as V_0 becomes smaller, the number of possible quantized energy states with energies smaller than V_0 decreases.   As in all potential-barrier problems, there is no quantization of the energy when $E > V_0$.

If the barriers were of different height on either side of the well, a continuum of states would appear at energies immediately above the lowest barrier. The variation of the energies of the bound energy levels, as V_0 increases, is shown schematically in Fig. 4–7. Note that as V_0 increases, more quantized states become possible, and their numerical values increase until at $V_0 = \infty$ they approach the values given by Eq. (4–23), and there is no longer any region of continuous energy states.

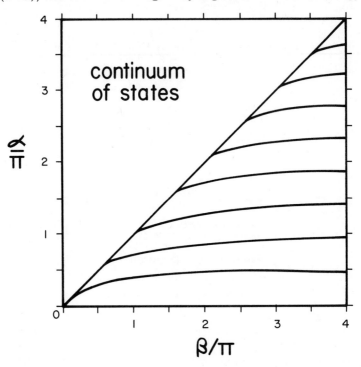

Fig. 4–7. Dependence of bound energy levels on the height of the potential well: $\alpha^2 = (2ma^2/\hbar^2)E$, $\beta^2 = (2ma^2/\hbar^2)V_0$. (After Bates, *Quantum Theory*, vol. 1, *Elements*, Academic Press, Inc., New York, 1961, p. 87.)

A second interesting result is shown in Fig. 4–8, where representative wave functions are drawn for two bound energy levels. It is seen that the general shapes of the wave functions are not dissimilar to those for the infinite-wall states; but an important difference is that the wave functions do not go to zero at the walls of the box, but instead extend into the classically forbidden region. We have already encountered this tunneling in other potential barriers that are not infinite in height. In those cases, also, the penetration diminishes as V_0 becomes larger, and when $V_0 = \infty$, the wave functions go to zero at the discontinuity.

Many other potential-barrier and potential-well problems could be constructed which might approximate interesting physical situations. They might be less idealistic if we were to approximate more closely the way in which V rises as a function of distance rather than employing the mathematically simpler vertical rise at the barrier. However, the results would not differ in their general characteristics. In any region not bounded by potential walls a continuum of possible energy states is found, but in a region completely bounded on all sides by a rise in potential energy that is greater than the energy of the particle only a limited number of quantized energy states are allowed. In both cases, so long as the potential barriers are not infinite or very large compared to the total energy, quantum-mechanical penetration of the classically forbidden

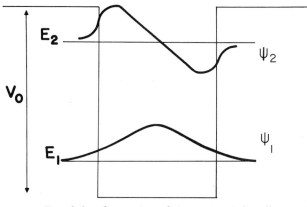

Fig. 4-8.   States in a finite potential well.

region is found. The extent of this tunneling depends on the height and thickness of the barrier. Finally, even for particles with energies greater than any existent barriers, there is a finite probability of reflection of particles at the barrier. As we have intimated, all these quantum phenomena become insignificant as the masses of the particles and the magnitudes of the distances involved become larger than those encountered on the atomic-molecular scale.

An interesting application of the simple particle-in-a-box problem is to the absorption spectra of long conjugated molecules such as the conjugated polyenes. Various properties such as the bond lengths and chemical reactivities of molecules with alternating double and single bonds have suggested that the electrons forming the double bonds in these molecules, the so-called π electrons, are not restricted to the regions indicated by the classical valence bond diagrams for these molecules, but are "delocalized" over the entire chain of atoms. Such conjugated systems show strong absorption of light in the visible and ultraviolet regions, many dye materials being such very long conjugated chains.

This simplified view of a conjugated molecule suggests the use of our quantum-mechanical model of a set of particles, the π electrons, in a one-dimensional box, the chain of conjugated carbon atoms. To keep the problem as simple as possible, let us assume that there is no interaction between the electrons, and that the potential energy is constant along the chain of carbon atoms and goes to infinity at the ends of the chain.

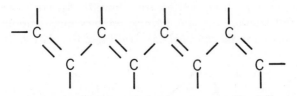

Although actual conjugated molecules are not linear, we will assume that the chain can be approximated by a one-dimensional potential well of length Nd, where N is the number of carbon atoms in the chain and d is half the sum of a carbon-carbon single-bond length and double-bond length. In a conjugated molecule of N atoms there will be N double-bond electrons. Introducing the molecular length into (4–23), we obtain

$$E_n = \frac{n^2 h^2}{8mN^2d^2},$$

$$\psi(x) = A' \sin \frac{n\pi x}{Nd}.$$

We must now consider how the energy levels are occupied by the electrons. Anticipating a familiar principle, which we will explore in more detail later, we will assume that two electrons may occupy a single energy level so long as their spin angular momentum vectors are opposite to each other (spins paired). Our N electrons will fill the levels from the lowest up, two electrons to each level, until the level $n = N/2$ has been filled. Now if energy is absorbed by the system, there will be a transition of an electron in the level $n = N/2$ to the next higher level $n = N/2 + 1$, from which we can state

$$h\nu = E_{N/2+1} - E_{N/2} = \frac{h^2(N+1)}{8md^2N^2} \simeq \frac{h^2}{8md^2N}.$$

We thus see that the frequency of absorption should be inversely proportional to the chain length. Short conjugated molecules absorb in the far ultraviolet region, but as the extent of conjugation increases by lengthening the chain and adding conjugating groups on the ends of the chain, the absorption shifts to longer and longer wavelengths (lower frequencies). This is seen clearly in the absorption data for the polyenes listed in Table 4–1. The larger of these absorb in the visible region. Although our predictions are verified qualitatively, the agreement is not exact. However, we might approach the problem more realistically by considering a non-constant potential energy along the chain, a non-linear chain, a potential barrier approximated by the ionization potential,

TABLE 4–1.   Absorption Bands of Polyenes

Compound	N	$\tilde{\nu}$ (cm^{-1})	λ (Å)
Ethylene	2	61,500	1625
Butadiene	4	46,080	2170
Hexatriene	6	39,750	2510
Octatetraene	8	32,900	3040
Vitamin A	10	30,490	3280
Axerophtene	10	28,900	3460
Tetrahexadecaene	12	27,780	3600
Anhydro vitamin A	12	27,100	3690
Dihydro-β-carotene	16	23,820	4200
α-Carotene	20	22,480	4450
β-Carotene	22	22,150	4510
γ-Carotene	22	21,750	4600
Dehydro-β-carotene	24	21,050	4750
Dehydrolycopene	30	19,850	5040

and similar factors. Such considerations have resulted in surprisingly accurate predictions. Although such a model is crude, it nevertheless has given us an insight into the nature of such molecules.

4.5   THE RIGID, FIXED ROTATOR

A very simple picture of a diatomic molecule is that of two masses m_1 and m_2 connected by a massless rod of constant length R, which is constrained to rotate in a plane about an axis through the center of mass of the molecule. Such a system is pictured in Fig. 4–9. The moment

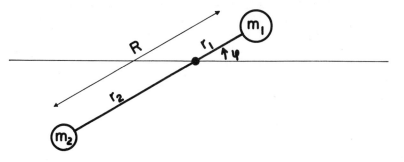

Fig. 4–9.   The fixed rigid rotator.

of inertia of this system is given by $I = m_1r_1^2 + m_2r_2^2$. This system is mechanically equivalent to a single particle of mass I rotating about the center of mass at unit distance from the axis. The classical Hamiltonian for such motion is

$$H = \frac{p_\phi^2}{2I},$$

where p_ϕ is the angular momentum. The Schrödinger equation is therefore

$$-\frac{\hbar^2}{2I}\frac{d^2\psi(\phi)}{d\phi^2} = E_\phi\psi(\phi),$$

since $V(\phi) = 0$. This differential equation is of the same form as (4–4) for the free particle, so a solution immediately is seen to be

$$\psi(\phi) = N_\phi e^{i(2IE_\phi)^{1/2}\phi/\hbar}.$$

However, in this situation the boundary conditions are somewhat different. For $\psi(\phi)$ to be continuous we must require that $\psi(\phi) = \psi(\phi + 2\pi)$. This can be so only if $(2IE_\phi)^{1/2}/\hbar$ is zero or integral, or in other words if

$$\psi(\phi) = N_\phi e^{im\phi},$$

where $m = 0, \pm1, \pm2, \ldots$. This requirement leads to an expression

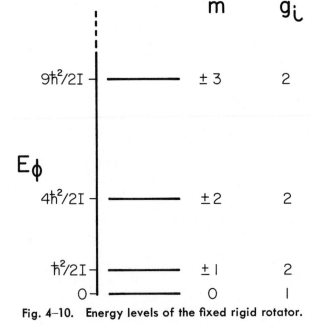

Fig. 4–10. Energy levels of the fixed rigid rotator.

for the energy

$$E = \frac{m^2\hbar^2}{2I}.$$

The positive and negative integers correspond to rotation in opposite directions, but with equal velocities, and therefore all the energy levels except $m = 0$ (no rotation) are doubly degenerate. Some of these levels are pictured in Fig. 4–10.

The normalization constant is obtained from

$$\int_0^{2\pi} \psi^*(\phi)\psi(\phi)\, d\phi = 1,$$

yielding

$$N_\phi = \frac{1}{(2\pi)^{1/2}},$$

$$\psi(\phi) = \frac{1}{(2\pi)^{1/2}}\, e^{im\phi}.$$

The rotating molecule that is not constrained to move about a fixed axis presents a more complex mathematical problem, to which we will return later.

4.6　THE LINEAR HARMONIC OSCILLATOR

In all the preceding problems we have assumed the potential energy to be constant over all space except for occasional discontinuities at potential barriers. A particularly interesting case in which the potential energy is not constant is that of the linear harmonic oscillator. In addition to being an extremely useful approximation to the vibrational motions of molecules, the harmonic oscillator also illustrates some of the more complex mathematical problems that arise when the potential-energy part of the Hamiltonian operator is not as simple as in the cases we have considered so far.

The classical linear harmonic oscillator is one in which a particle moves about an equilibrium position, the restoring force acting on the particle at some non-equilibrium position being proportional to its displacement, x, from the equilibrium point. As we have seen,

$$F_x = m\ddot{x} = -kx,$$

from which

$$V(x) = -\int F_x\, dx = \tfrac{1}{2}kx^2, \tag{4–25}$$

and solution of the classical equations of motion leads to

$$x = A\sin(2\pi\nu t + C),$$

where A, the amplitude of the wave form, and C, the phase factor, are constants and ν is the frequency of the oscillation. Also obtained from the classical equations are relations for the frequency of oscillation of the particle of mass m,

$$\nu = \frac{1}{2\pi}\left(\frac{k}{m}\right)^{1/2}, \tag{4-26}$$

and for the kinetic energy and the total energy of the oscillator,

$$T = \tfrac{1}{2}m\dot{x}^2,$$

$$E = \tfrac{1}{2}kA^2.$$

The constant k is commonly known as the force constant.

In terms of the quantum-mechanical equations of motion, the potential energy of Eq. (4–25) leads to the Schrödinger equation

$$-\frac{\hbar^2}{2m}\frac{d^2\psi(x)}{dx^2} + \tfrac{1}{2}kx^2\psi(x) = E\psi(x).$$

Introducing (4–26) for k and rearranging, we obtain

$$\frac{d^2\psi(x)}{dx^2} + (\lambda - \alpha^2 x^2)\psi(x) = 0, \tag{4-27}$$

where we have written $\lambda = 8\pi^2 mE/h^2$ and $\alpha = 4\pi^2 \nu\, m/h$ to simplify the manipulations.

In searching for a suitable well-behaved solution for this equation we find that no simple mathematical function is satisfactory. We turn then to more complicated possibilities, one useful approach being to try a power series in x as a possible solution, i.e., a function of the form

$$f(x) = a_0 + a_1 x + a_2 x^2 + a_3 x^3 + \cdots. \tag{4-28}$$

We can see immediately, however, that this simple series cannot itself be a satisfactory solution since it will not remain finite as x goes to infinity. In order to determine possible modifications of (4–28), it is therefore desirable to investigate asymptotic solutions of (4–27) at large values of x.

For large x we may neglect λ in comparison with $\alpha^2 x^2$ and thus obtain

$$\frac{d^2\psi(x)}{dx^2} = \alpha^2 x^2 \psi(x),$$

which has solutions

$$\psi(x) = e^{\pm \alpha x^2/2}.$$

Of these, only the negative exponential solution will be well-behaved, the positive solution going to infinity with increasing x.

Let us now see whether a solution of the form

$$\psi(x) = e^{-\alpha x^2/2} f(x) = e^{-\alpha x^2/2}[a_0 + a_1 x + a_2 x^2 + \cdots] \tag{4-29}$$

might be a well-behaved solution, since we have now modified our original power series with the asymptotic solution for large x.   Differentiation of (4–29) gives

$$\frac{d\psi(x)}{dx} = e^{-\alpha x^2/2} \sum_{n=0}^{\infty} [(n+1)a_{n+1} - \alpha a_{n-1}]x^n$$

and

$$\frac{d^2\psi(x)}{dx^2} = e^{-\alpha x^2/2} \sum_{n=0}^{\infty} [(n+2)(n+1)a_{n+2} - \alpha(2n+1)a_n + \alpha^2 a_{n-2}]x^n,$$

which yields on substitution into (4–27)

$$e^{-\alpha x^2/2} \sum_{n=0}^{\infty} [(n+2)(n+1)a_{n+2} + (\lambda - 2\alpha n - \alpha)a_n]x^n = 0.$$

This is again a power series in x, and in order for the series to vanish for all values of x it is necessary that the coefficient of each power of x separately be equal to zero.   Thus in general

$$(n+2)(n+1)a_{n+2} + (\lambda - 2\alpha n - \alpha)a_n = 0,$$

or

$$a_{n+2} = \frac{2\alpha n + \alpha - \lambda}{(n+2)(n+1)} a_n, \tag{4–30}$$

from which we see that for any arbitrary a_0 the values of a_2, a_4, . . . are all determined by (4–30), and similarly for any arbitrary value of a_1 the values of a_3, a_5, . . . are all determined.   The second-order differential equation requires only two arbitrary constants in the solution, and therefore (4–29) is satisfactory if it is well-behaved.   Equation (4–30), which generates coefficients in a series of this sort, is commonly known as a recursion formula.   All the foregoing relations are best verified by actually generating the series and performing all the operations.

Equation (4–29) is continuous and single-valued, but the series does not converge as x goes to infinity.   Comparison with the terms in the infinite series

$$e^{ax^2} = 1 + ax^2 + \frac{(ax^2)^2}{2} + \cdots + \frac{a^k x^{2k}}{k!} + \frac{a^{k+1}x^{2k+2}}{(k+1)!} + \cdots$$

shows that (4–29) diverges when x goes to infinity and therefore is not acceptable.   However, if the series should terminate after a finite number of terms, then (4–29) will approach zero for large values of x since the wave function will be dominated at large x by the exponential $(-\alpha x^2/2)$. The series can be made so to terminate if we set the numerator of the recursion formula (4–30) equal to zero, so that the final term in the series is a_n:

$$2\alpha n + \alpha - \lambda = 0, \tag{4–31}$$

from which

$$\lambda = 2\alpha(n + \tfrac{1}{2}). \tag{4-32}$$

There are two points we should note about this solution. First, n is an integer, as implied in the power series and by the restriction (4–31), which terminates the series. Second, if n is even, then a_1 must be set equal to zero to avoid the odd powers of x, which would not be terminated and would go to infinity with large x. Similarly, if n is odd, then a_0 must be set equal to zero.

Thus from the solution of the Schrödinger equation for the linear harmonic oscillator we obtain a set of functions, each of which consists of a terminated series of terms in integral powers of x multiplied by an exponential in $-x^2$. These solutions involve a set of related functions known as the Hermite polynomials, which follow a recursion formula of the form (4–30). We will not discuss the Hermite polynomials in detail here,[1] but will note that using the recursion formula we can easily calculate the first few simpler solutions. It is only necessary to remember that for a given function with a given value of n the series will terminate with the term containing a_n and will involve only even powers of x if n is even and only odd powers of x if n is odd. We can also apply the normalization condition to these functions to evaluate the normalization constant (which was not included explicitly in our discussion). The first few functions are listed below and are illustrated along with $|\psi|^2$ in Fig. 4–11:

$$\psi_0 = \left(\frac{\alpha}{\pi}\right)^{1/4} e^{-\alpha x^2/2},$$

$$\psi_1 = \left(\frac{4\alpha^3}{\pi}\right)^{1/4} x e^{-\alpha x^2/2},$$

$$\psi_2 = \left(\frac{\alpha}{4\pi}\right)^{1/4} (1 - 2\alpha x^2) e^{-\alpha x^2/2},$$

$$\psi_3 = \left(\frac{9\alpha^3}{\pi}\right)^{1/4} \left(x - \frac{2\alpha}{3} x^3\right) e^{-\alpha x^2/2}.$$

The energies of the states represented by these functions are found from (4–32) and the definitions of λ and α as

$$E_n = (n + \tfrac{1}{2})h\nu, \qquad n = 0, 1, 2, \ldots . \tag{4-33}$$

Since n must be zero or integral, this again brings to light a situation in which the possible energy states of the system are restricted to certain discrete values.

We observe that the functions of the harmonic oscillator are not dissimilar to those of the particle in a square potential well, and indeed the

---

[1] See Appendix D.

problems are similar mathematically except for the detailed behavior of $V(x)$. It will also be noted that even when the quantum number n for the harmonic oscillator is zero, there is still a physically significant wave function and an energy that is not zero. This non-zero energy is known as the zero-point energy and corresponds again to the uncertainty

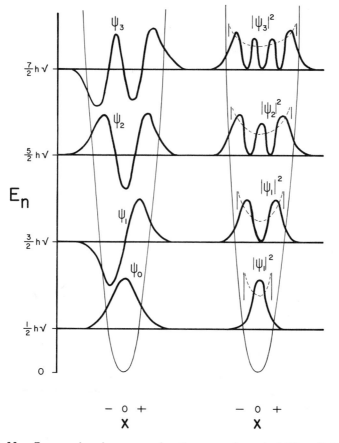

Fig. 4–11. Energy levels, wave functions, and probability distributions for the harmonic-oscillator potential well. The classical probability distributions are indicated by a dotted line.

in energy required by the localization of the oscillator in the region of the potential well. As the harmonic oscillator is a meaningful approximation to many real physical situations involving oscillation, it is worthwhile to note that this zero-point energy implies that even at the absolute zero of temperature, when all molecular motion is presumed to cease, molecules will still have a vibrational zero-point energy of $\frac{1}{2}h\nu$ for each coordinate of motion.

We will turn our attention to the application of these fundamental quantum-mechanical problems after discussing the problem of a large number of molecules in their possible quantum states. This must be done, since most experimental measurements are made on a large collection of atoms and molecules rather than on individual species.

SUPPLEMENTARY REFERENCES

Introductory

PAULING, L., and E. B. WILSON, *Introduction to Quantum Mechanics*, McGraw-Hill Book Co., New York, 1935.

EYRING, H., J. WALTER, and G. E. KIMBALL, *Quantum Chemistry*, John Wiley and Sons, New York, 1944.

KAUZMAN, W., *Quantum Chemistry*, Academic Press, New York, 1957.

PITZER, K. S., *Quantum Chemistry*, Prentice-Hall, Englewood Cliffs, N.J., 1953.

SHERWIN, C. W., *Introduction to Quantum Mechanics*, Holt, Rinehart & Winston, New York, 1959.

Intermediate

ROJANSKY, V., *Introductory Quantum Mechanics*, Prentice-Hall, Englewood Cliffs, N.J., 1946.

SCHIFF, L. I., *Quantum Mechanics*, McGraw-Hill Book Co., New York, 1955.

PROBLEMS

4-1. Show that, if for a free particle the potential energy V has any constant value, then our statements that p_x can be measured exactly, that x is indeterminate, and that the total energy may have positive continuous values are still true.

4-2. The wave function $\psi(x) = Be^{-i\alpha x}$, where $\alpha = (1/\hbar)\sqrt{2mE_x}$ and B is a constant, describes the motion of a particle of mass m in the $-x$ direction when there are no forces acting on the particle.

a. Show that this wave function is indeed a solution of Schrödinger's equation for this situation.

b. Find the expectation value of the momentum of such a particle from the wave function.

c. Show that if the momentum of the particle were measured, a definite value would be observed, and that this value is the same as the average calculated in (b).

d. Show that for this system no position is more probable for the particle than any other.

4-3. The wave equation $\psi(x) = Ae^{i\alpha x} + Be^{-i\alpha x}$ is a complete state function for a particle free to move in either direction along the x axis and not influenced by any forces.

a. Show that this wave function is a solution of Schrödinger's equation.

b. Find the expectation value of the momentum for such a system.

c. Find the expectation value of the square of the momentum $\langle p_x^2 \rangle$. Why is it different from $\langle p_x \rangle^2$?

4–4. It has been said that there are no isomers known that arise from differences in electron location alone, and that this is due to the small mass of the electron. Why does the small mass of the electron seemingly prevent such isomers? Under what conditions might such isomers exist?

4–5. Assume an electron in a box of sides $a = b = \frac{1}{3}c = 1\text{Å}$. Calculate the energies of the first six energy levels for the molecule (electron), and determine the degeneracies of each level. Repeat the calculation with all three sides equal to 1 Å. How does shortening the side affect the energies and degeneracies?

4–6. If N_2 molecules at 300°K are confined in a cube with a 10-cm edge, what is the separation between the lowest two adjacent energy levels for a molecule in such an enclosure? How does this compare in magnitude with the average kinetic energy of translation of these molecules as predicted by kinetic theory? Assuming for simplicity that $n_x = n_y = n_z = n$, what value of n corresponds to this average energy? Are a few or many translational states populated by a gas at room temperature? What is the probability distribution of molecules in the cube like?

4–7. If an electron is confined to a cube 3 Å along an edge, what is the separation of the lowest two adjacent energy levels? How does this compare with the results of the previous question? What is the significance of this difference?

4–8. For the lowest energy level of a particle in an infinite walled box calculate $\langle p_x \rangle$ and $\langle p_x^2 \rangle$, $\langle E \rangle$ and $\langle E^2 \rangle$, $\langle x \rangle$ and $\langle x^2 \rangle$. Discuss the results in terms of the uncertainty principle.

4–9. For the case of a potential well with finite potential walls and ranging from $x = -a$ to $x = a$, calculate the bound energy levels of a particle of mass m when

a. $V_0 = h^2/8\pi^2 ma^2$;

b. $V_0 = 4h^2/8\pi^2 ma^2$;

c. $V_0 = 12h^2/8\pi^2 ma^2$.

4–10. In benzene it is generally believed that the electrons in the π electron system are delocalized and can move anywhere around the ring of carbon atoms. Assuming interactions between electrons to be negligible and taking the average radius of the ring of carbon atoms to be 1.39 Å (that is, assuming a simple circle), derive an expression for the energy levels for the delocalized electrons. (If a point on a circle is located by the angle θ, the kinetic energy of a particle moving in a circle of radius R is $T = p_\theta^2/2mR^2$.)

4–11. Calculate the expectation values of x^2 and p_x^2 for the harmonic oscillator in the $n = 0$ and $n = 1$ states. From these obtain the average kinetic and potential energies in the two vibrational states, and compare with the classical values.

4–12. Apply the Bohr-Sommerfeld quantization rules (Chapter 2) to the determination of the energy levels of a harmonic oscillator, and compare with the results obtained in this chapter.

4–13. The infrared absorption spectrum of HCl^{35} shows a strong absorption at 2886 cm^{-1} and lines of decreasing intensity at 5668, 8347, and 10993 cm^{-1}.

a. Construct an energy-level diagram for the lowest vibrational levels of HCl.

b. Calculate the force constant of this molecule.

c. Set a lower limit to the binding energy of the molecule.

4–14. Verify the normalization constants of the harmonic-oscillator functions.

4–15. Show for the free particle that the wave function can be described in terms of a wavelength, λ, and that this wavelength corresponds to the de Broglie relation.

4–16. Since the momentum and energy of a free particle moving in one dimension can be known exactly, it would be expected that in this instance the momentum operator and Hamiltonian operator commute. Show that this is true.

4–17. Find the probability that an oscillator in the lowest energy state has a displacement greater than that bounded by the classical potential-energy curve.

4–18. A three-dimensional harmonic oscillator is described by

$$V = (x^2 + 4y^2 + 9z^2)10^4 \text{ g sec}^{-2}.$$

Calculate the six lowest energy levels and indicate their degeneracies.

4–19. Draw the energy levels for an isotropic three-dimensional harmonic oscillator and indicate their degeneracies.

5

Energy Levels, Statistical Mechanics, and Thermodynamics

5.1 THE NATURE OF THE STATISTICAL PROBLEM

We have dealt with several simple systems typical of atomic and molecular situations and have seen that the characteristic result of the quantum-mechanical treatment of a bound system is that only certain energy states, which we will call eigenstates, are predicted to be possible. As the potential energy terms vary from one situation to another, so also do the possible energy levels, their spacings, and their degeneracies vary. The existence of such stationary states is typical of all bound systems in quantum mechanics.

The cases we have chosen to study, and for that matter the cases it is at all possible to handle mathematically in quantum mechanics, have been limited to simple models. In each situation we have studied one atom or molecule, either from the standpoint of its translational motion in some potential field or with attention focused on its internal motions involving rotation or vibration. We have derived in this way simple expressions for the translational motion of free and bound particles, the eigenstates of a linear harmonic oscillator, and the possible energies of a rigid rotator, and we will study other situations subsequently. The results of these calculations have been strikingly verified by direct measurements, frequently spectroscopic, of the spacings and positions of the eigenstate energies of atomic and molecular systems.

The basic nature of quantum mechanics has already introduced us to the expectation that statistical ideas are an integral part of this approach to atomic and molecular structure. We have found it necessary to discuss the most probable location of a particle in a potential well, or its average position, rather than specify its location exactly. There is another important reason, however, why statistical methods are important to us, a reason which is fundamental to the application of quantum mechanics to chemical systems in the same way that statistical methods were necessary in classical physics.

Our equations have been for the possible states of a single atom or molecule. When we observe chemical systems, however, we are concerned with a large number of molecules, generally over 10^{20} of them, each of which may be in a different one of the possible energy states. The macroscopic behavior of the system, its pressure, its energy, its absorption spectrum, and other measurable quantities depend on the distribution of molecules in these available states and how this distribution changes with time. Somehow we must be able to predict how many

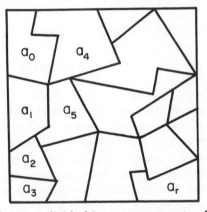

Fig. 5–1.   Box of area a divided into compartments of areas $a_0,$ $a_1,$ etc.

molecules out of a given number populate each available level and determine how this distribution affects other quantities such as the familiar thermodynamic functions. This is the problem approached by statistical mechanics.

Perhaps a simple geometrical model will help set the stage for the sort of problems with which statistical mechanics is concerned and give us an opportunity to discuss some of the basic concepts and methods. Consider a flat box which is divided into a number of compartments of arbitrary shape and size (Fig. 5–1). It will be assumed that the area of each compartment is given by $a_0, a_1, a_2, \ldots, a_r$, where the compartments have been numbered for the purpose of keeping track of them. The total area of the box must be

$$a = a_0 + a_1 + a_2 + \cdots + a_r.$$

Suppose that a total of n particles are put into the box in such a way that no portion of the box is favored initially over any other. This might be done by throwing the particles into a device which arbitrarily shakes the particle around and then drops it somewhere over the area of the box, no side, corner, or center portion of the box being favored. After n particles have been dropped into the box, it will be observed that there are a certain number of particles in each compartment, and it follows that the total number of particles is the sum of the particles in each compartment:

$$n = n_0 + n_1 + \cdots + n_r.$$

If the process of throwing n particles into the box is repeated, it is likely that a somewhat different distribution of particles in the compartments will be found; i.e., the separate n_i's will be different although their sum, of course, must remain the same (equal to n).   However, a large number of such trials will show that some distributions occur more frequently than others, and the one distribution which has occurred more frequently than any other will be the most probable distribution.   It is more likely that an additional trial will give this distribution as a result than one of the other distributions.

There are two factors operating to make one of the distributions more probable than the others.   The first of these is the probability that a given number of particles will land in each compartment.   The second is the number of ways the particles can be rearranged between the compartments while the number of particles in each compartment is kept the same.[1]

In this simple geometric example it is rather apparent that the larger the area of a compartment the greater the probability that a particle fall into that particular compartment.   In fact, it seems reasonable that the probability of a throw landing in compartment number i is the fraction of the total area of the box occupied by the area of compartment i. This assumed probability, called the *a priori probability* or the *statistical weight* for compartment i, is then

$$g_i = \frac{a_i}{a}.$$

All the g_i's add up to unity, which is consistent with the definition of probability.   If there are several throws, the probability that n_i particles fall into this compartment is $g_i{}^{n_i}$.   Thus the probability of a distribution with n_1 particles in compartment 1, n_2 particles in compartment 2, etc., all at the same time, is the product

$$D = g_0{}^{n_0} g_1{}^{n_1} g_2{}^{n_2} \cdots g_r{}^{n_r} = \prod_{i=0}^{r} g_i{}^{n_i}. \tag{5-1}$$

---

[1] The basic concepts in probability theory are outlined in Appendix C.

Although this product gives the probability of having the specified number of particles in each compartment, the total probability of obtaining this distribution is greater than this if the particles can be distinguished from one another, since the same distribution can then be obtained many times again by simply rearranging the particles in the compartments. As a simple example consider the distribution of three particles in three compartments with one particle in each compartment. There are six ways in which the three particles can be arranged in the three compartments, one in each:

Compartment	Particle number					
1	1	1	2	2	3	3
2	2	3	1	3	1	2
3	3	2	3	1	2	1

But if the distribution is $n_1 = 2$, $n_2 = 1$, $n_3 = 0$, then there are only three ways this distribution can be obtained:

Compartment	Particle number		
1	1,2	1,3	2,3
2	3	2	1
3	—	—	—

There is no significance to altering the order of the particles inside a compartment. The only way in which they can be distinguished from one another is by which compartment each is in. The distribution with all three particles in the first compartment, therefore, could be obtained in only one way. Thus we see that the distribution with one particle in each compartment can be obtained in more ways than any other distribution, so that with equal a *priori* probabilities for the compartments this distribution would certainly be the most probable.

Investigation of the arrangement of particles according to a certain distribution, as we have done here, gives the general result that the total number of ways in which particles in different cells may be exchanged while the number of particles in each compartment is kept constant is

$$P = \frac{n!}{n_0! n_1! \cdots n_r!} = \frac{n!}{\prod\limits_{i=0}^{r} n_i!}. \tag{5-2}$$

The terms in the denominator appear as a result if the fact that $n!$ arrangements are possible, but some of these merely correspond to rearrangements within a cell, a distinction that is meaningless.

The final probability of a given distribution is the product of the a *priori* probability of a distribution D, as given by Eq. (5-1), by the number of ways in which this distribution can be obtained by rearrangement of the particles in the cells, Eq. (5–2):

$$W = P \times D = \frac{n!}{n_0! n_1! \cdots n_r!} g_0{}^{n_0} g_1{}^{n_1} \cdots g_r{}^{n_r}$$

$$= n! \prod_{i=0}^{r} \frac{g_i{}^{n_i}}{n_i!}. \tag{5–3}$$

This may be easily verified by noting that the total probability for all distributions should be unity, i.e.,

$$\Sigma W = \sum n! \prod_{i=0}^{r} \frac{g_i{}^{n_i}}{n_i!} = 1.$$

From the polynomial theorem this sum is seen to be

$$(g_0 + g_1 + \cdots + g_r)^n = 1^n = 1.$$

Of particular interest to us is which of the possible distributions has the greatest probability. In general we will assume that a sample will contain a great many molecules, so that all the n_i's will be large and in fact so large that variations in the n_i's can be considered to be continuous. The purpose of finding the most probable distribution is that we shall assume that this distribution so far outweighs the effects of other possible distributions that the properties of the system can be determined by considering the most probable distribution alone. The error introduced by neglecting other distributions than the most probable will be discussed in more detail later.

We wish, then, to find the collection of n_i's that gives the maximum value of W. For reasons that will be apparent later, it is more convenient to find the distribution of n_i's that give a maximum in $\ln W$. The two, of course, are synonymous. From Eq. (5–3) we can express the natural logarithm of the probability of a given distribution as

$$\ln W = \ln \left(n! \prod_{i=0}^{r} \frac{g_i{}^{n_i}}{n_i!} \right),$$

which can be expanded to

$$\ln W = \ln n! + \sum_{i=0}^{r} n_i \ln g_i - \sum_{i=0}^{r} \ln (n_i!).$$

Stirling's approximation gives for the logarithm of a factorial for large x

$$\ln x! = x \ln x - x + \tfrac{1}{2} \ln x + \tfrac{1}{2} \ln 2\pi,$$

and if x is very large, this reduces further to

$$\ln x! = x \ln x - x,$$

so that for large values of the n_i's

$$\ln W = n \ln n + \sum_{i=0}^{r} n_i \ln \frac{g_i}{n_i}. \tag{5-4}$$

At the maximum value of $\ln W$ an arbitrarily small change in the n_i's will have no effect on $\ln W$, that is,

$$\delta(\ln W) = 0, \tag{5-5}$$

which from Eq. (5–4) is

$$\sum_{i=0}^{r} \ln \frac{g_i}{n_i} \delta n_i = 0. \tag{5-6}$$

This equation is subject also to the restriction that the total number of particles does not change:

$$\sum_{i=0}^{r} \delta n_i = 0. \tag{5-7}$$

These two conditions can be combined by Lagrange's method of undetermined multipliers. Multiplying Eq. (5–7) by the constant α and subtracting from Eq. (5–5) or (5–6), we obtain

$$\sum_{i=0}^{r} \left(\ln \frac{g_i}{n_i} - \alpha \right) \delta n_i = 0.$$

The changes in the n_i's are arbitrary, as can be seen by the fact that if α is chosen so as to make the first term in the sum equal to zero,

$$\ln \frac{g_0}{n_0} - \alpha = 0,$$

then δn_0 can be given any arbitrary value, and it follows that this is true also for all the other n_i's. Thus, in general, it is true that

$$\ln \frac{g_i}{n_i} - \alpha = 0,$$

or

$$n_i = g_i e^{-\alpha}.$$

Since α is a constant, the exponential is also a constant, and it can be evaluated by observing that

$$n = \sum_{i=0}^{r} n_i = \sum_{i=0}^{r} g_i e^{-\alpha} = e^{-\alpha} \sum_{i=0}^{r} g_i = e^{-\alpha},$$

so that

$$\frac{n_i}{n} = g_i,$$

which, from the original assumption defining the g_i's, says that the most probable numbers of particles in each compartment are proportional to the areas of the compartments. The result is intuitively obvious in this simple example, but in treating it in this manner we have illustrated several techniques and assumptions of the statistical approach.

The assumption has been made during our discussion that the most probable distribution far outweighs other possible distributions in its effect on the over-all properties of the system. Since the n_i's are large, small changes in the distribution are not different essentially from the most probable distribution, and the probability of larger deviations from the most probable distribution is assumed to be negligibly small.

Just for the purpose of verifying this assumption let us calculate the probability of a state that differs slightly in probability from the most probable distribution, and compare its probability with that of the most probable state. Consider a state that differs by a small amount δW from the most probable distribution. From Eq. (5–4) the probability of this distribution is

$$\ln (W + \delta W) = n \ln n + \sum_{i=0}^{r} (n_i + \delta n_i) \ln \left(\frac{g_i}{n_i + \delta n_i} \right),$$

and subtracting Eq. (5–4) from this, we obtain

$$\ln \frac{W + \delta W}{W} = \sum_{i=0}^{r} \delta n_i \ln g_i - \sum_{i=0}^{r} n_i \ln \frac{n_i + \delta n_i}{n_i} - \sum_{i=0}^{r} \delta n_i \ln (n_i + \delta n_i).$$

This expression can be arranged to contain explicitly the most probable distribution, whose probability is represented by $W_{\max}$, if we include Eq. (5–6) to obtain

$$\ln \frac{W_{\max} + \delta W}{W_{\max}} = - \sum_{i=0}^{r} n_i \ln \left(1 + \frac{\delta n_i}{n_i} \right) - \sum_{i=0}^{r} \delta n_i \ln \left(1 + \frac{\delta n_i}{n_i} \right). \quad (5\text{–}8)$$

This expression can be simplified by the approximation that, if δn_i is small compared to n_i, then the logarithm can be represented by the first one or two terms in the series

$$\ln (1 + x) = x - \tfrac{1}{2}x^2 + \tfrac{1}{3}x^3 - \cdots ,$$

which gives, from Eq. (5–8),

$$\ln \frac{W_{\max} + \delta W}{W_{\max}} = - \sum_{i=0}^{r} \delta n_i + \tfrac{1}{2} \sum_{i=0}^{r} \frac{(\delta n_i)^2}{n_i} - \sum_{i=0}^{r} \frac{(\delta n_i)^2}{n_i}$$

with higher powers of δn_i neglected. Since the total number of particles does not change, the first term in this sum is zero, so that the equation reduces to

$$\ln \frac{W_{\max} + \delta W}{W_{\max}} = - \tfrac{1}{2} \sum_{i=0}^{r} \frac{(\delta n_i)^2}{n_i}.$$

It can be seen from this result that no matter what the variations in the n_i's from the most probable distribution, the probability of the resulting distribution will be less than that of the most probable distribution. In most physical situations n_i will be large, so that small δn_i's appearing as a square term will give a negligibly small probability for an altered distribution compared with the most probable distribution. Suppose, for example, that there are only two compartments, each of the same area and therefore the same *a priori* probability. The most probable distribution would have the same number of particles in the two compartments. Suppose we consider that distribution which has 1 per cent of the particles in one compartment transferred to the other compartment. If the original distribution had 10^{20} particles in each compartment, then

$$\ln \frac{W_{\max} + \delta W}{W} = - \tfrac{1}{2} \frac{(10^{18})^2}{10^{20}} - \tfrac{1}{2} \frac{(10^{18})^2}{10^{20}} = -10^{16}$$

or

$$\frac{W_{\max} + \delta W}{W_{\max}} = e^{-10^{16}}$$

so that the slightly different distribution (1 per cent of the particles moved) is of negligible probability compared to the most probable distribution.

5.2   THE BOLTZMANN DISTRIBUTION LAW

We now turn our attention once again to the quantum states of atomic and molecular systems. Our problem is basically the same as the geometrical situation we have just considered. We wish to know, given a possible set of eigenstates, how a number of molecules will be distributed among these states. Our assumptions regarding large numbers of molecules and the most probable distribution representing the essential nature of the system should apply here as well as in our geometrical example.

In the geometrical case the *a priori* probability that a given compartment be occupied by chance was proportional to the area of the compartment. What can we assume about the *a priori* probability that a given eigenstate will be occupied? Although arguments of various sorts can be presented, we will state here simply that the *a priori* probabilities of all eigenstates are the same; i.e., *there is equal probability that any of the available quantum states can be occupied by a molecule or atom.*

For most purposes it is convenient to discuss specifically the possible energy levels for a system rather than the individual quantum states. If each energy level represents one quantum state, then our assumption is that the *a priori* probabilities of all the energy levels are the same. However, if two or more eigenstates have the same energy, then this degenerate energy level has a greater probability of occupancy. If it is twofold degenerate, obviously its probability of occupancy is twice that of a nondegenerate level since each quantum state has the same probability. On this basis *it is conventional to assign as the a priori probability of an energy level the degeneracy of that level.*

If, then, we consider the compartments of Sec. 5.1 to be available energy levels, the *a priori* probabilities to be the degeneracies of the energy levels, and again consider the total number of molecules to remain constant as the distribution is varied, then we have the same relations that must be satisfied for the state of maximum probability, namely

$$\sum_{i=0}^{r} \ln \frac{g_i}{n_i} \, \delta n_i = 0 \qquad (5\text{--}6)$$

and

$$\sum_{i=0}^{r} \delta n_i = 0. \qquad (5\text{--}7)$$

Now if we are to consider a system that is in equilibrium, not only must the total number of molecules in the system remain constant, but the total energy of the system must also remain constant. There is therefore an additional condition that must be satisfied, which is

$$\sum_{i=0}^{r} \epsilon_i \, \delta n_i = 0, \qquad (5\text{--}9)$$

where ϵ_i is the energy of level i.

We can again solve Eq. (5–6) with these two restraints by the Lagrangian method of undetermined multipliers. Multiplying Eq. (5–7) by the undetermined constant α and Eq. (5–9) by the constant β, we obtain, after subtracting the two results from Eq. (5–5) and (5–6),

$$\sum_{i=0}^{r} (\ln W - \alpha - \beta\epsilon_i) \, \delta n_i = \sum_{i=0}^{r} \left(\ln \frac{g_i}{n_i} - \alpha - \beta\epsilon_i \right) \delta n_i = 0. \quad (5\text{–}10)$$

If we consider the first two terms in this series,

$$\ln \frac{g_0}{n_0} - \alpha - \beta\epsilon_0 = 0,$$

$$\ln \frac{g_1}{n_1} - \alpha - \beta\epsilon_1 = 0,$$

we observe that we can choose α and β so that both equations are zero as written here. In this case δn_0 and δn_1 can vary arbitrarily without affecting (5–10). It also follows, therefore, that all the other δn's can also be varied without affecting the other terms since the only restriction is that the sum of all the δn_i's must be zero. Thus the distribution of maximum probability is represented by a series of equations of the form

$$\ln \frac{g_i}{n_i} - \alpha - \beta\epsilon_i = 0,$$

or

$$\frac{n_i}{g_i} = e^{-\alpha} e^{-\beta\epsilon_i}$$

The constant α can be evaluated by noting that

$$\sum_{i=0}^{r} n_i = n = \sum_{i=0}^{r} g_i e^{-\alpha} e^{-\beta\epsilon_i} = e^{-\alpha} \sum_{i=0}^{r} g_i e^{-\beta\epsilon_i},$$

so that

$$e^{-\alpha} = \frac{n}{\sum\limits_{i=0}^{r} g_i e^{-\beta\epsilon_i}}.$$

The denominator in this expression is known as the *partition function* or *sum over states* and is commonly given the symbol Q (or sometimes Z, or f):

$$Q = \sum_{i=0}^{r} g_i e^{-\beta\epsilon_i}. \quad (5\text{–}11)$$

We thus have for the fraction of molecules in energy level ϵ_i

$$\frac{n_i}{n} = \frac{g_i e^{-\beta\epsilon_i}}{Q}. \quad (5\text{–}12)$$

Additional arguments establish that the constant β is (Probs. 5–18, 5–19)

$$\beta = \frac{1}{kT},$$

where the constant k is the Boltzmann constant equal to R/N, so that Eq. (5–12) becomes

$$\frac{n_i}{n} = \frac{g_i e^{-\epsilon_i/kT}}{Q}, \tag{5–13}$$

which is the important Boltzmann distribution law. The extension of this law to give the ratios of molecules in two different energy levels of energies ϵ_i and ϵ_j is straightforward from (5–13):

$$\frac{n_i}{n_j} = \frac{g_i}{g_j}\, e^{-(\epsilon_i - \epsilon_j)/kT}. \tag{5–14}$$

The Boltzmann distribution law is of fundamental importance to physical chemistry since it allows us to determine immediately the most probable distribution of molecules among the available energy levels, the latter having been predicted by quantum-mechanical calculations and/or experiment. It will be necessary for us to find equations that connect the most probable distribution with measurable thermodynamic functions such as energy, entropy, and free energy. We will then have an intimate interdependence between our quantum-mechanical methods and such important thermodynamic quantities as heats of reaction and equilibrium constants.

There are several features of the quantities in the Boltzmann law which are useful to note in connection with solving practical problems. One of these is the nature of the summation in the partition function. The numerical value of k is 1.3803×10^{-16} erg deg^{-1} and it will be noted that if the separation in energy between two adjacent states is large compared to kT, then each exponential term, and hence each n_i, represents a distinct state which must be included in any summation such as that in the partition function.

On the other hand, if the separation between adjacent energy levels is very much smaller than kT, then for all practical purposes the sum of terms can be effectively replaced by an integral since, compared to kT, each energy state differs only infinitesimally from the next lower and next higher states. Thus we may write

$$\frac{dn}{n} = \frac{g e^{-\epsilon/kT}\, d\epsilon}{\int g e^{-\epsilon/kT}\, d\epsilon},$$

where dn/n is the fraction of molecules having an energy between ϵ and $\epsilon + d\epsilon$. In many cases it may be advantageous to convert these integrals from forms explicitly containing energy to integrals in terms of momenta and coordinates, in order to evaluate the integral with less difficulty. The ability to do this rests primarily on the premise that the separation between energy levels is small enough that the integral indeed represents the summation over all states.

An example of such a situation can be seen by considering the translational motion of a typical molecule in a macro-sized container. The average kinetic energy of helium atoms in a given direction at room temperature is about 2×10^{-14} g cm^2 sec^{-2} from kinetic theory. The mass of a helium atom is about 7×10^{-24} g, so that if the atoms are confined between walls that are 1 mm apart, the values of E given by Eq. (4–23) are

$$E_n = \frac{n^2 \times (6.6 \times 10^{-27})^2}{8 \times 7 \times 10^{-24} \times (.1)^2} = n^2 \times 7 \times 10^{-29} \text{ g cm}^2 \text{ sec}^{-2},$$

so that in view of the average kinetic energy of 2×10^{-14}, the average value of n^2 is about 3×10^{14}, or the average value of n is 1.7×10^7. We see that for finite containers and normal temperatures a large number of the available energy levels are occupied. Of more importance is the fact that the difference between the average level $n = 1.7 \times 10^7$ and the next highest level $n + 1$ is only of the order of 1×10^{-7} of the average energy, a fraction so small that for all practical purposes we can ignore quantization of the motion and consider the energy, momentum, velocity, etc., as continuously varying quantities.

There is also another case which is the extreme opposite of this situation. If the energies of the states are very large compared to kT, then the fraction of the molecules in the higher energy states may be so small as to be negligible, in which case it is only necessary to consider the ground state as containing all the molecules. In this case the partition function contains only one term, and if the ground state is arbitrarily chosen as the zero of energy relative to the higher states, then the partition function becomes unity, assuming the ground state is not degenerate.

This particular situation is typical of electronic energy levels at room temperature. The difference between the ground state of H_2 and its lowest excited state is 11.2 ev, or 263 kcal mole^{-1}. At room temperature kT is equivalent to .026 ev, so that essentially all hydrogen molecules are in their ground electronic state. In most molecules and many atoms the ground states are not degenerate, but it will be necessary to investigate this situation in more detail later.

Unfortunately, or otherwise, the spacing of many energy states may be such that we can neither ignore higher levels nor consider the energy to be continuous. Rotational levels, for example, are closely spaced with respect to kT at room temperature, but at lower temperatures the quantization of rotational energy cannot be ignored. Similarly, at room temperature and higher, the spacing of vibrational energy levels is generally such that the sum of states must be considered in detail.

In our derivation of the Boltzmann law we have made no assumptions concerning the nature of the energy levels. Thus this relation should be valid if we are considering the total energy states of a system or if we are investigating in particular the population of rotational states or the distribution of molecules only among translational states. In solving molecular and atomic problems in quantum mechanics it is often found that the degrees of freedom necessary to describe certain kinds of motion can be separated from one another and handled as independent problems. In the case of the translating particle in a box we were able to write the wave function, ψ, as a product of three functions, each a function of only one coordinate. The result of this procedure was that three separate Schrödinger equations, each one-dimensional, could be written if the stationary state energies were written as the sum of three energies, each an eigenvalue of the corresponding one-dimensional Schrödinger equation. In rectangular coordinates we had

$$E = E_x + E_y + E_z$$

where

$$E_x = \frac{h^2 n_x^2}{8ma^2}, \qquad E = \frac{h^2 n_y^2}{8mb^2}, \qquad E_z = \frac{h^2 n_z^2}{8mc^2}.$$

When the energy can be separated according to different degrees of freedom in this manner, then the Boltzmann relation can likewise be factored into separate terms, and in this case

$$Q = Q_x Q_y Q_z.$$

To a reasonable degree of approximation it is generally possible to separate the states of a molecule into separate terms giving the translational, rotational, vibrational, and electronic energies, so that for a given energy level we may write

$$\epsilon = \epsilon_{\text{trans}} + \epsilon_{\text{rot}} + \epsilon_{\text{vib}} + \epsilon_{\text{elec}},$$
$$Q = Q_{\text{trans}} Q_{\text{rot}} Q_{\text{vib}} Q_{\text{elec}},$$
$$g = g_{\text{trans}} g_{\text{rot}} g_{\text{vib}} g_{\text{elec}}.$$

In addition, these separate terms often can be separated further, as in the case of the three rectangular coordinates in translational motion. It is not always true that such a separation is strictly correct, for often the energy states corresponding to one degree of freedom do in fact depend on the energy states corresponding to other degrees of freedom. The rotational motions of a molecule, to cite a common case, have a measurable effect on the vibrational motions, and both affect to some

extent the electronic states, and vice versa.   In some cases these inter-
dependences prevent a valid separation of the energy into separate terms,
but for the most part the separation is sufficiently accurate for the calculation of thermodynamic quantities.

5.3   PHASE SPACE IN STATISTICAL MECHANICS

We have had the opportunity to observe several instances for which
the concept of phase space has been of aid in handling the mathematical
complexities of physical problems.   Nowhere has the phase-space
approach been more valuable than in considering problems in statistical
mechanics, both classical and quantum-mechanical.

The general statistical view is somewhat as follows: We have a system containing a certain number of molecules at a specified set of conditions, say of temperature and volume.   If the system is in equilibrium
with its surroundings, then the total energy of the system of molecules
is also constant and equal to a specific value.   We recognize that inter-
nally there are many different ways in which the positions and momenta
of the various molecules could be rearranged with the same over-all
macroscopic conditions of temperature, volume, and energy.   Statistically, we assert the fact that whichever macroscopic state could be
reproduced by the greatest number of microscopic rearrangements would
be the most probable state for this particular collection of molecules at
the specified temperature, volume, and energy.   Thus we set out to find
just how many different ways we could distribute our set of molecules
among the available energy states and still have the same external conditions that have been imposed.

Each hypothetical system that meets the requirements of the macroscopic state is called in statistical mechanics a microstate or complexion,
and the entire collection of complexions which can be conceived of that
satisfy the imposed external conditions is called an assembly of systems
or an ensemble.   Statistically, we envision the possibility that over a
period of time a real system might pass through all the possible complexions of the ensemble and it is assumed that the *a priori* probabilities
of all complexions are the same.   Thus in observing different possible
real macroscopic states of a system that differ in energy, pressure, or
some other quantity, but have the same temperature, volume, and number of molecules, we deduce that the macroscopic state that is represented
by the largest number of complexions duplicating that state will be the
most probable state of the system and will be the state from which variables such as energy, pressure, etc. can be calculated for the system.

Phase space is uniquely suited to consideration of the possible complexions making up the ensemble of a particular macroscopic state.   It

has already been pointed out that a particular system whose molecules have certain values of position coordinates and momenta is represented in phase space by a single point. The particular phase space in which this is true is one which for n particles, each of which requires f degrees of freedom, contains nf position coordinates and nf conjugate momenta as variables in phase space, giving a $2nf$-dimensional phase space which is known as γ-space.

It should be apparent that in γ-space each complexion of an ensemble is represented by a single point, since each complexion in the ensemble differs from other complexions in the assignment of positions and momenta to the individual molecules in the system. Although in classical mechanics it was assumed possible to determine precisely the positions and momenta of particles, we now know from Heisenberg's uncertainty principle that this is not really so. It is thus not possible to locate a given quantum state or complexion by a precise point in phase space. Instead, we can only specify that such a quantum state is somewhere in phase space in a cell of a certain size. The "volume" of such a cell can be determined from the uncertainty principle. For every coordinate q_i and its associated momentum p_i we know that $\Delta q_i \, \Delta p_i \simeq h$, so that with n particles and a $2nf$-dimensional phase space the uncertainty in the coordinates and momenta must be of the order of h^{nf}, this representing the volume in phase space in which a complexion can be located.

The volume in phase space of a quantum state can be most easily illustrated by a one-dimensional system that is represented by a two-dimensional phase space. One such system is the linear harmonic oscillator. We have already seen (Sec. 2.5) that the path of constant energy of such an oscillator in phase space is an ellipse, and that the areas between two ellipses representing quantum states which are an energy $h\nu$ apart is equal to h. The phase space of a linear harmonic oscillator was illustrated in Fig. 2–8.

A second simple case is that of the particle in a one-dimensional box. The energy states are given by Eq. (4–23) as $E_n = n^2 h^2 / 8ma^2$ where a is the length of the box. In the absence of a potential energy in the box, $p = \pm \sqrt{2mE_n} = \pm nh/2a$. Since the energy is constant for a given quantum state, each state is represented in phase space by a line of constant momentum between the bounds of the box. It will be recalled that each state represents motion in both the x and the $-x$ directions, so that in phase space each state actually consists of two lines of constant momentum, one with positive momentum and the other with negative momentum. The phase-space representation of a particle in a box is shown in Fig. 5–2. It is seen that the area between two adjacent stationary states is two rectangles (one in the positive momentum region and one in the negative), each of area $(h/2a)a = h/2$, so that the total area in phase space between two adjacent states (or the area which a state can be considered to occupy) is h.

The basic assumption regarding the *a priori* probabilities of quantum states is that all eigenstates are equally probable. In classical statistical mechanics it was assumed that the probability of finding the phase point in any one region of phase space is identical with that for any other region of equal volume, provided the regions correspond equally well to the conditions, such as constant energy, that are known to apply to the system. An extension of this assumption is that the probability that the

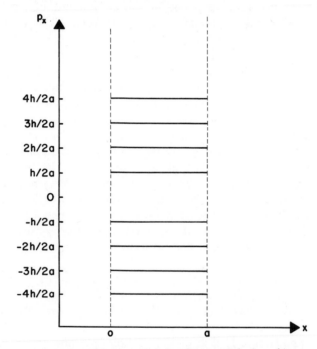

Fig. 5–2. Phase space for the particle in a box.

phase point for the system is in one of several regions of phase space is proportional to the volumes of these regions. Since each quantum state occupies a volume h^{nf} in phase space, it is seen that the equal *a priori* probabilities of quantum states correspond to the classical equal statistical weights of equal volumes in phase space. Our derivation of the Boltzmann distribution law was thus equivalent to the simple geometric problem of putting particles into compartments.

A second kind of phase space also is useful. This space, called μ-space, is made up of only the number of coordinates and their associated momenta required to describe a single molecule. Figures 2–8 and 5–2 are μ-spaces for the linear harmonic oscillator and a particle in a box. In μ-space each microstate or complexion is represented not by a single cell, but rather by a collection of cells, one for each molecule, each with volume h^f where f is the number of degrees of freedom necessary to describe the state of one molecule.

Finally, let us make a quantum-mechanical statement of our statistical model. We are supposing that our particles (atoms, electrons, molecules, etc.) are represented by coordinates q_1, q_2, . . . , q_n, and that there are available a total number k of eigenfunctions ϕ of the Hamiltonian operator describing the system such that $\phi_a(q_1)$, $\phi_b(q_2)$, . . . , $\phi_k(q_n)$ are the solutions of the Schrödinger equation for the n individual particles. The complete eigenfunction for the whole system may then be taken as

$$\psi = \phi_a(q_1)\phi_b(q_2) \cdot \cdot \cdot \phi_k(q_n),$$

where the normalizing constant has been omitted. If there are no further restrictions and the particles 1, 2, . . . , n are distinguishable, then this is only one eigenstate of the system. Any change in the distribution of the n particles among the k elementary wave functions ϕ_a, ϕ_b, . . . , ϕ_k would lead to a new value for ψ, and this would be another possible eigenstate corresponding to the same energy.

Later considerations of the fundamental nature of wave functions will place limitations on the possible eigenstates of a system, but for the present these will not be considered.

As a particular example of the use of phase space in handling statistical problems, consider the case of finding the translational partition function for an ideal gas. We have seen that the translational energy levels are so close together that the energy can be considered to be continuously variable. We can then write

$$Q = \int_0^\infty g e^{-\epsilon/kT} \, d\epsilon.$$

The translational energy of a molecule can be written in terms of classical theory as

$$\epsilon = \frac{p_x^2}{2m} + \frac{p_y^2}{2m} + \frac{p_z^2}{2m}.$$

In general, $d\epsilon$ will be large enough that several translational states are included in this range. In order to determine g we must then know how many energy states lie in the volume element $dx\,dy\,dz\,dp_x\,dp_y\,dp_z$ in phase space. We have seen that one eigenstate of a molecule occupies a volume h^f in phase space, or in this particular case h^3, so that the number of eigenstates in the volume element is given by

$$g = \frac{dx\,dy\,dz\,dp_x\,dp_y\,dp_z}{h^3}.$$

We can now write the partition function as

$$Q = \frac{1}{h^3} \int_{-\infty}^{\infty} \int_{-\infty}^{\infty} \int_{-\infty}^{\infty} \int_{0}^{x} \int_{0}^{y} \int_{0}^{z} e^{-(p_x{}^2 + p_y{}^2 + p_z{}^2)/2mkT} \, dp_x \, dp_y \, dp_z \, dx \, dy \, dz.$$

Since the coordinates are independent of the momenta, we have

$$\iiint dx \, dy \, dz = V,$$

the volume of the gas; and since the momentum components are also independent of one another, we have

$$\int_{-\infty}^{\infty} e^{-p_x{}^2/2mkT} \, dp_x = \sqrt{2\pi mkT}$$

with similar expressions for the p_y and p_z integrals. Thus

$$Q = (2\pi mkT)^{3/2} \frac{V}{h^3}.$$

It is thus possible to evaluate the partition function and related quantities relatively easily in many cases, using phase-space considerations.

5.4   THE PARTITION FUNCTION AND ITS RELATION TO THERMODYNAMIC FUNCTIONS

We have stated that our primary aim in applying statistical methods to quantum mechanics is to relate the microscopic behavior of molecules, i.e. their possible energy states and the way in which they are populated, to the macroscopic thermodynamic behavior, which we are able to measure and calculate by laboratory measurements that are largely thermal in nature. We are thus interested in seeing how the Boltzmann distribution law, and the partition function in particular, are related to the familiar thermodynamic functions.

Let us first consider the energy of a system using capital letters to denote molar quantities. The molar energy is

$$E = \sum_{i=0}^{r} n_i \epsilon_i = N\bar{\epsilon},$$

where the average energy of a molecule is

$$\bar{\epsilon} = \frac{\sum_{i=0}^{r} n_i \epsilon_i}{\sum_{i=0}^{r} n_i} = \frac{\sum_{i=0}^{r} g_i \epsilon_i e^{-\epsilon_i/kT}}{\sum_{i=0}^{r} g_i e^{-\epsilon_i/kT}} = \frac{\sum_{i=0}^{r} g_i \epsilon_i e^{-\epsilon_i/kT}}{Q}. \tag{5-15}$$

An investigation of Q discloses that

$$\left(\frac{\partial Q}{\partial T}\right)_V = \left(\frac{\partial \sum g_i e^{-\epsilon_i/kT}}{\partial T}\right)_V = \frac{1}{kT^2} \sum_i g_i \epsilon_i e^{-\epsilon_i/kT},$$

where the volume is held constant, so that the energies, ϵ_i, of the states will stay constant. Comparison with Eq. (5–14) shows that

$$\bar{\epsilon} = \frac{kT^2}{Q} \left(\frac{\partial Q}{\partial T} \right)_V = kT^2 \left(\frac{\partial (\ln Q)}{\partial T} \right)_V.$$

The partition function Q is for one molecule, so we would expect that the molar partition function for Avogadro's number, N, of molecules should be

$$Q_M = Q_1 Q_2 \cdots Q_N,$$

or since all the Q's are identical for a pure substance,

$$Q_M = Q^N.$$

Here, however, it is necessary to bring to light an additional point. In our discussions of distributions we have assumed that the particles under study were distinguishable; i.e., we have assumed that if two particles were interchanged in position and momentum (or in quantum states), although the macroscopic properties of the system would be the same, we could distinguish the two microscopic states as being in different cells in μ-space. In a large-scale experiment in which we can number balls or identify them by color or some other markings, we can indeed distinguish such rearrangements. In the case of atomic phenomena we can never see the behavior of the individual molecules. Rather we see their macroscopic result, and it is impossible in the case of molecules of a gas to distinguish that one particular molecule as opposed to another has a particular energy and position. Hence the rearrangements involving exchange of molecules among eigenfunctions is meaningless, and as a result the partition function for one mole is not the molecular partition function to the Nth power but instead is

$$Q_M = \frac{Q^N}{N!}.$$

Introducing the partition function for N molecules gives

$$E = kT^2 \left(\frac{\partial (\ln Q_M)}{\partial T} \right)_V = kT^2 \left(\frac{\partial (\ln Q^N)}{\partial T} \right)_V = RT^2 \left(\frac{\partial (\ln Q)}{\partial T} \right)_V. \quad (5\text{–}16)$$

We thus have found a simple relation between the molecular partition function and the molar energy.

In this derivation we have kept the volume constant and assumed the energy levels to remain constant. Suppose, however, that n parameters $x_1, x_2, \ldots, x_n$ might be varied, and that their variation can cause changes in the energy levels ϵ_i. These parameters could be any quantity that can have such an effect on the energy, such as the dimensions of the container, electric and magnetic fields, etc. A small change in the parameters will have an effect on each energy state by the relation

$$d\epsilon_i = \sum_{j=1}^{n} \frac{\partial \epsilon_i}{\partial x_j} \, dx_j.$$

Since the negative of the variation of the energy of state ϵ_i with respect to a parameter x_j is equal to the force, F_j, due to the change in that parameter,

$$F_j = -\frac{\partial \epsilon_i}{\partial x_j},$$

we can calculate the average force by the usual statistical method

$$\bar{F}_j = -\frac{\sum\limits_{i=0}^{r} (\partial \epsilon_i / \partial x_j) \, g_i e^{-\epsilon_i / kT}}{Q}.$$

We also note that from the definition of the partition function

$$\left(\frac{\partial Q}{\partial x_j}\right)_T = -\sum_{i=0}^{r} g_i \frac{1}{kT} e^{-\epsilon_i / kT} \frac{\partial \epsilon_i}{\partial x_j}.$$

Comparison with the preceding equation shows that

$$\bar{F}_j = \frac{kT}{Q} \left(\frac{\partial Q}{\partial x_j}\right)_T = kT \left(\frac{\partial (\ln Q)}{\partial x_j}\right)_T,$$

or in terms of N molecules,

$$N\bar{F}_j = kT \left(\frac{\partial (\ln Q_M)}{\partial x_j}\right)_T = RT \left(\frac{\partial (\ln Q)}{\partial x_j}\right)_T. \tag{5-17}$$

The work done on the system is given by the sum over all parameters of the products of the forces and the variations in the parameters,

$$\delta w = -\sum_{j=1}^{n} N\bar{F}_j \, \delta x_j = -\sum_{j=1}^{n} RT \left(\frac{\partial (\ln Q)}{\partial x_j}\right)_T \delta x_j$$

$$= -\sum_{j=1}^{n} kT \left(\frac{\partial (\ln Q_M)}{\partial x_j}\right)_T \delta x_j. \tag{5-18}$$

The first law of thermodynamics states that

$$dE = \delta q + \delta w.$$

Substituting Eqs. (5–16) and (5–18) yields

$$\delta q = d\left[RT^2\left(\frac{\partial(\ln Q)}{\partial T}\right)_V\right] + \sum_{j=1}^{n} RT\left(\frac{\partial(\ln Q)}{\partial x_j}\right)_T \delta x_j. \qquad (5\text{–}19)$$

The laws of calculus tell us that

$$d(\ln Q_M) = \left(\frac{\partial(\ln Q_M)}{\partial T}\right)_V dT + \sum_{j=1}^{n}\left(\frac{\partial(\ln Q_M)}{\partial x_j}\right)_T \delta x_j,$$

or

$$kT\, d(\ln Q_M) = RT\left(\frac{\partial(\ln Q)}{\partial T}\right)_V dT + RT\sum_{j=1}^{n}\left(\frac{\partial(\ln Q)}{\partial x_j}\right)_T \delta x_j.$$

Substituting in Eq. (5–19) gives

$$\delta q = d\left[RT^2\left(\frac{\partial(\ln Q)}{\partial T}\right)_V\right] + kT\, d(\ln Q_M) - RT\left(\frac{\partial(\ln Q)}{\partial T}\right)_V dT$$

$$= RT^2\, d\left[\left(\frac{\partial(\ln Q)}{\partial T}\right)_V\right] + 2RT\left(\frac{\partial(\ln Q)}{\partial T}\right)_V dT + kT\, d(\ln Q_M)$$

$$\hspace{4cm} - RT\left(\frac{\partial(\ln Q)}{\partial T}\right)_V dT$$

$$= RT^2\, d\left[\left(\frac{\partial(\ln Q)}{\partial T}\right)_V\right] + RT\left(\frac{\partial(\ln Q)}{\partial T}\right)_V dT + kT\, d(\ln Q_M)$$

$$= RT\, d\left[T\left(\frac{\partial(\ln Q)}{\partial T}\right)_V\right] + kT\, d(\ln Q_M)$$

$$= NkT\, d\left[T\left(\frac{\partial(\ln Q)}{\partial T}\right)_V\right] + kT\, d(\ln Q_M)$$

$$= kT\, d\left[\ln Q_M + NT\left(\frac{\partial(\ln Q)}{\partial T}\right)_V\right]$$

$$= kT\, d\left[\ln Q_M + T\left(\frac{\partial(\ln Q_M)}{\partial T}\right)_V\right].$$

For a system undergoing a reversible process in which the system is in equilibrium with its surroundings at all times,

$$dS = \frac{\delta q}{T} = kd\left[\ln Q_M + NT\left(\frac{\partial(\ln Q)}{\partial T}\right)_V\right].$$

It will be noticed that dS is an exact differential, as required for a thermodynamic function, since there is no temperature term multiplying the differential term on the right side of this equation.

Integrating yields

$$S - S_0 = k\left[\ln Q_M + NT\left(\frac{\partial(\ln Q)}{\partial T}\right)_V\right]. \qquad (5\text{–}20)$$

If it is possible to set the constant of integration equal to zero, we obtain

$$S = k \left[\ln Q_M + NT \left(\frac{\partial (\ln Q)}{\partial T} \right)_V \right]$$
$$= k \left[N \ln \frac{Q}{N!} + NT \left(\frac{\partial (\ln Q)}{\partial T} \right)_V \right].$$

This can be reduced by means of Stirling's approximation to

$$S = k \left[N \ln Q - N \ln N + N + NT \left(\frac{\partial (\ln Q)}{\partial T} \right)_V \right]$$

or

$$S = R \left[\ln \frac{Q}{N} + 1 + T \left(\frac{\partial (\ln Q)}{\partial T} \right)_V \right]. \tag{5-21}$$

Other thermodynamic functions can now be obtained readily from the expressions for E and S. The Helmholtz free energy is simply

$$A = E - TS = -kT \ln Q_M = -RT \left[\ln \frac{Q}{N} + 1 \right]. \tag{5-22}$$

The Gibbs free energy is

$$G = H - TS = A + PV.$$

This can be evaluated by noting that according to thermodynamics

$$P = - \left(\frac{\partial A}{\partial V} \right)_T = RT \left(\frac{\partial (\ln Q)}{\partial V} \right)_T \tag{5-23}$$

so that

$$G = -RT \left[\ln \frac{Q}{N} + 1 - V \left(\frac{\partial (\ln Q)}{\partial V} \right)_T \right]. \tag{5-24}$$

The enthalpy is

$$H = E + PV = RT^2 \left(\frac{\partial (\ln Q)}{\partial T} \right)_V + RTV \left(\frac{\partial (\ln Q)}{\partial V} \right)_T$$
$$= RT \left[\left(\frac{\partial (\ln Q)}{\partial (\ln T)} \right)_V + \left(\frac{\partial (\ln Q)}{\partial (\ln V)} \right)_T \right], \tag{5-25}$$

and the heat capacity at constant volume is readily obtained as

$$C_V = \left(\frac{\partial E}{\partial T} \right)_V = \frac{\partial}{\partial T} \left[RT^2 \left(\frac{\partial (\ln Q)}{\partial T} \right)_V \right]$$
$$= 2RT \left(\frac{\partial (\ln Q)}{\partial T} \right)_V + RT^2 \left(\frac{\partial^2 (\ln Q)}{\partial T^2} \right)_V, \tag{5-26}$$

or alternatively

$$C_V = -\frac{1}{T^2} \left(\frac{\partial E}{\partial (1/T)} \right)_V = \frac{R}{T^2} \left(\frac{\partial^2 (\ln Q)}{[\partial (1/T)]^2} \right)_V. \tag{5-27}$$

Other alternative forms of these functions can be derived, and the inner consistency of these expressions can be checked by means of the numerous thermodynamic relations interrelating them.

We see, then, that the thermodynamic functions can be derived if the partition function is known for a molecule. Since we can separate the partition function into translational, electronic, vibrational, rotational, and other contributing factors, we can likewise investigate the contribution of these terms to the thermodynamic properties of a system. We will study this procedure in more detail as various systems are investigated in the following chapters. In addition it now becomes possible to calculate ΔH, ΔS, ΔG, equilibrium constants, and similar quantities for chemical processes.

5.5   MOLECULAR CHAOS AND ENTROPY

The thermodynamic definition of the entropy function in terms of the heat absorbed in an idealized reversible process does not have any apparent significance in terms of molecular behavior, but in the previous section we derived an equation in which the entropy is related to the molecular partition function. It would be illuminating at this point to inquire further into the statistical interpretation of entropy.

We might first inquire again into the meaning of the phrase, "probability of a state." We mean by this the fraction of microscopic arrangements of atoms and molecules in their different possible eigenstates that correspond on a macroscopic scale to the state in which we are interested, out of all the different such microscopic arrangements of which it is possible to conceive. We have seen that a system may be represented by an ensemble of many complexions, each complexion being a particular distribution of the molecules among the available quantum states. Conceivably an infinite variety of complexions might be possible for a set of molecules if it were not for additional restrictions. One of the most important of such restrictions is the necessity that the total energy of a system in equilibrium be constant. In such a case the number of possible complexions that concur with this requirement will be somewhat less.

Even with this restriction, however, a large number of different distributions among the atomic and molecular eigenstates are possible. We have argued that the most probable distribution is the one from which we can determine the state of the system, and we can thus define the probability of this state as the fraction of all the complexions that correspond to this particular state. Since each complexion represents a different distribution of atoms and molecules among the available eigenstates, we might also define probability of a state as the total number of ways the atoms and molecules can be arranged among the available eigenstates and still produce the same macroscopic state. This latter probability is generally called the thermodynamic probability and is not really a probability in the true sense. The latter is a number always less than unity while the number of possible arrangements of atoms and molecules may be a very large number.

The nature of the relation between entropy and the thermodynamic probability can be illustrated by some examples. According to the third law of thermodynamics, the absolute entropy of a pure crystalline solid is zero at 0°K. On a molecular basis this situation corresponds to one in which each atom, ion, or molecule is located at a definite point in space with a definite energy. Actually, there cannot be considered to be a complete absence of motion, since even at the absolute zero there

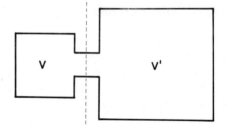

Fig. 5–3. Distribution of gas molecules between two containers of volumes V and V'.

remains a ground-state vibrational energy about the lattice site amounting to $\frac{1}{2}h\nu$ for each degree of freedom. Nevertheless, each molecule is in its ground state, and hence there is only one total wave function or one complexion corresponding to this macrostate. Thus the thermodynamic probability of this state is 1. Since the entropy is zero, we might infer that the entropy is related to the thermodynamic probability, W_T, by

$$S = k \ln W_T,$$

where k is a constant. As the temperature is raised and excited eigenstates can be occupied, the possibility of assigning different molecules and different numbers of molecules to these states increases, and hence the thermodynamic probability and the entropy increase.

Another example that throws light on the relation between entropy and probability is the effect of volume on the entropy of a gas. Consider two vessels of volumes V and V' connected as shown in Fig. 5–3, with N molecules of gas in the system. The probability of finding one molecule in the volume V is simply $V/(V + V')$ and the probability of having all N molecules in volume V is $[V/(V + V')]^N$. Obviously the probability of having all N molecules in the total volume $V + V'$ is unity since all the molecules are somewhere in the two containers.   Thus the ratios of the probability of having the N molecules in the volume $V + V'$ to that of having them in volume V is

$$\frac{W_{V+V'}}{W_V} = \frac{1}{[V/(V + V')]^N} = \left(\frac{V + V'}{V}\right)^N,$$

or

$$k \ln \frac{W_{V+V'}}{W_V} = k \ln \left(\frac{V + V'}{V}\right)^N = Nk \ln \frac{V + V'}{V}.$$

This equation can be related to entropy if it is recalled that simple thermodynamic arguments give for the expansion of an ideal gas

$$\Delta S = R \ln \frac{V_2}{V_1} = R \ln \frac{V + V'}{V} = Nk \ln \frac{V + V'}{V},$$

so that it is now apparent that the constant k can be identified with the Boltzmann constant, and it seems reasonable to assume again that

$$\Delta S = k \ln W_2/W_1, \quad S = k \ln W.$$

The formulation of this relation in a logarithmic ‛function is rather important, as the total probability of a combination of systems is equal to the product of the probabilities of the separate systems,

$$W_{tot} = W_1 W_2 \cdot \cdot \cdot ,$$

from which

$$\begin{aligned}
S_{tot} &= k \ln W_{tot} = k \ln (W_1 W_2 \cdot \cdot \cdot) \\
&= k \ln W_1 + k \ln W_2 + \cdot \cdot \cdot \\
&= S_1 + S_2 + \cdot \cdot \cdot ,
\end{aligned}$$

which is the expectation for an extensive thermodynamic function such as the entropy.

Let us now consider in general how one can determine the thermodynamic probability of a state.   We have defined this quantity as the number of complexions that correspond to the macroscopic state of interest.   For a system of distinguishable particles which can be distributed among eigenstates of equal statistical weight the thermodynamic probability is simply the number of ways the distribution corresponding to the macroscopic state of interest can be obtained:

$$W_T = \frac{n!}{n_0! n_1! \cdot \cdot \cdot n_r!}.$$

So long as the statistical weights are taken as the number of states with the same energy, the equal *a priori* probability energy levels have no effect on the thermodynamic probability.   If degeneracies are present, however, the thermodynamic probability, if expressed in terms of the available energy levels as is customary, is increased and is given by

$$W_T = \frac{n!}{n_0! n_1! \cdots n_r!} g_0{}^{n_0} g_1{}^{n_1} \cdots g_r{}^{n_r}.$$

Since we are usually concerned with thermodynamic systems in equilibrium, we are interested in the states of maximum probability, and

$$S = k \ln W_{T_{max}} = k \ln n! + k \sum_i n_{i_{max}} + k \sum_i n_{i_{max}} \ln \frac{g_i}{n_{i_{max}}},$$

where Stirling's approximation has been used.   The n_i's have already been evaluated from the Boltzmann distribution law, so that substitution into this equation would lead to an expression in terms of the partition function for the thermodynamic probability $W_{T_{max}}$ and for the entropy.

We have already indicated, however, that in most atomic and molecular systems the particles distributed among the different eigenstates are generally not distinguishable; hence the expression above for $W_{T_{max}}$ is unsatisfactory.   We wish, then, to derive an expression for the number of possible microstates when the particles are not distinguishable.   There are certain cases in which, because of the localization of the particles in space, the particles can be considered to be distinguishable.   A system of vibrating atoms in a solid crystalline lattice is such a localized system; for the eigenstates of the atoms can be identified with particular locations in the crystal, and an exchange of eigenstates between atoms would be distinguishable as a change in the locations of the eigenstates.   In the case of gaseous and liquid systems, however, such localization is absent and the particles must be considered as indistinguishable.

To determine the possible number of complexions we might first remember that at normal temperatures there are a large number of energy states available for molecules in a gas.   We have seen that the average state for translating atoms in a 1-mm box is of the order of the 10^7th state above the ground state, and for larger containers this will be even greater.   We thus recognize that if a very small increment in energy is considered, even if this increment is so small that for all practical purposes the energy can be considered constant in that interval, there are still a large number of translational quantum states in the interval.

Therefore let us choose an energy range small compared to kT, but sufficiently large that it will contain enough molecules that we can use

Stirling's approximation when convenient. If this range of energy is small, we can consider all the molecules and all the energy states in the interval as being of the same energy. The size of the interval is such that usually, although there are many molecules in the interval, there are many more quantum states in the interval which can be occupied than there are molecules occupying them. If we now consider how n_i molecules of energy ϵ_i can be distributed among the g_i eigenstates of energy ϵ_i (in the interval of energy for which the energy is said to be ϵ_i) we find that the number of permutations of the particles among the states is $(n_i + g_i - 1)!$ if the particles are not distinguishable. Again, however, the orders of the particles in the levels and of the levels among themselves are of no importance, so that the total number of significant arrangements is $(n_i + g_i - 1)!/n_i!(g_i - 1)!$. The thermodynamic probability for a complete distribution of n_0 molecules in g_0 states of energy ϵ_0, n_1 molecules in g_1 states of energy ϵ_1, etc., is then the product of the individual probabilities,

$$W_T = \prod_i \frac{(g_i + n_i - 1)!}{n_i!(g_i - 1)!},$$

or

$$\ln W_T = \sum_i [\ln (g_i + n_i - 1)! - \ln n_i! - \ln (g_i - 1)!].$$

Neglecting unity compared to n_i and applying Stirling's approximation yields

$$\ln W_T = \sum_i [(g_i + n_i) \ln (g_i + n_i) - (g_i + n_i) - n_i \ln n_i + n_i$$
$$- g_i \ln g_i + g_i]$$
$$= \sum_i [(g_i + n_i) \ln (g_i + n_i) - n_i \ln n_i - g_i \ln g_i].$$

By separating terms we have

$$\ln W_T = \sum_i [g_i \ln (g_i + n_i) + n_i \ln (g_i + n_i) - n_i \ln n_i - g_i \ln g_i],$$

and then, by recollecting,

$$\ln W_T = \sum_i \left[g_i \ln \frac{g_i + n_i}{g_i} + n_i \ln \frac{g_i + n_i}{n_i} \right]$$
$$= \sum_i \left[g_i \ln \left(1 + \frac{n_i}{g_i} \right) + n_i \ln \left(\frac{g_i}{n_i} + 1 \right) \right]$$
$$= \sum_i g_i \left[\ln \left(1 + \frac{n_i}{g_i} \right) + \frac{n_i}{g_i} \ln \left(\frac{g_i}{n_i} + 1 \right) \right].$$

The ratio n_i/g_i is small compared to unity, while g_i/n_i is large; and since for small x, $\ln(1 + x) \simeq x$, this becomes

$$
\ln W_T = \sum_i g_i \left[\frac{n_i}{g_i} + \frac{n_i}{g_i} \ln \frac{g_i}{n_i} \right]
$$

$$
= \sum_i g_i \left[\frac{n_i}{g_i} - \frac{n_i}{g_i} \ln \frac{n_i}{g_i} \right]
$$

$$
= \sum_i n_i \left[1 - \ln \frac{n_i}{g_i} \right].
$$

Therefore the entropy is given by

$$
S = k \ln W_T = k \sum_i n_i \left[1 - \ln \frac{n_i}{g_i} \right]. \tag{5-28}
$$

For the state of maximum probability we have, as before, the restrictions

$$
\delta(\ln W_T) = 0,
$$
$$
\Sigma \, \delta n_i = 0,
$$
$$
\Sigma \, \epsilon_i \, \delta n_i = 0,
$$

which, when combined by the Lagrangian method of undetermined multipliers, yield for the most probable distribution

$$
\frac{n_i}{g_i} = \frac{1}{e^\alpha e^{\beta \epsilon_i} - 1}.
$$

The assumption of indistinguishability of particles, with no limitations on the possible number of particles in each level, is known as Bose-Einstein statistics. A more detailed examination shows that this corresponds to a system in which the wave functions describing the states of the system are symmetric to the interchange of coordinates of any two identical particles. It is seen that the resulting most probable distribution differs from the Boltzmann distribution by the appearance of -1 in the denominator.

In those systems in which the possible states of the system are described by wave functions that are antisymmetric to the interchange of identical particles, the resulting statistics is known as Fermi-Dirac statistics. The restriction to states described by antisymmetric functions is equivalent to restricting the populations of the levels to one particle for each state. The resulting distribution is

$$
\frac{n_i}{g_i} = \frac{1}{e^\alpha e^{\beta \epsilon_i} + 1}.
$$

Under conditions for which g_i/n_i is large compared to unity, and

$$\frac{g_i}{n_i} + 1 \simeq \frac{g_i}{n_i} - 1 \simeq \frac{g_i}{n_i},$$

both the Bose-Einstein and Fermi-Dirac distributions reduce to that of the Boltzmann statistics. Experimentally, this condition is usually obtained if the temperature is high and the pressure low. Thus, many systems obey the Boltzmann law at ordinary temperatures, but will be described by one of the two quantum statistics at lower temperatures. The behavior of He^4 at low temperatures and of photons is explained by Bose-Einstein statistics. The nature of the conduction electrons in metals and the behavior of He^3 at low temperatures is described by Fermi-Dirac statistics.

By the assumption that the temperature and pressure are such that we can neglect unity as compared with the exponential, the distributions above become

$$\frac{n_i}{g_i} = e^{-\alpha}e^{-\beta\epsilon_i}.$$

The constant term is readily identified as before with N/Q, so that insertion of the fraction n_i/g_i into Eq. (5–28) yields

$$
\begin{aligned}
S &= k \sum_i \left[n_i + n_i \ln \frac{Q}{N} + \beta\epsilon_i n_i \right] \\
&= k \left\{ \Sigma_i \, n_i + \sum_i \left[n_i \ln \frac{Q}{N} + \beta\epsilon_i n_i \right] \right\} \\
&= k \left[N + N \ln \frac{Q}{N} + \frac{1}{kT} E \right].
\end{aligned}
$$

$$(5\text{–}29)$$

With Eq. (5–16) substituted for E, the equation for the entropy becomes

$$
\begin{aligned}
S &= k \left[N + N \ln \frac{Q}{N} + \frac{RT^2}{kT} \left(\frac{\partial(\ln Q)}{\partial T} \right)_v \right] \\
&= R \left[1 + \ln \frac{Q}{N} + T \left(\frac{\partial(\ln Q)}{\partial T} \right)_v \right],
\end{aligned}
$$

$$(5\text{–}30)$$

which is identical with Eq. (5–21).

Our usual association of an increase in entropy with temperature can be illustrated by observing that an equivalent expression to Eq. (5–30) is, from Eq. (5–29),

$$S = R \left[1 + \ln \frac{Q}{N} \right] + \frac{E}{T}$$

and that

$$\left(\frac{\partial S}{\partial T}\right)_V = R\left(\frac{\partial[\ln(Q/N)]}{\partial T}\right)_V + \frac{1}{T}\left(\frac{\partial E}{\partial T}\right)_V - \frac{E}{T^2}$$

$$= R\left(\frac{\partial[\ln(Q/N)]}{\partial T}\right)_V + \frac{1}{T}\left(\frac{\partial E}{\partial T}\right)_V - R\left(\frac{\partial[\ln Q]}{\partial T}\right)_V = \frac{1}{T}\left(\frac{\partial E}{\partial T}\right)_V$$

$$= \frac{C_V}{T}, \tag{5-31}$$

or

$$S = C_V \ln T + S_0 \tag{5-32}$$

where S_0 may be a function of volume. The increase in entropy with rising temperature results because, as the total energy of the system

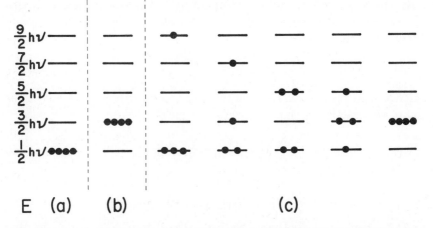

Fig. 5–4. The effect of available energy levels on the energy and entropy of four harmonic oscillators. Of interest is the number of distributions giving a total energy of $6h\nu$. (a) At 0°K only one level possible, no distribution gives $6h\nu$, only $2h\nu$ possible. (b) At slightly higher temperature, if two energy levels can be occupied, one distribution will give $6h\nu$. (c) At higher temperature, if five energy levels are available, there are five distributions having energy $6h\nu$. Thus, with more energy levels available, the number of possible microstates increases, with a resulting increase in the thermodynamic probability and the entropy. (Particles have been assumed here to be indistinguishable.)

becomes greater, more and more of the higher energy states can be occupied by more and more of the molecules, so that the number of ways in which a macroscopic state can be realized increases. Thus the thermodynamic probability of a macrostate is greater, and so also is the entropy. This is illustrated with a simple case in Fig. 5–4.

An increase in volume would also increase the number of available energy levels and hence also increase the number of possible microstates, so that an increase in volume will also result in a larger entropy.   Simple statistical arguments similar to those we have employed show that

$$\left(\frac{\partial S}{\partial V}\right)_T = \frac{R}{V},$$

which is consistent with the thermodynamic relations.

We are now able to understand the significance of the entropy function on a molecular basis perhaps more clearly than from a purely thermodynamic viewpoint.   At the absolute zero for a perfect crystal, only one microstate will describe the system.   If there are any irregularities, such as different molecular orientations in the lattice or mixtures of isotopes that permit more than a single microstate, then the entropy will be greater than zero.   If Eq. (5–31) is integrated in terms of the partition function, it becomes apparent that the constant of integration S_0 in Eqs. (5–32) and (5–20) is equal to the value of ln Q at 0°K which is simply g_0.   So long as $g_0 = 1$, then S_0 is zero, the assumption made by the third law of thermodynamics.   Generally, deviations from the calculation of the absolute entropy assuming $S_0 = 0$ can be calculated from entropy of mixing.   Finally, as the temperature and volume of a system increase, more energy levels are available, and hence many more complexions are possible for a given macrostate of the system.   Hence the thermodynamic probability and entropy increase.

5.6   THERMODYNAMIC FUNCTIONS FOR AN IDEAL GAS

Let us determine, by means of the equations we have derived, some of the common thermodynamic functions for a familiar case, the ideal monatomic gas.   In Sec. 5.3 we obtained an expression for the translational partition function as

$$Q = (2\pi mkT)^{3/2} \frac{V}{h^3}.$$

From this and Eq. (5–16) we obtain

$$E = \tfrac{3}{2}RT,$$

the familiar result from arguments in kinetic theory.

Although we can obtain C_V easily from this result, we note also it can be found by using Eq. (5–26), the result being

$$C_V = \tfrac{3}{2}R.$$

Also, from Eq. (5–25) we obtain, for the enthalpy of the monatomic gas,

$$H = \tfrac{3}{2}R + RT = \tfrac{3}{2}R + PV$$

which is again consistent with our result for E and the thermodynamic definition of enthalpy $H = E + PV$.

Less familiar is the result of applying Eq. (5–21), which yields

$$S = \frac{5R}{2} + \frac{3R}{2}\ln T + \frac{3R}{2}\ln M + \frac{3R}{2}\ln\left(\frac{2\pi k}{h^2}\right) + R\ln V - \frac{5R}{2}\ln N$$

which is commonly known as the Sakur-Tetrode equation. From this equation it is possible to calculate the absolute entropy of a perfect monatomic gas at some temperature T knowing only the molecular weight of the gas and its volume.

From Equations (5–22) and (5–24) it is verified also that

$$A = -RT\left\{\ln\left[\left(\frac{2\pi mkT}{h^2}\right)^{3/2}\frac{V}{N}\right] + 1\right\}$$

and

$$G = -RT\ln\frac{Q}{N} = -RT\ln\left[\left(\frac{2\pi mkT}{h^2}\right)^{3/2}\frac{V}{N}\right].$$

In later chapters we will study more complicated systems, evaluate partition functions for rotational and vibrational motions of molecules and for electronic states, and determine their effects on the calculation of thermodynamic functions, spectra, and related phenomena.

5.7 EQUILIBRIUM CONSTANTS

The equations which have been derived in this chapter would appear to indicate that it is possible to calculate unambiguous, absolute values for the partition function and for the various thermodynamic functions such as energy, enthalpy, and free energy. It is apparent from the definition of Q, however, that the numerical value of Q depends on the numerical values of the various energy levels of the system, and these, in turn, depend on the arbitrary selection of some zero of energy. For the purpose of statistical calculations it is convenient to select a zero of energy that makes all of the energy levels have a positive numerical value. In this way no ambiguity results concerning positive and negative sign. Frequently, the lowest energy level is chosen as zero, although other choices can be made as required for a given calculation. Thus the values of thermodynamic functions are actually calculated relative to the arbitrary energy zero and except for entropy are not absolute in the true sense of the word.

In many cases the thermodynamic functions themselves are of interest to the chemist. The absolute value of the entropy, for example, may give insight into the molecular configurations involved in a particular system. More often it is changes in energy or enthalpy during the course of a chemical or physical process which are of interest. If the partition functions for all reactants and products can be calculated, then the desired thermodynamic functions can be evaluated, and hence quantities such as ΔE, ΔH, and ΔG that indicate the heat of reaction under certain conditions and the spontaneity of the process.

From the change in free energy, thermodynamics predicts the degree of spontaneity of a process, and this is conveniently expressed in terms of the equilibrium constant. From our foregoing discussion it should be obvious that the equilibrium constant can be formulated in terms of the partition functions of the reactants and products. Hence the knowledge that can be gained from spectroscopic measurements about the energy levels for different substances ultimately can lead to the calculation of equilibrium constants for reactions involving these substances.

In the general case, the partition function for a molecule will be the product of several partition functions, most particularly those for translation, vibration, rotation, and electronic states,

$$Q = Q_{trans}Q_{rot}Q_{vib}Q_{elec}.$$

Of these, only the translational partition function depends on the volume of the system. All the others are governed by internal configurations and interactions. Hence in Eq. (5–24)

$$V\left(\frac{\partial(\ln Q)}{\partial V}\right)_T = V\left(\frac{\partial(\ln Q_{trans})}{\partial V}\right)_T = \frac{V}{V} = 1,$$

so that (5–24) becomes

$$G = -RT \ln \frac{Q}{N}. \tag{5–33}$$

If the standard state is specified, then

$$G^0 = -RT \ln \frac{Q^0}{N}. \tag{5–34}$$

The definition of the equilibrium constant for a process comes from the equation

$$\Delta G^0 = -RT \ln K,$$

from which it is apparent that K can be related to the partition functions of the reactants and products. Before this can be done, however, it must be recognized that the partition function for each species involved in the reaction normally is evaluated using a different energy zero point for each calculation. In order that the partition functions may all be used for a calculation of ΔG^0 it is necessary that a common zero point energy be chosen.   This can be done in any way that is most convenient (Fig. 5–5), and the partition function evaluated with respect to this zero

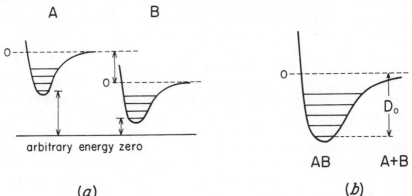

Fig. 5–5. Choice of energy zero. (a) Relation of potential-energy curves for different molecular species. (b) For the dissociation of a molecule into its atoms, ΔE_0^0 is the dissociation energy of the molecule.

point is easily related to that originally calculated, since the addition of some arbitrary increment E^0/mole can be factored out of the partition function.   That is,

$$Q = \Sigma \, g_i e^{-\epsilon_i/kT}$$
$$Q_{E_0} = \Sigma \, g_i e^{-(\epsilon_i + \epsilon_0)/kT}$$
$$= e^{-\epsilon_0/kT} \Sigma \, g_i e^{-\epsilon_i/kT}$$
$$= e^{-\epsilon_0/kT} Q$$
$$= e^{-E_0/RT} Q$$

where $E_0 = N\epsilon_0$ is the energy zero added per mole.   Thus Eq. (5–34) becomes

$$G^0 = -RT \ln \frac{Q_{E_0}^0}{N}$$

$$= -RT \ln \frac{Q^0}{N} + E_0^0. \tag{5–35}$$

It should be noted that E_0^0 represents the energy which one mole of molecules would have at 0°K since under those circumstances all the molecules would be in the lowest energy level.   Under these conditions it is also true that $E_0^0 = H_0^0$.   An alternative form of (5–35) is

$$\frac{G^0 - E_0^0}{T} = -R \ln \frac{Q^0}{N}.$$

The quantity on the left, often called the free-energy function, has been tabulated for many substances.

For a general reaction

$$aA + bB + \cdots \leftrightharpoons cC + dD + \cdots ,$$

it now follows that

$$\Delta G^0 = cG_C^0 + dG_D^0 + \cdots - (aG_A^0 + bG_B^0 + \cdots)$$
$$= -RT \ln \frac{(Q_C^0/N)^c(Q_D^0/N)^d \cdots}{(Q_A^0/N)^a(Q_B^0/N)^b \cdots} + \Delta E_0^0$$
$$= -RT \ln K,$$

from which

$$K = \frac{(Q_C^0/N)^c(Q_D^0/N)^d \cdots}{(Q_A^0/N)^a(Q_B^0/N)^b \cdots} e^{-\Delta E_0^0/RT}.$$

A particularly simple example is the dissociation of a diatomic molecule such as

$$H_2 \leftrightharpoons 2H,$$

for which

$$K = \frac{(Q_H^0/N)^2}{(Q_{H_2}^0/N)} e^{-\Delta E_0^0/RT}.$$

The choice of an energy zero is simple in this case, since the dissociation energy of H_2 into separate atoms is known. This represents the energy $D_0 = \Delta E_0^0$ shown in Fig. 5–5b, where the energy of the separate atoms is taken as the energy zero. The rotational and vibrational properties of many diatomic molecules have been studied extensively and can be used to evaluate the corresponding partition functions. Excited electronic states of the molecules and atoms commonly are so high in energy compared to kT that they do not have to be considered in the partition function.

In later chapters the partition functions for rotational, vibrational, and electronic states will be discussed in detail. Once these have been evaluated for the species of interest, calculation of quantities such as the equilibrium constant can be carried out readily.

SUPPLEMENTARY REFERENCES

Introductory

GURNEY, R. W., *Introduction to Statistical Mechanics*, McGraw-Hill Book Co., New York, 1949.

DOLE, M., *Introduction to Statistical Thermodynamics*, Prentice-Hall, Englewood Cliffs, N.J., 1954.

Rushbrooke, G. S., *Introduction to Statistical Mechanics*, Oxford University Press, London, 1949.

Pitzer, K. S., *Quantum Chemistry*, Prentice-Hall, Englewood Cliffs, N.J., 1953.

Intermediate

Mayer, J. E., and M. G. Mayer, *Statistical Mechanics*, John Wiley & Sons, Inc., New York, 1940.

Davidson, N., *Statistical Mechanics*, McGraw-Hill Book Co., New York, 1962.

Glasstone, S., *Theoretical Chemistry*, D. Van Nostrand, Princeton, 1944.

Eyring, H., D. Henderson, B. J. Stover, and E. M. Eyring, *Statistical Mechanics and Dynamics*, John Wiley & Sons, Inc., New York, 1964.

Hill, T. L., *Introduction to Statistical Thermodynamics*, Addison-Wesley Publishing Co., Reading, Mass., 1960.

Advanced

Fowler, R. H., and E. A. Guggenheim, *Statistical Thermodynamics*, Cambridge University Press, London, 1939.

Tolman, R. C., *Principles of Statistical Mechanics*, Oxford University Press, London, 1938.

PROBLEMS

5-1. Calculate the number of ways in which 16 balls can be distributed into four compartments for the following two distributions:

a. $n_1 = 2$, $n_2 = 6$, $n_3 = 6$, $n_4 = 2$;

b. $n_1 = 4$, $n_2 = 4$, $n_3 = 4$, $n_4 = 4$.

Assume the balls are distinguishable.

5-2. If the *a priori* probability of each compartment is $\frac{1}{4}$ in Problem 5-1 what are the probabilities of distributions (a) and (b)?

5-3. If the *a priori* probabilities in compartments 1, 2, 3, and 4 are $\frac{1}{4}$, $\frac{1}{4}$, $\frac{1}{3}$, and $\frac{1}{6}$, respectively, in Problem 5-1, what are the probabilities of distributions (a) and (b)?

5-4. Consider the following two distributions of molecules among the lowest five energy states of a molecule vibrating with frequency ν:

Distribution A		Distribution B	
State	n_i	State	n_i
0	17	0	16
1	8	1	8
2	2	2	4
3	2	3	2
4	2	4	1

a. Calculate the total number of molecules.

b. Calculate the total energy of each distribution.

c. Calculate the number of ways each distribution can be established, assuming that the molecules are distinguishable.

d. Which distribution is more probable?

5-5. Change both distributions A and B of Problem 5-4 by adding one molecule to state 1 from each of the energy states 0 and 2, thus maintaining the total energy constant.

a. Calculate again the number of ways each distribution can be established.

b. Which distribution, that of Problem 5-4 or that of 5-5 in each case (A and B), is the more probable?

5-6. Find C_V and C_p in terms of Q.

5-7. Compute the molar free-energy change of monatomic mercury atoms (assumed to be a perfect gas) in cooling from 400°C to 350°C at a pressure of 1 atmosphere.

5-8. Calculate the molar entropy of argon at 0°C and atmospheric pressure, and compare it with the experimental value.

5-9. Consider the simple case of the distribution of n molecules between two states of equal energy and equal *a priori* probability. Show that the most probable distribution has $n/2$ molecules in each state and that a distribution with x more molecules in one state and x less in the other has a probability reduced by a factor $\exp(-2x^2/n)$.

5-10. In terms of the Boltzmann energy distribution, what is the meaning of a negative absolute temperature? Is this hotter or colder than ordinary temperatures?

5-11. Derive an expression for the molar heat capacity C_V of a monatomic solid, assuming that each atom is vibrating with the same frequency ν along the three cartesian axes. This is the expression first obtained by Einstein. What does it predict about the temperature dependence of C_V and what are the limits of C_V at very high temperatures?

5-12. The fundamental vibrational frequency of N_2 is 2360 cm^{-1}. What fraction of N_2 molecules at 25°C have no vibrational energy apart from their zero-point energy?

5-13. Show that for a large box the distribution of energy levels becomes equivalent to the classical Maxwell-Boltzmann distribution of kinetic energies.

5-14. The first excited vibrational state of HCl is about 2990 cm^{-1} above the ground vibrational state. Explain why vibrational motions do not contribute to the heat capacity of HCl at normal temperatures.

5-15. Show that the vibrational partition function of a diatomic molecule at very high temperatures is $kT/h\nu$.

5-16. The translational partition function for a molecule is $(2\pi mkT)^{3/2}V/h^3$, and the rotational partition function for a rotating diatomic molecule such as HCl is $8\pi^2IkT/h^2$, where I is the moment of inertia of the molecule. Calculate from these partition functions the heat capacity of HCl gas, assuming that there is no vibrational contribution (calculate C_V).

5–17. Find $\ln Q$, E, and S per mole of F(g) atoms at 298.15°K from these data:[2]

Electronic State	Energy (cm⁻¹)	Degeneracy
$^2P_{3/2}$	0.0	4
$^2P_{1/2}$	404.0	2
Other	10^5	—

5–18. Leaving the partition function in the form of Eq. (5–11), with β undetermined, derive the partition function for translation and the molar energy of a monatomic gas. By comparison of the result with the kinetic-theory value for E, show that $\beta = 1/kT$.

5–19. Leaving the partition function in the form of Eq. (5–11), with β undetermined, derive an expression for the entropy function differential, dS, analogous to Eq. (5–20), and show that dS will not be an exact differential unless $\beta = 1/kT$.

5–20. Show that C_V for a monatomic solid should go to zero at 0°K (see Problem 5–11).

[2] Moore, *Atomic Energy Levels*, NBS 467 (1949).

6

The Hydrogen Atom

The simplest atomic system is the hydrogen atom, consisting of a positively charged proton and a negatively charged electron. We saw in Chapter 2 that Rutherford's experiments and the atomic spectra of atoms are both inconsistent with the well-established theoretical structure of classical physics. It was not until Bohr's radical introduction of Planck's and Einstein's quantum concepts that theoretical agreement was obtained with the well-known atomic spectrum of hydrogen. This theory was refined by the introduction of relativistic corrections, but its success was short-lived, for Bohr's simple quantum theory failed to agree with the observed properties of more complex atoms and molecules. It was this failure that led to a more thorough renovation of the fundamental postulates of physics and the development of quantum mechanics. We have already outlined the fundamental methods of quantum mechanics and studied the application of these methods to simple physical problems in Chapters 3 and 4. Let us now apply the postulates of quantum mechanics to a simple atom.

6.1 THE TWO-BODY PROBLEM

The proton-electron system constituting the hydrogen atom is mathematically a special case of the more general problem of the motion of two bodies which interact with each other by some type of attraction or repulsion that depends only on their separation. In the hydrogen atom, for example, the interaction between the two bodies is assumed to be the coulombic attraction of two equally but oppositely charged particles, $V(r) = -e^2/r$ where e is the electronic charge and r the distance between the charges. For a rigid but freely rotating diatomic molecule we could assume $V(r)$ is a constant or zero, while for a freely rotating harmonic oscillator $V(r) = \frac{1}{2}k(r - r_e)^2$ where r_e is the equilibrium separation between the two bodies.

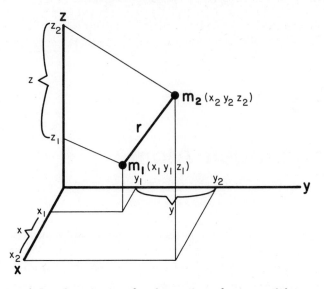

Fig. 6–1. Coordinates for the motion of two particles.

Consider two bodies in a cartesian coordinate system as illustrated in Fig. 6–1. Since the potential energy is not an explicit function of time, but only of distance, we are concerned with a conservative system and can employ the simpler time-independent Schrödinger equation. For two bodies this would be

$$\left(-\frac{\hbar^2}{2}\left[\frac{1}{m_1}\nabla_1{}^2 + \frac{1}{m_2}\nabla_2{}^2\right] + V(r)\right)\psi_T = E_T\psi_T,$$

where ψ_T is a function of x_1, y_1, z_1, the coordinates of particle 1, and x_2, y_2, z_2, the coordinates of particle 2, or

$$-\frac{\hbar^2}{2}\left[\frac{1}{m_1}\left(\frac{\partial^2\psi_T}{\partial x_1{}^2} + \frac{\partial^2\psi_T}{\partial y_1{}^2} + \frac{\partial^2\psi_T}{\partial z_1{}^2}\right)\right.$$
$$\left. + \frac{1}{m_2}\left(\frac{\partial^2\psi_T}{\partial x_2{}^2} + \frac{\partial^2\psi_T}{\partial y_2{}^2} + \frac{\partial^2\psi_T}{\partial z_2{}^2}\right)\right] + V\psi_T = E_T\psi_T. \quad (6\text{–}1)$$

It is possible to effect a separation of this equation into two simpler equations if we introduce the coordinates X, Y, and Z, which are the coordinates of the center of mass of the system:

$$X = \frac{m_1x_1 + m_2x_2}{m_1 + m_2},$$
$$Y = \frac{m_1y_1 + m_2y_2}{m_1 + m_2},$$
$$Z = \frac{m_1z_1 + m_2z_2}{m_1 + m_2}, \quad (6\text{–}2)$$

and the coordinates x, y, and z, which would be the coordinates of particle 2 if particle 1 were held fixed at the origin of the coordinate system:

$$x = x_2 - x_1,$$
$$y = y_2 - y_1,$$
$$z = z_2 - z_1. \tag{6-3}$$

If we assume that $\psi_T = \psi_t(X, Y, Z)\psi(x, y, z)$, we can separate Eq. (6-1) by substituting this equality into the equation and then dividing both sides of the equation by $\psi_T = \psi_t\psi$. After algebraic manipulations the result is

$$-\frac{\hbar^2}{2M}\frac{1}{\psi_t}\left(\frac{\partial^2\psi_t}{\partial X^2} + \frac{\partial^2\psi_t}{\partial Y^2} + \frac{\partial^2\psi_t}{\partial Z^2}\right)$$
$$-\frac{\hbar^2}{2\mu}\frac{1}{\psi}\left(\frac{\partial^2\psi}{\partial x^2} + \frac{\partial^2\psi}{\partial y^2} + \frac{\partial^2\psi}{\partial z^2}\right) + V(x, y, z) = E \tag{6-4}$$

where $M = m_1 + m_2$ is the total mass and $\mu = m_1m_2/(m_1 + m_2)$ is the reduced mass of the system.

The coordinates X, Y, and Z are independent of the coordinates x, y, and z, and since the sum of the terms in these coordinates equals a constant in Eq. (6-4), it must be true that the terms in each set of coordinates are independently equal to constants, so that

$$-\frac{\hbar^2}{2M}\left(\frac{\partial^2\psi_t}{\partial X^2} + \frac{\partial^2\psi_t}{\partial Y^2} + \frac{\partial^2\psi_t}{\partial Z^2}\right) = E_t\psi_t \tag{6-5}$$

and

$$-\frac{\hbar^2}{2\mu}\left(\frac{\partial^2\psi}{\partial x^2} + \frac{\partial^2\psi}{\partial y^2} + \frac{\partial^2\psi}{\partial z^2}\right) + V(x, y, z)\psi = E\psi, \tag{6-6}$$

where

$$E_t + E = E_T.$$

We recognize Eq. (6-5) as the equation of motion of a particle of mass M in free space. We have obtained the possible energies for this case and discussed the nature of the wave functions at some length in Chapter 4. It is apparent, then, that we have separated the general Schrödinger equation for the two-body system into an equation that describes the translational motions of the center of mass of the system and another that describes only the motions of the two bodies relative to each other. As the former case is easily understood, we are particularly interested in the second equation, which should allow us to deduce information about the internal nature of the system, such as the possible energy levels and distributions in space.

An additional manipulation is now desirable, in view of the symmetry of the two-body system. Although the potential energy can be expressed in cartesian coordinates, the resulting expression could be unduly complicated and unmanageable. Since the potential energy is most easily expressed in terms of a separation of the two particles, $V(r) = -e^2/r$ for the hydrogen atom, it would seem logical at this point to transform Eq. (6–6) into coordinates which would take advantage of this fact. In this case, spherical polar coordinates are the most obvious. Using the relations between coordinate systems discussed in Appendix B, Eq. (6–6) becomes

$$-\frac{\hbar^2}{2\mu r^2}\left[\frac{\partial}{\partial r}\left(r^2\frac{\partial\psi}{\partial r}\right) + \frac{1}{\sin\theta}\frac{\partial}{\partial\theta}\left(\sin\theta\frac{\partial\psi}{\partial\theta}\right)\right.$$
$$\left. + \frac{1}{\sin^2\theta}\frac{\partial^2\psi}{\partial\phi^2}\right] + V(r)\psi = E\psi \quad (6\text{–}7)$$

where ψ is now a function of r, θ, and ϕ.

This equation is mathematically equivalent to the equation of motion of a single particle of mass μ about the origin with a potential energy

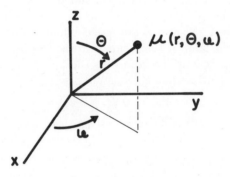

Fig. 6–2. Spherical polar coordinates for a particle of mass μ moving about the origin.

$V(r)$ which depends on its distance r from the origin (Fig. 6–2). We might note that in the hydrogen atom the mass of the proton is so much larger than that of the electron that the reduced mass is nearly equal to the mass of the electron. Thus, the model of an electron rotating around a fixed nucleus is not as extremely crude as we might imagine.

Although we have managed to eliminate all the motions except those relative motions which determine the internal energy of the system, it is obvious that Eq. (6–7) cannot be solved directly for the energy states of the system or for the wave functions describing these states. Instead, it will be necessary to separate (6–7) further into equations that are each dependent on only one of the three polar coordinates. That this is possible can be seen by again assuming that the wave function of (6–7) can be written as the product of three wave functions, each of which is dependent on only one coordinate:

$$\psi(r, \ \theta, \ \phi) = R(r)\Theta(\theta)\Phi(\phi). \tag{6-8}$$

Substituting (6–8) in (6–7), we obtain

$$-\frac{\hbar^2}{2\mu r^2 \sin^2 \theta} \left[\Theta\Phi \sin^2 \theta \frac{d}{dr} \left(r^2 \frac{dR}{dr} \right) + R\Phi \sin \theta \frac{d}{d\theta} \left(\sin \theta \frac{d\Theta}{d\theta} \right) \right.$$
$$\left. + R\Theta \frac{d^2\Phi}{d\phi^2} \right] + V(r)R\Theta\Phi = ER\Theta\Phi,$$

which can be rearranged, upon dividing by $\psi = R\Theta\Phi$, to

$$\frac{\sin^2 \theta}{R} \frac{d}{dr} \left(r^2 \frac{dR}{dr} \right) + \frac{\sin \theta}{\Theta} \frac{d}{d\theta} \left(\sin \theta \frac{d\Theta}{d\theta} \right) + \frac{1}{\Phi} \frac{d^2\Phi}{d\phi^2}$$
$$+ \frac{2\mu r^2 \sin^2 \theta}{\hbar^2} [E - V(r)] = 0. \tag{6-9}$$

Notice that one of the terms in this equation involves only the Φ function and the ϕ coordinate. Since this term is independent of variations in the other coordinates, and the other terms are similarly independent of variations in ϕ, then this term must be equal to a constant, and the sum of all the remaining terms must equal the negative of that constant in order that the sum of all terms will remain equal to zero. For reasons that will become more apparent soon, we will let this constant be $-m^2$, so that

$$\frac{d^2\Phi(\phi)}{d\phi^2} = -m^2\Phi(\phi). \tag{6-10}$$

Substituting this constant for the ϕ term in (6–9) and dividing by $\sin^2 \theta$, we obtain

$$\frac{1}{R} \frac{d}{dr} \left(r^2 \frac{dR}{dr} \right) + \frac{1}{\Theta \sin \theta} \frac{d}{d\theta} \left(\sin \theta \frac{d\Theta}{d\theta} \right) - \frac{m^2}{\sin^2 \theta} + \frac{2\mu r^2}{\hbar^2} [E - V(r)] = 0.$$

This equation now contains two terms dependent only on the variable θ and two terms dependent only on r. Again, since these two sets of terms are independent of each other, but their sum is a constant (0), then each set must also be equal to a constant. Setting the sum of the terms in θ equal to the constant $-\beta$, we have

$$\frac{1}{\sin \theta} \frac{d}{d\theta} \left(\sin \theta \frac{d\Theta}{d\theta} \right) - \frac{m^2}{\sin^2 \theta} \Theta + \beta\Theta = 0 \tag{6-11}$$

and

$$\frac{d}{dr} \left(r^2 \frac{dR}{dr} \right) - \beta R + \frac{2\mu r^2}{\hbar^2} [E - V(r)]R = 0. \tag{6-12}$$

Equations (6–10), (6–11), and (6–12) each depend on only one variable, and hence we may now attack the problem of obtaining solutions.

Notice that the energy of the system depends only on r, but that a complete description of the wave functions will require solving all three equations. It is also apparent that although different two-body systems will differ in their energy states and radial properties, they will have similar angular properties with respect to their wave functions.

6.2   THE Φ EQUATION

Turning our attention to Eq. (6–10), we observe that it is of the familiar form of Eq. (4–4), which we have already discussed in some detail. Thus a general solution of (6–10) is

$$\Phi_m = Ae^{im\phi} + Be^{-im\phi}.$$

In order that Φ be single-valued, it is necessary that $\Phi(\phi) = \Phi(\phi + 2\pi)$, or

$$Ae^{im\phi} + Be^{-im\phi} = Ae^{im(\phi+2\pi)} + Be^{-im(\phi+2\pi)}$$
$$= Ae^{im\phi}e^{im2\pi} + Be^{-im\phi}e^{-im2\pi},$$

which is possible only if $e^{\pm im2\pi} = 1$, which in turn requires that m be an integer.

An equally satisfactory form of this solution is

$$\Phi_m = Ae^{im\phi} \tag{6–13}$$

if we impose the restriction that the quantum number m can assume only the values

$$m = 0, \pm 1, \pm 2, \ldots .$$

In other words, for each numerical value of m except 0 there are two wave functions of the form of (6–13), one with positive m and one with negative m.

The wave functions (6–13) can be normalized easily by the integration

$$\int_0^{2\pi} \Phi_m^*(\phi)\Phi_m(\phi) \, d\phi = A^2 \int_0^{2\pi} d\phi = 1,$$

to give for the normalized functions

$$\Phi_m = \frac{1}{\sqrt{2\pi}} e^{im\phi}.$$

The solutions we have discussed so far have been complex functions, but for some purposes it is convenient to have alternative solutions which are real. These can be obtained readily, since our discussion in Chapter 3 has indicated that, if $\Phi = Ae^{im\phi}$ and $\Phi = Ae^{-im\phi}$ are solutions of Eq. (6–10), then linear combinations of these functions will also be solutions. Thus, for a given absolute value of m the sum and the difference of the two complex solutions will give us

$$\Phi_{|m|}(\phi) = \frac{1}{\sqrt{\pi}} \cos |m|\phi,$$

$$\Phi_{|m|}(\phi) = \frac{1}{\sqrt{\pi}} \sin |m|\phi. \tag{6–14}$$

The normalization constants were obtained in the usual way. For the particular value $m = 0$, there is only one real solution, which is

$$\Phi_0(\phi) = \frac{1}{\sqrt{2\pi}}.$$

The solution of the Φ equation has resulted in a particular restricted set of wave functions, denoted by a quantum number, in this case m, which can assume only certain values. This is a result which we have come to expect for bound systems in quantum mechanics. The quantum number m is often called the magnetic quantum number, and we will investigate its significance shortly. In the meantime we will delay further inquiry into the nature of the Φ functions until we have also obtained solutions for the Θ and R functions.

6.3   THE Θ EQUATION

Equation (6–11) does not have as obvious a solution as the simple differential equation we have just discussed. Since we are not concerned in this discussion with detailed mathematical techniques, we will not delve in detail into the solution of (6–11), but will instead note that this equation is of a form familiar to mathematicians as Legendre's equation, for which the solutions are well known. The solution of this equation can be treated also in a manner somewhat similar to our discussion of the harmonic oscillator in Chapter 4, and it is found that, in order that the solutions be well-behaved, the series of terms comprising the solution must be terminated at some point. This restriction results in the important relation

$$\beta = l(l + 1),$$

where $l = |m|, |m| + 1, \ldots$. Thus β and l are integers.

The solutions themselves are functions known to mathematicians as the associated Legendre functions, generally denoted by the symbol $P_l^{|m|}$. These functions are examined in more detail in Appendix D. For our purposes here we will simply state that they are functions of the variable $(\cos \theta)$ and have a specific functional form for given values of the quantum numbers l and m. Including the normalization constant, the Θ func-

TABLE 6–1. The Wave Functions $\Theta_{lm}(\theta)$

(The associated Legendre functions normalized to unity)

$l = 0$, s orbitals: $\quad \Theta_{00}(\theta) = \dfrac{\sqrt{2}}{2}$

$l = 1$, p orbitals: $\quad \Theta_{10}(\theta) = \dfrac{\sqrt{6}}{2} \cos \theta$

$\qquad\qquad\qquad \Theta_{1 \pm 1}(\theta) = \dfrac{\sqrt{3}}{2} \sin \theta$

$l = 2$, d orbitals: $\quad \Theta_{20}(\theta) = \dfrac{\sqrt{10}}{4} (3 \cos^2 \theta - 1)$

$\qquad\qquad\qquad \Theta_{2 \pm 1}(\theta) = \dfrac{\sqrt{15}}{2} \sin \theta \cos \theta$

$\qquad\qquad\qquad \Theta_{2 \pm 2}(\theta) = \dfrac{\sqrt{15}}{4} \sin^2 \theta$

$l = 3$, f orbitals: $\quad \Theta_{30}(\theta) = \dfrac{3 \sqrt{14}}{4} (\tfrac{5}{3} \cos^3 \theta - \cos \theta)$

$\qquad\qquad\qquad \Theta_{3 \pm 1}(\theta) = \dfrac{\sqrt{42}}{8} \sin \theta \, (5 \cos^2 \theta - 1)$

$\qquad\qquad\qquad \Theta_{3 \pm 2}(\theta) = \dfrac{\sqrt{105}}{4} \sin^2 \theta \cos \theta$

$\qquad\qquad\qquad \Theta_{3 \pm 3}(\theta) = \dfrac{\sqrt{70}}{8} \sin^3 \theta$

$l = 4$, g orbitals: $\quad \Theta_{40}(\theta) = \dfrac{9 \sqrt{2}}{16} (\tfrac{35}{3} \cos^4 \theta - 10 \cos^2 \theta + 1)$

$\qquad\qquad\qquad \Theta_{4 \pm 1}(\theta) = \dfrac{9 \sqrt{10}}{8} \sin \theta \, (\tfrac{7}{3} \cos^3 \theta - \cos \theta)$

$\qquad\qquad\qquad \Theta_{4 \pm 2}(\theta) = \dfrac{3 \sqrt{5}}{8} \sin^2 \theta \, (7 \cos^2 \theta - 1)$

$\qquad\qquad\qquad \Theta_{4 \pm 3}(\theta) = \dfrac{3 \sqrt{70}}{8} \sin^3 \theta \cos \theta$

$\qquad\qquad\qquad \Theta_{4 \pm 4}(\theta) = \dfrac{3 \sqrt{35}}{16} \sin^4 \theta$

$l = 5$, h orbitals: $\quad \Theta_{50}(\theta) = \dfrac{15 \sqrt{22}}{16} (\tfrac{21}{5} \cos^5 \theta - \tfrac{14}{3} \cos^3 \theta + \cos \theta)$

$\qquad\qquad\qquad \Theta_{5 \pm 1}(\theta) = \dfrac{\sqrt{165}}{16} \sin \theta \, (21 \cos^4 \theta - 14 \cos^2 \theta + 1)$

$\qquad\qquad\qquad \Theta_{5 \pm 2}(\theta) = \dfrac{\sqrt{1155}}{8} \sin^2 \theta \, (3 \cos^3 \theta - \cos \theta)$

$\qquad\qquad\qquad \Theta_{5 \pm 3}(\theta) = \dfrac{\sqrt{770}}{32} \sin^3 \theta \, (9 \cos^2 \theta - 1)$

$\qquad\qquad\qquad \Theta_{5 \pm 4}(\theta) = \dfrac{3 \sqrt{385}}{16} \sin^4 \theta \cos \theta$

$\qquad\qquad\qquad \Theta_{5 \pm 5}(\theta) = \dfrac{3 \sqrt{154}}{32} \sin^5 \theta$

tions, which are solutions of Eq. (6–11), can be written as

$$\Theta_{lm}(\theta) = \sqrt{\frac{2l + 1}{2} \frac{(l - |m|)!}{(l + |m|)!}} \, P_l^{|m|}(\cos \theta).$$

A few of the simpler solutions are listed in Table 6–1, where their functional form will be more apparent.

In the particular case of the hydrogen atom the quantum number l is often called the azimuthal quantum number. For the freely rotating and vibrating diatomic molecule, exactly the same solutions are obtained for Θ and Φ, since only the R equation contains the potential-energy term, which distinguishes one two-body problem from another. In this case the same quantum number is generally given the symbol J and is called the rotational quantum number. In either case the mathematical formalism is the same, and we will see that the physical interpretations are equivalent.

TABLE 6–2. Angular Factors for Two-Particle Wave Functions

$$l = 0, \, m = 0: \quad \Theta\Phi = \left(\frac{1}{4\pi}\right)^{1/2}$$

$$l = 1, \, m = 0: \quad \Theta\Phi = \left(\frac{3}{4\pi}\right)^{1/2} \cos \theta$$

$$l = 1, \, m = \pm 1: \Theta\Phi = \left(\frac{3}{8\pi}\right)^{1/2} \sin \theta \, e^{\pm i\phi},$$

$$\text{or} \left(\frac{3}{4\pi}\right)^{1/2} \sin \theta \cos \phi$$

$$\text{and} \left(\frac{3}{4\pi}\right)^{1/2} \sin \theta \sin \phi$$

$$l = 2, \, m = 0: \quad \Theta\Phi = \left(\frac{5}{16\pi}\right)^{1/2} (3 \cos^2 \theta - 1)$$

$$l = 2, \, m = \pm 1: \Theta\Phi = \left(\frac{15}{8\pi}\right)^{1/2} \sin \theta \cos \theta \, e^{\pm i\phi},$$

$$\text{or} \left(\frac{15}{4\pi}\right)^{1/2} \sin \theta \cos \theta \cos \phi$$

$$\text{and} \left(\frac{15}{4\pi}\right)^{1/2} \sin \theta \cos \theta \sin \phi$$

$$l = 2, \, m = \pm 2: \Theta\Phi = \left(\frac{15}{32\pi}\right)^{1/2} \sin^2 \theta \, e^{\pm 2i\phi},$$

$$\text{or} \left(\frac{15}{16\pi}\right)^{1/2} \sin^2 \theta \cos 2\phi$$

$$\text{and} \left(\frac{15}{16\pi}\right)^{1/2} \sin^2 \theta \sin 2\phi$$

The generality of these results, i.e., the independence of the angular wave functions from the nature of the radial potential-energy function, makes it convenient to consider the total angular function, which describes all the angular properties of the possible states of a two-body system. Such an angular wave function would be the product of the Θ and Φ functions, and these angular functions are commonly known as the spherical harmonics:

$$Y_{lm}(\theta, \ \phi) = \Theta_{lm}(\theta)\Phi_m(\phi).$$

A number of these functions are listed in Table 6–2.

One further point is that the spherical harmonic functions depend on both the quantum numbers l and m (as do the Θ functions, also). Both these quantum numbers are restricted to certain values, namely, 0, ± 1, ± 2, . . . for m and 0, 1, 2, . . . for l. In addition, an investigation of the associated Legendre functions discloses that the functions vanish for all cases in which the absolute value of m exceeds the value of l. Thus there do not exist angular wave functions for all possible values of l and m. In particular, for a given value of l, $|m|$ can have all values ranging from 0 to l, i.e., m can have values ranging from $-l$ up to $+l$. Since l is an integer and m can have only integral values, this means that for a given value of l there are $2l + 1$ different spherical harmonic functions, each having a different value of m ($m = -l$, $-l + 1$, $-l + 2$, . . . , 0, . . . , $l - 1$, l). This fact could also have been expressed the opposite way, in terms of given values of m and possible values of l for each m, but soon we will see that the physical interpretation of these quantum numbers makes it more convenient to discuss the states with different values of m as a subclass of a given value of l. Tables 6–1 and 6–2 have been arranged with this in mind. An examination of the tables should help clarify these points.

6.4   THE R EQUATION

The remaining equation to be solved is that containing the variable r. It is this equation that distinguishes one particular two-body problem from another and which, when solved, should predict the possible energy states of the system. The system of interest now is the hydrogen atom, for which $V(r) = -e^2/r$. A slightly more general problem of interest is the hydrogen-like atom (actually ion rather than atom), which consists of a nucleus of charge $+Ze$, where Z is the atomic number of the species, and a single electron. Such a system would be represented by ions like He^+, Li^{2+}, Be^{3+}, etc. In this more general model $V(r) = -Ze^2/r$. We will consider this general case, as the functional form is the same as for the hydrogen atom and differs only through the introduction of Z, which for hydrogen is unity.

For this potential-energy function, then, Eq. (6–12) becomes

$$\frac{1}{r^2}\frac{d}{dr}\left(r^2\frac{dR}{dr}\right) + \left[\frac{-l(l+1)}{r^2} + \frac{2\mu}{\hbar^2}\left(E + \frac{Ze^2}{r}\right)\right]R(r) = 0.$$

The solution of this equation is not difficult, but we will again reserve the details of the procedure for Appendix D and here merely indicate the method that may be used. The details are discussed in the references cited at the end of this chapter. To simplify the form of the equation, we introduce the symbols

$$\alpha^2 = -\frac{2\mu E}{\hbar^2} \quad \text{and} \quad \lambda = \frac{\mu Ze^2}{\hbar^2\alpha}, \tag{6–15}$$

and also a new variable ρ, which is defined as

$$\rho = 2\alpha r.$$

The R equation then has the simpler form

$$\frac{1}{\rho^2}\frac{d}{d\rho}\left(\rho^2\frac{dR}{d\rho}\right) + \left[-\frac{1}{4} - \frac{l(l+1)}{\rho^2} + \frac{\lambda}{\rho}\right]R = 0, \tag{6–16}$$

where R is now a function of the variable ρ. The behavior of this equation as ρ becomes infinite suggests a suitable asymptotic solution to be

$$R = e^{-\rho/2}.$$

It is therefore assumed that the solution of the general equation (6–16) is of the form

$$R = e^{-\rho/2}F(\rho),$$

and investigation of the behavior of this function in Eq. (6–16) at $\rho = 0$ leads to the substitution

$$F(\rho) = \rho^l \sum_{k=0}^{\infty} a_k\rho^k.$$

If the resulting expression for R is now substituted in (6–16), we obtain an infinite number of terms in increasing powers of ρ. Since the coefficients of all terms in a given power of ρ must vanish, it is possible to obtain a recursion formula for the a_k's by considering the coefficients for one power of ρ,

$$a_{k+1} = a_k\frac{k+l+1-\lambda}{(k+1)(k+2l+2)}. \tag{6–17}$$

It can then be shown that R does not remain finite as ρ becomes infinite unless the series terminates, and from (6–17) it is seen that, for termination of the series, we have

$$k + l + 1 - \lambda = 0, \tag{6–18}$$

which requires that λ be an integer. We shall henceforth denote λ by the symbol n, so that from (6–18)

$$n = k + l + 1. \tag{6–19}$$

It is apparent, then, from the restrictions on k (0, 1, 2, . . .) and l (0, 1, 2, . . .) that n can have any positive integral value 1, 2, 3,

TABLE 6–3. The Hydrogen-like Radial Wave Functions $R_{nl}(r)$

$$\left(\rho = \frac{2Z}{na_0} r \right)$$

$n = 1$, K shell: $l = 0$, $1s$, $R_{10}(r) = \left(\dfrac{Z}{a_0} \right)^{3/2} 2e^{-\rho/2}$

$n = 2$, L shell: $l = 0$, $2s$, $R_{20}(r) = \dfrac{(Z/a_0)^{3/2}}{2\sqrt{2}} (2 - \rho)e^{-\rho/2}$

$\qquad\qquad\qquad\ l = 1$, $2p$, $R_{21}(r) = \dfrac{(Z/a_0)^{3/2}}{2\sqrt{6}} \rho e^{-\rho/2}$

$n = 3$, M shell: $l = 0$, $3s$, $R_{30}(r) = \dfrac{(Z/a_0)^{3/2}}{9\sqrt{3}} (6 - 6\rho + \rho^2)e^{-\rho/2}$

$\qquad\qquad\qquad\ l = 1$, $3p$, $R_{31}(r) = \dfrac{(Z/a_0)^{3/2}}{9\sqrt{6}} (4 - \rho)\rho e^{-\rho/2}$

$\qquad\qquad\qquad\ l = 2$, $3d$, $R_{32}(r) = \dfrac{(Z/a_0)^{3/2}}{9\sqrt{30}} \rho^2 e^{-\rho/2}$

$n = 4$, N shell: $l = 0$, $4s$, $R_{40}(r) = \dfrac{(Z/a_0)^{3/2}}{96} (24 - 36\rho + 12\rho^2 - \rho^3)e^{-\rho/2}$

$\qquad\qquad\qquad\ l = 1$, $4p$, $R_{41}(r) = \dfrac{(Z/a_0)^{3/2}}{32\sqrt{15}} (20 - 10\rho + \rho^2)\rho e^{-\rho/2}$

$\qquad\qquad\qquad\ l = 2$, $4d$, $R_{42}(r) = \dfrac{(Z/a_0)^{3/2}}{96\sqrt{5}} (6 - \rho)\rho^2 e^{-\rho/2}$

$\qquad\qquad\qquad\ l = 3$, $4f$, $R_{43}(r) = \dfrac{(Z/a_0)^{3/2}}{96\sqrt{35}} \rho^3 e^{-\rho/2}$

$n = 5$, O shell: $l = 0$, $5s$, $R_{50}(r) = \dfrac{(Z/a_0)^{3/2}}{300\sqrt{5}} (120 - 240\rho + 120\rho^2 - 20\rho^3 + \rho^4)e^{-\rho/2}$

$\qquad\qquad\qquad\ l = 1$, $5p$, $R_{51}(r) = \dfrac{(Z/a_0)^{3/2}}{150\sqrt{30}} (120 - 90\rho + 18\rho^2 - \rho^3)\rho e^{-\rho/2}$

$\qquad\qquad\qquad\ l = 2$, $5d$, $R_{52}(r) = \dfrac{(Z/a_0)^{3/2}}{150\sqrt{70}} (42 - 14\rho + \rho^2)\rho e^{-\rho/2}$

$\qquad\qquad\qquad\ l = 3$, $5f$, $R_{53}(r) = \dfrac{(Z/a_0)^{3/2}}{300\sqrt{70}} (8 - \rho)\rho^3 e^{-\rho/2}$

$\qquad\qquad\qquad\ l = 4$, $5g$, $R_{54}(r) = \dfrac{(Z/a_0)^{3/2}}{900\sqrt{70}} \rho^4 e^{-\rho/2}$

. . . , but not 0. This quantum number is called the principal quantum number since it is related to the energy states of the system. This can be seen by introducing n into the defining equations (6–15) to obtain

$$\lambda = n = \frac{\mu Z e^2}{\hbar^2 \alpha}$$

and

$$E_n = -\frac{\hbar^2 \alpha^2}{2\mu} = -\frac{\mu Z^2 e^4}{2\hbar^2 n^2}, \quad n = 1, 2, 3, \ldots . \quad (6\text{–}20)$$

The radial functions themselves are known as the associated Laguerre functions and are discussed in Appendix D. Several of these are listed in Table 6–3, where the unit of distance a_0, the so-called Bohr-orbit distance or Bohr radius, is defined as

$$a_0 = \frac{\hbar^2}{\mu e^2} = .529 \times 10^{-8} \text{ cm.}$$

For a given value of the quantum number l, Eq. (6–19) restricts n to the values $l + 1, l + 2, \ldots .$ However, since it is the value of n that determines the energy of the system, it is more convenient to consider n as the fundamental number of the system, in which case we observe that for a given value of n we may have $l = 0, 1, 2, \ldots , n - 1$. We have already seen that for a given value of l we may have $m = -l, -l + 1, \ldots , l - 1, l$.

6.5   ENERGY LEVELS OF THE HYDROGEN ATOM

The possible energy levels for the hydrogen atom are given by Eq. (6–20) with $Z = 1$. This equation corresponds exactly with the result first obtained by Bohr, whose calculations, of course, agreed with experiment. Except for extremely small corrections which result from relativistic considerations, Eq. (6–20) accounts fully for the observed atomic spectrum of hydrogen. It should be noted that, if it is assumed that E is greater than zero (corresponding to an ionized atom), then solution of the R equation indicates that all positive energies are permissible. Thus the quantum-mechanical equation of state, the Schrödinger equation, predicts correctly all the possible energy states of the hydrogen atom. If the energy of the system is less than zero, a stable atom exists for which there are certain allowed energies. If the energy of the system is greater than zero, then the kinetic energies of the particles are too great to permit formation of an atom, and any positive kinetic energy is possible. It may be worthwhile to recall at this point that the setting of zero energy as complete ionization of the atom was initially completely arbitrary, but once decided upon, it leads automatically to negative energies for a stable system.

The coulombic potential-energy curve and the quantum-mechanically predicted energy states of the hydrogen atom are illustrated in Fig. 6–3. For hydrogen-like atoms with atomic number Z, the general features would be similar except that the potential well would be lower by a factor of Z and the quantum-mechanical energy levels would be displaced lower by a factor of Z^2.   It is apparent that increasing the nuclear charge has a large effect on the binding of an electron to an atom, most particularly electrons in the lower states.

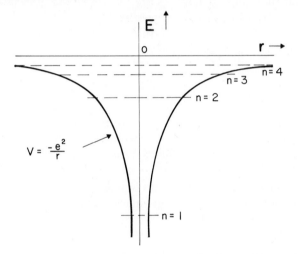

Fig. 6–3. The coulombic-potential-energy well and allowed energy levels of the hydrogen atom.

The total wave function describing any state of the hydrogen atom is, of course, the product of the R, Θ, and Φ functions, as we assumed in making our initial separation of the wave equation:

$$\psi_{nlm} = R_{nl}\Theta_{lm}\Phi_m \qquad (6\text{–}21)$$

Subscripts are included in (6–21) to indicate that different values of the quantum numbers n, l, and m result in different wave functions, which describe different states of the system.   Because the energies of the different states depend only on the principal quantum number n, many of the energy levels of the hydrogen atom are degenerate.   The complete hydrogen atom wave functions are listed in Table 6–4.

For the lowest, ground-state, level of hydrogen, $n = 1$.   The other two quantum numbers are in this case restricted to $l = 0$, $m = 0$, according to the relations we have just derived.   Hence the ground state is not degenerate.   But if we take the level for which $n = 2$, then we have several states which will have this energy; for we can have $l = 0$, for which it is necessary that $m = 0$, or we can have $l = 1$, for which it is possible to have $m = -1$, 0, or $+1$.   Each combination of the three quantum numbers represents a distinct state of the system; there are

TABLE 6–4.   Hydrogen-like Wave Functions

$$\left(\sigma = \frac{n}{2} \rho = \frac{Z}{a_0} r \right)$$

K SHELL

$n = 1, l = 0, m = 0$: $\psi_{1s} = \dfrac{1}{\sqrt{\pi}} \left(\dfrac{Z}{a_0} \right)^{3/2} e^{-\sigma}$

L SHELL

$n = 2, l = 0, m = 0$: $\psi_{2s} = \dfrac{1}{4\sqrt{2\pi}} \left(\dfrac{Z}{a_0} \right)^{3/2} (2 - \sigma)e^{-\sigma/2}$

$n = 2, l = 1, m = 0$: $\psi_{2p_z} = \dfrac{1}{4\sqrt{2\pi}} \left(\dfrac{Z}{a_0} \right)^{3/2} \sigma e^{-\sigma/2} \cos\theta$

$n = 2, l = 1, m = \pm1$: $\psi_{2p_x} = \dfrac{1}{4\sqrt{2\pi}} \left(\dfrac{Z}{a_0} \right)^{3/2} \sigma e^{-\sigma/2} \sin\theta \cos\phi$

$\psi_{2p_y} = \dfrac{1}{4\sqrt{2\pi}} \left(\dfrac{Z}{a_0} \right)^{3/2} \sigma e^{-\sigma/2} \sin\theta \sin\phi$

M SHELL

$n = 3, l = 0, m = 0$: $\psi_{3s} = \dfrac{1}{81\sqrt{3\pi}} \left(\dfrac{Z}{a_0} \right)^{3/2} (27 - 18\sigma + 2\sigma^2)e^{-\sigma/3}$

$n = 3, l = 1, m = 0$: $\psi_{3p_z} = \dfrac{\sqrt{2}}{81\sqrt{\pi}} \left(\dfrac{Z}{a_0} \right)^{3/2} (6 - \sigma)e^{-\sigma/3} \cos\theta$

$n = 3, l = 1, m = \pm1$: $\psi_{3p_x} = \dfrac{\sqrt{2}}{81\sqrt{\pi}} \left(\dfrac{Z}{a_0} \right)^{3/2} (6 - \sigma)\sigma e^{-\sigma/3} \sin\theta \cos\phi$

$\psi_{3p_y} = \dfrac{\sqrt{2}}{81\sqrt{\pi}} \left(\dfrac{Z}{a_0} \right)^{3/2} (6 - \sigma)\sigma e^{-\sigma/3} \sin\theta \sin\phi$

$n = 3, l = 2, m = 0$: $\psi_{3d_{z^2}} = \dfrac{1}{81\sqrt{6\pi}} \left(\dfrac{Z}{a_0} \right)^{3/2} \sigma^2 e^{-\sigma/3} (3\cos^2\theta - 1)$

$n = 3, l = 2, m = \pm1$: $\psi_{3d_{zx}} = \dfrac{\sqrt{2}}{81\sqrt{\pi}} \left(\dfrac{Z}{a_0} \right)^{3/2} \sigma^2 e^{-\sigma/3} \sin\theta \cos\theta \cos\phi$

$\psi_{3d_{yz}} = \dfrac{\sqrt{2}}{81\sqrt{\pi}} \left(\dfrac{Z}{a_0} \right)^{3/2} \sigma^2 e^{-\sigma/3} \sin\theta \cos\theta \sin\phi$

$n = 3, l = 2, m = \pm2$: $\psi_{3d_{x^2-y^2}} = \dfrac{1}{81\sqrt{2\pi}} \left(\dfrac{Z}{a_0} \right)^{3/2} \sigma^2 e^{-\sigma/3} \sin^2\theta \cos2\phi$

$\psi_{3d_{xy}} = \dfrac{1}{81\sqrt{2\pi}} \left(\dfrac{Z}{a_0} \right)^{3/2} \sigma^2 e^{-\sigma/3} \sin^2\theta \sin2\phi$

therefore four different states which have this energy, ψ_{200}, ψ_{210}, ψ_{21-1}, and ψ_{211}. The level $n = 2$ is thus fourfold degenerate. Obviously the higher levels will exhibit even greater degeneracy.

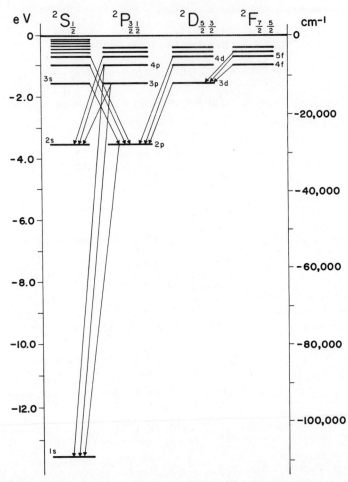

Fig. 6–4. Energy levels and some of the allowed emission transitions for atomic hydrogen.

In Chapter 2 we discussed the quantum-mechanical postulate that a system remains in a given state unless it can absorb or emit a quantum of radiation of exactly the energy to allow a transition to another state. Since the states themselves have fixed energies, the energy, and therefore the frequency, of the radiation will necessarily involve certain definite values. A more thorough study of the transitions between states will disclose that transitions are not possible between every possible pair of states. The restrictions on possible transitions are summarized in what are known as *selection rules*, and in the case of atomic spectra the selection rules are that n may change by any integer, l must change by ± 1, and m may change by ± 1 or not at all. We will return to the origin of these selection rules later.

The energy levels of the hydrogen atom and some of the possible transitions between these levels are illustrated in Fig. 6–4. For convenience in recognizing the states involved in these transitions, the states have been separated in columns according to the value of the azimuthal quantum number. In this way it is possible to apply the selection rule $\Delta l = \pm 1$ without difficulty. The degeneracy of the energy levels with respect to different values of l should be apparent from this diagram; however, no indication has been made here that, in addition, for a given value of l there are $2l + 1$ states having different values of m with the same energy. The terminology used in Fig. 6–4 for labeling the states will be discussed in the next section.

6.6 PROPERTIES OF THE HYDROGEN-LIKE WAVE FUNCTIONS

With some understanding now of the energy levels of the hydrogen-like atomic system, it is of interest to explore the nature of the wave functions that describe the states of this system. We are concerned with such questions as the electron distribution in space, the average distance of an electron from the nucleus, and other important physical quantities which can be deduced from the wave functions.

The method by which the Schrödinger equation was separated in the process of solution led us to the conclusion that the angular properties are the same for all two-body systems described by a potential energy dependent only on separation. The spherical harmonic functions describing these angular properties were listed in Table 6–2.

There are a number of ways in which we might view these functions. A quick examination of Table 6–2 discloses that for $l = 0$ there is no angular dependence of the wave function. That is, if we consider the numerical value of the wave function at a given distance from the origin, this value will remain constant through any changes in the angles θ and ϕ. For other values of l, however, the numerical value of the wave functions will depend on both θ and ϕ. In addition, the sign of the wave function will also change with a change of these angles, and at some angles the wave functions will vanish. This is illustrated in Fig. 6–5, where the sign of the spherical harmonic functions and the location of the nodal lines where the functions are zero are shown on the surface of a sphere about the origin. The shaded surfaces indicate a negative function.

More detail can be obtained if we plot some of the angular functions. This is done in Fig. 6–6. We notice in this figure that the function for $l = 0$ has no angular dependence, as could be determined from the function directly. For the case where $l = 1$, however, we observe very definite angular dependence, and we note that, although the shape of the function is similar for all values of the quantum number m, the orientation of the function with respect to cartesian coordinates is very markedly affected by this number. For $m = 0$ the function is distributed about the z axis and vanishes in the x-y plane. For $m = \pm 1$ the distribution is around the x-y plane and vanishes along the z axis. Similar behavior is observed for higher values of l.

Although the wave functions themselves are of considerable interest, the chemist perhaps would be most satisfied by some physical description of how the electron is located in space. The discussion in Chapter 3

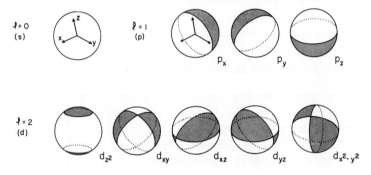

Fig. 6–5. Algebraic sign and nodal lines for the spherical harmonic functions.

disclosed that the probability of finding the system in a configuration denoted by a given set of coordinates is given by the square of the absolute value of the normalized wave function describing the system. Thus, the square of the spherical harmonic wave functions should show us the probability of finding an electron in a hydrogen-like atom as a function of the angles θ and ϕ. The actual electron distribution depends, of course, on the R function also. Inclusion of the radial function gives us a more accurate representation of the actual electronic distribution, but it is difficult to represent the result graphically. In Fig. 6–7 we have shown the regions in space within which the probability of finding an electron is large. In particular, the surfaces shown are those along which $\psi^*\psi$ is about one-tenth of the maximum value which $\psi^*\psi$ can have for each respective function. There is, of course, only positive probability since we are considering the square of the functions.

Inspection of Fig. 6–7 brings out many interesting features which are predicted by quantum mechanics and which may seem inconsistent with

our classical physical concepts.   It is rather apparent that our usual
conception of an electron revolving about the nucleus in a fixed orbit
is meaningless in quantum mechanics.   Figure 6–7 shows us that there
are some regions about the nucleus where the probability of finding an
electron is vanishingly small.   We should emphasize again, in fact, that
the quantum-mechanical approach to these atomic systems is an admis-
sion of the fact that it is impossible to locate an electron with certainty,
whether in a particular closed orbit or in any other kind of motion.   All
we can do is to make a statement concerning the probability that we can

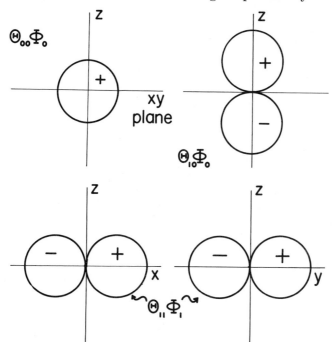

Fig. 6–6.   Polar diagrams of the angular wave functions for the hydrogen-
like atom.

find the electron in a certain region of space.   Because of this indetermi-
nateness, the particle of interest is often described in terms of a probability cloud in space rather than as a particle at a certain location.   This
viewpoint is indicated in Fig. 6–7.   In the probability cloud picture we
recognize that the space covered by the cloud is indicative of the region
in which the particle is likely to be found, and the density of the cloud
at any point is proportional to the actual probability of finding the
particle at that point.   In Fig. 6–7 we have rather roughly indicated
only the former aspect.

Although we are unable to pinpoint an atomic electron in a definite orbit around the nucleus, we have gained some important information from our quantum-mechanical probability picture.   We can see that the distribution of the electron in space has important directional properties. When the atom is in a given state, the electron is confined to regions in

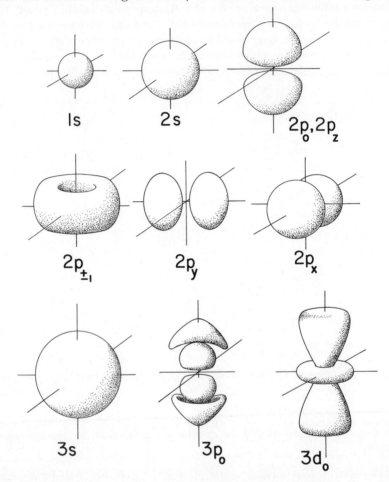

Fig. 6–7.   Representation of the shapes of hydrogen-like atomic orbitals. The surfaces of the figures are the contours along which the probability density of the electron is approximately one-tenth the maximum probability density.

space which are unique for that state.   It would not be surprising, there-fore, to find that the interaction of an atom under various conditions, such as the application of an electric field or the approach of another atom to form a chemical bond, may be quite different when the atom is in different electronic states.   These spatial distributions have an important bearing on the geometry of molecular systems and explain many features of molecular structure that earlier theories were powerless to describe.

We have already noted that the function with $l = 0$ is spherically symmetric about the origin. If we were to consider the functions with different values of the principal quantum number n, but all with $l = 0$, we would observe that they all have this same angular behavior, but the region in which the electron is expected to be found extends farther out from the origin with increasing values of n. Because all these functions have the same angular behavior regardless of their radial behavior, we will classify wave functions for the hydrogen-like atom according to the numerical value of the azimuthal quantum number. Thus, all atomic states with $l = 0$ are generally known as s states, a term arising from the nature of atomic spectra observed involving these states. All states for which $l = 1$ are called p states, those with $l = 2$ are called d states, those with $l = 3$ f states, and so on.

From Fig. 6–7 it can be seen that the probability distributions of the states $l = 1$, $m = +1$, and $l = 1$, $m = -1$ cannot be distinguished from one another. Since suitable eigenfunctions can be constructed by a linear combination of eigenfunctions, another convenient description of p states is possible if we construct the functions

$$p_x = \tfrac{1}{2}\sqrt{2}\,(p_{+1} + p_{-1})$$
$$p_y = -\tfrac{1}{2}\sqrt{2}\,(p_{+1} - p_{-1})$$
$$p_z = p_0.$$

Such combinations of functions are called *hybrid* functions. These are illustrated also in Fig. 6–7, where their interesting geometric properties can be seen clearly. In many instances these hybrid functions are more useful in constructing molecular wave functions from atomic functions since they have directional properties. These alternative functions are also given in Table 6–4. We see then that the primary spatial distinction between states with the same value of l, but with different m, is the orientation in space of the electron cloud. This is not strictly true, but is a useful approximation. We will shortly uncover a more fundamental distinction.

The angular properties of the hydrogen-like wave functions are not affected by the principal quantum number, but the radial functions depend not only on n, but also on the azimuthal quantum number. In order to make a physical interpretation of the radial wave function let us plot R^2 as a function of r. The resulting diagram, Fig. 6–8, then serves to tell us the density of the electron cloud per unit volume at any distance from the nucleus, i.e. the probability (neglecting the effects of the angular functions) of finding the electron in an infinitesimal volume element at a point which is at a distance r from the nucleus. While $R^2\,dr$ gives the probability density or probability per unit volume at distance r, we are also interested in the distribution from a slightly different point of view. If we multiply $R^2\,dr$ by the surface area of a sphere of radius r, we obtain the total probability of finding the electron at any point in the atom at a distance r from the nucleus. The quantity $4\pi r^2 R^2\,dr$, in other words, is proportional to the total probability of finding the electron

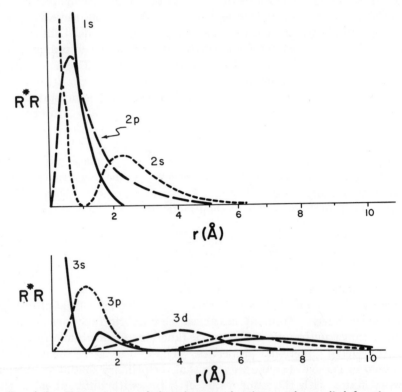

Fig. 6–8. Dependence of the electron density on the radial function, R^2, for several states of the hydrogen atom.

at a distance r from the nucleus. These functions are illustrated in Fig. 6–9. They are sometimes called the radial distribution functions.

A number of additional facts are disclosed by these diagrams. We notice, for example, that nodes occur in the distributions at certain values of r. At these points the probability of finding an electron is zero. We also observe that as the principal quantum number increases, the distance of maximum probability increases. This is most clearly seen in Fig. 6–9. This is not inconsistent with our classical expectations, since higher energies correspond to less tightly bound electrons, which are at greater distances from the positive charge.

The difference between $R^2\, dr$ and $r^2R^2\, dr$ is most clearly seen if we look for a moment at the radial distribution for the 1s state. We see in Fig. 6–8 that for this state the density of the electron cloud, i.e. the probability per unit volume, increases as we approach the nucleus. In fact, the probability density is *greatest at the nucleus*. This is certainly a non-

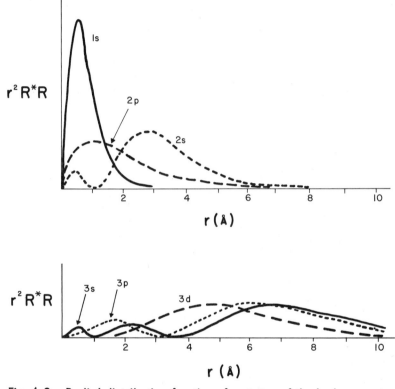

Fig. 6–9. Radial distribution functions for states of the hydrogen atom.

classical conclusion. At the same time, however, Fig. 6–9 shows that the probability of finding the electron at distance r from the nucleus is greatest not at the nucleus, but at $r = a_0$. The difference arises because as we progress outward from the nucleus, although the density per unit volume is decreasing as r increases, the total volume of the spherical element of radius r is increasing as r increases. The variation of the two leads to a maximum probability at a distance $r = a_0$, which then decreases again because the density per unit volume is decreasing more rapidly in this region than the spherical surface is increasing. There are times when both these views may be important. Some important phenomena depend directly on the probability density per unit volume at some point in space, say at the nucleus. In this case we would consider the value of R^2 at that point. On the other hand, we are often interested in such matters as the average distance of an electron from the nucleus, regardless of its angular position, or the most probable distance at which we would find an electron, and in this case the radial distribution function contains the desired information.

Incidentally, we observe in Fig. 6–9 that the most probable distance for an electron in the ground state, $r = a_0$, is numerically the same as the radius of the first Bohr orbit in the earlier quantum theory. Also the s states, which exhibit maximum electron density per unit volume at the nucleus, are the states for which the Bohr-Sommerfeld picture of elliptical orbits would have given straight-line orbits through the nucleus, with the azimuthal quantum number equal to zero.

Now that we have the wave functions for the hydrogen-like atom, it is possible to calculate the average value of other physical quantities, such as position and momentum, using the rules outlined in Chapter 3. The average distance of an electron from the nucleus, for example, would be calculated from the integral

$$\langle r \rangle = \int_0^{2\pi} \int_0^{\pi} \int_0^{\infty} \psi_{nlm}^* r \psi_{nlm} r^2 \, dr \, \sin \theta \, d\theta \, d\phi$$

with the appropriate limits of integration to include all space. For the $1s$ state $\langle r \rangle = \frac{3}{2} a_0$, which is the same as would be calculated for the Bohr orbit with $k = 0$. For many purposes of calculation involving various classical and quantum-mechanical interactions, it is necessary to obtain such quantities as $\langle 1/r \rangle$, $\langle 1/r^2 \rangle$, etc. A number of these are collected in Table 6–5 and can be verified by carrying out the integrations.

TABLE 6–5.   Average Values of r^k

$$\langle r \rangle = \frac{a_0 n^2}{Z} \left[1 + \frac{1}{2} \left\{ 1 - \frac{l(l+1)}{n^2} \right\} \right]$$

$$\langle r^2 \rangle = \frac{a_0^2 n^4}{Z^2} \left[1 + \frac{3}{2} \left\{ 1 - \frac{l(l+1) - \frac{1}{3}}{n^2} \right\} \right]$$

$$\left\langle \frac{1}{r} \right\rangle = \frac{Z}{a_0 n^2}$$

$$\left\langle \frac{1}{r^2} \right\rangle = \frac{Z^2}{a_0^2 n^3 (l + \frac{1}{2})}$$

$$\left\langle \frac{1}{r^3} \right\rangle = \frac{Z^3}{a_0^3 n^3 l (l + \frac{1}{2})(l + 1)}$$

$$\left\langle \frac{1}{r^4} \right\rangle = \frac{\frac{3}{2} Z^4 \{ 1 - l(l+1)/3n^2 \}}{a_0^4 n^3 (l + \frac{3}{2})(l + \frac{1}{2}) l (l - \frac{1}{2})}$$

Although the graphical representation of the electron probability density is difficult, we may obtain a rough idea of the distribution in some of the more important lower states.   Figure 6–10 is a representation of what the electron density ψ^2 would look like if viewed after slicing through the distribution in a plane through the nucleus.   In these figures both angular and radial properties can be seen.   We can observe, for example, the nodes in the distribution which for states higher than the 1s ground state occur both at certain angles and at certain radii.   The

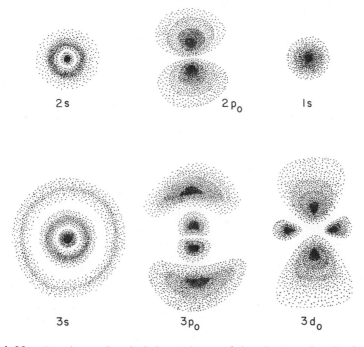

2 s   2 p$_0$ 1 s

3s   3p$_0$ 3 d$_0$

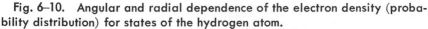

Fig. 6–10.   Angular and radial dependence of the electron density (probability distribution) for states of the hydrogen atom.

increase in the number of nodes with increasing n and l, the increasing extent of the distribution with increasing n, and similar features can be seen.

6.7   ANGULAR MOMENTUM

The importance of linear momentum, $\mathbf{p} = m\mathbf{v}$, in the analysis of physical systems has already been pointed out in our discussions of classical and quantum mechanics.   An equally important quantity is angular momentum, which is especially useful in the analysis of rotational motions.

If we consider the motion of a particle in a curved path about some point O (Fig. 6–11), the classical angular momentum of the particle is given by

$$\mathbf{M} = \mathbf{r} \times \mathbf{p} = m\mathbf{r} \times \mathbf{v}$$

and is represented by a vector perpendicular to both the radius and linear momentum vectors.

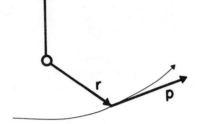

Fig. 6–11. Relation of the angular momentum vector to the radial and linear momentum vectors.

If a force is acting on a body so as to cause rotational effects, these effects are given by the torque, which is defined by the equation

$$\mathcal{L} = \mathbf{r} \times \mathbf{F}.$$

The relation between the torque acting on a body and the angular momentum is analogous to Newton's second law for linear motion:

$$\mathcal{L} = \frac{d\mathbf{M}}{dt}.$$

We could also describe the angular momentum, the radius vector, and the linear momentum in terms of their components along cartesian coordinate axes:

$$\mathbf{M} = M_x\mathbf{i} + M_y\mathbf{j} + M_z\mathbf{k},$$
$$\mathbf{r} = x\mathbf{i} + y\mathbf{j} + z\mathbf{k},$$
$$\mathbf{p} = p_x\mathbf{i} + p_y\mathbf{j} + p_z\mathbf{k}.$$

From the rules of vector multiplication the components of angular momentum can be shown to obey the relations,

$$M_x = yp_z - zp_y,$$
$$M_y = zp_x - xp_z,$$
$$M_z = xp_y - yp_x.$$

The scalar product of **M** with itself can also be shown to be

$$\mathbf{M} \cdot \mathbf{M} = M^2 = M_x{}^2 + M_y{}^2 + M_z{}^2,$$

or

$$M = (M_x{}^2 + M_y{}^2 + M_z{}^2)^{1/2}.$$

It is a simple matter to deduce the quantum-mechanical operators from these, using the rules outlined in Chapter 3. We obtain, in cartesian coordinates,

$$\hat{M}_x = -i\hbar \left(y\, \frac{\partial}{\partial z} - z\, \frac{\partial}{\partial y} \right),$$

$$\hat{M}_y = -i\hbar \left(z\, \frac{\partial}{\partial x} - x\, \frac{\partial}{\partial z} \right),$$

$$\hat{M}_z = -i\hbar \left(x\, \frac{\partial}{\partial y} - y\, \frac{\partial}{\partial x} \right),$$

$$\hat{M}^2 = \hat{M}_x{}^2 + \hat{M}_y{}^2 + \hat{M}_z{}^2;$$

and in spherical polar coordinates,

$$\hat{M}_x = -i\hbar \left[-\sin \phi\, \frac{\partial}{\partial \theta} - \cot \theta \cos \phi\, \frac{\partial}{\partial \phi} \right],$$

$$\hat{M}_y = -i\hbar \left[\cos \phi\, \frac{\partial}{\partial \theta} - \cot \theta \sin \phi\, \frac{\partial}{\partial \phi} \right],$$

$$\hat{M}_z = -i\hbar\, \frac{\partial}{\partial \phi},$$

$$\hat{M}^2 = -\hbar^2 \left[\frac{1}{\sin \theta}\, \frac{\partial}{\partial \theta} \left(\sin \theta\, \frac{\partial}{\partial \theta} \right) + \frac{1}{\sin^2 \theta} \left(\frac{\partial^2}{\partial \phi^2} \right) \right].$$

The importance of the angular-momentum operators in quantum mechanics may be discerned by examining some of their properties. In particular, we find that certain of these operators will commute while others will not. It can be shown, for instance, that

$$\hat{M}_x \hat{M}_y - \hat{M}_y \hat{M}_x = i\hbar \hat{M}_z,$$
$$\hat{M}_y \hat{M}_z - \hat{M}_z \hat{M}_y = i\hbar \hat{M}_x,$$
$$\hat{M}_z \hat{M}_x - \hat{M}_x \hat{M}_z = i\hbar \hat{M}_y,$$
$$\hat{M}^2 \hat{M}_x - \hat{M}_x \hat{M}^2 = 0,$$
$$\hat{M}^2 \hat{M}_y - \hat{M}_y \hat{M}^2 = 0,$$
$$\hat{M}^2 \hat{M}_z - \hat{M}_z \hat{M}^2 = 0.$$

We see that although none of the component angular-momentum operators commute with one another, all three component operators commute with $\hat{M}^2$. The physical significance of this is that, although it may be possible to know the total angular momentum and its component along one axis exactly, it is not possible to know its component along two coordinate axes at the same time. We will generally consider $\hat{M}^2$ and $\hat{M}_z$ as the two operators of interest since the expression for $\hat{M}_z$ is simple.

Another important property of the angular-momentum operators is that $\hat{M}^2$ and $\hat{M}_z$ commute with the Hamiltonian operator. In the case of the two-body system we have been discussing, this is seen easily. $\hat{M}^2$ and $\hat{M}_z$ have no effect on r, so it follows that

$$H = T + V = \frac{M^2}{2I} + V(r),$$

$$\hat{M}^2 \mathcal{H} = \hat{M}^2 \frac{\hat{M}^2}{2I} = \frac{\hat{M}^2}{2I} \hat{M}^2,$$

$$\hat{M}_z \mathcal{H} = \hat{M}_z \frac{\hat{M}^2}{2I} = \frac{\hat{M}^2}{2I} \hat{M}_z.$$

Thus, according to the arguments in Chapter 3 we conclude that it is possible to specify exactly the energy, the total angular momentum, and the component of angular momentum about one coordinate axis (conventionally the z axis) simultaneously.

The fact that $\mathcal{H}$, $\hat{M}^2$, and $\hat{M}_z$ all commute with one another then leads us to expect the spherical harmonic functions, which are eigenfunctions of the Hamiltonian operator, to be eigenfunctions of $\hat{M}^2$ and $\hat{M}_z$ as well. Operating on these functions, we obtain

$$\hat{M}^2 Y_{ml} = l(l + 1)\hbar^2 Y_{ml},$$
$$\hat{M}_z Y_{ml} = m\hbar Y_{ml}.$$

These two equations tell us that the only possible observable value of the angular momentum is $M = (M^2)^{1/2} = \sqrt{l(l + 1)}\,\hbar$, and the only observable value of the component of angular momentum along a specified axis is $m\hbar$. These results immediately highlight the significance of the quantum numbers n, l, and m. For a hydrogen atom in the state ψ_{nlm}, where the quantum numbers have specified values, we can state immediately that the energy of the state will be given by $E_n = -\mu e^4/2\hbar^2 n^2$, the total angular momentum of the atom will be $M = \sqrt{l(l + 1)}\,\hbar$, and the component of angular momentum about one coordinate axis will be $m\hbar$. The three quantum numbers thus not only serve as indices to classify the states of the atom, but also indicate definite information about the energy and the angular momentum.

It is interesting to view these conclusions in terms of our picture of the probability distribution for the various states. In the original Bohr-Sommerfeld model of atomic structure the interpretation was simple. The various states with different values of the azimuthal quantum number had the electron in elliptical orbits of varying degrees of eccentricity. The angular momentum was greatest in those orbits which were most nearly circular. The significance of the azimuthal quantum number in that model was therefore the same as we have just discussed; it was a measure of the angular momentum of the electron.　In our present picture, however, we are unable to follow the motion of an electron in such a definite manner.　We can only say that the electron will be found most probably in certain regions of space and that the angular momentum of these configurations is a certain value.　We see, for example, that the s states that are spherically symmetric about the nucleus have no angular momentum.

While l tells us something about the total angular momentum, m designates the component of angular momentum about a given coordinate axis, i.e. the projection of the classical angular momentum vector along a

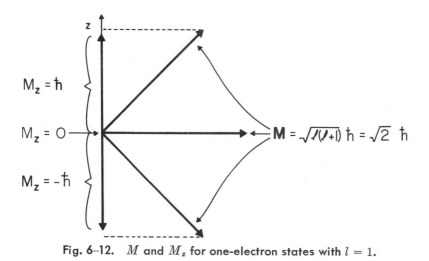

Fig. 6–12.　M and M_z for one-electron states with $l = 1$.

given axis.　We have observed that states with different m have different orientations with respect to the coordinate axes.　If a certain distribution has a certain total angular momentum, which in turn has a certain value about a coordinate axis, then different orientations of this distribution should be expected to have different components about the same coordinate axis.　This behavior is illustrated in Fig. 6–12.

In the absence of external forces, such as applied electric and magnetic fields, these different states with different orientations do not differ in energy.　In fact, in the model we have assumed, in which the radial force of attraction between the bodies is the only force acting in the system, the states of different total angular momentum do not have different energies either.　All these conclusions follow from the solution of the Schrödinger equation and the properties of the operators we have been discussing.

When there is more than one angular momentum, the total angular momentum can be calculated by applying the rules of vector addition. Thus,

$$\mathbf{M}_t = \sum_i \mathbf{M}_i,$$

$$\mathbf{M}_i = M_{xi}\mathbf{i} + M_{yi}\mathbf{j} + M_{zi}\mathbf{k},$$
$$\mathbf{M}_t = M_{xt}\mathbf{i} + M_{yt}\mathbf{j} + M_{zt}\mathbf{k},$$
$$M_{xt} = \sum_i M_{xi}, \quad M_{yt} = \sum_i M_{yi}, \quad M_{zt} = \sum_i M_{zi},$$

$$\mathbf{M}_t \cdot \mathbf{M}_t = M_t{}^2 = M_{xt}{}^2 + M_{yt}{}^2 + M_{zt}{}^2 \neq \sum_i M_i{}^2.$$

The total angular-momentum operators, which are obtained from the vectors in the usual way, obey the same sort of commutation relations as we have just outlined. That is, component angular-momentum operators such as $\hat{M}_{xt}$ and $\hat{M}_{zt}$ do not commute with each other but do commute with $\hat{M}_t{}^2$, and it can be shown that $\hat{M}_t{}^2$ and $\hat{M}_{tz}$ commute with the Hamiltonian operator so long as all interactions in the potential-energy term involve only forces that act along the line joining the particles.

6.8   RELATIVISTIC EFFECTS AND ELECTRON SPIN

Although the methods of quantum mechanics that we have outlined give excellent agreement with the observed spectra of atoms, there were early recognized a number of features of atomic spectra which were perplexing. These consisted most characteristically of small shifts in the expected frequencies of spectral lines and the resolution of many spectral lines into closely spaced multiplets of several lines. This multiplicity of lines, implying additional electronic states and transitions, is not predicted from the theory we have outlined.

An explanation for the multiplicity of spectral lines was advanced by Goudsmit and Uhlenbeck and others several years before quantum mechanics had been fully formulated. We will consider their model in the next section, when we examine some of the possible interactions between atomic particles besides the simple electrostatic attractions and repulsions. A really satisfactory prediction of these properties was not obtained until Dirac applied relativity theory to the quantum-mechanical formulation.[1] The mathematical considerations necessary in Dirac's treatment are far too complex to study here, but it would be worthwhile to examine briefly the consequences of his approach.

According to the theory of relativity the energy of a body depends not only on its kinetic and potential energies but also on its rest mass, i.e. its mass when it is stationary with respect to the frame of reference being

[1] Dirac, *Proc. Roy. Soc.*, **A117**, 610; **A118**, 351 (1928).

used to make measurements. If this energy term, in addition to the momentum and potential-energy terms, is inserted into the Hamiltonian operator in constructing the Schrödinger equation, it is found that the equation is of such a form that it cannot be solved without the introduction of several additional operators, whose nature we will not discuss here. In addition, the resulting equation cannot be solved as an ordinary differential equation, but requires the use of a more complex matrix formulation.

To appreciate the important results of the relativistic equation which Dirac solved, let us examine again the simple case of a single particle moving in one dimension and confined in a potential well with infinite walls (Fig. 4-4 with $V_0 = \infty$). With the non-relativistic Schrödinger equation, we found that only certain positive energy levels were possible. These were given by the equation

$$E_n = \frac{n^2h^2}{8ma^2}.$$

Solution of Dirac's equation gives

$$E_n = \left[m^2c^4 + \frac{c^2n^2h^2}{4a^2} \right]^{1/2}.$$

When the second term is small compared to the first, this becomes

$$E_n = mc^2 + \frac{n^2h^2}{8ma^2},$$

where it is obvious that the essential difference between the relativistic and non-relativistic solutions is that the former includes the relativistic rest-mass energy equivalent mc^2. Since transitions between states involve differences in energies, the constant mc^2 is not observed experimentally.

In our non-relativistic solution of the Schrödinger equation we found that for each energy level there is a single wave function describing the state of the system (4-22). The solution of the relativistic equation, however, gives the surprising result that there are *two* independent, orthogonal wave functions, which are solutions for each energy level. It is difficult to describe the significance of these two states with a simple physical picture. One clue as to their meaning may be as follows.

The expectation value for the operator $\hat{M}_z$ is a constant for the non-relativistic solution of the hydrogen atom, and the hydrogen atom wave functions are eigenfunctions of $\hat{M}_z$ with the eigenvalue $m\hbar$. An investigation of the operation of $\hat{M}_z$ on the relativistic solutions discloses that these solutions are *not* eigenfunctions of $\hat{M}_z$, however, which means that the z component of the orbital angular momentum of a state of the hydrogen atom does not really remain constant with time as we had predicted.

Although M_z is not a constant of motion, it is possible to construct another operator, of the form

$$\hat{J}_z = -i\hbar\frac{\partial}{\partial\phi} \pm \tfrac{1}{2}\hbar, \qquad (6\text{-}22)$$

for which the relativistic solutions are eigenfunctions. One of the two solutions is an eigenfunction of (6–22) with a positive sign on the second term, while the other is an eigenfunction with a negative sign on the second term. It will be noted that the first term in this operator is the same as the operator for the z component of the orbital angular momen-

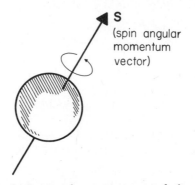

S
(spin angular momentum vector)

Fig. 6–13. The intrinsic angular momentum of the electron arising from spin.

tum. By analogy one speaks of J_z as representing the z component of the *total* angular momentum of the electron, and the second term as representing the z component of the *intrinsic* angular momentum of the electron.

One feels compelled to give a physical explanation for this self-contained angular momentum which the electron apparently possesses in addition to angular momentum arising from its orbital motions. A fairly obvious explanation, and one that is often easy to use in a semiquantitative way, is that the intrinsic angular momentum arises because of a spinning motion of the electron mass about an axis through its center. Such a rotational motion of mass would obviously give rise to angular momentum even though the particle might not itself be moving in some path about a central nucleus (Fig. 6–13). It is this picture that gives rise to the practice of calling the intrinsic angular momentum *spin* angular momentum or simply *electron spin*.

One should remember that this interpretation is not required by relativistic quantum mechanics. We have, in fact, introduced the idea of intrinsic angular momentum only by a process of analogy, comparing an operator which is a constant of motion in the relativistic case with the orbital angular-momentum operator from non-relativistic quantum mechanics. The danger of employing the term "angular momentum" at all in connection with the relativistic operator is emphasized by the fact that in cases such as the free particle moving in one dimension, and the one-dimensional particle in a box, we still obtain two wave functions for each energy level, even though there is no opportunity to make a direct analogy with angular momentum because the system has no classical angular momentum to begin with. Nonetheless, the concept of electron spin has proven useful and will be used from here on.

The concept of electron spin and the analogy used in examining the operator (6–22) lend a fairly obvious explanation to the nature of the two states that result from the relativistic equations. One corresponds to a system in which the intrinsic angular momentum of the particle is such that its z component is $+\frac{1}{2}\hbar$, while the other state has such a configuration that the z component of the intrinsic angular momentum is $-\frac{1}{2}\hbar$. We are assuming, in other words, that for all practical purposes the operator $\hat{J}_z$ can be separated into two operators, one of which gives the z component of *orbital* angular momentum and the other of which gives the z component of the *intrinsic* angular momentum. From this point on, we will use the symbols $\hat{M}^2$ and $\hat{M}_z$ only when discussing the general properties of angular momentum. Since we can now distinguish two kinds of angular momentum in atomic systems, we will use specific symbols to denote each kind. The symbols $\hat{L}^2$ and $\hat{L}_z$, defined as for $\hat{M}^2$ and $\hat{M}_z$, will be used for the orbital angular-momentum operators, and the orbital angular-momentum vector will be symbolized by **L**. We will give the symbols $\hat{S}^2$ and $\hat{S}_z$ to the spin angular-momentum operators.

Our discussion has pointed out that only J_z is a constant of motion. $\hat{L}_z$ and $\hat{S}_z$ are not actually operators which will give eigenvalues when operating on the relativistic wave functions of the system. For most purposes, however, the relativistic effects are small, and the difficulty of using the relativistic equations leads us to assume that the non-relativistic Schrödinger equation can be used. In the latter case, of course, L_z is a constant of motion. Because in most cases the energy effects of electron spin are relatively small, we will assume that we can continue to classify states such as those of the hydrogen atom with the non-relativistic quantum numbers, and then add to these solutions the additional facts which we have obtained about the spin angular momentum.

In the hydrogen-like atom, for example, we can assert that for each state ψ_{nlm} of the non-relativistic Schrödinger equation there are actually two states.   Although these states have (to a first approximation) the same energy, the same orbital angular momentum, and the same component of orbital angular momentum about the z axis, they differ in that they have different components of the intrinsic angular momentum about the z axis.   The simple consequence of the relativistic treatment, that there are only two such states for a single particle, leads to a handy designation of the two states as having spin up or spin down depending on whether the z component of the spin angular momentum is $+\frac{1}{2}\hbar$ or $-\frac{1}{2}\hbar$.

On the assumption that solution of the non-relativistic Schrödinger equation will give reliable information about all quantities except the spin angular momentum, we will continue to operate with Hamiltonian operators that do not include relativistic effects.   The resulting wave functions will not therefore include spin, but we can add our knowledge about spin by multiplying the non-relativistic functions by functions representing the possible spin states of the system.   In the case of the one-electron atom, for example, we can define two functions α and β as representing states with the electron spin either up or down.   That is, using the intrinsic angular-momentum operator for the component about the z axis $\hat{S}_z$, the functions α and β are such that

$$\hat{S}_z\alpha = \tfrac{1}{2}\hbar\alpha$$

and

$$\hat{S}_z\beta = -\tfrac{1}{2}\hbar\beta.$$

By analogy with the properties of $\hat{L}_z$, it is convenient to describe these two states by a quantum number m_s, which can have the values $\pm\frac{1}{2}$. That is,

$$\hat{S}_z(\text{spin function}) = m_s\hbar(\text{spin function}),$$

where m_s is $\frac{1}{2}$ when the spin function is α and is $-\frac{1}{2}$ when the spin function is β.

Because we now have two kinds of angular-momentum components, orbital and intrinsic, it is practical to avoid confusion by also giving a subscript to our quantum number m that designates the z component of orbital angular momentum.   We will refer to this quantum number from now on as m_l.

We can also define an operator $\hat{S}^2$, which has the eigenvalue $s(s + 1)\hbar^2$ when operating on α and β.   From the fact that m_s has only the values $\pm\frac{1}{2}$, it is reasonable to conclude that s has only the value $\frac{1}{2}$.   That is, the spin angular momentum of a single electron has only one value and only two possible orientations with respect to a fixed axis.

A complete description of a given state of the hydrogen atom would now include both the original non-relativistic function and a spin function. Thus for a state with a given principal quantum number n, a particular orbital angular momentum designated by l, a certain component of the orbital angular momentum about the z axis denoted by m_l, and a particular spin orientation we could describe the system by a wave function such as

$$\psi = \psi_{nlm_l} \cdot \text{(spin function } \alpha \text{ or } \beta),$$

or more compactly by the notation

$$\psi = \psi_{nlm_lm_s}.$$

The Dirac treatment brings out many more important relationships than we have discussed here. Some of these will be mentioned later, when we are concerned with atomic and molecular systems containing more than one electron and nucleus. The intrinsic angular momenta of particles are extremely important, and Dirac's analysis discloses important mathematical restrictions on systems in terms of these quantities.

In closing, we might mention one very interesting and unexpected result of relativistic quantum mechanics. In the problem of the free particle or the particle in a potential well, neither classical nor nonrelativistic quantum mechanics allows particles to have energies less than complete absence of motion or potential energy. Solution of the relativistic equations, however, permits both positive and negative energies relative to this zero. The significance of the latter is puzzling from a classical viewpoint. Dirac has proposed that all negative energy levels are completely filled by particles. If by some means, however, one of these negative-energy particles is excited up to a positive energy, a vacancy or hole will be left in this infinite "sea" of negative-energy particles. If the particle in question has an electrical charge, say an electron, then the hole will give the appearance of a similar particle of opposite charge. The negative-energy hole counterpart of the electron is the positron, a particle which has been verified experimentally. Such is the power of this mathematically complex treatment.

6.9 ELECTRIC AND MAGNETIC INTERACTIONS IN THE ATOM

The motion of the negatively charged electron about a central nucleus has been assumed to be governed solely by the one interaction, the electrostatic attraction between unlike charges. On this basis we set up a relatively simple wave equation which could be solved to obtain the energy levels of the system. Experimental evidence, however, suggests that the energy-level pattern is more complex. We can obtain some idea of what situation might result in such a one-electron atom if we consider some additional possible interactions that might have an effect on the energy.

Faraday's early experiments and Maxwell's brilliant mathematical theory of electromagnetic radiation showed a very intimate connection between electrical and magnetic phenomena. In the early stages of magnetic experimentation, the analogy between the equations describing the forces between electrical charges and the forces between permanent magnets led to the concept that, just as there are positive and negative

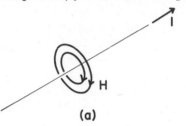

(a)

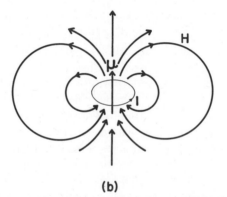

(b)

Fig. 6–14. (a) Magnetic field surrounding a current-carrying conductor. (b) Magnetic-dipole field surrounding a current-carrying coil.

electric charges, there are also positive and negative (or more conventionally, north and south) magnetic poles. So far as we know, there is in reality no such quantity as a magnetic pole. However, because the equations that describe the magnetic field around a permanent bar magnet are of the same form as those that describe an electric field around an electric dipole, it is often a convenient fiction to regard such a magnetic dipole as existing.

Magnetic fields are found to arise from the motion of electric charges. If we regard current flowing through a straight wire, for example, we observe a magnetic field surrounding the wire, as illustrated in Fig. 6–14a.

If we should bend the wire to form a circular coil, as in Fig. 6–14b, we would observe that at distances from the coil which are large in comparison with the diameter of the coil the magnetic field would be the same as that produced by a magnetic dipole at the center of the coil. It is likely that all magnetic fields are caused by such circulations of electric charge.

The magnitude of the magnetic-dipole moment which would produce the same field as the circulating current in a coil is given by the law of Biot and Savart as the product of the magnitude of the current by the area of the ring. With the current is esu and the magnetic-dipole moment in emu this would be, for a ring of radius r,

$$\mu = \frac{\pi r^2 I}{c},$$

where c is the velocity of light. The direction of the dipole with respect to the direction of current is as shown in Fig. 6–14b. If we consider an electron moving in a circular orbit of radius r about the nucleus, we have such a circulating current. If the velocity of the electron is v, the electron will complete rotation around the orbit $v/2\pi r$ times per second, and since the charge on the electron is $-e$, the current will be

$$I = -\frac{ev}{2\pi r},$$

so that

$$\mu = -\frac{erv}{2c}, \quad \text{or} \quad \mathbf{\mu} = -\frac{e}{2mc}\,\mathbf{r} \times \mathbf{p}.$$

The orbital angular momentum of the electron, however, is

$$L = mvr, \quad \text{or} \quad \mathbf{L} = \mathbf{r} \times \mathbf{p},$$

so that the magnetic dipole moment is related to the angular momentum of the electron by

$$\mathbf{\mu} = -\frac{e}{2mc}\,\mathbf{L}. \tag{6–23}$$

It is an idealization, of course, to picture the electron as moving in a simple circular orbit. However, we have seen that the various states of an electron in an atom have definite values of orbital angular momentum. If we assume, therefore, that Eq. (6–23) is a valid description of the relation between magnetic dipole moment and angular momentum, we will obtain, from the quantum-mechanical equation for orbital angular momentum $L = \sqrt{l(l+1)}\,\hbar$,

$$|\mathbf{\mu}| = \sqrt{l(l+1)}\,\frac{e\hbar}{2mc} = \sqrt{l(l+1)}\,\mu_B, \tag{6–24}$$

where μ_B, with m the mass of the electron and e the magnitude of its charge, is known as the Bohr magneton and is the atomic unit of electronic magnetic moment.   Note in (6–23) that, since the charge on the electron is negative, the magnetic-dipole moment is oriented in the opposite direction to the orbital angular-momentum vector.

We now recall that the various electronic states of the hydrogen atom for which the orbital angular momentum was the same, but for which m_l varied from $-l$ to $+l$, differed in that the component of the orbital angular momentum about the z axis varied from $-m_l \hbar$ to $+m_l \hbar$.   It is apparent that if the magnetic-dipole-moment vector arising from

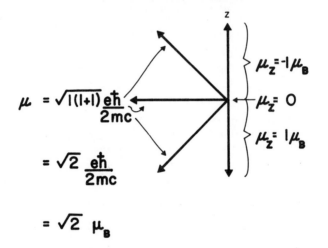

Fig. 6–15. Components of the magnetic dipole moment along the z axis.

orbital motion of the electron is antiparallel to the angular-momentum vector then the different orientations of the latter with different values of m_l will also result in different orientations of the magnetic dipole, and the magnetic-dipole moment can also be described in terms of its component along the z axis.   From the relationship between $\mathbf{L}$, L_z, l, and m_l, it follows that

$$\mu_z = -m_l \mu_B.$$

We see, then, that states with different values of l not only have different values of orbital angular momentum, but also have associated with them different magnetic fields which can be described as arising from a magnetic-dipole moment that is pointed in the opposite direction to the angular-momentum vector; the magnitude of the dipole is given by Eq. (6–24). In addition, states with different values of m_l have not only different components of the orbital angular momentum about the z axis, but also have different projections of the magnetic-dipole moment along the z axis. These facts are illustrated for a simple case in Fig. 6–15. Compare this with Fig. 6–12, which illustrates the angular momentum.

The existence of the magnetic-dipole moment arising out of the orbital motions of the electron does not in itself give rise to any changes in the energy levels of the atomic system. We could cause such changes easily, however, by applying a magnetic field to the atom. According to the classical electromagnetic theory, the energy of a magnetic dipole in a magnetic field is

$$E = -\mathbf{\mu} \cdot \mathbf{H} = -\mu H \cos \theta \tag{6–25}$$

where θ is the angle between the dipolar axis and the magnetic field. Since states with different values of m_l have different orientations of

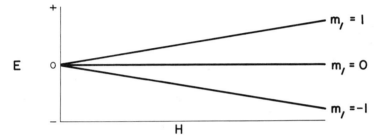

Fig. 6–16. Effect of a magnetic field on the energy of magnetic-dipole moments in states with $l = 1$.

the magnetic-dipole moment they will also have different energies in the applied magnetic field. If we assume the applied field is in the z direction, then

$$E = -\mu_z H = m_l \mu_B H, \tag{6–26}$$

and each of the formerly degenerate states now has a different energy. The actual energy of each level is seen to depend on the magnitude of the applied field. This new energy is added to the original energy of the system in the absence of the field. The effect of the magnetic field on the energy of a simple case is illustrated in Fig. 6–16.

The separation of energy levels in a magnetic field can be observed by several experimental techniques. The new levels immediately give rise to an increase in the number of transitions observed in atomic spectra since many levels are no longer degenerate. This phenomenon is known as the Zeeman effect (Fig. 6–17). It is also possible to observe transitions between the levels with the same values of n and l and different values of m_l and m_s by the technique of microwave absorption, which will be described in Chapter 11. Because the energy splittings are very much smaller than the separations between states of different n and l, the new lines in the optical spectra are closely spaced and appear as a multiplet structure of the main transition lines. This very small separation of energies also means that observation of direct transitions between states in microwave spectroscopy will require frequencies very much smaller than those in the optical region.

It is perhaps of some interest to describe the "motions" of the magnetic dipole moment in the applied magnetic field. When the magnetic-dipole

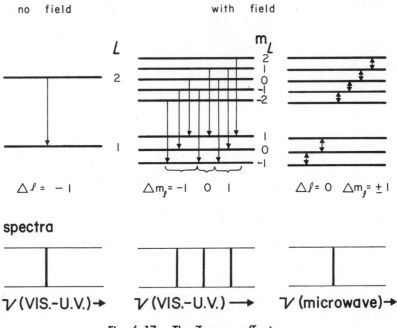

Fig. 6–17. The Zeeman effect.

moment is placed in the magnetic field, a torque is exerted by the field on the dipole

$$\mathcal{L} = \mathbf{\mu} \times \mathbf{H}; \quad |\mathcal{L}| = \mu H \sin \theta. \tag{6–27}$$

We have already mentioned that the torque is related to the rate of change of angular momentum of the system with time

$$\mathcal{L} = \frac{d\mathbf{L}}{dt}. \tag{6–28}$$

We know that the magnitude of the total orbital angular momentum and the component of the orbital angular momentum about the z axis do not change, since these quantities are constants of motion. Thus, the angular-momentum vector can change only in its direction, in such a way as to keep the component along the z axis constant. The torque applied to the magnetic dipole is perpendicular to both the field and the dipole. It thus tends to pull the dipole in a direction perpendicular to the plane of the field and the dipole vectors. The result is a precessional motion about the direction of the field as shown in Fig. 6–18. We can calculate the frequency of this precessional motion, known as the Larmor precessional frequency, in the following way: Equating the two expressions for the torque in (6–27) and (6–28), we obtain

$$\frac{d\mathbf{L}}{dt} = \mathbf{\mu} \times \mathbf{H}.$$

If we now substitute for $\mathbf{\mu}$ the expression relating the magnetic-dipole moment and the angular momentum, Eq. (6–23), we obtain

$$\frac{d\mathbf{L}}{dt} = -\frac{e}{2mc}\mathbf{L} \times \mathbf{H} = \frac{e}{2mc}\mathbf{H} \times \mathbf{L}. \tag{6–29}$$

The angular velocity of precession is related to the torque and the angular momentum by the equation

$$\mathbf{\mathfrak{L}} = \mathbf{\omega} \times \mathbf{L} = \frac{d\mathbf{L}}{dt},$$

so that by comparison with Eq. (6–29) we see that

$$\mathbf{\omega} = \frac{e}{2mc}\mathbf{H} = \frac{\mu_B \mathbf{H}}{\hbar} = \gamma\mathbf{H}. \tag{6–30}$$

This angular precessional velocity is represented by a vector which is perpendicular to both $\mathbf{\mathfrak{L}}$ and $\mathbf{L}$ and parallel to $\mathbf{H}$. We see that its magnitude is dependent on the strength of the magnetic field applied. We should observe that if we had been concerned with a positive charge rather than a negative electron, we would have found the magnetic-dipole moment to be parallel to the angular-momentum vector, and the sense of the precessional motion would have been in the opposite direction, so that the angular-frequency vector would be antiparallel to the field direction.

The ratio $\gamma = e/2mc = \mu/L$ is called the gyromagnetic ratio (or more properly the magnetogyric ratio) for electronic orbital angular momentum. The angular precessional frequency is in units of radians per second, but this may be easily converted to cycles per second by

$$\nu = \frac{\omega}{2\pi} = \frac{\mu_B}{\hbar}\mathbf{H} = \frac{\gamma}{2\pi}\mathbf{H}. \tag{6–31}$$

Although all these effects are of considerable interest, we have not as yet uncovered any interactions that result in changes in the energy levels of an undisturbed one-electron atom. We have neglected, however, one additional fact that was discussed in the last section. The solution of the relativistic Schrödinger equation suggested the existence of an intrinsic or spin angular momentum for the electron and other fundamental particles. The relativistic equations also disclose that these particles have an intrinsic magnetic-dipole moment.

The existence of the intrinsic magnetic-dipole moment should not be surprising; for if we consider that the intrinsic angular momentum of the electron arises from a spinning motion of the particle, this same spinning

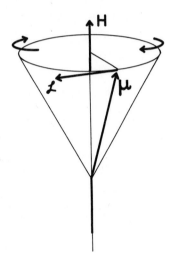

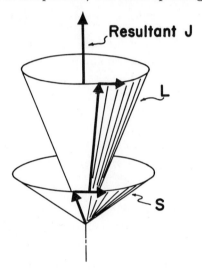

Fig. 6–18. Larmor precession of a magnetic-dipole moment in a magnetic field.

Fig. 6–19. Precession of spin and orbital angular momenta about the resultant total angular momentum vector.

motion of the charge of the particle should give rise to a magnetic-dipole field just as the orbital circulation was observed to do.

If we assume that relation (6–23) also holds for intrinsic angular momentum and the intrinsic magnetic moment, then we can derive equations exactly analogous to those preceding for the behavior of the magnetic dipole in a magnetic field. The relativistic equations, however, show that the simple classical explanation for the relation of angular momentum to magnetic-dipole moment is not quantitatively adequate. Instead, for all particles, we can state that the relation is of the form

$$\mathbf{\mu} = g_e \frac{e}{2mc} \mathbf{S}, \qquad (6\text{–}32)$$

where e is the charge and m the mass of the particular particle of interest. For the electron $g_e = 2.0023$. We have used the symbol introduced
in the last section for spin angular momentum. Since the charge of an
electron is negative, its spin magnetic moment is seen to be opposite in
direction to its spin angular-momentum vector.

In order to describe the states for an atom properly, we should indicate
both orbital and spin angular momentum. This can be done by introducing the concept of the total angular momentum as mentioned in the
last section. We represent the total angular momentum by the operator
$\mathfrak{J}$ which has the properties

$$\hat{J}_{xi} = \hat{L}_{xi} + \hat{S}_{xi},$$
$$\hat{J}_{yi} = \hat{L}_{yi} + \hat{S}_{yi},$$
$$\hat{J}_{zi} = \hat{L}_{zi} + \hat{S}_{zi},$$
$$\hat{J}_i{}^2 = \hat{J}_{xi}{}^2 + \hat{J}_{yi}{}^2 + \hat{J}_{zi}{}^2.$$

These equations follow the rules for the addition of angular momenta
as discussed in Sec. 6.7. The commutation properties of $\mathbf{J}$ are the same
as those already discussed for $\mathbf{L}$ and $\mathbf{S}$. $\hat{J}^2$ commutes with $\hat{J}_z$ (and with
the other component $\hat{J}$'s), and $\hat{J}^2$ and $\hat{J}_z$ both simultaneously commute
with the Hamiltonian operator. In addition, the eigenvalues of $\hat{J}^2$ have
the form $j(j + 1)\hbar^2$ where j is a quantum number analogous to l and s.
The eigenvalues of $\hat{J}_z$ are of the form $m_J\hbar$ where m_J may have the values
$-j, -j + 1, \ldots, j - 1, j$. Since m_s can only be $\pm\frac{1}{2}$ and m_l is integral,
we can see that m_J will be half-integral and therefore J also will be
half-integral.

The information we have accumulated about the orbital, spin, and
total angular momenta are displayed in Table 6–6, where the similarities

Table 6–6.   Angular-Momentum Properties

	Spin (S)	Orbital (L)	Total (J)
Operator	$\hat{S}^2$	$\hat{L}^2$	$\hat{J}^2$
Quantum number	s	l	j
Eigenvalues	$s(s + 1)\hbar^2$	$l(l + 1)\hbar^2$	$j(j + 1)\hbar^2$
Magnitude of angular momentum	$\sqrt{s(s + 1)}\,\hbar$	$\sqrt{l(l + 1)}\,\hbar$	$\sqrt{j(j + 1)}\,\hbar$
Possible values of quantum number for 1-electron atom	$s = \frac{1}{2}$	$l = 0, 1, \ldots, n - 1$	$j = l + s, \ldots, |l - s|$
Operator	$\hat{S}_z$	$\hat{L}_z$	$\hat{J}_z$
Quantum number	m_s	m_l	m_j
Eigenvalues	$m_s\hbar$	$m_l\hbar$	$m_j\hbar$
Magnitude of angular-momentum component along z axis	$m_s\hbar$	$m_l\hbar$	$m_j\hbar$
Possible values of	$m_s = \pm\frac{1}{2}$	$m_l = -l, \ldots, l$	$m_j = -j, \ldots, j$

between the operators, eigenvalues, and angular-momentum vectors will be more apparent.

The existence of two sources of magnetic-dipole fields in the atom now alters our consideration of the energy states of the system. Whereas the existence of only the orbital magnetic field required the application of an external magnetic field in order to change the energies of the degenerate states, the presence of the spin magnetic moment will automatically give rise to energy effects because of the interaction between the two magnetic-dipole fields.

We discussed with Eq. (6–25) the energy of interaction between a dipole and a magnetic field. For the purposes of determining the extent of interaction between the orbital and spin magnetic fields in the atom, we can consider the electron spin magnetic dipole and the magnetic field arising from the apparent circulation of the nuclear charge about the electron. The magnetic field produced at the electron by the moving positive charge depends on the electric field arising from that charge and can be shown to be

$$\mathbf{H} = -\frac{1}{r}\frac{\partial V}{\partial r}\frac{1}{mc}\mathbf{L},$$

where V is the electrostatic potential at the electron due to the nucleus and any other charged particles present. From Eqs. (6–25) and (6–32) it then follows that the spin-orbit interaction is

$$E_{so} = -\frac{ge}{2m^2c^2}\frac{1}{r}\frac{\partial V}{\partial r}\mathbf{L}\cdot\mathbf{S}. \qquad (6\text{–}33)$$

For the one-electron atom, the potential caused by the electric field of the nucleus is $V = Ze/r$ so that $(1/r)\,\partial V/\partial r = -Ze/r^3$.

The classical description of the motions of the angular momenta would be that the magnetic interaction exerts a torque on both magnetic dipoles, causing them to precess around a common axis, which is the direction of the total angular momentun as in Fig. 6–19.

The energy effects of this spin-orbit interaction are generally small (at least for smaller atoms), and it is often sufficient, as we have mentioned, to correct the non-relativistic energy levels for these effects rather than attempt to solve a completely general Schrödinger equation. In principle, one should include the spin-orbit interaction in the Hamiltonian operator before solving the Schrödinger equation. The suitable term can be obtained easily by using the appropriate operators for $\mathbf{L}$ and $\mathbf{S}$ in Eq. (6–33).

If we look in detail at the effects of the spin-orbit interaction on the individual energy levels, we see that the general effect is to split each energy level into two closely spaced levels. This is because for every value of l there are two possible orientations of the spin moment with respect to the orbital moment. Take, for example, the case $l = 1$. If $m_l = 1$, m_s can be $\frac{1}{2}$ or $-\frac{1}{2}$. If $m_l = 0$, m_s can be $\pm\frac{1}{2}$, and similarly for $m_l = -1$. For each of these orientations of **L** with respect to the z axis, the magnitude of the orbital angular momentum remains unchanged; only the direction of the angular-momentum vector has been altered. In turn, the spin-orbit interaction depends on the orientation of **S** with respect to **L**, and in each of the above cases there are two such possible mutual orientations of the spin moment with respect to the orbital moment. Thus there are two possible energies for the system, depending on whether the spin moment is approximately in the same direction as the orbital moment or in the opposite direction.

The one case in which this splitting of levels does not occur is in s states, where the atom has no orbital angular momentum. The result is thus only a single energy level.

The spin-orbit interaction is still not quite sufficient to predict the energy levels accurately for the hydrogen atom. Solution of the relativistic equations shows that in addition to the spin-orbit interaction there is another relativistic effect on all the energy levels, given approximately by

$$E_{\text{rel}} = \frac{E_n e^4}{4n^2 c^2 h^2}\left(\frac{4n}{l + \frac{1}{2}} - 3\right) + mc^2. \tag{6-34}$$

If we correct the energy levels which we obtained originally for the hydrogen atom, first with the spin-orbit correction and then with this relativistic correction, we finally obtain excellent agreement with the observed states. Although these effects are small and relatively unimportant in the bold features of the spectrum, they are a very fine test of our correct detailed knowledge of atomic structure. The resulting energy-level pattern for hydrogen is shown in Fig. 6–20.

In closing this discussion of the one-electron atom, it is relevant to point out that the development of quantum mechanics, as in all of science, consists very largely of new hypotheses, such as the Schrödinger equation, and successive attempts to refine theories so as to fit observations more accurately, as was done in quantum mechanics with relativistic corrections and the spin-orbit interaction. This process is never-ending and will lead to further refinements and new ideas. We could cite, for example, the fact that an additional splitting is observed in atomic spectra that cannot be explained by any of the effects we have discussed. Consideration of these splittings and of the concept of intrinsic angular momentum led to an understanding of the spin angular momenta of nuclei and the interactions of the nuclear magnetic-dipole moments with the electrons. Some of these effects will be discussed later, but it is worthwhile to observe that all fundamental theories are

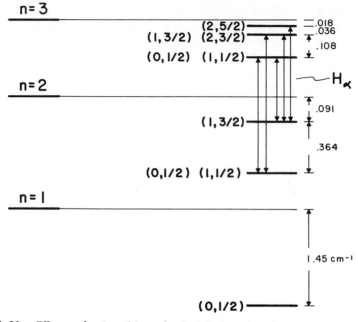

Fig. 6–20. Effects of spin-orbit and relativistic corrections on energy levels of the hydrogen atom. Values of l and j are indicated for each level. Splittings are greatly exaggerated for clarity.

in a state of flux, and the pictures used in explaining various phenomena should never be taken too literally.

6.10 SUMMARY

We have explored in some detail the quantum-mechanical picture of the one-electron atom. We began by setting up the Schrödinger equation for two particles, the positive nucleus and the negative electron. In doing so, we assumed that only the electrostatic attraction of the two charges need be considered. We were then able to separate the Schrödinger equation into three equations which depended separately on the spherical polar coordinates r, θ, and ϕ. We found that only the radial part of the equation involves the energy of the system. Solution of these equations gave us the complete wave functions for the one-electron atom and the possible energy levels.

We then considered the properties of the wave functions which we had obtained, and found that the states of the atom were very conveniently classified according to their orbital angular momenta and the component of orbital angular momentum along a fixed axis, as these were constants of motion. That is, the wave functions were eigenfunctions of $\hat{M}^2$ and $\hat{M}_z$. We found that the quantum number l gives an indication of the orbital angular momentum of a state, and m_l gives a measure of the component of this angular momentum about a fixed axis. In the absence of an external magnetic field, these states of different orientation are of the same energy, but they can be split by a magnetic field to give a multiplicity of lines in the atomic spectrum.

We then explored the results obtained from considering the requirements of relativity theory and found that additional states result from solution of the relativistic equations. These correspond to "up" and "down" orientations of the spin angular momentum of the electron with respect to the orbital angular momentum. We also saw that accompanying these spin and orbital angular momenta are magnetic-dipole fields which can interact with one another to result in different energies for the spin-up and spin-down states. These splittings are observed by a number of experimental techniques.

Although we have spent considerable time in examining the properties of angular momentum, electron spin, and similar quantities, we shall see that not only can these phenomena be explained most simply in the one-electron case, but the concepts and classifications introduced here continue to be used in more complex systems, where an exact analysis is more difficult. As we have mentioned, some of these interactions are extremely small compared to the relatively large separations of the simple energy levels that we first derived, and have little effect on the wave functions that we obtained from the elementary Schrödinger equation. Nevertheless, without a consideration of the fine structure of spectral lines and the use of relativistic quantum mechanics, the chemist would be without valuable information concerning electron spin and its properties, which play so important a part in chemical phenomena.

SUPPLEMENTARY REFERENCES

Introductory

COULSON, C. A., *Valence*, 2nd ed., Oxford University Press, London, 1962.

PAULING, L., and E. B. WILSON, *Introduction to Quantum Mechanics*, McGraw-Hill Book Co., New York, 1935.

KAUZMAN, W., *Quantum Chemistry*, Academic Press, Inc., New York, 1957.

EYRING, H., J. WALTER, and G. E. KIMBALL, *Quantum Chemistry*, John Wiley & Sons, Inc., New York, 1944.

PITZER, K. S., *Quantum Chemistry*, Prentice-Hall, Englewood Cliffs, N.J., 1953.

Intermediate

MARGENAU, H., and G. M. MURPHY, *The Mathematics of Physics and Chemistry*, D. Van Nostrand, Princeton, 1943.

BATES, D. R., *Quantum Theory*, vol. 1, *Elements*, Academic Press, Inc., New York, 1961.

RICHTMEYER, F. K., and E. H. KENNARD, *Introduction to Modern Physics*, 4th ed., McGraw-Hill Book Co., New York, 1947.

Advanced

SLATER, J. C., *Quantum Theory of Atomic Structure*, vol. 1, McGraw-Hill Book Co., New York, 1960.

DIRAC, P. A. M., *The Principles of Quantum Mechanics*, 4th ed., Oxford University Press, London, 1958.

PROBLEMS

6-1. Verify that Eq. (6–4) results upon substitution of (6–2) and (6–3) into (6–1).

6-2. From the transformations relating spherical polar coordinates and cartesian coordinates, derive Eq. (6–7) from (6–6) by carrying out the necessary differentiations.

6-3. What would be the error involved if the mass of the electron were used to calculate the energy of the hydrogen atom rather than the reduced mass of the atom? What would be the error in the calculated frequency of a spectral line?

6-4. Obtain the solutions (6–14) by the appropriate sum and difference of the solutions (6–13).

6-5. Verify the normalization constants for the various solutions of the Φ equation.

6-6. The electronic state of lowest energy, the $1s$ state, is the so-called ground state of the atom because in a collection of atoms most of the atoms will be in this lowest state. Calculate the fraction of hydrogen atoms which will be in the first excited state ($n = 2$) at room temperature. Do not neglect degeneracies. What temperature would be required to maintain 1 per cent of the atoms in the first excited state?

6-7. What is the ionization potential of a hydrogen atom from the state with $n = 2$?

6-8. A sample of hydrogen gas is illuminated with a source emitting monochromatic light of wavelength 1026 Å (corresponding to a line in the hydrogen Lyman series). If the hydrogen atoms re-emit the energy absorbed, what three wavelengths can one expect to find in the light radiated by the sample?

6-9. The first line in the Lyman series of atomic hydrogen lies at 1216 Å, in the Balmer series at 6563 Å. In the *absorption* spectrum of a certain star the Balmer line appears to have one-fourth the intensity of the Lyman line. Estimate the temperature of the star.

6-10. Calculate the wavelength to which the Balmer series converges.

6-11. What is the wavelength of the line in the spectrum of He^+ that corresponds to the first line in the Balmer series of hydrogen?

6–12. Calculate the energy of the quantum of radiation required to excite a hydrogen atom from the ground state to the $n = 2$ state. Also calculate the energy of Avogadro's number of such quanta. How does this energy compare with the average translational energy of hydrogen atoms at room temperature?

6–13. Calculate the expected lines in two or three series of the atomic spectrum of the He^+ ion.

6–14. Derive the equations in Sec. 6.6 for $\langle r \rangle$, $\langle r^2 \rangle$, $\langle 1/r \rangle$, and $\langle 1/r^2 \rangle$. Calculate the average radius for the $2s$ state for H and for He^+.

6–15. Calculate the average potential energy for an electron in the electric field of a proton in the ground state. What is the average kinetic energy?

6–16. An ordinary electron revolving around a positive electron (a positron) is called a positronium atom. Calculate the first four energy levels for this species. Is it proper to describe the motion in this case as an electron revolving around a fixed nucleus at the center of the atom? Explain.

6–17. The π^- meson is a nuclear particle whose charge is $-e$ and whose mass is 275 times the mass of an ordinary electron. In conjunction with a proton it forms a "mesic" atom. Calculate the energy of the ground state of this atom. Is it more or less stable than ordinary hydrogen?

6–18. Show that the wave functions for different energy levels of the hydrogen atom are orthogonal.

6–19. Unsold's theorem states that the sum of all the probability distribution functions for a given value of l is a constant, i.e.,

$$\sum_{m=-l}^{l} \Theta^*\Theta\Phi^*\Phi = \text{constant},$$

which is a mathematical way of stating that any closed-shell atom or ion has perfect spherical symmetry. Show that this theorem holds for the hydrogen states with $n = 2$, $l = 1$, and also for the states with $n = 3$, $l = 2$.

6–20. Calculate $\langle r \rangle$ for the first few values of n, all with $l = 0$, for the hydrogen atom.

6–21. What is the probability that the electron in a hydrogen atom (ground state) will be beyond 2 Å from the nucleus? What is the probability that it will be found between 0.9 and 1.0 Å?

6–22. Does $\hat{M}_z$ commute with $\hat{\mathbf{M}} = \hat{M}_x\mathbf{i} + \hat{M}_y\mathbf{j} + \hat{M}_z\mathbf{k}$? Interpret this in terms of the uncertainty principle.

6–23. Verify the eigenvalues of $\hat{M}^2$ and $\hat{M}_z$ when operating on the spherical harmonic wave functions.

6–24. What is the Larmor precession frequency of the electronic orbital angular momentum in a magnetic field of 5000 gauss? How does this compare with the frequency of radiation which would be required to cause a transition between two states with the same values of n and l, but with m_l differing by 1?

6–25. What is the Larmor precession frequency of the spin angular momentum of an electron in a magnetic field of 5000 gauss? How does this compare with the frequency required to cause a transition between the states $\psi(210 + \frac{1}{2})$ and $\psi(210 - \frac{1}{2})$?

6-26. Draw an energy-level diagram, neglecting spin and relativistic effects, in which the substates of different m_l's are shown, drawing them slightly separated, including states $1s$, $2s$, $3s$, $2p$, $3p$, $3d$. Indicate all transitions allowed by the selection rules for l and m_l. Will all these be observed as separate spectral lines? Indicate those which will be identical.

6-27. Derive the equations for $\hat{M}^2$, $\hat{M}_x$, $\hat{M}_y$, and $\hat{M}_z$ in spherical polar coordinates from those in cartesian coordinates.

6-28. The p_x and p_y wave functions locate the angular probability distribution more specifically than the p_1 and p_{-1} functions. Show that this advantage was gained by losing the definiteness of the angular-momentum orientation. (*Hint:* Show that p_x and p_y are not eigenfunctions of $\hat{M}_z$.)

6-29. Calculate the fraction of hydrogen atoms in the $1s$ ground state in which the electron might be located at a distance from the nucleus smaller than a_0.

7

Complex Atoms, Approximation Methods, and Spectral Transitions

7.1 THE SCHRÖDINGER EQUATION FOR THE HELIUM ATOM

No matter how complex a system may be, we find that initially it is not difficult to set up the problem. It is necessary to form the suitable Hamiltonian operator for the system, including a Laplacian term for each particle and an interaction term in the potential energy for every pair of interacting particles, plus terms for any other effects due to fields, etc. If we again assume that we can separate out the translational wave function and the translational energy of the center of mass of the system as we did for hydrogen in Sec. 6.1, then for helium, which has a nucleus of charge $+2e$ and two electrons (Fig. 7–1), the Hamiltonian operator would be

$$\mathcal{H} = -\frac{\hbar^2}{2}\left[\frac{\nabla_1{}^2}{m_1} + \frac{\nabla_2{}^2}{m_2}\right] - \frac{2e^2}{r_1} - \frac{2e^2}{r_2} + \frac{e^2}{r_{12}}. \tag{7-1}$$

Because the heavy nucleus is essentially the center of motion for the system, the masses m_1 and m_2 of the electrons have been used in place of reduced masses. We have also neglected spin effects at this stage.

Although it is a simple matter to set up the Schrödinger equation, it is not a simple matter to solve it. For the amplitude equation, using (7–1),

$$-\frac{\hbar^2}{2}\left[\frac{1}{m_1}\nabla_1{}^2\psi + \frac{1}{m_2}\nabla_2{}^2\psi\right] - \frac{2e^2\psi}{r_1} - \frac{2e^2\psi}{r_2} + \frac{e^2\psi}{r_{12}} = E\psi, \tag{7-2}$$

a separation of variables such as in the hydrogen case is not possible because of the potential-energy term containing r_{12}. In more complex atoms there will be additional interelectronic terms which also prevent the direct solution of the Schrödinger equation for the eigenstates and the wave functions that describe them. Thus it is necessary to turn to approximation methods with which we attempt to obtain solutions as close as possible to the correct energies and wave functions.

The difficulty we now face could be resolved if we could write the potential energy as the sum of two terms each of which depends only

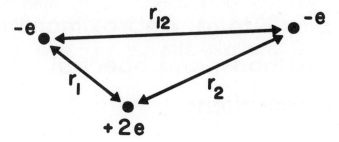

Fig. 7–1. Coordinates describing the helium atom.

on the position of one electron. In this case we would have

$$-\frac{\hbar^2}{2}\left[\frac{\nabla_1^2\psi}{m_1} + \frac{\nabla_2^2\psi}{m_2}\right] + V_1\psi + V_2\psi = E\psi, \tag{7-3}$$

which can be separated into two equations

$$-\frac{\hbar^2}{2m_1}\nabla_1^2\psi_1 + V_1\psi_1 = E_1\psi_1$$

and

$$-\frac{\hbar^2}{2m_2}\nabla_2^2\psi_2 + V_2\psi_2 = E_2\psi_2$$

if V_1 is a function of r_1 only and V_2 depends only on r_2. It is clear from the separation that $E = E_1 + E_2$. $V = V_1 + V_2$, and $\psi = \psi_1\psi_2$. The two equations, each depending on only one variable, can now be solved.

In such a formulation as this we are asserting that the two electrons in the system are statistically independent of each other. Stated in another way, we are saying that the electrons exert no forces on each other. Clearly this is not truly the case; the interelectronic repulsions play an important part in determining the energies and configurations of the various states of complex atoms. Nevertheless it has been found that considerable information can be gained about the configurations of electronic systems with this assumption as a starting point, and we will turn our attention briefly to how this can be done.

7.2   THE SELF-CONSISTENT FIELD APPROXIMATION

In a problem at the end of the previous chapter it is shown that if the configurations involving all the states of a given value of l are considered, the sum of the distribution functions is equal to a constant (Unsold's theorem). That is, such a probability distribution is spherically symmetric. Assuming that the angular dependence of the wave functions would not be altered appreciably by the presence of several electrons, this amounts to saying that if hydrogen-like states are filled with electrons, then the over-all distribution of a set of filled levels of the same value of l will be spherically symmetric. Thus in considering complex atomic structures we note that succeeding groups of states, as they are filled, will give over-all spherical symmetry to the electronic charge distribution. In fact, only a few electrons outside such completed sets ever need be considered as possibly having non-spherical distributions.

The spherical symmetry of closed electronic shells has an important consequence. Except for a few of the outermost electrons in an atom, we can consider the potential energy at any point to be that of a centrally located positive charge and a spherically symmetric electronic charge. In other words, any one electron in a complex atom can be considered approximately as being affected by a centrally symmetric potential energy. This means that, except for the detailed part of the solution involving the potential-energy term, we should expect solutions of the Schrödinger equation exactly like those of the hydrogen atom, which was also a centrally symmetric case. Since the potential-energy terms are involved only in the radial part of the Schrödinger equation, we should then expect spherical harmonic solutions for the angular wave functions of complex atoms, and the states would then differ from the hydrogen case only in the radial functions. Thus we could describe the structure of all atoms in exactly the same terms in which we describe the states of the hydrogen atom. The significance of the quantum numbers l and m_l with regard to the angular momentum and the angular dependence of the electronic distribution would be exactly the same. The important differences would lie in the radial distribution functions and the energies of the states.

These assumptions are the basis for the familiar language that chemists use to describe the structure of atoms. We explain the properties of the different elements in terms of electrons in s, p, d, and f orbitals, and we attribute the geometry of molecules to the shapes of those atomic orbitals that are involved in chemical bonds. The utility of this approach does not need to be emphasized here.

In deducing the structure of a complex atom according to this scheme, there is one additional factor which must be considered. On examining the fine structure of the spectrum of atomic hydrogen, we explained that relativistic quantum mechanics discloses an additional multiplicity of states which is not obtained from the non-relativistic Schrödinger equation. By analogy with the form of the mathematical equations involved, this effect has been associated with an additional property of electrons and other elementary particles—intrinsic angular momentum or "spin." An electron has associated with it a spin angular momentum, which can be represented by a vector, and coincident with this angular momentum there is also a magnetic dipole moment. The interaction of this magnetic moment with the magnetic moment arising from the orbital motions of the electron in the atom causes the energy of the system to differ for different relative orientations of the two angular momenta. In particular, two such orientations are possible for a single electron with a particular n, l, and m_l corresponding to $m_s = \pm\frac{1}{2}$.

The effect of relative spin and orbital angular momenta on the energies and configurations of atomic states will be considered shortly, but for the present we need only to recall the Pauli exclusion principle, which states that no two electrons in an atom may have the same four quantum numbers n, l, m_l, and m_s. This means, then, that two electrons can simultaneously occupy the hydrogen-like eigenstate with a certain n, l, and m_l if for one electron $m_s = +\frac{1}{2}$ while for the second $m_s = -\frac{1}{2}$. We therefore picture complex atoms in terms of hydrogen-like orbitals occupied, beginning with the orbital of lowest energy, with each level successively containing two electrons with opposite or "paired" spins. From this picture arises the familiar notation for atomic configurations as represented by $1s$ for hydrogen, $1s^2$ for helium, $1s^2 2s$ for lithium and so on.

For the moment we are not concerned with the details of this notation, but only with recognition of the fact that, as we consider more and more complex atoms, we progressively add electrons to hydrogen-like orbitals and successively fill complete "shells" of states that represent electronic distributions that are farther and farther from the central nucleus. That the collection of levels having the same value of n does correspond roughly to a shell of electronic distribution can be quickly verified by studying the radial distributions in Figs. 6–8 and 6–9. Although an increased nuclear charge will alter these distributions, the primary effect will be to draw the radii of maximum density in closer to the larger positive nuclear charge, and the general view of successive shells of negative charge is not altered essentially.

The existence of such shells has an important effect on our consideration of how electrons in the hydrogen-like orbitals will be affected by the nuclear charge and by the other electrons. We can see, for example, that the shells of inner electrons will effectively shield the outer electrons from the full effect of the positive nuclear charge. In some cases this shielding effect will be highly effective. From Fig. 6–9 it can be seen that a 1s electron would almost completely screen a 3p electron from one of the nuclear charges. On the other hand, a 2s electron would not be so effectively shielded because there is a significant probability that a 2s electron will "penetrate" the 1s distribution and be found close to the nucleus. A number of cases will be considered in detail in a later section.

On the basis of these qualitative ideas Hartree[1] turned to a well-known mathematical technique, the method of successive approximations. Hartree's approach, known as the self-consistent field (SCF) method, is essentially as follows: First, on the basis of qualitative reasoning such as we have just discussed, construct a tentative electronic distribution for the atom of interest. If this distribution is considered as an electron cloud spread about in space, then from the charge-density distribution it is possible to calculate a potential energy at every point in space arising from the electrons. If this charge density is spherically symmetric about the nucleus, then the potential energy at any point will depend only on r and will be independent of angle. We have already argued that all filled shells will have such spherically symmetric distributions, and Hartree, for the purpose of maintaining spherical symmetry, also averaged any non-spherical distributions over all angles on the assumption that this would not affect the validity of the results too seriously.

Now consider the potential field arising from the nucleus and all the electrons in the atom but one. As a first approximation, consider that this potential energy governs the motions of that single electron. Using this potential energy we can then solve the Schrödinger equation for the distribution function of the single electron. We can further single out each additional electron and calculate its distribution using for the potential energy in each case the charge distribution for all the other electrons except the one of interest. In this way we will obtain a new set of electronic distributions, each having been obtained by considering the effect of all the other electronic charges on that one electron. It would be hoped that the resulting distributions will be more accurate than the original estimates, since the effects of electronic charges have been taken into account more explicitly.

However, we now recognize that in calculating the new distribution for each electron we used in the beginning a total charge distribution which was a very approximate one and as yet uncorrected for the effects of all the other electrons. Hence it is now necessary to repeat the process using these new corrected electronic distributions to calculate the poten-

[1] Hartree, *Proc. Cambridge Phil. Soc.*, **24**, 89, 111, 426 (1928).

tial-energy functions which affect each electron. The resulting set of distributions again represents a more satisfactory solution, so that a more accurate potential-energy function should result using these newest distributions. Hence we repeat the calculation to obtain a third set of electronic distributions, use these to obtain new potential-energy functions, from which we can calculate a fourth set of distributions, and so on until there is no further change in the individual electronic distributions or their potential-energy fields. It is then said that these fields are self-consistent.

Mathematically the formulation of the SCF method is straightforward, but in practice it can be extremely laborious. It is assumed that the atomic wave function is a product of one-electron orbital functions,

$$\psi = \phi_1(1)\phi_2(2) \cdots \phi_n(n),$$

where the configurations are constructed by making use of the Pauli exclusion principle and approximating the proper electron distributions as nearly as possible at the start. $\phi_1^2(1)$ represents the probability distribution for electron 1, $\phi_2^2(2)$ that of electron 2 and so on.

At a given point in space (x_1, y_1, z_1), the average electrostatic interaction between electron 1 at that point and electron 2 is given by

$$V_1(x_1, y_1, z_1) = \iiint \left(\frac{e^2}{r_{12}}\right) \phi_2^2(2) \, dx_2 \, dy_2 \, dz_2,$$

where the integral is over all positions of electron 2. Similarly, the total potential at this point due to the nuclear charge and the interactions with all the other electrons 2, 3, . . . , n, is

$$V_1(x_1, y_1, z_1) = -\frac{Ze^2}{r_1} + \sum_{i \neq 1} \iiint \left(\frac{e^2}{r_{i1}}\right) \phi_i^2(i) \, dx_i \, dy_i \, dz_i.$$

This expression for V_1 is then used in the one-electron Schrödinger equation,

$$-\frac{\hbar^2}{2m_1} \nabla_1^2 \phi_1 + V_1\phi_1 = E_1\phi_1,$$

to solve for the energy of this electron and for ϕ_1.

The calculation is repeated for each additional electron; that is, for the jth electron,

$$V_j(x_j, y_j, z_j) = -\frac{Ze^2}{r_j} + \sum_{i \neq j} \iiint \left(\frac{e^2}{r_{ij}}\right) \phi_i^2(i) \, dx_i \, dy_i \, dz_i$$

and

$$-\frac{\hbar^2}{2m_j} \nabla_j^2 \phi_j + V_j\phi_j = E_j\phi_j.$$

For n electrons n such problems must be solved and the result will be a new set of n ϕ_i's, which should better represent the electron distribution than the original set. Once these new orbital functions have been obtained, the entire process is repeated to obtain a third set of ϕ_i's, and so on until there is no further change in the E_i's. At this point the functions are said to be self-consistent and the total energy of the atom is

$$E = \sum_{i=1}^{n} E_i.$$

There are several shortcomings of this simple approach. One is that the motions of the electrons are in a sense correlated. That is, because of repulsion, electron 2 will move in such a way as to avoid electron 1 as much as possible. This electron correlation can be incorporated into the method, but calculations become even more complex. Another difficulty is the fact that electrons in an atom are experimentally indistinguishable and cannot be assigned in such a definite manner to particular atomic orbitals. This problem, also, has been incorporated into the SCF technique.

As an example of the sort of results obtained by Hartree's method, let us examine the SCF electronic distributions for Rb. The configuration of Rb, atomic number 37, is $1s^2 2s^2 2p^6 3s^2 3p^6 3d^{10} 4s^2 4p^6 5s$. The radial charge densities of the different orbitals of this atom are shown in Fig. 7–2. Remember that there are two electrons with paired spins in every orbital except the $5s$. We see immediately that the general appearance of the radial densities is very similar to that of hydrogen. We see the same sequence of nodes and the general pattern of shells with increasing n. On comparison with Fig. 6–9, however, we also note that there are some striking dissimilarities, the most notable being that the wave functions for Rb are pulled much closer to the nucleus than in hydrogen. They have shrunk to such an extent that all the electrons except the $5s$ valence electron are contained in a volume hardly larger than the hydrogen atom.

Some of the consequences of the SCF approach can be illustrated by investigating this distribution in more detail. One point of interest is the radius of maximum charge density. We might expect that, since Rb has a nuclear charge of $+37e$, the electrons would have most probable radii $\frac{1}{37}$ of those in hydrogen. In Table 7–1 radii of several orbitals in Rb are given, and it will be noticed that the effect is not as great as first predicted. Although the radius of the $1s$ electron is nearly as small as $\frac{1}{37}$ of the hydrogen $1s$ radius, it can be seen that the electrons farther out apparently are not affected by the full nuclear charge. This is the screening effect of the inner electrons which was mentioned previously. The $1s$ electrons are little affected by the outer electrons, but the outer

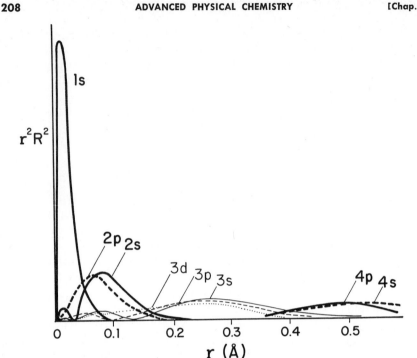

Fig. 7–2. SCF distribution functions for Rb. (After Slater, *Quantum Theory of Matter*, McGraw-Hill Book Co., 1951, p. 135.)

electrons are shielded to a greater or lesser degree from the full nuclear charge by the inner electronic charges. Again we might note the energies of these same Rb orbitals. We see in Table 7–2 that, as compared with the energies of the corresponding hydrogen orbitals, the electrons do not have as low energies as hydrogen-like orbitals experiencing a full nuclear charge of 37. This again can be accounted for by the shielding effect of the inner electrons.

One way of expressing this shielding effect would be to calculate an effective charge as a function of r so that $Z'(r)e$ becomes equal to Ze at

TABLE 7–1. Orbital Radii in Rb*

Orbital	$\dfrac{r_{max}}{a_0}$	$\dfrac{(r_H)_{max}}{(r_{Rb})_{max}}$
$1s$	.0273	36.6
$2p$	.122	32.8
$3d$	.405	22.2

* From Slater, *Quantum Theory of Matter*, McGraw-Hill Book Co., New York, 1951, p. 136; used by permission.

$r = 0$. This effective charge is the total charge, nuclear and electronic, contained within a sphere of radius r.   Simple electrostatic theory shows that the electrostatic field at radius r is that which would arise if the charge $Z'(r)e$ were concentrated at the nucleus.   This, of course, is the essential nature of the Hartree method, reducing the complex atom to a series of one-electron problems with centrally symmetric potential-energy functions governing their motion.   One method of discussing the effective charge is in terms of the difference between this charge and the full

TABLE 7-2.   Orbital Energies in Rb*

Orbital	Energy (ev)	$\dfrac{E_{\text{Rb}}}{E_{\text{H}}}$
$1s$	$-14{,}996$	33.3
$2p$	$-\ 1{,}799$	23.0
$3d$	$-\ \ \ 114.3$	8.75

* From Slater, *Quantum Theory of Matter*, McGraw-Hill Book Co., New York, 1951, p. 137; used by permission.

nuclear charge.   This difference is often called the shielding constant S. Mathematically, then,

$$S = Z - Z'.$$

The shielding constant provides a convenient means of indicating the environment of a given electron and is useful in at least one important method of obtaining orbital wave functions for complex atoms.

7.3   THE PERTURBATION METHOD

The atomic case, despite the large number of particles that may be involved, at least has the mathematical advantage of the centrally symmetric potential energy.   Unfortunately many other situations of interest cannot be handled by the SCF method.   There are many approximation techniques that can be used to obtain solutions of the Schrödinger equation under different circumstances, but we will confine our attention to two general methods that have been of primary usefulness in chemical problems, the perturbation method and the variation method.

The perturbation method is based on the behavior of equations and their solutions which are similar to but slightly "perturbed" from some simpler set of terms.   Suppose, for example, that for a particular problem we cannot solve the Schrödinger equation, but on examining the equation we note that except for one or two terms in the Hamiltonian operator it is the same as for some other problem that has been solved exactly. A simple example of such a case would be a potential-well problem for the system illustrated in Fig. 7-3. It will be noticed that, except for the small potential well in the center, this problem is identical with that of a potential well with infinite walls at $x = 0$ and $x = a$, for which we have obtained the energy levels and wave functions.

What will be the effect of the additional small well? First of all, it will change the potential-energy term in the Hamiltonian. It will also tend to lower the energy slightly and give a slightly larger wave function

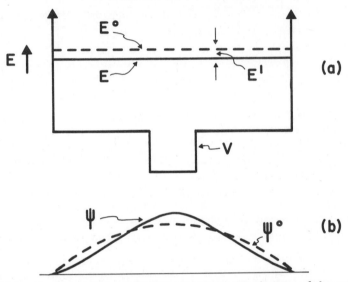

Fig. 7-3. Energy and wave function for the ground state of the perturbed potential well contrasted with the simple case.

in the region of the additional well as shown in Fig. 7-3. If this extra well is not large, then these changes will be small. The second well is then a "perturbation" on the simpler system, and the energies and wave functions of the perturbed system will differ only slightly from the simpler case.

Mathematically the perturbation method is handled as follows: We wish to solve the Schrödinger equation

$$\mathfrak{IC}\psi_n = E_n\psi_n, \tag{7-4}$$

where $\mathfrak{IC}$ is the complete Hamiltonian operator and the ψ_n are the wave functions which are solutions of the equation with eigenvalues (energies) E_n. We are assuming a conservative system and for the present will assume that none of the energy levels E_n are degenerate.

It may not be possible to solve (7–4) directly, but it may be possible to write the Hamiltonian operator in the form

$$\mathcal{3C} = \mathcal{3C}^0 + \lambda\mathcal{3C}' + \lambda^2\mathcal{3C}'' + \cdots, \tag{7–5}$$

where $\mathcal{3C}^0$ is the Hamiltonian for a situation for which we can solve the equation

$$\mathcal{3C}^0\psi_n^0 = E_n^0\psi_n^0 \tag{7–6}$$

exactly for the unperturbed energy levels E_n^0 and wave functions ψ_n^0, and where $\mathcal{3C}'$ and $\mathcal{3C}''$ are the perturbations which contain those terms that make the Hamiltonian of interest differ from the simpler solvable system. The symbol λ (*not* wavelength here) stands for a parameter whose value can be anywhere between 0 and 1. When $\lambda = 1$, the perturbation is operating at its greatest extent and (7–4) applies. When it is 0, the system is unperturbed and described by (7–6). We have introduced λ only as a mathematical device for obtaining the relations between E_n, E_n^0, ψ_n, and ψ_n^0. The question now is, what are E_n and ψ_n? If $\lambda = 0$, then the system is unperturbed and $E_n = E_n^0$, $\psi_n = \psi_n^0$. If λ increases from zero, we expect that E_n will deviate from E_n^0 and ψ_n from ψ_n^0 in a continuous manner. We assume that the energy can thus be written in the form

$$E_n = E_n^0 + \lambda E'_n + \lambda^2 E''_n + \cdots, \tag{7–7}$$

where E'_n and E''_n are correction terms which become more important as λ approaches 1. Note that, as required, $E_n = E_n^0$ when $\lambda = 0$. Similarly, we assume that

$$\psi_n = \psi_n^0 + \lambda\psi'_n + \lambda^2\psi''_n + \cdots. \tag{7–8}$$

With the full perturbation $\lambda = 1$, our problem is obviously to find E'_n, ψ'_n, etc., as far as is necessary to reach the desired accuracy. We would hope that perhaps terms in λ^2 and higher could be neglected, in which case we are concerned only with E'_n and ψ'_n. This degree of approximation is known as first-order perturbation theory. If we include the λ^2 terms, we are using second-order theory, and so on.

Considering only the $\mathcal{3C}'$ correction in $\mathcal{3C}$, we insert in Eq. (7–4) our expression for $\mathcal{3C}$ (7–5) and the series for E_n (7–7) and ψ_n (7–8). Rearranging terms in powers of λ, we obtain

$$(\mathcal{3C}^0\psi_n^0 - E_n^0\psi_n^0) + \lambda(\mathcal{3C}^0\psi'_n + \mathcal{3C}'\psi_n^0 - E_n^0\psi'_n - E'_n\psi_n^0)$$
$$+ \lambda^2(\mathcal{3C}^0\psi''_n + \mathcal{3C}'\psi'_n - E_n^0\psi''_n - E'_n\psi'_n - E''_n\psi_n^0)$$
$$+ \cdots = 0. \tag{7–9}$$

This equation must be true for all values of λ, and, provided the series is convergent, this requires that the coefficients of the powers of λ each vanish separately. For the term not containing λ (the zero-order term) we have $\mathcal{H}^0\psi_n{}^0 = E_n{}^0\psi_n{}^0$, which is simply the unperturbed equation (7–6).

Setting the coefficient of λ equal to zero, we obtain

$$\mathcal{H}^0\psi'_n - E_n{}^0\psi'_n = (E'_n - \mathcal{H}')\psi_n{}^0, \tag{7–10}$$

this being the first-order perturbation term. We know $\mathcal{H}^0$, $\mathcal{H}'$, and the $E_n{}^0$ and $\psi_n{}^0$. Thus we must determine the ψ'_n and the E'_n.

In Chapter 3 it was pointed out that any function can be constructed from a suitable expansion in terms of a complete set of orthonormal functions. Since we have such a complete set of functions from the solution of (7–6), and since the ψ_n will not differ greatly from the $\psi_n{}^0$, it seems logical that a reasonable way to obtain the first-order correction terms ψ'_n would be to form them by a series of the known $\psi_n{}^0$. Thus we write

$$\psi'_n = \sum_j a_{jn}\psi_j{}^0. \tag{7–11}$$

In other words, we are assuming that we can construct the first-order correction term for the wave function of the nth state of the perturbed system by a series of the unperturbed wave functions over *all* the states of the unperturbed system. In practice some of these states may have coefficients equal to zero and may not contribute to the correction term, but in theory we must include all the unperturbed states in order to have a complete set of orthogonal functions.

The utility of (7–11) becomes clearer when we substitute (7–11) into (7–10); for we see immediately that, because the $\psi_j{}^0$'s are eigenfunctions of $\mathcal{H}^0$, we have

$$\mathcal{H}^0\psi'_n = \mathcal{H}^0 \sum_j a_{jn}\psi_j{}^0 = \sum_j a_{jn}E_j{}^0\psi_j{}^0,$$

which gives us

$$\sum_j a_{jn}(E_j{}^0 - E_n{}^0)\psi_j{}^0 = (E'_n - \mathcal{H}')\psi_n{}^0. \tag{7–12}$$

In addition, the orthonormality of the functions is useful; for if we multiply from the left by $\psi_n{}^{0*}$ and displace all constant terms outside of the product of wave functions, we obtain

$$\sum_j a_{jn}(E_j{}^0 - E_n{}^0)\psi_n{}^{0*}\psi_j{}^0 = E'_n\psi_n{}^{0*}\psi_n{}^0 - \psi_n{}^{0*}\mathcal{H}'\psi_n{}^0,$$

which, upon multiplication by $d\tau$ and integration over all space, results in

$$\sum_j a_{jn}(E_j{}^0 - E_n{}^0) \int \psi_n{}^{0*}\psi_j{}^0 \, d\tau = E'_n \int \psi_n{}^{0*}\psi_n{}^0 \, d\tau - \int \psi_n{}^{0*}\mathcal{H}'\psi_n{}^0 \, d\tau.$$

The left side of this equation vanishes since, for $j = n$, the integral is unity (the $\psi_j{}^0$ are normalized) while $E_j{}^0 - E_n{}^0 = 0$ and, when $j \neq n$, the integral is zero (the ψ^0 are orthogonal). In addition, the first integral on the right side of the equation is unity. Thus, we are left with

$$E'_n = \int \psi_n^{0*} \mathfrak{IC}' \psi_n^0 \, d\tau = \langle n | \mathfrak{IC}' | n \rangle = H'_{nn}. \qquad (7\text{--}13)$$

We see that the first-order correction to the energy of the nth level of the unperturbed system to obtain the energy of the nth level of the perturbed system is simply the matrix element of the perturbation Hamiltonian over the unperturbed wave function for the nth state.

We also can find the coefficients a_{jn} required to evaluate ψ'_n if we multiply Eq. (7–12) by ψ_m^{0*}, the wave function for some state other than the nth state. We obtain upon integration

$$\sum_j a_{jn}(E_j^0 - E_n^0) \int \psi_m^{0*} \psi_j^0 \, d\tau = E'_n \int \psi_m^{0*} \psi_n^0 \, d\tau - \int \psi_m^{0*} \mathfrak{IC}' \psi_n^0 \, d\tau.$$

In this equation the left side is zero when $j \neq m$ because of the orthogonality of the wave functions, and when $j = m$, the integral is unity. Thus

$$a_{mn}(E_m^0 - E_n^0) = - \int \psi_m^{0*} \mathfrak{IC}' \psi_n^0 \, d\tau,$$

or

$$a_{mn} = - \frac{\langle m | \mathfrak{IC}' | n \rangle}{(E_m^0 - E_n^0)}, \quad m \neq n. \qquad (7\text{--}14)$$

From these results we see that for a non-degenerate energy level the first-order correction to the energy requires the evaluation of only one integral, but constructing the first-order correction to the wave function for that level may be very tedious, as a large number of a_{mn}'s may have to be evaluated. Once these have been obtained, they may be used in (7–11) to be added to the unperturbed wave function ψ_n^0. These calculations must be repeated for each energy level of interest; we have been describing all along only one level, the nth, of the perturbed system.

In case the first-order corrections are not sufficient, we can investigate the contribution of the term in λ^2 of Eq. (7–9). Setting the coefficient in parenthesis equal to zero, we can apply the same treatment to these terms and obtain expressions for E''_n and ψ''_n. The former is found to be

$$E''_n = \sum_j \frac{\langle n | \mathfrak{IC}' | j \rangle \langle j | \mathfrak{IC}' | n \rangle}{(E_n^0 - E_j^0)} + \langle n | \mathfrak{IC}'' | n \rangle \qquad (7\text{--}15)$$

with $j \neq n$. The complications in obtaining second-order corrections are obviously much greater than for a first-order calculation. In many cases a first-order calculation is sufficient, although for many interactions which have relatively small effects on the energy we shall see that second-order terms must be evaluated. Assuming, however, that only the first-order corrections are necessary, we can write

$$E_n = E_n{}^0 + \langle n|\mathcal{3C}'|n \rangle \tag{7-16}$$

and

$$\psi_n = \psi_n{}^0 - \sum_j \frac{\langle j|\mathcal{3C}'|n \rangle}{(E_j{}^0 - E_n{}^0)} \psi_j{}^0, \quad j \neq n. \tag{7-17}$$

The use of these two equations perhaps can be most clearly understood by examining a specific problem, the helium atom. In the general case in which the nucleus has a charge $+Ze$ and there are two electrons, we have the Schrödinger equation (7–2) with Z in place of 2 in two of the potential-energy terms. If we neglect the term containing r_{12}, then this equation can be treated as in (7–3), where $V_1 = -Ze^2/r_1$ and $V_2 = -Ze^2/r_2$. Thus, the total energy of the system without the interelectron repulsion would be twice that of a single hydrogen-like atom with charge $+Ze$; that is,

$$E_n{}^0 = 2Z^2E_H = \frac{-4Z^2\pi^2m_ee^4}{n^2h^2} = -108.24 \text{ ev.}$$

The perturbation in the atom with electronic repulsion is

$$\mathcal{3C}' = \frac{e^2}{r_{12}},$$

and the wave functions of the unperturbed atom are, for the lowest state,

$$\psi_{100,100}^0 = \psi_{100}(r_1, \theta_1, \phi_1)\psi_{100}(r_2, \theta_2, \phi_2),$$

where the subscripts indicate the values of n, l, and m_l for electrons 1 and 2. The analytical form of these functions is given in Table 6–4. Thus, the first-order correction to the energy of the lowest level is

$$E'_{100,100} = \left\langle 100, 100 \left| \frac{e^2}{r_{12}} \right| 100, 100 \right\rangle = \int \frac{e^2}{r_{12}} (\psi_{100,100}^0)^2 \, d\tau$$

since the wave functions are real. The integral represents the electrostatic energy of two overlapping, spherically symmetric clouds of charge. Evaluation of the integral is carried out in Appendix E. The result of the integration is that

$$E' = -\tfrac{5}{4} ZE_H = \frac{5Z\pi^2m_ee^4}{2h^2} = +33.82 \text{ ev.}$$

Thus, the energy of the ground state of the helium atom according to first-order perturbation theory is

$$E = E^0 + E' = -74.42 \text{ ev,}$$

which is not far from the experimentally measured value of -78.62 ev, an error of about 5.5 per cent.   The result is surprisingly good, considering the fact that in this case the perturbation is not really a small effect; it amounts to about 27 per cent of the unperturbed energy.   For ions with larger values of Z, the error is less and amounts to only about 0.4 per cent for the C^{+4} ion.

The first-order perturbation is primarily an accounting of the effect of changes in the potential-energy function for the electrons, and it will be noticed that in E' there are no terms involving the effect of one electron distribution on another.   In reality the electrons would tend to keep out of one another's way to some extent with a corresponding alteration of the electron distributions and energies.   This effect is often called *electron correlation*, and in the case of helium we can obtain some idea of the importance of electron correlation by comparing the first-order energy with the experimental value.   We see that taking electron correlation into account should lower the energy about 4.20 ev.   The second-order perturbation correction has such correlation matrix elements, but second-order calculations are extremely cumbersome in this system and good results are obtained more easily by the variation method to be discussed shortly.

We assumed in the derivation of the first-order perturbation terms that the energy level of interest was non-degenerate.   The reason for this is clear from Eq. (7–14), where we see that if another state m happens to have the same energy as the state n, then the coefficient a_{mn} becomes infinitely large.   This problem can be resolved, and for the sake of simplicity in notation we will consider an energy level which is only twofold degenerate.   The results can be expanded easily to higher degeneracies.

We will assume that the Hamiltonian operator can be written as in in (7–5), and that as the perturbation becomes smaller, the energy approaches that of the unperturbed system, so that the energies of the perturbed state can be written as a series just as in Eq. (7–7).   The question remains, however, what wave function should be used as the unperturbed wave function for a given energy level if the level is twofold degenerate.   In Chapter 3 it was observed that eigenfunctions corresponding to different energy levels are orthogonal, a property that was used in the earlier part of this section to derive the perturbation equations.   The wave functions of a degenerate level are not necessarily orthogonal, but we saw also that it is possible to construct a set of orthogonal functions from such degenerate functions.   Thus we will assume that the proper unperturbed function with which we should begin is a linear combination of the two degenerate eigenfunctions of the energy level of interest.   We will avoid numbering the energy level by a subscript in order to avoid confusion in the nomenclature, but remember that this discussion is concerned now only with one degenerate energy level. Following the approach taken in Eq. (7–8), we will then assume that the perturbed wave function is

$$\psi = c_1\psi_1{}^0 + c_2\psi_2{}^0 + \lambda\psi' + \lambda^2\psi'' + \cdots ,$$

where $\psi_1{}^0$ and $\psi_2{}^0$ are the degenerate eigenfunctions of the unperturbed energy level. In order that the linear combination of $\psi_1{}^0$ and $\psi_2{}^0$ be a normalized eigenfunction of the unperturbed Hamiltonian, it is necessary that

$$c_1{}^*c_1 + c_2{}^*c_2 = 1. \tag{7–18}$$

Substituting our expressions for $\mathcal{3C}$, E, and ψ into (7–4) as before, and arranging terms in powers of λ, we obtain

$$\mathcal{3C}^0(c_1\psi_1{}^0 + c_2\psi_2{}^0) - E^0(c_1\psi_1{}^0 + c_2\psi_2{}^0)$$
$$+ \lambda[(\mathcal{3C}^0 - E^0)\psi' - c_1(E' - \mathcal{3C}')\psi_1{}^0 - c_2(E' - \mathcal{3C}')\psi_2{}^0] + \cdots = 0.$$

Here again, the term in λ^0 is the Schrödinger equation for the unperturbed case. Setting the coefficient of λ equal to zero, we obtain

$$(\mathcal{3C}^0 - E^0)\psi' - c_1(E' - \mathcal{3C}')\psi_1{}^0 - c_2(E' - \mathcal{3C}')\psi_2{}^0 = 0. \tag{7–19}$$

We now express the first-order correction to the wave function, ψ', as a series of the basic orthonormal wave functions of the unperturbed system

$$\psi' = \sum_j a_j\psi_j{}^0. \tag{7–20}$$

It is noted that functions resulting from the operation of $\mathcal{3C}'$ on $\psi_1{}^0$, and $\psi_2{}^0$ could be found explicitly since both the wave functions and the perturbation Hamiltonian term are known. For purely mathematical convenience, however, we will also assume that these functions can be constructed from a series of the unperturbed wave functions, i.e.,

$$\mathcal{3C}'\psi_1{}^0 = \sum_j b_j\psi_j{}^0 \quad \text{and} \quad \mathcal{3C}'\psi_2{}^0 = \sum_j d_j\psi_j{}^0. \tag{7–21}$$

The coefficients of these series can be determined immediately from the orthonormality of the basis functions by the method used previously:

$$b_j = \langle j|\mathcal{3C}'|1\rangle = H'_{j1},$$
$$d_j = \langle j|\mathcal{3C}'|2\rangle = H'_{j2}.$$

Substitution of (7–20) and (7–21) into (7–19) gives us

$$\sum_j (E_j{}^0 - E^0)a_j\psi_j{}^0 - E'(c_1\psi_1{}^0 + c_2\psi_2{}^0) + \sum_j c_1H'_{j1}\psi_j{}^0 + \sum_j c_2H'_{j2}\psi_j{}^0 = 0,$$

where we have used the fact that the $\psi_j{}^0$ are eigenfunctions of $\mathcal{3C}^0$ and where $E^0 = E_1{}^0 = E_2{}^0$. This equation contains series of terms in $\psi_j{}^0$.

In order that the equation be true for arbitrary $\mathcal{K}'$, the coefficients of each ψ_j^0 must separately vanish. For ψ_1^0, then,

$$c_1 E' - c_1 H'_{11} - c_2 H'_{12} = 0, \qquad (7\text{--}22)$$

for ψ_2^0

$$c_2 E' - c_1 H'_{21} - c_2 H'_{22} = 0, \qquad (7\text{--}23)$$

for ψ_3^0

$$(E_3^0 - E^0)a_3 + c_1 H'_{31} + c_2 H'_{32} = 0,$$

and so on. A general expression for all the a_j's except a_1 and a_2 is found to be

$$a_j = \frac{c_1 H'_{j1} + c_2 H'_{j2}}{E^0 - E_j^0}, \qquad j \neq 1, j \neq 2.$$

To the first-order approximation, which we are considering here, the normalization requirements for ψ are that

$$c_1^* c_1 + c_2^* c_2 + \lambda(c_1^* a_1 + c_1 a_1^* + c_2^* a_2 + c_2 a_2^*) = 1,$$

and since the c's already satisfy the condition (7–18), it is necessary therefore that $a_1 = a_2 = 0$.

Coefficients c_1 and c_2 can be found from (7–22) and (7–23); for in these we have two simultaneous equations in c_1 and c_2, and except for the trivial solution $c_1 = c_2 = 0$ it is necessary that the determinant of the coefficients vanish:

$$\begin{vmatrix} H'_{11} - E' & H'_{12} \\ H'_{21} & H'_{22} - E' \end{vmatrix} = 0$$

which is

$$(H'_{11} - E')(H'_{22} - E') - H'_{21} H'_{12} = 0.$$

This equation is known as the *secular equation*, and the determinant as the *secular determinant*. We see that for a twofold degenerate energy level we obtain a 2×2 determinant equation, which has two roots. The magnitude of these roots may or may not be the same. If they are identical, then the resulting perturbed energy level $E = E^0 + E'$ obviously is still twofold degenerate, and we say that degeneracy has not been removed by the perturbation. On the other hand, if two different E''s are obtained, then the degeneracy has been removed by the perturbation.

Substitution of the E' back into (7–22) and (7–23) will immediately give the ratio c_1/c_2. We will not explore here the problem of obtaining the actual values of these constants, but the reader is referred to the literature cited at the end of the chapter. Our main concern is the perturbation of the energy levels.

In those cases in which we perturb an n-fold degenerate level, a treatment such as that carried out above results in an $n \times n$ determinant equation, which has n roots. Again, some of these roots may be identical, in which case not all of the degeneracy has been removed by the perturbation. Examples will be seen later.

A particularly convenient situation occurs when all the off-diagonal matrix elements in the secular determinant are zero. This determinant is said to be diagonalized, and it can be seen that the roots of the secular equation are simply H'_{11}, H'_{22}, etc.

$$
\begin{vmatrix}
H'_{11} - E' & 0 & 0 & \cdots & 0 \\
0 & H'_{22} - E' & 0 & \cdots & 0 \\
0 & 0 & H'_{33} - E' & \cdots & 0 \\
\cdots & \cdots & \cdots & \cdots & \cdots \\
0 & 0 & 0 & \cdots & H'_{nn} - E'
\end{vmatrix} = 0.
$$

As an illustration of the use of first-order degenerate perturbation theory let us make an approximate calculation of the energy of the valence electron in the Li atom. For the sake of simplicity, we will assume that two electrons are in the $1s$ state, that they experience the full nuclear charge of $+3e$, and that they are described by hydrogen-like wave functions. The radius of maximum probability for these electrons would then be $a_0/3$. This view is, of course, a gross oversimplification, as we have seen for the helium atom.

We will next assume that the valence electron is in the $n = 2$ level. When it is farther from the nucleus than $r = a_0/3$, it will be assumed that it experiences only a $+e$ charge because of the shielding by the inner electrons. We can calculate the energy of this electron using $V = -e^2/r$, the result being the same as for the hydrogen atom with $n = 2$. That is, $E^0 = -3.3825$ ev. But if we take into account the penetration of the $n = 2$ electron into the $1s$ cloud, this result will not be correct. Let us assume that, when $r < a_0/3$, this electron experiences the full nuclear charge, so that in this region $V = -3e^2/r$. We can handle this problem by assuming that there is a perturbation on our previously calculated energy in the region $0 < r < a_0/3$, which is described by $\mathfrak{K}' = -2e^2/r$.

Next we note that the $n = 2$ level for a hydrogen-like atom is fourfold degenerate; there are a $2s$ and three $2p$ states with the same energy. Hence the secular equation will be

$$
\begin{vmatrix}
H'_{11} - E' & H'_{12} & H'_{13} & H'_{14} \\
H'_{21} & H'_{22} - E' & H'_{23} & H'_{24} \\
H'_{31} & H'_{32} & H'_{33} - E' & H'_{34} \\
H'_{41} & H'_{42} & H'_{43} & H'_{44} - E'
\end{vmatrix} = 0 \quad (7\text{–}24)
$$

where the unperturbed hydrogen-like wave functions are $\psi_1^0 = \psi_{200}$, $\psi_2^0 = \psi_{210}$, $\psi_3^0 = \psi_{211}$, $\psi_4^0 = \psi_{21\,-1}$. It is found that in this circumstance all the off-diagonal matrix elements are zero, so that the roots of the secular equation follow immediately from H'_{11}, H'_{22}, H'_{33}, and H'_{44}. Each of these matrix elements is of the form $\langle j|\mathcal{3C}'|j\rangle$, where the integration is carried out only over the region $0 < r < a_0/3$, since the perturbation acts only in this region, i.e.,

$$H'_{11} = \langle 1|\mathcal{3C}'|1\rangle = \int_0^{2\pi} \int_0^{\pi} \int_0^{a_0/3} \psi_{200}^{0*} \left(-\frac{2e^2}{r} \right) \psi_{200}^0 r^2 \, dr \, \sin\theta \, d\theta \, d\phi.$$

Evaluation of the diagonal matrix elements results in

$$E'_1 = H'_{11} = .0275E_{\rm H},$$
$$E'_2 = H'_{22} = -.0029E_{\rm H},$$
$$E'_3 = H'_{33} = -.0029E_{\rm H},$$
$$E'_4 = H'_{44} = -.0029E_{\rm H}.$$

Thus the perturbation $\mathcal{3C}'$ has partially lifted the degeneracy of the $n = 2$ level. The 2s state, because of greater penetration, has a lower energy than the three 2p states, which remain degenerate to this degree of accuracy. Using the two values of E' obtained from the secular equation, we calculate the energies of the 2s and 2p states in lithium to be

$$E_{2s} = \tfrac{1}{4}E_{\rm H} + .0275E_{\rm H} = -3.3825 - .3721 = -3.7546 \text{ ev.}$$
$$E_{2p} = \tfrac{1}{4}E_{\rm H} - .0029E_{\rm H} = -3.3429 \text{ ev,}$$
and

$$E_{2p} - E_{2s} = +0.4117 \text{ ev,}$$

which can be compared with the experimental values $E_{2s} = -5.4001$, $E_{2p} = -3.5505$, and $E_{2p} - E_{2s} = +1.8496$ ev. The approximations made in setting up the problem are far too gross to expect very close agreement, but the primary effects are seen clearly.

7.4   THE VARIATION METHOD

It is frequently the case that the various interactions or boundary conditions are too extreme to be considered a small perturbation on a system for which the Schrödinger equation can be solved exactly. This is particularly true in molecular situations. In such cases it is necessary to make guesses at the form of the correct wave functions and test these functions to see whether they are good or not. One method of testing is based on the fact that for any arbitrary function it can be shown that the integral

$$W = \frac{\langle \phi|\mathcal{3C}|\phi\rangle}{\langle \phi|\phi\rangle}, \tag{7-25}$$

where $\mathcal{3C}$ is the complete Hamiltonian operator for the system of interest and ϕ is any arbitrary function, can approach but can never be less (lower, less positive, more negative) than the true energy, E, of the system. This is the equation upon which the variation method is based.

Inspection of Eq. (7–25) discloses that if ϕ were actually the correct wave function and hence an eigenfunction of the Hamiltonian operator, then W would be equal to E. If ϕ is not the correct wave function, then W will have some different numerical value, and it now remains for us to show that the value that will be obtained with some arbitrary function will necessarily be larger than the true energy of the system. Let us assume, as we have done before, that ϕ can be constructed by a complete series made up of the true orthonormal eigenfunctions of the Hamiltonian operator, even though we do not actually know what these functions are. Then

$$\phi = \sum_j a_j \psi_j{}^0, \qquad \sum_j a_j{}^* a_j = 1.$$

Substituting this expansion into (7–25), we note that the denominator is unity by virtue of the normality of the wave functions, leaving

$$W = \sum_j \sum_{j'} a_j{}^* a_{j'} \langle j | \mathcal{3C} | j' \rangle = \sum_j a_j{}^* a_j E_j. \tag{7–26}$$

The last step follows from the fact that the $\psi_j{}^0$'s are orthonormal and are also eigenfunctions of $\mathcal{3C}$ with eigenvalues E_j. If we now subtract the lowest energy level E_0 from both sides of (7–26), we obtain

$$W - E_0 = \sum_j a_j{}^* a_j (E_j - E_0). \tag{7–27}$$

E_0 is the lowest energy, and therefore $E_j - E_0$ must always be zero (if $E_j = E_0$) or positive. In addition the coefficients $a_j{}^* a_j$ are all zero or positive, so that the right-hand side of Eq. (7–27) is necessarily always zero or positive. Thus, we can state that

$$W \geqslant E_0,$$

which is the theorem we wished to prove.

The essential problem of the variation method is to find a function which gives the lowest possible value of W. If the functions tried are chosen with care, it may be possible to approach the true energy very closely. It obviously would be a tedious job to try many different arbitrary functions in order to pick out one which has the lowest W. Instead, it is more usual to construct a function with one or more variable parameters and then minimize W with respect to these variables. Generally, the more variables one has with which to operate, the closer the true energy can be approached.

As an example of the use of the variation method, let us again examine the ground state of the helium atom. We argued previously that the wave function for helium should not be unlike those for hydrogen electrons except for the effect of the shielding. A reasonable trial variation function might be constructed, then, from hydrogen $1s$ functions:

$$\phi = \phi_1\phi_2 = \frac{Z'^3}{\pi a_0^3} e^{-Z'r_1/a_0}e^{-Z'r_2/a_0}, \tag{7-28}$$

in which Z' is the effective nuclear charge with shielding included and is a variable parameter. The Hamiltonian operator is

$$\mathcal{3C} = -\frac{\hbar^2}{2m_e}(\nabla_1^2 + \nabla_2^2) - Ze^2\left(\frac{1}{r_1} + \frac{1}{r_2}\right) + \frac{e^2}{r_{12}}$$

where Z is the true atomic number.

Operating on the variation function with the Hamiltonian operator yields

$$\mathcal{3C}\phi = -\frac{\hbar^2}{2m}(\nabla_1^2 + \nabla_2^2)\phi_1\phi_2 - Ze^2\left(\frac{1}{r_1} + \frac{1}{r_2}\right)\phi_1\phi_2 + \frac{e^2}{r_{12}}\phi_1\phi_2$$

$$= -\frac{\hbar^2}{2m}[\phi_2\nabla_1^2\phi_1 + \phi_1\nabla_2^2\phi_2] - \frac{Ze^2}{r_1}\phi_1\phi_2 - \frac{Ze^2}{r_2}\phi_1\phi_2 + \frac{e^2}{r_{12}}\phi_1\phi_2. $$

$$\tag{7-29}$$

Since the variation functions ϕ_1 and ϕ_2 are hydrogen-like functions for nuclear charge $Z'e$, they must satisfy the equations

$$-\frac{\hbar^2}{2m}\nabla_1^2\phi_1 - \frac{Z'e^2}{r_1}\phi_1 = Z'^2E_H\phi_1$$

and

$$-\frac{\hbar^2}{2m}\nabla_2^2\phi_2 - \frac{Z'e^2}{r_2}\phi_2 = Z'^2E_H\phi_2.$$

Substitution of these expressions back into (7-29) and rearrangement of terms results in

$$\mathcal{3C}\phi = 2Z'^2E_H\phi_1\phi_2 + (Z' - Z)e^2\left(\frac{1}{r_1} + \frac{1}{r_2}\right)\phi_1\phi_2 + \frac{e^2}{r_{12}}\phi_1\phi_2.$$

Multiplication from the left by ϕ^* and integration then gives

$$W = \langle\phi|\mathcal{3C}|\phi\rangle$$

$$= 2Z'^2E_H + (Z' - Z)e^2\left\langle \phi_1\phi_2 \left| \frac{1}{r_1} + \frac{1}{r_2} \right| \phi_1\phi_2 \right\rangle + \left\langle \phi_1\phi_2 \left| \frac{e^2}{r_{12}} \right| \phi_1\phi_2 \right\rangle.$$

The first term above results immediately because the trial functions are normalized.   The first integral can be broken down into

$$e^2 \left\langle 1,2 \left| \frac{1}{r_1} + \frac{1}{r_2} \right| 1,2 \right\rangle = e^2 \left\langle 1 \left| \frac{1}{r_1} \right| 1 \right\rangle + e^2 \left\langle 2 \left| \frac{1}{r_2} \right| 2 \right\rangle$$

$$= 2e^2 \int \frac{\phi_1{}^2}{r_1} \, d\tau = -4Z'E_{\mathrm{H}},$$

since the two functions are identical except for subscripts and are normalized.   The last integral is identical with the one used in our first-order perturbation calculation for helium except that this integral contains Z' instead of Z.   Thus

$$\left\langle 1,2 \left| \frac{e}{r_{12}} \right| 1,2 \right\rangle = -\tfrac{5}{4}Z'E_{\mathrm{H}}.$$

Combination of these terms then gives us

$$W = [2Z'^2 + (Z' - 4Z)(-Z') - \tfrac{5}{4}Z']E_{\mathrm{H}}$$
$$= (2Z'^2 - 4Z'^2 + 4ZZ' - \tfrac{5}{4}Z')E_{\mathrm{H}}. \qquad (7\text{--}30)$$

To find the best value of Z', which is a variable parameter, we next minimize W with respect to Z', i.e., set

$$\frac{\partial W}{\partial Z'} = 0 = (4Z' - 8Z' + 4Z - \tfrac{5}{4})E_{\mathrm{H}}$$

from which it follows that

$$Z' = Z - \tfrac{5}{16}. \qquad (7\text{--}31)$$

This is the value of Z' that gives the lowest value of W and hence gives the best wave function of this form.   If (7–31) is substituted back into (7–30), we obtain

$$W = 2Z'^2 E_{\mathrm{H}} = 2(Z - \tfrac{5}{16})^2 E_{\mathrm{H}} = -77.45 \text{ ev.}$$

This is only about 2 per cent in error, so we see that it is possible to obtain reasonable accuracy with well-chosen variation functions.   Our result here is considerably better than we obtained with first-order perturbation theory.

It is possible to obtain even better results with a more flexible trial function.   If a second parameter c is introduced in the function:

$$\phi = A(1 + cr_{12})e^{-Z'r_1/a_0}e^{-Z'r_2/a_0}$$

and if W is minimized with respect to both Z' and c, we find that W is in error by only .34 ev.   In this case we find that $Z' = Z - .151$, which is a much smaller screening effect than found with (7–28).   This indicates that inclusion of the r_{12} term is a more effective way of taking electron correlation into account than to use Z' alone.   Inclusion of other polynomial terms in r_1, r_2, r_{12}, and Z' further narrows the difference between W and E. A 14-parameter function has given a value which agrees with the observed energy within .002 ev, and as many as 35 terms have been used in accurate calculations.

In searching for a suitable trial function, it is often found to be convenient to construct this function as a linear combination of functions:

$$\phi = c_1\phi_1 + c_2\phi_2 + \cdots + c_n\phi_n. \tag{7-32}$$

These functions may or may not be eigenfunctions of some particular Schrödinger equation. The only requirement is that they be well-behaved. If we introduce (7–32) into (7–25), we obtain

$$W = \frac{\sum\limits_{j=1}^{n} \sum\limits_{j'=1}^{n} c_j c_{j'} H_{jj'}}{\sum\limits_{j=1}^{n} \sum\limits_{j'=1}^{n} c_j c_{j'} S_{jj'}} \tag{7-33}$$

where

$$H_{jj'} = \langle j|\mathcal{H}|j'\rangle$$

and

$$S_{jj'} = \langle j|j'\rangle.$$

We have assumed that ϕ is real in the above equations. In order to find the minimum value of W and obtain the closest possible approximation to the true energy, it is necessary to differentiate (7–33) with respect to each c_j and set each expression for $\partial W/\partial c_j$ equal to zero. The result is a set of n equations in the c_j's, and algebraic theory shows that the determinant formed from the coefficients of the c_j's must vanish, i.e.,

$$\begin{vmatrix} H_{11} - S_{11}W & H_{12} - S_{12}W & \cdots & H_{1n} - S_{1n}W \\ H_{21} - S_{21}W & H_{22} - S_{22}W & \cdots & H_{2n} - S_{2n}W \\ \cdots & \cdots & \cdots & \cdots \\ H_{n1} - S_{n1}W & H_{n2} - S_{n2}W & \cdots & H_{nn} - S_{nn}W \end{vmatrix} = 0.$$

The lowest root of this equation, which is somewhat similar to the secular equation from perturbation theory, is the closest approximation to the energy E_0. Once the n roots of the determinant have been obtained, they can be substituted back into the set of equations that were obtained by taking the derivatives of W with respect to c_1, c_2, etc., and from the resulting equations the values of each of these coefficients can now be determined. Thus the complete wave function corresponding to each root can be constructed by putting these values of the coefficients in (7–32). Since we are interested primarily in the lowest value of W, it is the values of c_1, c_2, . . . obtained for this root that are of most interest.

Trial functions for the helium atom have been constructed in this way.

One of the most effective methods to construct trial functions of this type is to use, for ϕ_1, ϕ_2, etc., functions that represent the ground state and various excited states of the system. For helium the ground state is $1s^2$ and a suitable wave function is (7–28). One excited state of helium might be expected to be represented by a $2s^2$ configuration, in which case a suitable function would be of the form

$$\phi_2 = A\,\phi_{2s}(1)\,\phi_{2s}(2).$$

Using several such functions in a linear combination results in energies that are extremely close to the correct answer. It also seems apparent that the difficulties of calculation are likewise increased when many functions are used. The use of excited-state functions along with the approximate ground-state function is called *configuration interaction* and generally leads to more accurate ground-state energies.

The advantage of the use of orthonormal functions in the construction of a linear-combination variation function is seen here in that the off-diagonal terms of the secular determinant go to zero and the S_{ii} terms are unity.

In closing this discussion of approximation methods it should be mentioned that using the total energy as a criterion of the correctness of the wave function is particularly convenient but can be misleading. It is often possible to approach the true energy very closely, but one is usually dealing with very large numbers, so that even small percentage errors are significant on an absolute scale. Thus, many small interactions may be of the same order of magnitude as the error. In addition, many important atomic and molecular interactions can be calculated only if the wave functions are extremely accurate, and although the energy criterion may seem to indicate that we are very close to the correct energy, the wave function may still be grossly approximate with respect to that property of importance in the interaction. We will see a number of important cases in the following chapters.

We should also mention that many of the atomic and molecular "interactions" of which we often speak arise only because of our inability to write the exact wave functions for a system. Electron correlation is an example of such an effect. Upon trying a first-order perturbation calculation for the energy of helium, we found that the result was in error. The difference was ascribed to the fact that we had neglected interelectronic effects, electron correlation. But the fact is that we would never have introduced this concept if we had been able to write the correct wave function to begin with, in which case we would have obtained the correct energy immediately. These phenomena arising from our approximation procedures are often useful for comparison purposes, but should not be taken too literally.

7.5   SYMMETRY AND ELECTRON SPIN IN COMPLEX ATOMS

So far in our consideration of the structure of complex atoms, we have neglected the effects of the electronic spin angular momentum. We have seen that the spin-orbit interaction alters and splits the energy levels calculated without consideration of spin. These effects are very small for light atoms, however, especially to the degree of accuracy we have considered so far. Nonetheless, as we consider more electrons, or even the excited states of atoms such as helium, it is necessary to take into account two fundamental properties of quantum-mechanical systems which we have not yet discussed. These are the indistinguishability of identical particles and the symmetry requirements arising from relativistic quantum mechanics for particles with half-integral spin.

Consider first a simple case, two non-interacting particles contained in a potential well. If ϕ_j and ϕ_k are two wave functions (assumed to be real) that describe possible states of one electron in the potential well, then we have seen that a satisfactory solution of the Schrödinger equation for the two particles in the well would be

$$\psi_1 = \phi_j(q_1)\phi_k(q_2), \tag{7-34}$$

where q_1 and q_2 are the coordinates of the first and second particles. The probability distribution for the two particles would be

$$\psi_1{}^2 = \phi_j{}^2(q_1)\phi_k{}^2(q_2).$$

But this probability distribution implies, since ϕ_j and ϕ_k may be different, that particle 1 has a different probability distribution from that of particle 2. In other words, it would be possible to distinguish one particle from the other. If we interchanged the coordinates of the two particles so that the wave function for the system was

$$\psi_2 = \phi_k(q_1)\phi_j(q_2), \tag{7-35}$$

with a probability distribution

$$\psi_2{}^2 = \phi_k{}^2(q_1)\phi_j{}^2(q_2),$$

then we would be able to distinguish this arrangement from the previous one, as the particles have now interchanged probability distributions and remain unlike each other.

While both (7–34) and (7–35) are acceptable solutions of the Schrödinger equation for two particles in a potential well, they are not actually satisfactory because it is impossible experimentally to distinguish one particle from another (except, of course, on a macroscopic scale, where we can label things). Any experiment that we could perform could determine at best only the probability distribution for two particles with no identification of either particle separately. Thus our wave function for the system must also reflect the indistinguishability of the particles while retaining the over-all probability distribution. Such a function can be constructed since, if (7–34) and (7–35) are solutions, then a linear combination of them will also be a satisfactory solution. Thus, we write

$$\psi_s = \frac{1}{\sqrt{2}}(\psi_1 + \psi_2) = \frac{1}{\sqrt{2}}[\phi_j(q_1)\phi_k(q_2) + \phi_k(q_1)\phi_j(q_2)], \quad (7\text{–}36)$$

which we can see is unchanged if we interchange the coordinates of the two particles, i.e., change q_1 and q_2 to q_2 and q_1. Any function that remains unchanged by the exchange of the coordinates of two particles is said to be symmetric. We have labeled this symmetric function by the subscript s. It is clear that in this function the same distribution is implied for particle 1 as for particle 2. The constant term $1/\sqrt{2}$ is included to normalize the function.

It is possible also to construct another function from the difference of (7–34) and (7–35):

$$\psi_a = \frac{1}{\sqrt{2}}(\psi_1 - \psi_2) = \frac{1}{\sqrt{2}}[\phi_j(q_1)\phi_k(q_2) - \phi_k(q_1)\phi_j(q_2)]. \quad (7\text{–}37)$$

It can be seen that interchange of the particles in this function merely reproduces the same function but with a change in sign. Thus ψ_a^2 will not be affected by an exchange of particles in this function either, and the particles are again indistinguishable. A function that changes sign on interchange of the coordinates of the particles is antisymmetric.

In all the cases we have considered so far, we have not had to consider the possibility of distinguishing the particles, since in the ground state of helium both electrons were assumed to be 1s-like and thus automatically indistinguishable. Wave functions such as (7–36) and (7–37) will result, however, from a treatment of other cases, such as the excited states of helium in which one electron is in a 1s state while the second is in the $n = 2$ level. In the absence of the e^2/r_{12} term in the Hamiltonian operator, the zero-order energy of this excited state could be easily calculated by using hydrogen-like wave functions for $n = 1$ and $n = 2$, and it is found that

$$E^0 = 5\frac{Z^2}{4}E_H = -67.64 \text{ ev},$$

where E_H still stands for the ground-state energy of a hydrogen atom.

If we attempt to write all the simplest possible wave functions for the excited state without any regard for the indistinguishability of the electrons, we would find the unperturbed excited state to be eightfold degenerate:

$$
\begin{aligned}
\phi_1{}^0 &= 1s(1)2s(2), & \phi_5{}^0 &= 1s(1)2p_0(2), \\
\phi_2{}^0 &= 2s(1)1s(2), & \phi_6{}^0 &= 2p_0(1)1s(2), \\
\phi_3{}^0 &= 1s(1)2p_1(2), & \phi_7{}^0 &= 1s(1)2p_{-1}(2), \\
\phi_4{}^0 &= 2p_1(1)1s(2), & \phi_8{}^0 &= 2p_{-1}(1)1s(2).
\end{aligned}
$$

(A shortened nomenclature is used here in which $1s$ denotes the wave function ψ_{100} for a hydrogen-like atom and (1) indicates that the coordinates (r, θ, ϕ) are those for electron 1.)

We must therefore use perturbation theory for degenerate states, and from our discussion in Sec. 7.3 we can immediately write the 8×8 secular determinant which must be solved to find the perturbation energies. Most of the matrix elements in the determinant vanish as can be seen by investigating the symmetry properties of the terms in the integrands. The secular equation is found to have the form

$$
\begin{vmatrix}
J_s - E' & K_s & 0 & 0 & 0 & 0 & 0 & 0 \\
K_s & J_s - E' & 0 & 0 & 0 & 0 & 0 & 0 \\
0 & 0 & J_p - E' & K_p & 0 & 0 & 0 & 0 \\
0 & 0 & K_p & J_p - E' & 0 & 0 & 0 & 0 \\
0 & 0 & 0 & 0 & J_p - E' & K_p & 0 & 0 \\
0 & 0 & 0 & 0 & K_p & J_p - E' & 0 & 0 \\
0 & 0 & 0 & 0 & 0 & 0 & J_p - E' & K_p \\
0 & 0 & 0 & 0 & 0 & 0 & K_p & J_p - E'
\end{vmatrix} = 0, \quad (7\text{--}38)
$$

where the matrix elements are

$$
J_s = \left\langle 1s(1)2s(2) \left| \frac{e^2}{r_{12}} \right| 1s(1)2s(2) \right\rangle,
$$

$$
K_s = \left\langle 1s(1)2s(2) \left| \frac{e^2}{r_{12}} \right| 2s(1)1s(2) \right\rangle,
$$

$$
J_p = \left\langle 1s(1)2p(2) \left| \frac{e^2}{r_{12}} \right| 1s(1)2p(2) \right\rangle,
$$

$$
K_p = \left\langle 1s(1)2p(2) \left| \frac{e^2}{r_{12}} \right| 2p(1)1s(2) \right\rangle.
$$

In this problem the radial parts of all the $2p$ functions are the same, so it is not necessary to make any further distinction than we have done here. The J integrals are often called *Coulomb integrals* since they can be considered to represent the average Coulomb interaction energy of the two electrons in the probability distributions given by the two functions involved in the integral. The K integrals are generally known as *resonance integrals* or *exchange integrals* and can be seen to involve interchange of the coordinates of the electrons.

Solution of (7–38) results in four values for the perturbation energy. There must be eight states, however, since there was eightfold degeneracy to begin with. Therefore some of the perturbed energy levels are still degenerate to first order. From the values of E' it is possible to obtain the coefficients of the zero-order functions required to form the wave functions of the perturbed states. The calculated energy corrections and the corresponding wave functions from this first-order perturbation treatment are

$$E'_1 = J_s - K_s, \qquad \psi_1^0 = \frac{1}{\sqrt{2}}[1s(1)2s(2) - 1s(2)2s(1)],$$

$$E'_2 = J_s + K_s, \qquad \psi_2^0 = \frac{1}{\sqrt{2}}[1s(1)2s(2) + 1s(2)2s(1)],$$

$$E'_3 = E'_5 = E'_7 = J_p - K_p, \quad \psi_3^0 = \frac{1}{\sqrt{2}}[1s(1)2p_1(2) - 1s(2)2p_1(1)],$$

$$\psi_5^0 = \frac{1}{\sqrt{2}}[1s(1)2p_0(2) - 1s(2)2p_0(1)],$$

$$\psi_7^0 = \frac{1}{\sqrt{2}}[1s(1)2p_{-1}(2) - 1s(2)2p_{-1}(1)],$$

$$E'_4 = E'_6 = E'_8 = J_p + K_p, \quad \psi_4^0 = \frac{1}{\sqrt{2}}[1s(1)2p_1(2) + 1s(2)2p_1(1)],$$

$$\psi_6^0 = \frac{1}{\sqrt{2}}[1s(1)2p_0(2) + 1s(2)2p_0(1)],$$

$$\psi_8^0 = \frac{1}{\sqrt{2}}[1s(1)2p_{-1}(2) + 1s(2)2p_{-1}(1)].$$

$$(7\text{–}39)$$

The resulting functions can be seen to be linear combinations of the original zero-order functions. For example, $\psi_1^0 = (1/\sqrt{2})(\phi_1^0 - \phi_2^0)$ while $\psi_2^0 = (1/\sqrt{2})(\phi_1^0 + \phi_2^0)$. Also it is seen that all these wave functions are either symmetric or antisymmetric to interchange of the electrons, as we have just argued they must.

The resulting energy levels calculated from E^0 and the four E''s are illustrated in Fig. 7–4, where the contributions of the J and K integrals are separated. It can be seen that J_s is smaller than J_p, indicating that the repulsion of a $1s$ electron cloud with a $2s$ cloud is less than the repulsion of a $1s$ cloud with a $2p$ cloud. This results because, when a $2s$ electron penetrates a $1s$ cloud, the repulsion is reduced with that portion of the $1s$ cloud farther from the nucleus than the $2s$ electron. A $2p$ electron does not penetrate as effectively, and hence this reduction in repulsion is not as effective. From the absolute positions of the energy levels, after considering the J interactions, we can state this result in another way. The binding of an electron in a $2p$ level is less strong than the binding of a $2s$ electron. This is as we have argued because the $2s$ electron can penetrate the $1s$ cloud and feel the effect of the nuclear charge. In general, states with the same n and higher values of l are successively less tightly bound and therefore have a higher energy.

The exchange integrals can be seen from their definitions to depend on how extensively the two orbitals involved overlap with one another.

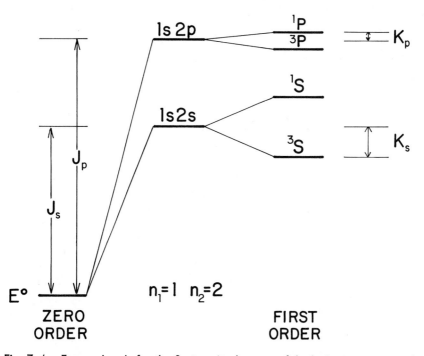

Fig. 7–4.   Energy levels for the first excited states of the helium atom according to first-order perturbation theory.

Since the $2s$ orbital penetrates the $1s$ more effectively, we expect K_s to be larger than K_p.

The neglect of electron spin has not been serious in so far as the energy is concerned. For atoms with small atomic numbers the spin-orbit interaction will have only small effects. The coulombic and exchange effects are by far the most important. It should be pointed out again, however, that these coulombic and exchange energies result from our approximation methods and can be used only qualitatively in comparing different orbitals in terms of overlap, penetration, and similar concepts. A second-order calculation not only will give better energies, but will change the magnitudes and interpretation of the J's and K's somewhat.

Before turning our attention to the important restrictions arising because of electron spin, it is worthwhile to point out an additional important property of the wave functions we have just calculated. The wave functions (7–39) are all eigenfunctions of the orbital angular momentum operator $\hat{L}^2$ and the operator for the z component orbital angular momentum $\hat{L}_z$. These operators can be constructed from the operators for a single particle as suggested in Sec. 6.7; and as mentioned there, they commute with the Hamiltonian operator, which means that the total orbital angular momentum and the z component of this angular momentum can be known exactly for the states of many-electron atoms as well as for single-electron atoms. The eigenvalues of the ground state and excited state wave functions with these two operators are listed in Table 7–3.

TABLE 7–3.   Eigenvalues of Helium Wave Functions with
Orbital Angular Momentum Operators

	Ground State	Excited States							
	ψ_0	ψ_1	ψ_2	ψ_3	ψ_4	ψ_5	ψ_6	ψ_7	ψ_8
$\hat{L}^2$	0	0	0	$2\hbar^2$	$2\hbar^2$	$2\hbar^2$	$2\hbar^2$	$2\hbar^2$	$2\hbar^2$
$\hat{L}_z$	0	0	0	$\hbar$	$\hbar$	0	0	$-\hbar$	$-\hbar$

For single-electron states we denoted the states by a quantum number l for which $|\mathbf{L}|^2 = l(l + 1)\hbar^2$ and the quantum number m_l for which $L_z = m_l\hbar$. In a similar way we can denote states of many-electron atoms by the quantum number L for which $|\mathbf{L}|^2 = L(L + 1)\hbar^2$ and by the quantum number M_L for which $L_z = M_L\hbar$. In addition, just as we described states with $l = 0, 1, 2, 3, \ldots$ as $s, p, d, f, \ldots$ states, so also we label states with $L = 0, 1, 2, 3, \ldots$ as $S, P, D, F, \ldots$ states. Inspection of Table 7–3 shows immediately that, for ψ_0, ψ_1, and ψ_2, $L = 0$, so that these would be described as S states. The remaining states all have $L = 1$ and are therefore P states. The energy levels in Fig. 7–4 were labeled with this nomenclature.

Now for the question of electron spin. Although the instrinsic angular momentum of the electron arises only from relativistic quantum mechanics, exact calculations cannot be made from the relativistic equation for complex systems. We must therefore add in the effect of electron spin by using suitable wave functions that depend only on spin and not on spatial coordinates. In Sec. 6.8 the functions α and β were introduced for this purpose, the former being the function for an electron whose z component of spin angular momentum is $\frac{1}{2}\hbar$ and the latter for an electron with a $-\frac{1}{2}\hbar$ component.

Let us again consider the helium atom, in which there are two electrons. As far as the spin of the electrons is concerned, there are apparently only four possible spin states, represented by the functions

$$\alpha(1)\alpha(2), \qquad \beta(1)\alpha(2),$$
$$\alpha(1)\beta(2), \qquad \beta(1)\beta(2).$$

These four combinations represent all the possible arrangements of the two spins. We note, however, that if we interchange the two electrons, two of these functions are unsatisfactory because they represent situations in which the two electrons could be distinguished from one another by virtue of their spin orientations. Thus we construct two new functions which keep the electrons indistinguishable, by taking the sum and difference of the two unacceptable functions, and this gives us for the four spin functions

$$\alpha(1)\alpha(2)$$
$$\frac{1}{\sqrt{2}}\left[\alpha(1)\beta(2) + \beta(1)\alpha(2)\right]$$
$$\beta(1)\beta(2) \tag{7-40}$$
$$\frac{1}{\sqrt{2}}\left[\alpha(1)\beta(2) - \beta(1)\alpha(2)\right]$$

The first three of these functions are symmetric to interchange of the electrons, while the fourth is antisymmetric. They are normalized and orthogonal.

If we now wish to combine these spin functions with the spatial functions for states of the helium atom, we can see that there are apparently many possibilities. In fact we can form 32 different complete wave functions for the excited states of helium from the eight spatial and four spin functions. Some of these wave functions will be symmetric with respect to electron interchange, while others will be antisymmetric. The question that concerns us is whether all of these 32 excited states of helium actually exist or not.

A number of important physical properties of atomic systems can be shown to depend on the symmetry of the wave functions describing the states of the system. A number of examples will be seen in our spectroscopic discussions. From a study of the spin-orbit interactions and the spectra of helium, it is found experimentally that apparently only those states of helium exist for which the wave functions are antisymmetric to the exchange of electrons. This means that only a few of the 32 wave functions obtained by combining all the spin functions and spatial functions for the excited states of helium need be considered.

Examination of the symmetry of the wave functions constructed above shows that only the following states are antisymmetric. In each, a symmetric spatial function is multiplied by an antisymmetric spin function or, conversely, an antisymmetric spatial function is multiplied by a symmetric spin function. The ground state of helium also is included here, and we have written the over-all configuration of the states to distinguish them more clearly:

$1s^2$

^1S $\psi = [1s(1)1s(2)] \dfrac{1}{\sqrt{2}} [\alpha(1)\beta(2) - \beta(1)\alpha(2)];$

$1s2s$

$^3S \begin{cases} \psi = \dfrac{1}{\sqrt{2}} [1s(1)2s(2) - 2s(1)1s(2)]\alpha(1)\alpha(2), \\[2ex] \psi = \dfrac{1}{\sqrt{2}} [1s(1)2s(2) - 2s(1)1s(2)] \dfrac{1}{\sqrt{2}} [\alpha(1)\beta(2) + \beta(1)\alpha(2)], \\[2ex] \psi = \dfrac{1}{\sqrt{2}} [1s(1)2s(2) - 2s(1)1s(2)]\beta(1)\beta(2); \end{cases}$

^1S $\psi = \dfrac{1}{\sqrt{2}} [1s(1)2s(2) + 2s(1)1s(2)] \dfrac{1}{\sqrt{2}} [\alpha(1)\beta(2) - \beta(1)\alpha(2)];$

$1s2p$

$^3P \begin{cases} \psi = \dfrac{1}{\sqrt{2}} [1s(1)2p_1(2) - 2p_1(1)1s(2)]\alpha(1)\alpha(2), \\[2ex] \psi = \dfrac{1}{\sqrt{2}} [1s(1)2p_1(2) - 2p_1(1)1s(2)] \dfrac{1}{\sqrt{2}} [\alpha(1)\beta(2) + \beta(1)\alpha(2)], \\[2ex] \psi = \dfrac{1}{\sqrt{2}} [1s(1)2p_1(2) - 2p_1(1)1s(2)]\beta(1)\beta(2); \end{cases}$

$^3P \begin{cases} \psi = \dfrac{1}{\sqrt{2}} [1s(1)2p_0(2) - 2p_0(1)1s(2)]\alpha(1)\alpha(2), \\[2ex] \psi = \dfrac{1}{\sqrt{2}} [1s(1)2p_0(2) - 2p_0(1)1s(2)] \dfrac{1}{\sqrt{2}} [\alpha(1)\beta(2) + \beta(1)\alpha(2)], \\[2ex] \psi = \dfrac{1}{\sqrt{2}} [1s(1)2p_0(2) - 2p_0(1)1s(2)]\beta(1)\beta(2); \end{cases}$

$^3P \begin{cases} \psi = \dfrac{1}{\sqrt{2}} [1s(1)2p_{-1}(2) - 2p_{-1}(1)1s(2)]\alpha(1)\alpha(2), \\[2ex] \psi = \dfrac{1}{\sqrt{2}} [1s(1)2p_{-1}(2) - 2p_{-1}(1)1s(2)] \dfrac{1}{\sqrt{2}} [\alpha(1)\beta(2) + \beta(1)\alpha(2)], \\[2ex] \psi = \dfrac{1}{\sqrt{2}} [1s(1)2p_{-1}(2) - 2p_{-1}(1)1s(2)]\beta(1)\beta(2); \end{cases}$

$$^1P \quad \psi = \frac{1}{\sqrt{2}}[1s(1)2p_1(2) + 2p_1(1)1s(2)]\frac{1}{\sqrt{2}}[\alpha(1)\beta(2) - \beta(1)\alpha(2)];$$

$$^1P \quad \psi = \frac{1}{\sqrt{2}}[1s(1)2p_0(2) + 2p_0(1)1s(2)]\frac{1}{\sqrt{2}}[\alpha(1)\beta(2) - \beta(1)\alpha(2)];$$

$$^1P \quad \psi = \frac{1}{\sqrt{2}}[1s(1)2p_{-1}(2) + 2p_{-1}(1)1s(2)]\frac{1}{\sqrt{2}}[\alpha(1)\beta(2) - \beta(1)\alpha(2)].$$

Our first-order perturbation treatment in Sec. 7.3 resulted in one ground-state energy level corresponding to the $1s^2\,^1S$ function. For the $n = 1$, $n = 2$ excited state, we have obtained four energy levels. The lowest of these corresponds to the spatial wave function contained in the three complete wave functions labeled $1s2s\,^3S$. We thus see that when we include spin in the wave function, this level turns out to be a "triplet" of degenerate states, each of the states having a different arrangement of the electron spins.

The next excited level was obtained for the state having the spatial function designated $1s2s\,^1S$, so we see that this level is not degenerate and has only one spin arrangement.

The next two levels correspond to the $1s2p$ configuration. The lowest of these represents the states labeled ^3P and we see that these correspond to three sets of "triplets." In this particular atom the degeneracy of the p orbitals makes this level more degenerate than might be found in other situations. Finally the highest level is again a degenerate level occupied by the ^1P states. This level can be considered to be three degenerate singlet states.

If we examine the properties of the spin functions (7–40) we find that these functions are eigenfunctions of the total spin angular momentum operators $\hat{S}^2$ and $\hat{S}_z$. By analogy with the notation for the spin angular momentum of a single particle and with other forms of angular momentum, the quantum numbers of interest are S for which $|\mathbf{S}|^2 = S(S + 1)\hbar^2$ and M_S for which $S_z = M_S\hbar$. The eigenvalues of the spin functions with these operators lead to the identification of the states by the quantum numbers S and M_S as follows:

Triplet states:

$$\alpha(1)\alpha(2), \qquad\qquad\qquad S = 1, \quad M_S = 1,$$

$$\frac{1}{\sqrt{2}}[\alpha(1)\beta(2) + \beta(1)\alpha(2)], \quad S = 1, \quad M_S = 0,$$

$$\beta(1)\beta(2), \qquad\qquad\qquad S = 1, \quad M_S = -1;$$

Singlet state:

$$\frac{1}{\sqrt{2}}[\alpha(1)\beta(2) - \beta(1)\alpha(2)], \quad S = 0, \quad M_S = 0.$$

These results should make clear the differences in the properties of the various states we have studied so far. The ground state of helium has no orbital angular momentum, being made up of two electrons that have no orbital angular momentum (s electrons). In addition, the spins of these electrons are opposed, so that the resulting atom has no net spin angular momentum either.

If one of the electrons is excited to the $n = 2$ level, several possibilities arise. The excited state of lowest energy is one in which the atom has no orbital angular momentum, since the two electrons are individually without orbital angular momentum. In this state, however, the atom does have a net spin angular momentum resulting from the coupling of the individual electron spins, so that they are "unpaired." This net spin angular momentum results in there being three states of this energy, each with a different component of the spin angular momentum along the z direction as denoted by the value of M_S in each case. We saw from our first-order perturbation calculation that this was the lowest excited state because of the penetration and overlap of the $1s$ and $2s$ electron clouds.

The next excited state also represents the $1s2s$ configuration, but in this level the electron spins are paired, so that there is no net spin angular momentum. Hence there is only one state for this level. At this stage we may well ask why the triplet state with unpaired electrons is of lower energy than the singlet state with paired electrons, especially since in chemical bonding we associate electron pairing with stable systems. The answer is seen in the symmetry of the functions for these two levels. When the electrons are paired, the spin function is antisymmetric, which requires a symmetric spatial function to retain antisymmetry of the complete wave function. We note that for a symmetric spatial function such as that in the singlet excited state, if the two electrons have the same coordinates (are at the same point in space), the wave function has a finite value. On the other hand, for an antisymmetric spatial function as found with unpaired electron triplet states, the wave function vanishes if the coordinates of the electrons are identical. In other words, there is an exceedingly small probability that the electrons can approach one another in a triplet state. Since electrons have the same charge sign they repel, and hence states in which electrons can come close together (the singlet state) should have a higher energy because of this repulsion energy than triplet states, where the antisymmetry of the spatial function keeps the electrons separated.

The higher excited states of helium can be interpreted in the same manner with a greater degree of degeneracy because the three $2p$ orbitals are degenerate.

The singlet-triplet character of the energy levels is also included in the nomenclature used to label these levels.   In particular the notation as to whether the level is singlet or triplet is put at the upper left-hand corner of the letter that denotes the value of L for the states in that level. Thus the ground state for helium is denoted ^1S and the excited states are ^3S, ^1S, ^3P, and ^1P respectively.   Note also that the singlet-triplet character can be found from the spin quantum number as equal to $2S + 1$.

In selecting these states for helium, we used experimental criteria for neglecting all the symmetric states.   A vast amount of experimental and theoretical evidence leads to an important postulate, which is actually a mathematical version of the *Pauli exclusion principle*.   This postulate says that the total wave function corresponding to any system occurring in nature must change sign on permutation of any pair of electrons in the system.   That is, all wave functions must be antisymmetric to the interchange of any two electrons.   Inspection of the wave functions for helium will disclose that this statement is equivalent to the more familiar one which says that no two electrons in an atom may have simultaneously the same four quantum numbers n, l, m_l, and m_s.

The Pauli exclusion principle and the antisymmetry of wave functions with respect to electron interchange are an extremely important factor governing the properties of matter.   The exclusion principle as stated above actually applies to all particles with half-integral spin.   Thus electrons, protons, neutrons, and nuclei with half-integral spin (odd mass numbers) are described by wave functions which are antisymmetric to interchange of these particles.   Particles with integral spin, such as deuterons, alpha particles, and photons, have symmetric wave functions. We shall observe a number of important consequences of these rules.

7.6   THE STATES OF COMPLEX ATOMS AND THE PERIODIC TABLE

We have dwelt at some length on the states of the helium atom because these can be calculated directly from simple hydrogen-like functions by perturbation and variation methods.   This investigation also allowed us to note in its simplest form some of the nomenclature and terminology involved with atomic states.   We will examine the extension of these ideas to more complex systems only very briefly.

Not the least of the problems involved is to write a suitable set of wave functions for a many-electron atom.   In the variation method many kinds of functions with variable parameters have been used, even including such things as Gaussian functions.   When using the perturbation method we select hydrogen-like functions which are solutions of the zero-order Schrödinger equation that does not include the electron repulsions.   We have seen that the particular energy level of interest in the atom may be manyfold degenerate, depending on the number of electrons and the number of orbitals used. In the helium atom it was possible to use the wave functions obtained by these various combinations, solve the secular equation directly for the perturbation energies, and then obtain the correct wave functions for these levels. In more complicated systems it may well not be possible to solve the secular equation, however. We can avoid much of the difficulty to begin with if we construct wave functions which already have the correct antisymmetry to exchange of the electrons. Slater has shown that for an energy level which places electrons 1, 2, 3, . . . , n in the orbitals whose wave functions are ϕ_a, ϕ_b, ϕ_c, . . . , ϕ_γ (some of these orbitals may be the same), a satisfactory antisymmetric function can be written as the determinant

$$\psi^0 = \frac{1}{\sqrt{n!}} \begin{vmatrix} \phi_a(1) & \phi_b(1) & \cdots & \phi_\gamma(1) \\ \phi_a(2) & \phi_b(2) & \cdots & \phi_\gamma(2) \\ \cdots & \cdots & \cdots & \cdots \\ \phi_a(n) & \phi_b(n) & \cdots & \phi_\gamma(n) \end{vmatrix},$$

where the ϕ's contain both the spin and the spatial properties. Thus for the ground state of lithium ($1s^2 2s$)

$$\psi^0 = \frac{1}{\sqrt{6}} \begin{vmatrix} 1s\alpha(1) & 1s\beta(1) & 2s\alpha(1) \\ 1s\alpha(2) & 1s\beta(2) & 2s\alpha(2) \\ 1s\alpha(3) & 1s\beta(3) & 2s\alpha(3) \end{vmatrix}.$$

Even with proper wave functions to begin with, the secular equation may not be diagonal, of course; for degeneracies may not be removed by the electronic repulsion perturbation. In getting the secular determinant into diagonal form, or as close to it as possible, use is made of the angular-momentum properties of the wave functions to sort out which states are which. Although this can be done in principle for any system, it is simpler to state the end results in a less complicated form in order to compare states and make predictions without detailed calculations.

The angular-momentum properties of atomic states are the most significant pieces of information. We have seen that the various kinds of angular momentum in a system can interact with one another in different ways. The important interactions are electrostatic or electrodynamic in nature, and their net result is to separate in energy states with different angular momenta. In Chapter 6 we observed that when a force is applied to a system having angular momentum, a torque is exerted on the angular momentum vector, causing it to precess. The important internal electrical forces in atoms can be considered to be the interaction of individual electronic orbital angular momenta with one another and the interaction of individual spin angular momenta with one another.

The interaction of the individual orbital angular momenta is such that they tend to precess about a common direction which represents the total orbital angular momentum of the atom. The relative orientations of these individual momentum vectors can assume different values, however, resulting in several possible states with different total orbital angular momentum. The interaction can be viewed rather simply by considering the individual orbital angular-momentum vectors and adding them according to the empirical rule (which follows from the observed properties of angular momentum and angular-momentum operators) that the total orbital angular-momentum quantum number can assume the values

$$L = l_1 + l_2, l_1 + l_2 - 1, l_1 + l_2 - 2, \ldots, |l_1 - l_2|. \quad (7\text{--}41)$$

In the case in which for electron one $l_1 = 1$ and for electron two $l_2 = 2$, the possible values of the total orbital angular-momentum quantum number would be $L = 3, 2, 1$. Or if $l_1 = 2$ and $l_2 = 2$, then $L = 4, 3, 2, 1, 0$ are possible. Other examples can be written out easily. The magnitudes of the angular momentum vectors are not actually l_1, l_2, etc., so that although we are adding the quantum numbers directly, the angular-momentum vectors are not actually aligned parallel to one another. We are really adding the z components, which leads us to the integral differences given by the rule. The angular-momentum vectors are precessing about a common direction as shown in Fig. 7–5, and along this direction $L\hbar$ is the maximum component ($L = M_L$) of the total orbital momentum. If there are more than two electrons, we can apply the rule of (7–41) to two of them, and then apply the rule a second time to each combination of the resultant L's with the third l, and so on.

If a state exists for which L has a certain value, then there must actually be $2L + 1$ states with that value of L, corresponding to the different possible orientations of **L** with respect to the z direction. We shall see shortly that this criterion is helpful in deciding which of several possible states are actually present.

The electrical interactions also cause the spin angular momenta of the electrons to couple by the same sort of rule as applies to orbital angular momenta, i.e.,

$$S = s_1 + s_2, s_1 + s_2 - 1, \ldots, |s_1 - s_2|. \quad (7\text{--}42)$$

In this case the problem is simpler because all the individual s's are $\frac{1}{2}$. Thus for two electrons $S = 1, 0$, for three electrons $S = \frac{3}{2}, \frac{1}{2}$, and so on. Again, for a given value of S there are $2S + 1$ states corresponding to the different orientations of **S** with respect to an external direction. The components of **S** along this direction are given by M_S, which can have the values $S, S - 1, \ldots, -S$.

Although (7–41) and (7–42) predict which states of a complex atom are possible, they do not determine whether all these states will actually exist. Use of the Pauli exclusion principle and consideration of the degeneracies arising from different values of M_L and M_S will help to solve this problem.

An example of how the possible states arising from a given electron configuration can be determined is illustrated by the case of two electrons

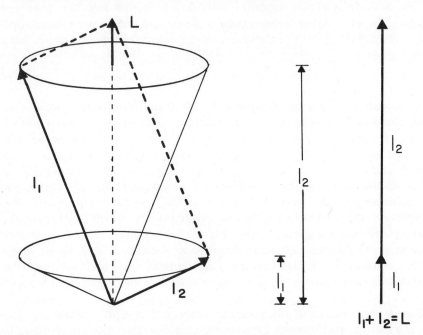

Fig. 7–5. Coupling of two electronic orbital angular momenta to give a resultant total orbital angular momentum for the atom.

in different p orbitals, say a $2p3p$ configuration. With $l_1 = 1$ and $l_2 = 1$ we expect that L can be 2, 1, or 0. Thus we may have D, P, and S states. In addition, with two spins we can have $S = 1$ and 0. Applying the relation mentioned in Sec. 7.5 that the multiplicity of a state is $2S + 1$, we then predict that we can have the following states: ^3D, ^1D, ^3P, ^1P, ^3S, ^1S. Are all these actually possible? If the two electrons are in different levels, then we do not have to be concerned with the Pauli exclusion principle, and all possible spin combinations should be possible. Thus we expect all the above states to be allowed. In addition, if we attempted a perturbation calculation for the $2p3p$ configuration, we would have nine spatial functions (each p orbital is threefold degenerate with p_0, p_1, and p_{-1}) times four spin functions (as for helium), or 36 degenerate zero-order functions. We thus expect 36 states in the perturbed atom, and they are as follows:

State	Number of Orbital Degeneracies $(2L + 1)$	Number of Spin Degeneracies $(2S + 1)$	Total Number of States
^3D	5	3	15
^1D	5	1	5
^3P	3	3	9
^1P	3	1	3
^3S	1	3	3
^1S	1	1	1
			36

Suppose, however, that the two p electrons were in the same shell, say $2p^2$. Immediately the Pauli exclusion principle becomes important. We know, for example, that if the two electrons are in the same orbital, they must have their spins paired. Thus, for the spatial functions $2p_0(1)2p_0(2)$, $2p_1(1)2p_1(2)$, $2p_{-1}(1)2p_{-1}(2)$ there can be no spin degeneracies; only the antisymmetric spin function is satisfactory in each case. In addition, if each electron is in a separate orbital, the spins may be paired or unpaired. For each pair of orbitals involved in the spatial part of the wave function, there are then four possible spin functions. There are three possible pairs of orbitals to be used and therefore 12 possible states including spin. Altogether this gives us only 15 possible states if both electrons are in the same shell.

It is not difficult to tell which states this involves. If $L = 2$, then there are five states corresponding to situations where $M_L = 2$, 1, 0, -1, -2. If this were a ^3D state, that would use up all our possible 15 states, and in addition our analysis using the Pauli principle shows that there are only nine possible states with unpaired spins. Therefore the state with $L = 2$ must be a ^1D state. There are now ten states left since the ^1D level is fivefold degenerate. Clearly from the nine possible unpaired electron arrangements, we can have a ^3P level. Here then we have states with $M_L = 1$, 0, and -1 with each threefold degenerate in spin, a total of nine states. There is only one state left and this then must be a ^1S which is not degenerate in spin or orbital components.

We will not attempt a more detailed analysis of these states, but the allowed multiplet terms for a number of cases are listed in Table 7–4 for reference and can be verified by these methods. The reader may consult to the references for more details.

In light atoms the coupling of spin angular momenta to form a total spin moment, and the coupling of orbital momenta to form a total orbital angular momentum, both by electrical mechanisms, is the most important interaction in terms of the energy levels of the different states. We have seen, however, that there is an additional interaction between spin and orbital angular momenta which is magnetic rather than electrical in nature. In atoms of small atomic number this interaction is small compared to the effects we have just discussed. As a result, we find that in the lighter atoms the strong electrical couplings give us a total spin and total orbital angular momentum, and the much smaller magnetic coupling is between these total spin and orbital moments rather than between individual electron moments. The nature of this interaction

TABLE 7–4. Multiplet Terms of Various Electron Configurations

EQUIVALENT ELECTRONS

s^2, p^6, and d^{10}	^1S
p and p^5	^2P
p^2 and p^4	^3P, ^1D, ^1S
p^3	^4S, ^2D, ^2P
d and d^9	^2D
d^2 and d^8	^3F, ^3P, ^1G, ^1D, ^1S
d^3 and d^7	^4F, ^4P, ^2H, ^2G, ^2F, ^2D, ^2D, ^2P
d^4 and d^6	^5D, ^3H, ^3G, ^3F, ^3F, ^3D, ^3P, ^3P, ^1I, ^1G, ^1G, ^1F, ^1D, ^1D, ^1S, ^1S
d^5	^6S, ^4G, ^4F, ^4D, ^4P, ^2I, ^2H, ^2G, ^2G, ^2F, ^2F, ^2D, ^2D, ^2D, ^2P, ^2S

NON-EQUIVALENT ELECTRONS

$s\ s$	^1S, ^3S
$s\ p$	^1P, ^3P
$s\ d$	^1D, ^3D
$p\ p$	^3D, ^1D, ^3P, ^1P, ^3S, ^1S
$p\ d$	^3F, ^1F, ^3D, ^1D, ^3P, ^1P
$d\ d$	^3G, ^1G, ^3F, ^1F, ^3D, ^1D, ^3P, ^1P, ^3S, ^1S
$s\ s\ s$	^4S, ^2S, ^2S
$s\ s\ p$	^4P, ^2P, ^2P
$s\ p\ p$	^4D, ^2D, ^2D, ^4P, ^2P, ^2P, ^4S, ^2S, ^2S
$s\ p\ d$	^4F, ^2F, ^2F, ^4D, ^2D, ^2D, ^4P, ^2P, ^2P

was discussed in Chapter 6 and the coupling via this mechanism gives rise finally to a total angular momentum for the atom as a result of the interaction of the spin and orbital angular momenta.

As with the other kinds of angular momentum, the total angular momentum is denoted by a quantum number J for which $|\mathbf{J}|^2 = J(J+1)\hbar^2$ and $J_z = M_J\hbar$ where $M_J = J,\ J-1,\ \ldots,\ -J$, as with the other z component quantum numbers. The properties of the angular momenta and their operators again result in the rule that states with a given value of L and a given value of S can couple in several different ways to give states with

$$J = L + S,\ L + S - 1,\ \ldots,\ |L - S|. \qquad (7\text{--}43)$$

As a result, any level with a given L and S will actually consist of several levels with different values of J given by (7–43), but the separation of these levels will be much smaller than the separation of levels with different values of L or S.

In heavier atoms the spin-orbit interaction becomes great enough that the coupling scheme described here begins to break down; that is, the spin and orbital momenta of the individual electrons tend to interact via the magnetic interaction to form a resultant **j** for the electron, and the individual **j**'s then interact electrically to form a total **J** for the atom. The former type of coupling is called Russell-Saunders or LS coupling

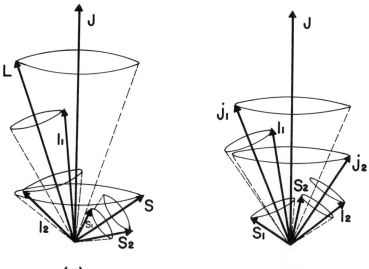

(a)   **(b)**

Fig. 7–6. (a) Russell-Saunders (LS) coupling of spin and orbital angular momenta. (b) jj coupling of spin and orbital angular momenta.

and is of the most importance in simple atoms. The latter, called jj coupling, and intermediate cases will not be considered here. These two types of coupling are illustrated in Fig. 7–6.

It is possible to make some general statements about the relative orders of the energies of states as predicted from the above procedures. The most convenient of these are included in what is known as Hund's rule, which states, in the order of decreasing importance as far as energy is concerned:

1. For the same value of L, states with higher S lie lower in energy;
2. For the same value of S, states with higher L lie lower;
3. When a shell of electrons is less than half full, states with lower J are lower in energy. When a shell is more than half full, states with higher J lie lower.

The first two of these rules have been verified earlier in this chapter for helium.

The generalized nomenclature for atomic states is extremely useful because it incorporates the most important properties of the states and points up similarities between different configurations.   It must be

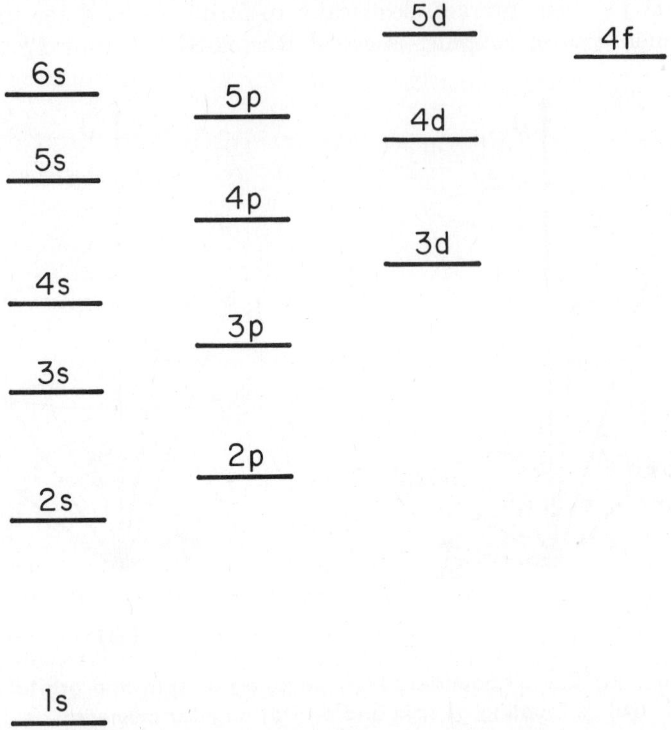

Fig. 7–7. Relative energies of hydrogen-like orbitals in a complex atom. Although the actual position of each level differs from atom to atom, this order represents the order in which the levels would be filled by successive addition of electrons, beginning with the one-electron hydrogen atom and progressing to more complex atoms.

remembered that in reality an atom in its ground state or some excited state is an entity having certain properties such as angular momentum which we may be able to measure.   In reality, we cannot say what the behavior of each individual electron in the system is.   We have merely used arguments as to how hydrogen-like electrons will be affected by all the attractions, repulsions, and other interactions.

Perhaps the most important factor in the behavior of atoms as far as the chemist is concerned is the periodic nature of atomic properties.   It is interesting to note that these properties would be quite different if nature did not behave in a way described by antisymmetric wave functions for electrons. It is because of this restriction that only two electrons will go in an s orbital, six in p orbitals, and so on. This is perhaps a misleading statement, since the properties of matter are what determine the theory which we use to explain those properties. Nevertheless, as far as a theoretical explanation is concerned, the Pauli exclusion principle is probably the most fundamental law of nature with regard to the properties of matter.

By considering the effects of electron penetration, repulsion, spin-orbit coupling, etc., physical chemists have established a fairly firm foundation for understanding the individual properties of atoms. The highly stable rare gases, alkali metal ions, and halide ions are verified by theory. The size of atoms, the order of the energies of hydrogen-like orbitals (Fig. 7–7), and similar properties can be predicted. It is possible also to offer explanations for the behavior of interesting systems, like the transition metals, on the basis of the relative energies of different orbitals. All these phenomena are discussed extensively in many textbooks on atomic structure and chemical bonding and will not be discussed at this time.

7.7   TIME–DEPENDENT PERTURBATION, TRANSITIONS, AND SELECTION RULES

By this time the power of quantum mechanics should be evident. Even though complex systems require approximation methods, a multitude of problems have resulted in solutions that agree remarkably with experiment. Quantum mechanics also provides a theoretical explanation for many phenomena that were even contrary to the expectation of earlier theories. There is, however, a major difficulty with the approach we have taken thus far. The eigenfunctions that are solutions of the time-independent Schrödinger equation represent states of systems whose energies are unchanging with time, and if a system does not change, then we are not likely to observe any phenomena of interest. Any piece of information we can obtain about an atomic or molecular system requires disturbing the system for a greater or lesser time and observing the changes that take place. These interactions may involve the application of electric or magnetic fields, collisions with other particles, electromagnetic radiation, or similar effects. Up to this time we have no assurance that these interactions will involve the stationary states we have studied in such a way that we can verify any of our conclusions.

Because perturbations such as those just mentioned will generally not remain constant with time, it is necessary to return to the general Schrödinger equation (3–5). Let us first assume that, for the system of interest unperturbed by the radiation or collisions which we will shortly use, we can solve the equation

$$\mathcal{H}^0 \Psi^0 = i\hbar \frac{\partial \Psi^0}{\partial t} \qquad (7\text{--}44)$$

for the stationary state wave functions and their energies. That is, in the absence of the perturbation, the potential energy is dependent only on position, and we can obtain the various time-independent wave functions ψ_j^0 from solution of

$$\mathcal{H}^0 \psi_j^0 = E_j^0 \psi_j^0.$$

The complete wave functions corresponding to these solutions would be given by

$$\Psi_j^0 = \psi_j^0 e^{-iE_j t/\hbar}.$$

Although each Ψ_j^0 represents a stationary state of the system, the most general solution of (7–44) would be

$$\Psi^0 = \sum_{j=0}^{\infty} a_j \Psi_j^0, \qquad (7\text{--}45)$$

where for normalization it is necessary that

$$\sum_j a_j{}^* a_j = 1.$$

It is recalled from Postulate V in Chapter 3 that $a_j{}^* a_j$ is a measure of the probability that upon measurement the system be found in the particular eigenstate Ψ_j^0 with energy E_j^0. Thus, although Ψ^0 is a general function, we can determine from the coefficients in its expansion (7–45) the probability that we shall find the system in each particular eigenstate.

Let us now assume that when the system is perturbed, the Hamiltonian operator can be written as the unperturbed Hamiltonian above, plus a perturbing term $\mathcal{H}'$, which may depend on time, the coordinates of the system, and momentum. Thus, the equation we wish to solve, including the perturbation, is

$$(\mathcal{H}^0 + \mathcal{H}')\Psi = i\hbar \frac{\partial \Psi}{\partial t}. \qquad (7\text{--}46)$$

The wave function Ψ is, of course, time-dependent, and to treat both the spatial and time dependence of this function would be an extremely difficult problem. Instead, we will take a simpler approach and assume that, at any time t, the wave function for the perturbed system can be written as

$$\Psi = \sum_j a_j(t)\Psi_j^0, \qquad (7\text{--}47)$$

where the coefficients $a_j(t)$ are dependent on time. In other words, instead of considering a complex function of unknown form, which depends on coordinates and on time, we will assume that the effect of the perturbation will be to change the probabilities that the system be in its different unperturbed eigenstates. In this way we can still describe the system in terms of the known $\Psi_j{}^0$'s, and need be concerned only with the time variation of the $a_j(t)$'s.

If the function (7–47) is substituted into the wave equation (7–46), we obtain

$$\sum_j a_j(t)\mathfrak{K}^0\Psi_j{}^0 + \sum_j a_j(t)\mathfrak{K}'\Psi_j{}^0 = i\hbar \sum_j \frac{da_j(t)}{dt}\Psi_j{}^0 + i\hbar \sum_j a_j(t)\frac{\partial\Psi_j{}^0}{\partial t},$$

in which the first and last terms cancel because the $\Psi_j{}^0$ are eigenfunctions of $\mathfrak{K}^0$. We are left, then, with

$$\sum_j \frac{da_j(t)}{dt}\Psi_j{}^0 = -\frac{i}{\hbar}\sum_j a_j(t)\mathfrak{K}'\Psi_j{}^0. \tag{7–48}$$

Taking advantage of the orthogonality of the unperturbed functions, we next multiply both sides of (7–48) by the function $\Psi_k{}^{0*}$ and integrate over all configuration space. Because of the orthonormality of the $\Psi_j{}^0$ we obtain

$$\frac{da_k(t)}{dt} = -\frac{i}{\hbar}\sum_{j=0}^{\infty} a_j(t)\langle k|\mathfrak{K}'|j\rangle, \quad k = 0, 1, 2, \ldots \tag{7–49}$$

Thus, when a perturbation has been applied, we can find the rate at which any one coefficient changes from an infinite sum of matrix elements involving all the unperturbed states. In addition, there will be an infinite number of such expressions, one for the time variation of each of the infinite number of coefficients.

This result is simplified if we can assume that, before the perturbation is applied the system is known with certainty to be in one particular quantum state $\Psi_n{}^0$. In this event all the a_j's are zero at $t = 0$ except $a_n(0)$, which is unity. If the perturbation $\mathfrak{K}'$ is small, then we can assume that even after a period of time $a_n(t)$ is still nearly unity, and only the state $\Psi_n{}^0$ contributes to Eq. (7–49). We can therefore neglect all the other terms. Thus the rate of change of the coefficient for the kth state becomes

$$\frac{da_k(t)}{dt} = -\frac{i}{\hbar}\langle k|\mathfrak{K}'|n\rangle = -\frac{i}{\hbar}H'_{kn}, \tag{7–50}$$

in which we have assumed $a_n(t) = a_n(0) = 1$ and have introduced the customary shorthand notation for the matrix element. If the matrix element is defined in terms of the time-independent wave functions $\psi_j{}^0$, then (7–50) becomes

$$\frac{da_k(t)}{dt} = -\frac{i}{\hbar} H'_{kn} e^{(E_k - E_n)it/\hbar}. \tag{7-51}$$

The situation confronting us therefore is as follows: In the absence of perturbing radiation or other interactions, we can solve a time-independent Schrödinger equation and obtain stationary-state energies and wave functions. If we construct a general solution, we can determine from the coefficients in its expansion the probability that we observe the system to be in a particular stationary state. For the sake of simplicity, however, we usually assume that we know that the system is initially in a particular stationary state, the nth, we apply the perturbation for a period of time, and then we look to see which of the stationary states now have finite coefficients. We interpret the appearance of a coefficient for these additional stationary states as a measure of the probability that transitions from the nth state to these states can be induced by the perturbation. This is illustrated schematically in Fig. 7–8.

From Eq. (7–51) we can see that transitions will take place from the nth state only to those states for which the matrix element H'_{kn} is finite. Such transitions are said to be *allowed* for the particular system and perturbation in question. If the matrix element connecting the initial and final states n and k is zero, then even after the perturbation has been applied for a period of time the probability that the system is now in the kth state will be zero and hence the transition is said to be *forbidden*. Because the wave functions for most systems have characteristic symmetry properties that are related to the quantum numbers describing the states, it is possible to deduce from an investigation of the matrix elements H'_{kn} which changes in the quantum numbers correspond to allowed or forbidden transitions. These shorthand descriptions are called *selection rules*. Our main problem, then, is to determine the selection rules for a given situation so that we can predict what transitions can take place and hence deduce what energy levels are involved in the observed phenomenon.

In view of our interest in spectroscopic methods, the most important perturbation to be considered is the interaction of electromagnetic radiation with matter. Although the recently expanding field of quantum electrodynamics has yet to solve rigorously all the problems of these interactions, we can make some approximate forays into the question and obtain some useful results.

The classical view of electromagnetic radiation is that light consists of oscillating electric and magnetic fields which are perpendicular to the direction of the propagating beam. We can deal with the interaction of this radiation by breaking it down into the interactions of the particles with the separate electric and magnetic fields. In order to construct a

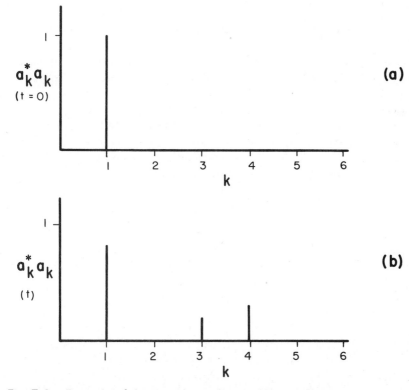

Fig. 7–8.   Example of the time dependence of the coefficients a_k.   At $t = 0$ it is assumed $a_1{}^*a_1$ is unity and all other a_k's are zero.   The system is thus known with certainty to be in the first state.   After a time t, several of the other states have finite a_k's, indicating that there is now a certain probability that the system initially in the first state may now be in one of these states, i.e., a transition has occurred.

Hamiltonian operator in quantum mechanics, however, it is more useful to use a more general formalism where the electromagnetic field is described by the vector potential **A** and the scalar potential ϕ (Appendix F).   These are related to the more familiar electric and magnetic field strengths, **E** and **H**, by the equations

$$ \mathbf{H} = \nabla \times \mathbf{A}; \qquad \mathbf{E} = -\frac{1}{c}\frac{\partial}{\partial t}\mathbf{A} - \nabla\phi. $$

A detailed analysis of the force exerted on a charged particle moving in an electromagnetic field results in the Hamiltonian operator

$$ \mathcal{H} = \frac{1}{2m}\left(-\hbar^2\nabla^2 + i\hbar\frac{e}{c}\nabla\cdot\mathbf{A} + 2i\hbar\frac{e}{c}\mathbf{A}\cdot\nabla + \frac{e^2}{c^2}|\mathbf{A}|^2 \right) + e\phi. $$

The first term in this Hamiltonian is the familiar kinetic-energy term for the particle, while the other terms represent the perturbations caused by the radiation. For several particles, we would have a summation of the above terms for each particle, and there would probably be an additional term, V, to represent the internal potential energy of the system of particles. Fortunately this Hamiltonian seldom needs to be used in its entirety. For the electromagnetic field associated with a light wave $\nabla \cdot \mathbf{A} = 0$ and $\phi = 0$. In addition the term $(e^2/c^2)|\mathbf{A}|^2$ can be neglected unless there are strong magnetic fields. Finally we note that $i\hbar\, \mathbf{A} \cdot \nabla$ is equivalent to $-\mathbf{A} \cdot \hat{\mathbf{p}}$. These considerations lead to a much simpler form for the perturbation Hamiltonian term,

$$\mathcal{H}' = -\sum_i \frac{e}{m_i c}\, \mathbf{A}_i \cdot \hat{\mathbf{p}}_i,$$

where the terms are summed over all the particles i in the system, and the unperturbed Hamiltonian is composed of the remaining terms:

$$\mathcal{H}^0 = -\sum_i \frac{\hbar^2}{2m_i}\, \nabla_i{}^2 + V.$$

Since $\mathbf{A}$ is a vector quantity, it can be described in terms of its components, and for the sake of simplicity let us assume for the moment that the radiation is plane-polarized, so that $\mathbf{A}_y$ and $\mathbf{A}_z$ are zero. In this case,

$$\mathcal{H}' = -\sum_i \frac{e}{m_i c}\, \mathbf{A}_{x_i}\hat{p}_{x_i}.$$

We also note at this stage that atomic and molecular dimensions are extremely small compared to the wavelength of visible light. Even though $\mathbf{A}$ may change with time, we may consider that at any instant $\mathbf{A}$ is constant over the space occupied by the atomic or molecular wave function. Thus, when considering the perturbation matrix elements containing $\mathcal{H}'$ we can regard $\mathbf{A}$ as constant over the space integration. Thus, a matrix element in (7–51) becomes

$$H'_{kn} = \langle k|\mathcal{H}'|n\rangle = \left\langle k \left| -\sum_i \frac{e}{m_i c}\, \mathbf{A}_{x_i}\hat{p}_{x_i} \right| n \right\rangle$$

$$= -\frac{e}{c}\, \mathbf{A}_x \sum_i \frac{1}{m_i} \langle k|\hat{p}_{x_i}|n\rangle$$

$$= \frac{e}{c}\, i\hbar\, \mathbf{A}_x \sum_i \frac{1}{m_i} \left\langle k \left| \frac{\partial}{\partial x_i} \right| n \right\rangle.$$

It is possible to show (Appendix G) that the matrix element in this equation is equivalent to a simpler integral

$$\left\langle k \left| \frac{\partial}{\partial x} \right| n \right\rangle = -\frac{m}{\hbar^2} (E_k - E_n) \langle k|x|n \rangle,$$

so that

$$\begin{aligned} H'_{kn} &= -\frac{e}{c}\frac{i}{\hbar} A_x (E_k - E_n) \sum_i \langle k|x_i|n \rangle \\ &= -\frac{1}{c}\frac{i}{\hbar} A_x (E_k - E_n) \langle k|e \sum_i x_i|n \rangle \\ &= -\frac{1}{c}\frac{i}{\hbar} A_x (E_k - E_n) (\mu_x)_{kn}. \end{aligned} \qquad (7\text{-}52)$$

The form of the operator in this matrix element is identical with the classical expression for the electric dipole moment of a system of point

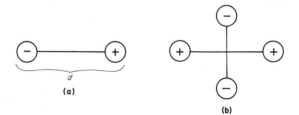

Fig. 7–9. Simple examples of (a) an electric dipole and (b) an electric quadrupole.

charges e. The simple and familiar case of an electric dipole is the arrangement of two charges $+q$ and $-q$ separated by a distance d, from which the dipole moment is defined as $\mu = qd$ (Fig. 7–9a). The electric field arising in space around the dipole has a characteristic magnitude and symmetry, which depends on μ and its orientation. For a system of point charges of magnitude e, the electric field surrounding the system can, at least in part (depending on the arrangement of the charges), be described as that arising from a dipole whose magnitude and direction are defined by

$$\boldsymbol{\mu} = e\mathbf{r} = e \sum_i \mathbf{r}_i,$$

or

$$\mu_x = e \sum_i x_i, \quad \mu_y = e \sum_i y_i, \quad \mu_z = e \sum_i z_i.$$

Magnetic fields of a symmetry similar to that of the electric field produced by an electric dipole moment are thought of as arising from a magnetic dipole moment, although we have observed that such a field does not actually result from a system of magnetic poles analogous to electric charges, but instead is the result of the circulation of electric charges. For a system of electronic point charges, the magnetic dipole moment is defined as

$$\mathbf{u}_m = \frac{e}{2mc}\,\mathbf{r} \times \mathbf{p} = \frac{e}{2mc}\,\sum_i \mathbf{r}_i \times \mathbf{p}_i.$$

The electric potential around a single charge (monopole) is proportional to $1/r$, while that of a dipole decreases with distance from the dipole more rapidly, as $1/r^2$. In a system of charges it may be found that the system has no dipole moment, but that the system is surrounded by an electric field which falls off as $1/r^3$. This collection of charges is called an electric quadrupole, and the quadrupole moment of the system is

$$eQ = e\mathbf{r}\mathbf{r} = \sum_i e_i\mathbf{r}_i\mathbf{r}_i,$$

where the last term is a sum of dyads (second-rank tensors). More simply,

$$eQ = \sum_i e_i\,\overline{(3z_i^2 - r_i^2)}.$$

A simple example of an electric quadrupole is illustrated in Fig. 7–9b.

Other distributions giving rise to other kinds of electric fields (such as the electric octapole field) can be defined, but they are relatively insignificant to the order with which we are concerned here. Any real system of charges is likely to have an electric field which is not purely that of a dipole or quadrupole or octapole, but which can be described as a combination of these kinds of fields, each defined as above.

For these reasons $(\mu_x)_{kn}$ in Eq. (7–52) is called the matrix element for the x component of the electric dipole moment. Inserting (7–52) into (7–51) we obtain

$$\frac{da_k(t)}{dt} = -\frac{1}{c\hbar^2}\,\mathbf{A}_x(E_k - E_n)(\mu_x)_{kn}e^{i(E_k-E_n)t/\hbar}.$$

As we remarked previously, if $(\mu_x)_{kn}$ vanishes, then da_k/dt is zero, and no transition from n to k can be caused by radiation polarized in the x direction.

If the radiation is of frequency ν, then the time dependence of $\mathbf{A}_x$ may be expressed as

$$\mathbf{A}_x = \mathbf{A}_x{}^0 \cos 2\pi\nu t = \tfrac{1}{2}\mathbf{A}_x{}^0(e^{2\pi i\nu t} + e^{-2\pi i\nu t}),$$

so that

$$\frac{da_k(t)}{dt} = -\frac{1}{2\hbar^2 c}\,\mathbf{A}_x{}^0(\mu_x)_{kn}(E_k - E_n)\{e^{i(E_k-E_n+h\nu)t/\hbar} + e^{i(E_k-E_n-h\nu)t/\hbar}\}.$$

To find $a_k(t)$, it is necessary to integrate this expression from $t = 0$ to t, remembering that $a_k(0) = 0$. We then obtain

$$a_k(t) = \frac{i}{2c\hbar} A_x^0(\mu_x)_{kn}(E_k - E_n) \left\{ \frac{e^{i(E_k - E_n + h\nu)t/\hbar} - 1}{E_k - E_n + h\nu} \right. $$
$$\left. + \frac{e^{i(E_k - E_n - h\nu)t/\hbar} - 1}{E_k - E_n - h\nu} \right\}. \quad (7\text{-}53)$$

If $E_k > E_n$, then the transition involves absorption of energy from the radiation field. We note that since $A_x^0(\mu_x)_{kn}$ is generally small, $a_k(t)$ in this case will be large only when $h\nu \simeq E_k - E_n$ and the denominator of the second term in the brackets approaches zero. The first term can then be neglected. If $E_n > E_k$, then $a_k(t)$ will be large only when $h\nu \simeq E_n - E_k$ and the denominator of the first term approaches zero, in which case the second term can be neglected.

In considering the first case, it is observed that a vanishing denominator leads to an indeterminate form, but the quantum-mechanical probability is $a_k^* a_k$; this gives the probability that the system is in the kth state at time t. Neglecting the first term in (7–53), we obtain for this probability

$$a_k^* a_k = \frac{t^2}{4c^2\hbar^4} |A_x^0|^2 |(\mu_x)_{kn}|^2 (E_k - E_n)^2 \frac{\sin^2 \{(E_k - E_n - h\nu)t/2\hbar\}}{\{(E_k - E_n - h\nu)t/2\hbar\}^2}$$
$$= \frac{t^2\pi^2}{c^2\hbar^2} |A_x^0|^2 |(\mu_x)_{kn}|^2 \nu_{kn}^2 \frac{\sin^2 \{(\nu_{kn} - \nu)\pi t\}}{(\nu_{kn} - \nu)^2 \pi^2 t^2}, \quad (7\text{-}54)$$

where $\nu_{kn} = (E_k - E_n)/h$.

This equation gives us the desired probability when radiation of the single frequency ν is used. If we use polychromatic radiation ("white" light), then we must integrate this expression over all frequencies. Depending on the source of the radiation, A_x^0 usually varies with frequency, some emitters being much more intense in some frequency regions than in others (see Fig. 2–7 for example). But since $a_k^* a_k$ is significant only when the frequency of the radiation is close to ν_{kn}, it is a reasonable approximation to assume that A_x^0 is a constant over the important frequencies around ν_{kn}; i.e., A_k^0 is a function of ν_{kn}, $A_x^0 = A_x^0(\nu_{kn})$. Integration of ν over all frequencies then gives

$$a_k^* a_k = \frac{\pi^2 \nu_{kn}^2}{c^2\hbar^2} |A_x^0(\nu_{kn})|^2 |(\mu_x)_{kn}|^2 t.$$

We see that the probability of finding the system in the kth state after irradiating the system which is initially in the nth state for time t depends on the electric dipole matrix element connecting the kth state with the initial state, on the intensity of the radiation (A_x^0), and on the frequency of the radiation, which, if monochromatic, must be close to ν_{kn}.

In general, the radiation will not necessarily be plane-polarized, and a general treatment shows that $a_k^* a_k$ is given by

$$a_k^* a_k = \frac{\pi^2 \nu_{kn}^2}{c^2 \hbar^2} \{ |A_x^{0}(\nu_{kn})|^2 |(\mu_x)_{kn}|^2 + |A_y^{0}(\nu_{kn})|^2 |(\mu_y)_{kn}|^2$$

$$+ |A_z^{0}(\nu_{kn})|^2 |(\mu_z)_{kn}|^2 \} t.$$

For isotropic radiation

$$|A_x^{0}|^2 = |A_y^{0}|^2 = |A_z^{0}|^2 = \tfrac{1}{3} |A^{0}|^2,$$

and from electromagnetic theory it is found that the radiation density $\rho(\nu_{kn})$ is related to the vector potential by

$$|A^{0}(\nu_{kn})|^2 = \frac{2c^2}{\pi \nu_{kn}^2} \rho(\nu_{kn})$$

so that

$$a_k^* a_k = \frac{2\pi}{3\hbar^2} \{ |(\mu_x)_{kn}|^2 + |(\mu_y)_{kn}|^2 + |(\mu_z)_{kn}|^2 \} \rho(\nu_{kn}) t$$

$$= \frac{2\pi}{3\hbar^2} |\mu_{kn}|^2 \rho(\nu_{kn}) t, \qquad (7\text{–}55)$$

where

$$|\mu_{kn}|^2 = |(\mu_x)_{kn}|^2 + |(\mu_y)_{kn}|^2 + |(\mu_z)_{kn}|^2 = |\langle k|e\mathbf{r}|n\rangle|^2.$$

The probability that a transition will take place in unit time from the state n to the state k, with an absorption of energy by the system from the radiation field, is seen from (7–55) to be

$$P_{k \leftarrow n} = \frac{2\pi}{3\hbar^2} |\mu_{kn}|^2 \rho(\nu_{kn}) = B_{k \leftarrow n} \rho(\nu_{kn}). \qquad (7\text{–}56)$$

The coefficient $B_{k \leftarrow n}$ is known as the Einstein transition probability coefficient for induced absorption.

We find similarly that for the emission of radiation induced by the electromagnetic field

$$B_{k \leftarrow n} \rho(\nu_{kn}) = B_{k \rightarrow n} \rho(\nu_{kn})$$

where $B_{k \rightarrow n}$ is the Einstein transition probability coefficient for induced emission.

We might well ask at this juncture how it is ever possible to conduct a spectroscopic experiment if the probability for induced absorption and emission of radiation are the same since, if this is true, it would mean that there is no net absorption or emission of radiation by a collection of atoms and molecules undergoing the induced transitions. There are several factors involved here. One is experimental. It is often possible to arrange our experiment so that the radiation all impinges on the sample from a given direction in a beam. Although radiation is emitted by the sample, it is emitted in all directions, and only a small fraction of the emitted radiation is in the same direction as the original beam. Hence even if as much radiation is emitted as absorbed, the amount of radiation observed coming from the sample in the same direction as the incident beam will be less than the amount of incident radiation, so that a net absorption appears to have occurred. It is often possible to arrange the experiment so that either absorption from the incident beam or emitted radiation at directions out of the path of the incident beam can be observed.

A more fundamental factor, however, is the fact that the total probability of transitions of a collection of atoms or molecules depends on the number of atoms or molecules in the initial state. If $B_{k \leftarrow n}\rho(\nu_{kn})$ is the probability that one atom or molecule undergoes an induced transition in unit time, then $N_n B_{k \leftarrow n}\rho(\nu_{kn})$ is the total probability that N_n molecules will undergo that transition. In addition, there is a probability that emission will occur spontaneously. Since there are generally more molecules in one state than another, the quantity of radiation absorbed will generally not be the same as that emitted.

If the perturbing interactions are not too great, then the number of molecules distributed among the various states will remain in the equilibrium established by the Boltzmann distribution law, i.e.,

$$\frac{N_k}{N_n} = \frac{e^{-E_k/kT}}{e^{-E_n/kT}} = e^{-h\nu_{kn}/kT}, \tag{7-57}$$

where we have neglected possible degeneracies of the levels. If this equilibrium is maintained, then it must be true that, while the system is being perturbed,

$$N_n B_{k \leftarrow n}\rho(\nu_{kn}) = N_k\{B_{k \rightarrow n}\rho(\nu_{kn}) + A_{k \rightarrow n}\}, \tag{7-58}$$

where the left side represents the number of transitions from n to k by induced absorption of radiation and the right side gives the number of transitions, both induced and spontaneous, from the upper to the lower state. $A_{k \rightarrow n}$ is the Einstein transition probability coefficient for spontaneous emission. Combining (7–57) and (7–58), we obtain

$$e^{-h\nu_{kn}/kT} = \frac{B_{k \leftarrow n}\rho(\nu_{kn})}{A_{k \rightarrow n} + B_{k \rightarrow n}\rho(\nu_{kn})},$$

which arranges to

$$\rho(\nu_{kn}) = \frac{A_{k \rightarrow n}e^{-h\nu_{kn}/kT}}{B_{k \leftarrow n} - B_{k \rightarrow n}e^{-h\nu_{kn}/kT}}$$

$$= \frac{A_{k \rightarrow n}/B_{k \rightarrow n}}{e^{h\nu_{kn}/kT} - 1}.$$

The energy density of radiation in equilibrium with a blackbody at temperature T is known from Planck's distribution law to be (Chapter 2)

$$\rho(\nu_{kn}) = \frac{8\pi h\nu_{kn}^3}{c^3} \frac{1}{e^{h\nu_{kn}/kT} - 1},$$

so that

$$A_{k \to n} = \frac{8\pi h \nu_{kn}^3 B_{k \to n}}{c^3},$$ (7-59)

or, from (7-56),

$$A_{k \to n} = \frac{32\pi^3 \nu_{kn}^3}{3c^3 \hbar} |\mu_{kn}|^2.$$

We have used in this development only the matrix element for the electric dipole moment between two states. This resulted from our assumption that **A** was constant over the extent of the molecule at a given instant. If this assumption is not true, then additional terms appear in the matrix element corresponding to interaction of the radiation with magnetic dipole, electric quadrupole, octapole, and other less symmetric charge distributions in the molecule. By considering only the first two, the coefficient for spontaneous emission becomes

$$A_{k \to n} = \frac{32\pi^3 \nu_{kn}^3}{3c^3 \hbar} \left\{ |\langle k|e\mathbf{r}|n\rangle|^2 + \left| \left\langle k \left| \frac{e}{2mc} \mathbf{r} \times \hat{\mathbf{p}} \right| n \right\rangle \right|^2 + \frac{3\pi^3 \nu_{kn}^2}{10c^2} |\langle k|e\mathbf{rr}|n\rangle^2. \right.$$

For radiation in the visible region the relative magnitudes of these three matrix elements (electric dipole, magnetic dipole, and electric quadrupole, respectively) are of the order of $1:10^{-5}:10^{-7}$, so that, unless the electric dipole matrix element vanishes between two states, the probability of spontaneous emission due to magnetic dipole or electric quadrupole effects is negligible.

It was assumed, in obtaining an estimate for $A_{k \to n}$, that the Boltzmann distribution is maintained. This may not be so if the intensity of radiation is great enough to induce transitions from the lower states to higher ones more rapidly than transitions downward can occur. In particular, we shall see that in radiofrequency spectroscopy electric-dipole transitions are not involved, and since spontaneous emission by magnetic-dipole transitions is extremely small, the downward transitions are limited to induced transitions. In this event the states do not remain populated according to the Boltzmann law.

In addition to knowing which transitions are possible, we find it convenient to be able to interpret the intensity of radiation absorbed from an incident beam of radiation. The familiar Beer-Lambert law for an absorbing solute in a non-absorbing solvent is

$$-dI = \epsilon(\nu)IC \, dl,$$ (7-60)

where I is the intensity of the beam, $\epsilon(\nu)$ is the molar absorption coefficient or molar extinction coefficient, C is the molar concentration of solute, and dl is an increment of distance in the solution. If the intensity of the radiation is I_0 before entering the sample and the thickness of the sample is l, then integration of (7–60) gives

$$\epsilon(\nu) = \frac{1}{Cl} \ln \frac{I_0}{I}.$$

Since radiation is generally absorbed over a small range of frequencies (a band), the total intensity of the band is found by integrating $\epsilon(\nu)$ over the frequency range of the band:

$$A = \int \epsilon(\nu) \, d\nu.$$

This A is called the integrated absorption coefficient.

In our previous discussion we observed that the number of molecules absorbing radiation depends on $B_{k \leftarrow n}\rho(\nu_{nk})$ and the number of molecules which are in the initial state. If we assume that the separation of energy levels is large (as it is in electronic states where the Beer-Lambert law is most commonly used), then essentially all the molecules are in the lower state. The amount of energy absorbed from the beam for each molecule undergoing a transition is $h\nu_{kn}$, and the intensity of the beam is reduced by this amount with each transition. If N' is the number of molecules per cubic centimeter in the sample, then

$$-dI = \frac{2\pi}{3\hbar^2} |\mu_{kn}|^2 \rho(\nu_{kn}) h\nu_{kn} N' \, dl$$

$$= \frac{2\pi}{3\hbar^2} |\mu_{kn}|^2 \rho(\nu_{kn}) h\nu_{kn} \frac{NC}{1000} \, dl$$

where N is Avogadro's number. The intensity I, which is the radiation energy flowing across a cross-sectional area of 1 cm² in 1 sec is,

$$I = c\rho,$$

so that

$$-dI = \frac{2\pi}{3\hbar^2} |\mu_{kn}|^2 \frac{I}{c} h\nu_{kn} \frac{NC}{1000} \, dl.$$

Comparison with (7–60) shows that

$$\epsilon(\nu) = \frac{2\pi}{3\hbar^2} |\mu_{kn}|^2 \frac{h\nu_{kn}}{c} \frac{N}{1000}$$

and

$$A = \frac{4\pi^2 N}{3000\hbar c} \nu_{kn} |\mu_{kn}|^2.$$

The connection between the band intensity and the electric-dipole matrix element is now apparent in this expression. Some examples of calculations of band intensities are given as exercises at the end of the chapter and in later sections.

7.8　SELECTION RULES IN ATOMIC SPECTRA

In order to interpret atomic absorption and emission spectra, it is necessary to know the selection rules governing transitions between the various electronic states of the atom. Following the discussion of the previous section, we must evaluate which of the electric-dipole-moment matrix elements are not zero. This is most easily done in terms of $(\mu_x)_{kn}$, $(\mu_y)_{kn}$, and $(\mu_z)_{kn}$ separately.

First we will consider the simple one-electron atom. Recalling that $\psi_{nlm_l} = R_{nl}(r)\ \Theta_{lm_l}(\theta)\Phi_{m_l}(\phi)$ and that $x = r\sin\theta\cos\phi$, $y = r\sin\theta\sin\phi$, and $z = r\cos\theta$, we note that an integral such as $(\mu_x)_{kn}$ can be broken up, into parts, each dependent on only one coordinate, such as

$$
\begin{aligned}
(\mu_x)_{kn} &= \int \psi^*_{n''l''m_l''} ex \psi_{n'l'm_l'}\, d\tau \\
&= e\left[\int_0^\infty R^*_{n''l''} r R_{n'l'} r^2\, dr \int_0^\pi \Theta^*_{l''m_l''}\sin\theta\, \Theta_{l'm_l'}\sin\theta\, d\theta \right. \\
&\qquad\qquad\left. \times \int_0^{2\pi}\Phi^*_{m_l''}\cos\phi\, \Phi_{m_l'}\, d\phi\right].
\end{aligned}
$$

Investigation of the radial functions for hydrogen discloses that the radial integral does not vanish for any combination of n' and n''. Thus, the selection rule for allowed transitions with respect to the principal quantum number is

$$\Delta n = 0,\ 1,\ 2,\ \ldots$$

Turning to the integral in Φ, we first consider the integral which is part of $(\mu_z)_{kn}$. For the z axis, $\phi = 0$, $\cos\phi = 1$, and

$$\int_0^{2\pi} e^{-im_l''\phi}e^{im_l'\phi}\, d\phi = \int_0^{2\pi} e^{i(m_l'-m_l'')\phi}\, d\phi,$$

which is zero unless $m_l' = m_l''$. For the contribution to $(\mu_x)_{kn}$,

$$
\begin{aligned}
\int_0^{2\pi} e^{-im_l''\phi}\cos\phi\, e^{im_l'\phi}\, d\phi &= \int_0^{2\pi} e^{-im_l''\phi}\tfrac{1}{2}(e^{i\phi}+e^{-i\phi})e^{im_l'\phi}\, d\phi \\
&= \tfrac{1}{2}\int_0^{2\pi}(e^{i\phi}+e^{-i\phi})e^{i(m_l'-m_l'')\phi}\, d\phi \\
&= \tfrac{1}{2}\int_0^{2\pi} e^{i(m_l'-m_l''+1)\phi}\, d\phi + \tfrac{1}{2}\int_0^{2\pi} e^{i(m_l'-m_l''-1)\phi}\, d\phi.
\end{aligned}
$$

The first integral is zero except when $m_l' - m_l'' = -1$, and the second vanishes unless $m_l' - m_l'' = 1$. Analysis of $(\mu_y)_{kn}$ gives the same results. Thus, the selection rule involving states with the quantum number m_l is that transitions are possible only between those states for which

$$\Delta m_l = 0 \text{ or } \pm 1.$$

For the Θ part of the matrix element, the analysis is slightly more difficult. For the z axis we have

$$\int_0^\pi \Theta^*_{l''m_l''}\cos\theta\, \Theta_{l'm_l'}\sin\theta\, d\theta,$$

and for the x and y axes

$$\int_0^\pi \Theta^*_{l''m_l''} \sin \theta \, \Theta_{l'm_l'} \sin \theta \, d\theta.$$

It will be recalled that the θ-dependent functions are normalized associated Legendre polynomials $P_l^{|m_l|}$ so that the integrals used for the purpose of discovering whether they vanish or not can be expressed as

$$\int_0^\pi P_{l''}^{|m_l''|} \cos \theta \, P_{l'}^{|m_l'|} \sin \theta \, d\theta$$

and

$$\int_0^\pi P_{l''}^{|m_l''|} \sin \theta \, P_{l'}^{|m_l'|} \sin \theta \, d\theta.$$

An analysis of the properties of the Legendre polynomials results in two recursion formulas which are of use here (Appendix D),

$$\cos \theta \, P_l^{|m_l|} = \frac{l - |m_l| + 1}{2l + 1} P_{l+1}^{|m_l|} + \frac{l + |m_l|}{2l + 1} P_{l-1}^{|m_l|}$$

and

$$\sin \theta \, P_l^{|m_l|} = \frac{(l + |m_l|)(l + |m_l| - 1)}{2l + 1} P_{l-1}^{|m_l|-1}$$
$$- \frac{(l - |m_l| + 1)(l - |m_l| + 2)}{2l + 1} P_{l+1}^{|m_l|-1}.$$

From an examination of these quantities in the required integrals, it is found that, for the z axis when $\Delta m_l = 0$ and for x and y when $\Delta m_l = \pm 1$, the integrals over θ vanish except when $l' = l'' \pm 1$, so the selection rule allows transitions for which

$$\Delta l = \pm 1.$$

The symmetry of the wave functions describing the states of a system has an important bearing on whether integrals such as these will vanish or not, and the selection rules can often be determined without recourse to a detailed evaluation of the integrals. All eigenfunctions for atoms have either even or odd parity, i.e., they are symmetric or antisymmetric to inversion of the coordinates of all the particles through the origin. The operator involved in the matrix element will also be even or odd. The electric-dipole-moment operator is odd because it changes sign upon inversion of the coordinates ($ex = -e(-x)$, etc.). If both ψ_k and ψ_n are even, then the integrand $\psi_k^* \mu_{kn} \psi_n$ in the matrix element will be odd, since the product of two even functions is even and the product of an even function with an odd function is odd. But if the integrand is odd, it will contribute equal positive and negative amounts to the integration over all values of the coordinates, and the integral will vanish. Similarly, two odd states and the odd dipole moment will result in an odd integrand, which results in turn in a vanishing integral. Only when one state is even and the other odd will the integrand be even and the integral finite. This behavior is summarized in the Laporte rule, which states that dipole radiation transitions can take place only from even to odd or from odd to even states. In our one-electron case it is seen by inspection that states with $l = 0, 2, 4, \ldots$ are even and states with $l = 1, 3, 5, \ldots$ are odd.

For complex atoms the Laporte rule is easily applied, for we have described the states of these atoms by the quantum number L, which is determined from one-electron l's. If the configuration of the atom consists of an odd number of electrons in orbitals with l odd, then the state is odd. For all other configurations the states are even. The states arising from a p^2 configuration, for example, would be even, but those corresponding to a p^3 configuration would be odd. The even-odd character of a state often is indicated in the term symbol by a subscript g (gerade, meaning "even") or u (ungerade, meaning "odd") to the right of the term symbol, or for odd states by a superscript 0 to the right of the term symbol.

We will not attempt the mathematical proof here, but it is found by the methods we have been discussing that for complex atoms in addition to the Laporte rule the selection rule for transitions between states of different L is

$$\Delta L = \pm 1.$$

Also only one electron can change its orbital in a single transition, and for that electron $\Delta l = \pm 1$.

A selection rule which holds except when $\mathbf{L} \cdot \mathbf{S}$ coupling becomes large is

$$\Delta S = 0.$$

This can be seen if we also consider the spin parts of the wave function in the matrix element and note that the α and β spin functions are orthonormal. Thus triplet-singlet transitions are forbidden although in heavy atoms such transitions are observed as weak lines in the spectrum.

It is found that application of the mathematical analysis used above limits the possible changes in the total angular momentum of the atom to the selection rule

$$\Delta J = 0 \text{ or } \pm 1,$$

with $J = 0 \rightarrow J = 0$ not allowed.

Finally, for M_J the selection rule is

$$\Delta M_J = 0 \text{ or } \pm 1,$$

as in the case of one electron. The particular case of $M_J = 0 \rightarrow M_J = 0$ is forbidden when $\Delta J = 0$.

Several examples of the energy levels and allowed transitions of complex atoms are illustrated in Figs. 7–10 and 7–11. Here can be seen the applicability of Hund's rules and the selection rules we have just discussed. Note that the states are grouped according to multiplicity to make the allowed transitions easier to portray ($\Delta S = 0$). States with different J but the same S and L are also separated into columns to show

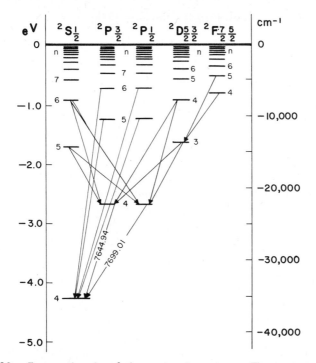

Fig. 7–10. Energy levels of the potassium atom. These states represent the ground-state configuration and excited configurations in which the outer *s* electron has been excited to higher levels. Some of the important emission-spectrum transitions are shown.

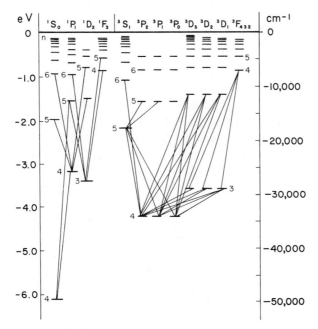

Fig. 7–11. Energy levels of the calcium atom.

the operation of the selection rules for J. Although these states are too close in energy to have noticeable differences in the diagram, their separation can be determined from the spectral frequencies given for the appropriate transitions. These transitions give rise to the multiplet fine structure observed in atomic spectra.

7.9 EFFECTS OF ELECTRIC AND MAGNETIC FIELDS

Although the various internal interactions in atoms cause states with different orbital, spin, and total angular momenta to have different energies, nevertheless in the free atom or ion, states with the same L, S, and J but different M_J remain degenerate. It was shown in Chapter 6, however, that such states have different energies if an external magnetic field is applied by virtue of the interaction between the external field and the magnetic dipole field associated with the angular momentum of the atom. This behavior, known as the Zeeman effect, was important historically in uncovering the various interactions we have mentioned and in providing an experimental area for the testing of theory.

Let us first consider a state of an atom in which there are no unpaired electron spins and $S = 0$. Then $J = L$ and the magnetic dipole moment associated with the atom in this state is, from Eq. (6–24),

$$\mu = \frac{e\hbar}{2mc}\sqrt{L(L+1)} = \frac{e\hbar}{2mc}\sqrt{J(J+1)}$$
$$= \mu_B\sqrt{J(J+1)}.$$

In a magnetic field the change in energy of the degenerate level is, from (6–25) and (6–26),

$$\Delta E = -\mathbf{\mu}\cdot\mathbf{H} = \mu_B M_J \mathsf{H}_z. \tag{7–61}$$

If we consider transitions between two states of different J when the atom is in a magnetic field H_z, we must observe the selection rules $\Delta M_J = 0$, ± 1. Such a situation was illustrated in Fig. 6–17 for non-spin states for which $J = 1$ and $J = 2$. It can be seen that the magnetic field splitting is the same for these two states since according to (7–61) it depends only on M_J. In applying the selection rule for ΔM_J, three lines result in the spectrum instead of the single line which would be observed in a field-free atom. (This line would actually be part of a closely spaced multiplet of lines in the field-free atom spectrum since states with different J are close in energy, and in the magnetic field each of these lines would be split as discussed here.) In the so-called normal Zeeman effect, which is observed for transitions between singlet states ($S = 0$), three lines are always observed, corresponding to the transitions with $\Delta M_J = -1$, 0, and 1.

In connection with our mathematical derivation of the selection rules, it is observed experimentally that the middle Zeeman line is plane-polarized in the direction parallel to the magnetic field (z) direction. This is consistent with the $\Delta M_J = 0$ selection rule, having arisen from a consideration of the integral containing μ_z. Similarly the lines corresponding to $\Delta M_J = \pm 1$ are plane-polarized perpendicular to the field. These facts are a satisfying aspect of our theoretical predictions.

For states with unpaired electrons, J is no longer equal to L. Instead,

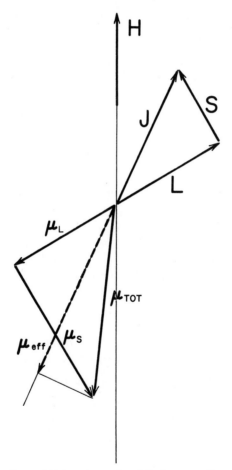

Fig. 7–12. Coupling of the spin and orbital magnetic moments. Because the spin moment is twice as large, relative to its corresponding spin angular momentum, as the orbital moment is, relative to its momentum, the total magnetic moment is not parallel to the total angular momentum vector. Hence, the precessional motion of these vectors yields a net effective magnetic moment μ_{eff} along the J axis.

$J = L + S, \ldots, |L - S|$. Calculation of the magnetic moment associated with such a state, and the splitting in a magnetic field now becomes more complicated because the orbital and spin angular momenta are not related to their associated magnetic moments in the same way. The intrinsic spin angular momentum is related to the spin magnetic dipole moment by Eq. (6–32), which is similar to (6–24) except for g_e, which is nearly equal to 2. Before relativistic quantum mechanics provided an explanation for these effects, the electron magnetic dipole moment was considered to be anomalous because it was twice as large as expected from the orbital case. The effect of the spin magnetic moment on the effective magnetic moment of the atom can be seen more clearly in a simple example.

In Fig. 7–12 are shown the addition of the orbital and spin angular momenta to form a total angular momentum. The magnitudes of these angular momenta are $\sqrt{L(L + 1)}\ \hbar$, $\sqrt{S(S + 1)}\ \hbar$, and $\sqrt{J(J + 1)}\ \hbar$, respectively. The magnetic moments associated with these momenta are shown, also, and at once it is seen that since $|\mathbf{\mu}_L| = \mu_B \sqrt{L(L + 1)}$, while $|\mathbf{\mu}_S| = 2\mu_B \sqrt{S(S + 1)}$, the resultant $\mathbf{\mu}_J$ is not antiparallel to the total angular momentum vector $\mathbf{J}$. In the $\mathbf{L} \cdot \mathbf{S}$ coupling interaction, the spin and orbital moments precess about the direction of $\mathbf{J}$ and hence the resultant $\mathbf{\mu}_J$ also precesses about $\mathbf{J}$. This precessional frequency is much more rapid in relatively weak fields than the precession of $\mathbf{J}$ about the direction of an external field. Thus, in the latter interaction it is the effective magnetic moment in the direction of $\mathbf{J}$, $\mathbf{\mu}_{\text{eff}}$, that is used in the calculation of energy changes.

The magnitude of this magnetic moment can be calculated from $\mathbf{\mu}_L$, $\mathbf{\mu}_S$, and $\mathbf{\mu}_J$ by simple trigonometric relations. Inspection of Fig. 7–13 shows that

$$
\begin{aligned}
\mu_{\text{eff}} &= \mu_L \cos (L, J) + \mu_S \cos (S, J) \\
&= \mu_B \sqrt{L(L + 1)} \cos (L, J) + 2\mu_B \sqrt{S(S + 1)} \cos (S, J) \\
&= \mu_B \left\{ \sqrt{L(L + 1)}\ \frac{J(J + 1) + L(L + 1) - S(S + 1)}{2[J(J + 1)]^{1/2}[L(L + 1)]^{1/2}} \right. \\
&\quad \left. + 2\sqrt{S(S + 1)}\ \frac{J(J + 1) + S(S + 1) - L(L + 1)}{2[J(J + 1)]^{1/2}[S(S + 1)]^{1/2}} \right\} \\
&= \mu_B \sqrt{J(J + 1)} \left\{ \frac{J(J + 1) + L(L + 1) - S(S + 1)}{2J(J + 1)} \right. \\
&\quad \left. + \frac{2J(J + 1) + 2S(S + 1) - 2L(L + 1)}{2J(J + 1)} \right\} \\
&= \mu_B \sqrt{J(J + 1)}\ \frac{2J(J + 1) + J(J + 1) + S(S + 1) - L(L + 1)}{2J(J + 1)} \\
&= \mu_B \sqrt{J(J + 1)} \left\{ 1 + \frac{J(J + 1) + S(S + 1) - L(L + 1)}{2J(J + 1)} \right\} \\
&= g\mu_B \sqrt{J(J + 1)}.
\end{aligned}
$$

The coefficient g is called the Landé g factor or spectroscopic splitting factor, and is not to be confused with g_e. Clearly the Landé factor differs for states with different L, S, and J. This means that the splitting of the degenerate M_J levels in a magnetic field will be different for different states, since

$$\Delta E = -\mathbf{\mu} \cdot \mathbf{H} = g\mu_B \sqrt{J(J+1)}\, \mathbf{H}.$$

A simple example of the anomalous Zeeman effect is the splitting observed for the sodium D lines (Fig. 7–13). Because the states are not

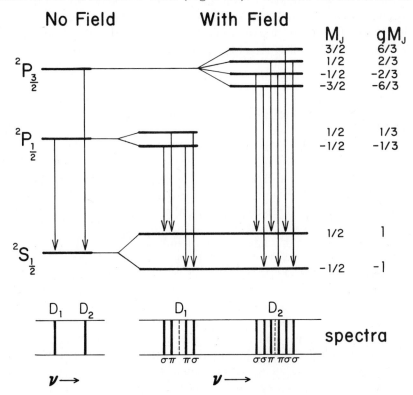

Fig. 7–13. Zeeman splitting of the D lines of sodium.

split by the same amount, the two transitions for $\Delta M_J = 0$ do not correspond to the same energy difference and hence are observed as separate spectral lines. Similarly for $\Delta M_J = -1$ and for $\Delta M_J = 1$ in the $J = \frac{1}{2} \rightarrow J = \frac{3}{2}$ transitions. Quite complicated patterns can result from these unequal splittings. The polarization of the lines is often a helpful means for identifying the transitions involved.

In strong magnetic fields only a normal Zeeman effect is observed, even when states with spin are involved. This phenomenon is known as the

Paschen-Back effect and results because the spin and orbital moments are decoupled by the strong field. The spin and orbital moments then precess independently about the field, and the splitting of the atomic levels can be considered as a splitting of the term into levels corresponding to different M_L, followed by a second splitting according to the different M_S.

Electric fields also have an effect on the energy levels of atomic states. The nature of this interaction, known as the Stark effect, is more complicated than the magnetic interaction of the Zeeman effect. The electric field does not act directly on the magnetic dipole moment of the atom, but acts instead to polarize the atom. This shifting of the centers of negative and positive charge from the center of the atom results in an induced electric dipole moment which is related to the electric field by

$$\mathbf{\mu}_{e_{\text{ind}}} = \alpha \mathbf{E}.$$

The proportionality constant α is known as the polarizability of the atom. This induced electric dipole is acted upon by the field in a $\mathbf{\mu}_e \cdot \mathbf{E}$ interaction, which causes the energy of the atomic state to be shifted. The energy of the polarized atom can be calculated in simple cases by perturbation theory, by considering the applied electric field as a small perturbation to the field-free atom. A problem is included at the end of this chapter in which the energy of a polarized hydrogen atom is calculated.

The electric field defines the z direction, of course, and the total angular momentum of the atom must be quantized with respect to this direction. States with different M_J have different induced electric dipole moments (different polarizabilities) and hence have different energies. Unlike the magnetic case in which the magnetic moment is permanent and always collinear with the angular momentum vector, the induced electric dipole is not necessarily coincident with the angular momentum, and its magnitude varies with M_J and with the other quantum numbers describing the field-free system. We will not attempt to derive general equations for the Stark effect, but it can be noted that, for a particular state with a given L, S, and J, the states with different M_J differ in energy, but states which differ only in the sign of M_J are degenerate. This is because the polarization depends only on the angle of the axis of the angular momentum to the field and not on the particular direction of the angular momentum vector. An example is shown in Fig. 7–14, where the energies of the states and the observed spectral lines can be seen.

In the Stark effect very large fields also result in a decoupling of the spin and orbital angular momenta. That is, the interaction with the field is greater than the strength of the $\mathbf{L} \cdot \mathbf{S}$ coupling and both the spin and orbital angular momenta precess separately about the field. The energy effects are interesting in this case, being partially indirect in nature. Consider a ^3D term for which there will be levels, slightly different in energy because of $\mathbf{L} \cdot \mathbf{S}$ coupling, corresponding to $J = 3, 2$, and 1.   Each of these levels is $2J + 1$ degenerate in the absence of a field as shown in Fig. 7–15.   If we now apply a strong electric field, there result three groups of levels corresponding to the electrical interaction between the field and the orbital angular momentum with $M_L = 0$, $M_L = \pm 1$, and $M_L = \pm 2$.   For $M_L = 0$, states with different M_S do not have different energies, since no electric dipole can be induced in the electron itself.

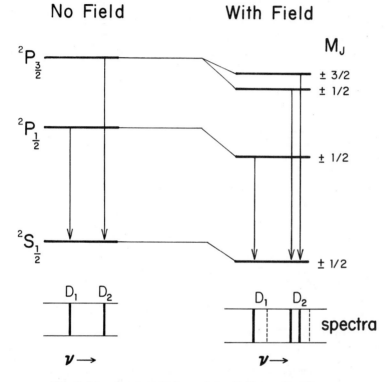

Fig. 7–14.   Stark splitting of the D lines of sodium.

But for $M_L = 1$, the electrical interaction of the field with the induced electric dipole causes a precession of the orbital angular momentum (and hence orbital magnetic moment) about the direction of the field, and this precession results in a magnetic field which can interact with the spin magnetic moment, giving a different energy for each orientation of the spin moment (each M_S).   Thus, for $M_L = 1$, there are three levels corresponding to $M_S = -1$, 0, and 1.   Similar results are obtained for $M_L = 2$.   A large variety of situations can arise, depending on the relative magnitudes of the applied field, and intermediate cases are not uncommon.

One does not need to apply an external electric field in order to observe the Stark effect. In fact, one of the most interesting areas in atomic spectroscopy, valence theory, and electron magnetic resonance spectroscopy is the investigation of atomic systems in which electric fields arise in the system itself by virtue of electrically charged ions in crystalline lattices around the atom of interest, or ionic and covalent bonding around an atom in a complex species. Among the more interesting of such systems are the transition metal ions in which the d orbitals are strongly affected by the electric fields in solids and complexes.

In a crystalline or molecular environment the electric fields acting on an atom are more complicated than when a uniform field is applied externally. Usually, however, there is some sort of symmetry involved

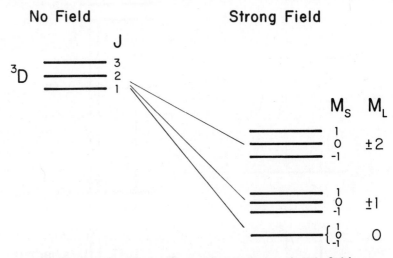

Fig. 7–15. The Stark effect with very large electric fields.

because of the regular arrangement of ions in the crystal lattice or in the ligands coordinated around a central atom. The transition metal ions form complexes of considerable symmetry, and we will consider briefly a particularly simple case, the arrangement of negative charges at equal distances along the x, y, and z axes about an atom at the origin (Fig. 7–16). The electric field at the central atom will have octahedral symmetry.

One can immediately write the potential energy at the origin due to the six charges from simple electrostatic theory and use this potential as a perturbation on the field-free states of the atom. It is also possible to draw some qualitative conclusions about the energies of the different d orbitals of an atom in such an environment. The d_{z^2} and $d_{x^2-y^2}$ orbital clouds lie along the x, y, and z axes, while the d_{xy}, d_{xz}, and d_{yz} clouds are pointed in directions between the axes (Fig. 6–7). It is clear that an electron in one of the former two orbitals would be more strongly repelled by the negative ions around the atom than one in the latter three.   The symmetry of the orbitals is such that the d_{z^2} and $d_{x^2-y^2}$ orbitals are affected energetically to the same degree, while the remaining three are affected equally to one another but differently from the first two.   The result is indicated schematically in Fig. 7–17.   The split levels are labeled according to their symmetry properties by a nomenclature used in group theory,

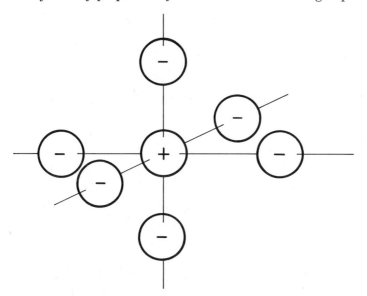

Fig. 7–16.   The arrangement of ions in an octahedral symmetry about a central point.   Two of the five d orbitals of an atom located at the center are oriented along the axes towards such ions, while the other three extend between the axes.

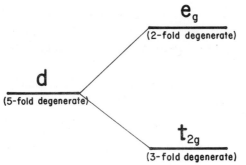

Fig. 7–17.   Splitting of the energy of the degenerate d orbitals by an electric field of octahedral symmetry.

which, we have already observed is a powerful mathematical tool for analyzing symmetric systems. One d electron in the octahedral field would occupy the lowest level, one of the three t_{2g} orbitals.

In this example repulsion by the negative ions results in an increase in energy of some of the levels. In other situations the energy might be lower, but the most important aspect here is the splitting of the ^2D level into two levels by the octahedral field. The magnitude of the splitting

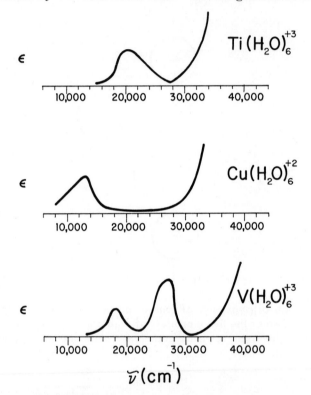

Fig. 7–18. Optical spectra of transition metal ions.

depends on the magnitudes and distances of the charges around the atom and hence is sensitive to changes in the environment of the atom.

An example of a d^1 configuration is the Ti^{+3} ion. In aqueous solutions the $Ti(H_2O)_6^{+3}$ ion is similar to the octahedral situation we have just described. Experimentally, it is found that this ion absorbs radiation at about 20,300 cm^{-1} or 5,000 Å (Fig. 7–18) corresponding to the transition of the single d electron from the lower t_{2g} level to the higher e level. This is in the green region of the visible spectrum, resulting in a gray-purple color for the solution.

A similar case is the Cu^{+2} ion which has a d^9 configuration.   Only a ^2D state is allowed by the Pauli exclusion principle for this configuration, and in a strong octahedral field the ^2D level is split as shown in Fig. 7–19. The inversion of the e_g and t_{2g} levels results from the difference in the repulsions when nine electrons rather than one occupy the d orbitals. This situation can be treated mathematically as a single positive charge rather than nine negative ones.   The nine electrons will then fill the e_g levels (four electrons), with five electrons in the upper level.

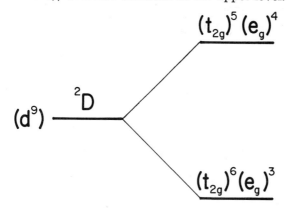

$$(t_{2g})^5 (e_g)^4$$

$$(d^9) \quad {}^2D$$

$$(t_{2g})^6 (e_g)^3$$

Fig. 7–19.   Splitting of the energy of the d^9 ^2D configuration by an electric field of octahedral symmetry.

In Fig. 7–18 it is seen that $Cu(H_2O)_6^{+2}$ absorbs in the red region of the visible spectrum, resulting in a blue solution.   This is the transition of an e_g electron to the empty t_{2g} orbital and represents a field splitting of 12,600 cm^{-1}.   In Table 7–5 are listed the absorption frequencies for several complexes of the Cu^{+2} ion, and it can be seen that each ligand causes splitting of the ^2D level by a different amount.   The colors of the transition metal ions and the remarkable color changes observed in different complex and crystalline forms of these ions are caused largely by this electric field splitting.   Ordinarily the spacing of electronic levels requires radiation of ultraviolet frequencies to excite electrons, but these crystal field splittings of the d states provide transitions of much lower frequencies, frequently in the visible region.

TABLE 7–5.   Absorption Frequencies for Complexed Cu^{+2}

Ligand	Frequency (cm^{-1})
H_2O	12,600
NH_3	15,000
Ethylene diamine	16,400

The situation we have pictured here is oversimplified in many ways. We have not mentioned spin-orbit coupling, for example. Environments of lower than octahedral symmetry result in more complicated splittings. In configurations with more than one and less than nine d electrons a number of field-free states are possible (Table 7–4), and the splitting of these states by an electric field often results in the crossing of these levels. In many cases the energy-level pattern is intermediate between the situation in which the various states arising from intra-atomic interactions are split slightly by the field and the situation in which the field is so strong that the states are determined solely by the field, except for small splittings caused by the intra-atomic interactions. An example is the

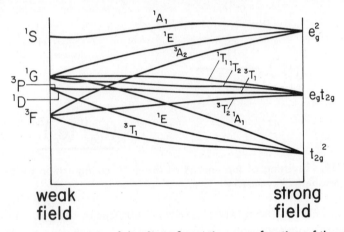

Fig. 7–20. Energy levels of the d^2 configuration as a function of the strength of an electric field of octahedral symmetry.

V^{+3} ion, which has been studied thoroughly and whose energy level pattern and absorption spectrum are shown in Figs. 7–20 and 7–18, respectively.

The V^{+3} ion has a d^2 configuration. In the absence of an electric field the interelectronic repulsions and the various possible arrangements of the two electrons in the d orbitals result in the states shown at the left of the energy-level diagram. In a weak field of octahedral symmetry some of these states are split as shown. Again, the states in the electric field are designated by group-theoretical symbols, which we will not discuss here. On the other hand in a very strong octahedral field only three energy levels are possible (right side of the diagram) corresponding to both electrons in the t_{2g} orbitals, one in a t_{2g} and one in an e_g orbital, and both in e_g orbitals. Unless the field is extremely large, however, the interelectronic repulsions will still have some effect, and the three levels will split slightly as shown. The intermediate case, where both internal interactions and external fields are comparable, a complex array of levels results. The ground state of V^{+3} should be t_{2g}^2, and the two peaks observed in the absorption spectrum of $V(H_2O)_6^{+3}$ are believed to be the $^3T_1 \rightarrow {}^3T_2$ and the $^3T_1 \rightarrow {}^3T_1(^3P)$ transitions.

The analysis of these systems is difficult, but a number of theoretical and experimental approaches have proved fruitful in this respect. Clearly the symmetry properties of the atomic wave functions and the symmetry of the electric field are an extremely important consideration. The ionic model, often called crystal-field theory, is not completely satisfactory. During the past decade molecular orbital and valence-bond methods have been developed in conjunction with the ionic approach and have proved highly successful. This modified theory has come to be known as ligand-field theory and is one of the most exciting developments in modern physical-inorganic chemistry.

7.10   SUMMARY

We have discussed in this chapter a number of fairly abstract approaches to the quantum mechanics of complex systems, and a backward glance may be desirable at this point. For very simple systems it is often possible to solve the Schrödinger equation exactly, but for more complex systems such as many-electron atoms, molecules, and even simple particles affected by complex potential energies, it is necessary to approximate the solution. We considered two approximation methods in detail and applied them to the simple case of the helium atom to illustrate how they function. The perturbation method begins with a system for which the wave functions and energies can be obtained exactly, and then considers the effect of a small perturbing term in the potential energy on these states. The resulting wave functions are constructed from the unperturbed wave functions, and the calculation can be carried to several degrees of approximation although the extensive number of manipulations required limits this in a practical way. The results of such a procedure are generally good, provided the perturbation is not too large.

The variation method is based on the fact that a matrix element of the sort $\langle \phi | \mathcal{H} | \phi \rangle$, where ϕ is any arbitrary function and $\mathcal{H}$ is the complete Hamiltonian operator for the system, cannot have a value which is any lower than the true energy of the system. The latter would be obtained from this matrix element if the correct eigenfunction of the operator were used. The problem in the variation method is to find a suitable function in order to obtain a value as close to the true energy as possible. In practice, one chooses a function as close to the symmetry of the system as possible, and introduces variable parameters which can be adjusted to bring the calculated energy as low as possible. It is often convenient to construct variation functions from a linear combination of familiar orthonormal functions from a similar system, and the calculation then becomes very similar to the perturbation method.

Numerous other approximation methods are used in calculations of this sort, depending on the nature of the problem, but the variation and perturbation treatments are among the most widely used, and we will return to them frequently in future chapters.

Although we may be able to predict the energy levels for atomic and molecular systems, verification of these predictions rests on experimental evidence, particularly spectroscopic information. A modification of perturbation theory to include time variations in the perturbation allows us to calculate the probability that a system initially in a particular state will be found in another state after a length of time under the influence of the perturbation. From these calculations we can obtain some idea of the intensity of the absorption band when the perturbation is electromagnetic radiation, and Bohr's frequency condition is found to be a natural consequence of this treatment.

These methods were applied briefly to atomic systems. The complexity of the problem leads us to search for rapid and consistent ways of finding suitable functions with which we can begin the solution. For atoms, the simplest choice is to construct the wave functions from hydrogen-like one-electron functions. In doing so, we can consider the resulting states of the atom in terms of successive interactions that lead from the simple hydrogen-like energy levels to the actual levels of the complex atom.

As a start, for example, we could consider each electron to have the energy of a hydrogen-like electron in the field of a nucleus with charge $+Ze$. The energy of the atom is then the sum of these energies. This is clearly in error, however, so we hasten to determine why. Two effects are immediately apparent: Electrons repel one another, and the configurations of the hydrogen-like orbitals are such that some electrons remain closer to the nucleus than others. The result is a shielding effect which causes outer electrons to be bound less strongly than in the hypothetical one-electron atom with nuclear charge $+Ze$. In the case of the carbon atom, for example, the $1s^2 2s^2$ configuration is a closed shell of electrons with no angular momentum, which very largely shields the $2p^2$ electrons from the full nuclear charge of $+6e$. The result is that the p electrons are somewhat higher in energy, as illustrated in Fig. 7–21.

The interelectronic interactions also result in a coupling of the electronic orbital angular momenta of the two p electrons to give several possible states, depending on the details of the coupling, i.e., on the individual angular momenta and their relative orientations when interacting. For the p^2 configuration we found that S, P, and D states are possible, each state having a different total orbital angular momentum. The energies of these states differ because the details of the electronic repulsions differ as the electrons occupy different pairs of the available p orbitals.

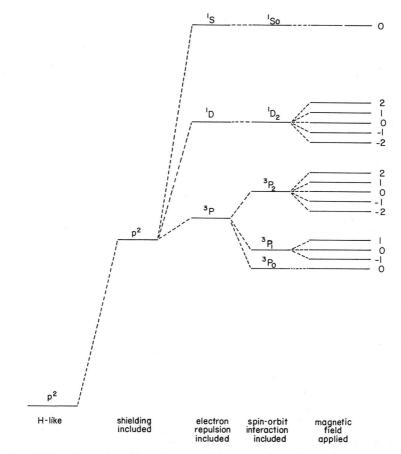

Fig. 7–21. Schematic view of successive interactions in the p^2 configuration. The separation of energy levels is not exact, and the spin-orbit and field splittings are magnified considerably.

The spin of the electrons is also important here because of the requirement that only states which are antisymmetric to the interchange of any two electrons are possible. The electrical interactions between the electrons also cause the spin angular momenta to couple, with several possible states of different net spin angular momentum resulting. The rules for angular momentum and the Pauli exclusion principle are used to determine what states are possible. For the p^2 configuration, the states resulting from these electrical interactions were found to be ^1S, ^3P, and ^1D. It is interesting that energy differences in these states depend more on the net spin angular momentum than on the net orbital angular momentum.   This results because the antisymmetry rules tend to keep the electrons unpaired and in different orbitals, in which case the repulsions are less. . Thus the ^3P state is the one of lowest energy, as shown in Fig. 7–21.   Although it is the properties of spin that control the configurations of the electrons, the actual energy effects still are electrical.

The shielding and electron repulsion effects are the largest and most important factors in the gross adjustment of the energy levels to the correct values, but other interactions of lesser magnitude can be observed. The direct magnetic interaction of the spin and orbital angular momenta, the $\mathbf{L} \cdot \mathbf{S}$ or spin-orbit coupling, results in a further shifting and splitting of the atomic states.   These also are shown for the p^2 configuration in Fig. 7–21.   Although we have not discussed other interactions in detail, we can mention that the spin angular momentum of the nucleus can interact with the electron orbital moment to produce a hyperfine splitting of the levels which is of even smaller magnitude than the $\mathbf{L} \cdot \mathbf{S}$ coupling, but which is extremely important in spectroscopic methods we will discuss later.   There is also a nuclear-electron spin-spin interaction, and if the nucleus has a quadrupole or octapole moment, these also interact with the electronic environment.   All these have been omitted from our discussion here because of their relatively small effects and the complications which arise in treating them.

We have thus approached the complete explanation of atomic states by considering smaller and smaller interactions.   We mentioned that in heavier atoms the spin-orbit interaction becomes much larger and may be more important than the coupling of orbital angular momenta with one another and spin angular moments with one another.   Although the resulting energy-level pattern is different, the approach is the same.

Finally we noted the effects that electric and magnetic fields produce on this field-free energy-level pattern.   In relatively weak fields the splitting of degenerate levels is simple, but in strong fields the interaction with the field may be much stronger than $\mathbf{L} \cdot \mathbf{S}$ coupling or even than the electron repulsion interactions and a quite different energy level pattern may result.   Among the most important considerations is the symmetry of the field, as this has a pronounced effect on the nature of the splitting.   Examples of such effects will be considered again in our discussion of other spectroscopic methods.

Space has prompted us to be somewhat brief in our discussion of the states of complex atoms, but more detailed discussions are found in the references listed.

SUPPLEMENTARY REFERENCES

PAULING, L., and E. B. WILSON, *Introduction to Quantum Mechanics*, McGraw-Hill Book Co., New York, 1935. Discusses the variation and perturbation methods and helium in some detail.

HERTZBERG, G., *Atomic Spectra and Atomic Structure*, Dover Publications, New York, 1944. A classic exposition based on the experimental aspects of spectra and the resulting theory.

KAUZMAN, W. J., *Quantum Chemistry*, Academic Press, Inc., New York, 1957. Considerable discussion of the states of helium and other complex atom calculations.

EYRING, H., J. WALTER, and G. E. KIMBALL, *Quantum Chemistry*, John Wiley & Sons, Inc., New York, 1944. A detailed examination of factoring the secular determinant, using angular momentum.

BATES, D. R., *Quantum Theory*, vols. 1 and 2, Academic Press, Inc., New York, 1961. Concise but thorough survey of the state of the art of atomic calculations.

SLATER, J. C., *Quantum Theory of Matter*, McGraw-Hill Book Co., New York, 1951. A useful introduction to numerous aspects of atomic and molecular theory.

SLATER, J. C., *Quantum Theory of Atomic Structure*, vols. 1 and 2, McGraw-Hill Book Co., New York, 1961. A much more detailed examination than the preceding of atomic calculations in particular.

PAULING, L., *Nature of the Chemical Bond*, 3rd ed., Cornell University Press, Ithaca, N.Y., 1960. Long-used, lucid, and imaginative discussion of chemical systems, with emphasis on structure.

ORGEL, L. E., *An Introduction to Transition-Metal Chemistry*, Methuen & Co., Ltd., London, 1960. A lucid discussion of the crystal-field, ligand-field approach to describing coordination compounds.

PROBLEMS

7–1. Using the concepts of penetration and shielding, explain why the $4s$ orbitals of K and Ca should fill before the $3d$ orbitals begin to fill, as for the transition series Sc to Zn.

7–2. The radii of the rare earth ions are essentially determined by the $5p$ electron. How do you account for their decrease in size with an increase in atomic number?

7–3. When an atom is placed in an electric field, it is polarized by the field; that is, the centers of negative and positive charge are separated, so that the atom has an induced electric dipole moment. This distortion has an effect on the energy of the atom and the wave functions describing the states of the system. The simplest case is that of a hydrogen atom placed in a uniform electric field **E** in the z direction, for which case the Hamiltonian operator is

$$\mathcal{H} = \mathcal{H}^0 + e\mathbf{E}z = \mathcal{H}^0 + e\mathbf{E}r \cos \theta,$$

where $\mathcal{H}^0$ is the Hamiltonian operator for a hydrogen atom in the absence of a field. Using first-order perturbation theory calculate the energy of the ground state of a hydrogen atom in an electric field **E**.

7–4. The use of second-order perturbation theory to determine the energy of a polarized hydrogen atom requires the calculation of many terms. The appropriate second-order equation can be rearranged, however, to the form

$$E''_n = \frac{(H'^2)_{nn}}{E_n{}^0} - \frac{(H'_{nn})^2}{E_n{}^0} + H''_{nn} + \sum_j \frac{E_j{}^0}{E_n{}^0} \frac{H'_{nj}H'_{jn}}{E_n{}^0 - E_j{}^0},$$

where $(H'^2)_{nn} = \langle n|\mathcal{3C}'^2|n\rangle$. In this case (atom in an electric field) there is no $\mathcal{3C}''$ perturbation term, so the third term in the above expression vanishes. It can also be shown that the signs and magnitudes of the terms in the summation are such that the entire summation can be neglected. Calculate the energy of a hydrogen atom in an electric field E according to this simplified second-order perturbation treatment.

7–5. Calculate the energy of the ground state of the hydrogen atom in an electric field E, using for a trial variation function $\phi = (1 + Ar \cos \theta)\psi_{1s}$ and minimizing the energy with respect to A. Neglect powers of E higher than E^2.

7–6. Calculate the energy of the ground state of the hydrogen atom in an electric field E, using for a trial variation function the linear combination $\phi = c_1\psi_{1s} + c_2\psi_{2p_0}$ and minimizing the energy with respect to c_1 and c_2.

7–7. The electric dipole moment of a polarized hydrogen atom in the above cases is simply $-ez$. The polarizability of an atom is the proportionality constant α in the equation $\mathbf{u} = \alpha E$, where $\mathbf{u}$ is the induced electric dipole and E the electric field. Calculate the dipole moment and the polarizability of hydrogen for each of the previous problems and compare with the experimental value $\alpha = \frac{9}{2}a_0{}^3 = .670 \times 10^{-24}$ cm^3.

7–8. Neglecting electron spin, calculate the effect of a magnetic field H in the z direction on the energy of the degenerate $2p$ level of a hydrogen atom. The perturbation term in the Hamiltonian operator is $\mathcal{3C}' = -\mu_{\text{mag}}H \cos \theta$.

7–9. Consider a particle of mass m in a spherical potential well of radius $r = a$. Inside the well $V(r) = 0$, while outside $V(r) = \infty$. As pointed out in Chapter 6, the solution of any spherically symmetric potential problem will result in the same angular solutions, namely the spherical harmonics. Using the R equation, then, but with $V(r) = 0$ in this case, obtain a solution by means of trial variation functions.

7–10. Show that, in the secular equation resulting from the variation method, $\langle i|\mathcal{3C}|k\rangle = \langle k|\mathcal{3C}|i\rangle$. Hint: Expand ϕ_i and ϕ_j as orthonormal sets of the true ψ^0's.

7–11. The harmonic oscillator is a problem which can be solved without difficulty by the variation method. Assume the potential energy is $V = \frac{1}{2}kx^2$. The first problem is to find a suitable trial function. Noting that the ground-state wave functions of all symmetric potential well problems are symmetric about the center, and remembering that a well-behaved wave function is finite, determine which of the following trial functions might be suitable to use:

$$Ae^{ax}, \; Ae^{-ax}, \; Ae^{a|x|}, \; Ae^{-a|x|}, \; Axe^{-a|x|}, \; Ae^{-ax^2},$$

$$A\frac{1}{x}e^{-ax^2}, \; A(\cos ax)e^{-x^2}, \; A(\sin ax)e^{-x^2}.$$

7–12. Using $Ae^{-2a|x|}$ as a trial variation function (A is a normalization constant and a a variable parameter), calculate the energy and the wave function for the ground state of the harmonic oscillator. How does this result compare with the exact solution in Chapter 4?

7–13. Using Ae^{-ax^2} as a trial variation function, calculate the energy and the wave function for the ground state of the harmonic oscillator. Is this a better function than the previous one? Why?

7–14. Suppose the potential energy of an anharmonic oscillator is given by

$$V = \tfrac{1}{2}kx^2 + ax^3.$$

If the x^3 term is considered to be a perturbation on the harmonic-oscillator potential, what is the effect of this perturbation on the energy levels of the harmonic oscillator?

7–15. Show that, for an electric charge e carrying out simple harmonic motion along the x axis, the selection rule for electric dipole transitions is $\Delta n = \pm 1$.

7–16. Verify the selection rules for n and l by calculating the transition moment integrals for hydrogen between the states $1s$ and $2s$, $1s$ and $2p$, $1s$ and $3p$, $1s$ and $4d$.

7–17. Verify that the determinantal wave function of a Li atom,

$$\psi = \begin{vmatrix} 1s\alpha(1) & 1s\beta(1) & 2s\alpha(1) \\ 1s\alpha(2) & 1s\beta(2) & 2s\alpha(2) \\ 1s\alpha(3) & 1s\beta(3) & 2s\alpha(3) \end{vmatrix},$$

is antisymmetric to the interchange of any two electrons.

7–18. If we attempted to put all three electrons of Li into the $1s$ orbital of the Li atom, the determinantal wave function could be

$$\psi = \begin{vmatrix} 1s\alpha(1) & 1s\beta(1) & 1s\alpha(1) \\ 1s\alpha(2) & 1s\beta(2) & 1s\alpha(2) \\ 1s\alpha(3) & 1s\beta(3) & 1s\alpha(3) \end{vmatrix}$$

or

$$\psi = \begin{vmatrix} 1s\alpha(1) & 1s\beta(1) & 1s\beta(1) \\ 1s\alpha(2) & 1s\beta(2) & 1s\beta(2) \\ 1s\alpha(3) & 1s\beta(3) & 1s\beta(3) \end{vmatrix}.$$

Show that these wave functions vanish.

7–19. Show that all closed-shell atomic configurations are in a ^1S electronic state. (Note that s^2, p^6, and d^{10} may be taken as examples of closed-shell configurations; also remember that the Pauli exclusion principle eliminates many possibilities.)

7–20. What is the connection between Unsold's theorem and the result of Problem 7–19?

7–21. Show that the same kind of electronic state arises from a p configuration as from p^5 configuration.

7–22. What states are possible for an sd configuration?

7–23. Find the lowest states for the elements O, Cl, Fe, La.

7-24. Show that the off-diagonal matrix elements of (7-24) are zero.

7-25. Complete the definite integrations outlined in Appendix E.

7-26. In Chapter 4 the spectra of conjugated hydrocarbons were treated by using the particle-in-a-box (free electron) model. Calculate the energy levels and wave functions for hexatriene, and determine the frequency of absorption for exciting an electron to the lowest unoccupied level. Using the appropriate wave functions, calculate $(\mu_x)_{mn}$ for this transition, and evaluate the integrated absorption coefficient. The observed value is $4.3 \times 10^{18} \sec^{-1} cm^{-1} mole^{-1}$ liter.

7-27. Perform the above calculations for octatetraene.

7-28. Using the variation function $\phi = Ae^{-kr}$, where k is a variable parameter, calculate the energy and the value of k giving the lowest energy for the hydrogen atom, and compare with the exact solution.

7-29. Find approximate energy levels for a particle attracted toward the origin by a force proportional to the third power of the distance.

7-30. Using the recursion formula for the Hermite polynomials (Appendix D), verify that the selection rule for the harmonic oscillator is $\Delta n = \pm 1$.

8

Molecules in Rotation and Microwave Spectroscopy

8.1 ENERGY STATES OF THE ROTATING DIATOMIC MOLECULE

From the difficulties that arise in attempting to understand the behavior of atomic systems, we well might expect the problems associated with molecular systems to be formidable indeed, and we shall not be disappointed in this expectation. One saving grace in the atomic problem is the centrally symmetric potential energy, which allows us to employ useful approximations at many stages. But this important symmetry property is immediately lacking even in the simplest molecule; for now there will be more than one massive nucleus, potential energies that are not centrally symmetric, and a complexity of motions of many particles that might appear to defy description.

Fortunately, the situation is not at all hopeless. It was suggested earlier that the energies of molecular systems can be separated conveniently into several parts with a reasonable degree of accuracy. This separation corresponds to our familiar way of analyzing the motions of many-particle systems into translation of the center of mass of the system, rotation of the system of masses about the center of mass, and movement of the individual particles with changes in their separations.

As in the atomic case, an extremely important factor is the tremendously large mass of a nucleus as compared with that of an electron. In atoms this results in the nucleus essentially being at the origin of the spherical polar coordinate system used to describe the system. In molecules it serves to make possible a separate consideration of the nuclear motions relative to one another and to the center of mass on one hand, and the motions of the electrons relative to the nuclei on the other. A complete molecular Schrödinger equation (neglecting spin effects for the moment) would include a ∇^2 term for each nucleus and for each electron and a potential-energy term for each electron-nuclear attraction, each electron-electron repulsion, and each nuclear-nuclear repulsion.

As in Chapter 6, some simplification results when the translation of the center of mass of this system is separated out. What is left is still unsolvable directly, but a detailed analysis of this problem by Born and Oppenheimer[1] showed that, to a first approximation, the Schrödinger equation can be separated into two parts. The first considers the nuclei to be fixed in space and is of the form

$$\left(-\frac{\hbar^2}{2m_e}\sum_i \nabla_i{}^2 + \sum_{i,i'}\frac{e^2}{r_{ii'}} - \sum_{i,j}\frac{Ze^2}{r_{ij}} + \sum_{j,j'}\frac{ZZ'e^2}{r_{jj'}}\right)\psi_{el} = E_{el}\psi_{el} \quad (8\text{--}1)$$

where i subscripts represent electrons and j subscripts nuclei. Notice that although all the potential-energy terms appear in this equation, there are kinetic-energy terms only for the electrons. If such an equation can be solved by suitable choice of coordinates and/or approximation methods, the results of the solution are the energies and wave functions for the electronic states of the molecule at a fixed internuclear separation $r_{jj'}$. These energies are calculated as a function of the internuclear distances and the minimum energy can be found by varying the $r_{jj'}$. This minimum energy represents the electronic energy of the molecule in its most stable configuration, which is that corresponding to the values of the $r_{jj'}$ at minimum energy. The solution of this equation will be discussed in more detail in Chapter 10. At this point we are primarily interested in the effect of these electronic energies on the remaining part of the problem. We have already mentioned that electronic states are generally so widely separated in energy that at room temperature only the lowest, the ground electronic state, need be considered. A typical curve showing the electronic energy of a stable molecular state for a diatomic molecule is illustrated in Fig. 8–1 as a function of the internuclear separation r_{AB}. The minimum of this curve represents the equilibrium nuclear separation r_e, and D_e represents the energy required to dissociate the molecule of this energy into separate atoms.

Equation (8–1), then, describes the electronic states of a molecule. The second equation contains all the remaining terms of the total molecular Hamiltonian and describes the nuclear motions and energies. It is of the form

$$\left[-\frac{\hbar^2}{2}\sum_j \frac{1}{m_j}\nabla_j{}^2 + E_{el}(r_{jj'})\right]\psi = E\psi. \quad (8\text{--}2)$$

Note that in this equation the electronic energy serves as the potential

[1] Born and Oppenheimer, *Ann. Physik*, **84**, 457 (1927).

energy governing the motions of the nuclei.   Thus, not only does the curve in Fig. 8–1 show how the electronic energy of the molecule varies with the separation of the nuclei, but also it represents the potential energy that governs these motions.   In the diatomic case (8–2) becomes particularly simple because E_{el} is a function of only one internuclear separation.

It would appear that in order to solve Eq. (8–2) for the nuclear motions (rotation and vibration), we must first solve (8–1) for the electronic

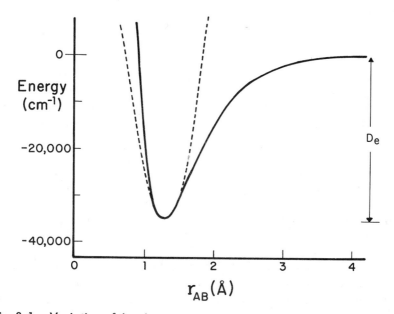

Fig. 8–1.   Variation of the electronic energy of HCl with internuclear separation.   The harmonic oscillator potential is shown for comparison.

energy, no small task even in simple cases.   Fortunately, this need not be.   The curve of Fig. 8–1 can be represented rather accurately by a number of analytical expressions the parameters of which can be determined by spectroscopic relations to be derived shortly.   One of the simplest equations was suggested by Morse (we will now use the conventional symbol $V(r)$ for the potential energy instead of $E_{el}(r)$):

$$V(r) = D_e[1 - e^{-a(r-r_e)}]^2. \qquad (8–3)$$

The relation of the parameters in this equation to the potential-energy curve is illustrated in Fig. 8–1.   The constant a is a measure of the curvature of the potential.

An even simpler potential function, which can be seen in Fig. 8–1 to be a fair approximation to the true potential-energy curve near the minimum, is the harmonic oscillator function,

$$V(r) = \tfrac{1}{2}k(r - r_e)^2.$$

This is a particularly convenient potential function since we are already familiar with many of the properties of the harmonic oscillator.

Let us now construct the Schrödinger equation for the nuclear part of the diatomic molecule problem, using the harmonic-oscillator potential-energy function. For two nuclei, A and B, we would have

$$\left\{ -\frac{\hbar^2}{2}\left(\frac{1}{m_A}\nabla_A{}^2 + \frac{1}{m_B}\nabla_B{}^2\right) + \tfrac{1}{2}k(r_{AB} - r_e)^2 \right\}\psi = E\psi.$$

If we consider this equation for a moment, it becomes apparent that it represents a two-body problem with a potential energy $V(r)$ that depends only on the separation of the two bodies. Therefore, the separation of variables discussed in Chapter 6 can be made immediately. That is, the two-body equation can be simplified by reformulating the equation in the coordinates of the center of mass of the nuclei and the reduced mass:

$$-\frac{\hbar^2}{2\mu}\nabla^2\psi + \tfrac{1}{2}k(r - r_e)^2\psi = E\psi, \qquad (8\text{--}4)$$

which describes the motion of a body of mass μ about the origin in spherical polar coordinates r, θ, and ϕ. In addition we can assume

$$\psi = R(r)\Theta(\theta)\Phi(\phi),$$

and because the potential energy depends only on r, the solution of (8–4) will yield exactly the same Θ and Φ functions as for the hydrogen atom. In Chapter 6 we discussed the properties of these functions in some detail, and we observed that the angular wave functions $Y_{m_l l} = \Theta\Phi$ have the important property that they are eigenfunctions of the operator for the square of the angular momentum and of the operator for the z-component of the angular momentum. The significance of the quantum numbers l and m_l is that $L = |\mathbf{L}| = \sqrt{l(l + 1)}\hbar$ and $L_z = m_l\hbar$.

For molecular states the quantum numbers l and m_l more often are given the symbols J and M_J, and for this reason we will use these designations here. It is unfortunate that some of the same letters should be used in several connotations, but so long as we confine our attention to atomic systems alone, or molecular systems alone, no confusion should arise. Thus, for the diatomic molecule we have

$$\hat{M}^2\Theta_{JM_J}\Phi_{M_J} = J(J + 1)\hbar^2\Theta_{JM_J}\Phi_{M_J}$$

and

$$\hat{M}_z\Theta_{JM_J}\Phi_{M_J} = M_J\hbar\Theta_{JM_J}\Phi_{M_J},$$

and we can immediately deduce the rotational angular properties of a molecular state from the quantum numbers J and M_J for that state.

We are left with the molecular equivalent of Eq. (6–12) to solve. With the harmonic-oscillator potential instead of the Coulomb potential this is

$$\frac{1}{r^2}\frac{d}{dr}\left(r^2\frac{dR(r)}{dr}\right)+\left[-\frac{J(J+1)}{r^2}+\frac{2\mu}{\hbar^2}\{E-\tfrac{1}{2}k(r-r_e)^2\}\right]R(r)=0.$$

The form of this equation can be simplified. First let us make the substitution

$$R(r)=\frac{S(r)}{r},$$

to obtain

$$\frac{d^2S(r)}{dr^2}-\frac{J(J+1)}{r^2}S(r)+\frac{2\mu}{\hbar^2}\left[E-\frac{k}{2}(r-r_e)^2\right]S(r)=0.$$

We will also write $q=r-r_e$, which results in

$$\frac{d^2S}{dq^2}-\frac{J(J+1)}{(q+r_e)^2}S+\frac{2\mu}{\hbar^2}\left[E-\frac{k}{2}q^2\right]S=0. \tag{8-5}$$

The denominator of the second term can be expanded as

$$\frac{1}{(q+r_e)^2}=\frac{1}{r_e^2}\left(1-\frac{2q}{r_e}+\frac{3q^2}{r_e^2}-\cdots\right), \tag{8-6}$$

and since the harmonic-oscillator potential is valid only at very small displacements from the equilibrium separation, we will neglect higher powers in (8–6). If we consider only the first term, we have

$$\frac{d^2S}{dq^2}-\frac{J(J+1)}{r_e^2}S+\frac{2\mu}{\hbar^2}\left(E-\frac{k}{2}q^2\right)S=0,$$

which rearranges to

$$\frac{d^2S}{dq^2}+\frac{2\mu}{\hbar^2}\left[\left\{E-\frac{\hbar^2J(J+1)}{2I_e}\right\}-\frac{k}{2}q^2\right]S=0, \tag{8-7}$$

where the moment of inertia of the molecule is $I_e=\mu r_e^2=\Sigma m_i r_i^2$, as in Fig. 8–2.

Since the second term in the brackets is constant and independent of q, this equation is essentially that which was considered in Sec. 4–6 for the harmonic oscillator. The boundary conditions in the simple harmonic-oscillator case were that the wave function must vanish at $q=-\infty$ and $q=+\infty$. In this case $S(r)=0$ at $q=0$ and $q=\infty$. Since the wave function has been seen not to extend far beyond the limits of the potential well, however, the limits $S(r)=0$ at $q=-\infty$ and $q=+\infty$

can be considered to apply here also. Thus (Sec. 4–6), the solution of (8–7) yields

$$E = \frac{J(J+1)\hbar^2}{2I_e} + (v + \tfrac{1}{2})h\nu_e, \quad v = 0, 1, 2, \ldots, \qquad (8\text{–}8)$$

where $\nu_e = (1/2\pi)\sqrt{k/\mu}$. The letter v has been used here in place of n to follow convention in describing molecular vibrational states.

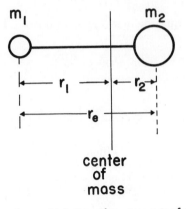

Fig. 8–2.   Parameters for calculating the moment of inertia of a diatomic molecule.

The second term in this expression obviously describes the energy-level pattern for a non-rotating harmonic oscillator. The first term is the equation for the energy levels of a rigid, freely rotating molecule. We could then express (8–8) as

$$E = E_{\text{rot}} + E_{\text{vib}},$$

which is an approximation we assumed in Chapters 2 and 5. The complete wave function for the rotating, vibrating molecule is thus

$$\psi = \Theta(\theta)\Phi(\phi)\psi_{\text{HO}}(r - r_e)r^{-1},$$

where ψ_{HO} is the harmonic-oscillator wave function discussed in Chapter 4. The relation of the vibrational and rotational energy states to the electronic energy is illustrated in Fig. 8–3. It is interesting to note that the lowest possible energy for the molecule is not the value of E_{el} at r_e but rather $E_{el} + \tfrac{1}{2}h\nu_e$ since there is a residual zero-point vibration energy even when $J = 0$ and $v = 0$.

Actual molecular parameters are such that the energy differences corresponding to changes in the quantum number v are much larger than those occurring for different values of J. At ordinary temperatures a large fraction of a collection of diatomic molecules will be in the lowest

($v = 0$) vibrational state. For this reason we will concern ourselves primarily with rotational states associated with the ground vibrational level. Neglecting the vibrational term in (8–8) entirely, the energy-level diagram for a freely rotating diatomic molecule is shown in Fig. 8–4a. Each one of these levels is ($2J + 1$)-degenerate since there are $2J + 1$ different M_J for a given J.

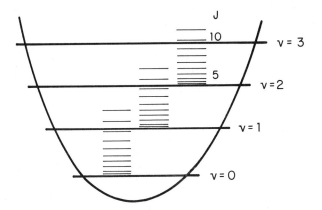

Fig. 8–3. Vibrational and rotational energy levels of a diatomic molecule. The lower rotational levels are crowded too closely to be observed separately.

A slightly more satisfactory result is obtained if the expansion (8–6) is cut off after the squared term rather than after the first term. Introducing this expression in (8–5) results in an equation which also can be manipulated into the form of the harmonic-oscillator equation by a suitable transformation of coordinates. The solution yields

$$E = (v + \tfrac{1}{2})h\nu_e + J(J + 1)\frac{\hbar^2}{2I_e} - \frac{J^2(J + 1)^2\hbar^4}{8\pi^2\nu_e^2 I_e^3}, \qquad (8-9)$$

in which the same terms appear, plus a third term, which takes into account the fact that, as the molecule rotates with greater energy, the centrifugal force tends to stretch the molecule, resulting in a greater moment of inertia and hence a slightly lower energy than if the centrifugal stretching did not occur. This effect is seen in the energy-level diagram (Fig. 8–4b) corresponding to Eq. (8–9) with the vibrational term again neglected. It is seen that the levels higher in energy (larger J) are the most affected.

Equation (8–9) is not entirely satisfactory for both vibrational and rotational levels, including excited states that are higher in energy. This is not surprising since the harmonic-oscillator potential is itself only fair near the potential minimum. For pure rotational transitions not involving higher vibrational states, however, (8–9) is generally satisfactory. We will investigate shortly the effect of the vibrational energy.

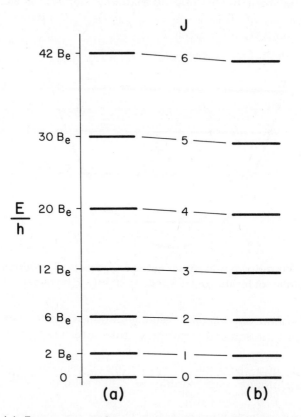

Fig. 8–4. (a) Energy levels for a rigid, freely rotating diatomic molecule. (b) Energy levels for a freely rotating diatomic molecule with centrifugal distortion.

Spectral transitions are conveniently measured in frequency units (sec^{-1} or cps), and hence a convenient expression for the rotational energy levels is

$$\frac{E}{h} = J(J+1)\frac{\hbar}{4\pi I_e} - \frac{J^2(J+1)^2\hbar^3}{16\pi^3\nu_e^2 I_e^3}$$
$$= J(J+1)B_e - J^2(J+1)^2 D, \tag{8–10}$$

where $B_e = \hbar/4\pi I_e$ and $D = 4B_e^3/\nu_e^2$. Spectroscopic energies are expressed also in units of cm^{-1} (ν/c), so that

$$\tilde{E} = \frac{E}{hc} = \tilde{B}_e J(J+1) - \tilde{D}J^2(J+1)^2.$$

It is obvious that $\tilde{B}_e = B_e/c$, $\tilde{D} = D/c$; and since we may define $\tilde{\nu}_e = \nu_e/c$, then $\tilde{D} = 4\tilde{B}_e{}^3/\tilde{\nu}_e{}^2$.   In these equations D and $\tilde{D}$ are not to be confused with the dissociation energy D_e.

8.2   SYMMETRY AND THE PARTITION FUNCTION FOR ROTATION

We have discussed the statistics of energy levels of atoms and molecules generally from the point of view that each higher level is less populated than the preceding lower level.   That this is not necessarily true

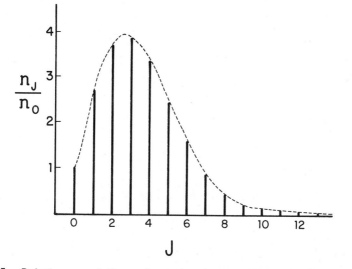

Fig. 8–5.   Relative populations of rotational energy levels for HCl at 300°K.

is strikingly apparent in the case of rotational levels.   The Boltzmann distribution law states that

$$\frac{n_i}{n_j} = \frac{g_i e^{-E_i/kT}}{g_j e^{-E_j/kT}} = \frac{g_i}{g_j}\,e^{-(E_i-E_j)/kT},$$

and the exponential term has been our justification for expecting a rapidly decreasing population of levels above the lowest levels except at high temperatures.   In the rotational case, however, two factors are responsible for a different behavior.

First of all, the separation of energy levels is small compared to kT, so that the change of population caused by the exponential is not great from one level to the next.   Also, the levels are degenerate, $g_J = 2J + 1$, and the degeneracy becomes greater with increasing J.   The combination of these two effects results in an increasing population of higher levels, which eventually levels off and then drops for succeeding higher levels. This is illustrated for HCl in Fig. 8–5.

The molecular partition function for the rotational levels of a diatomic molecule is, from (5–11),

$$Q_{rot} = \sum_{J=0}^{\infty} g_J e^{-E_J/kT} = \sum_{J=0}^{\infty} (2J+1)e^{-J(J+1)hB_e/kT}. \qquad (8-11)$$

For light molecules and at very low temperatures it is necessary to sum (8–11) directly, since the sum cannot be expressed in simple analytical form. When the energy differences are small compared to kT, however, the quantum number J can be considered a continuous variable and the sum replaced by

$$Q_{rot} = \int_0^{\infty} (2J+1)e^{-J(J+1)hB_e/kT}\, dJ. \qquad (8-12)$$

The integration is easily completed if we let $y = J(J+1)$; for

$$dy = d[J(J+1)] = d(J^2 + J) = (2J+1)\, dJ,$$

in which case (8–12) is equivalent to

$$Q_{rot} = \int_0^{\infty} e^{-hB_e y/kT}\, dy = \frac{kT}{hB_e}. \qquad (8-13)$$

From (5–13),

$$\frac{n_J}{n} = \frac{(2J+1)e^{-J(J+1)hB_e/kT}}{Q_{rot}} = \frac{(2J+1)hB_e}{kT}e^{-J(J+1)hB_e/kT}.$$

The partition function for rotation allows us to evaluate the contribution of rotation to the thermodynamic properties. The molar energy due to rotation, for example, is

$$E = \frac{RT^2}{Q}\left(\frac{\partial Q}{\partial T}\right)_V = \frac{RT^2 hB_e}{kT}\left(\frac{k}{hB_e}\right) = RT$$

and

$$C_V = R,$$

which was the contribution measured for diatomic gases as discussed earlier. For most cases of interest hB_e/kT is less than .3, in which case the partition function is given within .1 per cent or better by

$$Q_{rot} = \frac{kT}{hB_e}\left[1 + \tfrac{1}{3}\frac{hB_e}{kT} + \tfrac{1}{15}\left(\frac{hB_e}{kT}\right)^2 + \cdots\right].$$

In this discussion it has been assumed that all diatomic molecules are described by the energy-level equation (8–8) and the partition function (8–13). But we have neglected an important factor that was discussed in the previous chapter, the symmetry requirements which must be met by the wave functions describing the possible states of a molecule. In the atomic case these requirements are not difficult to handle since the massive nucleus locates the origin of the coordinate system, and it is only necessary to require that the wave functions be antisymmetric to the interchange of any two electrons. In the molecular case, however, there are two or more nuclei and several electrons, and all the particles must obey symmetry restrictions.

One symmetry property which was discussed in the preceding chapter is the symmetry of the atomic wave function with respect to inversion of the coordinates of all the electrons through the origin. Inspection shows that the Hamiltonian operator for a diatomic molecule is unchanged by the inversion of the coordinates of all the electrons and nuclei through the origin, and hence the total wave function for the molecule must be symmetric or antisymmetric to such an inversion.

We designate wave functions (and states) as $+$ or $-$ (even or odd), depending on whether the wave function remains the same or changes sign when all particles are inverted through the origin. We will now consider the symmetry of molecular states, including the rotational states. Since the total molecular wave function can be regarded as a product of electronic, vibrational, and rotational functions,

$$\psi = \psi_e \frac{\psi_v}{r} \psi_r,$$

we can consider the symmetry properties of each of these functions separately, and then deduce the symmetry of the total function.

A direct approach would be to examine the behavior of the functions directly upon the proper substitution of coordinates; that is, by replacing x, y, and z by $-x$, $-y$, and $-z$, or by replacing r, θ, and ϕ by r, $\pi - \theta$, and $\pi + \phi$, we can determine whether the sign of ψ changes or not. An often simpler approach is possible if we look at some of the general symmetry properties that we have discussed. The inversion of the particle coordinates, for example, can be viewed as the successive operations of rotating the molecule about an axis through its center and then reflecting the particles through the plane which passes through the molecule and is perpendicular to the C_2 axis of rotation (Fig. 8–6).

We have not yet discussed the symmetry of molecular electronic states, but we shall find that the ground electronic states of most diatomic molecules are even with respect to this inversion of the coordinates. The step of rotating the entire molecule 180° obviously leaves the electron-nuclear distances unchanged and hence ψ_e unchanged. For most molecules in their ground state it is found also that ψ_e remains unchanged on reflection through any plane passing through the nuclei. Electronic states that do not change sign upon such reflection are often labeled $+$ states, while those that change sign when reflected are called $-$ states.

The symmetry of electronic states will be considered in more detail in Chapter 10.

The vibrational function ψ_v/r is seen also not to change sign with the rotation and reflection operations because ψ_v/r is a function of $r - r_e$ and r only, and these quantities are not altered by the two procedures.

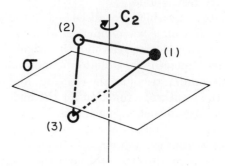

Fig. 8–6. Inversion of coordinates as successive operations of rotation and reflection.

Finally, from either substitution of the inverted coordinates into the rotational functions (Table 6–2) or investigation of the signs of these functions and their spatial distributions (Figs. 6–5 and 6–6) we can determine quickly that all rotational states with even values of J are unchanged by inversion, while those with odd J change sign. Thus for molecules with $+$ electronic states (the usual case) those states with even J are $+$ and states with odd J are $-$ (Table 8–1). This symmetry consideration

TABLE 8–1. Parity of Molecular States with Respect to Inversion Through the Origin

	Electronic State	
	$+$	$-$
J even	$+$	$-$
J odd	$-$	$+$

has an effect on the possible transitions that give rise to rotational spectra, as we shall see.

A particularly interesting situation arises with respect to homonuclear diatomic molecules. In addition to inversion symmetry we now have the requirement of symmetry of the wave function on exchange of the two identical nuclei. We are assuming that the electronic wave function is already antisymmetric to electron exchange as required for spin $\frac{1}{2}$ particles. It was mentioned in Chapter 7 that for particles with zero or integral spin the wave function must be symmetric to exchange. Many nuclei have an intrinsic spin angular momentum similar to that of electrons. For nuclei this spin angular momentum is given the symbol $\mathbf{I}$, and the nuclear spin quantum number I has exactly the same significance as does S for electrons ($|\mathbf{I}|^2 = I(I + 1)\hbar^2$, etc.). Common examples of nuclei with this property are O^{16} ($I = 0$), H^2 ($I = 1$), C^{12} ($I = 0$), N^{14} ($I = 1$). Such particles are often called *Bosons* since they follow the quantum statistics elaborated by Bose and Einstein. Particles with half-integral spin, so-called *Fermions*, must be described by wave functions antisymmetric to exchange of two identical particles. In addition

TABLE 8–2. Parity and Symmetry of Molecular States with Respect to Interchange of Identical Nuclei

	Electronic State			
	g^+	g^-	u^+	u^-
J even	$+$ Sym	$-$ Anti	$+$ Anti	$-$ Sym
J odd	$-$ Anti	$+$ Sym	$-$ Sym	$+$ Anti

to the electron, typical nuclear examples are H^1 ($I = \frac{1}{2}$), C^{13} ($I = \frac{1}{2}$), Na^{23} ($I = \frac{3}{2}$), Cl^{35} ($I = \frac{3}{2}$), and Mn^{55} ($I = \frac{5}{2}$).

As in the case of inversion symmetry, we can visualize the operation of exchanging two nuclei as the result of several successive operations. In this simple case two operations which would accomplish the desired result would be (1) inversion of all particles (nuclei and electrons) through the origin, followed by (2) inversion of the electrons alone back through the origin. This would leave only the nuclei interchanged. Since step 1 is identical with the inversion properties we just examined, it remains to determine the effect of step 2 on ψ_e. Again we must leave the details of electronic symmetry to a later chapter, but for simple homonuclear diatomic molecules it is found that all electronic states are either symmetric to inversion through the origin, in which case they are called g (gerade) states, or antisymmetric to inversion, in which case they are called u (ungerade) states.

For homonuclear molecules with $+$ electronic states we see, then, that on combining steps 1 and 2 the total wave function remains unchanged on exchange of nuclei for g states with even J and changes sign when J is odd. For u states, on the other hand, the sign of ψ remains the same for odd J and changes for even J. Exactly the reverse is found for $-$ electronic states. These statements are summarized in Table 8–2.

The effect of these considerations can now be deduced. We will first consider nuclei with $I = 0$. In this case the total wave function must be symmetric to nuclear exchange. Hence for homonuclear diatomic molecules consisting of such nuclei, if the electronic state is g^+, then only states with even J are allowed. States with odd J have antisymmetric wave functions and are not permitted. An example of such a molecule

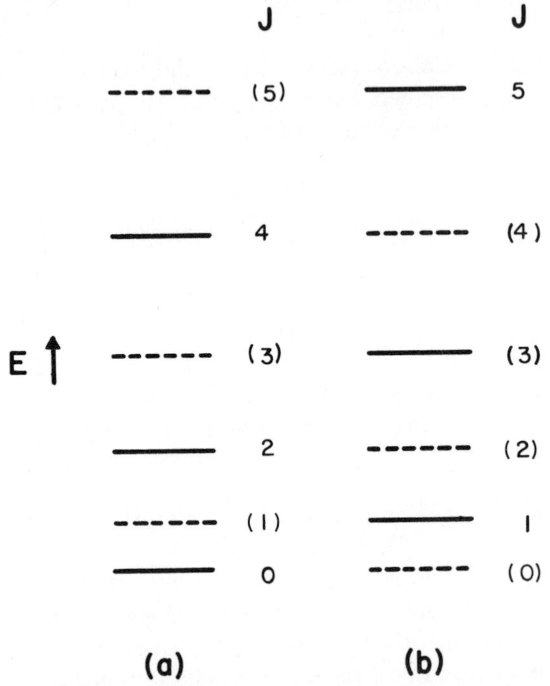

Fig. 8–7. Schematic representation of the rotational levels of (a) Hg_2^{200}, which has an electronic state even with respect to rotation, reflection, and inversion, (b) O_2^{16}, which has an electronic state even with respect to rotation and inversion, but odd with respect to reflection. Levels in dotted lines are not allowed by symmetry.

is Hg_2^{200}. The rotational levels for this molecule are shown in Fig. 8–7a, where the missing forbidden levels are indicated by dotted lines. Obviously, the symmetry requirements for nuclear exchange have an important bearing on the nature of the rotational states of the molecule.

If a molecule has a u^+ electronic state, the symmetry requirements restrict the molecule to rotational states with odd J. If the electronic function should be odd to the reflection operation, then our arguments are reversed from those of the preceding paragraph. An important example of this situation is O_2^{16}, which has a g electronic state, but which is odd to reflection through the plane of the nuclei. Thus for O_2 only odd rotational states are allowed. The energy levels of O_2 are illustrated in Fig. 8–7b.

The statistical weights of these rotational states have two contributions. The first of these is the $(2J + 1)$-degeneracy of the rotational levels. The second is any degeneracy that may arise because there is more than one way to pair nuclear spins in order to obtain a wave function of the correct symmetry to nuclear exchange. In the cases we have just described, since there is no nuclear spin, there is only one significant nuclear arrangement corresponding to each rotational state, and therefore the nuclear statistical weight for states permitted by symmetry is 1.

If we generalize our example now to a homonuclear diatomic molecule in which the nuclei have spin, the situation becomes slightly different because now the symmetry of the total wave function can be adjusted by constructing nuclear spin functions. We shall be concerned first with the simplest case, in which the nuclei have $I = \frac{1}{2}$. Since particles with half-integral spin are Fermions, the total wave functions for the states of this molecule must be antisymmetric to nuclear interchange. Consider, for example, a molecule in a g^+ electronic state. When the nuclear spins were zero, only rotational states with even J were allowed since only these wave functions were symmetric to nuclear exchange. If the nuclei have spin, however, then the total wave function will be given by

$$\psi = \psi_e \frac{\psi_v}{r} \psi_r \psi_{\text{nuclear spin}},$$

where it is assumed that the electron spin is already included in ψ_e. Recalling the approach taken with electron spin in complex atoms, we can construct four nuclear spin functions which are symmetric or antisymmetric to nuclear interchange. They are, omitting normalization,

$$\alpha(1)\beta(2) - \beta(1)\alpha(2)$$
$$\alpha(1)\alpha(2)$$
$$\alpha(1)\beta(2) + \beta(1)\alpha(2)$$
$$\beta(1)\beta(2)$$

where α denotes the spin function for $I_z = \frac{1}{2}$ and β that for $I_z = -\frac{1}{2}$.

The first of these functions is antisymmetric and therefore must go with a combination of $\psi_e \psi_v \psi_r$ which is symmetric in order to produce a total wave function which is antisymmetric as required for Fermions. In other words, for g^+ states, if there were no nuclear spin, we could not have a rotational level for each J, but when the nuclei have spin (half-integral in this case), then states with even J are possible if they contain the antisymmetric spin functions, while states with odd J are possible which contain the symmetric spin functions along with the antisymmetric

$\psi_e\psi_v\psi_r$. Since there are one antisymmetric nuclear spin function and three symmetric spin functions, there will be three times as many states with odd J as with even J. That is, the nuclear spin degeneracy of even J levels will be 1 and for odd J levels will be 3, so that the total degeneracy of even J levels will be $2J + 1$ and for odd J levels will be $3(2J + 1)$.

The foregoing description applies to the important molecule H_2 (H^1H^1), for which $I = \frac{1}{2}$ and for which the ground electronic state is a Σ_g^+ state.

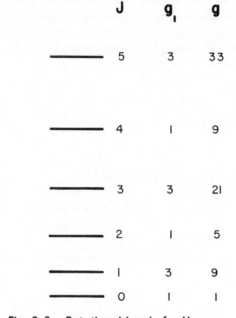

J	g_I	g
5	3	33
4	1	9
3	3	21
2	1	5
1	3	9
0	1	1

Fig. 8–8. Rotational levels for H_2.

The rotational levels of H_2 are sketched in Fig. 8–8, where the nuclear spin degeneracy, the rotational degeneracy, and the total statistical weights of the levels are indicated. Note that here, as contrasted with the $I = 0$ case, in which alternate levels are forbidden because of symmetry, all levels are possible, but their statistical weights alternate because of the singlet-triplet nature of even and odd J states.

The chemist generally regards such matters as nuclear spin and isotopic substitution as being relatively unimportant in chemical considerations, but from these results it should be apparent that these factors can have an important bearing on the properties of molecules. In terms of a physical model the singlet and triplet rotational states of H_2 correspond to molecules in which the two nuclear spins are oriented simultaneously in opposite directions (singlet) or in the same direction (triplet). There is a very strong selection rule which forbids transitions between states of different nuclear spin multiplicity. That is, molecular collisions, electrical fields, and similar perturbations cannot cause one of the nuclear spins in a hydrogen molecule to undergo a transition from one orientation to another. Only magnetic interactions, which are generally absent unless magnetic fields of the right sort are deliberately applied to the system or paramagnetic species are present, can cause such transitions. This means, in effect, that the nuclear singlet and triplet levels are essentially isolated from one another. In the absence of the necessary magnetic interactions, H_2 molecules with the two nuclear spins parallel will remain so, and those molecules with nuclear spins antiparallel will similarly remain with these spins opposed.

Since thermodynamic properties such as entropy, free energy, and heat capacity depend on the energy levels of a system, their degeneracies, and the populations of these states, it is seen that these two kinds of hydrogen molecules will exhibit different properties. The multiplicities of the even J levels are different from those of the odd J levels, for example, and the occupation of the respective sets of levels will differ in the two cases. The molecules occupying the odd J levels are traditionally known as ortho hydrogen and the even J species as para hydrogen. We can determine how many hydrogen molecules in a sample of H_2 should be ortho and how many should be para, as well as such quantities as the heat capacity of an equilibrium mixture.

If we denote the total nuclear spin by the symbol T ($T = 0$ for antiparallel, 1 for parallel spins of $I = \frac{1}{2}$), then the spin multiplicity of a level is $2T + 1$, and the partition function for rotation, including both rotational and nuclear spin degeneracy, is

$$Q_{\rm rot} = \sum_{J=0}^{\infty} (2J + 1)(2T + 1)e^{-J(J+1)hB_e/kT}. \qquad (8\text{--}14)$$

In the case of H_2 we know that when J is even, $T = 0$, and when J is odd, $T = 1$, so we can split this equation into

$$Q_{\rm rot} = \sum_{J \text{ even}} (2J + 1)e^{-J(J+1)hB_e/kT} + 3 \sum_{J \text{ odd}} (2J + 1)e^{-J(J+1)hB_e/kT}.$$
$$(8\text{--}15)$$

At high temperatures, when $hB_e \ll kT$, we can integrate rather than sum over states, and

$$\sum_{J \text{ even}} = \sum_{J \text{ odd}} = \frac{1}{2} \int_0^{\infty} (2J + 1)e^{-J(J+1)hB_e/kT} \, dJ$$
$$= \frac{kT}{2hB_e}.$$

From (8–15),

$$Q_{\rm rot} = \frac{kT}{2hB_e} + \frac{3kT}{2hB_e} = 2\frac{kT}{hB_e}. \qquad (8\text{--}16)$$

This is twice the value which we obtained in (8–13) without consideration of nuclear spin, and so before we come to any conclusions, we should investigate the heteronuclear case once again, this time with nuclear spin included.

If the nuclei in molecule AB have spins I_A and I_B, then there are $2I_A + 1$ possible orientations of spin A along an axis of quantization, and since the differences in energy of these orientations are negligible compared to the rotational energy differences we are considering here, they are all assumed to be of the same energy, giving a nuclear spin partition multiplicity of $2I_A + 1$ for A. Similarly, for B the nuclear spin partition multiplicity is $2I_B + 1$. The total partition function for the molecule AB is the product of the rotational partition function and the nuclear spin partition function:

$$Q_{rot} = \frac{kT}{hB_e} (2I_A + 1)(2I_B + 1). \tag{8-17}$$

For H_2, $I_A = I_B = \frac{1}{2}$, so that

$$Q_{rot} = 4 \frac{kT}{hB_e},$$

which is twice as great as the value we obtain in (8–16) when we impose the symmetry requirements on the homonuclear molecule. The difference between (8–16) and (8–17) can be corrected if we multiply the partition function (8–17) by $1/\sigma$, where σ, the symmetry number, is the number of non-equivalent ways in which the atoms of the molecule can be interchanged by rigid rotation of the molecule in space and remain completely indistinguishable from some other such orientational rearrangement,

$$Q_{rot} = \frac{1}{\sigma} \frac{kT}{hB_e} (2I_A + 1)(2I_B + 1). \tag{8-18}$$

For the AB molecule there is only one configuration, as no rotation would result in an indistinguishable orientation, and hence $\sigma_{AB} = 1$; but for the homonuclear molecule AA we cannot distinguish one orientation of the molecule from a second in which the molecule has been rotated 180° about an axis through the center of the molecule, and hence $\sigma_{AA} = 2$. With $\sigma = 2$ the partition function (8–18) reduces to the correct partition function (8–16). For the heteronuclear molecule there are no symmetry requirements, and (8–18) gives the correct result with $\sigma = 1$.

Strictly speaking, (8–18) must be used in all cases for studying in detail the distribution of diatomic molecules among rotational states. Fortunately, a simplification occurs when we consider chemical and physical processes and quantities such as ΔG, ΔS, and equilibrium constants. Since nuclear spin degeneracies appear in the partition functions of both reactants and products, and since the number and identities of the nuclei are unchanged, the nuclear parts of the reactant and product partition functions cancel out, leaving only the original partition functions (8–14) times $1/\sigma$. Therefore, for most chemical applications of statistical thermodynamics a satisfactory rotational partition function is

$$Q_{\text{rot}} = \frac{1}{\sigma} \frac{kT}{hB_e},\tag{8–19}$$

or a refinement thereof as required by the temperature.

Returning to the properties of H_2, we see from (8–15) that for even J

$$\frac{n_J}{n} = \frac{(2J+1)e^{-J(J+1)hB_e/kT}}{Q_{\text{rot}}},$$

and for odd J

$$\frac{n_J}{n} = \frac{3(2J+1)e^{-J(J+1)hB_e/kT}}{Q_{\text{rot}}},$$

so that if the nuclear spin states of hydrogen gas are in equilibrium,

$$\frac{(\text{ortho})}{(\text{para})} = \frac{3\sum_{\text{odd } J}(2J+1)e^{-J(J+1)hB_e/kT}}{\sum_{\text{even } J}(2J+1)e^{-J(J+1)hB_e/kT}}.$$

As the temperature becomes high, so that $hB_e \ll kT$, the two summations become identical, and

$$\frac{(\text{ortho})}{(\text{para})} = 3.$$

The equilibrium composition of hydrogen is shown in Fig. 8–9 as a function of temperature, and the predicted behavior is observed experimentally. The fact that nuclear spin reorientations are forbidden means that if hydrogen gas is cooled from room temperature, the ortho/para ratio of 3 will stay fixed, so that the distribution is no longer an equilibrium. At very low temperatures (20°K) the equilibrium ratio of ortho and para forms should be almost pure para hydrogen. This equilibrium can be attained if the hydrogen is brought into contact with charcoal, which catalyzes a dissociation-exchange process. If the gas is then warmed to room temperature, we obtain a non-equilibrium sample of nearly pure para hydrogen at room temperature. The thermodynamic properties of ortho, para, normal (25 per cent para), and equilibrium hydrogen can be calculated from the partition functions and measured experimentally. The heat capacities are shown in Fig. 8–10.

This discussion of the statistics of rotational states can be extended without difficulty to molecules in which the nuclei have $I > \frac{1}{2}$. The spin multiplicities become more complicated since more orientations of the nuclear spins are possible. Qualitatively the approach is the same, however. For homonuclear molecules containing nuclei with integral spin, the states must be symmetric to nuclear exchange. For nuclei with half-integral spin, the wave functions must be antisymmetric. The resulting levels with the higher total nuclear spin $(2I)$ are still called ortho states, and those with lower nuclear spin are the para form. In general, the

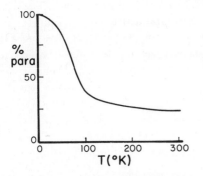

Fig. 8–9. Equilibrium composition of H_2 as a function of temperature. (After Davidson, *Statistical Mechanics*, McGraw-Hill Book Co., 1963, p. 135; used by permission.)

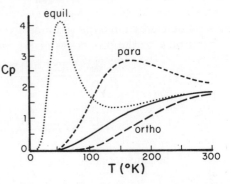

Fig. 8–10. Heat capacity of H_2. (After Herzberg, *Spectra of Diatomic Molecules*, 2nd ed., D. Van Nostrand Co., 1950, p. 470.)

high-temperature partition function for homonuclear diatomic molecules having nuclei with spin I is

$$Q_{rot} = (2I + 1)^2 \frac{kT}{2hB_e},$$

and the ortho/para ratio is $(I + 1)/I$. For heteronuclear diatomic molecules, all rotational states are possible, and there are no nuclear spin degeneracies to consider.

8.3 ROTATIONAL SPECTRA OF DIATOMIC MOLECULES

Thus far we have explored only the nature of rotational states for diatomic molecules. The quantum-mechanical picture is substantiated by the measurement of the temperature variation of thermodynamic quantities such as heat capacity and entropy. More directly, the existence and spacing of rotational energy levels can be verified by spectroscopic experiments. Rotational transitions can be induced by electromagnetic radiation whose frequency lies in the far infrared and microwave regions; transitions involving simultaneous vibrational and rotational changes are observed in the infrared region; and finally electronic transitions accompanied by vibrational and rotational transitions can be induced with radiation in the visible and ultraviolet regions. The interpretation of absorption and emission spectra in all these experiments strongly supports the quantum-mechanical theory, and extension to statistical treatments gives quantitative agreement with thermodynamic results. We are interested, therefore, in determining first of all the nature of rotational transitions and secondly the resulting nature of rotational absorption spectra.

In Chapter 7 we considered the time-dependent perturbation treatment of transitions, and it was seen that in order to predict possible electric dipole transitions induced by electromagnetic radiation, it is necessary to determine between which states the electric dipole moment matrix elements, μ_{kn}, are not zero. We have described the rotational states of diatomic molecules by the product functions, $\Theta\Phi$, these being the same spherical harmonic functions as were obtained in the solution of the hydrogen atom problem. In addition, we have already explored the dipole moment matrix elements for these functions in Sec. 7.8 in connection with atomic spectra. It was shown there that transitions are possible only between states for which $\Delta M_J = 0$ or ± 1 and for which $\Delta J = \pm 1$. It was also pointed out that the symmetry of the states and the dipole moment operator can be used to determine forbidden transitions, and we saw that electric dipole transitions are possible only from even to odd $(+ \rightarrow -)$ or odd to even $(- \rightarrow +)$ states. Since states with even J are even and states with odd J are odd, this also agrees with the rule $\Delta J = \pm 1$. Further, we have seen that, for homonuclear diatomic molecules, transitions cannot occur between symmetric (with respect to nuclear exchange) and antisymmetric states because of a strong selection rule that $\Delta I = 0$. In other words, electric dipole interactions do not provide a mechanism for changing nuclear spin orientation. The result of this restriction is that no electric dipole transitions between rotational states are possible at all for homonuclear diatomic molecules since any allowed transitions between two symmetric states or between two antisymmetric states would violate the selection rule $\Delta J = \pm 1$. Hence we cannot observe pure rotational spectra of homonuclear diatomic molecules.

This latter conclusion can also be reached from another viewpoint. The classical picture of the interaction of electromagnetic radiation with matter requires that there be a changing dipole moment for radiation to be emitted or absorbed. In the case of a rotating molecule, such a changing dipole moment can be viewed as resulting if the molecule has a permanent dipole moment, since the component of this moment in the direction of the electric field vector of the radiation will oscillate as the molecular dipole rotates. If the molecule has no permanent dipole, however, no such interaction is possible. Clearly any heteronuclear diatomic molecule will have an unsymmetric charge distribution, which will give the molecule a permanent electric dipole moment. The symmetry of homonuclear molecules precludes such a resultant moment. The necessity for a permanent molecular dipole moment for induced transitions can be seen also by inspecting the dipole matrix elements μ_{kn}. These integrals contain a dipole moment operator $\mathbf{u} = er$, and regardless of whether the rotational wave functions have the correct symmetries, the integral will still be zero if the dipole moment is zero. Hence we shall be concerned here only with the rotational spectra of heteronuclear diatomic molecules. Homonuclear molecules undergo rotational transitions simultaneously with vibrational and electronic transitions, and these can be observed, as will be seen in later chapters.

Applying the selection rule $\Delta J = +1$, corresponding to absorption of radiation, we obtain from the expression for rotational energy levels

$$\nu = \frac{\Delta E}{h} = 2B_e(J + 1) - 4D(J + 1)^3 \qquad (8\text{--}20)$$

and

$$\bar{\nu} = \Delta \tilde{E} = \frac{\Delta E}{hc} = 2\tilde{B}_e(J + 1) - 4\tilde{D}(J + 1)^3,$$

where J is the rotational quantum number for the initial (lower) state and can have the values $0, 1, 2, \ldots$. In most cases the centrifugal distortion effect is small, and the primary characteristics of the spectrum can be seen from the first term. We see that the frequencies of radiation absorbed correspond to $2B_e$, $4B_e$, $6B_e$, $\ldots$. The transitions corresponding to these frequencies are illustrated in Fig. 8–11. It is seen that the resulting spectrum consists of equally spaced lines, each separated by a frequency difference of $2B_e$. Both the frequencies of the lines and the separations of the lines thus allow us to calculate B_e for the molecule and hence to calculate the moment of inertia. In the diatomic molecule only the masses of the two atoms are further needed to calculate r_e.

A simple example of this case is HI, three rotational lines of which have been measured at .78, .39, and .26 mm. These correspond to frequencies of 3.85×10^{11}, 7.69×10^{11}, and 1.15×10^{12} sec^{-1}, respectively. The lowest-frequency line corresponds to the $J = 0 \rightarrow 1$ transition, as can be verified from the spacing of the lines giving $B_e = 1.93 \times 10^{11}$ sec^{-1}. From this it is easily found that $I_e = 4.34 \times 10^{-40}$ g cm^2. From the atomic masses of H and I the reduced mass is calculated to be 1.66×10^{-24} g, so that the equilibrium separation of the nuclei is

$r_e = 1.62 \times 10^{-8}$ cm. Some examples of diatomic molecules studied by microwave techniques are listed in Table 8–3 with calculated molecular parameters.

Experimentally, the details of obtaining pure rotational spectra are quite different from those encountered in more familiar spectroscopic techniques. The earliest pure rotational transitions were observed for

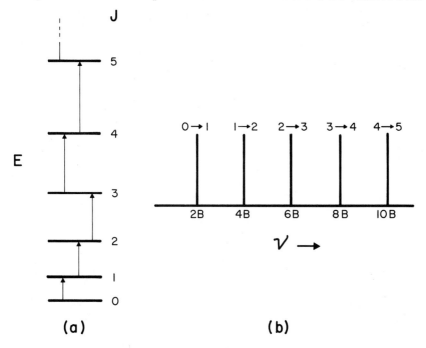

Fig. 8–11. (a) Allowed rotational transitions and (b) resulting absorption spectrum of a diatomic molecule.

relatively light molecules in the far infrared. Far infrared techniques involve the use of gratings and mirrors rather than prisms and lenses in order to avoid absorption of radiation by these media, and the light path must be evacuated for the same reason. Ultimately, production of sufficient radiation and detection of radiation becomes a severe difficulty at lower frequencies.

The development of generation and transmission mechanisms for microwave radiation was accelerated by World War II when radiation in this frequency region was utilized in radar systems. This development proved to be a boon to spectroscopists, who were now able to explore formerly inaccessible regions. The frequency range of interest is intermediate between more familiar radio frequencies and infrared and optical

TABLE 8–3.   Molecular Constants of Some Representative Diatomic Molecules*

Molecule	B_e (Mcps)	$\tilde{B}_e$ (cm⁻¹)	α_e (Mcps)	I_e (Å² × atomic mass units)	r_e (Å)	$\tilde{\nu}_e$ (cm⁻¹)	D (Mcps)	μ_e (Debyes)
H¹Cl³⁵	317,510	10.591	9050	1.592	1.275	2989.74	15.94	1.18
DI¹²⁷	(B_0 = 97,537.2)	(B_0 = 3.25348)	1840	(I_0 = 5.183)	1.604	1630	1.56	0.38
C¹²O¹⁶	57,897.5	1.93124	524.0	8.731	1.128	2170.21	0.1834	0.10
C¹³O¹⁶	55,344.9	1.84610	488.3	9.134	1.128	2074.81	0.1753	0.10
Cl³⁵F¹⁹	15,483.69	0.516479	130.67	32.65	1.628	793.2	0.02626	0.88
Cl³⁷F¹⁹	15,189.22	0.506657	126.96	33.28	1.628	778.6	0.02527	0.88
Br⁷⁹F¹⁹	10,706.9	0.357143	156.3	47.21	1.759	671	0.0121	1.29
Br⁸¹F¹⁹	10,655.7	0.355435	155.8	47.44	1.759	670	0.0121	1.29
K⁴¹Cl³⁵	3,767.394	0.125667	22.865	134.2	2.667	300	0.003	10.48
K³⁹Cl³⁵	3,856.370	0.128634	23.680	131.1	2.667	300	0.003	10.48
K³⁹Cl³⁷	3,746.583	0.124972	22.676	134.9	2.667	300	0.003	10.48
I¹²⁷Cl³⁵	3,422.300	0.114155	16.06	147.7	2.321	384.2	0.00121	0.65
I¹²⁷Cl³⁷	3,277.365	0.109320	15.05	154.2	2.321	376	0.00111	0.65

* From Townes and Schawlow, *Microwave Spectroscopy*, McGraw-Hill Book Co., 1955, p. 13; used by permission.

frequencies.   The experimental and theoretical treatment of microwave radiation reflects this dichotomy.   Microwave radiation is more accurately handled by electromagnetic equations than by simple optical equations.   It is also not so conveniently transmitted through space in beams in so far as spectroscopic applications are concerned.   At the same time the high frequencies involved do not allow transmission of energy through ordinary conductors as is the case for radio and lower frequencies.   Microwave radiation is most advantageously transmitted

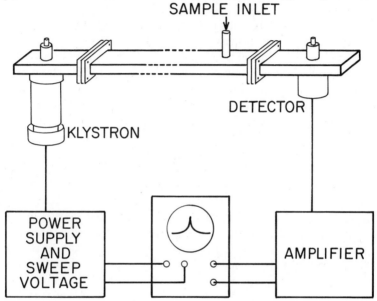

Fig. 8–12.   Essential components of a simple microwave spectrometer.

through hollow metallic conductors of such geometry that the electric and magnetic fields can be utilized to the greatest extent.   The hollow rectangular wave guide used for this purpose is now commonplace in chemical research facilities.

A special advantage gained in the microwave region (and also in the RF and lower regions) is that radiation of the desired frequency can be generated almost monochromatically by special electronic tubes, the klystron tube being the most used.   These klystron generators can be swept slowly over a limited range of frequencies, obviating the use of a dispersing prism or grating to single out successive frequencies.   The details of microwave spectrometers are extensive and varied, but the main features are shown in Fig. 8–12.   The radiation is generated by a klystron tube and passed through a wave guide, which contains the sample. The radiation not absorbed is then detected by a sensitive crystal detector or bolometer or similar detection device, which produces a voltage proportional to the intensity of the radiation detected. Because of the electrical properties of solids and liquids and because molecular collisions and similar interactions that occur in condensed phases severely limit the life times of rotational states, it is necessary to use gases at fairly low pressures in microwave experiments. Nevertheless, use of high and low temperatures greatly extends the types of molecules which can be studied.

It was noted in the previous section that the populations of rotational levels increase at first with increasing J. The most obvious effect on the microwave absorption spectrum is that the lines of progressively higher frequency will have progressively greater intensities since there are more molecules to undergo excitation in each succeeding state. Since both the absolute frequencies and the separation of the lines depend on B_e, it can be seen that molecules with small moments of inertia will have widely spaced lines at higher frequencies. The light hydrogen halide HCl is actually observed in the far infrared region rather than in the microwave range. Heavier molecules, on the other hand, will exhibit many closely spaced lines at lower frequencies in the microwave region.

In addition to the effect of rotational level population, line intensities also depend on the magnitude of the permanent electric dipole moment of the molecule, as is evident from the transition moment integral.

As resolution and sensitivity increase, the centrifugal term becomes more important. This is especially true for lines corresponding to large values of J. From (8–20) we see that the effect of the centrifugal distortion term is to lower the frequency of the higher lines slightly. Since this term is small for low J, measurement of the low-frequency line can be used to establish B_e, and measurement of higher lines then determines D. An alternative procedure is to use several frequencies to determine both B_e and D. The far infrared spectrum of HCl provides an excellent example of this sort of situation. The observed absorption lines for HCl are listed in Table 8–4. The experimental limitations prevented observation of the lowest transitions, but the separation of the lines allows one to deduce the frequency of the lowest line and the identification of all the observed lines. The separation of the lines is not constant, however, indicating centrifugal distortion. The values of B_e and D which give the best fit of the energy-level equation to all the observed lines are listed in Table 8–4.

The energy-level equation (8–9) was derived from the Schrödinger equation assuming a harmonic-oscillator potential. A more accurate potential function, such as the Morse potential, yields a more complicated expression which includes an additional term containing both the vibrational and rotational quantum numbers. This term arises from the anharmonicity of the vibrational motion, which because of its asymmetry about r_e results in a different equilibrium internuclear separation for each vibrational state.   This effect is illustrated in Fig. 8–13. The asymmetry of the potential function causes the internuclear separation to increase with higher and higher vibrational states.   Although the vibrational coupling is small, it is significant, considering the resolution of modern instrumentation, and for lower rotational lines is far more

TABLE 8–4.   Absorption Spectrum of HCl in the Far Infrared*

| | | | $\tilde{\nu}$ (calc.) | |
| | | | | $\tilde{B}_e = 10.395,$ |
J	$\tilde{\nu}$ (obs.)	$\Delta\tilde{\nu}$ (obs.)	$\tilde{B}_e = 10.34$	$\tilde{D} = .0004$
0	—		20.68	20.79
1	—		41.36	41.57
2	—		62.04	62.33
3	83.03		82.72	83.06
		21.1		
4	104.1⁵		103.40	103.75
		20.2		
5	124.30		124.08	124.39
		20.73		
6	145.03		144.76	144.98
		20.48		
7	165.51		165.44	165.50
		20.35		
8	185.86		186.12	185.94
		20.52		
9	206.38		206.80	206.30
		20.12		
10	226.50		227.48	226.55

* Herzberg, *Spectra of Diatomic Molecules*, D. Van Nostrand Co., 1951, p. 58.

important than centrifugal stretching.   With the anharmonicity term, which couples rotational and vibrational energies, the expression for the absorption frequency for a transition from state J becomes

$$\nu = 2B_e(J + 1) - 4D(J + 1)^3 - 2\alpha(v + \tfrac{1}{2})(J + 1), \qquad (8\text{–}21)$$

where $\alpha = 3h^2\nu_e/16\pi^2\mu r_e^2 D_e$.

D_e is the dissociation energy which appears in the Morse potential expression (8–3).   This expression can be put also into the form

$$\nu = 2B_v(J + 1) - 4D(J + 1)^3,$$

where $B_v = B_e - \alpha(v + \tfrac{1}{2})$.

If a significant number of molecules occupy vibrational levels other than the lowest $v = 0$ level, then these molecules will have slightly larger internuclear separations and hence larger moments of inertia. Thus each succeeding B_v will be slightly smaller than B_e. Actually, of course, the lowest-energy molecules will have the separation r_0 since the zero-point vibrational state is the lowest possible level. A common source of error is to proceed, as we have done up to this point, on the assumption

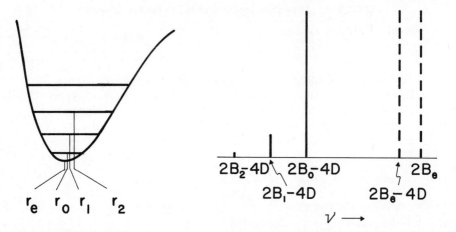

Fig. 8–13. Effect of anharmonicity of the potential energy on the average internuclear separation.

Fig. 8–14. Fine structure of a single rotational line for a diatomic molecule, with relative effects of centrifugal distortion and anharmonicity.

that the measured B corresponds to B_e when in fact it is B_0, which is slightly smaller. It is possible to calculate B_e and α, however, if more than one of the transitions involving the higher vibrational states can be observed. Employing the ground and first excited vibrational levels, for example, we find

$$B_0 = B_e - \alpha(\tfrac{1}{2}), \quad \tfrac{1}{2}\alpha = B_e - B_0,$$
$$B_1 = B_e - \alpha(\tfrac{3}{2}), \quad \tfrac{3}{2}\alpha = B_e - B_1,$$
$$\alpha = B_0 - B_1.$$

Then

$$B_e = \frac{B_0 + B_1 + 2\alpha}{2}$$
$$= \frac{B_0 + B_1 + 2B_0 - 2B_1}{2}$$
$$= \frac{3B_0 - B_1}{2}.$$

The net effect of centrifugal distortion and anharmonicity can be summed up in the following manner: The rigid freely rotating molecule would show a series of equally spaced lines at frequencies $2B_e$, $4B_e$, $6B_e$, ... Because of centrifugal distortion, however, these lines are slightly displaced to lower frequencies, $2B_e - 4D$, $4B_e - 32D$, $6B_e - 108D$, . . . , although the shift is significant only for higher lines. Inspecting the system in more detail, we note that the actual equilibrium separation of the molecule is that which occurs in the lowest vibrational level r_0, which is slightly larger than r_e because of the asymmetric potential curve. Hence the lines we actually observe are shifted still further to lower frequencies and are given by $2B_0 - 4D$, $4B_0 - 32D$, $6B_0 - 108D$, . . . , where $B_0 = B_e - \alpha/2$. Finally, we observe that higher vibrational states may be populated to some extent, and hence additional lines of decreasing intensity are also observed corresponding to B_1, B_2, . . . in these states. A schematic picture of the fine structure of one rotational transition is shown in Fig. 8–14. The magnitudes of the centrifugal distortion and anharmonicity effects can be seen in Table 8–3.

8.4   LINEAR POLYATOMIC MOLECULES

The equations derived for the rotational states of a diatomic molecule will be seen, on inspection, to apply to any linear molecule so long as coupling with vibrational motions is not considered. Thus, for a linear polyatomic molecule the absorption frequencies, to a first approximation, should be

$$\nu = 2B_e(J + 1),$$

so that observation of the absorption frequencies and their separations allows one to calculate B_e and the moment of inertia of the molecule. As pointed out, B_e is not actually observed directly from the spectrum, since most molecules are in the ground vibrational state. Hence the first line is actually at $2B_0$ (neglecting centrifugal distortion). B_e can be calculated if α is known, but often not enough data are collected to determine α, and hence B_0 is assumed for the calculation of I and r. This is an inherent limit in the accuracy of the internuclear distances that can be calculated. We will see in a moment why the calculation of α and B_e is more difficult for polyatomic molecules.

An obvious complication in the case of linear polyatomic molecules is that the moment of inertia depends on the separations of more than just two atomic masses. This is illustrated in Fig. 8–15 for the case of the triatomic molecule OCS. The rotational spectrum of any linear molecule gives one moment of inertia, but in terms of chemical bonds there are two internuclear separations to be determined.

From the diagram we can state

$$I = m_O r_O^2 + m_C r_C^2 + m_S r_S^2 = \Sigma \, m_i r_i^2,$$

where distances are measured from the center of mass of the molecule. Since $r_{OC} = r_O - r_C$, $r_{CS} = r_C + r_S$, and $r_{OS} = r_O + r_S$, it follows that

$$I = \frac{m_O m_C r_{OC}^2 + m_O m_S r_{OS}^2 + m_C m_S r_{CS}^2}{m_O + m_C + m_S}$$

$$= \frac{\frac{1}{2} \displaystyle\sum_i \sum_j m_i m_j r_{ij}^2}{\Sigma \, m_i}.$$

This equation holds for any linear molecule.

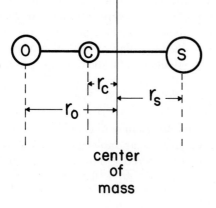

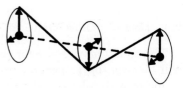

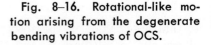

Fig. 8–15. Parameters for measuring the moment of inertia of a linear triatomic molecule OCS.

Fig. 8–16. Rotational-like motion arising from the degenerate bending vibrations of OCS.

The three internuclear distances in OCS are not independent, since $r_{OS} = r_{CS} + r_{OC}$, and hence there are only two independent unknowns, provided that all the masses are known. The simple assumption that the internuclear separations are unaffected by isotopic substitution is the key to escaping from this dilemma. It can be seen in Table 8–3 that in the diatomic case this assumption appears to be valid. If any one of the masses is changed by isotopic substitution, then we have two equations in two unknowns, and we can solve for the two internuclear distances. In many instances several peaks due to different isotopic combinations can be seen simultaneously so that a number of such measurements can be made without complication. In other cases careful synthetic work is necessary to carry out such an analysis.

Carbon oxysulfide provides a good example of this method. The existence of the isotopes O^{16} and O^{18}, S^{32} and S^{34}, and C^{12} and C^{13} provides a large number of measurements, any pair of which can be used to calculate the bond distances. Some of the absorption lines of OCS are listed in Table 8–5, and calculated bond distances are given in Table 8–6. It can be seen that the assumption that the bond distances remain constant upon isotopic substitution appears to be a reasonable one. With

TABLE 8–5.   Rotational Absorption Lines for OCS (in Mcps)*

Transition	$O^{16}C^{12}S^{32}$	$O^{16}C^{12}S^{34}$	$O^{16}C^{13}S^{32}$	$O^{16}C^{13}S^{34}$	$O^{16}C^{14}S^{32}$
$J = 1 \rightarrow 2$	24,325.92	23,731.33	24,247.82	23,646.92	24,173
$2 \rightarrow 3$	36,488.82				
$3 \rightarrow 4$	48,651.64	47,462.40			
$4 \rightarrow 5$	60,814.08				

* Townes, Holden, and Merritt, *Phys. Rev.*, **74**, 1113 (1948).

TABLE 8–6.   Internuclear Distances in OCS Calculated
from Various Isotopic Pairs*
(Zero-point vibrations are neglected)

Pair of Isotopic Molecules Used	O—C distance (Å)	C—S distance (Å)
$O^{16}C^{12}S^{32}$, $O^{16}C^{12}S^{34}$	1.1647	1.5576
$O^{16}C^{12}S^{32}$, $O^{16}C^{13}S^{32}$	1.1629	1.5591
$O^{16}C^{12}S^{34}$, $O^{16}C^{13}S^{34}$	1.1625	1.5594
$O^{16}C^{12}S^{32}$, $O^{18}C^{12}S^{32}$	1.1552	1.5653

* Townes, Holden, and Merritt, *Phys. Rev.*, **74**, 1113 (1948).

neglect of the zero-point vibrations of the molecule, calculated internuclear distances are usually correct within .01 Å.

The calculation of B_e for linear polyatomic molecules is a more complicated affair than with diatomic molecules because the vibrational motions of the former are more complex. The vibrations of a linear molecule consisting of N atoms can be described by combinations of $3N - 5$ normal modes of vibration. Each of these normal modes is characterized by its own frequency and force constant, although some of the vibrations may be degenerate either because of symmetry reasons or accidentally. If each vibration has a different coupling α_i with the rotational motions, then

$$B = B_e - \sum_i \alpha_i(v_i + \tfrac{1}{2}),$$

where the summation is over all the normal vibrations of the molecule.

Since any one of the levels of each normal mode can be occupied, a large variety of possibilities exists, although the lowest vibrational levels will be the most populated. It is evident, however, that B must be denoted by enough indices to show which level of each vibrational mode is occupied during the rotational transition in question.

For OCS there are $3N - 5 = 4$ normal modes of vibration, shown schematically in Fig. 9–11. Because of the symmetry of the molecule, two of these, corresponding to bending of the linear molecule, are degenerate. In this case three α_i's are needed to describe the rotational lines, and

$$B_{v_1 v_2 v_3} = B_e - \alpha_1(v_1 + \tfrac{1}{2}) - \alpha_2(v_2 + 1) - \alpha_3(v_3 + \tfrac{1}{2}) \qquad (8\text{--}22)$$

For each value of v_1, v_2, and v_3 there will be a different B and hence a different absorption line for any given rotational transition. Such effects have been observed in the spectrum of OCS and will be illustrated shortly.

Beside the multitude of vibrational levels that can be occupied by a polyatomic molecule, giving rise to many lines for each rotational transition, another rotational-vibrational interaction can occur which further complicates the spectrum. A full analysis of the motions of the atoms in a molecule must include terms for all the nuclear displacements relative to one another, force constants, masses, etc. In such an analysis the motions we have called rotations and normal vibrations are not entirely separable. We can describe these interactions qualitatively in many instances, and an important case that arises is the coupling of rotational motions and those vibrations of a linear molecule which are perpendicular to the bond axis, the so-called bending vibrations.

In OCS the two bending vibrations were described as degenerate because of the symmetry of the molecule. In an actual molecule the motions of the atoms are very complex, but can be described by a suitable linear combination of the normal modes of vibration. It is interesting to note that superposition of the two degenerate ν_2 vibrations in proper phase with one another results in rotational-like motions of a bent OCS molecule about the axis of the unbent molecule, as shown in Fig. 8–16. This motion effectively creates an angular momentum about the molecular axis.

If the rotation of the molecule about an axis perpendicular to the molecular axis is also considered, the ν_2 vibrations can no longer be assumed to be strictly degenerate. If, as in Fig. 8–16, we consider rotation about the x axis, then the vibration in the x-z plane is not exactly equivalent to the bending in the y-z plane because the effective moments of inertia about the x axis differ in the two cases. Hence the rotational energy levels are split slightly into two levels by this vibration-rotation coupling. Also important is the existence of Coriolis forces which arise on analysis of the vibrational motions in a rotating coordinate system. The Coriolis force acting on a particle with velocity v is given by

$$\mathbf{F} = 2\mathbf{v} \times \boldsymbol{\omega}, \qquad (8\text{–}23)$$

where ω is the angular velocity of rotation of the coordinate system.   For OCS the Coriolis forces acting on the atoms during vibrational motions as the molecule undergoes rotation are illustrated in Fig. 8–17.   Note that the Coriolis forces acting on ν_2 tend to move the atoms in directions which correspond to the normal vibration ν_3, and vice versa.   The vibrational motions of the atoms will thus not be exactly those which would occur in

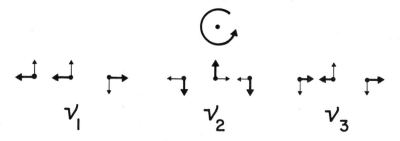

Fig. 8–17. Coriolis forces arising on vibration of a rotating molecule. The heavy arrows represent vibrational motion, the light arrows the Coriolis forces.

the absence of rotation.   On the other hand, ν_2 vibrations in the same direction as the axis of rotation will not give rise to Coriolis forces, since from (8–23) the velocity vectors are parallel to the angular velocity vector, which is along the axis of rotation.   Thus the two degenerate normal modes are not exactly similar in the presence of rotation.

The splitting of the rotational levels caused by the interactions we have just described is known as l-type doubling.   The rotational energy level equation can be derived, including these interactions, and for OCS (8–21) becomes

$$\nu = \left[2B \pm \frac{q_l}{2}\,(v_2 + 1) \right](J + 1) - 4D(J + 1)[(J + 1)^2 - l^2],$$

where B is given by (8–22) and the quantum number $l \leqslant J$ and can have the values v_2, $v_2 - 2$, $v_2 - 4$, . . . , $-v_2$.   This quantum number represents the angular momentum about the molecular axis due to vibration. The l-type doubling constant, q_l, has a value of approximately $2.6 B_e{}^2/\nu$ when $|l| = 1$.   For $|l| \geqslant 2$ the splitting is usually too small to observe.

The effects of different vibrational states and l-type doubling are illustrated in Fig. 8–18 for the $J = 1 \rightarrow 2$ transition of OCS.   The lines are labeled by the vibrational levels involved, and for those lines for which $v_2 > 0$ a superscript is added to show the value of $|l|$; i.e., $(v_1,\ v_2^{|l|},\ v_3)$. The l-type splitting is observed when $|l| = 1$, and the two resulting lines are distinguished by subscripts 1 and 2 after v_2.   In this spectrum the vibrational effects can be observed clearly.

Although a detailed accounting of such interactions as these allows calculation of the α's and B_e and should lead to more accurate determinations of internuclear distances, there are several reasons why such calculations are not frequently employed.   One difficulty is the experimental problem

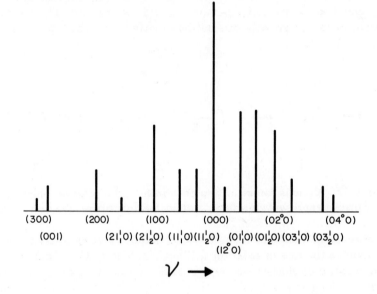

Fig. 8–18.   Fine structure of $J = 1 \rightarrow 2$ transition of OCS, showing vibrational and l-type doubling effects.   The lines are indicated by the values of $(v_1, v_2^{|l|}, v_3)$.   (After Townes and Schawlow, *Microwave Spectroscopy*, McGraw-Hill Book Co., 1953, p. 35; used by permission.)

of being able to conduct experiments at suitable temperatures and pressures so that the lines have sufficient intensity and can be resolved.   In addition, other effects such as quadrupole interactions (nuclear spin-rotational coupling), electronic-rotational angular momentum coupling, and Fermi resonance (an interaction of vibrational motions of similar frequencies, which can cause large line shifts) often complicate the spectra further.   Most microwave spectral data therefore neglect zero-point and higher vibrational effects and are correspondingly somewhat less accurate than theoretically possible.   Nevertheless, internuclear distances obtained from microwave data represent very accurate information.

The statistical treatment of linear polyatomic molecules is similar to that described for diatomic molecules since the rotational states depend on only one quantum number, J. Symmetrical molecules such as HCCH, OCO, NCCN, and DCCD will have no pure rotational spectra because they have no permanent electrical dipole moments. Statistically they will behave as their diatomic counterparts. The oxygen atoms in OCO, for example, have no spin, and hence only alternate rotational levels would be occupied, while the hydrogen atoms in HCCH have half-integral spin and will show a pattern similar to that of H_2. Rotational transitions of both symmetric diatomic and polyatomic linear molecules can be observed simultaneously with vibrational and electronic transitions. These will be discussed in later chapters.

8.5 SYMMETRIC TOP MOLECULES AND THEIR ROTATIONAL SPECTRA

Although relatively simple to treat, linear molecules represent only a small fraction of the variety of molecular species of interest to the chemist. The description of more complex molecules becomes more difficult but is simplified in many instances when a degree of symmetric order exists. We have seen that the moment of inertia is involved in the energy-level expression for molecules. The mass distribution of any molecule can be described completely by three moments of inertia along mutually perpendicular axes. The selection of three such axes is arbitrary, but the mathematical analysis is simplified considerably if a systematic approach is taken.

The moment of inertia of any rigid molecule about an axis passing through the center of mass of the molecule is

$$I = \sum_i m_i r_i^2,$$

where r_i is the perpendicular distance from mass m_i to the axis. The so-called momental ellipsoid of the molecule can be formed if a point is plotted a distance along this axis equal to $1/I^{1/2}$ from the center of mass and this procedure is repeated for all possible axes through the center of mass. The locus of such points is the surface of an ellipsoid, as illustrated for H_2CO in Fig. 8–19. The three perpendicular axes of this ellipsoid correspond to the principal axes of inertia of the molecule. It is conventional to label the major axis, the intermediate axis, and the minor axis A, B, and C respectively, in which case the principal moments of inertia about these axes are in the order $I_A < I_B < I_C$ since the lengths of the axes are inversely proportional to $I^{1/2}$.

The principal axes and the principal moments of inertia can be calculated without a laborious plotting procedure even if the choice of the principal axes is not obvious from the symmetry of the molecule. For an

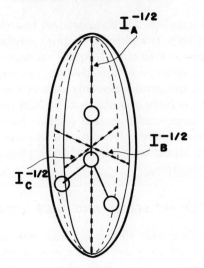

Fig. 8-19. Momental ellipsoid and principal moments of inertia of H_2CO.

arbitrary set of cartesian coordinates, the moments of inertia are defined as

$$I_{xx} = \sum_i m_i(y_i^2 + z_i^2),$$

$$I_{yy} = \sum_i m_i(x_i^2 + z_i^2),$$

$$I_{zz} = \sum_i m_i(x_i^2 + y_i^2),$$

and the products of inertia are

$$I_{xy} = \sum_i m_i x_i y_i,$$

$$I_{yz} = \sum_i m_i y_i z_i,$$

$$I_{xz} = \sum_i m_i x_i z_i.$$

The surface of the momental ellipsoid is generated by

$$I_{xx}x^2 + I_{yy}y^2 + I_{zz}z^2 - 2I_{xy}xy - 2I_{yz}yz - 2I_{xz}xz = 1,$$

and the principal moments, I, are the roots of the determinantal equation

$$\begin{vmatrix} I_{xx} - I & -I_{xy} & -I_{xz} \\ -I_{xy} & I_{yy} - I & -I_{yz} \\ -I_{xz} & -I_{yz} & I_{zz} - I \end{vmatrix} = 0.$$

In general the three principal moments of inertia will be unequal, in which case the molecule is said to be an asymmetric rotor or asymmetric top. The spectra of these molecules are the most difficult with which one can deal. In many instances, however, two or more of the principal moments of inertia may be equal. Such a situation occurs when the molecule has a high degree of symmetry. If two of the principal moments are equal, the molecule is said to be a symmetric top, while if all three are equal, the molecule is described as a spherical top. Inspection will show that linear molecules are a special case of the symmetric top, since two principal moments of inertia (about axes perpendicular to the molecular axis) are equal and one (about the axis of the molecule) is zero. Spherical tops will not give rise to pure rotational spectra, because their symmetry does not result in a permanent electric dipole moment.

If a molecule has a symmetry axis of rotation or a plane of reflection, these symmetry elements can be expected to coincide with one or more of the principal axes of inertia. This is seen in the case of CH_2O, for which the A axis corresponds to a twofold rotation axis of the molecule, and the B and C axes lie in reflection planes. Any molecule with an n-fold axis of symmetry with $n > 2$ will be a symmetric top, and two such axes will be found in a spherical top. $CHCl_3$ and CH_4, respectively, are examples. Which of the axes corresponds to the largest or smallest moment of inertia must be determined in each instance by calculation, but often this question can be resolved by inspection. In H_2CO, for example, I_A depends only on hydrogen atom masses and hence will be small compared to I_B and I_C.

For symmetric top molecules the third principal moment of inertia may be larger or smaller than the two equal moments. In the former case the molecule is said to be an oblate symmetric top. When the different moment is smaller than the other two the molecule is a prolate symmetric top. For the sake of uniformity it is always desirable to label the smallest moment of inertia I_A and the largest I_C as already mentioned. By this uniform convention, then, an oblate symmetric top is one for which $I_A = I_B < I_C$, while for a prolate top $I_A < I_B = I_C$. (Unfortunately one often finds in the literature that for symmetric tops the equal moments of inertia are given as $I_B = I_C$ while the unique moment is I_A regardless of whether it is smaller or larger than the two equal moments. In this convention an oblate top is one for which $I_A > I_B = I_C$, while, if $I_A < I_B = I_C$, it is prolate. We will use the first, more uniform convention here.)

The solution of the Schrödinger equation for a polyatomic molecule will not be attempted here, and the reader is referred to more detailed discussions. For a rigid polyatomic symmetric top molecule, the rotational energy levels are found to be given by

$$E = J(J + 1) \frac{\hbar^2}{2I_B} + K^2 \left(\frac{1}{I_A} - \frac{1}{I_B} \right) \frac{\hbar^2}{2}$$

or

$$\frac{E}{h} = J(J + 1)B + K^2(A - B) \tag{8-24}$$

when the molecule is prolate $(I_B = I_C)$, and

$$\frac{E}{h} = J(J + 1)B + K^2(C - B) \qquad (8\text{–}25)$$

for an oblate top $(I_A = I_B)$. The rotational constants A, B, and C are defined as

$$A = \frac{h}{4\pi I_A}, \quad B = \frac{h}{4\pi I_B}, \quad C = \frac{h}{4\pi I_C}$$

and will be recognized from the linear case. The quantum number J has the same significance as previously; i.e., the total rotational angular momentum of the molecule is $\sqrt{J(J + 1)}\, h$. The second quantum number K is an indication of the component of the total angular momentum along the molecular symmetry axis which is $\pm Kh$; for a given value of J, K can be $0, 1, 2, \ldots, J$. Finally, complete solution of the Schrödinger equation again results in the quantum number $M_J = 0, \pm 1, \ldots, \pm J$, which gives the component of the total angular momentum along an external direction fixed in space (the z axis). States with the same J and different M_J are degenerate in the absence of suitable orienting fields. Thus, when $K = 0$, each level is $(2J + 1)$-degenerate, but since K can have both positive and negative integral values, every other level is $2(2J + 1)$-degenerate. The energy levels corresponding to (8–24) and (8–25) are illustrated in Fig. 8–20, where levels are ordered in columns for different values of K. Since by our convention $A > B > C$, we see that for the prolate top the K^2 term is always positive, while in the oblate case it is always negative. Thus for a given value of J there are $J + 1$ levels corresponding to $K = 0, 1, \ldots, J$. Alternatively, for a given value of K there are an infinity of levels corresponding to $J = K, K + 1$, ... The spacing of this series of levels, since K is constant, is of exactly the same form as for a linear molecule. This latter picture is especially convenient when the selection rules for rotational electric dipole transitions are considered.

Analysis of the dipole moment matrix elements for symmetric top states shows that rotational transitions are possible only between states for which $\Delta J = \pm 1$, a result similar to that of the linear case. If the molecule has no permanent dipole moment, there will be no transitions induced. In addition, the symmetry of symmetric top molecules prevents any component of a permanent electric dipole moment perpendicular to the top axis. For this reason dipole radiation cannot excite or change the rotational motions of the molecule perpendicular to this axis. This leads to the additional selection rule $\Delta K = 0$. As a result of these rules, absorption spectra of symmetric top molecules will be given by

$$\nu = \frac{\Delta E}{h} = 2B(J + 1),$$

where J is the rotational quantum number of the initial lower state. This result is identical with that of the linear case, and although the simplicity of this result is welcome, it is accompanied by the restriction that only one of the moments of inertia, I_B, is obtained directly. For this reason a large portion of the spectral data on symmetric top molecules reports only the rotational constant B_0.

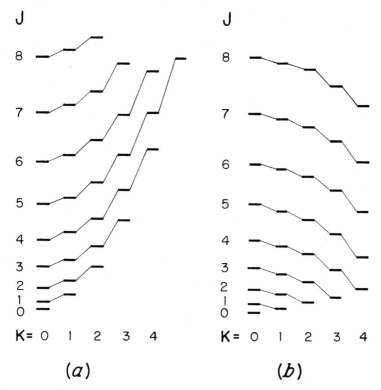

Fig. 8–20.   Energy levels of the symmetric rotor: (a) prolate; (b) oblate.

A great many of the symmetric top molecules which have been studied are of the trigonal pyramid structure (NH_3, NF_3, PH_3, $AsCl_3$, etc.) or a slightly more complicated threefold rotation symmetry (methyl halides, CH_3CN, PCl_3O, etc.). Both types are shown in Fig. 8–21. Although only one moment of inertia is obtained from the absorption spectrum, isotopic substitution provides enough parameters to determine the internuclear distances and angles. In the case of NF_3, for example, the moments of inertia are given by

$$I_C = 2m_1 r_{12}^2 (1 - \cos \theta),$$

$$I_B = m_1 r_{12}^2 (1 - \cos \theta) + \frac{m_1 m_2 r_{12}^2}{3m_1 + m_2} (1 + 2 \cos \theta),$$

so that two isotopic species will allow solution for both r_{12} and θ. The methyl halides are described in terms of two distances and one angle as in Fig. 8–21b. In this case

$$I_B = m_1 r_{12}^2 (1 - \cos \theta) + \frac{m_1(m_2 + m_3)r_{12}^2}{3m_1 + m_2 + m_3} (1 + 2 \cos \theta)$$

$$+ \frac{m_3 r_{23}}{3m_1 + m_2 + m_3} \left[(3m_1 + m_2)r_{23} + 6m_1 r_{12} \left(\frac{1 + 2 \cos \theta}{3} \right)^{1/2} \right],$$

and here three isotopic structures are needed to calculate r_{12}, r_{23}, and θ. Some examples of molecules of these two types are listed in Table 8–7.

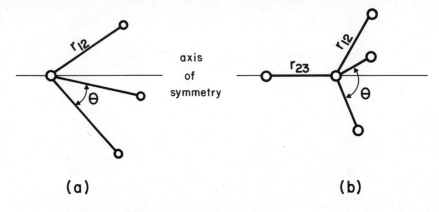

$$(a) \qquad\qquad\qquad\qquad (b)$$

Fig. 8–21. Parameters for determining the moment of inertia of symmetric top molecules: (a) NH_3 type; (b) CH_3Cl type.

Symmetric molecules are, of course, no more rigid than linear molecules, and a centrifugal stretching effect is observed in the former case as well as the latter. The expression for the rotational energy states for the non-rigid prolate symmetric top molecule is

$$\frac{E}{h} = BJ(J + 1) + (A - B)K^2 - D_J J^2 (J + 1)^2$$

$$- D_{JK}J(J + 1)K^2 - D_K K^4,$$

which for a transition from the initial state J, K gives

$$\nu = 2(J + 1)(B - D_{JK}K^2) - 4D_J(J + 1)^3 \qquad (8\text{--}26)$$

for the absorption frequencies. Since $\Delta K = 0$, the same result is obtained for the oblate top. D_J, D_{JK}, and D_K are small, but it can be seen that different values of K will result in slightly different absorption frequencies for the same J transition, whereas in the absence of centrifugal distortion the energy levels are of the same spacing regardless of the value of K. In the absence of high resolution these lines will result in a series of broad

TABLE 8–7.   Structure of Symmetric Top Molecules*

Molecule	B_0 (Mcps)	r_{12} (Å)	r_{23} (Å)	θ
NH_3	298,000	1.014		106°47′
NF_3	10,680.96	1.371		102°9′
PH_3	133,478.3	1.421		93°27′
PF_3	7,819.90	1.55		102°
PCl_3^{35}	2,617.1	2.043 ± 0.003		106° ± 20′
PBr_3^{79}	996.8	—		—
AsH_3	111,620	1.523		92°0′
AsF_3	5,878.971	1.712 ± 0.006		102° ± 2°
$AsCl_3^{35}$	2,147.2	2.161 ± 0.004		98°25′ ± 30′
$Sb^{121}H_3$	88,000	1.712		91°30′
$Sb^{121}Cl_3^{35}$	1,754	2.325 ± 0.005		99°30′ ± 1°30′
CH_3F	25,536.12	1.11	1.39	110°
CH_3Cl^{35}	13,292.95	1.113	1.781	110°31′
CH_3Br^{79}	9,568.19	1.113	1.939	111°14′
CH_3I	7,501.31	1.113	2.1392	111°25′
$Si^{28}H_3F$	14,327.9	1.46	1.5946	109°20′
$Si^{28}H_3Cl^{35}$	6,673.8	1.44	2.050	110°
$Si^{28}H_3Br^{79}$	4,321.72	1.57 ± 0.03	2.209 ± 0.001	111°20′ ± 1°
$Ge^{74}H_3Cl^{35}$	4,333.91	1.52	2.148	111°
$Ge^{74}H_3Br^{79}$	2,375.88	1.55 ± 0.05	2.297 ± 0.001	112° ± 1°
CF_3H	10,348.74	1.332	1.098	108°48′
CF_3Cl^{35}	3,335.56	1.32	1.77	109°
CF_3Br^{79}	2,098.06	1.33	1.91	108°
CF_3I	1,523.23	1.33	2.13	108°
$CCl_3^{35}H$	3,301.94	1.767	1.073	110°24′
$CHBr_3^{79}H$	1,247.61	1.930 ± 0.003	1.07	110°48′ ± 16′
SiF_3H	7,207.98	1.46	1.565	108°17′
$Si^{28}F_3Cl^{35}$	2,477.7	1.560	1.989	108°30′
$Si^{28}F_3Br^{79}$	1,549.9	1.56	2.15	109°
$Ge^{74}F_3Cl^{35}$	2,166.60	1.69 ± 0.02	2.067 ± 0.005	107°40′ ± 1°30′
PF_3O	4,594.25	1.52	1.45 ± 0.03	102°30′ ± 2°
PF_3S	2,657.63	1.53	1.87	100°20′
$PCl_3^{35}O$	2,015.20	1.99	1.45 ± 0.03	103°30′ ± 2°
$PCl_3^{35}S$	1,402.64	2.02	1.85 ± 0.02	100°30′ ± 2°
MnO_3F	4,129.11	1.586 ± 0.005	1.724 ± 0.005	108°27′ ± 7′
ReO_3F	3,566.75	—	—	—
ReO_3Cl^{35}	2,094.20	1.761	2.230	108°20′ ± 1°

* From Townes and Schawlow, *Microwave Spectroscopy*, McGraw-Hill Book Co., 1955, pp. 53, 55; used by permission.

absorption peaks, one such peak for each J.   In many instances, however, these lines have been resolved.   Inspection of (8–26) shows that for a given J there will be $J + 1$ lines as a result of centrifugal distortion effects. An example is shown in Fig. 8–22.

Rotational-vibrational couplings (α terms) are also present in symmetric top molecules and have been treated theoretically, but the complexity of vibrational motions ($3N - 6$ normal modes) and possible degeneracies makes it difficult to assign definite α's to definite vibrations. The phenomenon of l-type doubling involved with degenerate vibrational modes is also observed, but we will not attempt to describe a complex analysis of these interactions.

In our treatment of the statistics of rotational levels of diatomic and linear molecules we observed that a number of complications arise from different kinds of degeneracies, both rotational and nuclear, and from restrictions imposed on the symmetry of possible states because of the

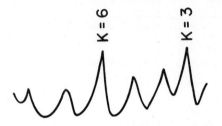

Fig. 8–22. Part of the centrifugal stretching fine structure of the $J = 8 \rightarrow 9$ line of CF$_3$CCH. (After Anderson, Trambarulo, Sheridan, and Gordy, *Phys. Rev.*, **82**, 58 (1957).)

presence of identical nuclei in symmetrical molecules. These restrictions apply, of course, to any molecule, so that we must expect similar problems in the case of the symmetric top. Analysis of the effects of nuclear spin and symmetry is complicated in this instance by the larger number of identical nuclei involved (such as the three hydrogen nuclei in CH$_3$Cl) and by the different types of molecular symmetry.

From the definition of the partition function and using the rigid-rotor energies we obtain for a prolate top

$$Q = \sum_{J=0}^{\infty} \sum_{K=-J}^{J} g_I(2J + 1)e^{-h[BJ(J+1)+(A-B)K^2]/kT},$$

where g_I is the degeneracy of each level arising from nuclear-spin symmetries. Note that, because the energy depends on both J and K, it is necessary to sum over all values of J and for each J sum over all possible values of K corresponding to that value of J. An alternative procedure would be to sum over all possible values of K and for each K sum over all J's corresponding to that value of K. This would lead to

$$Q = \sum_{K=-\infty}^{\infty} \sum_{J=|K|}^{\infty} g_I(2J + 1)e^{-h[BJ(J+1)+(A-B)K^2]/kT},$$

or

$$Q = \frac{1}{\sigma} \sum_{K=-\infty}^{\infty} e^{-h(A-B)K^2/kT} \sum_{J=|K|}^{\infty} (2J + 1)e^{-hBJ(J+1)/kT}, \qquad (8\text{–}27)$$

where σ is the symmetry number introduced previously. For linear molecules σ is either 1 or 2 depending on whether the molecule has twofold rotation symmetry about an axis perpendicular to the molecule. For non-linear molecules higher-fold symmetry axes are possible, and hence σ may assume other values. In the methyl halides, for example, there is a threefold symmetry axis through the C—X bond, and therefore there are three ways in which the rigid molecule can be rotated and remain indistinguishable from other orientations. Hence in this case $\sigma = 3$. If the halogen atom were replaced by another hydrogen atom, the resulting CH_4 molecule would have tetrahedral symmetry. Inspection will show that in this case there are twelve ways in which the molecule can be rotated (three rotations about each C—H bond), so that $\sigma = 12$. It was seen in our discussion of diatomic molecules that σ takes care of nuclear symmetry except for nuclear-spin degeneracy of $2I + 1$ for each nucleus.

We have seen that usually $hB \ll kT$, in which case the sums in the partition function can be replaced by integrals. On integrating over possible values of J it is not necessary that the lower limit of J be fixed exactly, so long as the integration begins in the neighborhood of $J = |K|$. For integration purposes it is convenient to choose this lower limit, J_{min}, so that $J_{min}(J_{min} + 1) = K^2$ or $J_{min} \simeq K - \frac{1}{2}$, in which case (8–27) becomes

$$
\begin{aligned}
Q &= \frac{1}{\sigma} \int_{-\infty}^{+\infty} e^{-h(A-B)K^2/kT} \left[\int_{J_{min}=K-1/2}^{\infty} (2J+1)e^{-hBJ(J+1)/kT} \, dJ \right] dK \\
&= \frac{1}{\sigma} \frac{kT}{hB} \int_{-\infty}^{\infty} e^{-hAK^2/kT} \, dK \\
&= \frac{\pi^{1/2}}{\sigma} \left(\frac{k^3 T^3}{\hbar^3 B^2 A} \right)^{1/2} \\
&= \frac{\pi^{1/2}}{\sigma} \left(\frac{2kT}{h^2} \right)^{3/2} I_B I_A^{1/2}.
\end{aligned}
\tag{8–28}
$$

The corresponding expression for an oblate top would replace I_A with I_C.

Thermodynamic functions can now be evaluated using (8–28) except at those temperatures at which the approximations made are invalid. The equilibrium population of various states E_{JK} are shown in Fig. 8–23, where the separate effects of J and K can be seen. The alternating differences in population of the rotational levels will lead to different line intensities. While the general pattern of increasing intensity for higher J transitions is observed, the alternating populations with respect to K will cause the centrifugal stretching fine structure lines to have different intensities, as can be seen in Fig. 8–22.

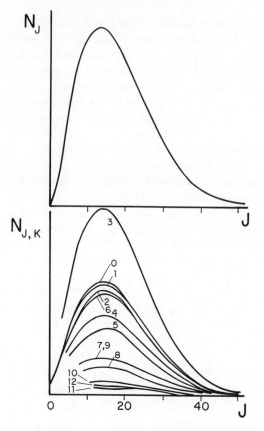

Fig. 8–23.   Thermal distribution of rotational levels of CH_3Cl at 300° K.   The top curve gives the total number of molecules for each value of J.   The bottom set of curves shows how these are distributed according to the value of K which labels each curve.   (After Herzberg, *Infrared and Raman Spectra of Polyatomic Molecules*, D. Van Nostrand Co., 1945, p. 30.)

8.6   ASYMMETRIC ROTORS

The asymmetric rotor has no two principal moments of inertia equal, and this lack of symmetry automatically results in a permanent dipole moment and a rotational spectrum.   As might be expected, the complexity of the rotational motions of such molecules increases, and it is not possible to solve the Schrödinger equation to obtain a general expression for the vibrational and rotational energy levels.   The total rotational angular momentum of an asymmetric rotor is found to be quantized and described by the quantum number J as in the more symmetric cases.   The component of this angular momentum along a fixed external direction, indicated by M_J, is also quantized.   However, the component of the angular momentum along some molecular axis is not quantized.   There is no molecular symmetry axis in such a molecule which is unique in this sense.

Although a complete analysis of the asymmetric molecule is prohibitively difficult, we might note that in terms of the principal moments of inertia, or the rotational constants, this case represents an intermediate situation between the prolate and oblate symmetric tops.   That is, for

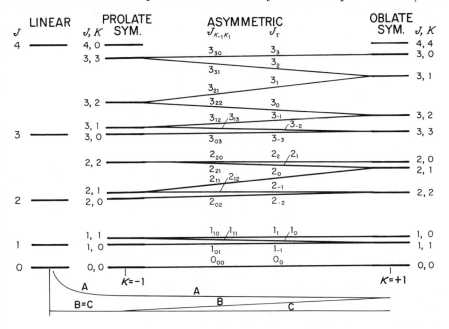

Fig. 8–24.   Correlation diagram of asymmetric top energy levels with prolate and oblate symmetric top levels.   The corresponding levels of a linear molecule are included for comparison, and the relative magnitudes of the rotational constants A, B, and C are shown below the correlation diagram.

the prolate top $A > B = C$, for the asymmetric top $A > B > C$, and for the oblate top $A = B > C$.   In the symmetric top cases we described the possible rotational states by J and K.   We can imagine many cases in which an asymmetric molecule may differ only very slightly from a symmetric top, and hence its energy-level pattern would not be expected to be greatly different.   The primary effect of a slight distortion from the symmetric case is to split the degenerate levels corresponding to $\pm K$ into two separate levels.   It is helpful, therefore, to use a correlation diagram to investigate the levels of asymmetric rotors.   Such a diagram is shown in Fig. 8–24, in which rotational levels for the linear molecule (a special case of the prolate symmetric top) are also shown. The variation of the rotational constants also is shown below the diagram.

The quantum number K has no real significance for the asymmetric rotor, but the correlation of symmetric and asymmetric states suggests the use of K to label asymmetric states. Two conventions have been used in the correlation diagram: In one, a subscript τ is given to J, and the states for a given J are labeled with values of τ ranging from $-J$ to $+J$ starting with the lowest state for that J. The three levels arising from the $J = 1$ levels of the symmetric tops, for example, are given in order as

TABLE 8–8.   Values of the Energy Parameter $E^J{}_{K_{-1}K_1}(\kappa)$
for Asymmetric Rotor States*

$J_{K_{-1}K_1}$	$E^J{}_{K_{-1}K_1}$
0_{00}	0
1_{10}	$\kappa + 1$
1_{11}	0
1_{01}	$\kappa - 1$
2_{20}	$2[\kappa + (\kappa^2 + 3)^{1/2}]$
2_{21}	$\kappa + 3$
2_{11}	4κ
2_{12}	$\kappa - 3$
2_{02}	$2[\kappa - (\kappa^2 + 3)^{1/2}]$

* From Townes and Schawlow, *Microwave Spectroscopy*, McGraw-Hill Book Co., 1955, p. 90; used by permission.

1_{-1}, 1_0, 1_1. The second convention, now more widely used, labels each J with two subscripts, the first giving the value of K for the prolate top level from which the asymmetric level arises, and the second giving the value of K for the corresponding oblate top level. In this notation the three $J = 1$ levels are denoted 1_{01}, 1_{11}, 1_{10}.

Asymmetric rotors can be described by an asymmetry parameter

$$\kappa = \frac{2B - A - C}{A - C},$$

which varies from -1 for a prolate top to $+1$ for an oblate top. In terms of this asymmetry parameter the energy levels of an asymmetric rotor can be expressed as

$$\frac{E}{h} = \tfrac{1}{2}(A + C)J(J + 1) + \tfrac{1}{2}(A - C)E^J_{K_{-1}K_1}(\kappa)$$

where the $E^J_{K_{-1}K_1}(\kappa)$ have been tabulated as a function of J, K_{-1}, and K_1. Some examples are listed in Table 8–8. Equations of similar form have been used to calculate the energies of slightly asymmetric molecules. Tables of appropriate functions are given in the references.

The primary selection rule for electric dipole transitions is $\Delta J = 0$, ± 1, and in this instance all the possible transitions have significance, even in absorption spectra, since many of the levels are no longer degenerate and overlap, so that levels with a particular value of J may actually be lower than some of those with a lower value of J. Again, symmetry considerations lead to determination of which transitions are possible among sublevels of a given J. In many instances there are essentially no restrictions on which levels may be involved, and as a result the spectra of asymmetric molecules contain many more lines than are seen in spectra

TABLE 8–9. Permitted Transitions Between Asymmetric
Rotor Levels of Low J Values*

(Numbers indicate ΔK_{-1} and ΔK_1; letter indicates axis along which molecular dipole moment must have a non-zero component for transition to occur)

	$0_{0,0}$	$1_{0,1}$	$1_{1,1}$	$1_{1,0}$	$2_{0,2}$	$2_{1,2}$	$2_{1,1}$	$2_{2,1}$	$2_{2,0}$
$0_{0,0}$	—	a 0,1	b 1,1	c 1,1					
$1_{0,1}$	a 0,−1	—	c −1,0	b 1,−1	a 0,1	b 1,1	c 1,0	—	a 2,−1
$1_{1,1}$	b −1,−1	c −1,0	—	a 0,−1	b −1,1	a 0,1	—	c 1,0	b 1,−1
$1_{1,0}$	c −1,0	b −1,1	a 0,1	—	c −1,2	—	a 0,1	b 1,1	c 1,0
$2_{0,2}$		a 0,−1	b 1,−1	c 1,−2	—	c 1,0	b 1,−1	a 2,−1	—
$2_{1,2}$		b −1,−1	a 0,−1	—	c −1,0	—	a 0,−1	b 1,−1	c 1,−2
$2_{1,1}$		c −1,0	—	a 0,−1	b −1,1	a 0,1	—	c 1,0	b 1,−1
$2_{2,1}$		—	c −1,0	b −1,−1	a −2,1	b −1,1	c −1,0	—	a 0,−1
$2_{2,0}$		a −2,1	b −1,1	c −1,0	—	c −1,2	b −1,1	a 0,1	—

* From Townes and Schawlow, *Microwave Spectroscopy*, McGraw-Hill Book Co., 1955, p. 98; used by permission.

of symmetric tops and linear molecules. Allowed transitions for small values of J are listed in Table 8–9. The vertical and horizontal columns list the initial and final states, and the entries in the table proper give the values of ΔK_{-1} and ΔK_1. In numerous cases transitions are not possible unless there is a component of the molecular dipole moment along a particular primary moment axis. When this requirement is present it is indicated by a prefix to the ΔK_{-1}, ΔK_1 notation indicating on which of the three axes the dipole moment must have a component. For the $0_{00} \rightarrow 1_{01}$ transition, for example, there must be a component of the dipole moment along the A axis, i.e., along the axis with the smallest moment of inertia.

It is apparent that these spectra are complex. They consist of many lines that are no longer arranged in compact, evenly spaced groups. Despite their complexity a great deal of information has been extracted from such spectra, particularly when data are available from other sources as well. The splitting of lines by the Stark effect also aids in determining which line corresponds to which transition.

Centrifugal distortion also has a large effect on asymmetric rotation lines, especially when any of the principal moments of inertia are small and for large values of J.   In HDS the correction to the line at 28,842.84 Mcps corresponding to the $12_{6,7} \rightarrow 12_{6,6}$ transition is 1008.25 Mcps, while for the low J lines it amounts to about 100 Mcps.   These are much larger effects than observed in symmetric top spectra where such corrections are of the order of 1 Mcps or less.   Since the lines for lower values of J are less affected, however, information about distortion usually can be obtained in order to interpret the higher transitions.   The details of quantitative treatments are given in the literature.

The partition function for the asymmetric rotor depends, as might be expected, on all three moments of inertia.   Neglecting the individual $(2I + 1)$ nuclear-spin multiplicities, this is

$$Q = \frac{\pi^{1/2}}{\sigma} \left(\frac{2kT}{\hbar^2}\right)^{3/2} I_A{}^{1/2} I_B{}^{1/2} I_C{}^{1/2},$$

where σ has the same significance as before.

8.7   ELECTRONIC AND NUCLEAR HYPERFINE STRUCTURE

In our survey of atomic structure and atomic spectra, we observed that there are a number of small but important interactions between orbital and spin angular momentum magnetic dipole fields.   Interactions of this sort are also important in molecular systems, although the nature of the electronic configurations in molecules is such that often there is no resultant electronic angular momentum.   Generally, stable molecules have all the electron spins paired and have no orbital electronic angular momentum. Thus, magnetic hyperfine effects are small in molecular systems except for molecules such as NO, ClO_2, NO_2, and O_2, which have unpaired electron spins and/or orbital angular momentum.   Nuclear magnetic moments also are involved in coupling effects of this type.

In molecules that have unpaired electrons or electronic orbital angular momentum, coupling interactions are found to be quite important. The electronic states of molecules will be discussed in Chapter 10, but we can observe now that molecular electronic states are described in terms similar to those used in atomic structure.   The net spin angular momentum of the electrons is denoted by S, which can have the values 0, $\frac{1}{2}$, 1, $\frac{3}{2}$, . . . , depending on the way in which the spins are coupled.   In the central field atomic case we also described electrons by their orbital angular momentum, using the symbol L to denote this quantity.   The molecular case is less straightforward because the torques acting on the electrons due to the presence of several nuclei prevent the electronic orbital angular momentum from remaining constant.   In linear molecules, however, the symmetry of the nuclear arrangement allows the component of $\mathbf{L}$ along the molecular axis to assume constant values.   This component is designated by the symbol Λ, which can have the values 0, ± 1, ± 2, $\ldots$ (corresponding to components of the electronic angular momentum along the molecular axis equal to 0, $\pm \hbar$, $\pm 2\hbar$, $\ldots$). The corresponding electronic states are said to be Σ, Π, Δ, $\ldots$ states. The spin angular momentum is affixed to this latter symbol by putting the spin multiplicity $(2S + 1)$ as a superscript to the left of the symbol. As in atoms the spin and orbital angular momenta may couple, giving rise to a total electronic angular momentum along the molecular axis which is $\Omega = \Lambda + \Sigma$,

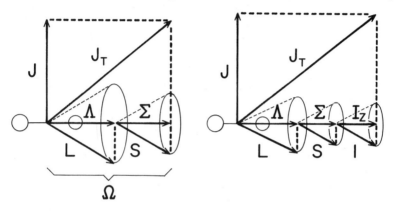

Fig. 8–25. (a) Coupling of electronic orbital angular momentum, electronic spin angular momentum, and molecular rotational angular momentum. (b) Coupling of nuclear spin angular momentum with electronic orbital and spin angular momenta and rotational angular momentum. These are only two of the simplest of such coupling possibilities.

where Σ is the projection of $\mathbf{S}$ on the molecular axis; i.e., the total electronic angular momentum quantum number can have the values $\Lambda + \Sigma$, $\Lambda + \Sigma - 1$, $\ldots$, $\Lambda - \Sigma$.

We have observed that several coupling schemes are possible in atomic systems, depending on the relative strengths of the interactions. The same is true in molecules, and because of the large number of possibilities we will make no attempt here to examine this problem in detail, but will illustrate only one or two typical cases. A common type of coupling (Fig. 8–25a) is one in which the electronic orbital angular momentum vector precesses about the molecular axis, to result in a constant component $\Lambda\hbar$ on that axis, while the total spin angular momentum similarly precesses about the molecular axis with a constant component $\Sigma\hbar$. The resulting vector along this molecular axis then couples with the vector representing the molecular rotational angular momentum $\mathbf{J}$, to result in a total rotational angular momentum $\mathbf{J}_T$. This situation is closely analogous to the symmetric top case where Ω has a significance similar to that of K in the absence of electronic angular momentum.   Frequently the electronic orbital angular momentum couples strongly with the rotational angular momentum of the molecule, giving a resulting momentum which then couples with the spin angular momentum.   These and other cases are discussed extensively in references cited at the end of the chapter.

The nuclear spin angular momenta also can couple with these other momenta.   A typical example (Fig. 8–25b) is that in which the nuclear spin angular momentum also precesses about the molecular axis along

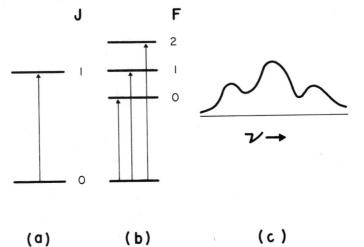

(a)   **(b)**   **(c)**

Fig. 8–26. Quadrupole splitting of the $J = 0 \to 1$ rotational line in DCN by the N nucleus. (After Simmons, Anderson, and Gordy, *Phys. Rev.,* **77,** 77 (1950).)

with the electronic orbital and electronic spin angular momenta, to give a total angular momentum which then couples with the rotational angular momentum J.   Again there are numerous other possibilities which we will not examine.

Because many stable molecules do not possess electronic spin and orbital angular momentum, the magnetic effects discussed above often are not important.   There is an additional interaction, however, which exists whenever a nucleus with a non-spherical charge distribution is placed in a non-uniform electric field.   Nuclei with $I \geqslant 1$ have an electric quadrupole moment Q which describes the nature of the charge distribution (Sec. 7.7).   In a non-uniform electric field, such as would be produced by a non-spherical electronic charge distribution about the nucleus, the system will have different energies with different orientations of the nuclear spin angular momentum relative to a given direction, say the axis of a linear molecule. A detailed discussion will be reserved until Chapter 11, but we can observe that this electrical interaction provides a mechanism by which nuclear spins can couple with the rotational angular momentum.

Representing the former by I and the latter by J (assuming no electronic angular momentum effects), this coupling gives a total angular momentum F which can have the values $F = J + I, J + I - 1, \ldots, J - I$. Thus the nuclear electric quadrupole interaction splits each J level into several levels corresponding to different nuclear spin orientations relative to the rotational angular momentum.

Analysis of the electric dipole transition matrix elements shows that transitions are possible for linear molecules when $\Delta J = 0, \pm 1, \Delta F = 0, \pm 1$. Quadrupole hyperfine splittings are observed in many rotational spectra. A simple linear case is DCN, in which a quadrupole coupling is observed for the N^{14} ($I = 1$) nucleus. The energy levels, transitions, and observed spectrum are illustrated in Fig. 8–26. More complicated cases are the rule rather than the exception, particularly when more than one nucleus in the molecule has a quadrupole moment. The theory has been strikingly successful, however, and a great deal can be surmised about electronic distributions in molecules from evaluation of quadrupole coupling constants in this manner.

8.8 THE ZEEMAN AND STARK EFFECTS

We have seen that the interaction of magnetic fields with atomic systems (Zeeman effect) can be readily measured and interpreted. Because molecular systems less often have unpaired spin or orbital electronic angular momentum the Zeeman effect is of less importance in microwave spectroscopy. It can be shown that even molecules in $^1\Sigma$ states give rise to a small magnetic dipole moment by virtue of rotation of the molecule, and this magnetic moment can interact with an external field. The effects are much smaller than Zeeman splittings in the atomic case, and often it is difficult to apply sufficiently large magnetic fields to make such splittings observable in molecular rotational spectra.

On the other hand, the Stark effect is an important phenomenon in molecular investigations. Marked splittings of rotational lines can be produced by moderate electric fields and interpreted simply. Many spectrometer systems actually use the Stark effect to modulate the signal and reduce system noise.

Since it is the orientation of J with respect to the direction fixed by the external field that has significance, it is apparent that molecules which have a component of their permanent electric dipole moment along the direction of J will interact with an electric field. Symmetric tops (except for $K = 0$) and asymmetric tops meet this requirement. We have already observed that the interaction is of the form

$$E' = -\mathbf{\mu}_e \cdot \mathbf{E}. \tag{8-29}$$

For a symmetric top molecule the component of $\mathbf{\mu}_e$ in the direction of $\mathbf{J}$ is

$$\mu_J = \frac{\mu_e K}{\sqrt{J(J+1)}}, \tag{8-30}$$

and if θ is the angle between $\mathbf{E}$ and $\mathbf{J}$, then (8–29) becomes

$$E' = -\mu_J E \cos \theta = -\mu_J E \frac{M_J}{\sqrt{J(J+1)}}. \tag{8-31}$$

Combining (8–30) with (8–31), we obtain

$$E' = -\mu_e E \frac{K M_J}{J(J+1)}.$$

From this result we see that the electric field has no effect when K or M_J is zero, but for all other states the energy shift is proportional to μE. For this reason this is often called the first-order Stark correction. For a transition governed by the selection rules $\Delta J = 1$, $\Delta K = 0$, $\Delta M_J = 0$ we obtain

$$\begin{aligned} \Delta E' &= E'(J+1, K, M_J) - E'(J, K, M_J) \\ &= -\mu_e E \left\{ \frac{K M_J}{(J+1)(J+2)} - \frac{K M_J}{(J+1)J} \right\} \\ &= 2\mu_e E \frac{K M_J}{J(J+1)(J+2)}, \end{aligned}$$

which represents the corrections to the non-field transition frequencies.

Strictly speaking we have assumed in the preceding derivation that the molecular electric dipole moment remains constant and is independent of the rotational state of the molecule. A more accurate approach would be to apply perturbation theory to the rotational wave functions with $-\mathbf{\mu}_e \cdot \mathbf{E}$ as the perturbation Hamiltonian. The first-order perturbation correction to the energy of a state was shown in Chapter 7 to be

$$E'_{JKM_J} = \langle JKM_J | \mathcal{K}' | JKM_J \rangle.$$

Substitution of the rotational wave functions results in

$$E'_{JKM_J} = -\mu_e E \frac{K M_J}{J(J+1)} \tag{8-32}$$

and

$$E'_{000} = 0,$$

which is identical with our previous arguments. The second-order perturbation correction is

$$E'' = \sum_{J' \neq J} \frac{\langle JKM_J | \mathfrak{K}' | J'KM_J \rangle \langle J'KM_J | \mathfrak{K}' | JKM_J \rangle}{E_J^0 - E_{J'}^0}$$

Since $\mathfrak{K}' = -\mu_e \cdot \mathbf{E}$, the electric field terms can be factored out and we are left with the dipole moment matrix elements

$$E''_{JKM_J} = \mathsf{E}^2 \sum_{J' \neq J} \frac{\langle JKM_J | \mu_e | J'KM_J \rangle \langle J'KM_J | \mu_e | JKM_J \rangle}{E_J^0 - E_{J'}^0} \quad (8\text{-}33)$$

We have observed that many dipole matrix elements between different states reduce to zero, so that the summation in (8–33) will contain only those matrix elements between states that correspond to allowed rotational transitions. Since $\mathfrak{K}'$ contains no differential operators, the two matrix elements in the numerator are equivalent, giving as a simpler equation

$$E''_{JKM_J} = \mathsf{E}^2 \sum_{J' \neq J} \frac{|\langle JKM_J | \mu_e | J'KM_J \rangle|^2}{E_{JK}^0 - E_{J'K}^0},$$

and since only the matrix elements corresponding to $\Delta J = 1$ will contribute to the summation, we obtain

$$E''_{JKM_J} = \mathsf{E}^2 \left[\frac{|\langle JKM_J | \mu_e | J-1, KM_J \rangle|^2}{E_{JK}^0 - E_{J-1,K}^0} + \frac{|\langle J-1, KM_J | \mu_e | JKM_J \rangle|^2}{E_{J-1,K}^0 - E_{JK}^0} \right],$$

which becomes

$$E''_{JKM_J} = \frac{\mu_e^2 \mathsf{E}^2}{2hB} \left[\frac{\{3K^2 - J(J+1)\}\{3M_J^2 - J(J+1)\}}{J^2(J+1)^2(2J-1)(2J+3)} - \frac{M_J^2 K^2}{J^3(J+1)^3} \right]$$
$$(8\text{-}34)$$

and

$$E''_{000} = -\frac{\mu_e^2 \mathsf{E}^2}{6hB}.$$

Except for the states with $K = 0$, where there is no first-order Stark effect, these second-order corrections are generally negligible, being of the order of .01 or less of the first-order effect. Hence the Stark effect in symmetric top molecules is adequately described by (8–32). For μ_e of the order of 1 Debye (10^{-18} esu) and E around 100 cm^{-1}, a first-order Stark splitting is of the order of $100/J$ and can be observed experimentally without difficulty. Values of the Stark shift are given in Table 8–10 for various transitions, and the resulting lines for several

TABLE 8–10.   Relative First-Order Stark Shifts
for Symmetric Top Molecules*
(Values of $2KM/J(J + 1)(J + 2)$)

					(K,M)					
	(1,1)	(2,2)	(2,1)	(3,3)	(3,2)	(3,1)	(4,4)	(4,3)	(4,2)	(4,1)
$J = 1 \to 2$	.3333									
$J = 2 \to 3$	.0833	.3333	.1666							
$J = 3 \to 4$	.0333	.1333	.0666	.3000	.2000	.1000				
$J = 4 \to 5$	.0166	.0666	.0333	.1500	.1000	.0500	.2666	.2000	.1333	.0666

* Bak, *Elementary Introduction to Molecular Spectra*, North-Holland Publishing Co., 1962, p. 73.

rotational transitions are shown schematically in Fig. 8–27.   As in this illustration, the experimental observation can be arranged so that Stark lines are viewed below the base line while normal no-field transitions are seen above the base line.

Linear molecules can be considered a special case of the symmetric top with $K = 0$.   Hence there is no first-order effect for linear molecules, and the second-order corrections must be considered.   Although the second-order effects are of the order of 1 Mcps or less for the small electric fields employed for observation of first-order splittings, it is possible to

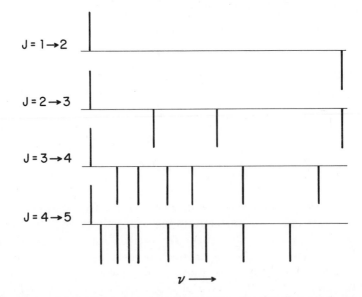

Fig. 8–27. First-order Stark lines for a symmetric top molecule. Only the high-frequency side of ν_0 is shown. (After Bak, *Elementary Introduction to Molecular Spectra*, North-Holland Publishing Co., 2nd ed., 1962, p. 73.)

TABLE 8–11. Relative Second-Order Stark Shifts
for Linear Molecules*
(Values of $\Delta[J(J + 1) - 3M^2]/J(J + 1)(2J - 1)(2J + 3)$)

	M			
	0	1	2	3
$J = 0 \rightarrow 1$	.5333			
$J = 1 \rightarrow 2$	−.1524	.1238		
$J = 2 \rightarrow 3$	−.0254	−.0071	.0476	
$J = 3 \rightarrow 4$	−.0092	−.0056	.0052	.0288

* Bak, *Elementary Introduction to Molecular Spectra*, North-Holland Publishing Co., 1962, p. 71.

utilize much larger fields in order to produce significant splittings. From (8–34) the splittings for a transition $\Delta J = 1$ are given by

$$\Delta\nu''_{J \neq 0} = \frac{2\mu_e^2 \mathrm{E}^2}{h^2\nu_0} \frac{3M_J{}^2(8J^2 + 16J + 5) - 4J(J + 1)^2(J + 2)}{J(J + 2)(2J - 1)(2J + 1)(2J + 3)(2J + 5)}$$

and

$$\Delta\nu''_{J=0} = \frac{8\mu_e^2 \mathrm{E}^2}{15h^2\nu_0},$$

where ν_0 is the frequency of the unperturbed zero-field line. Some values of these splittings and schematic spectra are shown in Table 8–11.

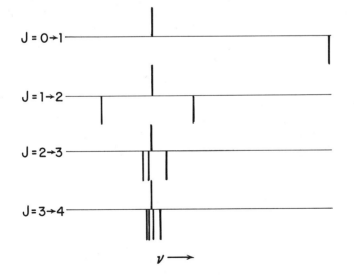

Fig. 8–28. Second-order Stark lines for a linear molecule. (After Bak, *Elementary Introduction to Molecular Spectra*, North-Holland Publishing Co., 2nd ed., 1962, p. 72.)

and Fig. 8–28.   One of the earliest observations of the Stark effect was the splitting of the rotational lines of OCS in an electric field.   One of these transitions is illustrated in Fig. 8–29.

A qualitative argument can be made for the non-existence of a first-order effect and the presence of a second-order effect for linear molecules.

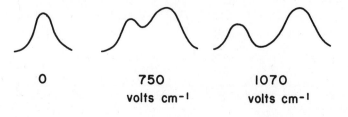

0   750   1070
            volts cm⁻¹   volts cm⁻¹

Fig. 8–29. Splitting by the Stark effect of a rotational line of OCS as observed from oscilloscope traces. (After Dakin, Good, and Coles, *Phys. Rev.*, 70, 560 (1946).)

When the permanent electric dipole is along the bond axis, as in Fig. 8–30, rotation of the molecule about J effectively averages out all the instantaneous orientations of μ_e with respect to the field direction. Hence there is no over-all first-order effect.   This averaging-out process is not complete, however; for the interaction of the field with the dipole tends to retard the motion of the rotating dipole when it is pointing

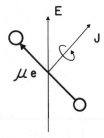

away from the field (θ large), while it speeds up the rotation when the dipole revolves toward the direction of E (θ small).   Thus the dipole actually spends a larger fraction of its time oriented away from E, and the energy of the dipole does not average to zero as it would if the rotational motion were uniform.   This "induced" second-order effect is that described by E''.

The Stark effect has proved to be a powerful tool for the calculation of the dipole moments of molecules. Even compounds such as the alkali halides can be vaporized sufficiently to determine μ_e by this method. Since the intensities and shifts of various lines depend on K and M_J, the Stark effect is often used also for identifying lines in complex spectra.

Fig. 8–30. Classical rotation of a linear molecule in an electric field.

8.9   OTHER MOLECULAR MOTIONS

Numerous other atomic and molecular transitions induced by electromagnetic radiation are found in the microwave region, but we will conclude our discussion of microwave spectra with two examples which are more closely related to the rotational effects of primary concern here. One of these involves torsional oscillations of groups of atoms about a bond axis, so-called internal rotation, and the other involves inversion of a molecule through some plane of symmetry, as in the umbrella-like inversion of the ammonia molecule.

In many molecules there are vibrational motions that cause one group of atoms to undergo an internal torsional motion with respect to another group of atoms, as in ethane, where one CH_3 group can twist about the C—C bond axis relative to the other CH_3 group. Although in some molecules these motions may be energetic enough to take place free of any hindering effects, it is generally the case that such internal oscillations and rotations are hindered by internal forces which cause some orientations of the molecular groupings to be more stable than others. In ethane, for example, the configurations in which the hydrogen atoms on opposite CH_3 groups are staggered, and hence as far away from one another as possible, are expected to represent a minimum-energy configuration, while eclipsed forms represent energy maxima. In this case there will be a periodic symmetry to the potential-energy curve representing internal rotation which is threefold, each maximum and minimum having the same value each time. Such a potential might be expressed by

$$V = \tfrac{1}{2}V_0(1 - \cos 3\theta). \qquad (8\text{--}35)$$

V_0 is the height of the barrier and θ is the azimuthal angle as shown in Fig. 8–31. In many instances the energy of the internal motion will be less than the maximum of the potential-energy curve. Classically, such a system would be bound to more restricted torsional oscillations within the potential well governing one orientational configuration. We have seen, however, that a quantum-mechanical phenomenon is also possible in cases in which a potential barrier is not too high or wide with respect to the energy of the system, namely quantum-mechanical "tunneling" through the barrier. This barrier penetration arises because of a finite probability that the system be found on both sides of the barrier. It is important in numerous cases of internal rotation.

An interesting situation results in the case of periodically repeating potential wells and barriers. This is most easily described in the case of two simple square wells (Fig. 8–32). If the potential barrier outside each well is infinitely high, then each well is an independent system, and the energy levels and wave functions are those described in Chapter 4. If the potential barrier separating the identical wells is finite, however, the two systems are no longer independent. There is a finite probability that each wave function will extend into the barrier region. In the case in which the barrier between the wells is narrow and not too high, the resulting states can be described very easily. We have already noted several cases in which suitable wave functions can be constructed by a linear combination of less general functions. In this instance, if the two wells are identical, a general solution to the problem is obtained from a linear combination of the functions for the two separate wells. As in the other cases we have studied, suitable solutions are obtained both for the sum and the difference of the two separate functions, i.e., both

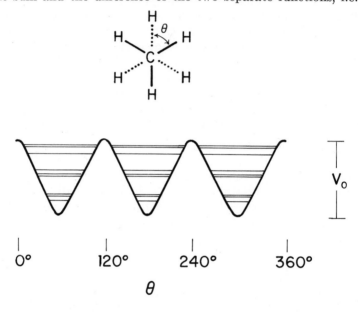

Fig. 8–31. A periodic potential energy as a function of the angle of torsion in ethane-like molecules.

symmetric and antisymmetric functions can be constructed, both of which are satisfactory solutions of the total system. A mathematical solution shows that the resulting symmetric and antisymmetric states do not have the same energy. The difference depends on the dimensions of the wells and the barrier. As a result, each of the levels which would exist for the separate wells is split into two more or less closely spaced levels, one corresponding to the symmetric state, the other to the antisymmetric state.

This simple picture can be extended to any number of wells in any number of dimensions. If there are three identical wells instead of two, for example, each level is split into three levels, and the wave functions for these states extend over all three wells. This model has been extremely successful in describing a number of physical situations where periodicity in the potential energy is believed to occur. The atoms in a metallic crystal, for example, are spaced in a regular manner and the electrostatic potential energy due to the nuclear charges varies periodically along a given direction. In the case of metals, the atomic levels corresponding to the valence electrons of the atoms are close enough to the top of the well, and the barriers are small enough, that this tunneling phenomenon is extremely important. As a result the valence electron energy levels are split many times, and the result is "bands" of electronic levels for electrons which can move readily throughout the entire lattice.

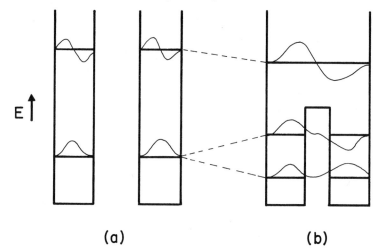

(a)   (b)

Fig. 8–32. The formation of symmetric and antisymmetric combinations of wave functions and the splitting of identical energy levels when two potential wells approach closely enough to interact.

In the case of internal rotation, the symmetric top is the most easily treated. The two molecular groups undergoing rotation about the molecular axis can be described by separate group moments of inertia about the molecular axis, I_1 and I_2. When the barrier V_0 is very large, the motion of one group relative to the other is essentially a torsional vibration, and the potential energy can be approximated by $V = \frac{1}{2}k\theta^2$. The torsional vibration frequency is then $\omega = (1/2\pi)\sqrt{k(I_1 + I_2)/I_1 I_2}$, and the energy of the combined rotational and torsional motions is simply

$$\frac{E}{h} = B[J(J + 1) - K^2] + CK^2 + \omega(v + \tfrac{1}{2}).$$

Each vibrational motion is triply degenerate in the threefold-symmetry case. Such splittings have been observed and a simple case is shown in Fig. 8–31. As the torsional levels become higher, the splitting is more pronounced, until levels above V_0 become essentially slightly restricted rotational levels. The extreme case is that in which there is essentially free rotation with no hindering potential whatsoever, and here the energy levels are given by

$$\frac{E}{h} = BJ(J + 1) - BK^2 + \alpha_1 k_1{}^2 + \alpha_2 k_2{}^2,$$

where $\alpha_i = \hbar/4\pi I_i$ and k_i is the angular-momentum quantum number for the ith group. If one of the groups possesses a component of dipole moment perpendicular to the molecular axis, then it can be shown that

TABLE 8–12. Barrier Height and Rotation-Vibration
Constant for Hindered Molecular Rotations*

Molecule	Barrier height (cm^{-1})	α (Mcps)
CH_3NO_2	2.10	—
CF_3SF_5	220	.05
CH_3CCl_3	950	—
CH_3SiF_3	410	4.2
CH_3OH	375	—
CH_3SH	400	—
CH_3SiH_3	558	30
CH_3CF_3	1200	—
CH_3CH_3	960	—
$(CH_3)_2O$	1000	—
CH_3CHF_2	1200	—
CH_3NH_2	685	—
H_2O_2	113	—

* Townes and Schawlow, *Microwave Spectroscopy*, McGraw-Hill Book Co., 1955, p. 323; used by permission.

the selection rules $\Delta K = 1$, $\Delta k_1 = 1$, and $\Delta k_2 = 0$ hold where group 1 has the perpendicular dipole moment. The frequencies of the allowed transitions are then

$$\nu = 2\alpha_1 k_1 + \alpha_1 - 2BK - B.$$

A truly symmetric molecule would not have such a dipole moment component, but often slightly asymmetric molecules can be treated as symmetric rotors with this property. Methanol, methyl amine, and nitromethane have been investigated successfully in this manner, and refinements have been made on the simple potential (8–35). Some examples of internal-rotation barriers studied by microwave techniques are listed in Table 8–12.

Related to internal-rotation phenomena is the interesting inversion of the ammonia molecule. If the nitrogen atom is inverted through the plane of the hydrogen atoms as in Fig. 8–33, an equally stable structure results which is not identical to any configuration that can be obtained by simple rotation of the molecule.   The energy of this inversion motion is not sufficient to cause the nitrogen atom to move over the energy barrier at the plane of the H atoms, but such motion can occur by quantum-mechanical tunneling.   Thus, the motions can be considered as a vibration in a double minimum-potential well, as indicated in Fig. 8–33. Again, the symmetry of the two potential wells and the low barrier between them result in a splitting of the levels, since symmetric and

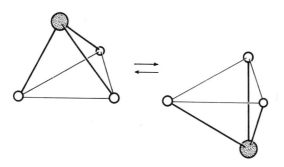

Fig. 8–33.   Inversion of the ammonia molecule.

antisymmetric combinations can be made of the wave functions for the separate wells.   This splitting, called inversion doubling, is small as contrasted with the separation of the vibrational levels and involves energy differences in the microwave region.   For NH_3 the splitting of the lowest vibrational level is 23,786 Mcps.   For the heavier ND_3 it is 1600 Mcps.   For most molecules the inversion barrier is too great for any significant interaction.   Spectra due to inversion are quite complex because the effects of centrifugal distortion and other interactions are all present.   Ammonia and its deuterated derivatives have been studied extensively by microwave spectroscopy and are understood in considerable detail.

8.10   THE SCOPE OF MICROWAVE SPECTROSCOPY

Although this branch of spectroscopy has not become uncomplicated enough to serve as a routine tool for the chemist, microwave methods have nonetheless grown in importance and have opened many avenues of investigation into molecular systems.   In this chapter we have emphasized its utility in the precise determination of interatomic distances. The ability to measure frequencies more precisely in this region than in the infrared–visible–ultraviolet region allows very accurate calculations if sufficient data can be collected and interpreted. Accuracy of the order of .001 to .005 Å is possible.

Details of atomic arrangement are not the only information obtainable as can be surmised from the many interactions we have discussed. Analysis of the effects of vibration-rotation coupling can lead, for example, to the parameters which describe E_{el} in some detail in the region near the minimum. In addition, numerous interesting motions such as internal rotation and inversion doubling can be studied.

The Stark effect has been utilized to determine molecular dipole moments, and phenomena such as the dielectric constant and dielectric dispersion can be measured. The hyperfine structure of microwave lines serves to measure nuclear spin angular momenta. Quadrupole effects also serve for such measurements, and if the quadrupole moments of the nuclei are known, information can then be deduced concerning the electric field gradients in the region of these nuclei. This in turn implies information concerning electronic distributions.

Microwave spectra can be used as an analytical tool. The quantitative measurement of isotope abundances is a simple example which should be obvious from our discussion. Since each molecular species is unique with respect to moments of inertia, anharmonicity effects, etc. exact molecular identification and analysis is possible. Although measurement is limited to molecules with fairly large dipole moments and reasonable structural simplicity, this does not restrict the field too seriously. Kinetic measurements also have been made from microwave line intensities.

The past decade has witnessed numerous new applications of microwave techniques in electronics. Many of these, such as the development of masers and radio astronomy, depend on molecular properties, and their development should not only permit the chemist to probe more deeply into molecular species, but also promise to allow man to explore even further into the far-flung galaxies.

SUPPLEMENTARY REFERENCES

Introductory

Bak, B., *Elementary Introduction to Molecular Spectra*, 2nd ed., North-Holland Publishing Co., Amsterdam, 1962.

Barrow, G. M., *Introduction to Molecular Spectroscopy*, McGraw-Hill Book Co., New York, 1962.

Brand, J. C. D., and J. C. Speakman, *Molecular Structure*, Edward Arnold, Ltd., London, 1960.

Intermediate

HERZBERG, G., *Spectra of Diatomic Molecules*, 2nd ed., D. Van Nostrand Co., Princeton, 1950; *Infrared and Raman Spectra*, D. Van Nostrand Co., Princeton, 1945. These texts survey the theory of spectra, as deduced from experimental measurements, and have very useful compilations of molecular and spectral data. There is little, however, on actual microwave measurements.

KING, G. W., *Spectroscopy and Molecular Structure*, Holt, Rinehart, & Winston, Inc., New York, 1964. This text provides a good survey of the many types of momentum coupling interactions and the basic aspects of rotational spectra. There are few numerical data, however.

Advanced

GORDY, W., W. V. SMITH, and R. F. TRAMBARULU, *Microwave Spectroscopy*, John Wiley & Sons, Inc., New York, 1953. The first text on the field and still very readable and informative.

INGRAM, D. J. E., *Spectroscopy at Microwave and Radio Frequencies*, Scientific Publications, London, 1958. A concise but useful compilation, particularly on experimental aspects.

TOWNES, C. H., and A. L. SCHAWLOW, *Microwave Spectroscopy*, McGraw-Hill Book Co., New York, 1955. The authoritative work in the field.

PROBLEMS

8–1. Calculate the moment of inertia of NO for which the equilibrium bond length is 1.151×10^{-8} cm.

8–2. The wavelength of some of the lines observed in the microwave spectrum of CO are reported to be .260 cm, .130 cm, .0877 cm, and .0650 cm. Calculate the internuclear separation of C and O from these lines.

8–3. The bond distance in ICl is 2.32 Å. Calculate the frequencies of the lowest three rotational transitions in Mcps and in cm^{-1}.

8–4. The rotational constants for $HC^{12}N^{14}$ and $DC^{12}N^{14}$ are 44,315.97 Mcps and 36,207.40 Mcps, respectively. Calculate the moments of inertia. Assuming the bond lengths to be unchanged by isotopic substitution, calculate the bond lengths in HCN.

8–5. Rotational constants found for several isotopic species of BrCN are

$Br^{79}C^{12}N^{14}$	4120.198 Mcps
$Br^{81}C^{12}N^{14}$	4096.788 Mcps
$Br^{79}C^{12}N^{15}$	3944.846 Mcps
$Br^{79}C^{13}N^{14}$	4073.373 Mcps
$Br^{81}C^{13}N^{14}$	4049.608 Mcps
$Br^{81}C^{12}N^{15}$	3921.787 Mcps.

Masses are

$$C^{13} = 13.00747 \text{ amu}$$
$$Br^{79} = 78.94365 \text{ amu}$$
$$Br^{81} = 80.94232 \text{ amu.}$$

Determine the Br—C and C—N bond lengths.

8–6. The rotational constants for several isotopic species of N_2O are measured to be

$N^{14}N^{14}O^{16}$	12,561.66 Mcps
$N^{15}N^{14}O^{16}$	12,137.30 Mcps
$N^{14}N^{14}O^{18}$	11,859.11 Mcps.

Masses are

$$N^{14} = 14.00751 \text{ amv}$$
$$N^{15} = 15.00489 \text{ amv.}$$

Calculate the N-N and N-O bond lengths.

8–7. Determine the values of the principal moments of inertia of a linear molecule ABA in which the mass of A is 6.0 amu and the AB bond is 3.0 Å.

8–8. Using symmetry considerations, determine the possible rotational levels and their degeneracies for CO_2, HCCH, D_2, and DCCD.

8–9. What is the symmetry number for octahedral SF_6?

8–10. Calculate the rotational partition function at 300°K for Cl_2, O_2, N_2, and HCl. What fraction of molecules are in the lowest state in each case?

8–11. At 300°K what fraction of a mole of HCl molecules are in the rotational state $J = 10$?

8–12. For $Br^{79}F$, $B_e = 10,706.95$ Mcps, $\nu_e = 671$ cm^{-1}, $\alpha_e = 156.3$ Mcps. Calculate the frequency of the $J = 5 \rightarrow 6$ transition for $v = 3$.

8–13. Calculate the rotational partition function at 300°K for OCS.

8–14. Sketch the locations and magnitudes of the principal moments of inertia of water, benzene, methyl chloride, and methane.

8–15. Given the values of bond distances and angles in Table 8–7, calculate the principal moments of inertia of NH_3, and plot several of the predicted rotational absorption lines.

8–16. Repeat the preceding exercise for CH_3F.

8–17. One mole of "normal" hydrogen gas has been cooled from room temperature to 20°K in the absence of any catalysts for ortho-para conversion. What fractions of the molecules are in rotational states corresponding to $J = 0$, 1, and 2 respectively?

8–18. The hydrogen of Problem 8–17 is now admitted to the presence of charcoal (an effective catalyst), and the ortho-para conversion proceeds to equilibrium. The temperature (20°K) and the pressure are kept constant during this process. What fractions of the molecules are now in rotational states corresponding to $J = 0$, 1, and 2? What quantity of heat (in calories) is evolved to the surroundings during this process? Compare with the molar heat of vaporization for hydrogen.

8–19. One of the rotational lines of OCS is observed to be split into two lines by an electric field. To which transition does this line correspond?

8–20. The permanent dipole moment of FCl is .88 Debye. Calculate the shift in the $J = 0$ and $J = 1$ energy levels in an applied field of 10,000 v cm^{-1}. Calculate the frequency of the splitting of the $J = 0 \rightarrow 1$ line of FCl in this field.

8–21. A rotational spectrum of a gas shows a series of equally spaced lines, two of which are located at adjacent wavelengths of 85.7 and 100 microns. The reduced mass of these molecules is 2×10^{-24} g. Calculate the interatomic distance, and determine which transitions are responsible for the lines cited.

8–22. Calculate the rotational partition function for NH_3 at 300°K.

8–23. In H_2O the O—H distance is .957 Å, and the bond angle is 105°.

(a) Take a set of cartesian axes through the center of gravity of the molecule. Calculate the moments and products of inertia of the molecule with respect to these axes.

(b) Show whether the axes chosen were the principal axes of the molecule. If they were not, calculate the principal moments.

8–24. (a) Repeat Problem 8–23a for HDO. Take the z axis at the bisector of the HOD angle.

(b) Calculate the principal moments of HDO and the angles which the principal axes make with the cartesian axes of part a.

8–25. What are the symmetry numbers of CH_4, CH_3D, CH_2D_2, CHD_3, and CD_4?

8–26. What are the symmetry numbers of benzene, toluene, 0-dichlorobenzene, and 1,3,5-trichlorobenzene?

8–27. What are the symmetry numbers of propane and cyclopropane?

8–28. If the principal moments of inertia of CH_4 are all 5.330×10^{-40} g cm², calculate the corresponding moments for CD_4.

8–29. Derive expressions for C_v and C_p of H_2 gas, assuming no vibrational contributions.

8–30. Derive expressions for C_v and C_p of a polyatomic gas, assuming no vibrational contributions.

8–31. Derive an expression for the contribution of rotation to the energy of a polyatomic gas.

8–32. Which of the following might be expected to have ortho-para forms, and what would be the high-temperature ratio of ortho to para? Which would be stable at 0°K? Li^6Li^6, Li^6Li^7, Li^7Li^7, Li^7H^1, Li^6H^1.

8–33. How many kinds of ortho and para deuterium (D_2) are there, and how are they differentiated? What J values are allowed for each, and why? What are the degeneracies, then, of the $J = 0$ and $J = 1$ levels?

8–34. Plot the distribution of CO molecules among rotational states at 200°K and at 2000°K. Calculate the rotational partition function in each case.

9

Infrared Spectroscopy—The Study of Molecular Vibrations and Rotations

9.1 SELECTION RULES AND VIBRATIONAL SPECTRA OF THE DIATOMIC MOLECULE

Because the separation of rotational energy levels is small compared to the spacing of vibrational energies, it is possible to conduct spectroscopic experiments that involve only changes in molecular rotational states by the use of suitably low-energy radiation, namely that of far infrared and microwave frequencies. The converse is generally never true—absorption of radiation of sufficient energy to cause vibrational transitions nearly always will induce simultaneous rotational changes. Hence absorption spectra in the infrared region may be considerably more complex in detail than microwave spectra. Nevertheless, an understanding of the main features of infrared spectra and the vibrational states of molecules can be realized if we first consider the vibrational energy levels alone.

On the assumption that the vibrational motions of a freely rotating diatomic molecule are governed by a harmonic oscillator potential function, we obtain Eq. (8–8), in which the second term clearly represents the possible vibrational states of the molecule since it is identical with the solution of the simple non-rotating harmonic-oscillator problem. This expression,

$$E_{\text{vib}} = (v + \tfrac{1}{2})h\nu, \quad v = 0, 1, 2, \ldots, \tag{9-1}$$

and the corresponding harmonic-oscillator wave functions are discussed in Chapter 4 and Appendix D. The vibrational energy levels are seen in Figs. 4–13 and 8–3 to be evenly spaced and separated by an energy $h\nu$, where ν is the classical vibrational frequency of the molecule.

Strictly speaking, the motions of a molecule cannot be described in classical terms, but the simple and familiar picture of rotation and vibration leads us to employ such a description. Although the forces holding a diatomic molecule together and influencing the motions of the nuclei are complex, we find apparently close agreement between the predictions of the harmonic-oscillator model and observed molecular spectra. Hence it is convenient for the molecular spectroscopist to describe the bond in a molecule in terms of a force constant, which is analogous to the force constant of a spring that obeys Hooke's law. We have already seen that the classical frequency of vibration of a Hooke's law system is related to this force constant and the masses on the ends of the spring by

$$\nu_{\text{vib}} = \frac{1}{2\pi} \sqrt{\frac{k}{\mu}},$$

where k is the force constant and μ the reduced mass of the system, assuming a massless spring. The extent of this classical vibration is governed by the potential-energy curve. The oscillatory motion of the atoms centers about the equilibrium separation, and the stretching and compression of the bond classically reaches its maximum at a separation corresponding to a point on this curve at which the kinetic energy is zero and the direction of motion reverses itself. At this point the potential energy is equal to the total energy of the system. Some idea of the extent of vibrational motion can be obtained from a typical case. In HCl $k = 4.8 \times 10^5$ dynes cm^{-1} and $\mu = 1.61 \times 10^{-24}$ gram, resulting in a vibrational frequency of 8.7×10^{13} sec^{-1} and a ground-state energy from (9–1) of 2.9×10^{-15} erg. The potential energy of the harmonic oscillator is $k(r - r_e)^2/2$, so that in the ground vibrational state

$$\tfrac{1}{2}k(r - r_e)^2 = \tfrac{1}{2}h\nu = 2.9 \times 10^{-15} \text{ erg}$$

from which $r - r_e = .11 \times 10^{-8}$ cm. The equilibrium separation of the nuclei in HCl is $r_e = 1.27 \times 10^{-8}$ cm, so that

$$\frac{r - r_e}{r_e} = \frac{.11}{1.27} = .087,$$

a little less than 10 per cent of the bond length. When a transition to a higher vibrational level occurs, the classical picture would be that the frequency of the vibration remains the same, but the amplitude of the motion is increased. There are limitations, of course, to such a classical view tacked on to quantum-mechanical predictions.

The partition function for the harmonic oscillator is easily calculated from (9–1):

$$Q_{\text{vib}} = \sum_{v=0}^{\infty} e^{-(v+1/2)h\nu/kT}$$

$$= e^{-h\nu/2kT} \sum_{v=0}^{\infty} e^{-vh\nu/kT}$$

$$= e^{-h\nu/2kT}(1 + e^{-h\nu/kT} + e^{-2h\nu/kT} + \cdots)$$

$$= \frac{e^{-h\nu/2kT}}{1 - e^{-h\nu/kT}},$$

from which expressions for the vibrational contribution to the energy, heat capacity, entropy, free energy, etc., can be obtained. Convenient tables of thermodynamic quantities expressed as a function of $h\nu/kT$ have been compiled for ease of calculation.

The distribution of a collection of molecules among the various levels is also easily obtained as

$$\frac{n_v}{n} = \frac{e^{-E_v/kT}}{Q_{\text{vib}}} = e^{-vh\nu/kT}(1 - e^{-h\nu/kT}),$$

or

$$\frac{n_{v'}}{n_v} = \frac{e^{-E_{v'}/kT}}{e^{-E_v/kT}} = e^{(v-v')h\nu/kT}.$$

For most molecules at normal temperatures $h\nu > kT$. This is apparent, for example, in the case of HCl. Thus, a very large fraction of the molecules will be in the ground vibrational state and will not be excited to higher vibrational levels by molecular collisions. In many instances the spacing of vibrational levels is so large compared to kT that there is essentially no vibrational contribution to the heat capacity. At higher temperatures, on the other hand, the vibrational contributions become important. At the limit, when $kT \gg h\nu$,

$$Q_{\text{vib}} \simeq \frac{kT}{h\nu} e^{-h\nu/2kT} \simeq \frac{kT}{h\nu}\left(1 - \frac{h\nu}{2kT}\right) \simeq \frac{kT}{h\nu},$$

and from this the classical contribution of R cal deg^{-1} mole^{-1} to the heat capacity is obtained. The vibrational contribution to several thermodynamic quantities is shown in Fig. 9–1 as a function of temperature.

The calculation of electric dipole moment matrix elements is now necessary in order to determine the selection rules governing infrared spectra. The direct calculation of $(\mu_x)_{mn} = \int \psi_n{}^* \mu_x \psi_m \, dx$ will not be attempted here, as manipulations of the harmonic-oscillator Hermite polynomials are required which become fairly complex in the general case (see, however, Appendix D and Problem 7–30). Instead, a more qualitative approach will be taken.

It has been seen that the dipole moment matrix element for rotational states is automatically zero if the molecule has no permanent dipole moment.   It is now of interest to determine the effect of a molecular dipole moment on vibrational transitions.   The actual calculation of a molecular dipole moment is a complex affair since it depends on the positions of all the particles, including the electrons.   If we assume that during the vibrational transitions there are no changes in the electronic state of the molecule, then the dipole moment of interest depends on

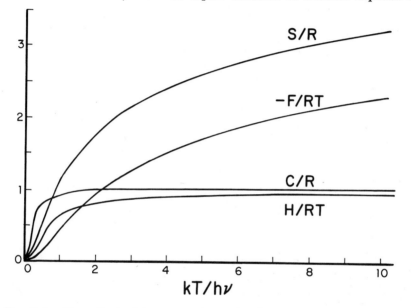

Fig. 9–1.   The effect of temperature on the thermodynamic functions of a harmonic oscillator.   (After Davidson, *Statistical Mechanics*, McGraw-Hill Book Co., 1963, p. 115; used by permission.)

the instantaneous internuclear separation r and is averaged with respect to all electronic coordinates.   That is, if $\psi_e(r)$ is the instantaneous electronic wave function at the separation r, then

$$\mu(r) = \int \psi_e^*(r)\mu_x\psi_e(r) \, d\tau_e,$$

where it is assumed for simplicity that the molecule is oriented along the x direction and $\mu_x = \Sigma \, ex$ as usual.

In lieu of a detailed knowledge of $\mu(r)$, we should expect that qualitatively, as r becomes very small, all charge separations would diminish and $\mu(r)$ would approach zero.   Similarly, if the molecule dissociates into neutral atoms, then $\mu(r)$ would also approach zero as r becomes very large.   The behavior of $\mu(r)$ would appear, then, approximately as shown in Fig. 9–2. Obviously a homonuclear diatomic molecule would have no dipole moment at any separation.

If the displacement of the atoms from the equilibrium separation r_e is small, then $\mu(r)$ can be approximated by

$$\mu(r) = \mu_{q=0} + \left(\frac{d\mu}{dr}\right)_{q=0} q + \tfrac{1}{2}\left(\frac{d^2\mu}{dr^2}\right)_{q=0} q^2 + \cdots, \qquad (9\text{–}2)$$

where we have let $q = r - r_e$ and where $\mu_{q=0}$ is the permanent electric dipole moment of the molecule in its equilibrium position. Neglecting all but the first two terms of (9–2), the dipole moment matrix element is

$$\mu_{mn} = \int \psi_m{}^*(q)\left[\mu_{q=0} + \left(\frac{d\mu}{dr}\right)_{q=0} q\right]\psi_n(q)\,dq,$$

where the wave functions are the harmonic-oscillator wave functions

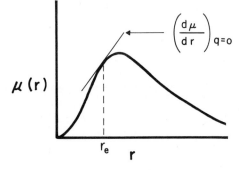

Fig. 9–2. Schematic view of the dependence of the molecular dipole moment on internuclear separation.

describing the vibrational states of interest. These functions are orthonormal. Hence the constant term $\mu_{q=0}$ does not contribute to the integral regardless of the states chosen. We conclude that a permanent dipole moment alone is not sufficient to permit electric dipole transitions between vibrational states. Instead, a change in the dipole moment with the vibrational motion is necessary. The integral of concern is thus

$$\mu_{mn} = \left(\frac{d\mu}{dr}\right)_{q=0} \int \psi_m{}^*(q)q\psi_n(q)\,dq,$$

and we can see immediately that since q is odd (antisymmetric to change of sign), the matrix element will vanish if both ψ_m and ψ_n are even or both are odd. A more detailed examination of the harmonic oscillator functions in Sec. 4.6 further reveals that the matrix element vanishes except when $\Delta v = \pm 1$. Hence transitions are possible between adjacent levels only. Since the harmonic oscillator levels are equally spaced, we deduce that a diatomic molecule should absorb at only one frequency in the infrared region, and since

$$\Delta E = h\nu = (v + 1 + \tfrac{1}{2})h\nu_{\text{vib}} - (v + \tfrac{1}{2})h\nu_{\text{vib}}$$
$$= h\nu_{\text{vib}}$$

t he frequency of absorption corresponds to the classical vibration frequency of the molecule. This would be expected from the classical picture of radiation interacting with an oscillating dipole, and thus this frequency is called the *fundamental* frequency. Clearly a homonuclear

TABLE 9–1.   Fundamental Frequencies and Force
Constants of Diatomic Molecules*

Molecule	$\tilde{\nu}$ (cm^{-1})	k (dynes/cm) $\times 10^{-5}$
H_2	4,159.2	5.2
D_2	2,990.3	5.3
HF	3,958.4	8.85
HCl	2,885.6	4.82
HBr	2,559.3	3.85
HI	2,230.0	2.93
CO	2,143.3	18.7
NO	1,876.0	15.5
F_2	892	4.5
Cl_2	556.9	3.2
Br_2	321	2.4
I_2	213.4	1.7
O_2	1,556.3	11.4
N_2	2,330.7	22.6
Li_2	246.3	1.3
Na_2	157.8	1.7
NaCl	378	1.2
KCl	278	.8

* From Barrow, *Introduction to Molecular Spectroscopy*, McGraw-Hill Book Co., 1962, p. 42; used by permission.

diatomic molecule for which $\mu_{q=0}$ and $(d\mu/dq)_{q=0}$ are zero does not absorb in the infrared.

The fundamental absorption bands of a number of heteronuclear diatomic molecules are listed in Table 9–1. Since the reduced masses of these molecules can be calculated easily from the atomic masses, the fundamental frequencies serve to calculate the classical force constants for the bonds. These are also listed in Table 9–1. While rotational spectra provide sufficient data for the calculation of an important structural parameter, the internuclear distance, the fundamental infrared frequency alone provides much less in the way of structural information, although the force constant certainly serves to give some insight into the strength of chemical bonds. If it is assumed that isotopic substitution causes no change in the bond force constant, then the fundamental frequency of an isotopically substituted molecule can be calculated from the change in reduced mass.   This effect is relatively small except in those cases for which the relative change in mass is large, as in the case of hydrogen-deuterium substitution.

Experimentally, the techniques of infrared spectroscopy are more akin to the familiar visible-UV methods than to the unique microwave wave-guide techniques.   Optical lenses and mirrors, gratings, and prisms are employed in various arrangements depending on the resolution, frequency region, and applications of interest.   Work in the far infrared region requires evacuated optical paths because of the interfering absorptions by water vapor and other impurity rotations and vibrations.   Even in the near infrared region it is often necessary to purge the system of

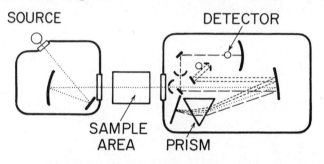

Fig. 9–3. A simple single-beam infrared spectrophotometer, in which the radiation is reflected through the dispersing prism twice for greater resolution. This is the basic optics of the Model 112 spectrophotometer manufactured by the Perkin Elmer Corporation.

water and CO_2, which absorb strongly.   A simple arrangement for observing infrared spectra is shown in Fig. 9–3.   Spectra are reproduced in a variety of ways in commercial instrumentation.   While it might be expected that a plot of per cent light absorbed as a function of frequency on a linear scale would be the most preferable (as in integrated absorption calculations, for example), many other conventions are found.   Hence scales linear in wavelength rather than frequency are commonly used, as well as per cent light transmitted, log per cent light absorbed, etc.   Some of these are dictated by the properties of the optical systems employed and others by other necessities or merely by tradition.

Although the single fundamental band is the most common characteristic of the infrared spectra of diatomic molecules, inspection shows that much weaker absorption bands often occur at higher frequencies. These are caused primarily by two effects: If the molecular dipole moment changes drastically with internuclear separation, it may be necessary to include the third term of Eq. (9–2) in the dipole moment matrix element, in which case transitions other than those for which $\Delta v = \pm 1$ will be predicted. A second important factor is the deviation of the potential-energy function from the harmonic-oscillator approximation.

It was shown in the previous chapter that a much more satisfactory approximation to the molecular potential-energy curve is the Morse potential, Eq. (8–3). The substitution of this potential function into Eq. (8–2) instead of the harmonic-oscillator function leads to a more complicated energy-level equation. Because it is somewhat cumbersome, the solution will not be attempted here, and the reader is referred to more detailed discussions. The resulting expression for the energy, equivalent to the harmonic oscillator result (8–9), is

$$E = (v + \tfrac{1}{2})h\nu_e + J(J + 1)\frac{\hbar^2}{2I_e} - (v + \tfrac{1}{2})^2\frac{h^2\nu_e^2}{4D_e}$$

$$- J^2(J + 1)^2\frac{\hbar^4}{8\pi^2\nu_e^2 I_e^3} - (v + \tfrac{1}{2})J(J + 1)\frac{3h^3\nu_e}{16\pi^2 I_e D_e}\left(\frac{1}{ar_e} - \frac{1}{a^2 r_e^2}\right).$$

Convenient expressions are those in units of sec^{-1},

$$\frac{E}{h} = (v + \tfrac{1}{2})\nu_e + J(J + 1)B_e - (v + \tfrac{1}{2})^2\chi_e\nu_e$$

$$J^2(J + 1)^2 D - (v + \tfrac{1}{2})J(J + 1)\alpha_e c,$$

and in units of cm^{-1},

$$\tilde{E} = \frac{E}{hc} = (v + \tfrac{1}{2})\tilde{\nu}_e + J(J + 1)\tilde{B}_e - (v + \tfrac{1}{2})^2\tilde{\nu}_e\chi_e$$

$$- J^2(J + 1)^2\tilde{D} - (v + \tfrac{1}{2})J(J + 1)\alpha_e, \quad (9\text{–}3)$$

where

$$\nu_e = \frac{a}{2\pi}\sqrt{\frac{2D_e}{\mu}}, \qquad \alpha_e = \frac{3h^2\tilde{\nu}_e}{16\pi^2 I_e^2 D_e}\left(\frac{1}{ar_e} - \frac{1}{a^2 r_e^2}\right),$$

$$B_e = \frac{\hbar}{4\pi I_e}, \qquad \tilde{\nu}_e = \frac{\nu_e}{c},$$

$$D = \frac{\hbar^3}{16\pi^3\nu_e^2 I_e^3}, \qquad \tilde{B}_e = \frac{B_e}{c},$$

$$\chi_e = \frac{h\nu_e}{4D_e}, \qquad \tilde{D} = \frac{D}{c},$$

and a and D_e are the Morse potential parameters. The first, second, and fourth terms in these expressions are identical with the harmonic-oscillator result discussed in the last chapter and represent the vibrational, rotational, and centrifugal stretching effects respectively. The last term, the vibration-rotation coupling effect, was discussed in Sec. 8.3. The term of interest here is the third term, which reflects the effect of anharmonicity on the vibrational levels. The net effect of this contribution is to lower the vibrational levels slightly, this lowering becoming more and more significant for higher states. The actual vibrational levels for H_2 are shown in Fig. 9–4, where the crowding of the higher levels is seen clearly. The wave functions for these states are similar to the HO functions, but are slightly distorted to give a slightly higher probability for $r > r_e$ than for $r < r_e$, as would be expected since the potential curve is displaced in this direction. On reflection, it will be realized that the

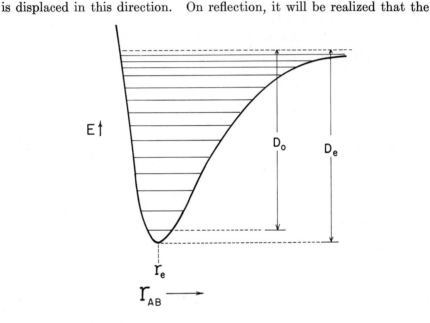

Fig. 9–4. The potential-energy curve and vibrational levels for H_2.

lowering of the energy levels is analogous to the lowering of the particle-in-a-box levels when the size of the box is increased.

With the anharmonic potential, selection rules are no longer limited to adjacent levels, and lines corresponding to $\Delta v = \pm 2, \pm 3, \ldots$ are predicted although with rapidly decreasing intensity. For evenly spaced levels, these transitions would result in lines at 2, 3, and other integral multiples of the fundamental frequency, and this is approximately what is observed. These weaker lines are called *overtones*. The lowering of the levels, however, causes each succeeding overtone to be at a slightly lower frequency than the corresponding integral multiple of the fundamental. This is illustrated in Fig. 9–5 for HCl, where the hypothetical and observed levels and spectral lines are both indicated. The frequencies of these lines are listed in Table 9–2.

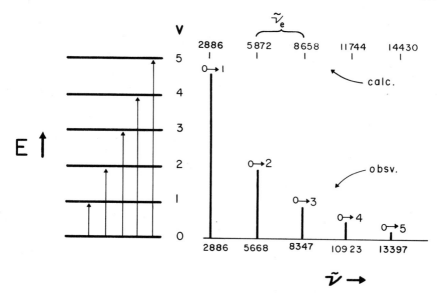

Fig. 9–5. Predicted and observed infrared transitions for HCl.

The deviations from simple integral multiples permit the calculation of the anharmonicity constant χ_e. Neglecting the rotational terms in (9–3),

$$\tilde{E} = (v + \tfrac{1}{2})\tilde{\nu}_e - (v + \tfrac{1}{2})^2 \chi_e \tilde{\nu}_e,$$

and for a transition from the ground state

$$\tilde{\nu} = \Delta\tilde{E} = \tilde{E}(v) - \tilde{E}(0) = v\tilde{\nu}_e - v(v + 1)\chi_e\tilde{\nu}_e. \tag{9-4}$$

$\tilde{\nu}_e$ and χ_e can be obtained by simultaneous solution of this equation,

TABLE 9–2. Infrared Bands of HCl*

v	$\tilde{\nu}$ (obs)	$\Delta\tilde{\nu}$ (obs)
		2885.9_0
$0 \to 1$	2885.9_0	
		2782.1_5
$1 \to 2$	5668.0_5	
		2678.9_3
$2 \to 3$	8346.9_8	
		2576.1_3
$3 \to 4$	10923.1_1	
		2473.4_4
$4 \to 5$	13396.5_5	

* Herzberg, *Spectra of Diatomic Molecules*, D. Van Nostrand Co., 2nd ed., 1950, p. 55.

using pairs of observed lines. In the case of HCl, a good fit of all the overtones is obtained with $\tilde{\nu}_e = 2988.90$ cm^{-1} and $\tilde{\nu}_e \chi_e = 51.60$ cm^{-1}. It will be observed that the calculated $\tilde{\nu}_e$ and the corresponding force constant ($k = 5.157 \times 10^5$ dynes cm^{-1}) are not the same as are obtained if the harmonic-oscillator potential is assumed.

For the harmonic oscillator the restoring force is always proportional to the displacement from equilibrium, and the force constant is the constant of proportionality. An anharmonic potential, however, results in a restoring force that depends on the displacement in a more complicated manner. This can be seen in a general way by considering a potential expressed as a series expansion, as in

$$V(q) = c_2 q^2 + c_3 q^3 + c_4 q^4 + \cdots . \tag{9-5}$$

In the harmonic-oscillator case $dV/dq = kq$ or $d^2V/dq^2 = k$, which would be equivalent to using only the square term of (9–5) with $k = 2c_2$. The force constant k is independent of q; but if the cubic term is included also, to provide a better fit for an anharmonic oscillator, then $d^2V/dq^2 = 2c_2 + 6c_3 q$, so that a restoring force constant defined as above would no longer be independent of q. But at $q = 0$, $k = 2c_2$, so that the significance of k for the anharmonic case is that it represents the curvature of the potential at its minimum, i.e., the restoring force in the region of the equilibrium position. With an accurate set of data, particularly if higher levels are observed, it is found that even higher terms may be required in the potential function. Several potential functions have been found to be more satisfactory than the Morse potential, but will not be discussed here. They lead to additional anharmonic terms such as $y_e \tilde{\nu}_e (v + \frac{1}{2})^3$ in the energy expression. The HCl lines, for example are well fit by $\tilde{\nu}_e = 2989.74$ cm^{-1}, $\chi_e \tilde{\nu}_e = 52.05$ cm^{-1}, $y_e \tilde{\nu}_e = .056$ cm^{-1}.

Another spectral feature that can result from the non-even spacing of levels is the observation of different absorption lines for the $\Delta v = +1$ transitions corresponding to $v = 0 \to 1$, $1 \to 2$, $2 \to 3$, etc. For the $v = 0 \to 1$ transition

$$\tilde{\nu} = \Delta \tilde{E} = \tilde{E}_1 - \tilde{E}_0 = \tilde{\nu}_e - 2\chi_e \tilde{\nu}_e,$$

while for $v = 1 \to 2$

$$\tilde{\nu} = \tilde{E}_2 - \tilde{E}_1 = \tilde{\nu}_e - 4\chi_e \tilde{\nu}_e,$$

and for $v = 2 \to 3$

$$\tilde{\nu} = \tilde{E}_3 - \tilde{E}_2 = \tilde{\nu}_e - 6\chi_e \tilde{\nu}_e.$$

These transitions and the resulting spectral lines are shown in Fig. 9–6. It is seen that each higher transition results in an absorption of slightly lower frequency. The spacing amounts to $2\chi_e \tilde{\nu}_e$. However, since the population of levels above the ground state is small, these lines are of considerably less intensity and fall off rapidly unless the sample is at elevated temperatures. These lines, when they can be identified, also serve to determine χ_e and $\tilde{\nu}_e$.

Although the force constant gives some indication of the strength of a bond, it does not actually represent the energy required to pull the molecule apart into separate atoms. Of considerable interest to the chemist, then, is the dissociation energy D_e or, since the molecule does not actually have a lower energy than the ground vibrational-state

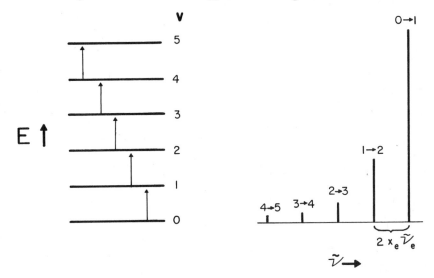

Fig. 9–6. Higher-level transitions for HCl with $\Delta v = 1$.

energy, D_0. In the harmonic-oscillator case these differ numerically by $h\nu_e/2$, but more exactly

$$D_e = D_0 + \tfrac{1}{2}\tilde{\nu}_e - \tfrac{1}{4}\chi_e\tilde{\nu}_e + \tfrac{1}{8}y_e\tilde{\nu}_e + \cdot\ \cdot\ \cdot\ .$$

From the Morse potential expression we obtain

$$D_e = \frac{\tilde{\nu}_e}{4\chi_e}.$$

This algebraic calculation can be made, or a graphical method can be employed. From Fig. 9–4 it is apparent that the vibrational levels converge to a limit corresponding to dissociation. If the energy of this convergence limit can be obtained, then

$$D_0 = E_{v_{\lim}} - E_{v=0}.$$

Defining the differences

$$\Delta\tilde{\nu}(v) = \tilde{\nu}(0 \to v + 1) - \tilde{\nu}(0 \to v),$$

we deduce from the HCl overtones

$$
\begin{aligned}
\Delta\tilde{\nu}(0) &= \tilde{\nu}(0 \to 1) &&= 2885.90 \\
\Delta\tilde{\nu}(1) &= \tilde{\nu}(0 \to 2) - \tilde{\nu}(0 \to 1) &&= 2782.15 \\
\Delta\tilde{\nu}(2) &= \tilde{\nu}(0 \to 3) - \tilde{\nu}(0 \to 2) &&= 2678.93 \\
\Delta\tilde{\nu}(3) &= \tilde{\nu}(0 \to 4) - \tilde{\nu}(0 \to 3) &&= 2576.13 \\
\Delta\tilde{\nu}(4) &= \tilde{\nu}(0 \to 5) - \tilde{\nu}(0 \to 4) &&= 2473.44
\end{aligned}
$$

from which the value of v at which these differences converge can be obtained by graphical extrapolation as in Fig. 9–7. The extrapolation gives $v_{\text{limit}} = 27.6$, from which

$$
\begin{aligned}
D_e = \tilde{E}(v_{\text{limit}}) &= \tilde{\nu}_e(v_{\text{limit}} + \tfrac{1}{2}) - \chi_e \tilde{\nu}_e (v_{\text{limit}} + \tfrac{1}{2})^2 \\
&= 43{,}144 \text{ cm}^{-1} \\
&= 123.35 \text{ kcal mole}^{-1}
\end{aligned}
$$

and

$$D_0 = 41{,}650 \text{ cm}^{-1}.$$

These values are probably too high, since a combination of accurately known values of $D_0(\text{H}_2)$, $D_0(\text{Cl}_2)$, and $\Delta H_f(\text{HCl})$ result in $D_0(\text{HCl}) =$

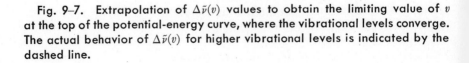

Fig. 9–7. Extrapolation of $\Delta\tilde{\nu}(v)$ values to obtain the limiting value of v at the top of the potential-energy curve, where the vibrational levels converge. The actual behavior of $\Delta\tilde{\nu}(v)$ for higher vibrational levels is indicated by the dashed line.

$37,212 \text{ cm}^{-1}$. This indicates that the higher levels actually converge at a more rapid rate than indicated by the lower levels. Infrared spectra alone are generally not sufficient to determine dissociation energies accurately, since the intensities permit observation of only a few of the low-lying transitions. In electronic spectra most of these higher vibrational states are observed, so that the true convergence to the limit can be observed. Both ground and excited electronic state dissociation energies can be calculated in this way.

9.2   VIBRATION–ROTATION FINE STRUCTURE

We observed at the beginning of this chapter that pure vibrational transitions are seldom observed in infrared spectra. In order to complete our description of diatomic molecules, we must now consider the result of simultaneous vibrational and rotational changes. Energy-level expressions containing both rotational and vibrational terms must now be used. In order to determine the selection rules, let us return to our consideration of the dipole moment matrix element.

The wave function for the diatomic molecule (assuming again the harmonic oscillator approximation) was seen to be

$$\psi = \Theta(\theta)\Phi(\phi)\psi_{\text{HO}}(r - r_e)r^{-1}.$$

Since $\mu_x = \mu(r) \sin \theta \cos \phi$,

$$\mu_{x_{mn}} = \int_0^\pi \Theta_m{}^*\Theta_n \sin^2 \theta \, d\theta \int_0^{2\pi} \Phi_m{}^* \cos \phi \, \Phi_n \, d\phi$$
$$\times \int_0^\infty \psi_{\text{HO}_m}{}^* \left[\mu_{r-r_e} + \left(\frac{d\mu}{dr}\right)_{r-r_e} (r - r_e) \right] \psi_{\text{HO}_n} \, dr.$$

The first two integrals are identical with those already discussed for the hydrogen atom and the rotating diatomic molecule. Together with the corresponding integrals for μ_y and μ_z, they yield the selection rules $\Delta J = \pm 1$ and $\Delta M_J = 0, \pm 1$. The third integral is the one which we have just discussed for the harmonic oscillator and which yields the selection rule $\Delta v = \pm 1$. Hence any transition should be possible that simultaneously obeys all these selection rules. The vibrational transitions involve much larger energies, so the effect of rotational changes will be to produce a fine structure which will consist of a large number of slightly separated lines since, as we have seen, a large number of rotational states are occupied at ordinary temperatures.

The ground and first excited vibrational levels of HCl are illustrated in Fig. 9–8 with the accompanying rotational levels. Employing the selection rules $\Delta J = \pm 1$ and $\Delta v = \pm 1$, a number of possible transitions are shown, with the corresponding spectral lines indicated below the energy-level diagram. A number of striking features are immediately apparent.

In pure rotational spectra only transitions with $\Delta J = +1$ were possible when radiation energy was absorbed, but now because the separation of vibrational energies is large, absorption of energy is possible for both $\Delta J = +1$ and $\Delta J = -1$. It is seen also that, since the transition $\Delta J = 0$ is forbidden for the diatomic molecule, there is no spectral line corresponding to a pure vibrational transition. As a result, there is a gap in the spectrum corresponding to this forbidden transition. The infrared

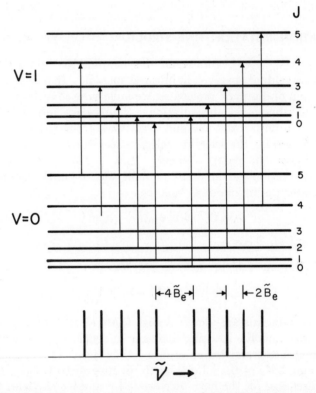

Fig. 9–8.   Rotational fine structure of the HCl fundamental.

frequencies listed in Table 9–1 were actually measured from this missing center position. (An exception is found in the case of molecules such as NO with unpaired electron spins, in which instance it was shown in Sec. 8.7 that $\Delta J = 0$ transitions are possible. These situations are rare enough that they will not be discussed here.)

The series of lines on the low-frequency side of the forbidden-transition gap all correspond to $\Delta J = -1$ and are commonly known as the P branch of the vibration-rotation band. The $\Delta J = +1$ lines on the high-frequency side are known as the R branch. In those cases in which a center absorption corresponding to $\Delta J = 0$ is observed the central line is called the Q branch.

Expressions for the frequencies of the vibration-rotation lines are easily obtained from the energy-level equation. Using (8–8), transitions for $\Delta v = +1$ and $\Delta J = -1$, the P branch, are given by

$$\tilde{\nu} = \Delta \tilde{E} = \tilde{\nu}_e - 2\tilde{B}_e J, \tag{9-6}$$

where J is the initial rotational state and can have the values 1, 2, 3, ... For the R branch, with $\Delta J = +1$,

$$\tilde{\nu} = \Delta \tilde{E} = \tilde{\nu}_e + 2\tilde{B}_e(J + 1), \tag{9-7}$$

where J can have the values 0, 1, 2, ...

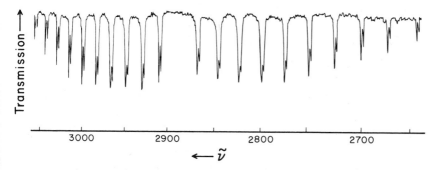

Fig. 9–9. The HCl fundamental band. The double peaks are caused by the presence of both HCl^{35} and HCl^{37}. (By permission from *Pure and Applied Chemistry*, **1**, 572 (1961).)

From these equations it is seen that the fine structure lines are separated by a frequency difference of $2\tilde{B}_e$, while the separation between the innermost lines of the P and R branches amounts to $4\tilde{B}_e$. Although the rotational fine structure is a complicating factor to infrared spectra, it is a fortunate circumstance for the molecular spectroscopist since the relation of the fine structure separations to the familiar rotational constant $\tilde{B}_e$ immediately allows one to determine an important molecular parameter from easily accessible infrared measurements. We will discuss this in more detail shortly.

Inspection of actual spectra shows that Eqs. (9–6) and (9–7) are only approximately correct. The fundamental band of HCl is shown in Fig. 9–9, and the frequencies of these lines as well as those in several of the overtone bands are listed in Table 9–3. A number of features are apparent. We have already observed that the overtone bands are not integral multiples of the fundamental because of the anharmonicity of the potential function and the resulting crowding of the upper vibrational levels.

It is also seen that the lines of the P and R branches in a given band are not actually spaced evenly. In the HCl fundamental the P branch is seen to spread out toward lower frequencies, while the R branch becomes more and more crowded at higher values of J. In addition, the spacing of the fine structure lines is not identical among the fundamental and overtone bands.

The reasons for these features have already been discussed in connection with rotation spectra and can be examined in this instance if we consider a more exact energy-level expression such as Eq. (9–3) derived from the Morse potential. First of all, we noted, in discussing the effect of vibration-rotation interaction on microwave spectra, that when the nuclear

TABLE 9–3. Absorption Lines of HCl^{35} (cm^{-1})*

	FUNDAMENTAL		
3059.32	2981.00	2863.02	2750.13
3045.06	2963.29	2841.58	2725.92
3030.09	2944.90	2819.56	2701.18
3014.41	2925.90	2796.97	2675.94
2998.04	2906.24	2773.82	2650.22
	FIRST OVERTONE		
5739.29	5706.21	5647.03	5602.05
5723.29	5687.81	5624.81	5577.25
	SECOND OVERTONE		
8412.25	8383.29	8326.10	8278.99
8398.70	8366.02	8303.39	

* Report of the Commission on Molecular Structure and Spectroscopy, IUPAC, *Pure and Applied Chemistry*, **1**, 573 (1961).

motions are governed by an anharmonic potential, the equilibrium interatomic separation becomes larger for higher vibrational states. Hence B depends on v, generally becoming smaller with larger values of v since the moment of inertia becomes greater as the molecule stretches. This effect is found in the last term of Eq. (9–3), and it was suggested in Chapter 8 that a simple expression giving B for each vibrational state could be constructed by combining the second and last terms of (9–3). That is,

$$\tilde{B}_v = \tilde{B}_e - \alpha(v + \tfrac{1}{2})$$

so that a simple harmonic oscillator-like energy expression

$$\tilde{E}_{v,J} = \tilde{\nu}_e(v + \tfrac{1}{2}) + \tilde{B}_v J(J + 1)$$

would more accurately describe the vibrational and rotational levels than would (8–8). The equation for a transition from the state v'', J'' to the state v', J' would then be

$$\begin{aligned}\tilde{\nu} &= \tilde{E}_{v',J'} - \tilde{E}_{v'',J''} \\ &= (v' - v'')\tilde{\nu}_e + \tilde{B}_{v'}J'(J' + 1) - \tilde{B}_{v''}J''(J'' + 1).\end{aligned} \qquad (9\text{-}8)$$

For the P branch, where $J' = J'' - 1$,

$$\tilde{\nu} = (v' - v'')\tilde{\nu}_e + (\tilde{B}_{v'} - \tilde{B}_{v''})J''^2 - (\tilde{B}_{v'} + \tilde{B}_{v''})J''; \qquad (9\text{-}9)$$

and for the R branch, where $J' = J'' + 1$,

$$\tilde{\nu} = (v' - v'')\tilde{\nu}_e + (3\tilde{B}_{v'} - \tilde{B}_{v''})J'' + (\tilde{B}_{v'} - \tilde{B}_{v''})J''^2 + 2\tilde{B}_{v'}. \qquad (9\text{-}10)$$

Since the average internuclear separation and therefore also the moment of inertia increase with v, it follows that $B_{v'} < B_{v''}$. Thus, the spacing between components of the P and R branches will not remain constant with different values of J'', but instead each line will be at a slightly lower frequency than predicted from (9–7), this effect becoming more and more significant with increasing J''. The low-frequency P branch will be stretched out, while the R branch will bunch up on the high-frequency side of the band center.

Consideration of Eqs. (9–9) and (9–10) along with Fig. 9–8 will show that the various rotational constants can be evaluated. If, for example, we consider the P and R components which correspond to transitions starting at the same value of J'' we have

$$\tilde{\nu}_R(J'') - \tilde{\nu}_P(J'') = 2\tilde{B}_{v'}(2J'' + 1). \qquad (9\text{-}11)$$

For the fundamental band this analysis gives us the value of $\tilde{B}_1$. If on the other hand we consider transitions that terminate at the same value of J', then

$$\tilde{\nu}_R(J'') - \tilde{\nu}_P(J'' + 2) = 2\tilde{B}_{v''}(2J'' + 3), \qquad (9\text{-}12)$$

yielding B_0 from an analysis of the fundamental band. These effects are not trivial, as is apparent from the non-uniform P and R branches. Typical values of molecular parameters obtained in this way are given in Tables 9–4 and 9–5. The increase in r_v can be seen clearly. It is also seen that for HCl the value of r_0 obtained from such an analysis agrees well with the values of r_e calculated from the far-infrared rotational spectrum (Table 8–2), where the difference between $\tilde{B}_e$ and $\tilde{B}_0$ was not considered. As mentioned in Sec. 8.3, more accurate calculations of $\tilde{B}_e$, $\tilde{B}_0$, $\tilde{B}_1$, etc. can be obtained from rotational spectra if the line frequencies are known precisely.

It is also interesting to note the effect of isotopic substitution. In the analysis of microwave and IR spectra, the assumption that bond distances are unaffected by isotopic changes is often used. From Table 9–5 it is evident that this assumption is more valid for r_e and $\tilde{B}_e$ than for the radii and rotational constants of higher vibrational levels. Hence accurate

TABLE 9–4. Rotational Constants of HCl in Different States of Vibration*

v	$\tilde{B}_v$ (cm^{-1})	$\Delta\tilde{B}_v$ (cm^{-1})
0	10.4400	
		.3034
1	10.1366	
		.3037
2	9.8329	
		.2986
3	9.5343	
		.3023
4	9.232	
		.299
5	8.933	

* Herzberg, *Spectra of Diatomic Molecules*, D. Van Nostrand Co., 2nd ed., 1950, p. 14.

TABLE 9–5. Vibrational Parameters for Diatomic Molecules*

Molecule	$\tilde{B}_e$	α_e (cm^{-1})	r_e (Å)	r_0 (Å)	r_1 (Å)
H_2	60.809	2.993	.7417	.7505	.7702
HD	45.655	1.993	.7414	.7495	.7668
D_2	30.429	1.049	.7416	.7481	.7616
HCl	10.5909	.3019	1.27460	1.2838	1.3028
DCl	5.445	.1118	1.275	1.282	1.295
CO	1.9314	.01748	1.1282	1.1307	1.1359
N_2	2.010	.0187	1.094	1.097	1.102

* From Barrow, *Introduction to Molecular Spectroscopy*, McGraw-Hill Book Co., 1962, p. 141; used by permission.

calculation of $\tilde{B}_e$ from fine structure components is highly desirable from this standpoint also.

It will be noted in Table 9–4 that the values of $\Delta\tilde{B}_v$ are not constant, indicating that the square terms in J in Eqs. (9–9) and (9–10) are not sufficient for a precise accounting of the observed lines. We have neglected from this discussion, however, the centrifugal stretching term, which plays such an important role in the analysis of pure rotational spectra. If the entire energy-level equation (9–3) is used, then the terms in $\tilde{D}$ will give cubic and quartic terms in expressions for $\tilde{\nu}_R - \tilde{\nu}_P$. In this way the effect of centrifugal stretching can be obtained from vibrational-rotational bands. It is usually sufficient to assume for this purpose that $\tilde{D}_{v''} = \tilde{D}_{v'}$ and employ only the cubic term.

A final feature of interest is the intensity pattern of the vibration-rotation lines. We have seen that at ordinary temperatures most molecules are in the ground vibrational state, and hence the fundamental band is considerably more intense than any other absorption in the infrared spectrum. On the other hand, a large number of rotational states are occupied. Because the degeneracies of the rotational levels increase with J, some of the higher rotational levels are more populated than the lowest ones. In general, we have seen that for the rotational states

$$\frac{n_J}{n} = \frac{(2J + 1)e^{-J(J+1)\hbar^2/2IkT}}{Q}.$$

It would be expected that the intensity of a given line in the vibration-rotation band would be proportional to the population of the initial rotational level, n_J/n, and this is borne out by experiment. The contour of an unresolved vibration-rotation band can be used, in fact, for an approximate calculation of the moment of inertia and hence of r. Or alternatively, one might estimate the temperature from the fine structure intensities. In detail, the transition probabilities also depend on J and ΔJ and can be taken into account if necessary.

9.3 POLYATOMIC MOLECULES AND NORMAL MODES OF VIBRATION

We have seen in numerous problems that a complete description of a system of N particles requires the use of $3N$ coordinates. Because the particles constituting atoms and molecules do not act independently of one another, it has been found convenient to define these coordinates in such a way that the Schrödinger equation can be separated into simpler and more familiar problems. Thus we have discussed the translation of the center of mass of a system of particles as a separate problem, leaving $3N - 3$ coordinates for an adequate accounting of all other motions. Rotation of the system required in turn 3 coordinates (2 in the case of linear molecules) leaving $3N - 6$ (or $3N - 5$) coordinates necessary for the internal or vibrational motions of the system.

The complete description of a polyatomic molecule is a complex affair even after separation of the electronic configuration energy by means of the Born-Oppenheimer approximation. If an arbitrary set of coordinates is used, say the ordinary cartesian coordinates of each particle, the expressions for kinetic and potential energy will in general be complicated.

The potential energy, for example, in its most general form, is

$$
\begin{aligned}
2V = {}& a_{11}x_1{}^2 + a_{22}y_1{}^2 + a_{33}z_1{}^2 + a_{44}x_2{}^2 + a_{55}y_2{}^2 + a_{66}z_2{}^2 + \cdots \\
& + 2a_{12}x_1y_1 + 2a_{13}x_1z_1 + 2a_{14}x_1x_2 + 2a_{15}x_1y_2 + 2a_{16}x_1z_2 + \cdots \\
& + 2a_{23}y_1z_1 + 2a_{24}y_1x_2 + 2a_{25}y_1y_2 + 2a_{26}y_1z_2 + \cdots \\
& + 2a_{34}z_1x_2 + 2a_{35}z_1y_2 + 2a_{37}z_1z_2 + \cdots \\
& + 2a_{45}x_2y_2 + 2a_{46}x_2z_2 + \cdots \\
& + 2a_{56}y_2z_2 + \cdots ,
\end{aligned}
$$

$$(9\text{–}13)$$

where the a_{ij} are constants. Even for a harmonic oscillator for which cubic and higher terms would not appear, it can be seen that the cross terms in x, y, and z yield a complex equation. The terms written above would completely describe a diatomic harmonic oscillator.

Fortunately the potential energy in a given case may not depend on all these terms. In the diatomic molecule, for example, the potential energy depends only on relative displacements of atoms, and not on translation and rotation of the system. For motion only along the x axis, (9–13) is reduced to

$$
2V = a_{11}x_1{}^2 + a_{44}x_2{}^2 + 2a_{14}x_1x_2.
$$

In addition, the symmetry of the diatomic molecule discloses that $a_{11} = a_{44} = -a_{14} = k$, giving

$$
2V = k(x_1 - x_2)^2,
$$

which will be recognized as the familiar harmonic-oscillator potential function. We have further reduced the complexity of this function by defining an internal displacement coordinate $q = x_1 - x_2$. An anharmonic potential can also be expressed in terms of q's and involves terms in q^3, q^4, etc.

We have observed that there are instances when the Schrödinger equation cannot be separated. In particular, this has occurred whenever terms appeared in the potential-energy expression that involve products of two or more coordinates simultaneously. Clearly, if the Schrödinger equation is set up in cartesian coordinates,

$$
\mathcal{3C} = -\frac{\hbar^2}{2}\left[\frac{1}{m_1}\frac{\partial^2}{\partial x_1{}^2} + \frac{1}{m_1}\frac{\partial^2}{\partial y_1{}^2} + \cdots + \frac{1}{m_2}\frac{\partial^2}{\partial x_2{}^2} + \cdots \right]
$$
$$
+ \tfrac{1}{2}\left[\frac{a_{11}}{2}x_1{}^2 + a_{12}x_1y_1 + \cdots \right],
$$

the cross terms such as $a_{12}x_1y_1$ will prevent separation of the equation into separate equations in x_1, y_1, etc. On the other hand, if the cross terms were missing, such a separation would be possible.

It can be shown mathematically that, given a set of $3N$ coordinates, x_1, y_1, z_1, x_2, y_2, z_2, . . . , it is possible to define a new set of coordinates q_1,

$q_2, \ldots, q_{3N}$ such that the potential and kinetic energies are given by expressions that involve no cross terms. In the case of the harmonic oscillator, then, such a set of coordinates would yield

$$2T = \dot{q}_1{}^2 + \dot{q}_2{}^2 + \dot{q}_3{}^2 + \cdots + \dot{q}_{3N}{}^2 \qquad (9\text{-}14)$$

and

$$2V = \lambda_1 q_1{}^2 + \lambda_2 q_2{}^2 + \cdots + \lambda_{3N} q_{3N}{}^2. \qquad (9\text{-}15)$$

Since there are no cross terms, the Hamiltonian operator

$$\mathfrak{K} = -\frac{\hbar^2}{2}\left[\frac{\partial^2}{\partial q_1{}^2} + \cdots\right] + \tfrac{1}{2}[\lambda_1 q_1{}^2 + \cdots] \qquad (9\text{-}16)$$

can be separated into $3N$ separate equations in $q_1, q_2, \ldots, q_{3N}$. Such a set of coordinates is known as the *normal coordinates* of motion.

Although it is an almost trivial case, the diatomic molecule is a helpful example for illustrating normal coordinates. Suppose we have an atom with mass m_1 described by coordinates x_1, y_1, z_1 and an atom with mass m_2 described by coordinates x_2, y_2, z_2. A possible set of normal coordinates for this system is

$$q_1 = \frac{\alpha_1 \alpha_2}{\beta}(x_1 - x_2),$$

$$q_2 = \frac{\alpha_1{}^2}{\beta} x_1 + \frac{\alpha_2{}^2}{\beta} x_2,$$

$$q_3 = \frac{\alpha_1 \alpha_2}{\beta}(y_1 - y_2),$$

$$q_4 = \frac{\alpha_1{}^2}{\beta} y_1 + \frac{\alpha_2{}^2}{\beta} y_2, \qquad (9\text{-}17)$$

$$q_5 = \frac{\alpha_1 \alpha_2}{\beta}(z_1 - z_2),$$

$$q_6 = q_{3N} = \frac{\alpha_1{}^2}{\beta} z_1 + \frac{\alpha_2{}^2}{\beta} z_2,$$

where

$$\alpha_1 = \sqrt{m_1}, \ \alpha_2 = \sqrt{m_2}, \ \beta = \sqrt{m_1 + m_2} = \sqrt{\alpha_1{}^2 + \alpha_2{}^2}.$$

Note that the masses are included in the definitions of the normal coordinates. This results in a simplification of the equations to be solved. Using these coordinates, we see that if we let $\lambda_1 = k(m_1 + m_2)/m_1 m_2$ with $\lambda_2 = \lambda_3 = \lambda_4 = \lambda_5 = \lambda_6 = 0$, then

$$\lambda_1 q_1{}^2 + \lambda_2 q_2{}^2 + \cdots + \lambda_6 q_6{}^2 = k(x_1 - x_2)^2 = 2V$$

and

$$\dot{q}_1{}^2 + \dot{q}_2{}^2 + \cdots + \dot{q}_6{}^2 = m_1(\dot{x}_1{}^2 + \dot{y}_1{}^2 + \dot{z}_1{}^2) + m_2(\dot{x}_2{}^2 + \dot{y}_2{}^2 + \dot{z}_2{}^2) = 2T,$$

which are the correct expressions in cartesian coordinates for the potential and kinetic energies of a linear harmonic oscillator lying along the x axis. Also, this can be seen if we carry out the alternative procedure of setting up the equations of motion in cartesian coordinates. Since the restoring force of a linear molecule lying along the x axis acts only along the x axis, we have

$$F_1 = m_1\ddot{x}_1 = \alpha_1{}^2\ddot{x}_1$$

or

$$-\frac{\partial V}{\partial x_1} = -k(x_1 - x_2) = \alpha_1{}^2\ddot{x}_1, \tag{9-18}$$

and

$$F_2 = m_2\ddot{x}_2$$

or

$$-\frac{\partial V}{\partial x_2} = -k(x_2 - x_1) = \alpha_2{}^2\ddot{x}_2. \tag{9-19}$$

From (9–17) we find that

$$x_1 = \frac{\alpha_2 q_1 + \alpha_1 q_2}{\alpha_1 \beta}$$

and

$$x_2 = \frac{\alpha_2 q_2 - \alpha_1 q_1}{\alpha_2 \beta},$$

so that (9–18) and (9–19) become

$$-k(\alpha_1{}^2 + \alpha_2{}^2)q_1 - \alpha_1{}^2\alpha_2{}^2\ddot{q}_1 - \alpha_1{}^3\alpha_2\ddot{q}_2 = 0$$

and

$$k(\alpha_1{}^2 + \alpha_2{}^2)q_1 + \alpha_1{}^2\alpha_2{}^2\ddot{q}_1 - \alpha_1\alpha_2{}^3\ddot{q}_2 = 0,$$

which yield

$$\ddot{q}_2 = 0 \tag{9-20}$$

and

$$k\beta^2 q_1 + \alpha_1{}^2\alpha_2{}^2\ddot{q}_1 = 0. \tag{9-21}$$

Since there is no restoring force in the y and z directions, it also follows that $\ddot{q}_3 = \ddot{q}_4 = \ddot{q}_5 = \ddot{q}_6 = 0$.

Equation (9–21) is a simple differential equation, with the solution

$$q_1 = a_1 \cos\left(\frac{\beta_1}{\alpha_1\alpha_2} k^{1/2}t + b\right)$$
$$= a_1 \cos\left(\lambda_1{}^{1/2}t + b\right),$$

where

$$\lambda_1 = \frac{\beta^2}{\alpha_1{}^2\alpha_2{}^2} k = \frac{m_1 + m_2}{m_1 m_2} k.$$

It is thus a periodic solution with frequency

$$\nu_1 = \frac{\lambda_1^{1/2}}{2\pi} = \frac{1}{2\pi} \sqrt{\frac{m_1 + m_2}{m_1 m_2}} k.$$

Equation (9–20) does not have a periodic solution, and hence $\lambda_2 = 0$ as also the corresponding coefficients for $q_3, \ldots, q_6$. Thus, of the six normal coordinates needed to describe the system, one corresponds to a vibrational motion while five are non-vibrational and represent translation and rotation of the molecule. These motions along the normal coordinates are called *normal modes* of motion.

The nature of the normal modes can now be pictured. q_1 is a periodic vibration (harmonic in this case since only q_1^2 is involved in V) which

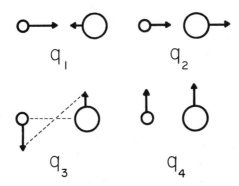

Fig. 9–10. Normal modes of motion of the diatomic molecule.

includes the simultaneous motion of particles 1 and 2 in opposite directions, as in Fig. 9–10. If no motion is involved along any other coordinate, then the relative amplitudes of the displacements of x_1 and x_2 can be determined from (9–17) by setting $q_2 = 0$, from which the relative displacements are $\alpha_2 a_1 / \alpha_1 \beta$ in x_1 and $-\alpha_1 a_1 / \alpha_2 \beta$ in x_2. The displacements are thus seen to be affected by the masses of the particles. The non-vibrational normal mode corresponding to normal coordinate q_2 is obtained by setting q_1 equal to zero, in which case the displacements are equal and in the same direction. This is clearly a translational motion along the x axis. Similarly, the displacements involved in the remaining normal modes can be analyzed and are found to correspond to translations and rotations.

A proof will not be given here, but it can be shown that for the general case there can always be found a set of normal coordinates that will result in a potential-energy expression which has no cross terms in these coordinates and a kinetic-energy expression which involves only square terms in the momenta along these coordinates. Any arbitrary motion of the system can be described by a superposition of several of the normal modes of motion along the normal coordinates. There are $3N$ independent modes of nuclear motion of N nuclei, of which six (or five if the molecule is linear) are non-periodic modes of rotational or translational motion. The remaining $3N - 6$ (or $3N - 5$) modes are periodic and correspond to simple harmonic vibrations if there are only square terms in the potential-energy equation. These periodic modes are thus known as normal modes of vibration.

From our discussion above we can see that a normal mode of vibration involves the displacement of the atoms always in phase with one another. That is, each atom reaches the maximum extent of its displacement simultaneously with the others, then reverses its motion back toward the equilibrium position and passes through the equilibrium position simultaneously with the others. We have seen that in general the amplitude of this displacement will differ for each atom, but in the normal coordinate system these periodic motions will always be in phase for a given normal mode of vibration.

The choice of normal coordinates and the resulting description of normal modes of motion seem fairly obvious in a simple system like the diatomic molecule. In polyatomic molecules the choice may not be so straightforward. The normal rotational and vibrational modes of two triatomic molecules CO_2 and SO_2 are illustrated in Fig. 9–11. In the linear CO_2 the $3N - 5 = 4$ normal modes of vibration are shown with the two rotational modes. In SO_2 it is seen that there are three rotational modes with a resulting $3N - 6 = 3$ normal modes of vibration. The relative displacements are again indicated by the arrows.

Some of the vibrational modes of these molecules can be seen to involve motion of the atoms along the axes that would be considered the chemical bonds, so-called stretching motions. In other modes the motions involve one or more atoms moving in some other direction and still others correspond to what would be called bending or flapping distortions. The relation of the force constant of such a vibrational mode to any physical quantity such as bond strength is less clear in these cases.

The two bending modes of the CO_2 molecule are seen to be identical with each other except for the direction of the motion. In both cases the symmetry of the molecule requires identical restoring forces and displacements. Hence the two vibrations are of the same frequency and the modes are said to be doubly degenerate. Because they are identical, the equations of motion would also be satisfied by any linear combination of the y and z displacements, the result being a simple harmonic motion of the same frequency in which the atoms follow elliptical or circular paths as was shown in Fig. 8–16.

Although one might not readily assume a correct set of normal coordinates for a molecule by merely glancing at the atomic configurations, it nevertheless seems clear from Fig. 9–11 that the symmetry of the molecule is an important factor in constructing such a set and deducing the possible degeneracies of the various modes of vibration in the set. We have observed on several occasions that molecular configurations can

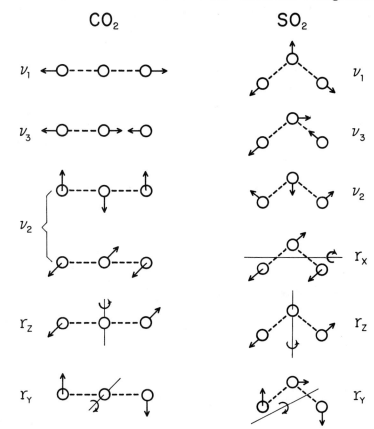

Fig. 9–11. Normal modes of vibration and rotation of CO_2 and SO_2.

be described in terms of symmetry operations. That is, molecular states can be designated according to the behavior of the wave functions to symmetry operations such as inversion, reflection, and rotation of coordinates. Molecules are often described as having certain symmetries when symmetry operations can be performed on the molecule which leave the relative positions of the atoms after the operation equivalent to their relative positions before the operation. The effect of several symmetry operations on CO_2 is shown in Fig. 9–12. In addition, a symmetry operation (if the molecule has or belongs to that symmetry) must leave the kinetic and potential energies of the molecule unchanged.

Just as one can examine the symmetry of a molecule with respect to atomic positions, one can also discuss the symmetry of atomic displacements. If the displacements are represented by vectors, then the relative magnitudes and orientations of these vectors can be observed as symmetry operations are performed, as in Fig. 9–13. Atomic displace-

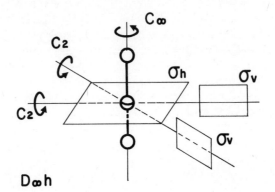

Fig. 9–12. The symmetry elements of CO_2.

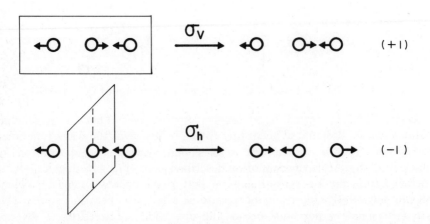

Fig. 9–13. The effect of symmetry operations on displacement vectors.

ments are best described in terms of normal coordinates, so that the Schrödinger equation can be separated for solution. Since the kinetic and potential energies are formulated in terms of these normal coordinates, the restriction cited above, that the potential and kinetic energies remain unaltered by a symmetry operation, requires that each normal coordinate must be symmetric or antisymmetric to operation by a symmetry operator. This follows because the potential and kinetic energies are written in terms of the squares of the normal coordinates and momenta as in Eqs. (9–14) and (9–15). Thus, for T and V to remain unchanged, each q must remain the same or at most change sign.

The symmetry of molecules and atomic displacements is an invaluable tool for determining a set of normal coordinates for a molecule, and the powerful techniques of group theory are again applicable. The details of normal coordinate analysis will not be extended here, but the reader is referred to several excellent discussions cited at the end of the chapter. The use of symmetry and group theory aids both the construction of normal coordinates and the determination of vibrational degeneracies. In addition, since molecular dipole moments depend on symmetry, these same techniques aid in establishing selection rules for the various vibrational modes.

We have emphasized the importance of normal coordinates in allowing a separation of the Schrödinger equation. With the Hamiltonian operator of the form of (9–16), the Schrödinger equation can be separated into $3N$ smaller equations of the form

$$-\frac{\hbar^2}{2}\frac{\partial^2\psi_i}{\partial q_i^2} + \tfrac{1}{2}\lambda_i q_i^2\psi_i = E_i\,\psi_i.$$

These normal coordinates for which $\lambda_i \neq 0$ correspond to vibrational modes of motion, so that the $3N - 6$ (or $3N - 5$) separate harmonic-oscillator solutions are

$$E_{v_i} = (v_i + \tfrac{1}{2})\frac{h\lambda_i^{1/2}}{2\pi} = (v_i + \tfrac{1}{2})h\nu_i$$

or

$$\tilde{E}_{v_i} = (v_i + \tfrac{1}{2})\tilde{\nu}_i.$$

Hence the total vibrational energy is the sum,

$$\tilde{E}_{\text{vib}} = \tilde{E}_{v_1} + \tilde{E}_{v_2} + \cdots,$$

and the vibrational wave function is the product of the separate eigenfunctions for the several normal modes of vibration. These wave functions differ from those already discussed only in that the normal coordinates are mass-weighted.

The vibrational energy levels for a typical triatomic molecule are illustrated in Fig. 9–14. Note that three quantum numbers are required, to designate each level, since there are three normal modes of vibration. In the non-linear molecule none of these levels is degenerate, although accidental degeneracies may occasionally occur. In the linear CO_2, however, degenerate levels would frequently occur since two modes are of the same frequency. It is also interesting to note that the zero-point vibrational energy can be considerable. In SO_2, for example, the lowest vibrational level (000) is 1515 cm^{-1} (4.30 kcal mole^{-1}) above the energy zero represented by the minimum of the potential-energy curve.

Selection rules are easily determined for electric dipole transitions. For the polyatomic molecule described in terms of normal coordinates,

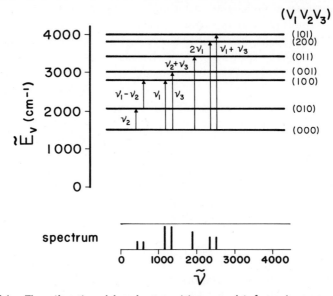

Fig. 9–14. The vibrational levels, transitions, and infrared spectrum of SO_2.

it is also convenient to express the dipole moment in terms of the same normal coordinates. Using an equation such as (9–2), we have

$$\mu = \mu^0 + \sum_{i=1}^{3N-6} \left(\frac{\partial\mu}{\partial q_i}\right)_{q_i=0} q_i + \frac{1}{2} \sum_{i=1}^{3N-b} \left(\frac{\partial^2\mu}{\partial q_i^2}\right)_{q_i=0} q_i^2 + \cdots ,$$

where μ^0 represents the equilibrium dipole moment of the molecule. To determine a dipole moment matrix element it is necessary to use a complete wave function, which for the polyatomic molecule will be a product of rotational and $3N - 6$ vibrational eigenfunctions. It is shown easily, as in the preceding section, that the permanent equilibrium dipole moment μ^0 gives rise to rotational transitions, while the second term is involved in vibrational changes. Each term in the summation would lead to matrix elements of the form

$$\left(\frac{\partial \mu}{\partial q_i}\right)_{q_i=0} [\int \psi_{v_1'}{}^*(q_1)\psi_{v_1''}(q_1)\ dq_1 \int \psi_{v_2'}{}^*(q_2)\psi_{v_2''}(q_2)\ dq_2$$
$$\cdots \int \psi_{v_i'}{}^*(q_i)q_i\psi_{v_i''}(q_i)\ dq_i \cdots]$$

where the $\psi_{v_i}(q_i)$ are simple harmonic oscillator functions. In each term in the sum, q appears only in the integral containing the corresponding ψ.

It is seen that the integrals will vanish except when $\Delta v_i = \pm 1$ and all other $\Delta v = 0$. It is necessary also that $\partial\mu/\partial q_i$ not vanish; that is, the vibration must involve a changing dipole moment in order to interact with the infrared radiation. The molecule, then, will absorb radiation at frequencies corresponding to the frequencies of vibration of the separate normal modes. It is as if the absorption of radiation excited the molecule in its ground state to vibrate with greater energy in one of its normal modes without exciting any other motions.

The $\Delta v_i = +1$ transitions for SO_2 are shown in Fig. 9–14, along with the resulting spectral lines. As in the simple diatomic molecule anharmonic dipole moments (terms in q^2, q^3, etc.) and anharmonic potential functions result in a breakdown of the simple selection rules. We observe as a result overtones ($\Delta v_i = +2$), combination bands (two normal modes excited simultaneously), and difference bands (one mode with $\Delta v = +1$, another with $\Delta v = -1$). Although overtones and other "forbidden" absorptions are generally less intense, it is frequently the case that some fundamental bands are so small in intensity that they may be the same order of magnitude. This can occur if $\partial\mu/\partial q_i$ is small for a given vibrational mode. Hence the most intense lines in the spectrum cannot automatically be assumed to be due to fundamental transitions. Other interactions can also occur between the classical vibrational modes that cause other complicating factors. Some of these additional transitions are shown in Fig. 9–14.

In summary, the motions of a molecule containing N atoms can be described in terms of $3N - 6$ (or $3N - 5$) normal modes of vibration. If a vibrational mode involves a changing dipole moment, then absorption of electromagnetic radiation can occur with $\Delta v = \pm 1$. The symmetry of the molecule may result in degeneracies and in motions with no changing dipole moment, in which cases still fewer frequencies of absorption will be observed. In addition, overtones, combinations, and difference bands are not uncommon for polyatomic species.

9.4 THE LINEAR POLYATOMIC MOLECULE

The combined phenomena of simultaneous vibrational and rotational transitions lead to a fine structure of the vibrational absorption lines much like the situation for the simple diatomic molecule. In discussing linear molecules it is pertinent to distinguish two types of vibrational motion. Reference to Fig. 9–11 shows that for CO_2 two of the normal modes of vibration involve atomic displacements which are parallel to the molecular axis. The corresponding infrared absorptions of such molecules are called *parallel bands*. The bending modes, on the other hand, involve displacements perpendicular to the molecular axis, and the corresponding IR bands are called *perpendicular bands*.

Some parallel motions, such as ν_1 for CO_2, involve no change in the molecular dipole moment and hence are not infrared-active. Vibrations that are symmetric to every symmetry operation of the molecule are called *totally symmetric* and are never active in the infrared. Other

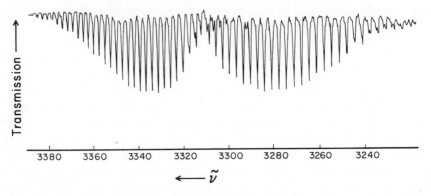

Fig. 9–15. The parallel fundamental band of HCN. (By permission from *Pure and Applied Chemistry*, 1, 568 (1961).)

parallel motions do involve dipole moment changes. The ν_3 vibration of CO_2 is clearly of this type. The selection rules for parallel vibrations are the same as those for the diatomic molecule; i.e., $\Delta v = \pm 1, \Delta J = \pm 1$. As a consequence, parallel infrared bands show the P and R branch structure. A thoroughly studied example is HCN, whose stretching fundamental is shown in Fig. 9–15. The measured frequencies of these lines are given in Table 9–6.

The analysis of the lines is similar to the diatomic problem. That is, it is assumed that $\tilde{B}$ depends on the vibrational state, so that the P and R separations in Fig. 9–15 depend on $\tilde{B}_0$ and $\tilde{B}_1$, where the subscripts refer to the ground and first excited states of this one particular normal mode of vibration. As in Eqs. (9–11) and (9–12), the P and R branch frequencies may be added and subtracted to give equations for the two rotational constants, from which $\tilde{B}_e$ can be calculated. Depending on the precision of measurement, it may be possible to calculate $\tilde{D}$. Although knowledge of $\tilde{B}_e$ is sufficient for the calculation of r_e for a diatomic

TABLE 9–6.   HCN Parallel Fundamental (cm^{-1})*

3385.55	3353.28	—	3277.82
3383.20	3350.64	—	3274.64
3380.83	3347.99	—	3271.44
3378.44	3345.31	3308.52	3268.22
3376.02	3342.60	3305.54	3264.98
3373.59	3339.88	3302.54	3261.72
3371.12	3337.14	3299.52	3258.44
3368.64	3334.37	3296.48	3255.14
3366.14	3331.58	3293.42	3251.82
3363.61	3328.77	3290.34	3248.48
3361.06	3325.94	3287.24	3245.12
3358.49	3323.09	3284.12	3241.75
3355.90	3320.22	3280.98	

* Report of the Commission on Molecular Structure and Spectroscopy, IUPAC, *Pure and Applied Chemistry*, **1**, 569 (1961).

molecule, it is not enough in the polyatomic case, since more than one internuclear distance must be obtained.   It was seen in Chapter 8 that isotopic substitution can be employed to obtain sufficient data for polyatomic parameters.

It is interesting that even symmetric molecules such as CO_2 and HCCH, which have no permanent dipole moment and no rotational spectrum, can absorb radiation in the infrared when they undergo vibrational motions that lead to momentary and changing dipole moments.   The totally symmetric stretching motion of CO_2 is not excited by infrared radiation because the dipole moment remains zero throughout all displacements of the atoms; but the asymmetric stretching mode does result in a continually changing dipole moment, and hence we observe absorption of radiation with the familiar pattern of P and R branches. The asymmetric band of CO_2 is shown in Fig. 9–16 with the expected

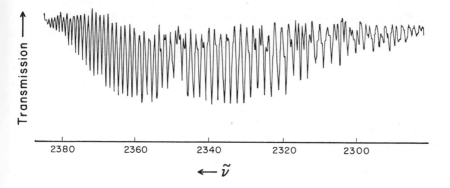

2380   2360   2340   2320   2300

Transmission →

$\leftarrow \tilde{\nu}$

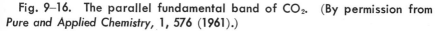

Fig. 9–16.   The parallel fundamental band of CO_2.   (By permission from *Pure and Applied Chemistry*, **1**, 576 (1961).)

fine structure. The measured frequencies are listed in Table 9–7. Inspection of these lines, however, discloses some features which are different from those we have predicted. Neglecting changes in $\tilde{B}$ with vibrational state, we have seen that the separation of fine structure lines is approximately $2\tilde{B}$, and with no Q branch the separation of the inner P and R lines would then amount to $4\tilde{B}$. In the CO_2 spectrum it will be seen that the gap is not twice the line separation but is only about half again as large as the line separation.

The cause of this difference was disclosed in our previous discussion of rotational states. It was seen in Sec. 8.2 that wave functions must meet certain symmetry requirements such as symmetry or antisymmetry

TABLE 9–7. CO_2 Parallel Fundamental (cm^{-1})*

2380.74	2364.15	2341.11	2315.21
2379.80	2362.85	2339.42	2313.18
2378.86	2361.51	2337.70	2311.12
2377.88	2360.16	2335.96	2309.05
2376.87	2358.77	2334.19	2306.95
2375.83	2357.37	2332.40	2304.84
2374.79	2355.94	2330.59	2302.69
2373.70	2354.48	2328.76	2300.50
2372.61	2353.00	2326.90	—
2371.47	2351.50	2325.01	—
2370.32	2349.96	2323.10	2294.45
2369.12	2347.62	2321.16	2293.10
2367.92	2346.03	2319.20	2291.62
2366.69	2344.41	2317.22	2290.23
2365.41	2342.77		

* Report of the Commission on Molecular Structure and Spectroscopy, IUPAC, *Pure and Applied Chemistry*, **1**, 577 (1961).

to inversion of coordinates. Among the most important of such properties is the symmetry with regard to exchange of two identical particles. Those with zero or integral spin angular momentum must leave the wave function unchanged when exchanged, while the wave function must be antisymmetric to exchange of two identical particles with half-integral spin. Thus in the case of the symmetric CO_2 molecule, exchange of the two oxygen nuclei $(I = 0)$ must leave the wave function unchanged. Since the ground vibrational wave function is symmetric and the ground electronic wave function is symmetric, only those rotational states can exist which are also symmetric. We predict, then, that in the ground vibrational state only states with even values of J are populated as shown in Fig. 9–17.

For the first excited vibrational state, the vibrational function is antisymmetric. Since the electronic state is unchanged, the possible rotational states of the molecule must now be antisymmetric in order that the total wave function be symmetric. Hence, only states with odd J are possible in the excited vibrational state. This situation also is shown in Fig. 9–17. Also shown are the resulting transitions obeying the selection rules $\Delta v = 1$, $\Delta J = \pm 1$.

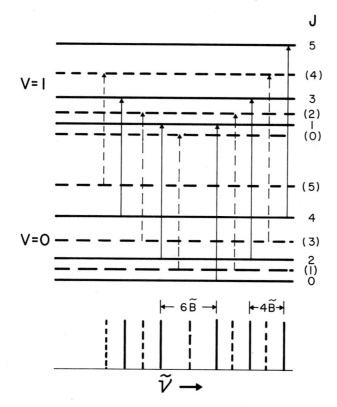

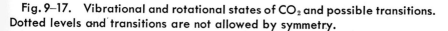

Fig. 9–17.   Vibrational and rotational states of CO_2 and possible transitions. Dotted levels and transitions are not allowed by symmetry.

It is immediately apparent from the diagram that, because a number of rotational states are missing, the corresponding transitions also are missing. Hence the spacing between the observed fine structure lines is approximately $4\tilde{B}$, while the separation of the inner P and R lines now amounts to $6\tilde{B}$. Other symmetric linear molecules such as acetylene show similar differences from the diatomic fine structure, although the details of the spacing may differ, depending on whether the nuclei involved are Bosons or Fermions.

The bending vibration of a linear triatomic molecule clearly results

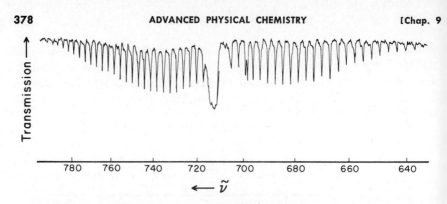

Fig. 9–18. The perpendicular fundamental band of HCN. (By permission from *Pure and Applied Chemistry,* **1,** 590 (1961).)

in a changing dipole moment perpendicular to the equilibrium bond axis, and this motion is infrared-active. For diatomic molecules and the parallel vibrations of linear molecules, only rotational transitions for which $\Delta J = \pm 1$ are allowed, but in all other cases the transitions for which $\Delta J = 0$ also are permitted. Hence lines corresponding to pure vibrational transitions, called the Q branch, are seen in the infrared spectra of all polyatomic molecules except for those vibrations of a linear molecule which are parallel to the molecular axis. The absence of a Q branch is thus an unambiguous indication that a molecule is linear and the vibration is parallel. The bending vibrations of linear polyatomic molecules are perpendicular to the rotational axes of the molecule, and the corresponding absorption bands are known as perpendicular bands.

The perpendicular band of HCN is illustrated in Fig. 9–18, where the presence of the Q branch is observed clearly. Lines are listed in Table 9–8. Unlike the P and R branch lines, the Q branch appears to be broad and asymmetric with some indication of fine structure. Letting $\Delta J = 0$

TABLE 9–8.   HCN Perpendicular Fundamental (cm^{-1})*

785.57	750.37	706.08	670.60
782.65	747.40	703.12	667.64
779.72	744.45	700.16	664.68
776.79	741.51	697.19	661.73
773.87	738.57	694.24	658.77
770.94	735.61	691.29	655.82
768.00	732.66	688.34	652.88
765.06	729.72	685.36	649.91
762.14	726.76	682.40	646.97
759.19	723.80	679.45	644.03
756.26	720.85	676.49	641.07
753.31	717.90	673.54	638.13

* Report of the Commission on Molecular Structure and Spectroscopy, IUPAC, *Pure and Applied Chemistry,* **1,** 591 (1961).

we find from Eq. (9–8)

$$\tilde{\nu} = \tilde{\nu}_e + (\tilde{B}_{v'} - \tilde{B}_{v''})J + (\tilde{B}_{v'} - \tilde{B}_{v''})J^2,$$

where J in this case stands for the value for both the initial and the final states.   From this result we see that since $B_{v'} \neq B_{v''}$ the $\Delta J = 0$ transitions corresponding to successively higher rotational states do not fall at exactly the same frequency, although the differences are indeed small. The vibrational-rotational interaction called l-type doubling also affects these lines.   The combination of the two degenerate bending vibrations leads to an effective angular momentum about the molecular axis.   The normal rotational levels are slightly split into pairs of levels corresponding to the two possible directions of this "vibrational" rotation.   As a result, the rotational-vibrational transitions are more complicated in detail, although the differences are small enough for us to neglect them here.

9.5　SYMMETRIC AND ASYMMETRIC TOP MOLECULES

The complexities that result when a polyatomic molecule is non-linear are offset to some extent when a high degree of symmetry exists in the molecular configuration.   The existence of a threefold or greater symmetry axis results in two of the three principal moments of inertia being equal, the symmetric top case.   It was shown in Chapter 8 that for such molecules both the total rotational angular momentum, represented by J, and the component of this angular momentum along the unique or figure axis of the molecule, denoted by K, are quantized.   The pattern of symmetric top rotational levels was illustrated in Fig. 8–20.

If the dipole moment matrix elements are examined for the combined rotational and vibrational wave functions, selection rules are deduced. It is found that these restrictions are different for vibrational modes that involve atomic motions parallel to the unique axis of the molecule and for vibrations that are perpendicular to this axis.   For parallel modes the selection rules are

$$\Delta K = 0, \Delta J = 0, \pm 1 \quad \text{when } K \neq 0$$

and

$$\Delta K = 0, \Delta J = \pm 1 \quad \text{when } K = 0.$$

Expressions for the frequencies of the parallel band lines follow from these rules and the energy-level expression (8–24), which can be rewritten as

$$\tilde{E}_v = \frac{E}{hc} = (v + \tfrac{1}{2})\tilde{\nu}_e + J(J + 1)\tilde{B}_\iota + K^2(\tilde{A}_v - \tilde{B}_v).$$

The subscript v is used to denote the vibrational level to which the rotational levels correspond. For the polyatomic molecule there should be $3N - 6$ numbers in this subscript for a complete description of the vibrational level, although they could be numbered consecutively or in some other manner. For the oblate top, by our convention, $\tilde{C} - \tilde{B}$ would appear in the last term of the above equation.

Insertion of the selection rules leads, for $K = 0$, to

P branch: $\quad \tilde{\nu} = \tilde{\nu}_e + J''^2(\tilde{B}_{v'} - \tilde{B}_{v''}) - J''(\tilde{B}_{v'} + \tilde{B}_{v''}),$

Q branch: $\quad$ absent,

R branch: $\quad \tilde{\nu} = \tilde{\nu}_e + 2\tilde{B}_{v'} + (3\tilde{B}_{v'} - \tilde{B}_{v''})J'' + (\tilde{B}_{v'} - \tilde{B}_{v''})J''^2;$

and for other values of K, to

$$P \text{ branch:} \quad \tilde{\nu} = \tilde{\nu}_e + (J''^2 - K^2)(\tilde{B}_{v'} - \tilde{B}_{v''}) - J''(\tilde{B}_{v'} + \tilde{B}_{v''})$$
$$+ K^2(\tilde{A}_{v'} - \tilde{A}_{v''}),$$

$$Q \text{ branch:} \quad \tilde{\nu} = \tilde{\nu}_e + (J''^2 - K^2)(\tilde{B}_{v'} - \tilde{B}_{v''}) + J''(\tilde{B}_{v'} - \tilde{B}_{v''})$$
$$+ K^2(\tilde{A}_{v'} - \tilde{A}_{v''}),$$

$$R \text{ branch:} \quad \tilde{\nu} = \tilde{\nu}_e + 2\tilde{B}_{v'} + J''(3\tilde{B}_{v'} - \tilde{B}_{v''}) + (J''^2 - K^2)(\tilde{B}_{v'} - \tilde{B}_{v''})$$
$$+ K^2(A_{v'} - A_{v''});$$

where, as usual, the double-primed terms are the initial states. The $\tilde{A}_v$ have been treated here in a manner analogous to the $\tilde{B}_v$ with respect to the equilibrium value of $\tilde{A}$.

Several things are to be noted regarding these expressions. For $K = 0$ transitions no Q branch appears, since $\Delta J = 0$ is forbidden. In addition it must be kept in mind that for transitions involving other values of K there are no states with $J < K$. Hence, if the P, Q, and R lines corresponding to different values of K are considered separately, as in Fig. 9–19, some of the inner lines of the P and R branches will be missing. Since K has a much smaller effect than J, it is seen in this figure that the resulting spectrum involving all possible transitions still resembles the perpendicular band of a linear molecule, except that in this case the various lines may be broadened enough by the non-overlapping lines corresponding to different K that the fine structure is obscured somewhat. This can be seen in the parallel band structure of CH_3Br illustrated in Fig. 9–20. When fine structure can be resolved, it is again possible to calculate values of $\tilde{B}$.

For symmetric top molecules the perpendicular bonds are the result of the selection rules

$$\Delta K = \pm 1, \quad \Delta J = 0, \pm 1.$$

A glance at the energy-level diagram for a symmetric top shows that the

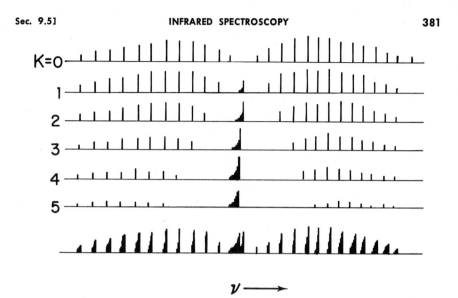

Fig. 9–19. Components of a parallel band of a symmetric top molecule showing contributions from each value of K and the total spectrum. (After Herzberg, *Infrared and Raman Spectra of Polyatomic Molecules*, D. Van Nostrand Co., 1945, p. 418.)

resulting fine structure will be considerably more complex than that of the parallel band. Some of the allowed transitions are shown in Fig. 9–21, along with the resulting spectral lines in Fig. 9–22. Again, the pattern corresponding to the value of K in the initial state is shown as well as the resulting spectrum. The Q branches in each case are the most prominent feature, and because many of the less intense P and R

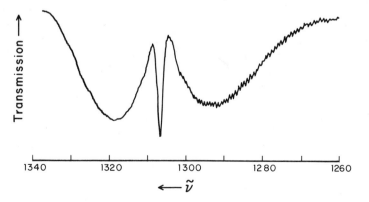

Fig. 9–20. The parallel absorption band of CH_3Br. (From Barrow, *Introduction to Molecular Spectroscopy*, McGraw-Hill Book Co., 1962, p. 153; used by permission.)

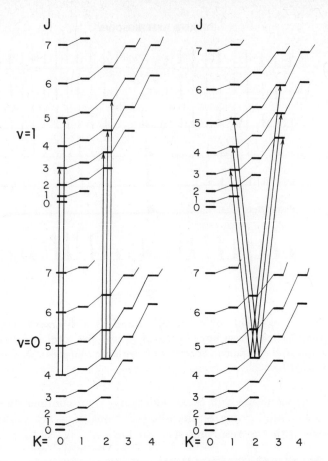

Fig. 9–21. Allowed transitions for a symmetric top molecule. For parallel bands $\Delta K = 0$ (vertical lines) while for perpendicular bands $\Delta K = \pm 1$.

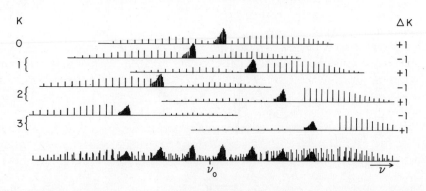

Fig. 9–22. Components of a perpendicular band of a symmetric top molecule showing contributions from each value of K and the total spectrum. (After Herzberg, *Infrared and Raman Spectra of Polyatomic Molecules,* D. Van Nostrand Co., 1945, p. 425.)

lines overlap in different ways, the pattern of Q lines is the most prominent feature in the resulting spectrum. This is seen in the spectrum of CH_3Cl, which is shown in Fig. 9–23. There are instances, however, where the P and R lines may be of sufficient intensity to mask even the Q lines, so that broad unresolved bands are observed.

The asymmetric molecule, because of its reduced degree of symmetry, becomes the most difficult case to treat in general terms. Fortunately a number of generalizations are possible. In particular, many of the motions can be discussed in terms of the three principal axes of the

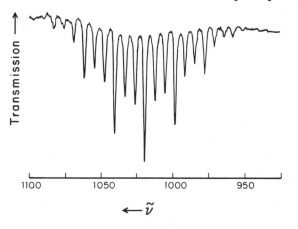

Fig. 9–23. Perpendicular band of CH_3Cl. The Q branches are the most prominent feature. There is an alternation of intensity because of the symmetry of the molecule, which leads to alternating statistical weights of the various levels. (From Barrow, *Introduction to Molecular Spectroscopy*, McGraw-Hill Book Co., Inc., 1962, p. 157; used by permission.)

molecule and selection rules deduced. The dependence of the energy levels on three rotational constants, however, causes complications and most cases must be treated in detail individually. We will not attempt to describe various cases here, and the reader is referred to more detailed monographs.

Many of the spectra illustrated in this chapter are of better resolution than obtained on typical commercial instruments. This fact, coupled with the overlapping of lines in less symmetric molecules, often results in a failure to distinguish between the rotational fine structure lines. Even so, band contours are observed, and these can lead to conclusions regarding the nature of the vibration and the symmetry of the molecule. Some typical rotational contours are illustrated in Fig. 9–24, where it is obvious that distinctions can be made if a little information is known about the molecule.

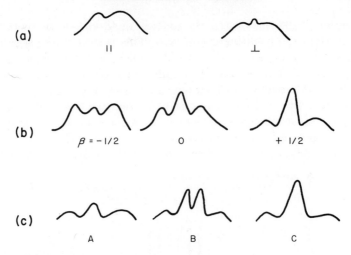

Fig. 9–24. Rotational contours for (a) linear molecule, (b) perpendicular mode of a symmetric top, (c) asymmetric top. The parameter $\beta = (I_B/I_A) - 1$. For the asymmetric top it is assumed $I_A:I_B:I_C = .69:.75:1$, and the bands A, B, and C correspond to vibrations parallel to the I_A axis, I_B axis, and I_C axis, respectively.

9.6 GROUP CHARACTERISTICS AND CHEMICAL EFFECTS

The increasing accuracy and precision of infrared measurements have made possible the determination of molecular parameters for many species. Even simple molecules such as CH_4 and NH_3 have been subjected to repeated study as techniques of measurement and computation have improved. The calculation of rotational constants is possible, however, only when rotational fine structure is present, and as in the case of microwave spectra, this condition holds only for gases at sufficiently low pressures that frequent molecular collisions do not limit the lifetimes of rotational states so severely that uncertainty broadening of the rotational lines occurs and washes out the fine structure. In condensed phases where such interactions are important, the rotational fine structure is no longer observed, and hence the direct calculation of rotational constants from infrared spectra is impossible. In addition, the presence of strong intermolecular forces alters the environment of the molecules so that the selection rules that cause some absorptions to be missing from the infrared gaseous spectrum may break down in liquids and solids because of a change in symmetry of the forces involved. Hence, in liquid spectra numerous lines, including combination and difference bands as well as overtones, are often present.

An example of the effect of condensation on the infrared spectrum is shown in Fig. 9–25, where the loss of fine structure and the addition of several bands can be observed. In the solid state the symmetry of the crystalline environment often reduces once again the multiplicity of bands and sharpens them considerably. It was mentioned previously that although overtone bands are considerably less intense than their fundamentals, some of the latter may be so weak that an overtone of some other mode is of comparable intensity. It is not always possible, then, to separate fundamental bands from others entirely on the basis of their intensities.

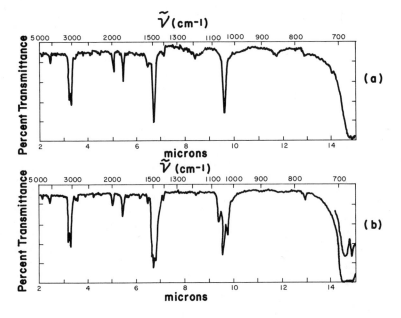

Fig. 9–25. Low resolution infrared spectra of benzene (a) vapor and (b) liquid.

Another feature often observed in infrared spectra is that some bands such as overtone and combination bands may be at considerably lower or higher frequencies than predicted by simple multiplication or addition of the fundamental frequencies. Very often this phenomenon is accompanied by two bands, not too distant from each other, of comparable intensity. These effects are believed to arise when two different absorptions are accidentally of almost the same frequency. It can be shown mathematically that an interaction occurs, which tends to mix the wave functions and separate the energy levels of the excited states involved. This is yet another resonance phenomenon and is known as *Fermi resonance*. The separation of the energy levels results in two different absorptions, which have frequencies more or less equally distributed

above and below the frequency predicted without the resonance interaction. In benzene, for example, two of the fundamentals at 1485 cm^{-1}
and 1585 cm^{-1} are expected to give a combination band at 3070 cm^{-1}.
This almost coincides, however, with the C—H stretching fundamental
frequency, and Fermi resonance results in two equally intense bands
at 3099 and 3045 cm^{-1}.

Despite the fact that the loss of rotational structure and the increasing
complexity of liquid spectra might appear to reduce the importance of
infrared spectroscopy, this technique has actually become one of the
most useful to the chemist both for analytical and identification purposes.
The spectra of polyatomic molecules are usually complex. Nevertheless,
since the frequencies of absorption depend specifically upon the structure,
symmetry, and forces in a specific molecule, the resulting infrared spectrum is very likely to be uniquely characteristic of that molecule, or at
least nearly unique. Given almost any change in the exact features of a
molecule, there will be decided effects on the infrared spectrum. The
lower-frequency region, in particular, which involves the general skeletal
motions of a complex molecule, will show decided differences from one
molecule to another. Hence, infrared spectra are utilized as "fingerprints" of molecules and serve as an invaluable aid for identification.

Another interesting correlation has been found. Although a normal
mode of vibration actually involves simultaneous motion of all or most
of the atoms in a molecule, it is possible to consider a bond in a complex
molecule approximately as similar to the bond in a diatomic molecule.
For the bond R—X, for example, where R is one group of atoms and X
another, we would write

$$\tilde{\nu} = \frac{1}{2\pi c} \sqrt{\frac{k}{\mu}}, \quad \mu = \frac{m_R m_X}{m_R + m_X}.$$

If $m_R \gg m_X$, then $\mu \simeq m_X$; and if the force constant of the R—X bond
does not depend on R, then the vibrational frequency is independent of
both m_R and the nature of R. This approximation is most valid when
the bond is a terminal one and X is hydrogen. It is, in fact, observed
that for all molecules containing a C—H bond there is an absorption
band in the range 2850–3050 cm^{-1}. Substitution of deuterium for
hydrogen lowers the frequency of these bands by a factor of $\sqrt{2}$ showing
that the molecular motions in this normal mode of vibration are primarily
the stretching motion of the C—H bond. Investigations of dilute
solutions (where intermolecular perturbations are small) of compounds
containing O—H and N—H bonds also disclose that there are absorptions
nearly always found in the regions 3600–3640 cm^{-1} and 3360–3500 cm^{-1}
respectively. Isotopic substitution is frequently a useful means for
identifying spectral lines with particular modes of motion.

The extension of this approximation to terminal bonds containing heavier atoms such as halogens is open to question, but a surprisingly large number of similar correlations have been found between infrared absorption frequencies and the presence of specific kinds of bonds. In addition to terminal bonds, there also seems to be a correlation with the presence of internal bonds such as $C=C$, $C\equiv C$, and others. The most useful correlations are those which involve bands at frequencies greater than about 1500 cm^{-1}. Below this frequency greater variation occurs, and more drastically affected motions such as bending and twisting modes are involved. Although specific types of bonds are not so readily identified in this lower-frequency region, it is here that the so-called skeletal absorptions occur; and despite the fact that each band cannot be definitely identified, the absorption patterns observed are quite specific for given molecules and can be used to identify molecular species or eliminate them as possibilities. For this reason the lower-frequency region of the IR spectrum is often called the "fingerprint" region.

Since accurate prediction of absorption frequencies cannot be made *a priori*, a great deal of effort has gone into the correlation and interpretation of experimental spectra. Several reviews and monographs cited at the end of the chapter have considered correlations of this sort with detailed discussions of variations in band frequencies and intensities. They provide an important source of information concerning a large number of experimental measurements and can lead to successful identifications in many instances. Some examples of infrared correlations are given in Table 9–9 and Fig. 9–26.

It becomes apparent upon studying correlations of infrared absorption with structure that many bands are sensitive to changes in the chemical nature of the environment. That is, changing substituents may alter electron densities in a given bond, such as an O—H bond or a $C=O$ bond, and hence change the force constant and absorption frequency. A good example of such effects is the correlation of the $C=O$ frequency of substituted benzoic acids with the Hammett sigma function, which relates the rate constant for esterification of benzoic acid to substituents on the benzene ring. The rate is supposedly affected by the electron-withdrawing properties of the ring substituents, and these same effects on the carbonyl bond are evident from the IR shifts, as shown in Fig. 9–27. Many interesting correlations have been recorded, showing the effects of various types of substitution on identified absorption bands, and these also frequently serve as an extremely useful diagnostic tool.

Some of the most striking infrared shifts are those caused when inter- and intra-molecular effects occur involving O—H and N—H bonds. The hydrogen-bonding interaction, in particular, causes large shifts of the OH stretching frequency to lower frequencies. In alcohols, for example

TABLE 9–9. Some Representative Group Stretching Frequencies (cm⁻¹)

—O—H	Stretch	(Lowered by hydrogen bonding)	3640–3600
$\diagdown$N—H$\diagup$	Stretch	(Lowered by hydrogen bonding)	3500–3380
—C—H	Stretch	In —C≡C—H	3305–3270
		Attached to aromatic ring	3030
		Attached to C=C	3090–3010
		In —CH₃ { Antisymmetric	2962
		{ Symmetric	2872
		In CH₂ { Antisymmetric	2926
		{ Symmetric	2853
—C≡N	Stretch		2260–2240
—C≡C—	Stretch	In —C≡CH	2140–2100
		In —C≡C—	2260–2190
$\diagdown$C=O$\diagup$	Stretch		1900–1580
$\diagdown$C=C$\diagup$	Stretch		1680–1630
—N$\diagup^{O}_{\diagdown O}$	Stretch	{ Antisymmetric	1560–1520
		{ Symmetric	1360–1340
		In NO₃⁻	1380–1350
—C$\diagup^{O}_{\diagdown O}$	Stretch	{ Antisymmetric	1610–1550
		{ Symmetric	1400–1300
$\diagdown$S=O$\diagup$	Stretch		1060–1045
$\diagdown$S$\diagup^{O}_{\diagdown O}$	Stretch	{ Antisymmetric	1335–1310
		{ Symmetric	1160–1130
		In SO₄²⁻	1130–1080
—C—F	Stretch		1350–1200
—P=O$\diagup$	Stretch		1300–1250
—Si—O	Stretch	In PO₄³⁻	1100– 950
			1100–1000
		In SiO₄²	1100– 900

(Fig. 9–28), the OH fundamental occurs at 3600 cm⁻¹, when the alcohol is diluted in an inert solvent in which no hydrogen bonds are formed. At higher concentrations bands are found at lower frequencies corresponding to hydrogen-bonded polymers. Similar phenomena are seen in solutions of carboxylic acids and compounds containing N—H bonds which can also be hydrogen-bonded. Under favorable circumstances integrated

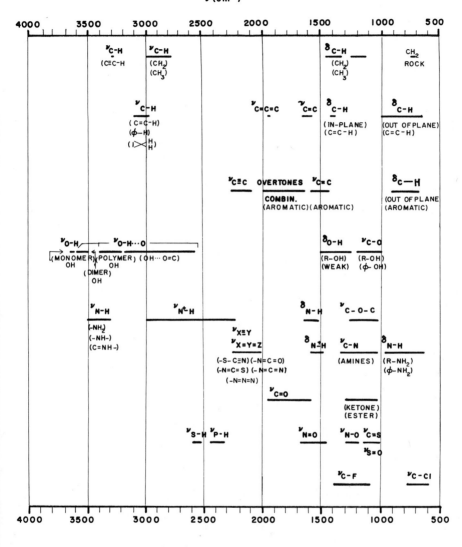

Fig. 9–26. Infrared-structure correlations.

intensities of the monomer and dimer peaks can be utilized to calculate equilibrium constants for the hydrogen-bonding equilibrium.

The infrared spectral region offers opportunities for obtaining many kinds of chemical information. In the case of gaseous molecules high resolution spectra disclose rotational fine structure, from which rotational constants can be calculated. It is possible to determine the infrared-active normal modes from symmetry considerations, and specific bands

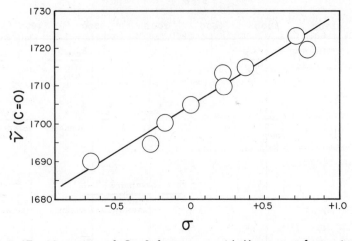

Fig. 9–27. Variation of C=O frequency with Hammet σ factor in various substituted benzoic acids dissolved in CH_3OH. From left to right the substituents are NH_2, OCH_3, CH_3, H, p-Cl, Br, m-Cl, m-NO_2, p-NO_2. (Data from Flett, *Trans. Faraday Soc.*, **44**, 767 (1948).)

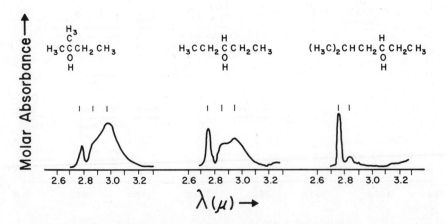

Fig. 9–28. The OH stretching absorption of three alcohols at approximately the same concentrations in CCl_4. In the simplest alcohol, peaks attributed to monomers, dimers, and polymers are observed. As the OH group becomes more hindered, the larger polymers are less abundant. In the most hindered molecule most of the molecules are not hydrogen-bonded at all.

can be identified according to the nature of their fine structure or relative order of frequency. Stretching modes, for example, are generally of higher frequency than bending modes. The reverse procedure is an obvious extension; the presence and absence of bands of particular structure can be used to rule out certain types of molecular symmetry. In addition, details concerning the potential-energy function can be obtained from overtones and combination bands.

In liquids, although rotational structure is lost and some of the symmetry restrictions may vanish, infrared spectra nevertheless retain many important features. Again, the relative frequencies of bands (as well as intensities) may serve to distinguish the motions involved. Since the extremely helpful rotational fine structure is missing, one relies largely on extensive correlations of infrared lines in order to associate bands with particular molecular features. At higher frequencies such correlations serve to identify nearly unambiguously certain structural groups such as O—H bonds and C≡C groupings. At lower frequencies the skeletal absorptions serve as unique fingerprints of over-all molecular configurations. A number of the problems at the end of the chapter illustrate these methods.

The uniqueness of infrared spectra and the ability to identify certain structural features result in this branch of spectroscopy being one of the most useful to chemists. Routine infrared spectra obtained on reliable commercial instrumentation are taken as a matter of course to serve for identification. In addition, the observed bands can be used in a quantitative way, by assuming the Beer-Lambert law or determining the effect of concentration on extinction coefficients more precisely, to measure equilibria, rates, and similar effects. Finally, the dependence of absorption frequencies on intra- and inter-molecular perturbations throws light on interactions of chemical interest. Numerous examples of such problems as well as details on experimental methods can be obtained from monographs in the field.

Although a number of symmetric vibrations that do not involve changing molecular dipole moments are missing in the infrared spectrum, it is possible to supplement IR data with a closely allied technique, Raman spectroscopy. The Raman phenomenon involves the scattering of radiation which is energetic enough to excite the molecule momentarily out of the ground electronic state. When the radiation is reemitted, the molecule may end up in an excited rotational and/or vibrational state, in which case the frequency of the emitted radiation will be displaced from that of the incident radiation. These shifts can then be used to determine the vibrational and rotational parameters of the molecule. The Raman effect depends on the polarizability of the molecule rather than its dipole moment, and since many vibrations that have no dipole moment do have an effect on the polarizability, many infrared-inactive transitions are seen in Raman spectra. This very valuable spectroscopic method is discussed in several of the references cited below.

SUPPLEMENTARY REFERENCES

BARROW, G. M., *Molecular Spectroscopy*, McGraw-Hill Book Co., New York, 1962. The basic features of vibrational spectra are introduced, followed by a lucid description of group theory and its use in solving for the normal coordinates of a polyatomic molecule. Introductory.

HERZBERG, G., *Spectra of Diatomic Molecules*, D. Van Nostrand Co., Princeton, 1950; *Infrared and Raman Spectra*, D. Van Nostrand Co., Princeton, 1945. Considerably more detail is given on the many complicated features of diatomic and polyatomic spectra. Useful compilations of data are included. Intermediate.

COTTON, F. A., *Chemical Applications of Group Theory*, John Wiley & Sons, Inc., New York, 1963. A very readable introduction to group theory and its use, with a chapter on molecular vibrations.

WILSON, E. B., J. C. DECIUS, and P. C. CROSS, *Molecular Vibrations*, McGraw-Hill Book Co., New York, 1955. A detailed discussion of the mathematics of normal coordinate analysis with useful discussions of group theory. Advanced.

ALLEN, H., and P. C. CROSS, *Molecular Vib-Rotors*, John Wiley & Sons, Inc., New York, 1964. Considers in some detail advances in the mathematical analysis of vibrational-rotational interactions and spectra. Advanced.

BELLAMY, L. J., *Infrared Spectra of Complex Molecules*, John Wiley & Sons, Inc., New York, 1958. One of the most useful compilations of spectra-structure correlations.

WEISSBERGER, A. (ed.), *Physical Methods of Organic Chemistry*, vol. 9, Interscience Publishers, Inc., New York, 1956. An excellent chapter devoted to chemical applications of infrared spectra and structure correlations.

BAUMAN, R. P., *Absorption Spectroscopy*, John Wiley & Sons, Inc., New York, 1962. A useful survey of experimental and theoretical aspects of infrared, visible, and ultraviolet spectroscopy. The theoretical material is detailed but compact. Very useful discussions of qualitative and quantitative analytical problems are included.

NAKANISHI, K., *Infrared Absorption Spectroscopy—Practical*, Holden-Day, Inc., New York, 1962. Similar to Bellamy, with emphasis on correlations of spectra with structural groupings. Many illustrative spectra are included.

PROBLEMS

9-1. The fundamental vibration frequency of H_2 is 4,159.2 cm^{-1}. Calculate the vibration frequency of D_2.

9-2. For the CH radical $\bar{\nu}_e = 2073.4$ cm^{-1} and $\chi_e\bar{\nu}_e = 57.0$ cm^{-1}. Calculate the band centers of the fundamental and first overtone.

9-3. For FCl^{35} $\bar{\nu}_e = 313.5$ cm^{-1}, $\chi_e = .00706$. What is the force constant of the Cl—F bond? What is the band-center frequency of the third-overtone band?

9–4. From the infrared spectrum of HCl^{37} it is calculated that $\tilde{B}_0 = 10.43$ cm^{-1}, $\tilde{B}_1 = 10.12$ cm^{-1}, $\tilde{B}_2 = 9.78$ cm^{-1}. From these determine $\tilde{B}_e$ and r_e, and compare with the values for HCl^{35}. Show that this is an expected result.

9–5. From the rotation-vibration lines in Table 9–6 calculate all possible $\tilde{B}_v$ for HCN. Compare with the rotational constants calculated from the perpendicular vibration, and between the two calculate $\tilde{B}_e$ for HCN.

9–6. The oxide of nitrogen, N_2O, could possibly exist in one of several configurations. It could have the structural formula N—N—O or N—O—N and could be linear or bent. In the infrared spectrum of gaseous N_2O three strong bands are observed. The lowest-frequency band is at 579 cm^{-1} and has P, Q, and R branches. A band at 1285 cm^{-1} has only P and R branches and the third at 2224 cm^{-1} also has only P and R branches. Several weaker bands are observed, two of these being at 2563 cm^{-1} and 2798 cm^{-1}. On the basis of these observations what is the probable structure of N_2O? What vibrations can be assigned to the above-mentioned bands?

9–7. The high-frequency fundamental of N_2O shows fine structure, some of which are, in cm^{-1},

2219.49,	2224.59,
2220.38,	2225.48,
2221.22,	2226.24,
2222.03,	2227.03,
2222.90,	2227.82.

Calculate all possible B_v for N_2O.

9–8. Sketch the expected normal modes of vibration for H—C≡C—H. Three strong bands are observed in the IR spectrum, 3287 cm^{-1}, 1327 cm^{-1}, and 729 cm^{-1}. The 729-cm^{-1} band has a strong Q branch. To which vibration does it belong? Which vibration or vibrations will have no infrared absorption? If the 3287-cm^{-1} band is a combination band, to what transitions could it correspond?

9–9. Several of the fine structure lines observed in the vibrational absorption of CO are, in cm^{-1},

2127.79,	2147.19,
2131.74,	2150.97,
2135.65,	2154.71,
2139.53,	2157.41.

Calculate $\tilde{B}_e$ and r_e for CO and compare with the results from microwave spectra.

9–10. Calculate the partition function and the vibrational contribution to C_v of HCl at 300°K, 1000°K, and 5000°K.

9–11. Calculate the heat capacity of HCl at 300°K, 1000°K, and 5000°K from all contributions (except electronic).

9–12. Draw schematically the expected relative intensities of the lines in the P and R branches of CO at 300°K and at 1000°K.

9–13. From a spectroscopic analysis of a group of electronic bands of CO, the vibrational levels can be represented by the equation

$$\tilde{E}_v = 2170.21 \ (v + \tfrac{1}{2}) - 13.461 \ (v + \tfrac{1}{2})^2 + .0308 \ (v + \tfrac{1}{2})^3.$$

From Table 9–5, $r_e = 1.128$ Å. Calculate $\tilde{D}_e$, $\tilde{E}_0$, k_e, and sketch the potential-energy curve.

9–14. Assuming for simplicity that HCl is completely ionic and can be represented by point charges at the locations of the nuclei, calculate the dipole moment of HCl in its equilibrium configuration (1 Debye $= 10^{-18}$ esu/cm). The measured dipole moment is 1.03 D. What formal charge on each nucleus would produce this result?

9–15. Using the result from Problem 9–14 calculate $(\partial \mu / \partial q)$ near the equilibrium distance, and from this determine the dipole moment transition probability and molar extinction coefficient.

9–16. Find the classical amplitude of vibration of HCl in the ground and first excited states. Express displacement in angstroms and as a percentage of the normal bond length.

9–17. As an approximation CCl_4 can be assumed to be a spherical molecule of diameter 4.75 Å. Assuming CCl_4 can be treated as an ideal gas in the liquid state, find the average time between collisions for CCl_4 at 300°K. From the Heisenberg uncertainty principle estimate the half-width of a vibrational absorption. Most liquids have half-widths ranging from 2.5 to 25 cm^{-1}.

9–18. Assuming a spring were available with a force constant the same as that of N_2, calculate the displacement of a 1-ft spring with a load of 10 kg. The vibrational frequency of N_2 is 2360 cm^{-1}. Is such a mechanical spring a practicality?

9–19. Calculate the molal entropy S°_{298} (in cal mole^{-1} deg^{-1}) of H_2 in the perfect gas state corresponding to each of the following conventions, using the rigid-rotator, harmonic-oscillator approximation:

a. The so-called "absolute" entropy, which includes the contributions from the nuclear-spin states.

b. The value to be expected from conventional application of the third law of thermodynamics to experimental heat-capacity data for "normal" H_2 (in which conversion is very slow) from 10°K up to room temperature.

c. The "practical" entropy, to be used for the ordinary calculations of chemical thermodynamics.

9–20. Repeat Problem 9–19 for D_2.

9–21. Consider an assembly of four independent harmonic oscillators a, b, c, d, each of the same frequency ν. Let the assembly be isolated with a total energy of $7h\nu$; i.e., five quanta are shared by four oscillators.

a. There are 56 ways (complexions) of distributing the total energy in this assembly. Make a table listing the values of the four quantum numbers v_a, v_b, v_c, v_d for each of these 56 complexions.

b. A distribution is defined by specifying the numbers n_i of oscillators with each value of the quantum number v; e.g., the set $n_0 = 2$, $n_1 = 0$, $n_2 = 1$, $n_3 = 1$ defines one of the possible distributions in the assembly here considered. List the values of n_i for each of the six possible distributions of this assembly, and give the number of complexions corresponding to each. Verify that these agree with the formula $N!/\pi_i(n_i!)$.

c. Show that the total number of complexions (56) of the assembly is given by the coefficient of z^5 in the power-series expansion of $(\sum_{n=0}^{\infty} z^n)^4$ with $z < 1$. (For $z < 1$ the sum $\sum_{n=0}^{\infty} z^n$ equals $1/(1 - z)$.)

d. Referring to your table of (a), find the numbers of complexions for which the quantum number v_a of oscillator a has each of its possible values from 0 to 5. Assigning equal weight to each complexion, calculate the probabilities of finding a given oscillator with each of the possible values of v. When multiplied by N, these probabilities give the average numbers $\bar{n}_v$ of oscillators with quantum numbers v.

e. Find the numbers n_v* describing the "most probable" distribution of energy among the oscillators, obtaining the temperature in terms of $h\nu/k$. Compare these results with (d) by plotting $\bar{n}_v$ and n_v* against v. Why is agreement not exact?

9-22. Given:

Molecule	$\bar{\nu}$ (cm^{-1})	r_e (Å)	$D_0{}^0$ (ev)
H_2	4395	.7416	4.476
Li_2	351.4	2.672	1.03
LiH	1405.6	1.595	2.50

$$I_H = \tfrac{1}{2} \qquad I_{Li} = \tfrac{3}{2}$$
$$M_H = 1.008 \qquad M_{Li} = 6.940$$

a. Write general expressions for the total partition functions of the three molecules. Assume that ground electronic states have no degeneracy. (Note that D_0 includes the zero-order vibrational energy, so that the latter should not be included in the vibrational partition function.)

b. Obtain an expression for the equilibrium constant for the dissociation $2LiH \rightleftharpoons Li_2 + H_2$ and evaluate it at 800°K and 1000°K.

9-23. Calculate the molal entropy of HCl gas at 298.1°K, and compare with thermodynamic values.

9-24. Calculate the molal entropy and heat capacity of HCN at 298.1°K.

9-25. The parallel bands for symmetric top molecules were analyzed in Fig. 9-19. Derive expressions for the P and R branch origins (the innermost lines) as a function of K.

9-26. Derive expressions for the P, Q, and R branches of a perpendicular band of a symmetric top molecule.

9–27. In the spectra of Fig. 9–29 identify the various absorptions as to molecular motions:

     a. CS_2.

     b. C_2H_5OH.

     c. *n*-hexane.

     d. CCl_4.

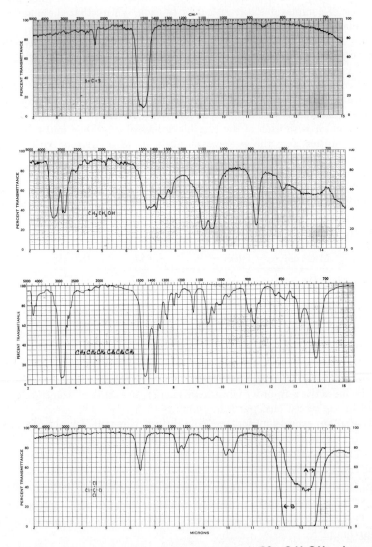

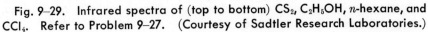

Fig. 9–29. Infrared spectra of (top to bottom) CS_2, C_2H_5OH, *n*-hexane, and CCl_4. Refer to Problem 9–27. (Courtesy of Sadtler Research Laboratories.)

9–28. For the spectra in Fig. 9–30 identify the probable substance or the structure if a formula is given:

   a. A commercial polymer.

   b. C_6H_{14}.

   c. $C_{14}H_{14}$.

   d. N_2H_4CS.

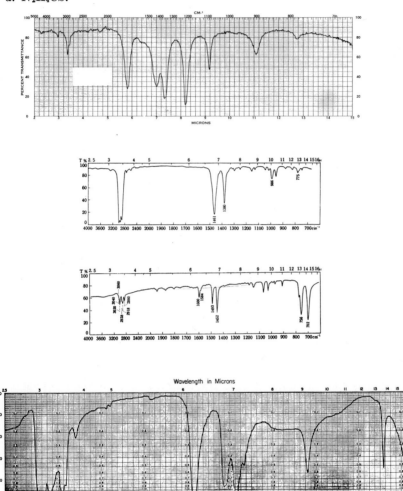

Fig. 9–30. Infrared spectra for Problem 9–28. (Top spectrum courtesy of Sadtler Research Laboratories. Second and third spectra reprinted with permission from Nakanishi, *Infrared Absorption Spectroscopy—Practical*, Holden-Day, Inc., 1962.)

10

Electronic States of Molecules and Molecular Spectra

Microwave and infrared spectral studies have played a major role in our attempt to understand the structures of molecules. Yet it might well be said that our discussion has failed thus far to show that quantum mechanics can directly predict the existence and stability of any particular molecular species. It was implied in our discussions of the hydrogen atom and of many-electron atoms that in principle one needs only the particles involved and the interactions between them in order to construct the Schrödinger equation, from which one should be able to extract the wave functions, energy levels, and other details. We will now consider molecules from this standpoint.

10.1 THE H_2^+ ION

The problem, of course, lies in the mathematical difficulties that arise when one leaves the simpler centrally symmetric case of atoms. Hence few molecular examples can be discussed without recourse to approximation methods. We will begin with the simplest of all cases, the H_2^+ ion, which is a stable molecular species and which consists of two protons and an electron. Although this molecule is relatively unimportant to the chemist, we can illustrate here several characteristics of the molecular problem.

The first step in the problem is to construct the Hamiltonian operator, which for the H_2^+ system (Fig. 10–1) is

$$\mathcal{H} = -\frac{\hbar^2}{2}\left(\frac{1}{m_A}\nabla_A{}^2 + \frac{1}{m_B}\nabla_B{}^2 + \frac{1}{m_e}\nabla_e{}^2\right) + \left(-\frac{e^2}{r_A} - \frac{e^2}{r_B} + \frac{e^2}{r_{AB}}\right).$$

It was shown, however, by Born and Oppenheimer (Chapter 8 and Appendix H) that the nuclear motions could be separated from the electronic, so that, if the internuclear separation r_{AB} is considered to be a variable parameter, the electronic problem reduces to the much simpler Hamiltonian,

$$\mathcal{3C} = -\frac{\hbar^2}{2m_e} \nabla_e^2 + \left(-\frac{e^2}{r_A} - \frac{e^2}{r_B} + \frac{e^2}{r_{AB}} \right).$$

Thus the Schrödinger equation to be solved is

$$-\frac{\hbar^2}{2m_e} \nabla_e^2 \psi + \left(-\frac{e^2}{r_A} - \frac{e^2}{r_B} + \frac{e^2}{r_{AB}} \right)\psi = E\psi.$$

We have seen on several occasions that a great simplification of the problem results if the Schrödinger equation can be separated by a judicious

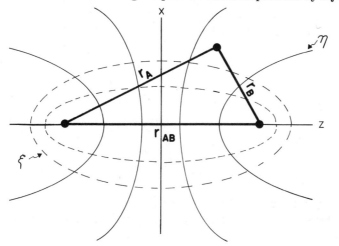

Fig. 10–1. Coordinates of the H_2^+ molecule ion. The ellipses and hyperbolas are contours along which the coordinates ξ and η, respectively, remain constant.

choice of coordinates so that the total wave function, which is a function of several variable coordinates, can be written as the product of several simpler functions, each of which is a function of only one variable. The use of spherical polar coordinates proved invaluable, for example, in the spherically symmetric hydrogen atom. The H_2^+ model can be described by a coordinate system which allows such a separation of variables. In this case it is separable in confocal elliptical coordinates ξ and η and the azimuthal angle ϕ about r_{AB} as shown in Fig. 10–1. The coordinates ξ and η are given by

$$\xi = \frac{r_A + r_B}{r_{AB}},$$

$$\eta = \frac{r_A - r_B}{r_{AB}};$$

and if the Laplacian operator is rewritten in these coordinates, the Schrödinger equation becomes

$$\frac{\partial}{\partial \xi} \left\{ (\xi^2 - 1) \frac{\partial \psi}{\partial \xi} \right\} + \frac{\partial}{\partial \eta} \left\{ (1 - \eta^2) \frac{\partial \psi}{\partial \eta} \right\} + \left(\frac{1}{\xi^2 - 1} + \frac{1}{1 - \eta^2} \right) \frac{\partial^2 \psi}{\partial \phi^2}$$
$$+ \frac{2 m_e r_{AB}^2}{\hbar^2} \left\{ \frac{E}{4} (\xi^2 - \eta^2) + \frac{e^2}{r_{AB}} \xi \right\} \psi = 0.$$

With $\psi(\xi,\ \eta,\ \phi)$ replaced by $\psi(\xi,\ \eta,\ \phi) = \Xi(\xi)\mathrm{H}(\eta)\Phi(\phi)$, this equation is separable into

$$\frac{d^2 \Phi}{d\phi^2} = -m^2 \Phi, \tag{10-1}$$

$$\frac{d}{d\eta} \left\{ (1 - \eta^2) \frac{dH}{d\eta} \right\} + \left(\lambda \eta^2 - \frac{m^2}{1 - \eta^2} - \mu \right) H = 0, \tag{10-2}$$

$$\frac{d}{d\xi} \left\{ (\xi^2 - 1) \frac{d\Xi}{d\xi} \right\} + \left(-\lambda \xi^2 + 2D\xi - \frac{m^2}{\xi^2 - 1} + \mu \right) \Xi = 0. \tag{10-3}$$

The parameters λ and D in these equations are given by

$$\lambda = - \frac{m_e r_{AB}^2 E}{2\hbar^2}$$

and

$$D = \frac{r_{AB}}{a_0}$$

so that it can be seen that the energy will be a function of r_{AB}. To find the energy of the stable molecular species, we would vary r_{AB} to find a minimum in E.

The first of these three equations, (10-1), is recognized as one that is solved easily. It will be recalled that there are solutions for Φ corresponding to $m = 0, \pm 1, \pm 2, \ldots$ It is then necessary to find the relations between λ and μ that allow a satisfactory solution of (10-2) and then proceed with this relation to finding solutions to Equation (10-3) which would give characteristic values of λ and therefore of the energy of the electronic configuration. We will not attempt to follow these calculations, but the equations have been solved at several levels of accuracy, and an exact solution agrees perfectly with the spectroscopic equilibrium distance of 1.060 Å and dissociation energy of 2.791 ev.[1] Exact calculations also have been made of a number of the excited states. The electron distribution of the ground state of H_2^+ is shown in Fig. 10-2, where it is seen that the most probable region for the electron is located between the two nuclei, as would be expected on simple electrostatic grounds.

Unfortunately, the separability of the Schrödinger equation in the case of H_2^+ is exceptional. Just as the addition of a second and third electron

[1] Jaffé, *Z. Physik,* **87,** 535 (1934).

to the hydrogen atom makes exact solution of the atomic case impossible, so also does the addition of more electrons and nuclei to the H_2^+ model complicate the situation tremendously.   For this reason it becomes necessary to employ approximation methods.   Since the H_2^+ case is relatively simple to handle, it is worthwhile to illustrate these methods here.

Our investigation of the use of approximation methods in the case of the helium atom disclosed that the deviations of the actual potential-energy terms from a solvable case are often so large that a first-order perturbation treatment does not give particularly accurate results.   The variation method has proven to be a generally more effective and popular

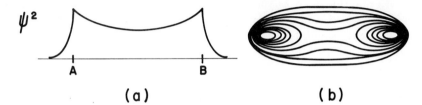

Fig. 10–2. The electronic probability distribution for the ground state of H_2^+.   (a) The ψ^2 profile along the AB axis.   (b) ψ^2 contours in any plane containing both nuclei.

approach.   It will be recalled that in this method one constructs a variation function which has one or more adjustable parameters, and on applying the true Hamiltonian operator for the system of interest these parameters are adjusted for a minimum in the calculated variation energy.   In many cases the known energies of the species of interest serve as a guide to the success of the trial functions.

In the H_2^+ case there are several possibilities as to a trial function.   One could use, for example, any arbitrary function which displays the proper symmetry properties and the generally expected shape of the true function.   One used by James[2] was

$$\psi = e^{-b\xi}(1 + c\eta^2), \qquad (10\text{–}4)$$

where b and c were adjusted to minimize the energy.   This function gives a dissociation energy of 2.786 ev, which is very close to the true value, and the internuclear distance corresponding to this energy is 2.06 Å.   The values of the parameters in this case are $b = 1.35$, $c = .447$.

There are not too many problems of simple enough symmetry to be able to use arbitrary trial variation functions in this manner, although there has been considerable success in some instances from using a variety of simple functions such as combinations of Gaussian functions, exponentials,

[2] James, *J. Chem. Phys.*, **3,** 9 (1935).

and others. In complex molecules, particularly, it is helpful to consider what related information we already have that might be of help in constructing the trial function. Perhaps most helpful, as well as most obvious, is the chemists' view of molecules as structures which are made up of atoms held together by various interactions. It certainly behooves us to investigate the possibility that molecular wave functions might be constructed successfully from the wave functions of the atoms from which the molecule is constituted.

One point should be made clear at the outset, that this approach is clearly an approximation. The configurations of the electrons in molecules are not the same as they are in isolated atoms. Nevertheless the atomic situations would hopefully at least give us a starting point. We will investigate several ways in which atomic functions can be used and will attempt to interpret some of the quantities that arise in these methods. But it must be remembered that although one method may give more satisfactory results than another in any given calculation, one should not mistake one method as giving the "true" picture of the bonds in a molecule, the others being "false." The methods are a means to an end. It is only the molecules themselves that have any real meaning.

As a start let us consider H_2^+ in terms of the species from which it could be formed or into which it might dissociate. If we should pull the two hydrogen nuclei further and further apart, it seems reasonable that the electron would tend to remain in the vicinity of one or the other, but not both, of the nuclei since the hydrogen atom itself is a very stable configuration. We might suspect, then, that the wave function of a single hydrogen atom might serve as a reasonable starting point. Using a hydrogen atom $1s$ wave function as our trial variation function, we wish then to evaluate the integral

$$W = \frac{\langle 1s|\mathcal{3C}|1s \rangle}{\langle 1s|1s \rangle}.$$

If we use the normalized $1s$ function (Table 6–4), the denominator is unity and the numerator becomes

$$W = \left\langle 1s_A \left| -\frac{\hbar^2}{2m_e} \nabla_e^2 - \frac{e^2}{r_A} \right| 1s_A \right\rangle + \left\langle 1s_A \left| -\frac{e^2}{r_B} + \frac{e^2}{r_{AB}} \right| 1s_A \right\rangle,$$

where we have made a separation of the Hamiltonian operator into two parts. We are taking the nucleus A as the proton contained in the hydrogen atom. The Hamiltonian operator in the first integral is then that for a hydrogen atom with A as the nucleus. Thus

$$\left\langle 1s_A \left| -\frac{\hbar^2}{2m_e} \nabla_e^2 - \frac{e^2}{r_A} \right| 1s_A \right\rangle = E_{1s}\langle 1s_A|1s_A \rangle = E_{1s}.$$

This result follows because ψ_{1s} is an eigenfunction of the operator in the first integral and is also already normalized. The second integral can be further divided:

$$\left\langle 1s_A \left| -\frac{e^2}{r_B} + \frac{e^2}{r_{AB}} \right| 1s_A \right\rangle = \left\langle 1s_A \left| -\frac{e^2}{r_B} \right| 1s_A \right\rangle + \left\langle 1s_A \left| \frac{e^2}{r_{AB}} \right| 1s_A \right\rangle.$$

The operator in the second of these integrals has no effect on ψ_{1s_A}, which contains only r_A, and since the wave function is normalized, this term is simply e^2/r_{AB}. The first integral, often called a coulomb integral, commonly denoted by the symbol J. The variation energy of the H_2^+ molecule is thus given by

$$W = E_{1s} + \frac{e^2}{r_{AB}} + J.$$

The coulomb integral J is so called because it represents the electrostatic energy of a unit charge at a distance r_{AB} from the center of an electron cloud whose charge density is $\psi_{1s}{}^*\psi_{1s}$. This term can be evaluated by using confocal elliptical coordinates (Appendix E). The result of this evaluation is

$$J = e^{-2r_{AB}/a_0} \left(\frac{e^2}{a_0} + \frac{e^2}{r_{AB}} \right) - \frac{e^2}{r_{AB}}, \tag{10-5}$$

so that

$$W = E_{1s} + e^{-2r_{AB}/a_0} \left(\frac{e^2}{a_0} + \frac{e^2}{r_{AB}} \right).$$

W is clearly a function of r_{AB}, and inspection reveals that there is no minimum in W. As r_{AB} is made smaller, W increases continuously. Using this trial function, we have predicted that there is no stable species H_2^+.

In retrospect we could have ascertained in the beginning that the single 1s function is unsatisfactory as a trial function. We know from James' trial function (10–4) that the wave function is symmetric about the center of r_{AB}, as is the Hamiltonian operator for the molecule. But the 1s function is not symmetric about the center of the molecule and hence is unsatisfactory. In other words, the actual electron distribution in the molecule allows for the electron to be on either nucleus or in between them, while our trial function restricted the electronic positions to one nucleus.

A much more satisfactory function would be one that recognizes the symmetry of the Hamiltonian, that is, the association of the electron with with both nuclei. Such a function can be constructed by a linear combination of two hydrogen atom functions as in

$$\psi = c_1(1s_A) + c_2(1s_B). \tag{10-6}$$

The use of a trial function which is a linear combination of functions was discussed in Sec. 7.4 where it was shown that minimizing W with respect to c_1 and c_2 leads to a secular determinant,

$$\begin{vmatrix} H_{AA} - S_{AA}W & H_{AB} - S_{AB}W \\ H_{BA} - S_{BA}W & H_{BB} - S_{BB}W \end{vmatrix} = 0,$$

where H_{ij} is the matrix element $\langle i|\mathfrak{IC}|j\rangle$ and S_{ij} is the integral $\langle i|j\rangle$. In this particular problem the normality of the hydrogen functions allows us to determine that

$$S_{AA} = S_{BB} = 1, \quad S_{AB} = S_{BA}, \quad H_{AB} = H_{BA}, \quad H_{AA} = H_{BB}.$$

Substituting these into the secular determinant, we obtain

$$(H_{AA} - W)^2 = (H_{AB} - WS_{AB})^2,$$

from which

$$W = \frac{H_{AA} \pm H_{AB}}{1 \pm S_{AB}}. \tag{10-7}$$

If this is substituted into the two equations which led to the secular determinant, we find that

$$c_1 = \pm c_2,$$

so that there are two suitable trial functions of the type (10–6). Including normalization, these are

$$\psi_S = \frac{1}{[2(1 + S)]^{1/2}} (\psi_{1s_A} + \psi_{1s_B}) \tag{10-8}$$

and

$$\psi_A = \frac{1}{[2(1 - S)]^{1/2}} (\psi_{1s_A} - \psi_{1s_B}), \tag{10-9}$$

where S_{AB} is shortened to S. The energies of these states are given by (10–7). The evaluation of the integrals is relatively straightforward. For example,

$$H_{AA} = \langle A|\mathfrak{IC}|A\rangle = E_{1s} + \frac{e^2}{r_{AB}} + J,$$

as we have already observed. The two-center integral is

$$H_{AB} = \langle A|\mathfrak{IC}|B\rangle = \left\langle A \left| -\frac{\hbar^2}{2m_e} \nabla^2 - \frac{e^2}{r_B} \right| B \right\rangle + \left\langle A \left| -\frac{e^2}{r_A} + \frac{e^2}{r_{AB}} \right| B \right\rangle$$

$$= \langle A|E_{1s}|B\rangle + \left\langle A \left| \frac{e^2}{r_{AB}} \right| B \right\rangle + \left\langle A \left| -\frac{e^2}{r_A} \right| B \right\rangle$$

$$= E_{1s}S_{AB} + \frac{e^2}{r_{AB}} S_{AB} + K.$$

The integral K is often called a resonance or exchange integral because it involves the possibility of electron motion around both nuclei. Using confocal elliptical coordinates, K is evaluated to be (Appendix E)

$$K = -\frac{e^2}{a_0} e^{-r_{AB}/a_0} \left(1 + \frac{r_{AB}}{a_0}\right).$$

The integral S_{AB} is known as a non-orthogonality or overlap integral, since it vanishes when r_{AB} is large and becomes significant when the electron densities around A and B overlap considerably at a smaller internuclear

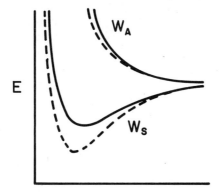

Fig. 10–3. The ground and first excited states of H_2^+ as compared with the simple variation calculation. Solid lines are the calculated energies.

distance. This integral, also simplified by elliptical coordinates, is evaluated in Appendix E:

$$S_{AB} = S = e^{-r_{AB}/a_0} \left(1 + \frac{r_{AB}}{a_0} + \tfrac{1}{3} \frac{r_{AB}^2}{a_0^2}\right).$$

Thus the energies of the symmetric and antisymmetric states of H_2^+ are found to be

$$W_S = E_{1s} + \frac{e^2}{r_{AB}} + \frac{J + K}{1 + S}$$

and

$$W_A = E_{1s} + \frac{e^2}{r_{AB}} + \frac{J - K}{1 - S}$$

respectively. These are shown as a function of r_{AB} in Figure 10–3 along with the accurate solution discussed previously.

Several facts are disclosed by these results. First of all, choice of a trial function with different symmetry from that of the system (Hamiltonian) resulted in no satisfactory solution. Choice of a function with the proper symmetry, however, leads to the prediction that H_2^+ should be a stable species. In addition, we can see in the expressions for the energy that the mathematical factors that differ in the two cases are the exchange integral, K, and the overlap integral S. It is obvious that the larger (more negative) the exchange integral becomes and the larger the overlap, the more stable the species that results. In other words, by allowing the electron to move around both nuclei we have produced a stable configuration—a chemical bond. The importance of the introduction of this exchange of the electron between two nuclei has led to a description in which the molecule is said to be stabilized by the "resonance" of the molecule between the two structures represented by $1s_A$ and $1s_B$. The energies of each of these structures (atom plus proton) we have seen to be high, actually unstable as a molecular configuration; but when the electron is exchanged from one nucleus to another, i.e., the molecule "resonates" between the two structures, stabilization occurs. This situation is analogous to the double-minimum potential well (Sec. 8–9) and is mathematically equivalent to the resonance phenomenon when vibrating systems are coupled. It is important to note, however, that this phenomenon, as well as the exchange and overlap integrals, appears only because (a) we used an approximate trial function rather than the exact wave function, (b) the trial function was constructed from a linear combination of free-atom wave functions. When the correct wave function is used to begin with, the correct energy and electron distribution are obtained immediately. One must take care not to believe in approximate mathematical models as if phenomena (in this case resonance structures) actually exist. Nevertheless, since we find it convenient to use atomic functions as a starting point, these concepts are of considerable utility in qualitative and semiquantitative discussions.

The bond energy, 1.76 ev, calculated with this trial function is not in very good agreement with the actual energy of 2.79 ev, and the calculated equilibrium internuclear distance of 1.32 Å is rather much larger than 1.06 Å. This is not surprising, in view of the crude approximation with which we began. Several methods can be employed to improve the situation, one of which is to introduce a variable parameter Z' into the wave function, much like the shielding parameter discussed in the atomic case.[3] Writing the hydrogen functions more explicitly and introducing Z', we would have the form

$$\psi = c_1 e^{-Z'r_A} + c_2 e^{-Z'r_B} \tag{10–10}$$

neglecting normalization. A Z' of 1.228 gives a bond energy of 2.25 ev and an internuclear separation very close to 1.06 Å when the variation treatment is carried out with (10–10). Still better agreement with experiment is obtained if hydrogen $2p$ orbital wave functions (directed along the

[3] Finkelstein and Horowitz, *Z. Physik*, **48**, 118 (1928).

bond axis) are used as well as the $1s$ functions. The introduction of p functions, which already have electron density in the desired direction along the internuclear axis, might be included in a manner such as

$$\psi = 1s_A(Z') + 1s_B(Z') + c[2p_A(Z'') + 2p_B(Z'')]$$

where it is recognized that the functions for nuclei A and B will have equal weight and two different parameters, Z' and Z'', are used in the exponential parts of the functions. With a function of this sort the energy is approached within .05 ev.[4]

The excited states of H_2^+ can be obtained by similar LCAO (linear combination of atomic orbitals) wave functions. The antisymmetric function (10–9), in fact, represents the first excited state above the ground state. It is clearly repulsive (non-binding) in nature. This can be correlated with the electron distribution described by the antisymmetric function which removes electron density from between the nuclei. Similar excited states could be approximated by functions such as $2s + 2s$, $2p + 2p$, $2s - 2s$, etc. They can also be obtained by exact solution, but again the use of atomic orbitals in this case illustrates methods more generally applicable to complicated systems. Notice that the LCAO functions constructed in this way involve all the nuclei (in this case only two) in the molecule. For this reason these states are often called molecular orbital (MO) states since they represent states of the molecule as a whole. As in the case of atomic orbitals, a nomenclature has been devised to describe these various states. This nomenclature is based largely on the symmetry properties of the molecular orbital functions and will be illustrated with a few simple examples.

10.2 H_2^+ MOLECULAR ORBITALS

Investigation shows that there are four convenient operators which commute with the Hamiltonian operator of H_2^+ for all values of r_{AB}. Any function that is an eigenfunction of one of these operators must therefore also be an eigenfunction of the others (Chapter 3). The eigenvalues of the MO wave functions, when operated on by these operators, and their significance are:

a. $\hat{L}_z$, the component of angular momentum along the internuclear axis (the axis about which the azimuthal angle ϕ is measured). If the eigenvalues are $0, 1, 2, 3, \ldots$ times $\hbar$, then the molecular orbitals are denoted as $\sigma, \pi, \delta, \phi, \ldots$ orbitals. Note the similarity between this terminology and that for atomic states ($s, p, d, f, \ldots$). It is not difficult to deduce the eigenvalues of $\hat{L}_z$ for simple cases from a pictorial consideration of how the molecular orbitals are formed from atomic orbitals. Consider the formation of the ground state orbital

[4] Dickinson, *J. Chem. Phys.*, **1**, 317 (1933).

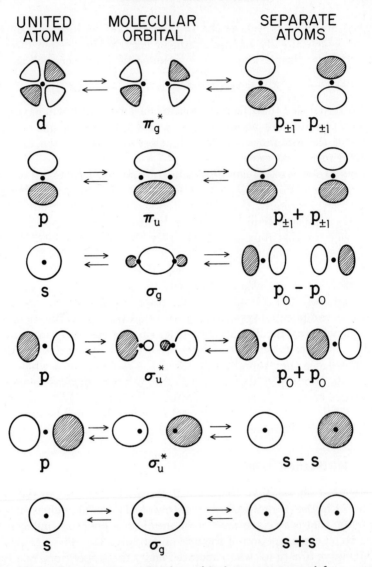

UNITED ATOM	MOLECULAR ORBITAL	SEPARATE ATOMS

Fig. 10–4. One-electron molecular orbitals as constructed from combined-atom and separated-atom atomic orbitals. Shaded regions represent the areas over which ψ is negative.

of H_2^+ as an example. The 1s state of hydrogen is one which has no angular momentum and no component about any given direction. We will arbitrarily take the internuclear axis as the z direction. When the ground state MO is formed from the overlap of two 1s wave functions, the resulting wave function, being cylindrically symmetric about the z direction, will also have no component of angular momentum about the z direction (Fig. 10–4). Hence the ground state orbital is a σ orbital. In a similar fashion, the antibonding antisymmetric excited state formed by $1s - 1s$ will also be cylindrically symmetric about the z direction and will be a σ state. The situation obviously will be similar for all s orbital combinations. Several possibilities arise in the case of p orbitals, however. Although the p orbitals have angular momentum, it is seen that the combinations of p_z orbitals (Fig. 10–4) lead to σ states, while those of p_x and p_y orbitals lead to states which are not cylindrically symmetric about the bond. We will not attempt to picture more complicated δ and ϕ states here. It is clear, however, that the nomenclature based on $\hat{L}_z$ alone is not sufficient to distinguish all the differences between molecular orbitals completely.

b. $\hat{\imath}$, the inversion of the electronic coordinates through the center of the internuclear axis. Because of the symmetry of the H_2^+ molecule, such an inversion of coordinates will either change the sign of the wave function or leave it unchanged. Hence the eigenvalues of $\hat{\imath}$ operating on a H_2^+ MO will be ± 1. If the eigenvalue is $+1$ (sign of the wave function unchanged), then the molecular orbital is said to be a g state (from the German *gerade* meaning even), while an eigenvalue of -1 signifies a u state (German *ungerade* meaning odd). A perusal of the states we have thus far described reveals readily the behavior of the functions on inversion, and the states are labeled accordingly in the diagrams.

c. $\hat{\sigma}_d$, reflection of the electronic coordinates through the plane which is perpendicular to the molecular axis and midway between the nuclei. Again, the molecular wave function will either change sign or remain the same upon such a reflection. When the eigenvalue of $\hat{\sigma}_d$ is $+1$, the state is not denoted by any special symbol, but when the eigenvalue is -1 (the MO function changes sign on reflection), then an asterisk is appended to the symbol as a superscript. The proper nomenclature for each of the s and p combinations is given also in Fig. 10–4 and can be verified by inspection.

d. $\hat{\sigma}_v$, reflection of the electronic coordinates through a plane passing through the nuclei and perpendicular to the σ_d plane. In this case states which do not change sign (eigenvalue $+1$) are denoted $+$ states and those with eigenvalue -1 are denoted $-$ states.

Not all the symbols described here are always used if they are not necessary to an adequate description. In the case of H_2^+, there is little difficulty in identifying the states. Several of these are listed in Table 10–1.

TABLE 10–1.   MO States of H_2^+ Molecule (LCAO)

MO	$\hat{L}_z$	Eigenvalues for		$\hat{\sigma}_v$	Symbol
		$\hat{\imath}$	$\hat{\sigma}_d$		
$1s_A + 1s_B$	0	1	1	1	$\sigma_g 1s$
$1s_A - 1s_B$	0	-1	-1	1	$\sigma_u{}^*1s$
$2s_A + 2s_B$	0	1	1	1	$\sigma_g 2s$
$2s_A - 2s_B$	0	-1	-1	1	$\sigma_u{}^*2s$
$2p_{1A} + 2p_{1B}$	1	-1	1	-1	$\pi_u 2p$
$2p_{1A} - 2p_{1B}$	1	1	-1	-1	$\pi_g{}^*2p$
$2p_{0A} + 2p_{0B}$	0	-1	-1	1	$\sigma_u{}^*2p$
$2p_{0A} - 2p_{0B}$	0	1	1	1	$\sigma_g 2p$

Several qualitative considerations are useful for investigating more complicated cases. We have observed, for example, that the stable bonding molecular orbital of H_2^+ has a high electron density between the nuclei, while the state with an absence of electrons in this region is repulsive or

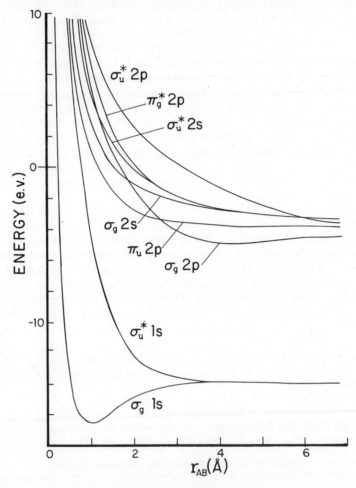

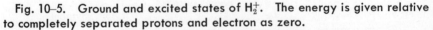

Fig. 10–5. Ground and excited states of H_2^+. The energy is given relative to completely separated protons and electron as zero.

antibonding. On this basis we notice that those wave functions that change sign on reflection through a plane perpendicular to the bond axis (σ_d) should be unstable. We can thus denote orbitals with an asterisk as antibonding orbitals, while those which are unstarred are bonding orbitals.

The actual energies of various states of H_2^+ are shown in Fig. 10–5, where it becomes obvious immediately that the distinction of bonding and antibonding molecular orbitals is not of much significance in H_2^+. The only excited state of H_2^+ that has any stability at all, relative to a separate proton and hydrogen atom, is the $\sigma_g 2p$ state. We will see, however, that the most common bonding situation with two electrons with two nuclei is conveniently described in this way.

We have approached the formulation of molecular orbitals from what is often called the separated-atoms viewpoint. That is, we have considered the nature of orbitals formed when two atoms come together from large separations. The illustration of the energies of these states is an accurate representation of how the energies of the states change with internuclear separation. In particular, the nuclear-nuclear repulsions come into prominance when the atoms come together at short distances. It is useful, however, to consider the situation that might occur if in the absence of internuclear repulsions the nuclei continued to approach each other and finally merged into a single nucleus, thereby creating a single atom with its accompanying atomic orbital states. Or alternatively, we could consider what would happen to the atomic orbitals of an atom if the nucleus were separated into two equal parts and these were pulled apart to some distance corresponding to the separation of the nuclei in the H_2^+ ion. This approach is called the combined-atom or united-atom viewpoint and leads to a second nomenclature for molecular orbitals. In the H_2^+ case the combined atom would be one with a nucleus containing two protons, so that the energy levels of the atomic orbitals would be those of the helium ion.

As an example consider the ground state molecular orbital of H_2^+ which was formed in the separated atoms picture by the overlap of two $1s$ wave functions. If we continue to bring the nuclei together, we see that the resulting atomic orbital will also have spherical symmetry about the nucleus and will hence be an s atomic orbital. Since we are dealing with the lowest state of the separated atom and molecule, it would be a helium $1s$ orbital. We have already designated the MO in question as σ_g, and in the combined-atom description this term is prefixed by the symbol for the combined atom state from which it is formed. Thus the ground state of H_2^+ would be denoted $1s\sigma_g$. In the separated-atom picture it was $\sigma_g 1s$.

Similarly, the merging of the σ_u^* MO into a single united atom results in an atomic p orbital ($2p$ is the lowest). Thus we denote this state as the $2p\sigma_u^*$ MO. The separated atom designation was $\sigma_u^* 1s$, so that between the two descriptions we have a complete picture of the properties of the molecular orbital. We can further illustrate the collapse of the $\sigma_g 2s$ and $\sigma_u^* 2s$ into $2s\sigma_g$ and $3p\sigma_u^*$ states, respectively, as well as the formation of $4p\sigma_u^*$ from $\sigma_u^* 2p$, $3d\sigma_g$ from $\sigma_g 3s$, $2p\pi_u$ from $\pi_u 2p$, $3d\pi_g^*$ from $\pi_g^* 2p$, etc.

It is interesting to note that the united-atom model is not restricted solely to a qualitative description of molecular states. Matsen[5] has car-

[5] Matsen, *J. Chem. Phys.*, **21**, 928 (1953).

ried out a perturbation calculation using atomic orbitals centered at the middle of r_{AB} and the Hamiltonian

$$\mathcal{3C} = -\frac{\hbar^2}{2m_e}\nabla_e^2 - \frac{Ze^2}{r} + \left(\frac{Ze^2}{r} - \frac{1}{r_A} - \frac{1}{r_B}\right)$$

where r is the distance from the center of the bond to the electron. The first two terms comprise $\mathcal{3C}^0$, the unperturbed Hamiltonian for the simple united atom with nuclear charge Z ($Z = 2$ for the united-atom states of H_2^+), and the remaining three terms are the perturbation $\mathcal{3C}'$, which results

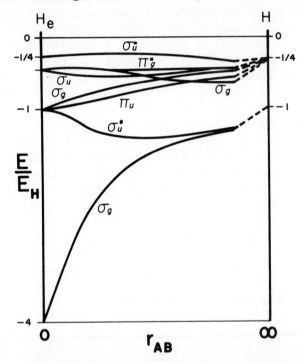

Fig. 10–6. Correlation diagram of H_2^+ molecular orbitals from separated-atom atomic orbitals to combined-atom atomic orbitals. Internuclear repulsions are neglected.

when the nucleus is pulled apart a distance r_{AB}. Best results were obtained for a variable Z which could be used to minimize the energy, and the calculated energies are reasonably good, particularly for excited states where the electron density is spread far away from the nuclei.

Although such a diagram does not represent the true energies of molecular and atomic systems going through various configurations, it is convenient to connect the separated atomic orbital energy levels with the combined-atom orbitals by means of a correlation diagram which shows the relative orders of the energies of the MO's that exist between the two extremes. A diagram of this sort is shown in Fig. 10–6, which can be contrasted with Fig. 10–5 by the absence of repulsion at short distances. Study of this diagram with respect to the symmetries of the separate and combined atomic orbitals and the intermediate molecular orbitals is well repaid, and we will return to the utility of the correlation diagram when considering more complicated diatomic molecules.

10.3　THE MOLECULAR–ORBITAL TREATMENT OF H_2

Next to H_2^+ the simplest molecular species is diatomic hydrogen itself. It differs from our preceding case by the addition of a second electron to the problem. Thus from Fig. 10–7 we construct the Hamiltonian

$$\mathcal{3C} = -\frac{\hbar^2}{2m}\left(\nabla_1{}^2 + \nabla_2{}^2\right) + \left(-\frac{e^2}{r_{A1}} - \frac{e^2}{r_{A2}} - \frac{e^2}{r_{B1}} - \frac{e^2}{r_{B2}} + \frac{e^2}{r_{AB}} + \frac{e^2}{r_{12}}\right)$$

for the electronic states of H_2. The Schrödinger equation written with

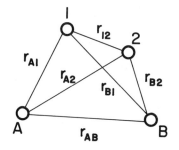

Fig. 10–7.　Coordinates of the H_2 molecule.

this Hamiltonian cannot be separated, even in confocal elliptical coordinates, because of the term containing r_{12}. We must thus resort to approximation methods again, notably the variation method. We must therefore decide on a trial function.

One approach presents us with an attractive possibility. We have described in some detail the one-electron molecular orbitals of the H_2^+ molecule ion. By analogy with the atomic case we might expect that, although the details would be altered, the hydrogen molecule might be accurately described in terms of putting two electrons into an H_2^+-like molecular orbital, just as the H^- ion could be approximated as consisting of two electrons in an H-like atomic orbital. Since we now have two electrons, we must be careful to construct total wave functions (spatial part times spin part) which are antisymmetric to the interchange of the two electrons, but as in the atomic case this can be done simply, and the spin functions will be assumed to be relatively unimportant in evaluating the various integrals inherent in the variation method.

Let us consider for a moment that both electrons are in the ground state σ_g MO. As per previous methods we might designate this as a $(1s\sigma_g)^2$ configuration. The spatial wave function would then be the product of two σ_g wave functions, one with the coordinates in terms of electron 1 and the other with electron 2, i.e.,

$$\psi = \sigma_g(1)\sigma_g(2) \times \text{spin function.}$$

From our experience with many-electron atoms, the spin function is constructed easily. Since the spatial function above is symmetric to exchange of the electrons, the spin function must be antisymmetric. Thus our total wave function is

$$\psi = \sigma_g(1)\sigma_g(2) \times \frac{1}{\sqrt{2}}\,[\alpha(1)\beta(2) - \beta(1)\alpha(2)].$$

If the individual MO functions are normalized, then the total function is also normalized. Neglecting the spin part, we obtain by the variation method

$$W = \langle \sigma_g(1)\sigma_g(2)|\mathcal{3C}|\sigma_g(1)\sigma_g(2)\rangle.$$

The integral is less difficult to evaluate if we divide the Hamiltonian operator into parts so as to obtain integrals of known form. If we let

$$\mathcal{3C} = \mathcal{3C}^0(1) + \mathcal{3C}^0(2) + \frac{e^2}{r_{AB}} + \frac{e^2}{r_{12}},$$

where

$$\mathcal{3C}^0(1) = -\frac{\hbar^2}{2m}\,\nabla_1{}^2 - \frac{e^2}{r_{A1}} - \frac{e^2}{r_{B1}}$$

and

$$\mathcal{3C}^0(2) = -\frac{\hbar^2}{2m}\,\nabla_2{}^2 - \frac{e^2}{r_{A2}} - \frac{e^2}{r_{B2}},$$

then

$$W = \langle 1,2|\mathcal{3C}^0(1)|1,2\rangle + \langle 1,2|\mathcal{3C}^0(2)|1,2\rangle + \left\langle 1,2\left|\frac{e^2}{r_{12}}\right|1,2\right\rangle + \frac{e^2}{r_{AB}}$$

$$= W_{(\mathrm{H_2^+})_1} + W_{(\mathrm{H_2^+})_2} + \frac{e^2}{r_{AB}} + H_{12},$$

where $H_{12} = \langle 1,2|e^2/r_{12}|1,2\rangle$ and the $W(H_2^+)$ terms are the energies of the H_2^+ molecular orbitals neglecting the r_{AB} terms. The actual evaluation of these integrals depends, of course, on the trial functions used for the original molecular orbitals. The excellent fit of James' trial function would suggest this as a possible choice, and the results obtained are a bond energy of 3.096 ev and an equilibrium $r_{AB} = .738$ Å which compares with

4.745 ev and .740 Å as the known values.[6] This result can be improved by introducing additional variable terms, but the results are not greatly improved. It is also possible to use other kinds of variation functions which have the proper symmetry characteristics and a large number of adjustable parameters. We will not delve into such functions except to mention one significant point. It appears that good results are obtained only if terms in r_{12} are included in the function. This reflects the fact that the repulsion between the electrons will affect the over-all electronic distribution, and hence allowance for this fact needs to appear in the functions themselves. Inclusion of terms to take this into account is often called *electron correlation.*

We have also investigated molecular orbitals constructed by a linear combination of atomic orbitals, the LCAO-MO method. We might use, therefore, for our trial function for H_2 the LCAO-MO for the σ_g orbital, or

$$\psi = \frac{1}{2(1 + S)} (1s_A + 1s_B)(1)(1s_A + 1s_B)(2) \times \text{spin function.} \quad (10\text{--}11)$$

The evaluation of H_{12}, which can be broken down into smaller integrals upon substitution of $1s_A + 1s_B$ for σ_g, is complicated in practice, and we will not attempt to explore this problem in detail. Using the symbol A for $1s_A$ and B for $1s_B$ yields

$$H_{12} = \langle [A(1) + B(1)][A(2) + B(2)] \left| \frac{e^2}{r_{12}} \right| [A(1) + B(1)][A(2) + B(2)] \rangle$$

$$= \langle A(1)A(2) + A(1)B(2) + A(2)B(1) + B(1)B(2) \left| \frac{e^2}{r_{12}} \right|$$

$$A(1)A(2) + A(1)B(2) + A(2)B(1) + B(1)B(2) \rangle$$

$$= 2e^2 \int \frac{[A(1)]^2[A(2)]^2}{r_{12}} \, d\tau + 2e^2 \int \frac{[A(1)]^2[B(2)]^2}{r_{12}} \, d\tau$$

$$+ 8e^2 \int \frac{[A(1)]^2 A(2)B(2)}{r_{12}} \, d\tau + 4e^2 \int \frac{A(1)A(2)B(1)B(2)}{r_{12}} \, d\tau.$$

The expansion results in 16 different integrals but because of the similarity of the functions (e.g., $A(1)^2A(2)^2/r_{12} = B(1)^2B(2)^2/r_{12}$) the total number of integrals that must be evaluated is reduced to these four different kinds. The first of these is the same coulomb integral discussed in the He atom problem. The second is a two-center coulomb integral, the fourth an exchange integral, and the third a hybrid coulomb-exchange integral. Evaluation of the latter is difficult, and the reader may consult the references at the end of the chapter. The result, using (10–11) as the trial function for H_2, is a dissociation energy of 2.681 ev and an internuclear distance of .850 Å.[7] This result is clearly not very accurate, but we have

---

[6] Coulson, *Trans. Faraday Soc.*, **33**, 1479 (1937); *Proc. Cambridge Phil. Soc.*, **34**, 204 (1938).

[7] *Ibid.*

already observed that the LCAO construction of trial functions is a very crude one. The results are qualitatively correct, however, for a stable molecule is predicted. As in the case of H_2^+, this LCAO function can be improved by introducing a variable Z' into the $1s$ functions and minimizing the energy by varying this parameter.[8] This one improvement leads to an energy of 3.470 ev and a bond distance which is only .008 Å in error.

Further improvement also is possible by the inclusion of excited H_2^+-like MO's in the construction of the trial function for H_2. This process, called *configuration interaction*, allows the true electron density to be more closely approximated by the combination of different molecular orbitals with different spatial properties. In the present example a suitable MO function might be

$$\psi = c_1 1s\sigma_g(1) 1s\sigma_g(2) + c_2 2p\sigma_u^*(1) 2p\sigma_u^*(2),$$

where $1s\sigma_g$ and $2p\sigma_u^*$ are the LCAO functions $1s_A + 1s_B$ and $1s_A - 1s_B$. This trial function results in a bond energy of 3.21 ev and a bond length of .884 Å.[9] If a variable Z' parameter is introduced in the $1s$ function, an energy of 4.00 ev and a bond length of .748 Å are obtained.[10] Clearly these results are considerably better, although further improvement is still necessary.

The LCAO functions can be further improved, as was mentioned earlier in connection with other types of MO functions, by including terms in the function which take into account the repulsion of the two electrons—the electron correlation terms. The function

$$\psi = \sigma_g(1)\sigma_g(2)(1 + ar_{12}),$$

for example, yields a dissociation energy of 4.11 ev, which clearly is better than for the simpler function (10–11).[11] The problem of electron correlation is of considerable importance when extremely accurate results are sought.

In closing this description of the molecular orbital approach to solving the H_2 case, an important point must be made. In principle the MO approach is perhaps the most reasonable to solving a molecular problem since all the nuclei and electrons are included in the configuration. The energy of H_2 has been approached well within experimental error by wave functions that take advantage of the symmetry and interaction parameters. The 15-parameter functions of James and Coolidge[12] are the classical

[8] *Ibid.*
[9] Weinbaum, *J. Chem. Phys.*, **1**, 593 (1933).
[10] *Ibid.*
[11] Frost and Braunstein, *J. Chem. Phys.*, **19**, 1133 (1951).
[12] James and Coolidge, *J. Chem. Phys.*, **1**, 825 (1933).

examples of calculations of this sort. But such functions are difficult to construct for more complicated systems, and hence for diatomic molecules the use of H_2^+ functions is a convenient approach. The results are less satisfactory, but only because the trial functions are a grosser approximation. In both diatomic and polyatomic molecules the use of the LCAO method is particularly useful because it relies on more readily obtained functions and inherently contains some chemical intuition built in as the MO functions are constructed. But this approach generally yields only semiquantitative results unless configuration-interaction and electron-correlation terms are also included. In other words, it is the LCAO construction that is approximate, and not the hypothesis that the molecule in its ground state can be described by a single molecular wave function. After investigating another approach to constructing suitable functions, we will return to some of the ways in which the LCAO-MO approach, as well as other descriptions, can be used in complex molecules.

10.4   THE VALENCE–BOND DESCRIPTION OF H_2

The science of chemistry made considerable progress in the eighteenth and nineteenth centuries without any sophisticated theoretical foundation such as quantum mechanics, and undoubtedly a good deal more progress will be made in many ways without quantitative quantum-mechanical calculations. By a long line of logical reasoning the idea of the chemical bond evolved and found its most useful formulation in the concept by Lewis and Kossel that a stable covalent bond is formed between two atoms when two electrons are shared by two atoms. The prediction of when and how many such bonds could be formed relies on other generalities such as Langmuir's octet rule. The value of the concept of the covalent bond is unquestionable, and in view of its utility it would seem advantageous to explore how it might aid in the construction of wave functions in quantum mechanics.

For H_2 we might consider a function that places one electron on nucleus A and the second on nucleus B. Such a function, neglecting the spin part,

$$\psi_I = 1s_A(1)1s_B(2),$$

then yields an energy which has a minimum of about .4 ev at 1 Å. A similar result would be obtained with $\psi_{II} = 1s_A(2)1s_B(1)$. Although a stable species is predicted, these functions are obviously unacceptable. Investigation shows that they are not symmetric or antisymmetric to inversion of the electronic coordinates through the center of the molecule. Since the picture of the covalent bond is that the electrons are shared by both nuclei, and by analogy with the way in which a satisfactory function was first constructed for H_2^+, an alternative form is suggested:

$$\psi = (c_1\psi_I + c_2\psi_{II}) \times \text{spin function}$$
$$= [c_1 1s_A(1)1s_B(2) + c_2 1s_A(2)1s_B(1)] \times \text{spin function}.$$

This function was first employed by Heitler and London[13] and is commonly called the valence-bond approach (VB) since it emphasizes the sharing of two electrons between two nuclei. Because this approach was subsequently elaborated by Slater and Pauling, this method is also called the Heitler-London-Slater-Pauling (HLSP) method. Note that there are no terms corresponding to ionic structures in this wave function.

The variation method requires minimizing W with respect to c_1 and c_2, so that the secular equation

$$\begin{vmatrix} H_{I\,I} - W & H_{I\,II} - S_{I\,II}W \\ H_{II\,I} - S_{II\,I}W & H_{II\,II} - W \end{vmatrix} = 0$$

must be solved, where

$$H_{I\,I} = \langle 1s_A(1)1s_B(2)|\mathcal{H}|1s_A(1)1s_B(2)\rangle,$$
$$H_{I\,II} = \langle 1s_A(1)1s_B(2)|\mathcal{H}|1s_A(2)1s_B(1)\rangle,$$
$$S_{I\,II} = \langle 1s_A(1)1s_B(2)|1s_A(2)1s_B(1)\rangle, \text{ etc.}$$

From symmetry it can be seen that $H_{I\,I} = H_{II\,II}$, $H_{I\,II} = H_{II\,I}$, and $S_{I\,II} = S_{II\,I}$. The secular equation then gives

$$W = \frac{H_{I\,I} \pm H_{I\,II}}{1 \pm S_{I\,II}} \tag{10-12}$$

for the energy. The integrals are evaluated more easily if we arbitrarily divide the Hamiltonian into

$$\mathcal{H} = \mathcal{H}_A(1) + \mathcal{H}_B(2) + \mathcal{H}_{\text{int}},$$

where

$$\mathcal{H}_A(1) = -\frac{\hbar^2}{2m}\nabla_1^2 - \frac{e^2}{r_{A1}},$$
$$\mathcal{H}_B(2) = -\frac{\hbar^2}{2m}\nabla_2^2 - \frac{e^2}{r_{B2}},$$

and

$$\mathcal{H}_{\text{int}} = -\frac{e^2}{r_{B1}} - \frac{e^2}{r_{A2}} + \frac{e^2}{r_{12}} + \frac{e^2}{r_{AB}}.$$

Simplification results because $1s_A(1)$ is an eigenfunction of $\mathcal{H}_A(1)$ and

[13] Heitler and London, *Z. Physik*, **44**, 455 (1927).

$1s_B(2)$ is an eigenfunction of $\mathcal{K}_B(2)$. Thus

$$H_{I\,I} = \langle 1s_A(1)1s_B(2)|\mathcal{K}_A(1)|1s_A(1)1s_B(2)\rangle$$
$$+ \langle 1s_A(1)1s_B(2)|\mathcal{K}_B(2)|1s_A(1)1s_B(2)\rangle$$
$$+ \left\langle 1s_A(1)1s_B(2) \left| -\frac{e^2}{r_{A2}} - \frac{e^2}{r_{B1}} + \frac{e^2}{r_{12}} + \frac{e^2}{r_{AB}} \right| 1s_A(1)1s_B(2) \right\rangle$$
$$= 2E_{1s} + \frac{e^2}{r_{AB}} + 2\left\langle 1s_A(1)1s_B(2) \left| -\frac{e^2}{r_{B1}} \right| 1s_A(1)1s_B(2) \right\rangle$$
$$+ \left\langle 1s_A(1)1s_B(2) \left| \frac{e^2}{r_{12}} \right| 1s_A(1)1s_B(2) \right\rangle$$
$$= 2E_{1s} + \frac{e^2}{r_{AB}} + 2J + e^2 \int \frac{|1s_A(1)1s_B(2)|^2}{r_{12}}\, d\tau,$$

where

$$J = \left\langle 1s_A(1) \left| -\frac{e^2}{r_{B1}} \right| 1s_A(1) \right\rangle.$$

The coulomb integral J is identical with that encountered in the H_2^+ problem and is given by (10–5). The integral in r_{12} is the same as the two-center coulomb integral found in the LCAO-MO treatment. The other integrals in $H_{I\,II}$, etc., may be similarly evaluated. We will not attempt to do this here.

Substitution of the two energy expressions into the secular equation leads to $c_1 = \pm c_2$, so that corresponding to the two energies of (10–12) are the wave functions

$$\psi_S = \frac{1}{\sqrt{2 + 2S}}\,[1s_A(1)1s_B(2) + 1s_A(2)1s_B(1)] \qquad (10\text{–}13)$$

and

$$\psi_A = \frac{1}{\sqrt{2 + 2S}}\,[1s_A(1)1s_B(2) - 1s_A(2)1s_B(1)]. \qquad (10\text{–}14)$$

The function symmetric in the spatial part leads to a stable molecular configuration. At an internuclear separation of .869 Å, a minimum energy of 3.140 ev is obtained. As with the MO functions, the VB function can be improved by the introduction of a variable effective nuclear charge Z' ($r_{AB} = .743$ Å, $W = 3.76$ ev)[14] and/or by the inclusion of p orbitals as well as $1s$ orbitals.[15] Since these functions do not include any "ionic" structures, it would also be expected that inclusion of terms of the type $1s_A(1)1s_A(2)$ might help also. As in the MO case, such adjustments do improve the results, but the correct energy is closely approached only by complicated functions that involve many parameters and are based on symmetry and interactions rather than on the MO or VB formulation

[14] Wang, *Phys. Rev.*, **31**, 579 (1928).
[15] Rosen, *Phys. Rev.*, **38**, 2099 (1931).

directly. By the time either the MO or the VB functions are improved with these stratagems, they are practically indistinguishable from one another and give very similar results. In the H_2 case, at least, the simple VB formulation has some advantage in the evaluation of integrals.

We have given only the spatial functions. Recognition of the requirement that the total wave function must be antisymmetric to the exchange of electron pairs enables us immediately to write four functions from (10–13) and (10–14):

$$\text{Singlet} \quad \psi_{\text{sym}} \times \frac{1}{\sqrt{2}} [\alpha(1)\beta(2) - \beta(1)\alpha(2)]$$

$$\text{Triplet} \quad \begin{cases} \psi_{\text{anti}} \times \alpha(1)\alpha(2) \\ \psi_{\text{anti}} \times \frac{1}{\sqrt{2}} [\alpha(1)\beta(2) + \beta(1)\alpha(2)] \\ \psi_{\text{anti}} \times \beta(1)\beta(2) \end{cases}$$

The first of these, corresponding to the stable ground state of H_2, shows that the electrons must have opposite spin orientation to form a stable covalent bond. The remaining three are degenerate in energy, to the degree of accuracy we will consider here, and correspond to the triplet excited state of H_2 in which the electron spins are unpaired.

10.5 EXCITED STATES OF HYDROGEN

In the process of determining the ground state configuration of H_2 by the VB method, we have also obtained an unstable excited triplet state described by the spatial function (10–14). It should be possible to construct the wave functions of other excited states of H_2 in the same manner, using different combinations of atomic orbitals for atoms A and B. Some of the resulting states would be stable, others unstable. Actually the VB method has not been used extensively to describe the excited states of diatomic molecules, since the MO picture readily lends itself to these systems. For this reason we will consider the excited states of H_2 from the MO viewpoint.

The ground state of H_2 we found to have a $(1s\sigma_g)^2$ configuration; i.e., both electrons can be considered to be in the lowest MO. The spatial wave function for the ground state,

$$\psi = (1s\sigma_g)(1)(1s\sigma_g)(2),$$

is symmetric to interchange of the electrons, and hence the spin part of the total wave function must be antisymmetric to such an exchange. Thus the total MO wave function for the ground state of H_2 is

$$\psi = (1s\sigma_g)(1)(1s\sigma_g)(2) \frac{1}{\sqrt{2}} [\alpha(1)\beta(2) - \alpha(2)\beta(1)].$$

In the VB treatment, also, the necessary pairing of electron spins to obtain an antisymmetric function resulted.

We might expect that the next lowest excited state of H_2 would result if one of the two electrons were elevated to the $2p\sigma_u{}^*$ MO. In this case the spatial function

$$\psi = (1s\sigma_g)(1)(2p\sigma_u{}^*)(2) \tag{10-15}$$

is unacceptable because it implies that we can identify the electron in the $1s\sigma_g$ orbital as electron 1 and the electron in the higher MO as electron 2, while in actuality the electrons are experimentally indistinguishable. This situation was noted also in the case of helium, and suitable functions were constructed by linear combinations of functions such as (10–15). We obtain in this manner four possible states for the $(1s\sigma_g)(2p\sigma_u{}^*)$ configuration when we consider the spin functions also. These are

$$[(1s\sigma_g)(1)(2p\sigma_u{}^*)(2) + (1s\sigma_g)(2)(2p\sigma_u{}^*)(1)][\alpha(1)\beta(2) - \alpha(2)\beta(1)],$$
$$[(1s\sigma_g)(1)(2p\sigma_u{}^*)(2) - (1s\sigma_g)(2)(2p\sigma_u{}^*)(1)]\alpha(1)\alpha(2),$$
$$[(1s\sigma_g)(1)(2p\sigma_u{}^*)(2) - (1s\sigma_g)(2)(2p\sigma_u{}^*)(1)][\alpha(1)\beta(2) + \alpha(2)\beta(1)],$$
$$[(1s\sigma_g)(1)(2p\sigma_u{}^*)(2) - (1s\sigma_g)(2)(2p\sigma_u{}^*)(1)]\beta(1)\beta(2),$$
$$\tag{10-16}$$

where normalization constants are omitted. The first represents a singlet excited state, the last three a degenerate triplet excited level. According to Hund's rule (Chapter 7) the triplet states should be of lower energy than the singlet, since the electrons tend to occupy different regions of space when their spins are parallel. This is actually found to be true in the case of these states of H_2. Their relative energies are shown in Fig. 10–8. In addition, we might expect that none of these states would be stable, since one electron is in a bonding MO and the other in an antibonding MO. This is seen to be true for the triplet states, but the higher-energy singlet state has a small minimum. This is apparently because in this excited state the separation of the molecule into two parts would not necessarily result in two hydrogen atoms. If the spatial function (10–16) is written in terms of LCAO MO's, we have

$$\psi = (1s_A + 1s_B)(1)(1s_A - 1s_B)(2) + (1s_A + 1s_B)(2)(1s_A - 1s_B)(1)$$
$$= 1s_A(1)1s_A(2) - 1s_A(1)1s_B(2) + 1s_B(1)1s_A(2) - 1s_B(1)1s_B(2)$$
$$\quad + 1s_A(2)1s_A(1) - 1s_A(2)1s_B(1) + 1s_B(2)1s_A(1) - 1s_B(2)1s_B(1)$$
$$= 2[1s_A(1)1s_A(2) - 1s_B(1)1s_B(2)],$$

which corresponds to ionic structures. At large distances two oppositely charged species would be attractive, while the repulsions from the antibonding orbital would be important only at short distances. We also note that the minimum in the energy for this state is at a similar separation close

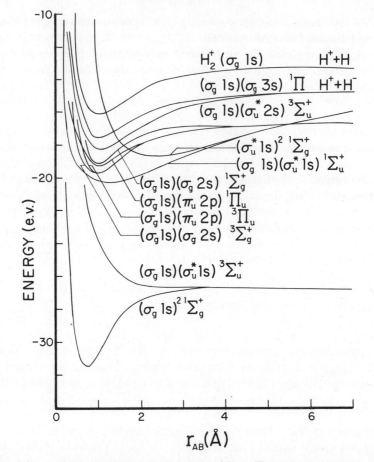

Fig. 10–8. Ground and excited states of H₂. The energy is given relative to completely separated electrons and protons as zero. These states can be compared with those of H_2^+ in Fig. 10–5, which is drawn to the same scale and with the same zero of energy.

to that of H_2^+, which dissociates into H^+ and H. Other excited states can be constructed by a similar combination of MO functions. For example, the $(1s\sigma_g)(2s\sigma_g)$ configuration would lead again to singlet and triplet states:

$$[1s\sigma_g(1)2s\sigma_g(2) + 1s\sigma_g(2)2s\sigma_g(1)][\alpha(1)\beta(2) - \beta(1)\alpha(2)],$$

$$[1s\sigma_g(1)2s\sigma_g(2) - 1s\sigma_g(2)2s\sigma_g(1)] \begin{cases} \alpha(1)\alpha(2) \\ [\alpha(1)\beta(2) + \alpha(2)\beta(1)] \\ \beta(1)\beta(2), \end{cases}$$

and so on for any combination of orbitals. In all cases, triplet states are found to be lower in energy than singlet states.

As in the case of many-electron atoms, there are a very large number of possible excited states, many of which may be stable and many of which are similar to one another with regard to symmetry, angular momentum, and other observable properties.   Although the configuration $(1s\sigma_g)(2s\sigma_g)$ tells us something about the nature of an excited state, it is not a particularly complete description since there is more than one excited state resulting from this configuration, and states of other configurations such as $(1s\sigma_g)^2$ may have similar properties that are not apparent.   A generalized nomenclature has been devised to designate the particular properties of molecular electronic states.   This description is similar to that for states of many-electron atoms.

The basis for atomic state symbols is the total orbital angular momentum of the electrons about the nucleus.   In linear molecules the total orbital angular momentum of the electrons about the nuclei is not a constant of motion ($\hat{L}^2$ does not commute with the electronic Hamiltonian).   However, the component of electronic angular momentum about r_{AB} is exactly known and hence can serve as a basis for our symbolism.   If the eigenvalue of $\hat{L}_z$ (the internuclear axis is taken in the z direction) is given by the integers 0, 1, 2, . . . (times $\hbar$), then the electronic state is described by the symbol Σ, Π, Δ, Φ, ...   As in the case of atoms of low Z, we will neglect spin-orbit interactions, in which case the spin angular momentum operator $\hat{S}^2$ communtes with $\mathcal{3C}$ and the spin quantum number S is a good quantum number.   As in the atomic case, the multiplicity of the state is given by $(2S + 1)$ and is affixed to the greek letter symbol as a superscipt on the left side.   The behavior of the wave functions upon operation by $\hat{i}$ and $\hat{\sigma}_v$ is used in a manner similar to its use with individual MO's.   If the eigenvalue on operation by $\hat{i}$ is $+1$, the state is denoted by a subscript g, while if it is -1, a subscript u is used.   Similarly, if operation on the wave function by $\hat{\sigma}_v$ results in the eigenvalue $+1$, the state is given the superscript $+$, and if it is -1, the superscript $-$.   This latter symbol has significance only for Σ states.

These rules can be illustrated with some simple cases.   Although the nature of electronic states can be deduced from electronic band spectra, we will consider here the possibility of predicting these properties from the MO configurations.   The simplest case is that in which both electrons are in σ orbitals.   Since neither MO has a component of angular momentum, the total state obviously will not, and therefore all σ^2 and $\sigma\sigma$ configurations will give rise to Σ states.   In addition, if both electrons are in the same MO (i.e., σ^2), then the Pauli exclusion principle requires that the electron spins be paired and only a singlet state, $^1\Sigma$, will be possible.   On the other hand, if each electron is in a different σ orbital, $^1\Sigma$ and $^3\Sigma$ states will arise. An obvious extension of these considerations shows that all $\sigma\pi$ configurations will result in $^1\Pi$ and $^3\Pi$ states, since only one electron has angular momentum about the bond.   The other symmetry properties of the states also can be determined.   It is verified easily that $\hat{\sigma}_v$ leaves σ orbitals unchanged, and therefore Σ states arising from such orbitals will be $+$. Investigation also shows that, since $\hat{\imath}$ changes the sign of a MO which is u, if there are an odd number of electrons in u states, then the sign of the total wave function will be changed, but for an even number of u MO's the total state will be g.   Thus, the following states are deduced:

Configuration	States
σ_g	$^2\Sigma_g{}^+$
$(\sigma_g)^2$	$^1\Sigma_g{}^+$
$\sigma_g\sigma_g$	$^1\Sigma_g{}^+$ $^3\Sigma_g{}^+$
$\sigma_g\sigma_u{}^*$	$^1\Sigma_u{}^+$ $^3\Sigma_u{}^+$
$(\sigma_u{}^*)^2$	$^1\Sigma_g{}^+$
$\sigma_g\pi_u$	$^1\Pi_u$ $^3\Pi_u$
$\sigma_g\pi_g{}^*$	$^1\Pi_g$ $^3\Pi_g$

These states can be described most thoroughly if the MO configuration is given, along with the electronic state symbol.   The ground state of H_2^+ would be $(1s\sigma_g)$ $^2\Sigma_g^+$.   That of H_2 would be $(1s\sigma_g)^2$ $^1\Sigma_g^+$.   For two of the excited states of H_2 the descriptions would be $(1s\sigma_g 2p\sigma_u{}^*)$ $^1\Sigma_u$ and $(1s\sigma_g 2p\sigma_u{}^*)$ $^3\Sigma_u$, and so on for other configurations.   The reader should consult the references for a more detailed examination of this terminology.

10.6   COMPARISON OF THE METHODS

Before turning our attention to more complex situations, it will be worthwhile to summarize some of the important facts arising from calculations on H_2^+ and H_2.   The initial problem in any such calculation is the choice of a suitable trial function (assuming the variation method is to be used).   A great many possibilities present themselves.   Arbitrary functions of suitable symmetry have been used.   SCF and similar methods have been employed.   We have chosen to discuss two of the most straightforward methods, the VB method (which uses AO's to construct a variation function) and the MO method (particularly the LCAO approach). For the ground state of H_2 the former starts with the spatial function

$$\psi_{VB} = A[1s_A(1)1s_B(2) + 1s_A(2)1s_B(1)],$$

while the LCAO-MO technique begins with

$$\psi_{MO} = B[1s_A(1) + 1s_B(1)][1s_A(2) + 1s_B(2)].$$

A and B are normalization constants.

Using either of these functions, we find that a stable molecular species is predicted, but the energies calculated are not very accurate by either method. The fact that for H_2 the VB function gives slightly better results is not very significant. The lack of accuracy is a result of the attempt to use AO's in such a simple manner.

There are basic similarities between the two functions as well as differences. We note in the VB function that in both terms the electrons are shared equally by $1s_A$ and $1s_B$. Thus, the VB function can be said to represent a *covalently bound* molecule. If we expand the LCAO-MO function

$$\psi_{\text{MO}} = B[1s_A(1)1s_A(2) + 1s_A(1)1s_B(2) + 1s_A(2)1s_B(1) + 1s_B(1)1s_B(2)],$$

we see that two of the terms are identical with the VB function while two others, $1s_A(1)1s_A(2)$ and $1s_B(1)1s_B(2)$, represent *ionic* structures, in which the two electrons are simultaneously on the same nucleus ($H_A^- H_B^+$ and $H_A^+ H_B^-$ respectively). The failure of both the simple VB and the MO functions arises from the fact that the VB function does not contain any ionic terms, while the MO function has far too great a contribution from such terms.

It seems reasonable to expect therefore that a function such as

$$\psi = c_1\psi_{\text{VB}} + c_2\psi_{\text{ionic}},$$

where $\psi_{\text{ionic}} = 1s_A(1)1s_A(2) + 1s_B(1)1s_B(2)$, would be more satisfactory. The optimum with these simple functions is reached when the ionic contribution is about 20 per cent.

Another approach, which reaches the same result, could be obtained in a quite different way. The antibonding $2p\sigma_u{}^*$ excited state of H_2 is described by the LCAO-MO:

$$\psi'_{\text{MO}} = C[1s_A(1) - 1s_B(1)][1s_A(2) - 1s_B(2)].$$

Inspection will show that the ionic terms can be reduced in the combination

$$\psi = c_3\psi_{\text{MO}} + c_4\psi'_{\text{MO}}.$$

The process of "mixing-in" excited state functions with the function of interest is configuration interaction. We conclude from this example that there is essentially no difference between the VB function with ionic terms added and the LCAO-MO function with configuration interaction included.

VB functions can be improved also by including terms that describe other excited states of the molecule. In both the VB and the MO treatments configuration interaction is important not only because of the ionic terms, but also because the resulting functions more closely represent the actual electronic configurations, which the simple overlapping AO's only roughly approximate.

Another very important consideration, which we have mentioned several times, is the mutual interaction of the electrons that causes their motions to be correlated. The inclusion of electron correlation in the trial functions is most directly accomplished by the inclusion of terms containing r_{12} but frequently methods are sought that cause less difficulty with the evaluation of the resulting integrals.

TABLE 10–2. Comparison of Methods for Hydrogen

Wave Function	D_e (ev)	Parameters
MO		
$(1s\sigma) =$		
$e^{-r_A} + e^{-r_B}$	2.681	$(Z = 1)$
$e^{-Zr_A} + e^{-Zr_B}$	3.470	$Z = 1.197$
$e^{-Z(r_A+r_B)}\left[1 + a\dfrac{(r_A - r_B)^2}{r_{AB}^2}\right]$	3.096	$Z = 0.535$ $a = 0.23342$
$e^{-Zr_A} + e^{-Zr_B} + (2p\sigma_u{}^*)^2$	4.00	$Z = 1.193$
VB		
(Atomic orbital) $=$		
e^{-r_A}	3.14	$(Z = 1)$
e^{-Zr_A}	3.76	$Z = 1.166$
$e^{-Zr_A}(1 + aZr_A \cos\theta_A)$	4.02	$Z = 1.17$ $aZ = 0.123$
$e^{-Zr_A - Z'r_B}$	4.04	$Z = 1.081$ $Z' = 0.131$
Other		
$[1s_A(1) + 1s_B(1)][1s_A(2) + 1s_B(2)][1 + ar_{12}]$	4.10	$Z = 1.285$ $a = 0.28$
$1s_A(1)1s_B(2)[1 + \alpha Z^2(x_{A1}x_{B2} + y_{A1}y_{B2}) + \beta^2(z_{A1}z_{B2})]$ $+ 1s_A(2)1s_B(1)[1 + \alpha Z^2(x_{A2}x_{B1} + y_{A2}y_{B1}) + \beta^2(z_{A2}z_{B1})]$ $+ \gamma[1s_A(1)1s_A(2) + 1s_B(1)1s_B(2)]$	4.25	$Z = 1.195$ $\alpha = -0.05735$ $\beta = -0.06944$ $\gamma = 0.3334$
One-center functions	4.39	—
James-Coolidge (13 parameters)	4.7198	—
Observed	4.7451	—

Numerous mathematical and computational techniques are employed to carry out these refinements. As we have mentioned, the actual evaluation of the integrals is by far the most difficult problem in molecular calculations. Frequently modified AO's, such as those proposed by Slater, aid in reaching an accurate answer more promptly. Some comparisons of results are shown in Table 10–2.

Finally, it is instructive to consider the factors which actually lead to a stable molecular configuration, a chemical bond. The situation in the formation of H_2 from separate atoms is qualitatively similar to the case discussed in Sec. 8.9 for two identical potential wells.   In this case a potential well represents the stable configurations of an electron in the coulomb field of a proton.

When the two atoms are infinitely far apart, the two systems are completely independent, but as the nuclei approach each other, the barrier between the wells becomes smaller, and the entire system is represented by wave functions which encompass both nuclei.   It is interesting to note that at relatively large separations, when this interaction first becomes significant, the system is not stabilized by a lowering of the potential

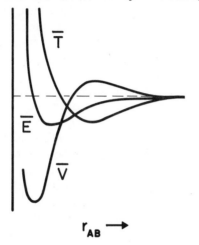

$r_{AB} \longrightarrow$

Fig. 10–9.   Variation of the potential energy, the kinetic energy, and the total energy with internuclear separation.

energy of the electrons.   That is, the additional electrostatic attraction of a second nucleus for an electron is not sufficient to give additional stability to the system.   In fact, quite the opposite is true.   This is because, as the electronic charge moves into the region between the nuclei, the attraction of an electron by its own nucleus is actually reduced, and the system is electrostatically less stable, i.e., the potential energy rises. This is shown schematically in Fig. 10–9.

If the potential energy actually begins to increase, then why is the molecule more stable at this separation than two separate atoms?   The answer lies in the kinetic energy, which is decreased because each electron can now occupy a greater region of space.   Recall that the energy levels of a potential well go down as the width of the well is increased.   In this case we have increased the effective area accessible to an electron from the size of an isolated atom to the size of an elongated molecule.   This lowering of the kinetic energy is more than enough to offset the increasing potential energy, so a net decrease in the total energy results. This is the primary significance of the exchange integral in the energy expressions for H_2.

As the nuclei come even closer together, the situation changes rapidly, and very soon the coulomb attractions lower the potential energy rapidly, resulting in a very stable configuration. By the time the equilibrium separation is reached, the potential energy has decreased by a large amount, and the kinetic energy is now increasing because the space available to the electrons is decreasing again as the nuclei come together. It is apparent, in fact, that although the nuclei will repel when brought very close together, the primary cause of the repulsion of the atoms at smaller separations than the minimum is the rapidly increasing kinetic energy in this region. The potential energy still continues to be low until very close separations are reached.

The case of attracting ions is different in one respect. The mutual coulomb attraction of positive and negative ions causes a lowering of the potential energy immediately as the ions approach. The kinetic energy is not important because in ions the electrons remain localized around their respective nuclei. But at very close separations the kinetic energy rises rapidly as the space available is squeezed up, and again the primary cause of repulsion at close approach is not electrostatic but is caused by the rapidly increasing kinetic energy in this region. These are clearly rather different pictures from the oft-encountered descriptions of electrostatic nuclear-nuclear repulsion in molecules and electrostatic electron-cloud repulsions in neighboring ions.

In the double potential-well picture we also were confronted with the fact that the separate-well energy levels are split when the wells overlap, and the lower and higher levels are represented by symmetric and antisymmetric combinations of the separate-well functions. This is exactly what we have observed for both H_2^+ and H_2.

10.7 DIATOMIC MOLECULES AND CORRELATION DIAGRAMS

We have found it convenient to use the correlation diagram of the molecular orbitals of the one-electron system H_2^+ as a guide to describing the configurations of a two-electron molecule, H_2. This usefulness extends even further to more complex diatomic molecules. It must be recognized, of course, that as nuclear charges, electronic interactions, and internuclear distances change, the energies corresponding to these hypothetical one-electron molecular orbitals will be altered from one case to the next. Nevertheless, it is possible to construct a correlation diagram such as the one for H_2^+ that indicates the approximate order in terms of energy of the one-electron MO's and the changes in their order that may occur with different nuclear charges and separations. Such a diagram is shown in Fig. 10–10 for homonuclear diatomic molecules. Although the behavior of the levels with increasing r_{AB} is rather arbitrary, some effort is made to cross states in a manner consistent with experimental results.

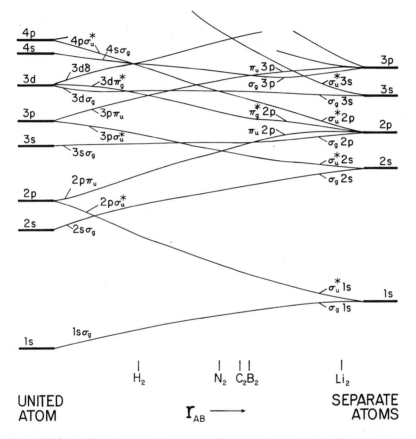

Fig. 10–10. Correlation diagram of molecular orbitals for homonuclear diatomic molecules. Note that the scale of internuclear separation is not linear, but that rough estimates can be made of bond distances in order to obtain the proper sequence of levels.

In order to use such a diagram, we must recall the Pauli exclusion principle, which requires that for two electrons to occupy the same orbital, their spins must be paired. To find the ground state of a molecule, we then proceed to fill the successive MO's, two electrons in each, beginning with the lowest. A rough correlation should exist between the number of electrons in bonding and antibonding orbitals and the stability of the molecule. If the numbers of antibonding and bonding electrons are the same, or if there are more of the former than the latter, then no stable molecule would be predicted. On the other hand, more bonding electrons than antibonding should lead to a stable diatomic species.

Several methods of listing MO's in such a scheme are found in the literature. Two of these we have discussed—the separated- and combined-atom viewpoints. The former is perhaps more convenient in considering the formation of molecules from two atoms. Also in use is the procedure of retaining the σ, π, δ, . . . notation but denoting only the energetic order of the orbitals with no reference to atomic orbitals. Beginning with the lowest orbital, we could write 1σ, 2σ, 3σ, ... Letters also have been used instead of numbers for this purpose, but

TABLE 10–3. MO's of Diatomic Molecules
(Lowest energy states at bottom)

σ^*2p_0	$u\sigma$	6σ
$\pi^*2p_1,\ \pi^*2p_{-1}$	$v\pi$	2π
$\pi2p_1,\ \pi2p_{-1}$	$w\pi$	1π
$\sigma2p_0$	$x\sigma$	5σ
σ^*2s	$y\sigma$	4σ
$\sigma2s$	$z\sigma$	3σ
σ^*1s	—	2σ
$\sigma1s$	—	1σ

because nearly all cases have the first two orbitals filled, these are often considered as unimportant to the bonding, and the lettering begins with the σ_g2s MO, which is called $z\sigma$, followed (with increasing energy) by $y\sigma$, $x\sigma$, ... The relation between these systems is shown in Table 10–3.

The use of the correlation diagram is illustrated by considering some of the first elements in the periodic table:

H_2^+: $(\sigma1s)$. A bonding orbital, which we have seen to be stable.

H_2: $(\sigma1s)^2$. Two electrons with opposite spins in a bonding orbital. The excited state $(\sigma1s)(\sigma^*1s)$ is unstable, with one electron in a bonding orbital and the other antibonding.

He_2^+: $(\sigma1s)^2(\sigma^*1s)$. Only two electrons allowed in the lowest MO; therefore the third is in the next highest. Two bonding electrons vs. one antibonding and expected to be stable. This species is observed experimentally.

He_2: $(\sigma1s)^2(\sigma^*1s)^2$. With as many bonding electrons as antibonding, we do not expect stability, a well-known fact. It is interesting, however, that excited states such as $(\sigma1s)^2(\sigma^*1s)(\sigma2s)$ might (and do) exist.

Li_2: Using the notation KK for $(\sigma1s)^2(\sigma^*1s)^2$, which is not likely to affect the over-all bonding now that atomic electrons further from the nuclei are involved, we have $KK(\sigma2s)^2$, which should be stable with two extra electrons in a bonding orbital.

Be_2: $KK(\sigma 2s)^2(\sigma^* 2s)^2$. No experimental evidence for Be_2, as would be inferred from equal numbers of bonding and antibonding electrons. Zn_2, Cd_2, and Hg_2 are known to exist, but have extremely small dissociation energies. There are no known dimers of other Group II elements.

B_2: $KKLL(\pi_u 2p)^2$. The crossing of the $2p$ MO's is uncertain at this point, but B_2 is known experimentally and is known to be in a $^3\Sigma_g^-$ state. Hence the $\pi_u 2p$ MO is drawn lower at this separation. Any of the proximate MO's would predict stability, however, with two extra bonding electrons.

C_2: $KKLL(\pi_u 2p)^4$. Again stability is predicted because of four extra bonding electrons. The $\pi_u 2p$ orbitals are degenerate and hence can hold a total of four electrons. Spectroscopic evidence indicates that the $KKLL(\pi_u 2p)^3(\sigma_g 2p)$ state differs by less than .1 ev. Since the energies of the MO's are close, stability is gained in this latter configuration because a triplet state can be formed.

N_2: $KKLL(\sigma 2p)^2(\pi_u 2p)^4$. With six extra bonding electrons, a very stable molecule is predicted. Alternative notations would be $KK(z\sigma)^2(y\sigma)^2(x\sigma)^2(w\pi)^4$ and $(1\sigma)^2(2\sigma)^2(3\sigma)^2(4\sigma)^2(5\sigma)^2(1\pi)^4$. There is now evidence that the $(\sigma 2p)$ level is actually the highest since the singly ionized N_2^+ ion has the configuration $KKLL(\pi_u 2p)^4(\sigma 2p)$.

O_2: $KKLL(\sigma 2p)^2(\pi 2p)^4(\pi^* 2p)^2$. With two of the bonding $2p$ electrons now canceled by the two $\pi^* 2p$ antibonding orbitals, the molecule should be less stable than N_2, but should still be a quite secure entity. An interesting point arises in this molecule, for since the $\pi^* 2p$ orbitals are doubly degenerate, the two electrons should go into the separate orbitals with their spins unpaired (Hund's rule). This would lead us to expect a triplet state for O_2 (observed) and paramagnetism due to the unpaired electron magnetic moments. The latter property is well known for O_2.

F_2: $KKLL(\sigma 2p)^2(\pi 2p)^4(\pi^* 2p)^4$. Now down to two excess bonding electrons, but still stable.

Ne_2: $KKLL(\sigma 2p)^2(\pi 2p)^4(\pi^* 2p)^4(\sigma^* 2p)^2$. Now we are back to the same number of bonding and antibonding electrons, which leads us to predict no stability for this species.

The electronic states of these molecules, along with a résumé of the configurations, are listed in Table 10–4. It is interesting, of course, that the predicted behavior of these molecules (relative stability, etc.) fits the observations so well. It is even more interesting that such unexpected phenomena as the paramagnetism of O_2 are automatically predicted in this description. Another interesting connection is the relation between the number of excess bonding electrons and our chemical notions about bonds. The idea of two electrons in a bond, with resultant double and triple bonds when there are four and six such electrons, is nicely matched by the MO picture. We would thus draw the classical bonds Li—Li, B—B, C=C, N≡N, O=O, F—F, etc. from the MO description. In addition, we note that single bonds appear to involve the bonding electrons in a σ^2 configuration. In a double bond it is $\sigma^2\pi^2$, while in a triple bond it is $\sigma^2\pi^4$. These configurations immediately tell us more than the fact that

TABLE 10–4. Summary of Properties of Ground States for Diatomic Molecules*

Molecule	Electronic Configuration	State	N_b (bonding electrons)	N_a (antibonding electrons)	Bonds $\frac{1}{2}(N_b - N_a)$	Dissociation Energy (ev)	Dissociation Energy (kcal.)	r_{AB} (Å)	k (dyne cm^{-1} × 10^{-5})
H_2^+	$(\sigma_g 1s)$	$^2\Sigma_g^+$	1	0	$\frac{1}{2}$	2.648	61.06	1.06	1.56
H_2	$(\sigma_g 1s)^2$	$^1\Sigma_g^+$	2	0	1	4.476	103.24	0.7415	5.60
He_2^+	$(\sigma_g 1s)^2(\sigma_u {}^*1s)$	$^2\Sigma_u^+$	2	1	$\frac{1}{2}$	(3.1)	—	1.08	3.13
He_2	$(\sigma_g 1s)^2(\sigma_u {}^*1s)^2 (= KK)$	$^1\Sigma_g^+$	2	2	0	—	—	—	—
Li_2	$KK(\sigma_g 2s)^2$	$^1\Sigma_g^+$	2	0	1	1.03	25	2.672	0.25
Be_2	$KK(\sigma_g 2s)^2(\sigma_u {}^*2s)^2$	$^1\Sigma_g^+$	2	2	0	—	—	—	—
B_2	$KK(\sigma_g 2s)^2(\sigma_u {}^*2s)^2(\pi_u 2p)^2$	$^3\Sigma_g^-$	4	2	1	(3.0)	69	1.589	3.60
C_2	$KK(\sigma_g 2s)^2(\sigma_u {}^*2s)^2(\pi_u 2p)^3(\sigma_g 2p)$	$^3\Pi_u(^1\Sigma)$	6	2	$2\frac{1}{2}$	(5.9)	150	1.3117	9.55
N_2^+	$KK(\sigma_g 2s)^2(\sigma_u {}^*2s)^2(\pi_u 2p)^4(\sigma_g 2p)$	$^2\Sigma_g^+$	7	2	$2\frac{1}{2}$	8.73	—	1.116	20.1
N_2	$KK(\sigma_g 2s)^2(\sigma_u {}^*2s)^2(\pi_u 2p)^4(\sigma_g 2p)^2$	$^1\Sigma_g^+$	8	2	3	9.756	225.0	1.0976	23.1
O_2^+	$KK(\sigma_g 2s)^2(\sigma_u {}^*2s)^2(\pi_u 2p)^4(\sigma_g 2p)^2(\pi_g {}^*2p)$	$^2\Pi_g$	8	3	$2\frac{1}{2}$	6.48	—	1.1227	16.6
O_2	$KK(\sigma_g 2s)^2(\sigma_u {}^*2s)^2(\pi_u 2p)^4(\sigma_g 2p)^2(\pi_g {}^*2p)^2$	$^3\Sigma_g^-$	8	4	2	5.080	117.96	1.20741	11.8
F_2	$KK(\sigma_g 2s)^2(\sigma_u {}^*2s)^2(\pi_u 2p)^4(\sigma_g 2p)^2(\pi_g {}^*2p)^4$	$^1\Sigma_g^+$	8	6	1	(1.6)	36	1.418	4.45
Ne_2	$KK(\sigma_g 2s)^2(\sigma_u {}^*2s)^2(\sigma_g 2p)^2(\pi_u 2p)^4(\pi_g {}^*2p)^4(\sigma_u {}^*2p)^2$	$^1\Sigma_g^+$	8	8	0	—	—	—	—

* Kauzmann, *Quantum Chemistry*, Academic Press, Inc., 1957, p. 406.

we have one, two, or three electron pairs between the atoms. They also tell us the geometry of the electron distributions, and we can conveniently picture the bonding electrons in B_2, C_2, and N_2 in terms of the spatial distributions σ and π bonds. These distributions are important because they have a bearing on many chemical and physical properties of the molecule. Finally, we might also note that species with odd numbers of electrons as in H_2^+ and He_2^+ can be accommodated in the MO treatment, while they are excluded from the electron-pair VB viewpoint.

Heteronuclear diatomic molecules also can be treated by the MO correlation-diagram approach. These cases are complicated by the fact that the same atomic orbitals will not be involved on both atoms, because of size, energy, and directional differences. The atomic orbitals that are involved must have the same σ, π, . . . properties and energies that are not too different, or they are not likely to find a combined configuration more stable. In the case of reasonably similar atoms it is possible to draw a correlation diagram such as that in Fig. 10–11, in which the separated atomic orbitals have different energies and the g, u symmetry disappears because the nuclear charges are different, but in which the angular momentum properties are retained. If we consider a molecule such as CO, for example, the 14 electrons (6 from C and 8 from O) would form the configuration $KK(z\sigma)^2(y\sigma)^2(x\sigma)^2(w\pi)^4$, using the lettering type of nomenclature. With three extra pairs of bonding electrons, we would thus predict a stable molecule with a $^1\Sigma$ ground state. The molecules N_2 and BF would be of a similar structure except, of course, for the distribution of the electrons, which would be distorted toward the nucleus with the greatest electron affinity. The molecule NO would be $KK(z\sigma)^2(y\sigma)^2(x\sigma)^2(w\pi)^4(v\pi)$ and would hence be less stable ($v\pi$ is antibonding), and the unpaired electron would result in a doublet ground state.

A more detailed study of these cases reveals that many of our intuitive ideas about bonding are useful. The LiH molecule has been very thoroughly investigated, and not only has the total energy been calculated with great accuracy, but the wave functions have given a dipole moment that agrees quite well with experimental measurements. With the H $1s$ electron and the Li $1s^2 2s$ electrons, we would proceed to fill the MO's in the correlation diagram. Two of the four electrons could occupy the lowest σ orbital, and two more the next σ orbital. Calculation of the energies of these MO's shows that the energy of the lowest σ orbital is very nearly the same as that of the $1s$ orbital in a Li atom. Thus, an equally satisfactory description of the bonding would be that the inner $1s$ electrons in Li remain confined to the Li nucleus, while the $2s$ electron interacts with the H $1s$ electron to form the bond.

Simple wave functions based on covalent structures would be expected to be only very approximate, as they were even for the more symmetrical homonuclear systems. Hence inclusion of ionic terms along with covalent terms would be expected to improve the description. Suppose, for example, a purely covalent wave function ψ_C is written for HCl similar to the VB function for H_2, but using H $1s$ and Cl $2p_z$ orbitals. One could

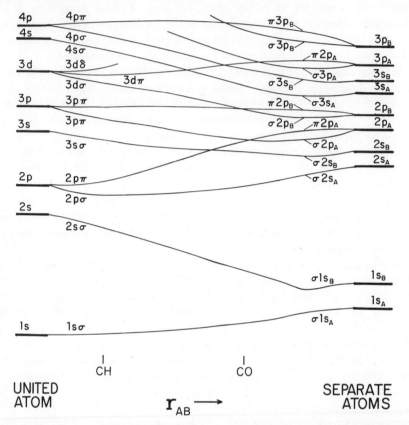

Fig. 10–11. Correlation diagram for heteronuclear diatomic molecules. Since the separate atoms are not identical, the energies of the separate atomic orbitals are not identical, as was the case for homonuclear molecules. Otherwise, the scheme of filling successively higher molecular orbitals is the same.

calculate the variation energy for such a function as we have illustrated. It is also possible to write a function, ψ_I, which includes terms such as $2p_{z\text{Cl}}(1)2p_{z\text{Cl}}(2)$ that are clearly of an ionic nature. Again, the variation energy can be calculated using ψ_I as the variation function.

In the general case neither ψ_C nor ψ_I would alone be adequate. Hence a linear combination

$$\psi = c_C\psi_C + c_I\psi_I$$

might be expected to yield better results. The energy for this variation function would be found from the secular determinant

$$\begin{vmatrix} H_{CC} - W & H_{CI} - S_{CI}W \\ H_{IC} - S_{IC}W & H_{II} - W \end{vmatrix} = 0.$$

The matrix element H_{CC} is the energy which would have been obtained by using ψ_C alone, and hence represents the energy which HCl would have if purely covalent in nature. H_{II} in turn would then represent the energy of a purely ionic species H^+Cl^-.

The values of H_{CC} and H_{II} could be calculated or estimated. H_{CC} for example could be estimated from covalent bond energies of H_2 and Cl_2 and related elements. The ionic energy in turn could be estimated from the ionization potential of H, the electron affinity of Cl, and the coulomb attraction of the resulting H^+ and Cl^- ions. Qualitatively, it is known that neither H_{CC} nor H_{II} can be any lower than W, and if either one of them is equal to W, then there is no contribution from the other. Several examples are shown in Fig. 10–12. In general, W will be lower, so that both ψ_C and ψ_I are needed in some proportion to yield the most stable system. This is another example of the resonance concept involving two different structures.

In the case of HCl, we see that the energy is lowered from H_{cc}, the purely covalent energy, by the inclusion of ionic terms. That is, W is lower than H_{cc}. The amount of "ionic character" of the bond in HCl could be estimated from the relative magnitudes of c_I and c_C. Pauling suggested that the relative electron-attracting power of different atoms could be expressed in terms of atom electronegativities, which could be defined as

$$(H_{CC} - W) = (X_A - X_B)^2,$$

where X_A and X_B are the electronegativities of atom A and B, and the utility of this concept has led to wide usage of electronegativities in a semiquantitative way. Electronegativities can be related to bond energies, dipole moments, and similar quantities. Some representative electronegativities are listed in Table 10–5.

From Fig. 10–12 it can be seen that HI is nearly completely covalent. In turn, the electronegativities of H and I are very close. On the other hand completely ionic Na^+Cl^- is formed when Na and Cl atoms are brought together. As would be expected, the electronegativities are quite different.

In general, the quantitative treatment of heteronuclear diatomic molecules is considerably more difficult than the homonuclear case. Fortunately, however, the correlations between bond energies, dipole moments, ionization potentials, electronegativities, and other measurable phenomena have aided greatly in ordering our knowledge of such species.

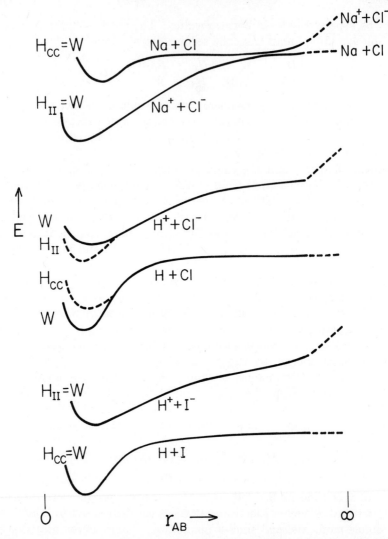

Fig. 10–12. Ionic and covalent resonance energies of several diatomic molecules. The ground state of HI is essentially covalent, while the ground state of HCl is best described by a combination of covalent and ionic terms. The stable configuration of NaCl is completely ionic, although at large separations Na and Cl atoms are more stable than Na^+ and Cl^- ions.

With very dissimilar atoms we are more likely to revert to a qualitative picture. In HCl, for example, the large nuclear charge of the Cl atom probably eliminates the chlorine $n = 1$ and $n = 2$ electrons from consideration, because their energies are much lower than the hydrogen $1s$ energy. On geometric grounds, the $3p$ orbitals are not all favorable,

TABLE 10–5.   Electronegativities of the Elements*

Atom	Thermochemical Pauling	Thermochemical Haissinsky	Force Constants Gordy (i)	Electric Potential at Covalent Boundary Gordy (ii)	Electron Affinity, Ionization Potential χ_P	"Best" Value
Ag	—	1.8	1.9	.91	$1.36s$	1.7
Al	1.5	—	1.5	1.48	$1.81sp^2$	1.5
B	2.0	—	1.9	1.91	$2.01sp^2$	1.8–2.0
Ba	.9	.85	.9	.93	—	.9
Be	1.5	—	1.45	1.38	$1.46sp$	1.4–1.5
Bi	—	1.8	1.8	1.83	—	1.8
Br	2.8	—	2.75	2.68	$2.76p$	2.8
C	2.5	—	2.55	2.52	$2.63sp^3$	2.5–2.6
Ca	1.0	—	1.0	1.03	—	1.0
Cd	—	1.5	1.1	1.13	$[1.4sp]$	1.4
Cl	3.0	—	2.97	3.00	$3.00p$	3.0
C	—	1.7	—	—	—	—
F	4.0	—	3.95	3.94	$3.91p$	3.9
Ga	—	1.6	1.4	1.48	$1.95sp^2$	1.6
Ge	1.7	—	1.7	1.77	—	1.8–1.9
H	2.1	—	2.13	2.17	$2.28s$	2.1
I	2.5	2.6	2.65	2.36	$2.56p$	2.5
K	.8	—	.80	.82	$.80s$	.8
Li	1.0	—	1.0	.96	$.94s$	1.0
Mg	1.2	—	1.2	1.16	$1.32sp$	1.2–1.3
N	3.0	—	3.0	3.01	$2.33p$	3.0
Na	.9	—	.9	.90	$.93s$	.9
Ni	—	1.7	—	—	—	—
O	3.5	—	3.45	3.47	$3.17p$	3.5
P	2.1	—	2.1	2.19	$1.81p$	2.1
S	2.5	—	2.53	2.58	$2.41p$	2.5–2.6
Sb	1.8	—	1.8	1.82	$[1.65p]$	1.9
Se	2.4	2.3	2.4	2.35	$2.23p$	2.4
Si	1.8	—	1.8	1.82	$2.44sp^3$	1.8–1.9
Sn^{IV}	1.7	1.8	1.7	1.61	—	1.8–1.9
Te	2.1	—	2.1	2.08	$2.10p$	2.1–2.2
Zn	—	1.5	1.2	1.21	$1.49sp$	1.5

* From Pritchard and Skinner, *Chem. Rev.*, **55**, 767 (1955).

because the $3p_x$ and $3p_y$ orbitals are of the wrong symmetry type (π). Visual inspection will verify that overlap of orbitals with different symmetries (say s with πp) results in two regions of overlap which have different algebraic signs and which therefore cancel each other for no net result. Hence the $3p_z$ orbital can give maximum overlap with the hydrogen $1s$ orbital to form a stable bond. If we write an MO wave function as

$$\psi_{HCl} = [c_1 1s_H(1) + c_2 3p_{zCl}(1)][c_1 1s_H(2) + c_2 3p_{zCl}(2)],$$

we would find $c_1 < c_2$, with the electron distribution moved toward the more electronegative chlorine. This loss of electrical symmetry would lead to a permanent electric dipole moment.

10.8 ELECTRONIC SPECTRA OF DIATOMIC MOLECULES

Although diatomic molecules are not of everyday interest to most practicing chemists, the study of such molecules has played an integral part in understanding more complicated systems and having a basis for describing them.   Not only have the electronic spectra of diatomic species served as a starting point for understanding electronic transitions in molecules, but the relation of electronic spectra to infrared and microwave spectra immediately made clear many of the important facts we have been discussing in this text.

Experimentally, UV-visible spectroscopy is not unlike IR instrumentation.   That is, prisms and gratings are used to produce monochromatic radiation, and the radiation can be focused and directed in the desired configurations by mirrors.   Both photographic and photoelectric measurement of intensities is employed.   Far-UV spectroscopy requires vacuum systems to prevent absorption by molecules such as O_2, O_3, and other atmospheric species.

Despite the differences inherent among different diatomic molecules, we have discussed a number of convenient descriptions and properties that are of aid in illustrating and understanding their spectra.   We have seen that the ground and excited states can be described approximately by MO functions with consideration of the net angular momentum, spin, and other symmetry properties.   In addition, these states can be described energetically by electronic potential-energy curves such as those drawn for H_2^+ and H_2 earlier.   The minima of these curves represent the equilibrium internuclear distances for molecules in the various states.   Since the electronic energies represent the potential energies that govern the vibrational motions of the molecule, the vibrational levels for each electronic state can also be drawn as in Fig. 10–13.   Finally, it is possible also to include rotational states corresponding to each electronic and vibrational level.

In discussing the electronic spectra of diatomic molecules, our problem is threefold: First, what are the selection rules which govern the transitions of molecules from one electronic state to another when the molecule interacts with electromagnetic radiation?   Secondly, what sort of vibrational and rotational transitions can occur simultaneously with such an electronic transition?   And finally, what will the resulting electronic spectrum look like?   We will not attempt to describe all the possible molecular transitions that are possible, since electronic spectra are

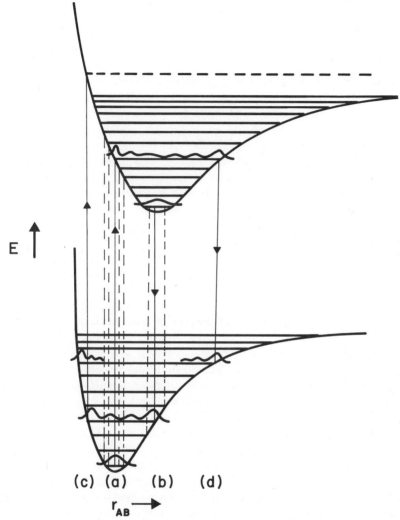

Fig. 10–13. Electronic transitions obeying the Franck-Condon principle: (a) absorption transitions from the ground electronic and ground vibrational state; (b) emission from the lowest vibrational level of the excited electronic state; (c) absorption from an excited vibrational state leading to dissociation; (d) emission directly from a higher vibrational level of the excited electronic state.

immensely complex and varied, but we will survey some of the major features.

Although the exact nature of selection rules for electronic transitions depends on the interaction of electronic and rotational energies, it is generally true for most cases that electronic transitions are governed by the selection rule

$$\Delta\Lambda = 0, \pm 1.$$

This means that transitions such as $\Sigma \rightarrow \Sigma$, $\Pi \rightarrow \Pi$, $\Sigma \rightarrow \Pi$, $\Pi \rightarrow \Delta$, etc., are possible, but not transitions such as $\Sigma \rightarrow \Delta$, $\Sigma \rightarrow \Phi$, etc. In addition, symmetry restrictions permit only $g \rightarrow u$ or $u \rightarrow g$. As in the case of atomic spectra, it is found that the spin multiplicity does not change during a molecular electronic transition, i.e., $\Delta S = 0$. Thus transitions between singlet and triplet states are forbidden. This is an important property of electronic systems since often a molecule may be excited into a triplet state by a combination of mechanisms. Once a molecule is in such a state, however, it cannot return to a singlet ground state by the simple emission of radiation, since this transition is "forbidden" by the selection rule $\Delta S = 0$. Hence the molecule is "trapped" in the excited triplet state. The properties of triplet states have an important bearing on the reactivity of many molecules, particularly those involved in photochemical processes.

The electronic spectra of even simple diatomic molecules prove to be exceedingly complex (Fig. 10–14). Investigation of the frequencies of the various spectral lines and bands indicates that the complexity arises primarily from the multiplicity of vibrational and rotational transitions which can occur during a single electronic transition. Comparison of the fine structure frequencies with the respective infrared spectra indicate, moreover, that although for pure vibrational transitions the selection rule $\Delta v = \pm 1$ holds, vibrational transitions accompanying changes in electronic state are not similarly restricted and are affected by quite different factors.

If we regard the molecular wave function to be made up of electronic, vibrational, and rotational functions, then the dipole moment integral for a transition would be given by

$$\mu_{mn} = \int \psi'_e \psi'_v \psi'_r \hat{\mu} \psi''_e \psi''_v \psi''_r \, d\tau.$$

The rotational contributions can be separated out in a manner similar to that discussed in Chapter 8. Similarly, the dipole moment operator can be separated into two terms, one summing over the nuclei, the other over the electrons

$$\hat{\mu} = \hat{\mu}_e + \hat{\mu}_n.$$

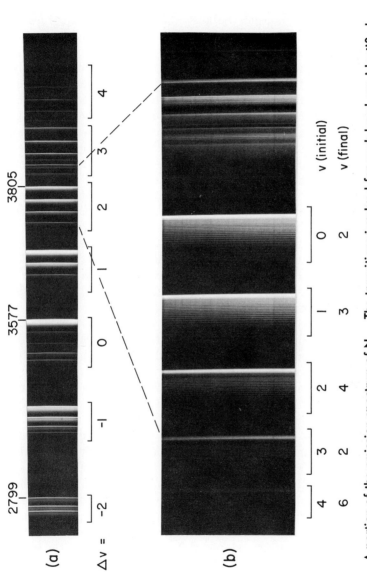

Fig. 10-14. A portion of the emission spectrum of N_2. The transitions involved for each band are identified, and the rotational fine structure can be seen in the enlarged portion. (Spectra courtesy of J. A. Marquisee, Case Institute of Technology.)

Thus

$$\mu_{mn} = \int \psi'_e \hat{\mu}_e \psi''_e \, d\tau_e \int \psi'_v \psi''_v \, d\tau_n + \int \psi'_e \psi''_e \, d\tau_e \int \psi'_v \hat{\mu}_n \psi''_v \, d\tau_n.$$

The second term vanishes because the electronic wave functions are orthogonal, and if we consider one particular electronic transition, the first integral in the first term is constant. The vibrational integral in the first term does not vanish, because the vibrational states involved are associated with different electronic states and are therefore governed by different potential-energy curves, so that these are not necessarily orthogonal functions. We can state, however, that the vibrational integral will be extremely small, or will vanish altogether, if the wave functions ψ'_v and ψ''_v do not overlap. Thus if the probability of finding the nuclei at the same internuclear separation is the same in both states, the probability of a vibrational transition occurring simultaneously with the electronic change is large. Consideration of the Schrödinger equation reveals that the momentum of the nuclei also must be similar in the two vibrational states in order for a transition to occur.

These results are expressed qualitatively by the Franck-Condon principle,[16] which states that since an electronic transition occurs rapidly with respect to nuclear motions, the transition will involve a change to a vibrational state in the new electronic configuration in which the positions and momenta of the nuclei are essentially the same as in the initial state. The Franck-Condon rule can be illustrated by means of potential-energy diagrams. In Fig. 10–13 are illustrated hypothetical potential-energy curves for an electronic ground state and one excited state. Note that the internuclear distances at which the minima are found do not coincide for both states—a common occurrence. Vibrational levels also are shown for each electronic state and the nuclear probability distributions are sketched for some of these states.

In the absence of radiation most of the molecules will be in the ground electronic state and also in the lowest vibrational state. If enough energy is absorbed to transfer the molecule to the excited electronic state, to what vibrational level would the transition occur? From the diagram we see that, in order to maintain the internuclear separation approximately constant, we must follow a vertical line directly up from the ground state. It follows immediately that, unless the equilibrium separations are the same in the two electronic states, the transition will put the molecule in an excited vibrational state of the higher electronic state. The particular vibrational states involved can be deduced if we observe that, although the ground vibrational state has maximum probability near r_e, in the higher vibrational states the wave functions have their greatest probability

[16] Franck, *Trans. Faraday Soc.*, **21**, 536 (1926); Condon, *Phys. Rev.*, **28**, 1182 (1926); **32**, 858 (1928).

at the extremes of the vibrational motions, i.e., in the regions near the potential-energy curve. These separations also correspond to points in the classical picture of molecular vibration where the motion of the nuclei is slow and therefore momentum is zero or is very small. Thus, in order to provide maximum overlap of the initial- and final-state wave functions, as well as to cause little change in nuclear momentum, the vibrational transition will terminate in a vibrational level which the vertical line meets at the potential-energy curve, as shown in Fig. 10–13. Actually, transitions will occur to a number of vibrational states coming close to meeting these restrictions, and since the ground vibrational state has a relatively low momentum and high probability over most of the region between the potential-energy curve, a band of transitions will be involved as shown in the diagram. The Franck-Condon principle thus explains the appearance of a number of bands in the electronic absorption spectra. These bands correspond to transitions to different vibrational levels. It would be expected that maximum wave-function overlap would cause the transition with $r_{AB} = r_0$ of the ground electronic state to be the most important.

Several features of electronic spectra can be explained by means of this picture. Note in Fig. 10–13 that the distribution and intensities of the vibrational bands is greatly affected by the relative positions and shapes of the two electronic potential-energy curves. In addition, emission spectra, which are obtained at high temperatures by means of flames, arcs, and similar excitation mechanisms, are likely to be quite different from absorption spectra, which are generally observed at much lower temperatures. Because of the high temperatures involved, the excited molecules are likely to be in a variety of excited vibrational states, and hence a number of transitions back to the ground electronic state are possible, as illustrated in Fig. 10–13. A thorough examination of all the vibrational bands in an electronic spectrum allows a detailed accounting of the vibrational energy levels in both ground and excited electronic states, which is an aid in determining the nature of the potential-energy curves for these states. Quite often the shallowness of the potential curves for excited states permits the observation of vibrational states all the way up to the dissociation limit of the species.

Examination of the vibrational bands in an electronic transition reveals additional fine structure which arises from rotational changes. We have already considered the case in which the rotational part of the Schrödinger equation can be separated out, i.e., there is no coupling between electronic and rotational angular momenta. For that simple case the selection rule $\Delta J = 0, \pm 1$ has already been derived. Only the case $\Delta J = +1$ was considered previously since it corresponded to absorption of energy in a pure rotational transition. In combined electronic-vibration-rotation transitions of diatomic molecules a detailed examination of the dipole moment integrals shows that for transitions between Σ states only changes are allowed for which $\Delta J = \pm 1$. If we denote the sum of vibrational and electronic energy changes by $\tilde{\nu}_0$, then

$$\frac{\Delta E}{hc} = \tilde{\nu}_0 + \tilde{B}'_v J'(J' + 1) - \tilde{B}''_v J'' + 1),$$

and if the transitions with $\Delta J = -1$ are considered from the initial state J, then

$$\frac{\Delta E}{hc} = \tilde{\nu}_0 - (\tilde{B}'_v + \tilde{B}''_v)J + (\tilde{B}'_v - \tilde{B}''_v)J^2,$$

which corresponds to the P branch in vibration-rotation spectra. For $\Delta J = +1$ from the initial state J, then

$$\frac{\Delta E}{hc} = \tilde{\nu}_0 + 2\tilde{B}'_v + (3\tilde{B}'_v - \tilde{B}''_v)J + (\tilde{B}'_v - \tilde{B}''_v)J^2$$

which is analogous to the R branch in vibration-rotation spectra. We note, however, that both the terms $\tilde{B}'$ and $\tilde{B}''$ are involved in these expressions, and the moment of inertia of the molecule may be quite different in

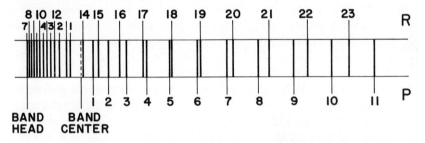

Fig. 10–15. A rotational band head in an electronic spectrum.

various electronic states. If $\tilde{B}' = \tilde{B}''$, the familiar P and R branches symmetrical about $\tilde{\nu}_0$ would result (neglecting any centrifugal distortion effects). But if $\tilde{B}' \neq \tilde{B}''$, then the term in J^2 may become significantly large with increasing values of J to cause the series of lines in one or the other of the branches to turn back on itself. This results in what is called a *band head*. This behavior is illustrated in Fig. 10–15 for a typical case. Again, an analysis of the lines in these bands results in the information about $\tilde{B}'$ and $\tilde{B}''$ and hence about internuclear separations in various electronic states. Obviously a wealth of information can be obtained from carefully analyzed electronic spectra.

If one or both of the electronic states has an orbital electronic angular momentum, then the selection rule $\Delta J = 0$ also is applicable, and hence a

Q branch,

$$\frac{\Delta E}{hc} = \tilde{\nu}_0 + (\tilde{B}'_v - \tilde{B}''_v)J + (\tilde{B}'_v - \tilde{B}''_v)J^2,$$

arises from these transitions as well. In addition, coupling of electronic and rotational angular momentum results in further complications. These were discussed for rotational spectra in Chapter 8. If the component of electronic angular momentum along the molecular axis is given by the quantum number Ω, then the energy levels are given by

$$\frac{E}{hc} = B_v J(J + 1) + A\Omega^2,$$

which has previously been noted to be of the form of the symmetric top energy expression, except that the angular momentum about the molecular axis is electronic rather than nuclear. If the $A\Omega^2$ term is included in the electronic part of E and ΔE, then we must restrict J to $\Omega + 1$, $\Omega + 2$, . . . , and as a result one or more of the lines beginning the P and R branches will be missing in the electronic spectrum.

The electronic spectra of diatomic molecules, particularly in the gaseous state, have been exceedingly useful for determining molecular parameters and correlating theoretical predictions. The spectra of liquid and solid species are interesting also, but in many respects are less informative. Because the lifetimes of the states are severely limited by molecular collisions in the condensed phases, the rotational, and sometimes the vibrational fine structure, is obscured, and hence much useful information is lost.

10.9 HYBRIDIZED ORBITALS, DIRECTED VALENCE, AND MULTIPLE BONDS

The prediction of molecular stability and the correlation of experimental data such as energies of dissociation, electronic band spectra, dipole moments, infrared spectra, and much other information was a considerable triumph for quantum mechanics. High-speed computer techniques have allowed a great advancement toward accurate calculations of parameters for atoms and diatomic molecules. Despite the fact that such calculations can be only approximate for more complicated polyatomic species, quantum mechanics provides us with numerous concepts and methods that aid in a semiquantitative understanding of molecular architecture. Not the least of these is the prediction of the geometry of molecules.

A classic example is that of water (Fig. 10–16). We have predicted that an oxygen atom in its ground state should have a $1s^2 2s^2 2p^4$ configuration in which two electrons, each in a separate p orbital, are unpaired.

This was also described as a ^3P state. A hydrogen atom has a $1s$ configuration, a ^2S state. If oxygen forms a covalent bond with a hydrogen atom, we expect (a) a pairing of electrons, to result in no net spin angular momentum, and (b) a maximum overlap of hydrogen and oxygen wave functions. This can be accomplished if one hydrogen atom overlaps with one of the p orbitals and a second hydrogen atom overlaps with the second p orbital. Maximum overlap (and hence minimum energy according to the equations for H_2) results if the H—O—H angle is 90°, since the oxygen p orbitals are at right angles to each other. This is essentially a qualitative

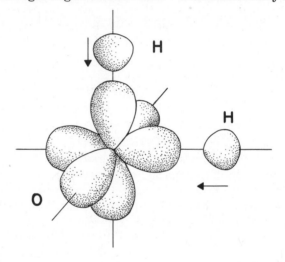

Fig. 10–16. Overlap of hydrogen $1s$ orbitals with oxygen $2p$ orbitals in the formation of a water molecule. This diagram is schematic only, since three oxygen p orbitals have completely spherical symmetry. They have been separated here for clarity.

VB picture of H_2O and correctly pictures both the formula and approximate shape of the molecule. We could also construct MO's from a LCAO using the O and two H wave functions. The result would be essentially the same.

The crudity of such a picture is apparent if we pry into any particular known facts: We cannot calculate the energy of H_2O relative to 2H and O with appreciable accuracy; the dipole moment cannot be evaluated; the actual bond angle is closer to 110°; and so on with other problems. Nevertheless, this qualitative description is helpful. Furthermore, better agreement can be obtained by improving the wave functions. We have discussed a variety of ways in which this might be done. Such improvements can range all the way from an observation that two H atoms, both positive ends of bond dipoles, will repel each other and so lead to a widening of the bond angle from 90° (in H_2S, where the H atoms are farther apart to begin with and less likely to interact, the bond angle *is* 90°) to a use of atomic functions, ionic and covalent terms in the molecular wave functions, careful accounting of the unbonded oxygen p electrons in calculating the dipole moment, etc. Thus we have established a fair degree of confidence in our predictions.

But one does not have to search far to find further discrepancies. The classic example is carbon. Using the ground state configuration (which is the correct one), $1s^2 2s^2 2p^2$, we would predict that a carbon atom can form two covalent bonds by sharing the two unpaired p electrons with other atoms, say two H atoms. Unfortunately divalent carbon, as evidenced by the predicted CH_2, is a rarity in nature, while tetravalent carbon, as in CH_4, is the rule rather than the exception. Furthermore the 90° bond angles we would predict from the p orbitals do not agree with the considerable amount of evidence that in saturated organic molecules the bonds are all 109° apart, that is, directed to the corners of a regular tetrahedron.

In order to form four covalent bonds, we expect carbon to have four unpaired electrons. This can be attained if one of the carbon $2s$ electrons is excited to the third p orbital so that we have a sp^3 configuration in the valence shell. It can be argued that the energy gained in the formation of four covalent bonds is more than sufficient to provide for the excitation of the $2s$ electron. We are still in difficulty, however, for the three p orbitals are mutually perpendicular, while the s orbital has no directional properties at all. This would not appear to result in four equivalent bonds.

A solution to this problem was suggested by Pauling, who pointed out that four new equivalent atomic orbitals can be constructed by taking suitable linear combinations of the s and p orbitals. The resulting orbitals are called *hybrid* orbitals, and in the case of the four equivalent carbon sp^3 hybrid orbitals it is found that they are directed to the corners of a regular tetrahedron as desired. The construction of the four hybrid orbitals can be illustrated as follows: Four arbitrary linear combinations would be

$$\psi_1 = a_1\psi_{2s} + b_1\psi_{2p_x} + c_1\psi_{2p_y} + d_1\psi_{2p_z},$$
$$\psi_2 = a_2\psi_{2s} + b_2\psi_{2p_x} + c_2\psi_{2p_y} + d_2\psi_{2p_z},$$
$$\psi_3 = a_3\psi_{2s} + b_3\psi_{2p_x} + c_3\psi_{2p_y} + d_3\psi_{2p_z},$$
$$\psi_4 = a_4\psi_{2s} + b_4\psi_{2p_x} + c_4\psi_{2p_y} + d_4\psi_{2p_z}.$$

The orthogonality and normalization requirements lead to the relations

$$a_i^2 + b_i^2 + c_i^2 + d_i^2 = 1 \quad (i = 1, 2, 3, 4),$$
$$a_i a_j + b_i b_j + c_i c_j + d_i d_j = 0 \quad (i \neq j = 1, 2, 3, 4),$$

a total of ten equations in sixteen unknowns. As a matter of convenience let us choose $a_1 = b_1 = c_1 = d_1$, in which case the hybrid orbital ψ_1 will extend in the direction of the $(1, 1, 1)$ corner of the cube shown in Fig. 10–17. Normalization of ψ_1 requires $a_1 = \frac{1}{2}$. The remaining hybrid orbitals must be orthonormal to ψ_1, and it can be verified that such a set is obtained if

$$a_1 = a_2 = a_3 = a_4 = b_1 = b_2 = -b_3 = -b_4 = c_1 = -c_2 = c_3 = -c_4$$
$$= d_1 = -d_2 = -d_3 = d_4 = \tfrac{1}{2}.$$

The resulting four hybrid orbitals are directed toward the alternate corners of the cube as in Fig. 10–17, which is the same as being directed to

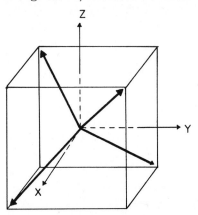

Fig. 10–17. The tetrahedral spatial orientation of sp^3 hybrid orbitals.

the corners of a regular tetrahedron. Each one is equivalent in shape along its axis. Thus four equivalent orbitals have been obtained with a satisfactory geometry.

We might notice that in addition to their equivalent properties, the shape of a single sp^3 hybrid orbital is quite different from that of either an s or a p orbital. The former extends mostly in one direction (Fig. 10–18), and in fact it can be shown that not only are the tetrahedrally placed hybrid orbitals equivalent, but the wave function for each has a larger maximum value along its respective axis than does a p orbital or an s orbital. In other words, for a given separation of atoms greater overlap is possible between a sp^3 hybrid orbital with another atomic wave function than can result with an s or a p orbital. We are led to expect, then, not only four bonds but also stronger bonds than we would obtain with s and p orbitals. Experimentally the sp^3 ^5S state has been observed to be about 96 kcal above the ground-state s^2p^2 configuration. This is only about half the energy gained by the formation of two additional C—H bonds, and the extension of the hybrid orbitals in one direction from the nucleus leads to stronger overlap with other wave functions than would be possible with the original unhybridized orbitals.

A word of caution at this point: It may appear that we have engaged in some convenient sleight of hand in order to fit quantum mechanics into the proper experimental situation. In point of fact, we have done just that. We should expect difficulties any time we begin to describe molecular situations by using hydrogen-like atomic orbitals as a starting point. The carbon atom in its ground state is not completely described by hydrogen-like orbitals. More important, a carbon atom in a molecular configuration hardly resembles a free carbon atom. Quite different forces, arising from additional nuclei and electrons, are involved. We might be better off to try to solve the Schrödinger equation for CH_4 directly, and this has been done by using a variety of centrally symmetric variation

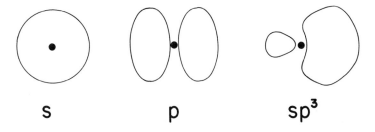

$$s \qquad\qquad p \qquad\qquad sp^3$$

Fig. 10–18. Comparison of the spatial extension of s, p, and sp^3 orbitals.

functions. But in most molecular cases such simple symmetry is not present, and the LCAO approach is a most attractive alternative since we have chemical facts which we can relate to the problem. Thus, we are simply following the procedure of constructing as satisfactory a variation function as possible when we form the hybrid orbital wave functions from the simpler atomic functions. The known symmetry (or at least the fact that we need four equivalent orbitals) guided us in our construction. It is for this reason that the concept of hybridization is a useful fiction.

The sp^3 hybrid orbitals so constructed, we find, are still very crude, indeed. They can be further improved by also including $3s$, $3p$, . . . orbitals as well, but obviously the complexity of calculation becomes immense. We thus use the simple hybrid orbital description extensively, but we must always keep in mind its qualitative nature.

Hybridized atomic orbitals can be formed from any combination of atomic orbitals, and such hybrid states are frequently a better starting point for describing molecular configurations. A list of some typical examples is included in Table 10–6, where the number of bonds and the resulting geometry of the hybrid orbitals is indicated. Undoubtedly the utility of these descriptions is already familiar to the reader. Although we are not able to explore the subject here, group-theoretical methods are extremely powerful in constructing suitable hybridized orbital wave functions when molecular symmetries are known or suspected.

Multiple bonds also can result from combinations of hybrid atomic orbitals. The familiar example of carbon will suffice to illustrate this. In addition to the sp^3 hybrid orbitals, it is also possible for only three orbitals to be used in the formation of three equivalent sp^2 hybrid orbitals.

TABLE 10–6.   Examples of Some Hybridized Orbitals

Number of Bonds	Hybrid	Geometry
2	sp	Linear
	dp	Linear
	ds	Angular
3	sp^2	Trigonal plane
	dp^2	Trigonal plane
	ds^2	Trigonal plane
4	sp^3	Tetrahedral
	d^3s	Tetrahedral
	dsp^2	Tetragonal plane
	d^2p^2	Tetragonal plane
	dp^3	Irregular tetrahedron
5	dsp^3	Bipyramid
	d^2sp^2	Tetragonal pyramid
6	d^2sp^3	Octahedron

The third p orbital is not used in the construction of these hybrids. A satisfactory set of wave functions for this situation is

$$\psi_1 = \frac{1}{\sqrt{3}}\,\psi_{2s} + \frac{\sqrt{2}}{\sqrt{3}}\,\psi_{2px},$$

$$\psi_2 = \frac{1}{\sqrt{3}}\,\psi_{2s} - \frac{\sqrt{2}}{2\sqrt{3}}\,\psi_{2px} + \frac{\sqrt{2}}{2}\,\psi_{2py},$$

$$\psi_3 = \frac{1}{\sqrt{3}}\,\psi_{2s} - \frac{\sqrt{2}}{2\sqrt{3}}\,\psi_{2px} - \frac{\sqrt{2}}{2}\,\psi_{2py}.$$

The orthogonality of these functions is easily verified. These three equivalent orbitals are found to lie in a plane with an angle of 120° between adjacent orbitals, as shown in Fig. 10–19. If we consider the possibility of two carbon atoms, each with an sp^2 hybrid configuration, coming together to form a bond, we see that a normal σ bond results from the overlap of the two hybrid electron clouds. The remaining sp^2 orbitals can form additional covalent bonds which will be 120° apart. We still have unpaired electrons in each of the unused p orbitals, and if these overlap as in Fig. 10–19, a bond will result.   This overlap of the p orbitals will be significant only if all the sp^2 orbitals remain in the same plane.   In this way the geometry, hindrance to rotation about the C—C bond, and stability of the unsaturated C=C molecules such as ethylene are explained. Although the sp^2 hybrid orbitals do not provide as much overlap as the sp^3 hybrids, the additional overlap of the unhybridized p orbitals which form the π bond contribute to make the C=C bond more stable than in saturated compounds such as ethane.   The species is nevertheless more reactive since the π electron clouds are spatially more susceptible to distortion and rearrangement by intruding atoms.

The linear C≡C configuration found in acetylene can be described in a similar manner by utilizing sp hybridized orbitals with overlap of the two

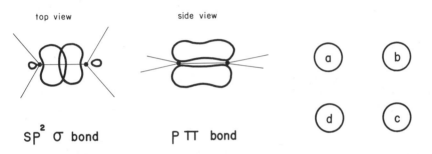

top view   side view

SP^2 σ bond   P π bond

Fig. 10–19. The formation of multiple *sigma* **and** *pi* **bonds from the overlap of hybridized orbitals and of unused** p **orbitals.**

Fig. 10–20. The hypothetical H₄ molecule.

remaining sets of unhybridized p orbitals.   Again, the total bonding configuration is more stable but also more reactive.

10.10 POLYATOMIC MOLECULES

Some insight into the VB and MO methods for treating polyatomic molecules can be gained by studying a simple hypothetical case, the molecule H_4.   Suppose that we have four hydrogen atoms placed, for simplicity, at the corners of a square as in Fig. 10–20.   The problem thus consists of four nuclei and four electrons.   We can write the Hamiltonian operator for this system without difficulty.

From the MO viewpoint we would consider the possibility that a single electron might be associated with all four nuclei, and hence we would attempt to construct molecular orbitals for the molecule and then fill these orbitals in order to see what the over-all properties of the species are like. For convenience' sake, we use hydrogen $1s$ orbitals and construct LCAO MO's.   The method followed is that suggested by Hückel, and for this reason the MO's are often called Hückel MO's or HMO's. The simplest method of accomplishing this task is to use the symmetry properties of the nuclear configuration and apply group theory in order to obtain a set of orthonormal functions of the proper symmetry. In lieu of this, we will observe that by analogy with the H_2^+ and H_2 MO's, which we have studied, we might expect the lowest-lying MO to be

$$\psi = c_a\psi_a + c_b\psi_b + c_c\psi_c + c_d\psi_d.$$

We must therefore solve the secular equation

$$\begin{vmatrix} H_{aa} - S_{aa}W & H_{ab} - S_{ab}W & H_{ac} - S_{ac}W & H_{ad} - S_{ad}W \\ H_{ba} - S_{ba}W & H_{bb} - S_{bb}W & H_{bc} - S_{bc}W & H_{bd} - S_{bd}W \\ H_{ca} - S_{ca}W & H_{cb} - S_{cb}W & H_{cc} - S_{cc}W & H_{cd} - S_{cd}W \\ H_{da} - S_{da}W & H_{db} - S_{db}W & H_{dc} - S_{dc}W & H_{dd} - S_{dd}W \end{vmatrix} = 0, \quad (10\text{--}17)$$

where $H_{ij} = \langle i|\mathcal{H}|j\rangle$ and $S_{ij} = \langle i|j\rangle$.

Since the atomic orbital functions used are all hydrogen $1s$ functions, we have $S_{ii} = 1$. At this point one other approximation is often made in the Hückel method. Although the overlap integrals S_{ij} are not actually zero, it will be assumed for simplicity in calculation that they vanish or are negligibly small when $i \neq j$. In practice, it appears that, although all S_{ij}'s are not zero, there are canceling effects which make their neglect not too serious for qualitative arguments. Thus we have

$$\begin{vmatrix} H_{aa} - W & H_{ab} & H_{ac} & H_{ad} \\ H_{ba} & H_{bb} - W & H_{bc} & H_{bd} \\ H_{ca} & H_{cb} & H_{cc} - W & H_{cd} \\ H_{da} & H_{db} & H_{dc} & H_{dd} - W \end{vmatrix} = 0.$$

A convention that has arisen in treatments by the HMO approach is to give the coulomb integrals H_{ii} the symbol α_i. We note that in this particular problem all the α_i's will be the same, and they represent the energy of a hydrogen $1s$ orbital. The matrix elements H_{ij} are often called bond integrals or resonance integrals and are given the shorthand symbol β_{ij}. For the purpose of easy mathematical handling, an assumption is frequently made that β_{ij} is negligible except in those cases in which atoms i and j are adjacent and can interact significantly. For our hypothetical square planar H_4 molecule, this would mean

$$\beta_{ac} = \beta_{ca} = \beta_{bd} = \beta_{db} = 0,$$
$$\beta_{ab} = \beta_{ba} = \beta_{bc} = \beta_{cb} = \beta_{cd} = \beta_{dc} = \beta_{ad} = \beta_{da} = \beta.$$

The equalities result from the similarity of the atomic orbitals involved. With the HMO nomenclature and the assumptions regarding S_{ij} and β_{ij}

we now have the secular equation

$$\begin{vmatrix} \alpha - W & \beta & 0 & \beta \\ \beta & \alpha - W & \beta & 0 \\ 0 & \beta & \alpha - W & \beta \\ \beta & 0 & \beta & \alpha - W \end{vmatrix} = 0.$$

At this state the determinant is easily decomposed into

$$(\alpha - W)^4 - 4\beta^2(\alpha - W)^2 = 0,$$

the solutions of which are found if we let $x = (\alpha - W)/\beta$, so that this

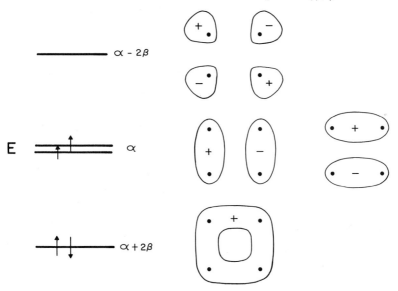

Fig. 10–21.   Energy levels and molecular orbitals for the H_4 molecule.

equation is simply $x^4 - 4x^2 = 0$.   The solutions are $x = 0, 0, +2, -2$.
From the definition of x this gives us

$$W = \alpha, \alpha, \alpha - 2\beta, \alpha + 2\beta.$$

Since β is negative, an orbital is said to be bonding if the coefficient of β
is positive in the energy expression.   If the coefficient is zero, the orbital
is nonbonding, and if negative, antibonding.

Substitution of these solutions results in the coefficients in the LCAO
functions corresponding to these energies.   The MO levels and the corresponding wave functions are shown in Fig. 10–21.   Since the integrals
α and β will both be negative, the order of the lowest MO will be that

with $W = \alpha + 2\beta$, which corresponds to the ground-state MO function

$$\psi = \frac{1}{\sqrt{4}} \left(\psi_a + \psi_b + \psi_c + \psi_d \right).$$

Note that two states are degenerate, so that, if Hund's rule and the Pauli exclusion principle are followed, the four electrons will lie in the orbitals indicated, with the resultant molecule in a triplet state. In addition, the wave functions indicate that the degenerate MO's are non-bonding, i.e., the bonding part of the wave function is canceled by an antibonding part, and the upper state is antibonding. Finally, since the coulomb integral α is approximately the energy of a hydrogen $1s$ orbital, the bonding energy of H_4 would be

$$E_{H_4} - 4E_H = 4\alpha + 4\beta - 4\alpha = 4\beta.$$

If a similar HMO treatment is carried out for H_2, we have

$$\psi = c_a \psi_a + c_b \psi_b,$$

$$\begin{vmatrix} H_{aa} - S_{aa}W & H_{ab} - S_{ab}W \\ H_{ba} - S_{ba}W & H_{bb} - S_{bb}W \end{vmatrix} = 0,$$

$$\begin{vmatrix} \alpha - W & \beta \\ \beta & \alpha - W \end{vmatrix} = 0,$$

$$(\alpha - W)^2 = \beta^2,$$

$$W = \alpha \pm \beta.$$

With both electrons in the lowest $(\alpha + \beta)$ level,

$$E_{H_2} = 2\alpha + 2\beta;$$

and since $\alpha \simeq E_H$,

$$E_{H_2} - 2E_H = 2\alpha + 2\beta - 2\alpha = 2\beta,$$

or

$$E_{2H_2} - 4E_H = 4\beta.$$

On comparison with H_4, we see that our hypothetical H_4 is no more stable relative to four H atoms than are two H_2 molecules. Before making too many hasty conclusions from these results, however, one must appreciate the large number of assumptions that were made regarding overlap integrals and similar quantities. These often have serious consequences on such qualitative predictions.

The VB approach also can be used to explore the nature of our hypothetical H_4 molecule. It will be recalled that the VB wave functions are constructed to emphasize the sharing of two electrons by two nuclei. VB functions are often called bond orbitals in contrast to the molecular orbitals we have just discussed. In discussing H_2^+ and H_2 it was a simple matter to study the spatial part of the wave functions separately, since the effect of the spin part was easily added by considering the symmetry of the functions on exchange of two electrons.   With more nuclei and electrons, however, this becomes more difficult, and often it is found desirable to construct wave functions that contain the spatial and the spin parts simultaneously.   In our four-atom case a function that indicates electron-pair bonds (with spins antiparallel) between nuclei a and b and between c and d would be

$$\psi = (a\alpha)_1(b\beta)_2(c\beta)_3(d\alpha)_4,$$

the subscripts indicating which electron is in each atomic orbital.   But since the energy of the system would be unchanged by exchange of any two electrons, an equally satisfactory function would be

$$\psi = (a\alpha)_2(b\beta)_1(c\beta)_3(d\alpha)_4,$$

and similarly many other permutations of the pairs of electrons would be possible.   Thus a truly satisfactory wave function for the valence bond structure

$$\begin{matrix} a\text{---}b \\ d\text{---}c \end{matrix} \qquad\qquad A$$

(where the lines indicate covalent bonds) would be a sum of a number of functions such as these described above.   In addition, the sum must be made in such a manner that the total wave function is antisymmetric to interchange of any two electrons.   In our discussion of complex atoms it was mentioned that Slater pointed out that such antisymmetric functions could be formed by writing them in determinantal form.   In this case, for example, a wave function describing structure A would be

$$\psi_I = \frac{1}{\sqrt{4!}} \begin{vmatrix} a\alpha_1 & b\beta_1 & c\alpha_1 & d\beta_1 \\ a\alpha_2 & b\beta_2 & c\alpha_2 & d\beta_2 \\ a\alpha_3 & b\beta_3 & c\alpha_3 & d\beta_3 \\ a\alpha_4 & b\beta_4 & c\alpha_4 & d\beta_4 \end{vmatrix}. \tag{10-18}$$

If this determinant is expanded, it will be seen that all the permutations of electrons 1, 2, 3, and 4 are included in the sum of terms.

The function (10–18) is not yet adequate, however, since the electron at each nucleus can have spin α or β.   There are, in fact 2^n different ways of arranging the α and β spin functions among n nuclei, 16 in the case of four atoms.   Thus we should construct a total wave function that is a sum of 16 determinants such as (10–18), and the solution of the secular equation would seem to be hopelessly complicated.   Fortunately, we can take advantage of some fundamental chemical intuition and simplify our problem.   We expect, for example, that there should be no unpaired electrons remaining if each is involved in a covalent bond.   Hence, we will consider only those determinantal functions for which the number of electrons having spin α is equal to the number with β spin. The problem is reduced immediately to six determinantal functions, the arrangements of spin being

ψ	a	b	c	d
I	α	β	α	β
II	α	α	β	β
III	α	β	β	α
IV	β	α	α	β
V	β	α	β	α
VI	β	β	α	α

From these six functions we can now construct so-called bond eigen-functions, which are based on the possible ways of pairing the available electrons. For structure A, we find by inspection that only I, III, IV, and V have a and b with opposite spins, and c and d with opposite spins, as is required for a covalent bond. Hence, a linear combination of these four functions can be used to construct a function for structure A. The linear combination must result in an antisymmetric function, and this can be assured if I is taken as positive, and then each of the other functions is given a change in sign for every interchange in the order of α and β necessary to convert I into that function. For example, to convert I to III an exchange of spin is necessary between c and d, and hence III will appear in the wave function for structure A with a negative sign. For the conversion of I to V we must interchange the spins of A and B, and also of C and D. Hence V appears in A with a positive sign. Our resulting wave function, including approximate normalization, is

$$\psi_A = \frac{1}{\sqrt{4}} \, (\psi_I - \psi_{III} - \psi_{IV} + \psi_V).$$

For the bonding structure

$$\begin{array}{cc} a & b \\ | & | \\ d & c \end{array} \qquad\qquad B$$

a similar analysis results in the function

$$\psi_B = \frac{1}{\sqrt{4}} \, (\psi_I - \psi_{II} + \psi_V - \psi_{VI}),$$

and for the only remaining way to bond two pairs of atoms

$$C$$

we have

$$\psi_C = \frac{1}{\sqrt{4}}\,(\psi_{II} - \psi_{III} - \psi_{IV} + \psi_{VI}).$$

We note, however, that all three functions are not independent, and that $C = A - B$. Hence there are two independent bond functions describing structures with non-crossing bonds. These structures are known as canonical structures.

Now we are in a position to apply the variation method. We construct the variation function by a linear combination of the bond functions:

$$\psi = c_A\psi_A + c_B\psi_B.$$

Our method of constructing the determinantal and bond functions has assured us that the function will be antisymmetric to electron exchange. In order to determine the energies and the coefficients we must solve the secular equation,

$$\begin{vmatrix} H_{AA} - S_{AA}W & H_{AB} - S_{AB}W \\ H_{BA} - S_{BA}W & H_{BB} - S_{BB}W \end{vmatrix} = 0. \tag{10–19}$$

This is mathematically a much simpler problem than the solution of a 16×16 determinant, as would have been necessary if we had used all the possible permutations of electrons and electron spins. This does not mean that there is no complicated mathematics left, however, since each bond function is a sum of four determinantal functions, each of which is a product of four atomic spatial and spin functions. Hence, evaluation of the matrix elements in (10–19) is likely to be cumbersome. Several simplifications can be made. We find, for example,

$$H_{AB} = H_{BA}, \quad S_{AB} = S_{BA}.$$

Evaluation of the matrix elements then requires expanding A and B in terms of their component functions. As an example,

$$\begin{aligned} H_{AA} &= \langle A|\mathcal{3C}|A\rangle = \langle I - III - IV + V|\mathcal{3C}|I - III - IV + V\rangle \\ &= \tfrac{1}{4}[\langle I|\mathcal{3C}|I\rangle + \langle III|\mathcal{3C}|III\rangle + \langle IV|\mathcal{3C}|IV\rangle + \langle V|\mathcal{3C}|V\rangle] - 2[\langle I|\mathcal{3C}|III\rangle \\ &\quad + \langle I|\mathcal{3C}|IV\rangle + \langle III|\mathcal{3C}|V\rangle + \langle IV|\mathcal{3C}|V\rangle - \langle I|\mathcal{3C}|V\rangle - \langle III|\mathcal{3C}|IV\rangle], \end{aligned}$$

and if we consider just one of these integrals,

$$\begin{aligned} \langle I|\mathcal{3C}|I\rangle &= \langle a_1b_2c_3d_4|\mathcal{3C}|a_1b_2c_3d_4\rangle \\ &\quad - \langle a_1b_2c_3d_4|\mathcal{3C}|c_1b_2a_3d_4\rangle - \langle a_1b_2c_3d_4|\mathcal{3C}|a_1d_2c_3b_4\rangle, \end{aligned}$$

where the spin parts of the functions have been separated out and those containing terms such as $\langle \alpha|\beta\rangle$ that are zero because of the orthogonality of α and β are dropped out. We will not attempt to describe in detail the evaluation of integrals of this type. A number of rules have been worked out for following a graphic counting procedure for evaluating the various matrix elements, and these methods usually involve neglecting certain terms such as overlap integrals between non-bonded orbitals. These are outlined in several of the references cited at the end of the chapter. Group theory is a powerful tool for utilizing the symmetry of the system in constructing suitable functions. It is found that there are two energy levels corresponding to $c_A = c_B$ and $c_A = -c_B$, and the energies of these levels are

$$W = \pm 2\alpha,$$

where α is here an exchange integral between adjacent atoms and is negative. By this method the energy of one H_2 molecule is calculated to be α, so that according to this method H_4 has the same energy as $2H_2$. Since the entropy of H_4 would be much lower than that of $2H_2$, the free-energy differences between these structures would rule out the stability of H_4 relative to two H_2 molecules.

It should be noted that the α's and β's of the LCAO-MO secular determinant are not the same as those of the VB determinant. But since energies are expressed in terms of these quantities, it should be approximately true that α arising from the VB treatment is directly related to the β from LCAO-MO's.

In such MO and VB calculations as the preceding, hybrid orbitals may be used, as well as simple atomic orbitals, and will give better results when the geometry of the molecular configurations are better described by hybrid functions. Molecules with non-equivalent atoms can be treated, also. Such calculations generally require additional assumptions about the electronic distributions and other factors. One of the most fruitful applications of methods such as these has been the study of molecules containing multiple bonds and in particular molecules in which conjugation of the double-bond system is possible. In these systems the primary chemical and physical properties result largely from the π bond electrons, which are easily polarized, easier to excite, and more mobile. Thus the underlying bond skeleton of the molecule is assumed, and only the interaction of the p electrons that may be involved in the π bonding is considered.

The cyclobutadiene molecule

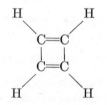

involves, after taking care of the σ bond structure, four electrons in four carbon p orbitals, and we can use either the MO or the VB approach to determine what bonding will occur and what energies will be involved. Note that this situation is very similar to the four-electron, $1s$ orbital problem we have just considered, differing only in the numerical values which would be obtained for the various integrals, since we would use $2p$ orbitals instead of $1s$. Thus, the HMO picture would predict four possible MO's, the lowest of which would include all four carbon atoms, the others being localized between pairs of atoms or on individual atoms. The energies of these orbitals would be $\alpha + 2\beta$ and $\alpha - 2\beta$ (where α and β are determined by using carbon $2p$ orbitals). The total energy of the four-electron π system would thus be $4\alpha + 4\beta$. In the VB picture the two bond structures involving different pairs of atoms would be used to form the variation function, and the energy levels of the resulting configuration would be found to be 2α and -2α, where again $2p$ orbitals are used in the evaluation of the integrals. The stability of cyclobutadiene could then be inferred by comparison with isomeric structures which are known to exist.

It is of interest to contrast the cyclic cyclobutadiene problem with the linear *cis* 1,3-butadiene

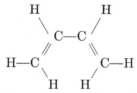

in which the number of π electrons is the same after all the C—H and C—C σ bonds have been considered. If we should assume here also that

$$\psi = c_1\psi_1 + c_2\psi_2 + c_3\psi_3 + c_4\psi_4,$$

where the ψ_i now refer to carbon p orbitals, the secular equation to be solved is identical with (10–17). But in this case carbon atoms 1 and 4 are at opposite ends of the chain, so that $\beta_{14} = \beta_{41} = 0$. The simplified secular determinant, after neglect of the S_{ij}, is thus

$$\begin{vmatrix} \alpha - W & \beta & 0 & 0 \\ \beta & \alpha - W & \beta & 0 \\ 0 & \beta & \alpha - W & \beta \\ 0 & 0 & \beta & \alpha - W \end{vmatrix} = 0,$$

which has the roots

$$W_1 = \alpha + 1.618\beta,$$
$$W_2 = \alpha + .618\beta,$$
$$W_3 = \alpha - .618\beta,$$
$$W_4 = \alpha - 1.618\beta.$$

In this example there are no degenerate levels, and hence two of the four electrons are in W_1 and two are in W_2. From these roots the coefficients c_i can be calculated and, for W_1, are found to be

$$c_1 = c_4 = .3717,$$
$$c_2 = c_3 = .6015.$$

The level W_2 yields the coefficients

$$c_1 = -c_4 = .6015,$$
$$c_2 = -c_3 = .3717.$$

As opposed to the cyclic case, the coefficients are not the same for each atom. The VB approach also can be used for this model, but will not be carried through here.

These two methods lead to two alternative descriptions of electronic systems that find considerable utility among chemists. The MO picture leads to a picture of "delocalized" electrons which encompass several nuclei, as in the lowest MO of cyclobutadiene. Such a delocalization of electrons in conjugated and aromatic systems, for example, accounts for many phenomena such as the equivalence of different nuclei with respect to reactivity, uniform bond lengths which are intermediate between single and double bond distances, and transmission of electronic effects over several atoms. The VB picture, on the other hand, begins with the concept of localized covalent bonds and combines these structures to form a suitable wave function. Because this procedure is mathematically similar to descriptions of physical resonance phenomena, these structures are familiarly known as resonance structures, or sometimes mesomeric structures, and the molecule is said to "resonate" back and forth between these different structures. Actually, there is no evidence that these structures do exist in the molecule described by a combination of such structures. They are postulated on the basis of normal covalent bonds and serve as a starting point for the formulation of a better wave function for the molecule than any one covalent structure alone represents. It is interesting that the superposition of the resonance structures, as is done in the total VB variation function, leads to a delocalized picture similar to the MO description. The concept of resonance structures, however, is a simple and convenient one for a multitude of purposes.

In addition to the descriptions of molecular structures which the MO and VB theories support, there is another important consequence of these calculations which strengthens their utility. If one calculates the energy by either the MO or the VB method, and then compares the result with the energy obtained by the same method for a similar molecule in which the electrons are localized in normal two-electron two-atom covalent bonds (as in a single resonance structure), one generally finds that the energy of the molecule that contains delocalized MO's or combines several resonance structures is lower.   That is, the energy lowering caused by delocalization or resonance stabilizes the molecule.   This corresponds experimentally to measuring the dissociation energy into separate atoms and comparing this with the calculated energy using normal single-, double-, and triple-bond dissociation energies.   The latter energies are generally less than the former.   Actually, of course, the stabilization by delocalization or resonance is fictitious.   The real molecule does not consist of normal covalent bonds.   We are led to these concepts by the concept of electron-pair bonds but it is not likely that we shall abandon these useful ideas, since more direct calculations are next to impossible.

Previous reference was made to another picture of molecular properties that has proved useful in some respects.   In Chapter 4 we discussed briefly the assumption that the electrons in a conjugated system can be treated as free particles in a potential well (which may be linear, circular, or as required by molecular geometry).   By means of refinements in the shape of the potential well, quite reasonable calculations have been made of electronic absorption frequencies, magnetic properties, and other effects. In many respects this model, often called the free-electron model, is similar to the MO picture, but in the free-electron approach no use is ever made of atomic orbitals.

The MO and VB treatments of polyatomic molecules have been elaborated upon and extended in many ways.   The extreme simplifications we have considered, such as the use only of simple AO's, neglect of the overlap integrals, neglect of electron-electron repulsions and correlations, and similar effects, must be carefully considered in accurate calculations. Even so, it remains difficult to account for many of the spectral properties of molecules.   Nonetheless, semiquantitative correlations have been made which have been very successful.   These correlations have included chemical and physical properties, comparisons of reactivities, geometry, and similar factors.

Extensive use has been made of approximate methods for calculating the behavior of conjugated systems, both linear and cyclic.   Particular emphasis has been placed on spectral properties, bond lengths, and the geometry of chemical reactivity.   In such calculations it is necessary to assume the underlying σ-bond structure of the molecule.   Needless to say, the calculation from first principles of the complete structural properties of even simple molecules such as H_2O, NH_3, and CH_4 is a difficult problem.

We have observed a number of properties that can be correlated to electronic structure.   In Table 10–4, for example, the shortening of bond length with increasing numbers of bonding electrons was shown.   Also, the C—C, C=C, and C≡C bonds show a similar shortening, in the order given.   The description of multiple bonds has taken various forms, one of the most useful being the mobile bond order, a number which can be based on the coefficients arising from VB and MO calculations. A convenient definition of the bond order of a bond between atoms i and j is

$$P_{ij} = \Sigma \; c_i c_j,$$

where the summation is over all states that are occupied by electrons. In the case of 1,3-butadiene $c_1 c_2 = (.3717)(.6015)$ for the ground state and

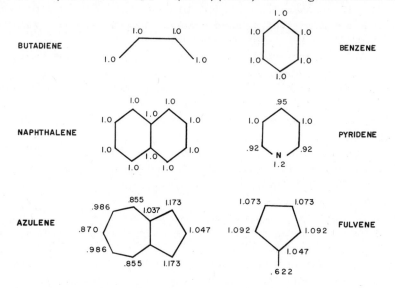

Fig. 10–22. π electronic charge densities for several conjugated molecules.

$(.6015)(.3717)$ for the excited state. Since there are two electrons in the ground state and two in the excited state,

$$P_{12} = 2(.3717)(.6015) + 2(.6015)(.3717) = .894.$$

By similar calculation $P_{12} = P_{34}$ and $P_{23} = .447$. For comparison $P_{ij} = 0$ in a saturated compound and is 1 in an isolated double bond, as in ethylene. The conjugation effect is seen very clearly in this case. By contrast, the bond orders are identical for all four bonds in cyclobutadiene, although again they are intermediate between saturated and isolated double-bond values. Bond orders have been related to a number of physical parameters such as bond lengths and vibrational frequencies.

Another useful parameter is the π-electronic charge density around atom i,

$$q_i = \Sigma \; c_i^2,$$

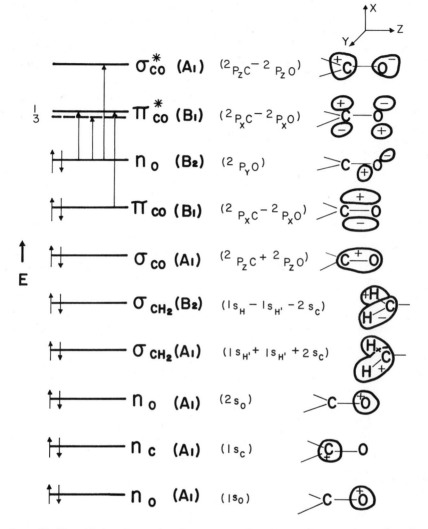

Fig. 10–23. Molecular orbitals, energy levels, and transitions for the formaldehyde molecule H_2CO. The symmetries of the various orbitals are indicated. These are influential in determining selection rules.

where the summation is again over all occupied states. For butadiene,

$$q_i = \Sigma\, c_i{}^2 = 2(.3717)^2 + 2(.6015)^2 = 1 = q_2 = q_3 = q_4.$$

It is found that the charges are equal in conjugated systems unless a ring has an odd number of atoms or the molecule contains heteroatoms. It would be expected that in these latter cases chemical reactivity would be affected by whether an atom had an excess negative or positive charge. Some examples are shown in Fig. 10–22.

If we pick one atom in a molecule and sum the bond orders of all the bonds of which this atom is one end, we would find that for conjugated hydrocarbons this sum cannot be greater than 1.732. If the sum is less than this, there is essentially some non-coupled electron density around the atom, and this can be measured by the free-valence number of atom i,

$$F_i = 1.732 - \Sigma P_{ij}.$$

For butadiene,

$$F_1 = 1.732 - .894 = .84 = F_4,$$
$$F_2 = 1.732 - (.894 + .447) = 0.39 = F_3.$$

The concepts of π-electronic charge and free-valence number have proved useful in the prediction and correlation of reactions.

The nomenclature of electronic states of polyatomic molecules is in many ways less concise than for our previous examples. In cases of high symmetry, as in CH_4 or C_6H_6, it may be possible to use suitable symmetry notation to describe states of the molecule as a whole. More often, states are designated according to particular features of interest, and frequently molecular orbital terminology is used, but localized to particular bonds in the molecule. An example is formaldehyde, H_2CO.

The MO's for this molecule are listed and illustrated in Fig. 10–23. They can be constructed by means of symmetry consideration, using group theory. The orbitals are designated by a letter giving the symmetry type. The numbers simply list orbitals of the same symmetry in a consecutive order (of increasing energy). These orbitals also are given a name according to the familiar diatomic-molecule MO symbolism, with the atoms primarily involved indicated with the symbol. The total configuration of H_2CO is

$$(1S_C)^2(1S_O)^2(2S_O)^2(\sigma_{CH})^2(\sigma_{CH'})^2(\sigma_{CO})^2(\pi_{CO})^2(n_O)^2$$

10.11 ELECTRONIC SPECTRA OF POLYATOMIC MOLECULES

The electronic spectra of polyatomic molecules are understandably more complex than those of diatomic molecules. Considerable use has been made of the spectra of relatively simple molecules in the gas phase, in which electronic, vibrational, and rotational lines can be resolved. Much of the use of ultraviolet and visible spectroscopy by chemists, however, has been concerned with absorption spectra of solutions. In this situation much of the fine structure is lost, and absorption spectra generally consist of relatively broad absorption envelopes which may or may not contain some indication of vibrational bands. Another important feature of such spectra is that, since the energy of the radiation in the visible and near-UV regions is relatively low compared to the energies required to excite electrons in strong σ bonds, typical absorption spectra reflect transitions occurring between states involving more weakly held electrons such as nonbonding electrons (as in the unbonded electrons on an oxygen or nitrogen atom), π-bond electrons, and antibonding π electrons.   In other words, aromatic molecules, conjugated systems, carbonyl compounds, cyanides, nitro compounds, azo compounds, and similar species characteristically involve absorption of radiation in a convenient spectral region.   In fact, many are colored, indicating absorption in the visible region.   Since the energy levels are sensitive to structural changes and electrical interactions, shifts in UV absorption bands prove to be extremely useful for studying chemical systems.

The determination of selection rules for electronic transitions is also a more complicated matter in the case of polyatomic molecules.   The quantization of electronic orbital angular momentum with respect to the molecular axis in diatomic and linear molecules is a convenient basis for electronic selection rules, but in non-linear molecules this particular quantity has no significance.   On the other hand, the over-all symmetry properties of the electronic states are fundamental in a consideration of such transitions.   We have mentioned several times the power of group theory in obtaining wave functions of the proper symmetry in a number of different cases.   Not only can group theory simplify the selection of functions in constructing MO and VB wave functions, but also the possible electronic transitions can be predicted from the symmetries of the various states.   A general rule of thumb is that a change in symmetry is required for an electronic transition.   As in diatomic molecules, transitions are possible only when $\Delta S = 0$, so that singlet-triplet transitions are considered forbidden.   Actually, of course, many so-called forbidden transitions actually may be observed, but the intensity of absorption will be considerably smaller than in allowed cases.   A large number of forbidden transitions are observed in UV spectra because vibrational motions can destroy the supposed symmetry of the electronic states to some extent.

Despite the infinite variety of visible-UV transitions, molecular spectra can be discussed as belonging to one of several general types.   The first of these comprises transitions from a bonding orbital in the ground state to a higher-energy antibonding orbital.   These are classified as $N \rightarrow V$ transitions, and most cases of interest involve $\sigma \rightarrow \sigma^*$ or $\pi \rightarrow \pi^*$ transitions. Since the former involve very large energies and are seen only in the vacuum UV (CH_4 absorbs at 125 mμ), the latter are of most common interest.   The second class, known as $N \rightarrow Q$ transitions, involves the change of a non-bonding electron on an atom such as O, N, or Cl to a higher antibonding orbital.   Both $n \rightarrow \pi^*$ and $n \rightarrow \sigma^*$ transitions are observed, the latter usually in the far UV (CH_3NH_2 at 213 mμ).   The $n \rightarrow \pi^*$ transitions are forbidden by symmetry, but are often observed as weak absorptions.   Finally, transitions from a ground-state orbital to one of very high energy, close to actual ionization of the molecules, are called $N \rightarrow R$ transitions.   Because of the high energies involved, they also are observed only in the vacuum UV region.

In the convenient visible-UV region, therefore, a great many of the observed absorption bands, especially in organic molecules, are due to $\pi \rightarrow \pi^*$ and $n \rightarrow \pi^*$ transitions.   The former are allowed by selection rules and result in intense absorption, while the latter are weak forbidden bands.   In addition, since the bonding π orbitals are generally lower in energy than the non-bonding orbitals (as in Fig. 10–23), the $n \rightarrow \pi^*$

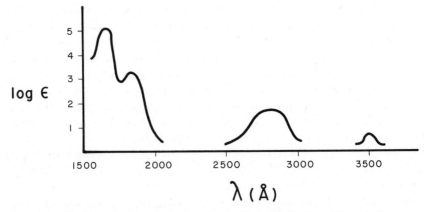

Fig. 10–24.   Carbonyl absorption in the visible-ultraviolet region.

transitions are expected at lower frequencies (longer wavelength) than the $\pi \rightarrow \pi^*$ bands.

A simple example of such transitions is afforded by formaldehyde.   The highest filled orbital is the non-bonding lone-pair oxygen orbital, and below this is the π_{CO} bonding orbital.   The lowest empty orbital is a π_{CO}^* antibonding orbital, and a higher empty orbital is a σ_{CO}^* antibonding orbital.   We might expect, then, to observe $n \rightarrow \pi^*$, $n \rightarrow \sigma^*$, and $\pi \rightarrow \pi^*$ transitions.   Only the latter is rigorously allowed, and hence it will give the only intense band.   The absorption spectrum of carbonyl compounds such as formaldehyde is shown in Fig. 10–24.   Three of the bands can be relatively easily identified, the highest-frequency (lowest-wavelength) band being the most intense.   This is the $\pi \rightarrow \pi^*$ transition.   At a slightly lower energy is the $n \rightarrow \sigma^*$, and at a much lower energy the $n \rightarrow \pi^*$ absorptions.   The absorption at 3500 Å is very weak and is also an $n \rightarrow \pi^*$

transition.   Recall that, when there are two electrons in separate orbitals, both singlet and triplet states are possible.   The low-energy transition is to the triplet π^* state since triplet states lie lower than singlet.   Singlet to triplet transitions are both symmetry- and spin-forbidden, however, so there is only a slight absorption of radiation at this frequency.

Molecular configurations with isolated double bonds such as carbonyl groups in aldehydes and ketones, NO and NO_2 groups, $C\!=\!C$ bonds, and similar structures give rise to characteristic absorption frequencies if the groups are not conjugated with another portion of the molecule.   Such groups are known as *chromophores*.   UV-visible spectra are therefore useful for identifying the presence of structural groups of these types.   Interactions such as hydrogen bonding and inductive and resonance effects by substituents cause changes in the energies of the electronic states and therefore in shifts of absorption bands to higher or lower frequencies.   We have observed that, in polymers and aromatic molecules, absorption frequencies are sensitive to parameters such as chain length and extent of conjugation.   Structural groups that cause shifts in the normal ranges of absorption of chromophores in a molecule are called *auxochromes*.   Although the absorptions caused by such groupings can be only roughly described, the presence of absorption bands in certain regions can be used for identification if care is taken to identify such groups.   Examples of chromophores and auxochromes are given in Table 10–7.

Another interesting phenomenon giving rise to absorption in the visible and near UV regions is the formation of charge-transfer complexes.   These are associations of molecules with high-electron affinity with others which have a low ionization potential.   In such associated species, electrons are easily excited to a state in which an electron is transferred from one molecule to the other.   These transitions are characterized by absorption at frequencies much lower than those of the non-complexed molecules and by extremely intense absorption.   Charge-transfer bands are also generally broad.   Since charge-transfer absorption is often in the visible region, these complexes are characteristically identified by color changes.   Typical examples are the highly colored picrates of alkyl benzenes, the shift of color of iodine, which is purple in inert solvents but brown in aromatic solvents, and the intense color of ferric ion–thiocyanate ion complexes.

The sensitivity of electronic energies to structural changes and interactions such as tautomeric equilibria, acid-base equilibria, and steric changes leads to useful changes in UV-visible spectra which can be analyzed to interpret such effects.   The use of the Beer-Lambert relation, when applicable, allows quantitative studies as well as qualitative estimates.

The intensities of electronic bands are difficult to predict in detail, particularly in the case of emission spectra, where many excited states may

TABLE 10–7.   Chromophores and Auxochromes*

Group	Example	σ $(10^3\ cm^{-1})$	λ $(\mathring{A})$	α $(l\ mole^{-1}\ cm^{-1})$
$C{=}C$	$H_2C{=}CH_2$	55	1825	250
		57.3	1744	16,000
		58.6	1704	16,500
		62	1620	10,000
$C{\equiv}C$	$H{-}C{\equiv}C{-}CH_2{-}CH_3$	58	1720	2500
$C{=}O$	H_2CO	34	2950	10
		54	1850	Strong
$C{=}S$	$CH_3{-}\overset{\overset{S}{\|}}{C}{-}CH_3$	22	4600	Weak
$-NO_2$	$CH_3{-}NO_2$	36	2775	10
		47.5	2100	10,000
$-N{=}N-$	$CH_3{-}N{=}N{-}CH_3$	28.8	3470	15
		>38.5	<2600	Strong
(benzene ring)		39	2550	200
		50	2000	6300
		55.5	1800	100,000
$-Cl$	CH_3Cl	58	1725	—
$-Br$	CH_3Br	49	2040	1800
$-I$	CH_3I	38.8	2577	—
		49.7	2010	1200
$-OH$	CH_3OH	55	1830	200
		67	1500	1900
$-SH$	C_2H_5SH	43	2320	160
$-NH_2$	CH_3NH_2	46.5	2150	580
		52.5	1905	3200
$-S-$	$CH_3{-}S{-}CH_3$	44	2280	620
		46.5	2150	700
		49.3	2030	2300
$C{=}C{-}C{=}C$	$H_2C{=}CH{-}CH{=}CH_2$	48	2090	25,000
(naphthalene)		32	2110	250
		37	2700	5000
		45	2210	100,000
(anthracene)		28	3600	6000
		40	2500	150,000
$O{=}$(ring)$={=}O$		23	4400	20
		34	3000	1000
		40	2500	15,000
$C{=}C{-}C{=}O$	$H_2C{=}C{-}\overset{\overset{O}{\|}}{C}{-}H$	30	3330	20
		27.5	2100	12,000

TABLE 10-7 (Continued)

Group	Example	σ (10^3 cm^{-1})	λ (Å)	α $(\text{l mole}^{-1}\text{cm}^{-1})$
⬡–C(=S)–CH₃ (with O)		16.5	6000	—
⬡–N=N–⬡ (with O)		22.5	4400	500
		31	3200	20,000
		43	2300	10,000

* Bauman, *Absorption Spectroscopy*, John Wiley & Sons, Inc., 1962, p. 318.

be involved. In principle only the populations of the initial states and the dipole moment matrix elements are needed for a calculation, but since accurate wave functions are seldom available, such calculations are only qualitative.

The relation between the molar extinction coefficient, the integrated absorption coefficient, and μ_{mn} was shown in Chapter 7. A very simple, but qualitatively useful, approach to estimating absorption coefficients for electronic absorption spectra is to assume that a bound electron in a molecule can be considered as a three-dimensional harmonic oscillator. Since an electron is affected by coulombic forces and the polarizability of a molecule is seldom isotropic, this is clearly a very crude approximation.

Using harmonic-oscillator wave functions and the selection rule $\Delta v = 1$, it is found that for one-dimensional oscillator

$$|\mu_{10}|_x = \frac{1}{\sqrt{2}\,\alpha}\left(\frac{d\mu}{dx}\right)_{x=0}$$

where $\alpha = \sqrt{m_e k}/\hbar$. For the electron $\mu_x = ex$ so that $d\mu/dx = e$. In addition, the mass of the electron is small compared with the rest of the molecule, so that m_e has been used in place of the reduced mass.

Assuming the oscillation to be isotropic for a three-dimensional oscillator, we have

$$|\mu_{10}|_x = |\mu_{10}|_y = |\mu_{10}|_z,$$

giving

$$|\mu_{10}|^2 = \frac{3e^2\hbar}{4\pi m\bar{\nu}c},$$

so that

$$A = \frac{Ne^2}{1{,}000cm} \ \text{sec}^{-1} \ \text{cm}^{-1} \ \text{mole}^{-1} \ \text{liter},$$

or

$$\tilde{A} = \frac{Ne^2}{1{,}000c^2m} \ \text{cm}^{-2} \ \text{mole}^{-1} \ \text{liter}$$

$$= 2.31 \times 10^8 \ \text{cm}^{-2} \ \text{mole}^{-1} \ \text{liter}$$

$$= \int \alpha(\tilde{\nu}) \ d\tilde{\nu}.$$

The *oscillator strength* is defined as the ratio of the observed integrated absorption coefficient to this value,

$$f = 4.33 \times 10^{-9} \int a(\tilde{\nu}) \ d(\tilde{\nu}).$$

For many electronic transitions f is near unity. In the case of "forbidden" transitions, very much smaller oscillator strengths are observed. It is interesting that even absorptions of weak intensity (low f) can cause visible colors in solutions. This is the case, for example, in the colors of many transition metal-ion solutions. On the other hand, transitions such as those observed for charge-transfer complexes actually involve very large electronic displacements, and the absorption lines are very intense. Calculation of oscillator strengths is thus very useful for interpreting the nature of absorption bands.

We have put some emphasis here on absorption spectra, although historically the study of emission spectra has been extensive. We have cited, however, some of the characteristics of electronic emission lines as contrasted with absorption lines of the same species. There are several emission phenomena also related to absorption of energy and of considerable importance in chemical systems. One of the most familiar of these is the observation of *fluorescence*, i.e., radiation emitted at frequencies different from the frequency of radiation absorbed by the molecule. Fluorescence is understood if one examines typical potential-energy curves for ground and excited electronic states. Although such diagrams cannot be drawn for many-atom molecules because of the large number of dimensions required, a qualitative understanding can be obtained with simple curves such as those in Fig. 10–25. We have seen that absorption of radiation excites molecules to a higher electronic state and to vibrational states which depend on the relative shapes and positions of the potential-energy curves. Transitions back to the lower state are possible, but if they do not occur immediately, then molecular collisions will cause the molecules to lose vibrational energy rapidly, as illustrated in Fig. 10–25a. By the time radiation is emitted, the molecules may be in the lowest vibrational

level of the excited electronic state, and hence the emission will involve
quite different frequencies from the original absorption.   The radiationless loss of vibrational energy, followed by the emission of the fluorescent
radiation to return to the ground electronic state, generally occurs within
10^{-8} sec of excitation.

Closely related to fluorescence is *phosphorescence*, the emission of radiation after a time interval somewhat longer than that required for fluorescence.   In some instances the phosphorescent radiation may continue for

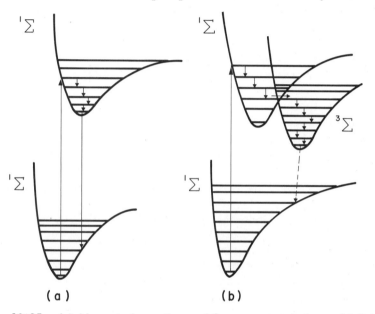

(a)   (b)

Fig. 10–25.   (a) Normal absorption and fluorescent emission.   (b) Internal
conversion from a singlet excited state to a triplet excited state via vibrational
motion.   The forbidden transition from the triplet state back to the singlet
ground state can take place only very slowly, resulting in phosphorescence.

seconds or even minutes after the initial irradiation of the molecule.
Although several mechanisms have been proposed for this delayed process,
it appears that the most reasonable explanation is that the molecules
become trapped in an excited triplet state, so that return to the ground
singlet state, being forbidden by $\Delta S = 0$, is much slower.   It is also
unlikely, of course, that a molecule be excited to the triplet state from a
singlet state directly by absorption of radiation.   There is, however,
another common mechanism by which the excited triplet state can be
occupied.   Many of the potential-energy curves of electronic states are
found to overlap in various ways as shown schematically in Fig. 10–25b.
We have already noted that rapid molecular collisions deactivate the

higher vibrational states. During this deactivation process, if a molecule should happen to have the vibrational energy and internuclear separation corresponding to a point at which the potential curves of two electronic states cross, then the vibrational deactivation may easily continue in the second electronic state instead of the original one. Recall that, at the internuclear separation corresponding to a point on the potential curve, the vibrational motions have brought the nuclei to a momentary standstill. Hence no large changes in nuclear motions and no change in energy are required at that point to transfer from one state to the other if their potential curves overlap at that point.

Such a radiationless process, known as *internal conversion*, is apparently a common occurence in electronic processes. The most important point in the case of phosphorescence is that, if the second electronic state, to which the molecule has been transferred by internal conversion, is a triplet state, then the molecule has become effectively trapped and the further radiation of energy after the vibrational levels have been completely deactivated by collisions is delayed. Note also that, if two or three internal conversions are involved in deactivating the molecule to a triplet state, the minima in the potential curves of the excited triplet and ground singlet states are likely to be at very different interatomic separations, so that the frequency of the phosphorescence may be considerably different (and generally lower) than that of the radiation originally absorbed by the molecule. The long lifetimes of triplet states thus occupied and the greater reactivity of configurations with unpaired electrons result in a great deal of interest in excited triplet states. Many processes involving electron transfer in photochemical reactions are believed to involve excited triplet states. There is special interest in this area of research because of the biological implications of such processes.

In discussing the interaction of electromagnetic radiation with matter, our emphasis has been on the quantum-mechanical picture of energy levels and transitions between these levels, i.e., the spectroscopic experiment. There are, of course, many electrical, magnetic, and optical properties of matter which are not spectroscopic in nature and can be discussed, at least qualitatively, from a classical viewpoint. We will mention some magnetic phenomena in the following chapter.

Familiar electrical and optical interactions of interest to the chemist include dielectric absorption and dispersion, optical rotation, optical rotary dispersion, birefringence, and similar phenomena. Some discussion of dipole moments and dielectric constants is usually included in undergraduate courses, and we will not attempt a lengthy description of polarization and dispersion here. These effects, however, are also of utility in uncovering detailed information about electronic configurations and interactions in molecules.

10.12   THE EXTENT OF MOLECULAR KNOWLEDGE

At this point it would not be surprising if the reader is somewhat frustrated by the extent of topics we have *not* discussed in this chapter. After all, the whole of chemistry is intimately linked to calculations of equilibrium bond lengths, dissociation energies, thermodynamic functions, electronic distributions, charge densities, and the like.   Although microwave spectroscopy until recently has not been as accessible to the average chemist as an IR spectrometer or visible-UV spectrophotometer, the mathematical treatment of rotational states and transitions is relatively straightforward, and we were able to explore several simple cases in some detail.   In our review of vibrational states of molecules, space and mathematical limitations required that we leave normal coordinate analysis and group-theoretical methods to more comprehensive monographs.

The situation with regard to electronic states and electronic spectra is even more difficult.   Extensive discussion could be made of the many observed features of spectra and how these can be correlated with other properties and with theory.   This is done in a number of excellent review articles and texts.   The most serious limitation, however, is the very nature of a molecular calculation itself.   It is almost impossible to describe even simple molecules exactly from theory.   Nearly every conceivable variation in approximating the mathematical problem has been explored. Semiempirical methods have been used to settle questions regarding approximations, and measurement of numerous molecular properties is important in this respect.   Even the simplest of cases, H_2 and LiH for example, require mathematical techniques that far outdistance the usual chemist's everyday preparedness.

For these reasons we have chosen to look closely at two simple molecules, H_2^+ and H_2, and we have explored two general techniques (with variations on the theme) for making as accurate calculations as possible. In the process, we have tried to understand some of the basic concepts involved in such calculations.

Recognizing that approximations and semiquantitative results are all we can expect at present as far as an extensive use of theory is concerned, we then proceeded to explore some basic concepts in discussing more complex diatomic and polyatomic molecules.   Again, our purpose has been to note the basic significance of such widely used terms as hybridization and resonance rather than attempt to explore all the possible ways in which these concepts have been used.   There is a wealth of such information in the more specifically oriented monographs cited below.   The seemingly infinite variety of spectral features also has precluded our ranging very far in this introductory examination.

It is perhaps appropriate to ask under the circumstances what progress has been made in quantum-mechanical calculations, and what is destined for the future. To the first point we can answer that although exact solutions have been obtained for few cases, the total usefulness of energies, transitions, reactivities, and all the rest calculated by quantum mechanics has been overwhelming. There is no doubt that we better understand, or can at least better predict and correlate, than before the advent of quantum mechanics.

Most calculations on molecular systems begin from either a VB or MO viewpoint. This is not always true, however. The symmetry of some systems is such that single functions expanded about some point or points of symmetry can be used. Since electron densities are largest in the region between atoms, some calculations start with functions centered between atoms rather than around the nuclei themselves. In addition, simple minimization of the variation energy by changing different parameters is not always sufficient to obtain good results. Frequently approximate electron distributions are further improved by SCF calculations and similar techniques. Nevertheless, the use of simple atomic orbitals in either a VB or MO wave function is a very convenient and often-used starting point.

Despite the variation of techniques, we have observed some of the things which must be done if accurate results are to be obtained. To cite a typical sequence:

1. Use AO's to construct a wave function (VB or MO), or use parts of an orbital if useful for the purposes of calculation.

2. If the geometry of the molecule is known, improve the function by forming hybrid orbitals of appropriate symmetry from the AO's instead of using the simple AO's themselves.

3. Improve the electron distribution over that which results from simple overlap and exchange of such orbitals by mixing in excited state functions with the function being used. This is configuration interaction.

4. Improve the electron distribution by including terms that show the interaction of pairs of electrons as they move through space. This is electron correlation.

5. Use every possible device, e.g. electronic computers, to calculate the resulting integrals exactly rather than make approximations.

6. Use not merely the energy, but every measurable physical and chemical property to test the resulting functions.

In spite of our optimism about quantum mechanics, it is a simple fact that the most extensive and useful correlations of theory with experiment in electronic spectra dependent on electronic configuration are those which are only semiquantitative. (This is quite a contrast with the situation for pure rotational spectra, for example.)   Thus, the Hückel MO approach and refinements thereof have been used widely as have analogous VB calculations.   The usual site of approximation is in the evaluation of integrals, where arbitrary decisions are made about what to neglect or what numerical value to assign to an integral.   Often such decisions are based on accumulated experience, and routine formulas have been worked out.   Fortunately the sometimes serious errors that result are nearly the same from one molecule to the next, so that correlations, trends, and ratios are not in serious disagreement with fact, and the methods are thus highly useful.

As for the future, there seems little doubt that the situation will improve.   It is interesting that at present theoretical chemists are divided between two prevailing schools.   The first is concerned with exact calculations and thus limits study to small molecules, to computer techniques, and to newer sophisticated mathematical foundations that may be of use either in the formulation of quantum mechanics or in computation.   The second school is interested in more approximate methods that can be directly applied to problems of chemical interest.   Molecular geometry, reactivities, spectral properties, carcinogenesis, and many other aspects of chemical science have been put to the test, and the successes have been exciting.   There is certainly no reason why both approaches should not be considered valid, and as time progresses, the two should continue to complement one another.

G. N. Lewis is said to have once defined physical chemistry as "anything which is interesting."   It would seem that the rapidly increasing numbers of organic, inorganic, and bio-chemists who talk in terms of delocalization and ligand fields and free valences, and label their research as physical-organic, physical-inorganic, and physical biochemistry, attest to the accuracy of Lewis' definition.

SUPPLEMENTARY REFERENCES

Quantum-Mechanical Calculations

PITZER, K. S., *Quantum Chemistry*, Prentice-Hall, Englewood Cliffs, N.J., 1953.   A concise but perceptive survey of calculations, spectra, and properties.

EYRING, H., J. WALTER, and G. E. KIMBALL, *Quantum Chemistry*, John Wiley & Sons, Inc., New York, 1944.   Many of the integrals encountered here are examined, along with descriptions of some of the valence-bond techniques and the use of group theory.

KAUZMANN, W., *Quantum Chemistry*, Academic Press, Inc., New York, 1957.   A good summary of the factors that must be considered in constructing accurate wave functions.   There is also a good development of theories relating to the interaction of radiation with matter.

ROBERTS, J. D., *Molecular Orbital Calculations*, W. A. Benjamin, Inc., New York, 1961. An elementary introduction to the use of the Hückel MO method to organic molecules.

STREITWEISER, A., *Molecular Orbital Theory for Organic Chemists*, John Wiley & Sons, Inc., New York, 1961. A more thorough treatment than the preceding.

SANDORFY, C., *Electronic Spectra and Quantum Chemistry*, Prentice-Hall, Englewood Cliffs, N.J., 1964.

DAUDEL, R., R. LEFEBVRE, and C. MOSER, *Quantum Chemistry—Methods and Applications*, Interscience Publishers, Inc., New York, 1959.

Both these texts review numerous computational methods and compare them with experimental measurements of various kinds.

COULSON, C. A., *Valence*, Oxford University Press, London, 1963. A non-mathematical and readable description of chemical bonding.

SLATER, J. C., *Quantum Theory of Molecules and Solids*, McGraw-Hill Book Co., New York, 1963. An advanced treatment.

Spectra

BAUMAN, R. P., *Absorption Spectroscopy*, John Wiley & Sons, Inc., New York, 1962. A useful survey of both experimental and theoretical aspects of spectrophotometry.

KING, G. W., *Spectroscopy and Molecular Structures*, Holt, Rinehart & Winston, Inc., New York, 1964. A concise summary of the interactions and selection rules giving rise to spectral features.

RAO, C. N. R., *Ultraviolet and Visible Spectroscopy*, Butterworths Scientific Publications, London, 1961. This small monograph is a useful survey of the main features, correlations, and uses of visible-UV spectroscopy.

HERZBERG, G., *Spectra of Diatomic Molecules*, D. Van Nostrand Co., Princeton, 1950; and *Infrared and Raman Spectra*, D. Van Nostrand Co., Princeton, 1945. These texts contain detailed accounts of spectral features and include useful tables of data.

BARROW, G. M., *Introduction to Molecular Spectroscopy*, McGraw-Hill Book Co., New York, 1962. An elementary and readable discussion. Includes a very useful discussion of symmetry and group theory.

Physical and Chemical Properties

KETELAAR, J. A. A., *Chemical Constitution*, 2d. ed., Elsevier Publishing Co., Amsterdam, 1958.

HARVEY, K. P., and G. B. PORTER, *Introduction to Physical Inorganic Chemistry*, Addison-Wesley Publishing Co., Reading, Mass., 1963.

Both these well-written books are a valuable supplement to the theoretical topics treated in this text. Both contain numerous tables of properties, correlations, and discussions of structure and theory.

PROBLEMS

10–1. Apply the variation principle to James' function for the H_2^+ molecule ion and calculate D_e and r_e. (Use confocal elliptical coordinates.)

10–2. Carry through any missing steps in the derivation of the J, K, and S integrals for H_2^+ outlined in Appendix E.

10–3. Using the expressions derived for the J, K, and S integrals, plot the energy of H_2^+ as a function of r_{12} and determine r_e and D_e.

10–4. Calculate r_e and D_e for the MO variation function of H_2^+ without using a graphical method.

10–5. Using data for D_e and $\bar{\nu}_e$ from previous chapters, plot the Morse potential curve for H_2.

10–6. With the expressions given for the integrals arising in the MO and VB treatments of H_2, plot the potential-energy curves for both these approximations and compare with the Morse potential.

10–7. Predict the electronic configurations of $O_2^=$, O_2^-, O_2, and O_2^+, and predict the relative order of bond lengths and dissociation energies for these species.

10–8. Predict the electronic configurations of CO, BF, and BeF. What would you expect would happen to bond lengths in these molecules?

10–9. How should the dissociation energy and interatomic distance in CN compare with that in N_2? With that in CN^-?

10–10. Verify that the four sp^3 hybrid orbitals constructed in this chapter are orthonormal.

10–11. Plot a diagram of an sp^3 orbital.

10–12. Verify that the three sp^2 hybrid orbitals are orthonormal. Are they orthogonal to the unused p orbital?

10–13. Construct two sp hybrid orbitals, starting only with the assumption that they must be equivalent. Show that they lie 180° apart.

10–14. Derive an expression for the energy levels of H_4, assuming that S_{ij} is finite for adjacent atoms but zero for atoms that are diagonally opposed (not adjacent). If these S_{ij}'s are of the order .25, how does this change the energy-level pattern as contrasted with the simple Hückel treatment, in which all S_{ij}'s are assumed to be zero?

10–15. Expand $H_{I\ II}$ for the Heitler-London treatment of H_2.

10–16. Calculate the coefficients for the AO's corresponding to each of the energy levels resulting from the treatment of H_4.

10–17. Verify the coefficients given for the two LCAO-MO's of 1,3-butadiene.

10–18. Show that in cyclobutadiene all four bonds have the same mobile bond order.

10–19. Calculate the π-electron charge on each carbon atom of cyclobutadiene.

10–20. Apply the HMO method to benzene, C_6H_6. Calculate the energy levels and the corresponding wave functions, show the occupancy of the levels, and calculate the π-electron charges and bond orders.

10–21. On the basis of electronic configuration why does N_2 not readily form N_2^-?

10–22. Predict the electronic configurations of P_2, K_2, and S_2.

10–23. Give electronic configurations of two excited states of He_2 that might be stable even though the ground state is unstable. Explain your reasoning.

10-24. From data given in this and previous chapters complete Fig. 10–26, and discuss the significance of each quantity.

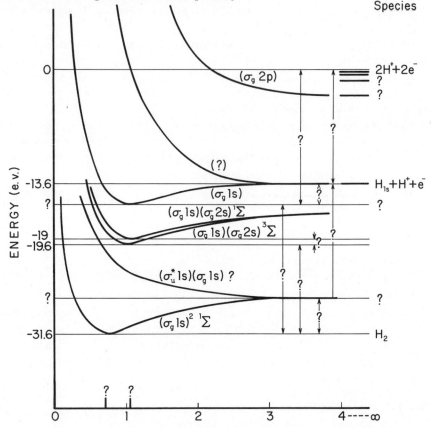

Fig. 10–26. Comparison of several states of hydrogen atoms, the hydrogen molecule ion, and the hydrogen molecule.

10-25. Minimize the energy for H_2^+ by varying the parameters in the James function.

10-26. Show that for large values of r_{AB} the variation energies of the symmetric and antisymmetric LCAO H_2^+ states are approximately $W_S = E_{1s} + K$ and $W_A = E_{1s} - K$.

10-27. Evaluate the integrals obtained in the simple VB treatment of H_2.

10-28. Verify the normalization constant for the symmetric and antisymmetric H_2^+ LCAO functions.

10-29. Verify the decomposition of the H_{AA} integral for the H_4 VB calculation as indicated on page 457.

10-30. Explain why the dissociation energies of the diatomic alkali metal molecules decrease in going from Li_2 (25 kcal mole^{-1}) to Cs_2 (10.4 kcal mole^{-1}).

10-31. Discuss the expected change in bond lengths in Cl_2 and Cl_2^+.

11

Magnetic Phenomena and Magnetic-Resonance Spectroscopy

11.1 MAGNETIC FIELDS AND MAGNETIC SUSCEPTIBILITY

We have seen in our brief investigations of atomic and molecular phenomena that magnetic fields and interactions between magnetic fields play an important role in determining the properties of atomic and molecular systems. Not only do these interactions lead to observable spectroscopic effects such as the fine structure of atomic energy levels and the Zeeman effect, but they result also in bulk magnetic properties for a collection of atoms or molecules which can be investigated by non-spectroscopic means. These properties had, in fact, been discovered and studied long before our understanding of atomic and molecular structure had advanced far enough to provide an adequate explanation of their existence. Among the more important of these bulk properties of matter is the magnetic susceptibility.

Magnetic materials were well known to the ancients, who discovered that freely suspended bodies made of certain materials tended to orient themselves in the direction of the earth's north and south poles (more accurately the earth's magnetic poles rather than the geographic poles). These magnetic bodies also interact with one another, either attracting or repelling one another depending on their relative orientations. It is perhaps unfortunate that certain similarities between electrical and magnetic phenomena led to definitions of magnetic quantities in a manner corresponding to those of known electrical quantities. Just as the presence of a force acting on an electrical charge is interpreted as the presence of an electrical field which acts on the charge, so also a force being exerted on a magnetic body is interpreted in terms of a magnetic field in space at that point.   And just as an electric field is created in space by the existence of an electric charge, it was convenient to assume that a similar magnetic quantity, the magnetic pole, gives rise to a magnetic field.   Although electric charges, or *monopoles* as sometimes called, exist, there is no reality to a magnetic monopole.   The simplest magnetic quantity is the magnetic dipole.   As in the case of the electric dipole moment, the magnetic dipole moment can be defined as the product of the magnitude of two equal magnetic poles by the distance between them; but since there is no reality to the magnetic monopole, this is not a satisfactory approach.   At the present time, magnetic fields are defined conveniently in terms of the force exerted on a current-carrying wire and, conversely, the magnitude of a magnetic dipole moment can be determined from the strength of the magnetic field at a given distance and direction from the dipole.   We have seen that a magnetic field identical with that which would be produced by a magnetic dipole, such as a permanent magnet, can be formed by a circulating electric charge.   It may well be that all magnetic dipole moments arise from such a charge circulation.   However, there is no real evidence that the spin angular momentum and magnetic moment of the fundamental atomic particles arise in this way, since mathematically they exist only on consideration of relativistic effects.

If a substance is placed in a magnetic field of strength $\mathbf{H}$, then the magnetic induction in the medium is given by

$$\mathbf{B} = \mathbf{H} + 4\pi\mathbf{M}, \tag{11-1}$$

where $\mathbf{M}$ is the intensity of magnetization of the medium, or the magnetic moment per unit volume of the substance.   In simple isotropic substances $\mathbf{M}$ is proportional to $\mathbf{H}$, and the ratio is known as the magnetic susceptibility per unit volume

$$\chi_V = \frac{\mathbf{M}}{\mathbf{H}}. \tag{11-2}$$

If $\mathbf{\mu}_m$ is the magnetic dipole moment of a molecule, and there are n molecules per unit volume in the sample, then

$$\mathbf{M} = n\bar{\mathbf{\mu}}_{\text{mol}},$$

where $\bar{\mathbf{\mu}}_{\text{mol}}$ is the average value of $\mathbf{\mu}_m$ in the direction of $\mathbf{H}$.

It is found generally that the volume susceptibility is proportional to density, and therefore more convenient quantities are the magnetic susceptibility per gram,

$$\chi_g = \frac{\chi_V}{d},$$

and the molar susceptibility,

$$\chi_M = M\chi_g = \frac{M\chi_V}{d},$$

where d is the density of the substance and M the molecular weight.

The magnetic susceptibility may be positive or negative.   In the former case, the substance is said to be *paramagnetic*, while in the second, which is more common, the substance is *diamagnetic*.   Experimentally, these two conditions are manifested in the behavior of the substance when

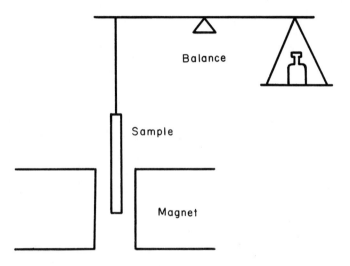

Fig. 11–1.   The Guoy method of measuring magnetic susceptibilities.

placed in a magnetic field.   A paramagnetic substance will tend to move in the direction of increasing field strength, while a diamagnetic material will experience a force in the opposite direction.   This behavior is utilized in a variety of experimental methods for determining the magnetic susceptibility of substances, the most direct and familiar of these being the method devised by Guoy.   In this technique the sample is suspended between the poles of a magnet in the form of a long rod of uniform cross-section or, if a powder or fluid, in a glass tube of uniform cross-section (Fig. 11–1).   The sample is suspended from one arm of a sensitive balance, so that any force acting on the sample in the vertical direction can be measured.   The lower end of the sample is placed near the center of the field between the two pole faces, while the upper end of the sample is a good distance from the magnet and thus in a much weaker magnetic field. An analysis of this situation reveals that the total force acting on the sample is approximately

$$F = \frac{\chi_2 - \chi_1}{2} A(\mathsf{H}^2 - \mathsf{H}_0{}^2),$$

where χ_2 and χ_1 are the volume susceptibilities of the specimen and the surrounding medium, which is usually air, A is the cross-section area of the sample, and H and H_0 are the magnetic field strengths in the center of the field at the bottom of the sample, and outside the magnet at the upper end of the sample, respectively. In the usual experiment H may be several thousand gauss while H_0 is of the order of less than 100 gauss, so that a convenient approximation is to neglect H_0. Also, the force is measured conveniently by balancing the balance arm while no magnetic field is present, and then balancing it again after the field has been applied. The difference in mass, m, represents the magnetic force on the specimen; hence

$$\frac{\chi_2 - \chi_1}{2} A\mathsf{H}^2 = mg,$$

from which the susceptibility of the sample can be calculated. We will not explore the various other techniques that may be utilized to determine magnetic susceptibilities; they are summarized in several of the references cited at the end of the chapter.

The susceptibilities of a large number of substances and solutions have been measured and tabulated, and numerous empirical methods have been devised to correlate experimental results. It is also of considerable interest to attempt a theoretical explanation for diamagnetism and paramagnetism in atoms and molecules.

Our previous studies of atomic and molecular systems have disclosed that many atoms and molecules have a net angular momentum arising from orbital and/or spin angular momenta of the electrons and nuclei in the system. We have seen also that, associated with the angular momenta of charged particles, there is a magnetic dipole field, the magnitude of which can be predicted from the angular momenta. Thus any atom or molecule with a net spin and/or orbital angular momentum will possess a permanent magnetic dipole moment. It is this permanent dipole moment that gives rise to the phenomenon of paramagnetism; for, when placed in a magnetic field, these permanent magnetic dipoles will tend to orient with respect to the field, resulting in a net magnetization of the sample which is in the same direction as the applied field. However, there is also an interaction between the electronic system of an atom or molecule with an applied magnetic field, which will give rise to a small induced magnetic dipole that is opposed to the applied field. This induced dipole field, which will be produced whether the system has a permanent magnetic dipole or not, is the cause of diamagnetism. Although all substances are diamagnetic, the magnitude of the paramagnetic effect in the case of permanent dipoles is several orders of magnitude larger than the diamagnetic effect, so that the latter is of importance only in non-paramagentic substances.

11.2 DIAMAGNETISM

A simple picture of the effects giving rise to diamagnetism is to consider the effect of a magnetic field on an atom which has a permanent magnetic dipole moment. In Sec. 6.9 we found that in the presence of a magnetic field a magnetic dipole that is associated with angular momentum will precess about the direction of the applied field with an angular velocity

$$\omega_L = \frac{e}{2mc} \mathsf{H},$$

where e is the charge. This motion is known as the Larmor precession. Although we have described this motion as being that of a magnetic dipole, it can be described also as an imposition, on the motions of the electrons in the system, of an angular velocity ω_L in addition to that angular velocity which they already possess by virtue of their orbital motions and which gives rise to the permanent magnetic dipole moment. The original angular velocity of the electrons is calculated easily from the equation for the orbital angular momentum on page 187 upon substitution of the identity

$$v = r\omega,$$

where r is the distance of the electron from the center of rotation. This leads to

$$L = m\omega r^2.$$

If the electron is not in a circular orbit, so that r and ω are not constant with time, we may replace their product by its average value, so that

$$L = m \overline{\omega r^2}. \tag{11-3}$$

The magnetic dipole moment associated with this motion was given by Eq. (6–23), which on combination with (11–3) becomes

$$\mu = -\frac{e \overline{\omega r^2}}{2c}.$$

We have described the effect of the applied magnetic field on this system as the addition of an angular velocity ω_L to the system. Thus, in the presence of this field the total angular velocity of the electron is $\omega_T = \omega + \omega_L$, and the total magnetic dipole moment of the system becomes

$$\mu_T = -\frac{e\,\overline{r^2(\omega + \omega_L)}}{2c}.$$

The effect of the magnetic field, therefore, has been to change the magnetic dipole moment of the system by an amount

$$\Delta\mu = -\left[\frac{e\,\overline{r^2(\omega + \omega_L)}}{2c} - \frac{e\,\overline{r^2\omega}}{2c}\right] = -\frac{e\,\overline{r^2\omega_L}}{2c},$$

which, on introducing (6–30), becomes

$$\Delta\mu = -\frac{e^2\,\overline{r^2}\,\mathsf{H}}{4mc^2}.$$

The effect of the applied magnetic field, therefore, has been to induce a magnetic dipole that is opposed to the applied field.

For a system of i orbits oriented at random to the field, the mean-square radius of an orbit perpendicular to the applied field becomes $\frac{2}{3}\,\overline{r_i^2}$, where $\overline{r_i^2}$ is now simply the mean-square radius of an orbit in any direction. For a gram-atom we thus have, for the induced magnetic moment,

$$\Delta\mu = -N\,\frac{e^2\mathsf{H}}{6mc^2}\sum_i r_i^2,$$

and for the susceptibility per gram atom,

$$\chi_M = \frac{\Delta\mu}{\mathsf{H}} = -N\,\frac{e^2}{6mc^2}\sum_i r_i^2. \tag{11–4}$$

It is not altogether clear from this derivation that an atomic system which has no permanent magnetic dipole moment should be affected by an external magnetic field. Langevin showed, however, that even in the classical case the effect of a magnetic field is to induce this precessional motion even though the system may have no angular momentum to begin with. The phenomenon is analogous to the situation described by Lenz's law, which states that when a magnetic field is applied to a current-carrying wire, the motion of the perturbed current will be such as to oppose the applied field.

A more exact derivation of Eq. (11–4) is obtained by solving the Schrödinger equation with the magnetic field interactions included in the Hamiltonian operator. Since the latter are relatively small, we can use first-order perturbation theory and regard the interaction terms as a perturbation, $\mathcal{K}'$, to the simpler Hamiltonian. In Chapter 7 we introduced this perturbation expressed in terms of the vector potential $\mathbf{A}$ and the scalar potential ϕ, which are related to the more familiar electric and magnetic field strengths **E** and **H**. This perturbation operator is

$$\mathfrak{K}' = \sum_i \left[\frac{1}{2m_i} \left(i\hbar \frac{e}{c} \nabla_i \cdot \mathbf{A}_i + 2i\hbar \frac{e}{c} \mathbf{A}_i \cdot \nabla_i + \frac{e^2}{c^2} |\mathbf{A}_i|^2 \right) + e_i\phi_i \right].$$

In the present situation we are interested in a system that is in a uniform magnetic field, which is conveniently taken to be along the z axis. In this case it is found that

$$A_{x_i} = -\tfrac{1}{2}H_z y_i; \quad A_{y_i} = \tfrac{1}{2}H_z x_i; \quad A_z = 0; \quad \phi = 0,$$

from which

$$\nabla_i \cdot \mathbf{A}_i = 0,$$

$$|\mathbf{A}_i|^2 = \frac{H_z{}^2}{4}(x_i{}^2 + y_i{}^2),$$

$$\sum_i \mathbf{A}_i \cdot \nabla_i = \frac{H_z}{2} \sum_i \left(x_i \frac{\partial}{\partial y_i} - y_i \frac{\partial}{\partial x_i} \right) = \frac{H_z}{2} \frac{i}{\hbar} \hat{L}_z,$$

resulting in the form

$$\mathfrak{K}' = -\frac{e}{2mc} H_z \hat{L}_z + \frac{e^2 H_z{}^2}{8mc^2} \sum_i (x_i{}^2 + y_i{}^2)$$

for the perturbation Hamiltonian operator. If the interaction of the magnetic field with the electron spin is included, we have

$$\mathfrak{K}' = -\frac{e}{2mc} H_z (\hat{L}_z + 2\hat{S}_z) + \frac{e^2 H_z{}^2}{8mc^2} \sum_i (x_i{}^2 + y_i{}^2). \qquad (11\text{–}5)$$

Let us now consider a system which has no orbital or spin angular momentum in the uniform magnetic field H_z. The Hamiltonian operator describing the system will be $\mathfrak{K}^0 + \mathfrak{K}'$, where $\mathfrak{K}^0$ is the Hamiltonian operator for the system in the absence of a field. Applying first-order perturbation theory as discussed in Chapter 7, we find that the perturbation on the energy of the system is simply

$$E' = \frac{e^2 H^2}{8mc^2} \sum_i \overline{(x_i{}^2 + y_i{}^2)}.$$

The first term in (11–5) has no effect in this case since the system has no angular momentum in the absence of a field. To a first approximation, the system is spherically symmetric, so that $x_i{}^2 = y_i{}^2 = z_i{}^2 = \tfrac{1}{3}r_i{}^2$, and we obtain

$$E' = \frac{e^2 H^2}{8mc^2} \tfrac{2}{3} \sum_i \overline{r_i{}^2}.$$

The resulting magnetic dipole moment is found quantum-mechanically by the differentiation

$$\mu = - \frac{\partial \mathcal{3C}'}{\partial \mathsf{H}} = - \frac{\partial E'}{\partial \mathsf{H}},$$

giving for this case

$$\mu = - \frac{e^2 \mathsf{H}}{6mc^2} \sum_i \overline{r_i^2}$$

and

$$\chi_{\text{mol}} = - \frac{e^2}{6mc^2} \sum_i \overline{r_i^2}$$

which is converted easily to the molar susceptibility and is identical with our previous result (11–4). In essence, the quantum-mechanical result

TABLE 11–1. Gram-Atomic Susceptibilities of the Inert Gases*
$(-\chi_M \times 10^6)$

	He	Ne	Ar	Kr	Xe
Observed (av.)	1.9	7.0	19.0	28.6	43.2
Slater (calc.)	1.853	5.7	18.9	31.7	48.0
Pauling (calc.)	1.54	5.7	21.5	42	66
Hartree (calc.)	1.90	8.6	24.8	—	—

* From Selwood, *Magnetochemistry*, Interscience, 1956, p. 72.

is that although the system may not have an angular momentum in the absence of a magnetic field, it does have angular momentum in such a field, and this gives rise to the observed diamagnetism.

Using the expression obtained in Table 6–5 for the average value of r^2 for a hydrogen-like orbit, and collecting all the constant terms, we obtain for the susceptibility

$$\chi_M = -.790 \times 10^{-6} \left[\frac{5n^4 - 3n^2 l(l + 1) + n^2}{2Z^2} \right]. \qquad (11–6)$$

The experimental determination of diamagnetic susceptibilities is difficult, particularly in the light of errors caused by such factors as dissolved paramagnetic oxygen in the samples. In addition, there are few monatomic gases for which the preceding treatment would be valid. Reasonably accurate measurements have now been made of the susceptibilities of the inert gases, and these are collected in Table 11–1. In order to use Eq. (11–6), it is necessary to modify the expression for interelectronic effects. This is most easily done by the introduction of $Z - S$ in place of Z, where S is the Slater screening constant. The results obtained by summing such expressions over all the electrons in the atom, with appropriate values of the screening constants, are shown in Table 11–1 along with results obtained by other theoretical models for determining $\overline{r_i^2}$ such as the Hartree self-consistent field method. It can be seen that the results are reasonable, at least for smaller atoms, where errors in $\overline{r_i^2}$ are not as serious.

The theoretical calculations for ions are similar, but unfortunately it is not possible to measure the susceptibilities of ions except in mixtures of cations and anions. Numerous methods have been used to estimate the relative contributions of cations and anions in a system to the measured susceptibility. The disagreement between these methods leaves the question in doubt, but for practical purposes it is possible to obtain a self-consistent set of ionic susceptibilities that can be added together in solutions of cations and anions to obtain estimates of molar susceptibilities. In solids large deviations from additivity are often observed, as would be expected in the case of the strong interactions that are present between the ions in a crystal lattice.

The calculation of diamagnetic susceptibilities of molecules is a formidable problem compared to the corresponding atomic situation. When the electric field which acts on the electrons in a molecule is not spherically symmetric as in atoms, then the Larmor precession does not strictly apply. This lack of symmetry in effect hinders the electronic circulations and reduces the total diamagnetism. In addition, the diamagnetism of molecules may be highly anisotropic. That is, the observed diamagnetic susceptibility is a function of the orientation of the molecule with respect to the applied magnetic field. This effect again arises because of the hindered and localized circulations of the electrons, which may be more effective in one orientation of the molecule than in another. Anisotropy is particularly important in crystals, where such angular dependence may be quite marked because of the regular alignment of the molecules. In solutions anisotropies tend to be averaged out by the rapid molecular motions, but many effects, such as chemical shifts in nuclear magnetic resonance spectra, can still be observed.

Quantum-mechanically, the effect of the non-symmetric fields in molecules is to cause mixing-in of the excited states of the molecule with the ground state. In other words, the distorted molecule in the magnetic field can be described by a wave function that is made up of the ground-state wave function in the absence of a field plus excited-state wave functions. This is the essence of the perturbation method. We will not consider in detail the means of obtaining an expression for molecular diamagnetism, but will briefly describe the equation obtained by Van Vleck, using second-order perturbation theory.[1] The molar susceptibility of a

[1] Van Vleck, *Electric and Magnetic Susceptibilities*, Oxford University Press, London, 1932.

polyatomic molecule with no net electron spin moment is given by

$$\chi_M = -\frac{Ne^2}{6mc^2} \sum_i \overline{r_i^2} + \frac{Ne^2}{2m^2c^2} \sum_{n \neq 0} \frac{|\langle 0|\hat{L}_z|n\rangle|^2}{E_n - E_0},$$

(11–7)

where in the first term the sum is over all electrons in the molecule, and in the second term the sum is over all excited electronic states of the molecule.

The first term in this equation is seen immediately to be identical with the expression for the atomic case, and the sign of the second term is seen to diminish the magnitude of the diamagnetism by virtue of the restriction in electronic currents in the molecule. For this reason the second term is often called the second-order paramagnetic term or temperature-independent paramagnetic term. This second term depends on the matrix elements connecting electronic angular momentum components of excited states with the ground state and on the energies of the excited states. We note that if the energies of any excited states are low-lying, then there may be an appreciable contribution from the second-order paramagnetic term to the total susceptibility of the molecule.

Our previous experience with the electronic states of molecules suggests to us that the practical application of Eq. (11–7) is limited. Not only are satisfactory wave functions for polyatomic molecules lacking, but information about the wave functions and energies of excited states are particularly scant. Unfortunately the paramagnetic term above is very sensitive to these parameters. Numerous attempts have been made to simplify this equation in terms of average excitation energies and localized electronic currents, and some of these have been more or less successful. The most elaborate calculation was made by Witmer[2] on hydrogen, using James-Coolidge wave functions; the theoretical calculation from Eq. (11–7) gave for H_2 a susceptibility of -3.8×10^{-6} as compared with the experimental value of -4.005×10^{-6}. The results of such calculations for more complicated systems is considerably less satisfactory.

These difficulties inherent in theoretical calculations of susceptibility have led to more empirical schemes, one of the most successful being that due to Pascal. In Pascal's method individual susceptibilities are assigned to atoms, and it is assumed that the molar susceptibility can be calculated by adding together all the atomic susceptibilities plus a constitutive correction constant which depends on the nature of the bonds between the atoms; that is,

$$\chi_M = \sum n_A \chi_A + \lambda.$$

(11–8)

A few Pascal constants are listed in Table 11–2. As an example of their use consider the susceptibility of n-butyl alcohol. From Eq. (11–8) and

[2] Witmer, *Phys. Rev.*, **48**, 380 (1935); **51**, 383 (1937).

Table 11–2 we write

$$\chi_M = 4\chi_C + 10\chi_H + \chi_O = -57.9 \times 10^{-6},$$

which compares reasonably with the experimental -56.15×10^{-6}.

TABLE 11–2. Pascal Constants for Diamagnetic Susceptibility*
($\times 10^6$)

H	-2.93	Aromatic	
C	-6.00	Cl	-17.2
N (open chain)	-5.57	Br	-26.5
N (in ring)	-4.61	I	-40.5
N (monoamides)	-1.54		
N (diamides, imides)	-2.11	Aliphatic	
O (alcohols, ethers)	-4.61	F	-6.4
O (aldehyde, ketone)	1.66	Cl	-19.9
O (carboxyl—both atoms)	-7.95	Br	-30.4
S	-15.0	I	-44.6
Se	-23.2		
B	-7.3		
Si	-13		
As	-21		
P	-10		

λ Corrections for Bonds

C=C	5.5	C=N	8.15
C≡C	0.8	C≡N	.8
C=C—C=C	10.6	N≡N	1.85

λ Corrections for Rings

Cyclopropane	3.4	Piperazine	7.5
Cyclobutane	1.1	Each C, aromatic	$-.24$
Cyclohexane	3.1	Each C member of two	
Cyclohexene	7.2	aromatic rings	-3.1
Cyclohexadiene	10.7	Pyridine	.5

λ Corrections for Halogen Bonds

Cl bound to C	3.1
Br bound to C	4.1
I bound to C	4.1

* From Selwood, *Magnetochemistry*, Interscience, 1956, p. 92.

The uses of atomic and molecular diamagnetic susceptibilities in the study of molecular structure and molecular interactions have been manyfold. The susceptibilities of atomic and ionic systems can be used to test wave functions and electronic distributions. In addition, deviations of susceptibilities from additivity and from predicted trends have been used to investigate the nature of interactions such as hydration, crystal interactions, and similar effects. The use of Pascal's constants to predict molecular susceptibilities has suggested the study of possible electronic tautomer structures of molecules by comparing predicted and measured values.　Reaction rates can be followed by changes in susceptibility.　In recent years closely related nuclear magnetic resonance techniques have increased interest in understanding the fundamental nature of diamagnetism in molecules, and there is promise of extensive development in describing electronic configurations and currents during the next few years.

It was mentioned previously that particularly in regular crystals anisotropy of the magnetic susceptibility is observed.　Notable for such behavior are aromatic-like ring molecules such as benzene, naphthalene, anthracene, graphite, and similar structures.　Anisotropies result when

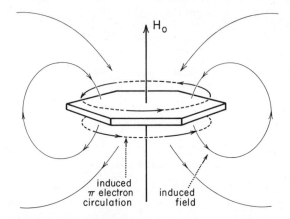

Fig. 11–2.　Anisotropic susceptibility of benzene caused by induced π-electron currents in a magnetic field H_0.

the induced electronic currents and the restrictions on them vary with the orientation of the molecule with respect to the field.　In the case of aromatic rings, the delocalized π electrons are easily induced to move by the field when the field is perpendicular to the plane of the ring, but not when the field is directed along the plane (Fig. 11–2).　Thus, Pauling[3] suggested that in the former case it could be assumed that six electrons can move in a ring of average diameter 1.39 Å, in which case the simple equation (11–4) could be used, while in the latter case there will be no extra effects due to the π electrons.　In this way he calculated an anisotropy of -49.2×10^{-6} for benzene as compared with the measured -54×10^{-6}.　More recently, refinements have been made in this treatment to take more accurately into account the actual spatial distribution of the π electrons around the ring and to determine the effects in condensed ring systems.　We will consider magnetic anisotropies in more detail in our later discussion of nuclear magnetic resonance and chemical shifts.

[3] Pauling, *J. Chem. Phys.*, **4**, 673 (1936).

11.3　PARAMAGNETISM

The presence of a permanent molecular magnetic dipole moment associated with spin or orbital angular momentum drastically alters the magnetic behavior of a substance. Classically, paramagnetism can be treated in a manner completely analogous to the calculation of the dielectric properties of a substance containing permanent electric dipoles. We would thus assume that a collection of molecules having molecular dipole moments $\mathbf{\mu}_{mol}$ would tend to align with an applied magnetic field except that thermal motions distribute the orientations over a variety of angles. Using the Boltzmann distribution, we can calculate the resultant total moment in the direction of the field, this representing the intensity of magnetization of the sample. Such a calculation, made by Langevin in the early part of the century, was successful in accounting for the gross behavior of paramagnetic substances.

From experiment and quantum-mechanical theory, we are now aware of the quantization of angular momentum and its effect on quantities such as the magnetic moment. Also we have observed the complications that can arise, depending on the coupling energy of spin and orbital angular momenta with one another and with the applied field. The most applicable case in atomic systems we have seen to be the situation known as Russell-Saunders or LS coupling, in which the total orbital angular momentum and total spin angular momentum interact to give a total angular momentum, which in turn interacts with an applied magnetic field. Generally states of different J (electronic) are widely enough separated in energy, as compared with kT, that only the ground state need be considered.

If we apply the magnetic-interaction Hamiltonian perturbation (11–5) to a system of permanent magnetic dipoles, we generally find that the diamagnetic energy discussed in the previous section is very much smaller than the paramagnetic term, so that as a first approximation we will neglect the second term in the operator. For a completely aribitrary magnetic field $\mathbf{H}$, the paramagnetic term is

$$\mathcal{3C}' = -\frac{e}{2mc}(\mathbf{H}\cdot\hat{\mathbf{L}} + 2\mathbf{H}\cdot\hat{\mathbf{S}}),$$

and for an atom in a state characterized by the quantum numbers L and S, we find that the perturbation energy, to first-order approximation, is

$$E'(L,\,S) = -\frac{e}{2mc}(\mathbf{H}\cdot\mathbf{L} + 2\mathbf{H}\cdot\mathbf{S}),$$

where $\mathbf{L}$ is a vector of magnitude $\sqrt{L(L+1)}\,\hbar$ and $\mathbf{S}$ is a vector of magnitude $\sqrt{S(S+1)}\,\hbar$. As before, the magnetic moment is found by taking the derivative of E' with respect to the field

$$\mathbf{u}(L,\ S) = \frac{e}{2mc}\ (\mathbf{L} + 2\mathbf{S}) = \frac{\mu_B}{\hbar}\ (\mathbf{L} + 2\mathbf{S}).$$

We can also define a vector $\mathbf{J}$ representing the total electronic angular momentum having magnitude $\sqrt{J(J+1)}\ \hbar$. The component of the dipole along this vector can then be found in terms of the projections of $\mathbf{L}$ and $\mathbf{S}$ along $\mathbf{J}$, or

$$\mathbf{u}_J(L,\ S) = \frac{\mu_B}{\hbar}\ \{\mathbf{L}\cos(\mathbf{L},\ \mathbf{J}) + 2\mathbf{S}\cos(\mathbf{S},\ \mathbf{J})\} = \frac{g\mathbf{J}\mu_B}{\hbar},$$

where g, known as the Landé splitting factor, is shown from trigonometric relations (Chapter 7) to be

$$g = 1 + \frac{J(J+1) + S(S+1) - L(L+1)}{2J(J+1)}.$$

In order to find the average component of the magnetic moment of an atom along the direction of the applied magnetic field, we must now consider the distribution of dipoles among the various states with different values of M_J, i.e., with different orientations with respect to the applied field. Assuming that only the ground electronic state need be considered, we obtain from the Boltzmann distribution law

$$\bar{\mu} = \frac{\displaystyle\sum_{M_J=-J}^{J} gM_J\mu_B \exp(gM_J\mu_B\mathsf{H}/kT)}{\displaystyle\sum_{M_J=-J}^{J} \exp(M_J\mu_B\mathsf{H}/kT)}.$$

This expression can be simplified by expanding the exponentials in series and retaining only the first two terms, on the assumption that for small values of H the remaining terms represent a negligible contribution. This gives us

$$\bar{\mu} = \frac{\displaystyle g\mu_B \sum_{M_J=-J}^{J} M_J + (g^2\mu_B{}^2\mathsf{H}/kT)\sum_{M_J=-J}^{J} M_J{}^2}{\displaystyle\sum_{M_J=-J}^{J}(1 + g\mu_B M_J\mathsf{H}/kT)}.$$

Recognizing that $\Sigma_{M_J}\ 1 = (2J+1)$, $\Sigma_{M_J}\ M_J = 0$, and

$$\sum_{M_J} M_J{}^2 = \frac{J(J+1)(2J+1)}{3},$$

we note that this expression can be reduced to

$$\bar{\mu} = \frac{J(J+1)g^2\mu_B{}^2}{3kT}\ \mathsf{H},$$

which immediately allows us to obtain the molar magnetization

$$\mathsf{M} = N\bar{\mu} = \frac{NJ(J+1)g^2\mu_B{}^2}{3kT}\,\mathsf{H}$$

and the molar susceptibility

$$\chi_M = \frac{\mathsf{M}}{\mathsf{H}} = \frac{NJ(J+1)g^2\mu_B{}^2}{3kT}. \tag{11–9}$$

To be more correct, the diamagnetic contribution, which is always present, should be included, so that our expression for the molar susceptibility of a paramagnetic atomic system would be

$$\chi_M = \frac{NJ(J+1)g^2\mu_B{}^2}{3kT} - \frac{Ne^2}{6mc^2}\sum_i \overline{r_i{}^2}.$$

For atoms with $J = 0$, the paramagnetic contribution to the susceptibility vanishes, as we expect. In those cases where $L = 0$ (S states), $J = S$, and the paramagnetism is due entirely to unpaired electrons. Most molecules have zero orbital angular momentum and no unpaired spins in their ground state and hence are not paramagnetic, but many atomic systems exhibit one or both kinds of paramagnetism. Without deriving the equations in full, we can observe that in those cases where the multiplet splittings are of the same order as kT, and states of various J must be included in the distribution, the molar susceptibility is given by a more complicated expression in which g's and energies are summed over various possible J's. In the case in which the individual couplings of the orbital and spin angular momenta with the applied field are much stronger than with one another, and the multiplet splittings are small compared to kT, the simple result is

$$\chi_M = \frac{N\mu_B{}^2}{3kT}\{4S(S+1) + L(L+1)\}.$$

Equation (11–9) is generally in accord with experimental findings, and the diamagnetic term or second-order terms can be added when necessary. The well-known law of Curie, for example, that the paramagnetic susceptibility is inversely proportional to temperature, is predicted by (11–9). This dependence on temperature is used experimentally to distinguish the paramagnetic and diamagnetic contributions to the susceptibility, the latter being temperature-independent.

A direct test of (11–9) would best be made on a paramagnetic monatomic gas which is dilute enough that interatomic interactions can be avoided. Unfortunately, few systems meet these requirements. The most obvious type of atom to investigate in this respect would be the alkali metals which have a single unpaired electron. The ingenious experiments of

Stern and Gerlach[4] were designed to measure the magnetic moments of such atoms directly and were an early substantiation of the existence of electron spin. In their experiments a beam of atoms produced by heating the alkali metal in a furnace, and collimated with a series of slits, is passed through an inhomogeneous magnetic field (Fig. 11–3). While in the inhomogeneous field the magnetic dipoles are aligned by the field, and they experience a force in the direction of increasing field strength. Thus the beam is deflected from its original path. The deflection of the beam depends, however, on the component of the magnetic dipole along the

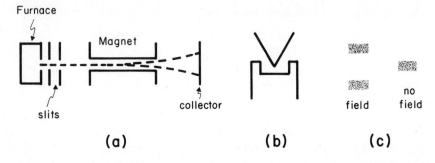

Fig. 11–3. The Stern-Gerlach experiment: (a) schematic of the apparatus; (b) cross-section of the magnet gap; (c) traces of undeflected and deflected beams of silver in an atomic beam experiment.

direction of the field, and as we have seen, there are $2J + 1$ (or in the case of spin-only moments $2S + 1 = 2$) orientations with respect to the field. Thus the field splits the beam into two beams, one corresponding to one orientation of the electron spins, and the other corresponding to the opposite orientation. In the absence of the field, the beam will be neither deflected nor split.

The original atomic beam experiment actually was done with Ag, which is also in a ^2S ground state. Other Group I elements subsequently were investigated and the spin magnetic moment confirmed. Accurate measurement of the field inhomogeneity and beam deflections permit calculation of the magnitude of the moment, but such measurements are difficult in the direct deflection method. More recently, other techniques have been developed which are more sensitive and can also detect nuclear spin effects.

A large amount of data has been collected on the susceptibilities of the rare earth ions in crystals and in solutions. These systems are especially convenient for the test of theory since their chemical and physical simi-

[4] Stern, *Z. Physik,* **7,** 249 (1921); Gerlach and Stern, *Ann. Physik,* **74,** 673 (1924); **76,** 163 (1925).

larities have suggested that the electrons of interest, the f-electrons, are so deeply embedded in the electron cloud that they should be little influenced by environment, even in the strong electric fields of a crystal. In Table 11–3 are listed the measured and calculated magnetic moments of the rare earth ions, and it will be seen immediately that the agreement is

TABLE 11–3. Paramagnetism of Rare Earth Ions*

Ion	Number of $4f$ Electrons	Normal State	S	L	J	g	μ_{eff} Theory	μ_{eff} Experiment
La^{+++}	0	$^1S_0$	0	0	0	—	0	0
Ce^{+++}	1	$^2F_{5/2}$	$\frac{1}{2}$	3	$\frac{5}{2}$	$\frac{6}{7}$	2.54	2.4
Pr^{+++}	2	$^3H_4$	1	5	4	4	3.58	3.5
Nd^{+++}	3	$^4I_{9/2}$	$\frac{3}{2}$	6	$\frac{9}{2}$	$\frac{8}{11}$	3.62	3.5
Gd^{+++}	7	$^8S_{7/2}$	$\frac{7}{2}$	0	$\frac{7}{2}$	2	7.94	8.0
Tb^{+++}	8	$^7F_6$	3	3	6	$\frac{3}{2}$	9.72	9.5
Ds^{+++}	9	$^6H_{15/2}$	$\frac{5}{2}$	5	$\frac{15}{2}$	$\frac{4}{3}$	10.65	10.7
Ho^{+++}	10	$^5I_8$	2	6	8	$\frac{5}{4}$	10.61	10.3
Er^{+++}	11	$^4I_{15/2}$	$\frac{3}{2}$	6	$\frac{15}{2}$	$\frac{6}{5}$	9.58	9.5
Tu^{+++}	12	$^3H_6$	1	5	6	$\frac{7}{6}$	7.56	7.3
Yb^{+++}	13	$^2F_{7/2}$	$\frac{1}{2}$	3	$\frac{7}{2}$	$\frac{8}{7}$	4.54	4.5
Lu^{+++}	14	$^1S_0$	0	0	0	—	0	0

* Pitzer, *Quantum Chemistry*, Prentice-Hall, 1953, p. 376.

excellent. The magnetic moments listed are in units of effective magnetons, defined as

$$\mu_{eff} = \left(\frac{3kT\chi_{mol}}{N\mu_B{}^2} \right)^{1/2}.$$

Combined with Eq. (11–9), the theoretical equation is then

$$\mu_{eff} = g \sqrt{J(J+1)}.$$

Another interesting group of ions are those of the transition region. It has been found that many of the calculated moments do not agree with experiment unless the assumption is made that the paramagnetism is due only to spin angular momentum. Stoner has suggested that the orbital angular momentum in most of these ions is "quenched" by the strong action of crystalline electric fields. That is, the interaction with the electric field is so strong that the oribital angular momentum does not respond to the application of a magnetic field. In this case only the spin angular momentum is effective. These conclusions seem consistent with a large number of experimental facts.

The use of measurements of paramagnetism in matter for the study of structural problems is widespread and has gained in importance in recent years with the development of electron magnetic resonance techniques. It is possible, for example, to obtain evidence about crystal-defect structures in solids, the effects of radiation, the participation of triplet states in luminescence, free radicals, and similar phenomena by studying magnetic susceptibilities and magnetic resonance absorption. One of the most satisfying and familiar of such applications is the determination of the geometry and electron bonding in coordination compounds containing transition metal ions. Extensive discussions are found in inorganic chemistry texts of the concepts introduced by Pauling to correlate the stereochemistry of complex ions of Fe^{+3}, Ni^{+2}, and similar ions. Although the more recent ideas of crystal field theory and ligand field theory have modified Pauling's simple ionic and covalent explanations of coordination, the usefulness of magnetic susceptibility measurements in helping to understand the nature of the bonding and the geometry has not been diminished. The general field of coordination chemistry and paramagnetism is discussed in several of the references given at the end of the chapter.

Although most molecules have non-magnetic ground electronic states, there are a number of important molecules that are paramagnetic because of unpaired electron spins and/or orbital angular momenta. The most familiar of such species is molecular oxygen, which we have seen to have two unpaired electrons. Magnetic susceptibility measurements verify a two-spin-only contribution, showing that the predicted $^3\Sigma$ state is correct. The susceptibility of oxygen is given by Eq. (11–9) with $S = 1$ in place of J. The paramagnetism of oxygen, incidentally, provides a simple and accurate method for oxygen analysis, since few other common gases are similarly paramagnetic. Sulfur vapor has also been shown to be paramagnetic, as we might anticipate from its similarity to oxygen.

Another thoroughly studied paramagnetic molecule is NO, whose behavior is complicated by the fact that the $^2\Pi_{1/2}$ and $^2\Pi_{3/2}$ levels lie close together. However, calculated susceptibilities agree well with experiment. Numerous other examples could be given of paramagnetic molecular species. Many of these are free radicals. The application of susceptibility measurements to the identification of free radicals in chemical reactions and to the verification of electronic states for molecules is obvious, and the interested reader can find many detailed accounts in the literature.

11.4 MAGNETIC RESONANCE

The behavior of atomic and molecular systems is described most exactly in terms of quantum mechanics. We often resort to more classical pictures, however, in order to provide an easier means for visualizing phenomena. In the case of magnetic phenomena, it should have become apparent by now that many of the interactions that exist in atomic and molecular systems can be described by classical equations, at least to a first approximation.

In Chapter 6 we investigated the relation between angular momentum and the magnetic fields that arise from electronic motions. From the interaction of the fields arising from orbital and spin momenta, we were able to predict the splitting of energy levels and spectral lines in the one-electron atom, and we then extended these findings to more complex atomic and molecular states. The effects of nuclear and electron spin on various other phenomena also have been described. We will now examine in more detail the nature of nuclear and electron spin angular momenta, their interactions with one another and with external fields, and the various spectroscopic techniques that are based on these effects. In order to keep our description as simple as possible, we will first take the semiclassical approach.

Associated with the intrinsic angular momentum of a particle is a magnetic dipole field. For an electron we have seen this field to be given by (6–32):

$$\mathbf{\mu} = -g_e \frac{e}{2m_e c} \mathbf{S}; \qquad |\mathbf{\mu}| = g_e \frac{e}{2m_e c} \sqrt{S(S+1)}\, \hbar, \qquad (11\text{–}10)$$

where $S = \frac{1}{2}$. Because the electronic charge is negative, the spin dipole is oriented in the direction opposite to that of the spin angular momentum. In terms of the Bohr magneton defined in Eq. (6–24), we also write

$$\mu = g_e \mu_B \sqrt{S(S+1)} = \tfrac{3}{4} g_e \mu_B = \tfrac{3}{2} \mu_B, \qquad (11\text{–}11)$$

where we have introduced the fact that g_e for the electron is almost exactly equal to 2. It is seen from the nature of S and m_S that the component of the electronic magnetic moment along the z direction is approximately

$$\mu_z = \pm \mu_B.$$

In the case of nucleons such as the proton and neutron, or complex nuclei, the spin angular momentum is described by the quantum number I, the total spin angular momentum being $|\mathbf{I}| = \sqrt{I(I+1)}\, \hbar$. For the proton and neutron $I = \frac{1}{2}$, while for heavier nuclei the nucleon spins may couple to give a net spin which may be zero, half-integral, or integral. Nuclei for which both the atomic number (number of protons) and the mass number (number of protons and neutrons) are even have no intrinsic angular momentum, and I is zero. Nuclei with even atomic number have only integral values of I, while those with odd atomic number have half-integral I. For such particles we can also write, as in (11–10) and (11–11),

$$\mathbf{\mu} = g_n \frac{e}{2m_p c} \mathbf{I}; \qquad |\mathbf{\mu}| = g_n \mu_n \sqrt{I(I+1)}, \qquad (11\text{–}12)$$

TABLE 11-4. Properties of Nuclear Species*

Isotope	ν_0 for 10,000-gauss Field	Natural Abundance (%)	Relative Sensitivity for Equal Numbers of Nuclei		μ (in units of μ_N)	I (in units of $\hbar$)	Electric Quadrupole Moment Q (in units of $e \times 10^{-24}$ cm²)
			At Constant Field	At Constant Frequency			
n^1	29.167	—	.322	.685	-1.91315	$\frac{1}{2}$	—
H^1	42.576	99.9844	1.000	1.000	2.79268	$\frac{1}{2}$	—
H^2	6.5357	1.56×10^{-2}	9.64×10^{-3}	.409	.85738	1	2.77×10^{-3}
B^{11}	13.660	81.17	.165	1.60	2.6880	$\frac{3}{2}$	3.55×10^{-2}
C^{13}	10.705	1.108	1.59×10^{-2}	.251	.70220	$\frac{1}{2}$	—
N^{14}	3.076	99.635	1.01×10^{-3}	.193	.40358	1	7.1×10^{-2}
N^{15}	4.315	.365	1.04×10^{-3}	.101	$-.28304$	$\frac{1}{2}$	—
O^{17}	5.772	3.7×10^{-2}	2.91×10^{-2}	1.58	-1.8930	$\frac{5}{2}$	-4×10^{-3}
F^{19}	40.055	100	.834	.941	2.6273	$\frac{1}{2}$	—
Na^{23}	11.262	100	9.27×10^{-2}	1.32	2.2161	$\frac{3}{2}$	.1
Al^{27}	11.094	100	.207	3.04	3.6385	$\frac{5}{2}$	.149
P^{31}	17.236	100	6.64×10^{-2}	.405	1.1305	$\frac{1}{2}$	—
Cl^{35}	4.172	75.4	4.71×10^{-3}	.490	.82091	$\frac{3}{2}$	-7.9×10^{-2}
Mn^{53}	11.00	—	.361	5.41	5.050	$\frac{7}{2}$	—
Co^{59}	10.103	100	.281	4.83	4.6388	$\frac{7}{2}$	.5
Sn^{119}	15.87	8.68	5.18×10^{-2}	.373	-1.0409	$\frac{1}{2}$	—
Tl^{205}	24.57	70.48	.192	.577	1.6115	$\frac{1}{2}$	—
Pb^{207}	8.899	21.11	9.13×10^{-3}	.209	.5837	$\frac{1}{2}$	—
Free electron	27.994	—	2.85×10^8	658	-1836	$\frac{1}{2}$	—

* From NMR Table, 4th ed., courtesy of Varian Associates, Palo Alto, Calif.

μ_n being the nuclear magneton calculated with the mass of the proton. For the proton g_n is 5.58490, while for other nuclei g_n assumes a characteristic value for each nuclear species. These constants must be determined experimentally, as they cannot be predicted from theory.

Again, the component of the nuclear magnetic dipole moment along the z axis will be

$$\mu_z = g_n m_I \mu_n$$

where m_I can assume the values $-I$, $-I + 1$, . . . , I. The product $g_n(e/2mc)$ is often called the magnetogyric or gyromagnetic ratio and is

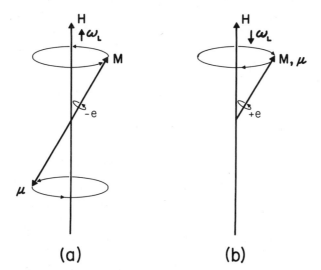

Fig. 11–4. Precession of (a) electronic and (b) nuclear spin angular momenta and magnetic moments in a magnetic field.

given the symbol γ. The origin of this name is seen from Eq. (11–12), which can be rearranged to

$$\gamma = \frac{\mu}{I}.$$

Characteristic constants for a number of nuclear species are collected in Table 11–4.

When placed in a magnetic field, the torque acting on the electronic or nuclear magnetic dipole moment was seen to produce a precessional motion of the dipole about the direction of the field. Because the relation between the magnetic dipole and the spin angular momentum differs, depending on the sign of the charge of the particle, the sense of this precession will differ in the case of electron spins and nuclear spins. Both these cases are illustrated in Fig. 11–4. The direction of the angular momentum vector, the magnetic dipole vector, and the angular velocity vector can be verified from the relations derived in Sec. 6.9 and in this section. For the electron and nuclear spins in a magnetic field we have

$$\omega_e = g_e \frac{e}{2m_e c} \mathbf{H} = g_e \frac{\mu_B}{\hbar} \mathbf{H} = \gamma_e \mathbf{H} \tag{11-13}$$

and

$$\omega_n = -g_n \frac{e}{2m_p c} \mathbf{H} = -\frac{g_n \mu_n}{\hbar} \mathbf{H} = -\gamma_n \mathbf{H}. \tag{11-14}$$

The magnitude of the angular velocity will be of more importance for most of our considerations rather than the direction.

It is important to note that according to these calculations the frequency of precession of the spin dipole depends only on the magnetic moment (and hence on the spin angular momentum) and the strength of the magnetic field. In the classical case we know nothing of the quantization of angular momentum and would thus predict that, regardless of the angle between the direction of the magnetic dipole and the field, the frequency of precession would be the same. In addition, this angle is not changed by the precession. Since the energy of a dipole in a magnetic field is a function of the angle between them ($E = -\mathbf{\mu} \cdot \mathbf{H}$), the energy of the system will remain constant during the precessional motion. In other words, no energy will be absorbed or emitted from a system of isolated magnetic dipoles in a magnetic field, even though they are experiencing precessional motion; and regardless of the angle of the dipole from the field, the precessional velocity will be the same for all identical species.

A system that does not emit or absorb energy is spectroscopically uninteresting and we now search for some means to cause changes in the energy of the system so that we can measure the radiation absorbed or emitted and obtain information about the system. A simple mechanism for causing such changes can be found. Imagine a second magnetic field, much smaller than the first, oriented in the x-y plane perpendicular to the z axis and the original steady field. The dipoles will also interact with this second field and will attempt to precess about both fields simultaneously. This can happen continuously, however, only if the second field rotates about the z axis in the same direction and with the same angular velocity as the precessing dipoles; otherwise, the interaction of the dipoles with the small field will cancel out as the angle between them changes with precession about the static field. When the small field rotates at the same velocity as the dipole, however, the angle between them is maintained, and the interaction allows the dipole to precess about the rotating field while it continues to precess about the static field.

An investigation of these motions will disclose quickly that the net effect is a continual tilting up and down of the dipoles with respect to the

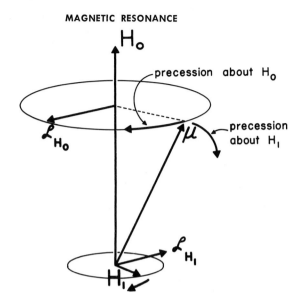

Fig. 11–5. Effect of a rotating magnetic field H_1 on a magnetic dipole precessing about a static field H_0.

static field while they are precessing. The resulting change in angle between the dipoles and the large field then results in a change in energy of the system (Fig. 11–5).

In a practical experiment we could produce such a rotating field perpendicular to the primary field, but it is considerably easier to produce a linearly oscillating field by applying an oscillating voltage to a coil of wire which has its axis perpendicular to the main field (Fig. 11–6). Mathematically, the oscillating field that results can be considered to consist of

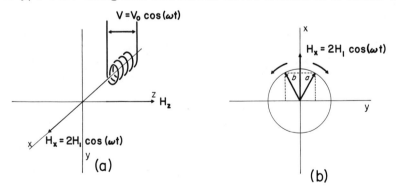

Fig. 11–6. (a) Production of a linearly oscillating magnetic field in the x direction by an alternating current through a coil of wire. (b) Rotating fields equivalent to the oscillating field.

two fields rotating with the same angular velocity but in opposite directions. If the oscillating field is described by the equation

$$H_x = 2H_1 \cos \omega t,$$

then the equivalent rotating fields will be

(a) $H_x = H_1 \cos \omega t$, $H_y = H_1 \sin \omega t$, $H_z = 0$;
(b) $H_x = H_1 \cos \omega t$, $H_y = -H_1 \sin \omega t$, $H_z = 0$;

one of which will be rotating in the same direction as the precessing dipole and will effectively interact with it. The other will have no effect.

If the angle between the dipoles and the large field increases, then energy must be absorbed from the radiation, that is from the rotating field. Thus, what we are accomplishing is in essence a spectroscopic experiment, and in order to calculate the frequency of the radiation (the precessing or oscillating field) required, it is necessary only to convert (11–13) and (11–14) to frequency units, to obtain

$$\nu_e = \frac{\omega_e}{2\pi} = g_e \frac{\mu_B}{h} H_z = \frac{|\gamma_e|}{2\pi} H_z \tag{11-15}$$

and

$$\nu_n = \frac{\omega_n}{2\pi} = g_n \frac{\mu_n}{h} H_z = \frac{\gamma_n}{2\pi} H_z. \tag{11-16}$$

Because the energy changes only when the frequency of the radiation is exactly the same as the frequency of precession, i.e., only when the two frequencies are "in resonance," this type of experiment is generally known as a magnetic resonance experiment.

In order to put the quantities involved into perspective, we will calculate the frequencies required to cause absorption of energy from an oscillating field when an electron or proton is placed in a static field of 10,000 gauss. Introducing the proper values for the charge and mass of these particles, we find that for a magnetic field of 10,000 gauss $\nu_e = 27.994$ kMcps while $\nu_p = 42.577$ Mcps. Thus, in easily attainable laboratory fields the frequency required to cause absorption of energy by electrons is in the microwave frequency region while for protons, which have a much larger mass, the frequency lies in the radiofrequency region of the electromagnetic spectrum. It is these frequencies, particularly the latter, that often cause magnetic resonance experiments to appear somewhat different from the usual spectroscopic methods. We do not require a monochromator, for example, since we can produce a monochromatic radiation field of any desired frequency by means of a radiofrequency oscillator or microwave klystron tube. In addition, although microwave energy can be piped around in a manner at least resembling optical beams, radiofrequency energy can be transmitted via wires. Thus in the typical nuclear magnetic resonance spectrometer we have radiofrequency oscillators, coils, and similar items rather than prisms, mirrors, and photocells.

Before proceeding with a description of a magnetic resonance experiment, let us also describe this phenomenon in quantum-mechanical terms. We will now concern ourselves only with nuclear spins, the electronic case being exactly analogous.   The Hamiltonian operator for the interaction

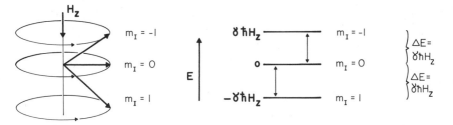

Fig. 11–7.   Energy levels and magnetic moment orientations for a nucleus with $I = 1$ in a magnetic field H_z with allowed transitions.

of a nuclear spin I with a magnetic field **H** is

$$\mathcal{3C} = -|\gamma|\hbar\hat{\mathbf{I}} \cdot \mathbf{H}, \tag{11–17}$$

which we know from the properties of these operators will have the eigenvalues

$$E_m = -\gamma\hbar m_I H_z = -\mu_z H_z. \tag{11–18}$$

For a given spin represented by I there will thus be $2I + 1$ energy levels in the magnetic field H_z.   Each of these levels can be thought of as representing a different orientation of the nuclear magnetic moment with respect to the field, as illustrated in Fig. 11–7.   According to the classical picture, these dipoles would be precessing around H_z while maintaining the proper constant component along z.

If a small oscillating field H_x is now applied, we can treat this new field as a small perturbation on the system, with the perturbation Hamiltonian given by

$$\mathcal{3C}' = \mu_x H_x = 2\mu_x H_1 \cos 2\pi\nu t,$$

which in terms of the component of spin angular momentum along the x direction would be

$$\mathcal{3C}' = 2\hbar\gamma\hat{I}_x H_1 \cos 2\pi\nu t. \tag{11–19}$$

Application of time-dependent perturbation theory then gives, for the probability of a transition between the states with quantum number m_I and m'_I,

$$P_{m_I m'_I} = \gamma^2 H_1^2 |\langle m'_I|\hat{I}_x|m_I\rangle|^2 \delta(\nu_{mm'} - \nu) \tag{11–20}$$

where δ is the Dirac delta function, which has the value 1 when $\nu_{mm'} = \nu$ and is zero when $\nu_{mm'} \neq \nu$, $\nu_{mm'}$ is the frequency corresponding to the difference in energy between the states m_I and m'_I, and ν is the frequency of the oscillating H_x field. From our previous experience with angular momentum operators and their eigenfunctions, we expect the result that the matrix element of I_x between states m_I and m'_I will vanish except when $m'_I = m_I \pm 1$, so that the selection rule for the absorption of radiation from the oscillating field is $\Delta m_I = 1$, while for the induced emission of radiation the selection rule is $\Delta m_I = -1$. From the separation of these levels we see that

$$\Delta E = \gamma \hbar \mathsf{H}_z = h\nu_{mm'}$$

or

$$\nu_{mm'} = \frac{\gamma}{2\pi} \mathsf{H}_z. \tag{11-21}$$

We see also from the properties of the Dirac delta function in (11-20) that the probability of a transition is finite only when the frequency of the oscillating field is the same as $\nu_{mm'}$, so that the frequency of radiation that will induce transitions between the magnetic levels is also given by Eq. (11-21). This is exactly the same result as we deduced from the classical picture. Since the energy levels are equally spaced, the different possible transitions will all give rise to absorption at the same frequency.

It is interesting to note that in the case of $I = \frac{1}{2}$ it is possible to calculate the motions of a magnetic moment in a time-varying magnetic field directly, without recourse to perturbation theory, and from the results it is clear that the probability of transitions is important only when the frequency of radiation is the same as the Larmor precession frequency.

The g-factor differs for each nuclear species, and hence for a given static magnetic field, say 10,000 gauss, the frequency of radiation giving rise to observable transitions will differ for each kind of nucleus. These frequencies are listed in Table 11-4 for a few important nuclei. From Eq. (11-20) it is apparent that the probability of a transition, and hence the intensity of the absorption, also depends on g. Some indication of the expected sensitivities is shown also in Table 11-4.

11.5 POPULATION OF NUCLEAR MAGNETIC ENERGY LEVELS AND RELAXATION

The nature of the nuclear magnetic resonance experiment and the features of the spectral lines depend on several factors. Among the most important of these are the relative transition probabilities from lower-energy to higher-energy states and vice versa, the relative populations of the different states, and electrical and magnetic interactions that may affect the states.

All our previous discussions of spectroscopy have dealt with interactions which are basically electrical dipole interactions. For this type of transition we obtained equations giving the transition probabilities both for induced absorption and emission and for spontaneous emission. We found the first two to be equal, so that in the absence of other effects the rates of transition up and down in energy depend on the relative populations of the levels. We also found that for electric dipole transitions the probability for spontaneous emission is high. This is an extremely important phenomenon in spectroscopy because it continually allows atomic and molecular systems to return to the ground state, thus keeping the ground state more highly populated than the excited states and giving rise to a net absorption of energy from a directed beam of radiation.

It was observed, however, that the probability of spontaneous emission is several orders of magnitude less for magnetic dipole and electric quadrupole radiation transitions. The nuclear magnetic resonance experiment is seriously affected by this fact. In the absence of spontaneous emission we find that the equal probabilities of upward and downward transitions result in only a very slight net absorption of energy, and continued radiation of the sample may eventually lead to an equalization of the upper and lower states, so that there is no absorption of energy at all. In the nuclear resonance experiment we cannot direct a beam of radiation toward the sample and observe the intensity passing through. We are forced by the nature of the equipment to detect all energy absorbed and emitted. Hence, if there is no net absorption, the transitions cannot be detected.

To appreciate the magnitudes involved, we can calculate the relative populations of nuclear magnetic levels. Taking the simplest case of $I = \frac{1}{2}$ we calculate

$$\frac{n\left(\frac{1}{2}\right)}{n\left(-\frac{1}{2}\right)} = e^{-[\epsilon_{1/2} - \epsilon_{-1/2}]/kT}$$

$$= e^{-\gamma \hbar H_z / kT} = 1 + \frac{\gamma \hbar H_z}{kT} = 1 + \frac{g\mu_n H_z}{kT}.$$

If we introduce g for the proton and let the field be 10,000 gauss, we find that at room temperature the ratio is approximately $1 + (7 \times 10^{-6})$. That is, for every million nuclei in the upper level there will be one million and seven in the lower. The differences in population of nuclear magnetic levels are thus extremely small.

It is also interesting to note that, since there is a difference in population, there will result a net magnetization of the sample caused by the greater number of nuclear magnets oriented in the direction of the field (the lower energy state) than in the direction opposed to the field. This can be calculated by summing the number of nuclei in each state times the z component of the magnetic moment of each state. The result of such a calculation is

$$\mathsf{M} = \frac{N}{3kT} \, g^2 \mu_n{}^2 I(I + 1)\mathsf{H}$$

for the nucleus of spin I. Because the nuclear magneton is very much smaller than the Bohr magneton, this kind of paramagnetism is much smaller than even electronic diamagnetism. At low temperatures, however, the nuclear contribution becomes more important, and direct measurements of the nuclear magnetization have actually been made on solid hydrogen.

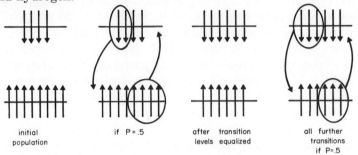

initial population   if P = .5   after transition levels equalized   all further transitions if P=.5

Fig. 11–8. Simplified view of saturation of nuclear magnetic energy levels. If $P = \frac{1}{2}$, then twice as many transitions will occur upward (4) as downward (2) since there are initially twice as many spins in the lower state. Once the levels are equalized, there will be the same number (3) transferred up and down, with no net change in energy.

With such a small difference in populations it is not difficult to see that in the absence of spontaneous emission of energy the upper and lower states may quickly become equalized in population upon continued irradiation with the oscillating magnetic field. The total probability of transition, or the total number of transitions in unit time, is the product of the probability of a single transition by the population in the initial state. The single-transition probabilities are the same both up and down. Since there are more nuclei in the lower state, this means that there will be more nuclei undergoing a transition up than down. The net result will be a decrease in the population of the lower state and an increase in the upper. Finally, a continuation of this process results in equal populations in the two levels, equal numbers of transition up and down, and no net absorption or emission of energy. This phenomenon is known as *saturation* of the nuclear resonance line (Fig. 11–8).

Even without spontaneous emission as a mechanism for losing energy, transitions between rotational, vibrational, and electronic states can take place as a result of collisions between molecules. Molecules are continually experiencing the varying electric fields caused by the motions of neighboring molecules. We have seen that these interactions are sufficient to destroy the fine structure in spectra by limiting the lifetimes of the various states. Magnetic interactions between nuclei are much smaller, however. Each nucleus is almost completely isolated from magnetic fields of nuclei in neighboring atoms, and many of the nuclei in the same molecule are likely to have no magnetic moment at all. The isolation is not complete, however. Various interactions, although often small, can contribute to maintaining the ground-state population at a higher number than the upper states. Such mechanisms are called *relaxation* processes.

An important mechanism of this sort is known as the *spin-lattice relaxation*. It arises from the interaction of the nuclear magnetic moment with the electrons and other nuclei surrounding it (the lattice), and an analysis shows that the interaction involves the magnetic fields arising from electronic moments and other nuclear moments in the region of the nucleus in question. If we consider the motions of atoms and molecules in a fluid or solid, we recognize that many rotational, vibrational, and translational motions may be possible. Many of these which have magnetic moments associated with them will give rise to a time-varying magnetic field at the point in space occupied by a nucleus. Although these fields will be complex, they can be analyzed mathematically by the procedure of expanding the time dependence in a Fourier series, and it will be found that among the component frequencies there will be one corresponding to the frequency required to cause transitions between magnetic states of the nucleus of interest. Even in the absence of an externally applied oscillating field, then, there will be at the vicinity of the nucleus a time-varying field of the necessary frequency to cause transitions, and this field will serve to induce transitions from the higher states back down to the ground state. The energy lost by the spins in going back to the lower state will be absorbed by the lattice. In this way thermal equilibrium (the Boltzmann distribution) is maintained.

Some of the mathematical restrictions on such a relaxation process can be obtained by investigating the relation of transition probability and the excess population in the lower state. The result is that if a nuclear system in equilibrium with the lattice is disturbed by changing the magnetic field, the new equilibrium distribution will be approached exponentially with time; that is,

$$\frac{dn}{dt} = 2P(n_0 - n),$$

or

$$n = n_0 \left[1 - \frac{n_0 - n_i}{n_0} e^{-2Pt} \right],$$

where n is the number of nuclei per unit volume in excess in the lower state at any time, n_i is the initial excess population in the lower state, n_0 is the final equilibrium excess population, and P is the probability per unit time of a transition. The excess population thus approaches the equilibrium value with the characteristic time constant $1/2P$, which for nuclei with $I = \frac{1}{2}$ can be defined to be the spin-lattice relaxation time T_1:

$$T_1 = \frac{1}{2P}, \quad (I = \tfrac{1}{2}).$$

The spin-lattice relaxation time has two predominant effects on the spectral lines. If T_1 is very long, i.e., if the spin-lattice interactions are very weak and a long time is taken to reach equilibrium, than the irradiation of the sample may cause transitions to take place at a rate faster than the rate by which the spin-lattice relaxation can bolster the population of the lower level. In this case the difference between absorption and emission will decrease, as will the line intensity. If the relaxation is too slow, then the populations may be equalized, and no net signal will be observed except perhaps at the first moment of resonance. The spin-lattice relaxation times in liquids are of the order of 10^{-2} to 10^2 sec, although for magnetically isolated nuclei they may be longer. In the presence of paramagnetic ions, which will produce strong fluctuating fields in the sample, the relaxation time may be as short as 10^{-4} sec. In a resonance experiment, therefore, the irradiation field, $\mathbf{H}_1$, must be kept small enough to prevent saturation, although the signal-to-noise ratio of the equipment may preclude reducing $\mathbf{H}_1$ to a very low level.

If T_1 is extremely short, the energies of the magnetic states may become uncertain because of the Heisenberg relation between the lifetime of the state and its energy. In this case there will be a broadening of the spectral line similar to other cases of uncertainty broadening which we have observed previously.

Relaxation of nuclear spins also can be caused by what is known as *spin-spin relaxation*. Although a mathematical description of the interactions causing spin-spin relaxation will not be given here, we can describe approximately the nature of these phenomena and their effect on the spectrum. One type of spin-spin interaction depends primarily on the fact that, if a nucleus is precessing about the static magnetic field at its Larmor frequency, it will produce at the location of another similar nucleus a rotating magnetic field of the same frequency, as shown in Fig. 11–9. This rotating field will be of the precise frequency to cause a transition of the second nuclear spin. The reverse effect will also operate, and the net result will be that the two nuclear spins will both flip to another orientation and will have thus exchanged energy. Although this has not altered the over-all distribution of spins among the magnetic levels, it will have shortened the lifetimes of the states and thus caused an uncertainty in the energies of the states. The result is again a broadening of the spectral line if the lifetimes are short enough.

An additional spin-spin interaction arises from the static component

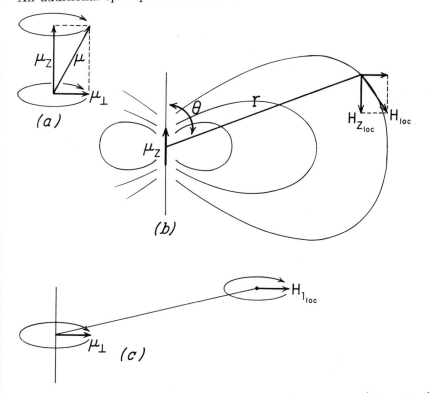

Fig. 11–9. (a) Resolution of a nuclear magnetic dipole moment into moments along the external z field direction and a direction perpendicular to the field. (b) The local field at a distance r from a magnetic dipole, arising from the z component of a magnetic dipole. (c) The rotating local field produced by the rotating perpendicular component of a precessing magnetic dipole moment.

of the magnetic field of the nuclear dipole along the direction of the applied field, as illustrated in Fig. 11–9. When a nucleus undergoes transitions from one magnetic state to another, this component field at the location of another nucleus will change. Over a period of time the second nucleus will experience a field in the z direction that varies from a value slightly more than the applied field to a value slightly less. As a result, the second nucleus will have a Larmor precession frequency and a separation of magnetic energy levels that can assume several values. Molecular motions in fluids will tend to average out all these different values, but in solids such effects may be quite significant. The result of these spin-spin interactions is again a broadening of the spectral line, since different fields at the nucleus will require different radiation frequencies to cause resonance.

The distribution of resonance frequencies about the simple isolated spin Larmor frequency can be expressed by multiplying the single-frequency transition probability (11–20) by a shape function, $g(\nu)$, which modifies the expression to give a finite probability of transition at frequencies other than the interaction-free Larmor frequency, and which indicates the relative probabilities of transitions at these other frequencies.

The effect of spin-spin relaxation in bringing a nuclear system to equilibrium in a given magnetic field can be described mathematically in a manner similar to that employed for the spin-lattice relaxation process. The characteristic relaxation time in this case is given the symbol T_2, and it can be shown that the spin-spin relaxation time is related to the absorption line shape by

$$T_2 = \tfrac{1}{2} g(\nu)_{\max}$$

and

$$\frac{1}{T_2} = \Delta\nu_{1/2},$$

where $g(\nu)_{\max}$ is the value of the shape function at the center of the resonance line, and $\Delta\nu_{1/2}$ is the half-width of the line in frequency units at half the peak height. These are both illustrated in Fig. 11–10. If the variation in local fields due to other dipoles is H_{loc}, then from the relation between field and frequency (11–21),

$$T_2 = \frac{1}{\gamma H_{loc}}.$$

Whether local fields are averaged out effectively or not depends on the motions that the molecules undergo, and hence the spin-spin relaxation time is sensitive to the state of molecular motions in a sample. The mutual spin-exchange phenomenon is also dependent upon the proximity of similar nuclei, so that in systems containing only a few nuclei of a given kind, say C^{13} nuclei at natural abundance, this mechanism of relaxation will be ineffective.

It should be mentioned that other factors may contribute to relaxation and line-broadening. Nuclei that have a quadrupole moment (all nuclei with $I \geqslant 1$ have quadrupole moments) can interact with non-symmetric electric fields in a molecule to cause transitions, even in the absence of magnetic interactions. Thus in many molecules the relaxation time is very short by virtue of electrical interactions rather than magnetic ones. In addition, the relaxation times in liquids often give rise to line shapes that are much narrower than the experimentally attainable homogeneity of the applied magnetic field across the sample, so that the observed lines are broader than expected from T_1 and T_2.

Equations relating relaxation times, H_1, and transition probabilities to obtain line shapes have been derived in a variety of ways. Some of the most useful equations are those derived by Bloch.[5] By considering the

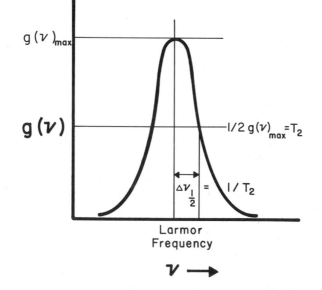

Fig. 11–10. Relation of the line shape function and the spin-spin relaxation time.

effects of the H_1 field and the relaxation processes on the total magnetization of the sample, Bloch was able to deduce equations giving the energy absorbed as a function of the frequency of the H_1 field as well as related quantities such as the frequency-dependent magnetic susceptibilities of the sample. The Bloch equations are useful for obtaining estimates of the effects of different relaxation times and irradiating fields on the line characteristics. Other more elaborate and general cases have been treated.

Experimentally, there are two fundamental approaches to observing nuclear magnetic resonance. The first is the most obvious experiment, to measure the energy absorbed. A schematic diagram of the electronic components required for this is shown in Fig. 11–11.

Because it is difficult to construct a variable-frequency oscillator of high stability, it is more convenient to use a fixed-frequency signal genera-

[5] Bloch, *Phys. Rev.*, **70**, 460 (1946).

tor and vary the magnetic field of the sample until the Larmor condition is met and resonance occurs.   The field can be varied easily by controlling the current through the coils of an electromagnet.   The current can be adjusted until the field is just below the correct field for resonance, and then a secondary field can be applied by means of a current through a pair of Helmholtz sweep coils placed against the faces of the magnet poles. This secondary field can then be increased to give a total field at the sam-

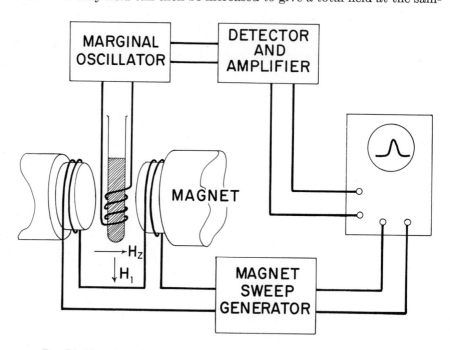

Fig. 11–11.   A nuclear magnetic resonance absorption experiment.

ple of any value below, on, or above the resonance condition.   The sweep-coil generator also can be used to control the sweep of an oscilloscope.

A useful means for observing the absorption of energy by the sample at resonance is to make the coil that generates the oscillating H_1 field part of a carefully tuned oscillator circuit, so that when energy is absorbed and the characteristics of the sample inside the coil change, the oscillator circuit will become detuned and the level of oscillation will drop.   This change in the oscillator circuit can be detected by means of a voltmeter, an oscilloscope, or a recorder.   If a sawtooth voltage is applied to the sweep coils, the field at the sample will repeatedly pass through the resonance condition, and each time it does so, the oscillator level will change, while the condition of resonance is maintained.   Another similar absorption spectrometer relies on the unbalance of a bridge circuit when energy is absorbed by the sample from the H_1 field.

A second approach, employed widely in commercial instrumentation, is based on the magnetic properties of the sample as a whole. Bloch's equations show that the net magnetization of the sample in the static magnetic field is affected by the oscillating H_1 field in such a way that there is produced a precession of the net magnetic moment about the H_z

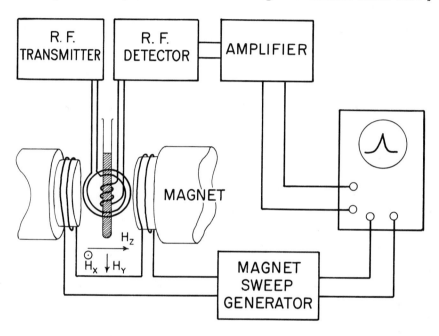

Fig. 11–12.   A nuclear magnetic resonance induction experiment.

direction, with resulting components in the x-y plane which rotate about z with the precessional frequency. If a coil of wire is placed on the y axis, this changing component of magnetization will induce a voltage in the coil, and this voltage can be detected, amplified, and displayed. When the resonance conditions are not met, there is no net magnetization in the x-y plane, and no signal is induced. There are many variations in the electronic techniques that can be used to detect the induced signal. A simple schematic of a nuclear induction spectrometer is shown in Fig. 11–12. The nature of the induced signal has been shown to be directly related to the absorption of energy, so that the two methods described are essentially equivalent. The use of one technique or another depends on particular experimental factors.

11.6 . NUCLEAR MAGNETIC RESONANCE IN SOLIDS

The phenomenon of nuclear magnetic resonance would be generally uninteresting to chemists if nuclei were isolated in space from one another. The NMR experiment would then serve primarily to establish accurate values of g_n for different nuclear species by measurement of the field and frequency at which resonance occurs. Nuclei, however, are not isolated. They exist in atomic and molecular situations surrounded by electrons, and they exert forces on one another. It is these interactions that give rise to interesting effects.

In solids, the motions of atoms and molecules are more or less restricted to rotations and vibrations about equilibrium positions in the crystal lattice. In the absence of suitable motions, the local magnetic fields produced by neighboring magnetic dipoles will not be averaged out, and a particular nucleus in the solid will experience, in addition to the external H_z field, a local field in the z direction, which may assume several values as the nuclear moments producing this local field undergo transitions between their different nuclear magnetic states.

Suppose that we have a single crystal of a substance which contains as the only magnetic nuclei the species A and B, each of which has a spin $I = \frac{1}{2}$. We will assume for the sake of simplicity that A and B occur in pairs, separated by a distance r_{AB}, and that the distance from one pair to another is very large compared to r_{AB}. In addition, we will assume that the crystal is oriented with respect to the externally applied static field in such a way that the angle between r_{AB} and the direction of the field is θ. This situation was shown in Fig. 11–9.

Let us now apply an external magnetic field of such a magnitude that we can observe the resonance condition for nucleus A. We will give the symbol H_0 to the external field which would cause resonance if A were completely isolated from all other effects, and from (11–16) we calculate that the frequency of the H_1 field required to cause resonance in this case would be $\omega_A = \gamma_A H_0$. But in the crystal the magnetic field at nucleus A is not simply H_0, but also includes a local field caused by the fact that nucleus B has a magnetic dipole moment. The frequency actually required for resonance would thus be given by

$$\omega_A = \gamma_A H_A = \gamma_A (H_0 + H_{loc})_z.$$

Our problem is to find $(H_{loc})_z$. This can be done if we know the component of the magnetic moment of B in the z direction. Classically, the field at any point arising from a magnetic dipole is given by

$$(H_{loc})_z = \mu_{Bz} r_{AB}^{-3} (1 - 3 \cos^2 \theta)$$

where θ is still the angle between r_{AB} and H_0 (which is along the z axis).

In the presence of a magnetic field, however, we know that $\mathbf{\mu}_B$ is quantized and can assume only two values since $I_B = \frac{1}{2}$. Thus, from our previous description of the z component of the magnetic moment, we have

$$(\mathsf{H}_{\text{loc}})_z = \frac{1}{2}\gamma_B \hbar r_{AB}^{-3}(1 - 3\cos^2\theta).$$

This means, then, that the actual magnetic field H_A at nucleus A will be $\mathsf{H}_0 + \frac{1}{2}\gamma_B \hbar r_{AB}^{-3}(1 - 3\cos^2\theta)$ or $\mathsf{H}_0 - \frac{1}{2}\gamma_B \hbar r_{AB}^{-3}(1 - 3\cos^2\theta)$ depending on the particular orientation of nucleus B. If we look at all the pairs of nuclei in the crystal, we expect to find nearly equal populations of the upper and lower states of nucleus B, so that approximately half of the A nuclei will experience one field and half the other. The result of our experiment will be that we will observe two resonances, one corresponding to each different local field situation, and the separation of the two resonances is equivalent to the field difference $2(\mathsf{H}_{\text{loc}})_z$. If we examined the resonance of nucleus B, we would observe a similar effect. The magnetic field 1 Å from a proton is about 10 gauss, so that in solids we may well expect resonance lines split 15–20 gauss in this manner.

This semiclassical picture is qualitatively correct, but ignores a number of important factors such as the effect of the rotating component of the dipole field in stimulating spin-exchange. We must turn then to a quantum-mechanical description for more exact details.

In the absence of internuclear interactions the Hamiltonian operator for a system of nuclear spins in a magnetic field H_0 is written easily from (11–17):

$$\mathcal{H}^0 = -\hbar \mathsf{H}_0 \cdot \sum_i \gamma_i \hat{\mathbf{I}}_i = -\mathsf{H}_0 \cdot \sum_i \mathbf{\mu}_i. \tag{11–22}$$

The local interactions can be described by a perturbation Hamiltonian, which is

$$\mathcal{H}' = -\sum_i \mathbf{\mu}_i \cdot \sum_{j>i} [\mathsf{H}_{\text{loc}}(j)]_i,$$

where $[\mathsf{H}_{\text{loc}}(j)]_i$ is the local field caused by nucleus j at the position of nucleus i. The local field is simply the field of a magnetic dipole given by

$$[\mathsf{H}_{\text{loc}}(j)]_i = -\frac{\mathbf{\mu}_j}{r_{ij}^3} + 3\frac{(\mathbf{\mu}_j \cdot \mathbf{r}_{ij})\mathbf{r}_{ij}}{r_{ij}^5},$$

which gives for $\mathcal{H}'$

$$\mathcal{H}' = \sum_i \sum_{j>i} [\mathbf{\mu}_i \cdot \mathbf{\mu}_j r_{ij}^{-3} - 3(\mathbf{\mu}_i \cdot \mathbf{r}_{ij})(\mathbf{\mu}_j \cdot \mathbf{r}_{ij})r_{ij}^{-5}].$$

The evaluation of the perturbation term is straightforward but tedious. The result for nuclei that are dissimilar is the same as we derived classically, but for nuclei that are identical the spin exchange leads to a narrowing of the splitting. In the case of two identical spins with $I = \frac{1}{2}$, for example, solution of the perturbed system of two spins leads to four possible energy levels, as we would expect for two spins each of which can have two values of M_I. The levels are shown in Fig. 11–13 along with the levels predicted from (11–22) in the absence of the perturbation.

The selection rules, when worked out, show that only two transitions are possible (singlet-to-triplet transitions are not allowed, as usual). These transitions have equal intensity and can be seen to give rise to

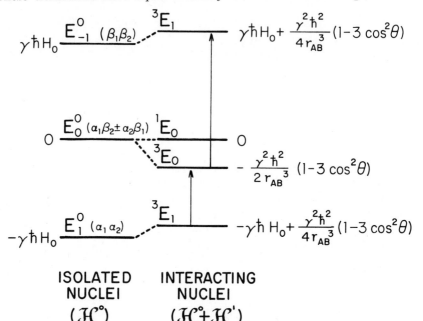

ISOLATED NUCLEI
$(\mathcal{H}^\circ)$

INTERACTING NUCLEI
$(\mathcal{H}^\circ + \mathcal{H}')$

Fig. 11–13. Energy levels and allowed transitions for a pair of nuclei with spin $\frac{1}{2}$.

two absorptions, equally spaced from the expected line in the absence of interactions.

The case we have considered here is actually an idealization in that, although two magnetic nuclei may be very much closer to each other than to other such pairs, the latter will still have some effect on the local fields at the pair of interest. Thus, the observed lines will be broadened somewhat by these additional smaller fields.

If a crystal containing nuclear pairs, all with the same orientation with respect to the crystal axes, is now rotated at different angles to the applied magnetic field, then the angle between r_{AB} and the field will change, as will the splitting of the nuclear resonance absorption. From

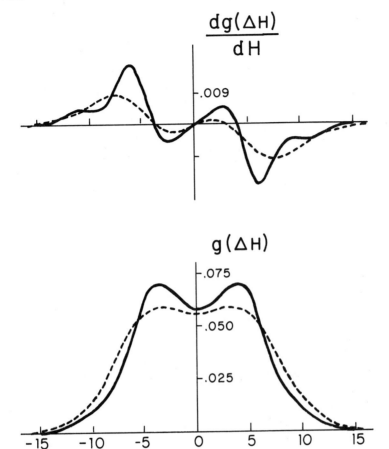

Fig. 11–14. Calculated absorption line shapes and the derivatives of the absorption lines for the proton magnetic resonance in solid powdered $CaSO_4 \cdot 2H_2O$. The separation of the proton pair in a single water molecule is assumed to be 1.54 Å. The full curves represent the lines for the case in which the average distance from one proton pair (water molecule) to its nearest neighbor is 2.80 Å. For the dotted curves this next-nearest-neighbor separation is assumed to be 1.96 Å.

this information one can calculate both the separation of the nuclei and their orientation with respect to the axes of the crystal.

In many instances single-crystal experiments are not feasible, but information can still be obtained from powdered samples; for the primary difference is that now the $\cos^2 \theta$ term has been averaged over all values of θ because of the completely random orientations of r_{AB} with respect to the field in the powdered sample. The expected line shape can thus be easily calculated since all angles are equally probable. In addition it is again necessary to include the effects of more distant magnetic nuclei on the local fields. Calculated line shapes for the proton pair in $CaSO_4 \cdot 2H_2O$ are shown in Fig. 11–14 for cases with different distant-neighbor interactions. The experimental techniques used to measure resonance absorption in solids generally involve modulation of the static field by an audiofrequency field, with detection of the signal by a lock-in

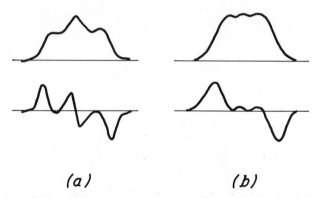

(a)   (b)

Fig. 11–15. Absorption curves and derivatives for (a) three-spin systems such as the H_3O^+ ion, the —CH_3 group, etc., and for (b) four-spin systems such as the NH_4^+ ion.

system which displays the first harmonic of the absorption signal, i.e., the derivative of the absorption curve, rather than the absorption itself. The derivative of the line shape for a proton pair is also shown in Fig. 11–14.

It is possible to extend these calculations, using the perturbation Hamiltonian we have just discussed as a basis, to spin groups containing three or four nuclei. Examples of the line shapes for such groupings are illustrated in Fig. 11–15. NMR spectroscopy has proved to be an extremely useful supplement to x-ray analysis since the latter cannot locate light atoms such as protons. The NMR spectra, especially in the case of single crystals, allow verification of certain proton groupings and orientations as well as calculation of the interproton distances. Many hydrates have been studied in this manner, one of the most interesting findings being the verification of the H_3O^+ ion structure in hydrates of strong acids such as $HNO_3 \cdot H_2O$.

In practice the direct calculation of line shapes is too difficult except in the simplest cases of only two or three interacting species. Van Vleck has developed an analytical method, however, which is particularly useful for samples containing a number of interacting nuclei.[6] If we express the shape function in terms of the magnetic field rather than frequency, it is possible to define *moments* of the line shape.   The definition for the nth moment is

$$\langle H^n \rangle = \int_{-\infty}^{\infty} (\Delta H)^n g(\Delta H) \, d\Delta H,$$

or in terms of the derivative of the shape function

$$\langle H^n \rangle = -\frac{1}{n+1} \int_{-\infty}^{\infty} (\Delta H)^{n+1} \frac{dg(\Delta H)}{d\Delta H} \, d\Delta H.$$

For interactions that are small ($\mathcal{3C}' \ll \mathcal{3C}^0$, $\mathcal{3C}' \ll kT$), the second moment is calculated to be

$$\langle H^2 \rangle = \tfrac{3}{2}I(I+1)N_s^{-1}\gamma^2\hbar^2 \sum_i \sum_{j>i} (1 - 3\cos^2\theta_{ij})^2 r_{ij}^{-6}$$
$$+ \tfrac{1}{3}N_s^{-1}\hbar^2 \sum_i \sum_f \gamma_f^2 I_f(I_f+1)(1 - 3\cos^2\theta_{if})^2 r_{if}^{-6}.$$

In this equation I and N_s refer to all of the N_s nuclei at resonance, while the I_f refer to all the other spins whose moments give rise to fields at the resonant nuclei.   In powdered samples the $(1 - 3\cos^2\theta)^2$ terms can be replaced by their average $\tfrac{4}{5}$.

Comparisons of second moments calculated from the observed line shapes with second moments calculated from assumed values of the molecular distances have been used widely to determine various molecular parameters and to establish structural arrangements in the solid state. The planarity of the urea molecule, for example, has been verified by both single-crystal and powdered-sample studies, which show that the NH_2 protons do not lie outside the plane of the rest of the molecule.

One of the most interesting applications of wide-line NMR has been the study of molecular motions in solids.   Various types of motions, such as internal rotation of structural groups in molecules, and rotations of molecules about fixed axes in the crystal lattice, have a pronounced effect on line shapes because they average out part of the $1 - 3\cos^2\theta$ term.   This averaging is not generally isotropic, however, because the motions are restricted about certain axes in the molecule or crystal. Once these axes have been identified, it is possible to calculate the line width to be expected for a given type of motion and compare it with experiment.   Motions of this sort reduce the line widths, and the observation of such motional narrowings can be employed to observe the onset of these motions at different temperatures.

Theory indicates that, only if the frequency of motion in the molecular system is of the order of H_{loc} or greater, will line-narrowing occur.   For

[6] Van Vleck, *Phys. Rev.*, **74**, 1168 (1948).

this reason it is dangerous to make too much of the actual temperatures at which the onset of motion appears to occur. These temperatures may or may not coincide with similar motional transitions observed by other methods such as dielectric-constant measurements or heat-capacity measurements. Each method is able to detect such motions with a characteristic sensitivity and response time.

An excellent example of motional narrowing is in 1,2-dichloroethane, which contains two symmetric proton pairs. The line widths have been

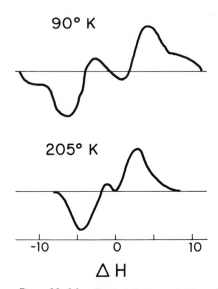

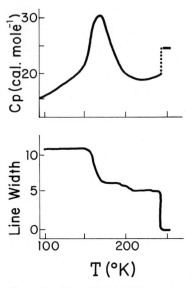

Fig. 11–16. Derivative curves of the proton magnetic resonance absorption line in 1,2-dichloroethane at 90°K and 205°K.

Fig. 11–17. Line width versus temperature and heat-capacity curves for 1,2-dichloroethane. (By permission from Gutowsky and Pake, J. Chem. Phys., 18, 162 (1950).)

studied in the solid state as a function of temperature, and two typical derivative curves are shown in Fig. 11–16. It is obvious that some motion is taking place at the higher temperature which is not present at the lower. Line widths are plotted as a function of temperature in Fig. 11–17.

Calculations show that the line width observed up to about 160°K corresponds to the splitting expected for a rigid proton pair in the CH_2Cl group. Thus one concludes that at these temperatures there are no molecular motions, at least none with a rotational frequency as great as 50 kcps. Above 160°K the line width drops to approximately half its previous value, and this corresponds to a reorientation of the proton pairs about an axis perpendicular to the line joining the proton pairs on each group in the molecule. In all likelihood such reorientations are what we would describe as internal rotation. Above the melting point, complete random motion of the molecules reduces the line width to the very small values characteristic of liquids.

Another interesting case is that of the motions in $Co(NH_3)_6Cl_3$. Experimental line shapes are plotted in Fig. 11–18 along with calculated line shapes for three possible kinds of motion. At 100°K this motion in all likelihood corresponds to rotation of the NH_3 groups about the

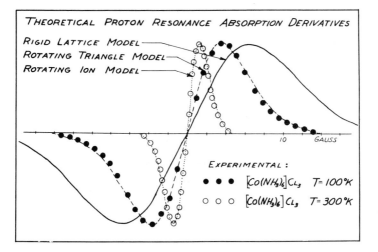

Fig. 11–18.   Theoretical and experimental proton line shape derivatives in $Co(NH_3)_6Cl_3$. (Courtesy of Professor John S. Waugh.)

threefold axis joining them to the central atom, while at 300°K random tumbling of the entire ion appears to be occurring.

The most thorough and informative studies of motions in solids include not only the observation of line widths but also the calculation of second moments and relaxation times as a function of temperature. With detailed information of this sort one is able, for example, to distinguish diffusion in the solid from rotational motions. It is possible to distinguish the motions of segments of polymer molecules and to observe the onset of new types of chain motions at different temperatures. From the second moment one can also infer the frequencies of various motions as a function of temperature and obtain in this way an Arrhenius plot giving approximate activation energies for these motions. NMR studies of the solid state are certain to explore new areas in the future, considering the great interest in this area at the present time.

11.7 CHEMICAL SHIFTS AND HIGH RESOLUTION NMR

Although the physicist and the physical chemist find many interesting areas to explore via wide-line NMR methods, there is no doubt that the development of high-resolution NMR instrumentation opened up those realms of greatest interest to the organic and inorganic chemist. The amazing rapidity of development and acceptance of high-resolution methods is emphasized when we realize that the first NMR experiments on bulk matter were carried out only in 1945, and the first commercial spectrometer was introduced in the early 1950's. Today the inclusion of NMR data in research papers is as commonplace as reports of vibrational spectra and chemical structure proofs.

Even with the inhomogeneous magnetic fields used in the early magnetic-resonance experiments, relatively precise measurements could be

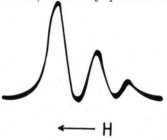

Fig. 11–19. Proton magnetic resonance spectrum of CH_3CH_2OH under conditions of low resolution. (After Arnold, Dharmatti, and Packard, *J. Chem. Phys.*, **19**, 507 (1951).)

made of the frequency and field relationships for different nuclei at resonance, and in this way accurate values of g_n for nuclei could be determined. Such activities were hardly of interest to chemists, however, until the homogeneity of the fields became good enough that it was possible to observe different resonance conditions for the same nucleus in different chemical environments. The classic example is ethanol, which was observed to display three resonance peaks at different applied fields, as shown in Fig. 11–19.

An inspection of the ethanol molecule reveals that there are three different kinds of protons in the molecule, those in the CH_3 group, two in a CH_2 group, and a single OH proton. The relative areas of the three observed peaks strongly suggest identifying each peak with one of these three kinds of protons.

It may be worthwhile at this point to review again briefly the nature of the NMR experiment by which this spectrum was obtained so that we can appreciate the significance of the different resonance peaks and their relative positions. We have stated the typical experiment involves irradiation of the sample with a fixed-frequency H_1 field while the magnetic field H_0 is varied until resonance is observed. As the magnetic field is slowly increased, we reach the field at which resonance occurs for the OH protons, and then pass on through the resonance condition, so that no signal is produced until the field at length becomes great enough for the CH_2 protons to resonate, and finally until the CH_3 protons

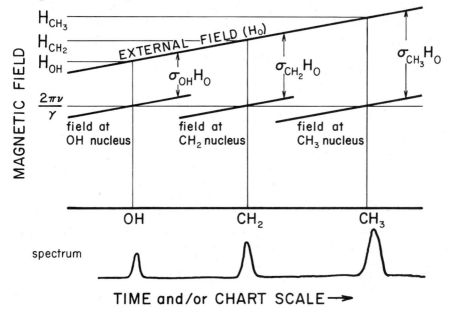

Fig. 11–20. Relation of the externally applied magnetic field and the local fields at different nuclei in a nuclear magnetic resonance experiment with ethanol.

give rise to a signal. These conditions are illustrated in Fig. 11–20, and it can be seen that the spectrum simply tells us that a greater magnetic field is required to produce resonance of the CH_3 protons than is required for the CH_2 protons to resonate or for resonance of the OH proton.

If these protons had been isolated without electrons around them, we would have observed a single resonance for all of them at a magnetic field which we can calculate from the value of g_n for the proton. For an H_1 frequency of 42.5 Mcps, for example, we would require H_0 to be 10,000 gauss. Since the protons in the molecule do not all experience resonance at the same magnetic field, we can deduce only that the electron environment must in some way change the magnetic field experienced by the nuclei, so that a different external field must be applied in each case to make the field actually experienced by each nucleus be the resonance field.

That the electrons in the molecule can influence the field at the nucleus should be no surprise, since in our discussions of magnetic effects in atoms and molecules and of diamagnetism we found that in a magnetic field electronic distributions are affected in such a way that their circulations give rise to a secondary magnetic field that is opposed to the externally applied field. Not only do we observe this secondary field externally as a diamagnetic magnetization, but the nuclei in the system experience the same secondary field, and since it is opposed to the external H_0 field, we immediately recognize that the external field will have to be increased above the resonance condition in order that the nuclei experience the H_0 required for resonance.

This effect is generally called *shielding* since the electrons are in a sense shielding the nuclei from the full effect of the external field. The changing electronic environment in different atomic and molecular groupings leads to a different electronic shielding for the nuclei in these environments. The different external fields required to cause resonance in each of these cases is commonly referred to as the *chemical shift* effect. We conclude that in the case of ethanol the electrons around the proton in a methyl group produce a greater diamagnetic field and thus more effectively shield the methyl-type proton from the external field than do the electrons in the CH_2 group or the OH group. It is therefore necessary to apply a greater magnetic field to the sample in order that the methyl protons experience the requisite resonance field.

The electronic shielding is conveniently expressed mathematically by the relation

$$H_i = H_0(1 - \sigma_i), \tag{11-23}$$

where H_i is the field actually existent at nucleus i and σ_i is the shielding coefficient. Since the shielding effect is caused by the same phenomenon as gives rise to diamagnetism, we expect a direct relation of σ to the equations we have derived in Sec. 11.2, and such is the case.

The theoretical problem is to find the perturbation on the energy of a spin system due to the joint action of the external field H and a parallel magnetic dipole $\mathbf{u}$ at the position of the nucleus in question arising from other electronic circulations in the molecule. The Hamiltonian operator representing this situation can be written

$$\mathcal{H}_1 + \mathcal{H}_2 = \frac{e}{mc} \sum_j \mathbf{A}_j \cdot \hat{\mathbf{p}}_j + \frac{e^2}{2mc^2} \sum_j |\mathbf{A}_j|^2,$$

where $\mathbf{A}_j$ is the vector potential at the position of electron j and $\mathbf{p}_j$ is the momentum of electron j. The change in energy of the system equivalent to the chemical shift is given by second-order perturbation theory as

$$\delta E = \langle 0|\mathfrak{K}_2|0\rangle - \sum_{n\neq 0} \frac{\langle 0|\mathfrak{K}_1|n\rangle\langle n|\mathfrak{K}_1|0\rangle}{E_n - E_0},$$

where the second term is summed over all excited states. The similarity to Van Vleck's equation for molecular diamagnetism is seen clearly. Ramsey has evaluated expressions for σ in these terms and obtained several equations giving σ as a function of the wave functions and energies of the excited states.[7] Since the latter are difficult to evaluate, he has also suggested a simpler form, which is

$$\sigma = \frac{e^2}{3mc^2}\left\langle 0\left|\sum_k \frac{1}{r_k}\right|0\right\rangle - \frac{4}{3\Delta E}\left\langle 0\left|\sum_{jk} \frac{\hat{\mathbf{L}}_j{}^0 \cdot \hat{\mathbf{L}}_k{}^0}{r_k{}^3}\right|0\right\rangle, \qquad (11\text{--}24)$$

where $\hat{\mathbf{L}}_j{}^0$ and $\hat{\mathbf{L}}_k{}^0$ are the orbital angular momentum operators for electrons j and k respectively and r_k is the distance from the shielded nucleus to electron k. ΔE is the average value of $E_n - E_0$ for all the excited states. In this expression, if the ground-state wave function is known accurately, then all that is required is a good estimate of ΔE to obtain values for σ. Unfortunately, even this limitation is serious, and only a few simple systems have been analyzed in a satisfactory manner.

The first term in (11–24), the so-called Lamb correction, corresponds to the shielding in a spherically symmetric system such as an isolated atom. The summation of matrix elements in this term gives the potential at the nucleus due to the surrounding electrons. The second term, because it decreases the extent of shielding, is often called the paramagnetic term. For molecular hydrogen, calculations using different forms of (11–24) lead to a shielding $\sigma = 32.1 \times 10^{-6}$ for the first term and a paramagnetic term of -5.5×10^{-6}, so that the net shielding constant for H_2 is $\sigma = 26.6 \times 10^{-6}$. From (11–23) we can see that, if H_2 is placed in a magnetic field of 10,000 gauss, the actual field at the location of a proton will be on the average only 9,999.734 gauss. Such a difference may seem small, but the precision and stability of radiofrequency oscillators and the ability to produce field homogeneities of the order of one part in 10^9 over small sample volumes results in such small shieldings being highly significant and easily measured.

The chemical shifts measured for other nuclei such as F^{19} and B^{11} are of the order of 100 times as great as proton shieldings, so that measurements are even more simply made for these elements. Calculation of proton chemical shifts is complicated by the fact that in molecules the paramagnetic shifts and anisotropies may often be of the same order of

[7] Ramsey, *Phys. Rev.*, **78**, 699 (1950).

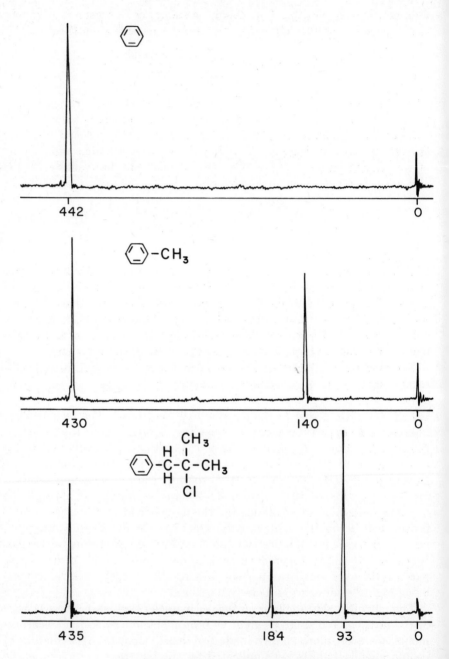

Fig. 11–21.   Nuclear magnetic resonance spectra of proton
from tetramethylsilane as zero.   All spectr

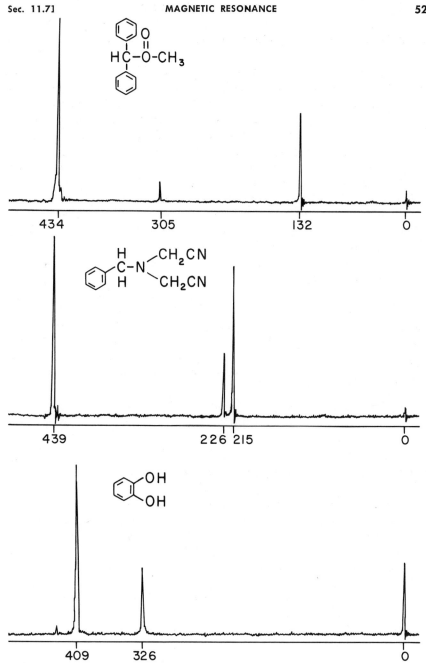

measured at 60 Mcps.   Chemical shifts are measured in cps
are with increasing magnetic field to the right.

magnitude as the diamagnetic term, so that simple estimates are not made easily.

Although theoretical calculations of chemical shifts in proton-containing molecules are rudimentary, empirical correlations have nonetheless been highly successful. Experimentally, it is found that in spite of small shifts in different molecules many structural units containing protons show resonance at characteristic fields, and the presence of resonance peaks with certain chemical shifts is an indication of these structural groups in the sample. This is seen most clearly in an example. In Fig. 11–21 are shown several proton magnetic resonance spectra. The small peak at the highest magnetic field is caused by a small amount of tetramethylsilane, $Si(CH_3)_4$, which has been dissolved in the sample to serve as an internal reference. All chemical shifts are then measured from the tetramethylsilane peak.

It can be seen that in all the aromatic compounds there is a resonance peak near the same location, and the same is true of all the compounds with a CH_3 group or a CH_2 group. Since the energy absorbed from the radiation field, or the voltage induced in the receiver coil, should be proportional to the number of nuclei undergoing resonance, the integrated area of each peak should be proportional to the number of nuclei of the corresponding type. From relative areas and chemical shifts of observed resonance lines one can begin to deduce the number of kinds of protons in a sample.

The measurement and reporting of chemical shifts in the literature has been marred unfortunately by considerable confusion. In the first place, the precision in measuring differences in chemical shift is not nearly matched by an ability to measure an absolute value of the magnetic field for a resonance peak, and the lack of theoretical values of the shielding constant does not help this problem. In addition, the chemical shift depends on the strength of the magnetic field applied to the sample, as can be seen from Eq. (11–23). If the separation of two resonance peaks which arise because of two different shielding constants σ_1 and σ_2 are measured at a field of 9396 gauss and 40 Mc (for protons), it will be found that the separation in gauss between the peaks will be two-thirds ($\frac{40}{60}$) as great as the separations observed at 14,094 gauss and 60 Mc. If chemical shifts are to be reported in absolute field units, or the frequency units to which they are equivalent, then the value of the static field and the frequency of the oscillating field must be carefully specified so that the shielding constants can be calculated.

Some degree of agreement has been reached concerning the measurement and reporting of shifts in NMR spectra. Since shifts are proportional to the applied field, it is desirable to report them in field-independent units, and to do this the chemical shift is often reported relative to a standard resonance peak, often in parts per million (ppm) of the static field, as

$$\delta = (\sigma_r - \sigma_i) \times 10^6 = \frac{H_i - H_r}{H_0} \times 10^6, \qquad (11\text{--}25)$$

where H_i is the strength of the magnetic field at which resonance occurs for the kind of nucleus being described, H_r is the field at which a reference peak resonates, and H_0 is the approximate value of the static field and is essentially equal to both H_i and H_r since these are nearly the same. From the proportionality between field strength and resonance frequency we can also write

$$\delta = \frac{\nu_i - \nu_r}{\nu_0} \times 10^6. \qquad (11\text{--}26)$$

This equation is particularly useful because, although the resonance peaks are generally displayed in a spectrum as a function of the applied magnetic field, the actual experimental measurement of chemical shifts is very conveniently carried out by a method that determines the frequency difference. This method is based on the fact that if either the H_1 field or the static field is modulated by introducing an audiofrequency voltage from an audio oscillator, then sidebands will be produced on either side of each resonance peak, and these sidebands will be spaced from the resonance peak by a distance in frequency units exactly equal to the frequency of the modulating signal. Since the latter can be measured exactly by means of an electronic counter, the sidebands can then be used to determine the separation of resonance peaks from one another by extrapolation, interpolation, superposition, and similar techniques.

In the early days of high resolution NMR, a number of convenient compounds such as benzene, water, and cyclohexane were used as reference compounds. As the precision of measurements increased, however, it became apparent that additional effects were of a consequential magnitude. In addition to shielding of a nucleus by the electrons in a molecule, the field at the molecule is also affected by the bulk magnetic susceptibility of the sample itself, which alters the field as in Eqs. (11–1) and (11–2). It is actually the magnetic induction that is experienced in a bulk medium. In addition, the susceptibility of any container surrounding the sample will affect the field at the molecule. Corrections to the chemical shift can be made if the susceptibilities of all the media are known, but a simpler method of automatically taking these effects into account is to use a dilute reference compound which is dissolved in the sample and which experiences all the same effects as the molecules of interest. For protons a suitable reference appears to be tetramethylsilane (TMS; see Fig. 11–21). For this reason the recent literature most often refers to TMS as the internal reference compound.

The resonance of tetramethylsilane is found to be at a higher field than almost all other types of hydrogen, and for this reason Eqs. (11–25) and (11–26) will give negative chemical shifts for most compounds. To avoid negative numbers an additional chemical shift, τ, has been suggested, which uses TMS as the reference compound and then assigns to TMS a positive shift of 10.00 ppm. Thus,

$$\tau = 10.00 + \delta, \tag{11–27}$$

where δ and therefore τ are expressed in ppm. Although the τ system is being employed widely, recent commercial instrumentation has employed chart paper calibrated with shifts measured from TMS as zero and with a positive shift for peaks at a lower field than TMS. Comparison of shift measurements in the literature will therefore continue to require careful examination for the basis of the reported shifts.

One of the most promising developments in recent years has been the introduction of commercial instrumentation which by means either of highly stable permanent magnets or of lock-in circuits is able to reproduce spectra as a function of the applied field and displays the spectra on chart paper already calibrated in terms of frequency and ppm shifts. This type of instrumentation should encourage even more widespread use of NMR by chemists.

Some examples of chemical shifts observed for protons are given in Table 11–5. Extensive compilations of shifts and spectra, some of which are found in the references at the end of this chapter, provide comparisons between the shifts of different structural types of protons as well as shifts of the same type of protons in different molecules. Not only do such comparisons lead to deductions about the electronic distributions in molecules, but they also provide an extremely useful basis for deciding on an exact structure of a molecule from measured shifts.

Many correlations have been made between chemical shifts and such factors as the electronegativities of substituents in the molecule, resonance effects, steric effects, and hydrogen bonding. It has been noticed, for example, that the electronegativity of substituents attached to an ethyl group can be correlated to the difference in chemical shift between the CH_2 and CH_3 protons. For protons such correlations are not always satisfactory because the paramagnetic effects of nearby atoms or groups on the shielding and anisotropies in the shielding are an important contribution to proton shifts. The chemical shifts of protons in benzene, for example, might be expected to be somewhat like those found in olefins, but instead the benzene resonance is at a considerably lower applied field. Examination of Fig. 11–2 discloses an explanation of this anomaly; for we see there that, when the molecule is perpendicular to the static field, the induced motions of the π electrons produce a secondary

TABLE 11–5. Typical Chemical Shifts of H^1

Compound	Shift (τ) (ppm)	Compound	Shift (τ) (ppm)
Methyl Protons		$(CH_3)CCHCH_2Br$	8.20
$(CH_3)_4Si$	10.000	Bicyclo[2.2.1]heptane	7.81
$CH_3(CH_2)_3CH_3$	9.15	Bicyclo[2.2.1]hepta-2,5-diene	6.53
$(CH_3)_4C$	9.08		
CH_3CH_2OH	8.83	*Olefinic Protons*	
CH_3CH_2Cl	8.60	$(CH_3)_2C=CH_2$	5.4
CH_3CH_2Br	8.34	$(CH_3)_2C=CHCH_3$	4.79
$(CH_3)_2C=CH_2$	8.299	1-Methyl cyclohexene	4.70
CH_3CN	8.026	$(C_6H_5)_2C=CH_2$	4.60
$(CH_3)_2S$	7.942	Cyclohexene	4.43
CH_3COOH_3	7.915	Cyclohexa-1,3-diene	4.22
CH_3I	7.84	$CH_3CH=CHCHO$	3.95
$CH_3C_6H_5$	7.66	Cyclopentadiene	3.58
CH_3Br	7.38	$Cl_2C=CHCl$	3.55
CH_3Cl	7.00	Bicyclo[2.2.1]hepta-2,5-diene	3.35
$(CH_3)_2O$	6.73	*cis*-Stilbene	3.51
CH_3OH	6.62	*trans*-Stilbene	3.01
$CH_3OC_6H_5$	6.27		
CH_3F	5.70	*Acetylenic Protons*	
CH_3NO_2	5.72	$HOCH_2C\equiv CH$	7.67
		$CLCH_2C\equiv CH$	7.60
Methylene Protons		$C_6H_5C\equiv CH$	7.07
Cyclopropane	9.78	$CH_3COC\equiv CH$	6.83
$CH_3(CH_2)_4CH_3$	8.75		
Cyclohexane	8.56	*Aromatic Protons*	
Cyclopentane	8.49	Pyrrole (β)	3.93
Bicyclo[2.2.1]hepta-2,5-diene	8.05	Furan (β)	3.72
Cyclopentanone	7.98	Pyrrole (α)	3.47
1.3-Cyclohexadiene	7.74	Mesitylene	3.36
$(CH_3CH_2)_2CO$	7.61	Thiophene (β)	2.94
$(CH_3CH_2)_2N$	7.58	Toluene	2.91
$CH_3COCH_2COOCH_3$	6.52	Thiophene (α)	2.83
$(CH_3CH_2)_2O$	6.64	Benzene	2.73
$CH_3COCH_2COCH_3$	6.45	Furan (α)	2.64
CH_3CH_2OH	6.41	C_6H_5CN	2.46
Tetrahydrofuran	6.37	Naphthalene	2.27
$HC=CCH_2Cl$	5.91	Pyridine (γ)	2.64
$HC\equiv CCH_2OH$	5.82	(β)	3.015
$C_6H_5CH_2OH$	5.61	(α)	1.50
Methine Protons		*Aldehydic Protons*	
Chlorocyclopropane	7.05	$(CH_3)_2N-CHO$	2.16
$(CH_3)_2CHNH_2$	7.05	CH_3OCHO	1.97
Chlorocyclohexane	6.08	$(CH_3)_2CHCHO$	.44
$(CH_3)_2CHOH$	6.05	$C_6H_5CH=CHCHO$	.37
$(CH_3)_2CHCl$	5.88	CH_3CHO	.284
$(CH_3)_2CHBr$	5.83	p-$CH_3OC_6H_4CHO$	.199
		C_6H_5CHO	.035

field at the protons in the plane of the molecule, which is in the same direction as the applied field. When the molecule is parallel to the field, there are no such secondary fields. The net result over all possible orientations is that on the average the benzene protons will experience secondary field which tends to "unshield" the protons compared to the shielding that exists when such π electron circulations are not possible.

Precise measurements of proton chemical shifts have emphasized the need for a more thorough understanding of electronic circulations in

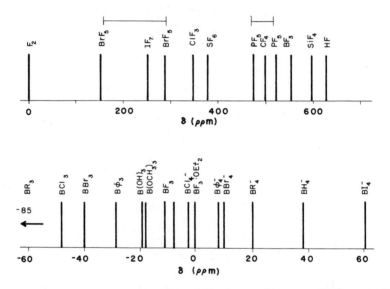

Fig. 11–22. Typical chemical shifts of fluorine and boron. Shifts are given in ppm with increasing magnetic field to the right.

molecules. As mentioned in the discussion of diamagnetism, recent studies have been concerned with breaking the total effect into smaller localized effects, and these attempts have been promising not only from the standpoint of reliable predictions, but also because they may lead to useful means of visualizing the effects of bond anisotropies, ring currents, hydrogen bond formation, and similar phenomena in specific cases.

Chemical shifts have also been studied extensively for other magnetic nuclei, and examples of typical results have been collected in Fig. 11–22. In the shifts for F^{19} the effect of the electronegativity of the attached atom can be clearly seen. Calculations of the chemical shift of fluorine have been moderately successful because the primary effects are caused by the single p electron involved in the bonding. In the case of B^{11} not only are electronegativity effects observed, but changes in hybridization can be seen to be important. Comparison of such shifts permits deductions about "back donation," double-bond formation, and other interactions of chemical interest. Discussion of these factors in the literature is extensive, and the reader may examine the references for more information. Elements for which such shifts have been measured include H^1, B^{11}, C^{13}, N^{14}, O^{17}, F^{19}, Si^{29}, P^{31}, Sn^{119}, and others.

11.8   FINE STRUCTURE AND SPIN–SPIN INTERACTIONS

With the development of magnetic fields with a very high degree of homogeneity it became apparent that there are more significant details in nuclear magnetic resonance spectra than the different peaks observed because of chemical shift effects. It was found, for example, that in the PO_3F^{-2} ion, although there is structurally only one kind of phosphorus atom and one kind of fluorine atom, the F^{19} resonance spectrum consists of two peaks separated by about 860 cps, and the P^{31} resonance spectrum also consists of two lines separated by the same amount. In addition, it is found that, unlike chemical shifts which are proportional to the applied magnetic field, these splittings of 860 cps are independent of the magnetic field at which the resonances are observed. Clearly some new interaction is involved.

Another example of such fine structure splittings of NMR lines is found in HD. The H^1 resonance (observed, say, at 42.577 Mcps and 10,000 gauss) consists of three lines with the separation between adjacent lines amounting to 43 cps. The H^2 resonance (which could be observed also at 10,000 gauss but at a frequency of 6.536 Mcps) consists of two lines also separated by 43 cps.

In both these cases the identical splittings suggest that there is some interaction between the unlike nuclear spins. We further note that there is a similarity between the number of lines observed for one nucleus and the possible orientations $(2I + 1)$ of the other nuclear spin in a magnetic field. In the first example, both the fluorine and the phosphorus nuclei have a spin of $\frac{1}{2}$, and both lines are split into doublets. In the second case, the proton has a spin of $\frac{1}{2}$, and the deuterium resonance is split into a doublet, while the deuterium nucleus has a spin of 1, and the proton spectrum is split into three peaks.

Nuclear spin-spin interactions of this sort are not confined to unlike nuclear species. In Fig. 11–23 we see the proton magnetic resonance spectrum of acetaldehyde, CH_3CHO, as observed at 60 Mcps. We can immediately identify the larger peak as that arising from the resonance of the methyl protons and the smaller peak at low field as the aldehydic proton. In addition to the chemical shift effects we can see a splitting of both resonances. The CH_3 peak is split into a doublet with the splitting amounting to 2.85 cps, while the aldehyde resonance is a quartet of the same splitting. It appears that, so long as two nuclei are in different magnetic environments, we can observe their interaction with each other, but for completely equivalent nuclei we cannot. Thus, in H_2 or in H_2O no splittings are observed.

A search for the possible cause of these splittings reveals that they cannot be caused by direct nuclear dipole-dipole interactions, as we might infer from the connection between the nuclear spin orientations and the number of lines produced, because the random motions of molecules in liquids and gases will carry the spin pairs through all possible orientations

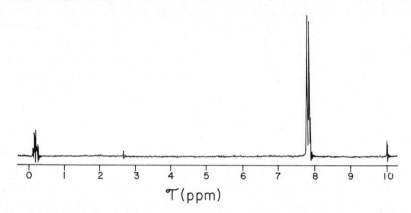

$\mathcal{T}$ (ppm)

Fig. 11–23. Proton magnetic resonance spectrum of acetaldehyde, CH_3CHO, measured at 60 Mcps and 14,100 gauss.

with respect to the field and average out any such splittings. In addition, we do not observe splittings for pairs of identical nuclei.

Ramsey and Purcell[8] suggested that these effects are caused by an indirect nuclear spin-spin interaction which is transmitted by the electron spins in the molecule. The hyperfine structure of atomic spectra disclosed that there are nuclear-electron spin interactions in which the nuclear spin orientations have an effect on the energies of the possible electron spin orientations. Thus, with a nuclear spin in a certain state, the electron spin associated closely with that nucleus will also be in an energetically preferred spin state. In a molecule the interactions of electron spins are commonly such that the spins of electrons involved in a covalent bond will be paired with opposite spins. In other words, the orientation of one electron spin will determine which orientation of the other electron will be preferred. The interaction of this electron with a second nucleus will again transmit a particular magnetic field at the nucleus for a particular electron spin orientation. If the orientation of the first nuclear spin changes, then this will be transmitted via the

[8] Ramsey and Purcell, *Phys. Rev.*, **85**, 143 (1952).

nuclear-electron, electron-electron, and electron-nuclear interactions, to result in a different local field at the second nucleus. In this way the second nucleus will experience a slightly different field with each orientation of the first nucleus, and since this is caused by internal interactions, the orientation of the molecule and the magnitude of external fields will have no effect on the resulting differences in energy of the nuclear system. This mechanism is shown schematically in Fig. 11–24 for HD.

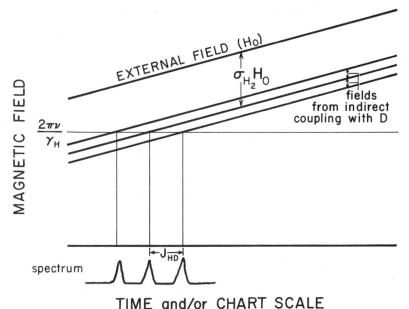

Fig. 11–24. Relation of magnetic fields caused by electronic shielding and indirect nuclear spin-spin interaction in HD (H[1] resonance experiment).

In this illustration it can be seen that the split lines will be of equal intensity, since the differences in energy of various spin orientations are so small that in a large number of molecules each spin state will be equally populated and hence equal numbers of the other nucleus will experience each of the different possible local fields. In molecules with more than one nucleus of a given structural type, this will not be so. In the case of acetaldehyde, for example, the two possible orientations of the aldehyde proton spin will cause two different local fields at the methyl protons via the indirect coupling and thus cause two resonance lines (Fig. 11–25). If we consider the possible spin orientations of the methyl protons, we observe that, all the ways in which we can combine the orientations of the three methyl spins, there will result four different net spins in the z direction, and hence there will be produced four different local fields at the aldehyde proton and four resonance lines for the aldehyde proton. But there are three different ways in which two of these net spins states can be produced, depending on which spins are oriented up and which are down, while for the two states with both spins in the same direction only one possibility exists for obtaining each. Thus we expect that three times as many aldehyde protons will experience the local fields produced by the former two of the spin combinations of the

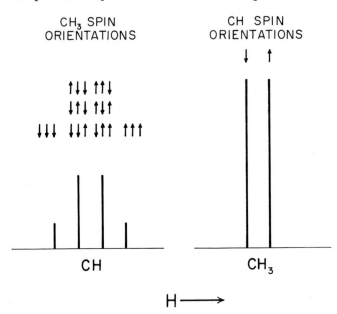

Fig. 11–25. Spin-spin splittings in acetaldehyde.

methyl protons as will experience the latter two fields. This gives rise to the intensities, which are seen to be in the ratio $1:3:3:1$.

This qualitative picture of nuclear spin-spin interactions is sufficient for understanding many typical magnetic resonance spectra of even greater complication. In Fig. 11–26, for example, we see the simultaneous splitting of the CH_2 protons in ethanol by both the methyl and the OH protons. The splittings are not quite equal in these two cases, so that a fairly complex pattern is obtained.

While the qualitative arguments used in analyzing spin-spin splittings of NMR spectra are often correct, a study of many spectra shows that not only are the spacings and intensities of many lines not exactly the same as predicted by this method, but additional lines are often present that are unexplained in this simple model. We must turn again to a more exact quantum-mechanical explanation.

The theoretical derivation of an expression for the coupling of nuclear spins is not simple, and we will here only indicate the nature of its formulation. If we consider all the possible interactions between electrons and nuclei in an atomic or molecular system, we find that the Hamiltonian operator describing the motions of the electrons in the field of

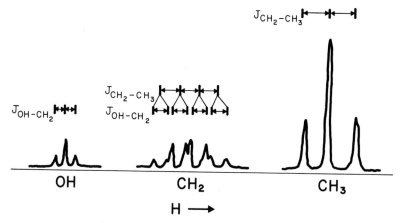

Fig. 11–26.   Spin-spin splittings in ethanol.

the nuclei can be expressed as

$$\mathcal{H} = \mathcal{H}_1 + \mathcal{H}_2 + \mathcal{H}_3,$$

where the first term is

$$\mathcal{H}_1 = \sum_k \frac{1}{2m_e} \left(\frac{\hbar}{i} \nabla_k + \frac{e}{c} \sum_N \hbar \gamma_N \hat{\mathbf{I}}_N \times \frac{\mathbf{r}_{kN}}{r_{kN}^3} \right)^2 + V + \mathcal{H}_{LL} + \mathcal{H}_{LS} + \mathcal{H}_{SS}.$$

We recognize in this term the kinetic energy of the electrons, k, and their interaction as moving charged particles in the magnetic field of the nuclei, N. The remaining parts, V, $\mathcal{H}_{LL}$, $\mathcal{H}_{LS}$, and $\mathcal{H}_{SS}$ are the electrostatic potential energy (terms in e^2/r) and the electron orbital-orbital, spin-orbital, and spin-spin interactions. The forms of these interactions have not been written here because they do not include the nuclear spin and hence are not of interest in the present question.

The second term, $\mathcal{H}_2$, of the general Hamiltonian operator represents the dipole-dipole interactions between the nuclear magnetic moments and the electronic magnetic moments and has the form

$$\mathcal{H}_2 = 2\mu_B \hbar \sum_k \sum_N \gamma_N [3(\hat{\mathbf{S}}_k \cdot \mathbf{r}_{kN})(\hat{\mathbf{I}}_N \cdot \mathbf{r}_{kN}) r_{kN}^{-5} - (\hat{\mathbf{S}}_k \cdot \hat{\mathbf{I}}_N) r_{kN}^{-3}].$$

The final term, $\mathfrak{3C}_3$, is

$$\mathfrak{3C}_3 = \frac{16\pi\mu_B\hbar}{3} \sum_k \sum_N \gamma_N \delta(\mathbf{r}_{kN}) \hat{\mathbf{S}}_k \cdot \hat{\mathbf{I}}_N,$$

where $\delta(\mathbf{r}_{kN})$ is the Dirac delta function, which considers only the value $\mathbf{r}_{kN} = 0$ in any integration over the coordinates of electron k, and which therefore is concerned with the properties of the electrons at the location of the nucleus. It was derived from relativistic quantum mechanics by Fermi and is often called the Fermi contact term. It is this term that is of primary significance in the indirect spin-spin coupling.

The analysis of these interactions requires second-order perturbation theory. Part of the interaction is found to arise via the contact coupling term. The total interaction is found to have the form

$$\Delta E = hJ_{NN'}\mathbf{I}_N \cdot \mathbf{I}_{N'},$$

and expressions have been derived for calculating $J_{NN'}$, the coupling constant, which is measured in units of cycles per second. The calculation of coupling constants again involves detailed knowledge of wave functions and energies of different states of the molecule, and hence few detailed calculations have been possible. There have been a number of useful studies using both molecular-orbital and valence-bond methods which have disclosed interesting estimates of coupling constants and their dependence on various factors of molecular geometry. These will be discussed shortly. In the meantime we will recognize the reality that most information about coupling constants comes directly from experimental measurements rather than theory.

For a collection of nuclear spins, then, we can write a Hamiltonian operator which describes both the effects of the applied field and the smaller perturbing effects of the indirect spin-spin coupling. The unperturbed Hamiltonian for a system of spins is formed easily from Eq. (11–17), which gave the Hamiltonian for a single spin in a magnetic field. The result is

$$\mathfrak{3C}^0 = -\sum_i \gamma_i\hbar\hat{\mathbf{I}}_i \cdot \mathbf{H}_i = -\hbar \sum_i \gamma_i \mathsf{H}_i \hat{I}_z(i), \tag{11–28}$$

where H_i is the magnetic field (assumed as usual to be in the z direction) actually experienced by nucleus i and can be determined from the applied field H_0 and the screening constants by Eq. (11–23). The unperturbed energy of the system of spins is simply the sum of all the individual energies with the effects of electronic screening included.

The indirect coupling is then given by the perturbation Hamiltonian

$$\mathcal{H}' = -\hbar \sum_{i<j} \sum J_{ij} \hat{\mathbf{I}}_i \cdot \hat{\mathbf{I}}_j, \qquad (11\text{-}29)$$

where all possible pairs of nuclei are included in the summation.

We have not attempted to discuss in detail the form of spin angular momentum operators because they are not simply derived from classical expressions as in the case of orbital angular momentum. They are conveniently expressed in the form of 2×2 matrices. We do know, however, that they have certain properties in common with all angular momentum operators, and we also know that suitable spin wave functions for a system must be eigenfunctions of $\hat{S}^2$, $\hat{S}_z$, $\hat{I}^2$, and $\hat{I}_z$. We have used the symbols α and β to describe spin functions for electron spins, and the same terminology will here be used for nuclear spins. That is, α is the spin function which for a nucleus with $I = \frac{1}{2}$ will be an eigenfunction of $\hat{I}_z$ with the eigenvalue $\frac{1}{2}\hbar$, while β is the spin function for a nucleus with the eigenvalue $-\frac{1}{2}\hbar$. These eigenvalues are the magnitudes of I_z for these two possible spin states of the nucleus with $I = \frac{1}{2}$.

In the unperturbed system described by $\mathcal{H}^0$ we could construct wave functions that are eigenfunctions of the Hamiltonian operator and obtain the corresponding energies. Let us consider the simple system of two spins both with $I = \frac{1}{2}$. We will also consider that they are not identical nuclei. A set of suitable wave functions would be

$$\psi_1 = \alpha(A)\alpha(B),$$
$$\psi_2 = \alpha(A)\beta(B),$$
$$\psi_3 = \beta(A)\alpha(B),$$
$$\psi_4 = \beta(A)\beta(B),$$

and from Eqs. (11–28) and (11–18) the energies of the pair of spins described by each one of these wave functions would be

$$E_1 = -\gamma_A \hbar (\tfrac{1}{2}) \mathsf{H}_A - \gamma_B \hbar (\tfrac{1}{2}) \mathsf{H}_B,$$
$$E_2 = -\gamma_A \hbar (\tfrac{1}{2}) \mathsf{H}_A + \gamma_B \hbar (\tfrac{1}{2}) \mathsf{H}_B,$$
$$E_3 = +\gamma_A \hbar (\tfrac{1}{2}) \mathsf{H}_A - \gamma_B \hbar (\tfrac{1}{2}) \mathsf{H}_B,$$
$$E_4 = +\gamma_A \hbar (\tfrac{1}{2}) \mathsf{H}_A + \gamma_B \hbar (\tfrac{1}{2}) \mathsf{H}_B.$$

If the two nuclei are not the same either because they are different species or because different electronic shieldings result in different H_i's, then the two terms in the energy expressions will not be equal, and four energy levels will result. These are illustrated in Fig. 11–27. If the two spins are completely identical, then, of course, the wave functions describing the system must take into account their indistinguishability, and the familiar singlet and triplet states would result with only three possible energies for the system. These are illustrated also in Fig. 11–27.

If we now conduct a nuclear resonance experiment and apply a small oscillating field sufficient to cause transitions from one spin state to another, we must add a second perturbation term to the Hamiltonian

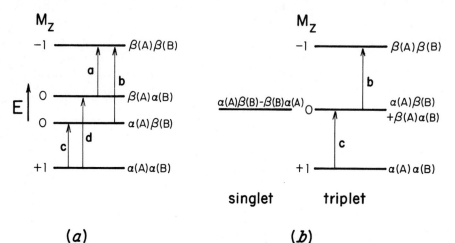

Fig. 11–27. Energy levels for a pair of nuclei with spin $\frac{1}{2}$ in the absence of spin coupling interactions: (a) non-equivalent nuclei; (b) equivalent nuclei.

of the form given in (11–19), where we now express the interaction of the field with the net nuclear moment of the nuclei in the x direction:

$$\mathcal{K}'' = 2H_1\hat{M}_x \cos 2\pi\nu t,$$

where

$$\hat{M}_x = \hbar \sum_i \gamma_i \hat{I}_x(i).$$

The result of applying this additional perturbation is that transitions can take place only between states that differ in one of the spins i and also $\Delta M_I = \pm 1$, where $M_I = \Sigma_i M_I(i)$. In the two-spin system we are considering, the allowed transitions are illustrated in Fig. 11–27, and the resulting spectral lines are shown schematically in Fig. 11–28. It can be seen that in the absence of the coupling perturbation the transitions are exactly what we would have predicted from considering each nucleus by itself. The spacing of the energy levels in Fig. 11–27 and the separation of the lines in Fig. 11–28 depend, of course, on the non-equivalence of the two nuclei. If they are completely different species, then the separation of the lines will be of the order of at least several Mcps, and in a practical experiment we would observe the resonance line for only one of the nuclei and would have to alter the experiment to a quite distant frequency to observe the other. If, on the other hand, the difference arises only because of shielding effects on the same species, then the separation of the lines will be small enough that both can be observed at some fixed frequency with only a moderate sweep of the magnetic field, or at the same field with only a small change in frequency.

What if we now introduce $\mathcal{3C}'$, which describes the perturbation caused by the nuclear-electron-nuclear indirect spin coupling? We will find in

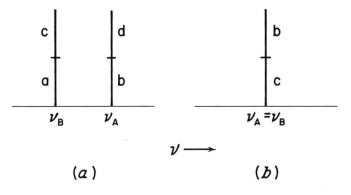

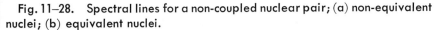

Fig. 11–28. Spectral lines for a non-coupled nuclear pair; (a) non-equivalent nuclei; (b) equivalent nuclei.

this case that our simple product spin functions are no longer eigenfunctions of the new Hamiltonian ($\mathcal{3C}^0 + \mathcal{3C}'$). In order to obtain spin functions that properly describe the possible states in this new system, we might apply the variation method and use as our wave functions linear combinations of the simple first-order functions.

Recalling the principles involved in the variation method, we would then construct a trial function of the form

$$\psi = c_1\psi_1 + c_2\psi_2 + c_3\psi_3 + c_4\psi_4,$$

insert this function in the variation integral

$$W = \int \psi^*(\mathcal{3C}^0 + \mathcal{3C}')\psi \, d\tau,$$

then take the derivative of W with respect to each of the four coefficients, set each derivative equal to zero to obtain a minimum in W, and thus approach as nearly as possible the correct energy. The four derivatives will result in four simultaneous equations, giving us a 4×4 secular determinant which can be solved for the energies of the states. From the properties of the spin operators and the spin functions most of the off-diagonal matrix elements are found to be zero, and for the two-spin case

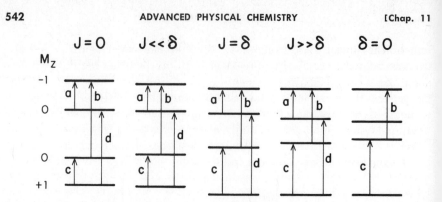

Fig. 11–29. Energy levels for the coupled two-spin system for various ratios of coupling constant and chemical shift.

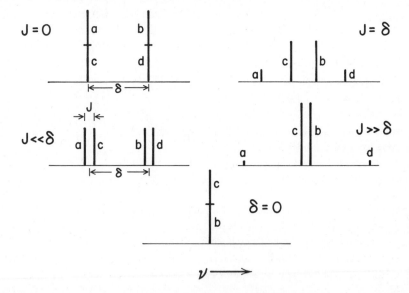

Fig. 11–30. Theoretical spectra for the two-spin system for various values of J and δ.

the result is shown in Fig. 11–29 along with the levels for the non-coupled case. The energies are indicated in the figure for each state. The selection rules upon application of the resonance perturbation $\mathcal{H}''$ are again found to be $\Delta M = \pm 1$, with the spin of one nucleus changing. The probabilities of these transitions are no longer equal, however, and the resulting line intensities will be altered. We will not attempt to discuss calculation of these intensities here, but they are indicated in the schematic spectra shown in Fig. 11–30. It is obvious from the equations for the energy levels that the spacings will alter with the relative magnitudes of the differences in H_i for the two nuclei (and hence with the value of δ) and the spin-spin coupling constant J. These effects also are shown in Figs. 11–29 and 11–30. It is apparent from these diagrams why coupling nuclei which have identical electronic environments, and thus have the same chemical shift, do not give rise to splittings of their own resonance line.

Analyses such as this can be extended to more complex systems to determine the line positions and intensities even when several spins are interacting. Such analyses have been highly successful, and recent high-speed computer programs have enabled calculations of many possible cases of shift and coupling ratios. Programs have even been devised that introduce an artificial line shape, so that spectra can be printed by the computer and then compared with experimental results.

The magnitudes of spin-spin couplings depend on many factors. For protons they are generally small, as are proton chemical shifts. Other nuclei show spin-spin splittings which may be much larger. Although it is generally true that couplings are stronger for adjacent nuclei in a molecule, there are many interesting cases of rather long-range interactions in molecules. Experimental and theoretical studies have been able to relate coupling constants to such parameters as the dihedral angle between adjacent C—H bonds and the amount of s-character in the atomic orbital of an atom. In addition, therefore, to being useful for identifying two nuclei as being in a certain configuration in a molecule, the spin-spin coupling constants can provide an interesting tool for understanding the specific electronic properties of a molecular system. Some examples of typical couplings are given in Table 11–6.

For practical structural determinations the combination of chemical shift data and spin-spin splitting information often is sufficient to determine unambiguously the structure of a molecule, often even to the extent of deciding upon the existence of *cis* or *trans* isomers or a particular ring conformation. In the case of ethanol, for example, the chemical shifts of the three main resonance peaks suggest the identification of CH_3, CH_2, and OH protons, while the splittings both confirm these assignments and also fix the CH_2 between the OH and CH_3 group by virtue of the two interactions. Even in extremely complex molecules, certain characteristic groupings can often be identified, with useful information resulting therefrom. The analysis of NMR spectra requires some practice, and the reader is referred to the problems at the end of the chapter as well as to the references for a number of typical examples. The most thorough analyses will include a complete study of the shift-splitting ratios and their effects on line positions and intensities.

TABLE 11–6. Typical Spin-Spin Coupling Constants

Coupling	Constant (cps)	Coupling	Constant (cps)	
Proton-Proton	J_{HH}	*Proton-Fluorine and Fluorine-Fluorine*	$J_{HF}(X = H)$	$J_{FF}(X = F)$
	12–15		44–81	158
CH—CH	2–9	CX—CF	7–13	—
CH—(C)$_n$—CH	0	CX—C—CF	0	11
	0–3.5		1–8	33–58
	6–14		12–40	115–124
	11–18	*o* / *m* / *p*	6–10 / 5–6 / 0	20 / 2–4 / 12–15
	4–10	*Others*		
		BH_4^-	$J_{BH} = 81$	
	0.5–2.0	$(BH)_3(NH)_3$	$J_{BH} = 136$	
		PF_3	$J_{PF} = 1400$	
C=CH—CH=C	10–13	PF_5	$J_{PF} = 930$	
		$(CH_3)_4Si$	$J_{CH} = 120$	
o / *m* / *p*	7–10 / 2–3 / 1	$CHCl=CHCl$	$J_{CH} = 203$	
CH—C≡CH	2–3	C_6H_6	$J_{CH} = 159$	

11.9 THE STUDY OF RATE PROCESSES BY NMR

The brief discussion of relaxation processes in Sec. 11.5 suggested that the rate at which the magnetic environment of a nucleus changes has an important bearing on the nature of the NMR absorption, particularly with respect to line width and intensity.   These effects, while sometimes a disturbing factor in trying to apply spectral features to the determination of structure, can be employed advantageously to obtain information about the rates of processes that have an effect on nuclear environments.

A simple example of such rate factors is seen in the proton resonance

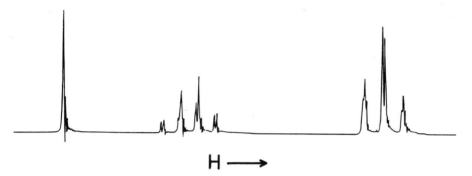

H ⟶

Fig. 11–31. Proton magnetic resonance spectrum of acidified ethanol. This can be compared with the spectrum of pure ethanol in Fig. 11–26.

spectrum of ethanol (Fig. 11–26).   Here the OH proton resonance is split into a triplet by the spin-spin coupling interaction with the CH_2 protons. If a trace of H^+ or OH^- is added to the ethanol, a marked change takes place, and the resulting spectrum appears as shown in Fig. 11–31.

The most distinctive changes have occurred in the OH and CH_2 absorptions.   The former is now a single peak, and the latter a quartet.   These features are consistent with the assumption that the OH-CH_2 coupling has been removed, and only the CH_2-CH_3 coupling remains.   It will be noticed that there are still more details in the CH_2 and CH_3 peaks than are accounted for by simple qualitative arguments.   These are second-order splittings which can be predicted from the more complete quantum-mechanical treatment of the spin-spin interactions.

The explanation for this disappearance of the OH-CH_2 coupling in acidified alcohol is that the H^+ ions enhance the rate of exchange of protons from one molecular environment to another, the rate being so great in acidified systems that a particular OH proton does not spend sufficient time in the environment of one molecule to respond to that environment, but instead can respond only to an average of all the environments that it experiences.   Even if the environment does not differ significantly from one molecule to another, the lifetime of a given nucleus in a given spin state in a given molecule is too short to establish the spin-spin coupling interaction, so that neither the OH protons which are exchanging nor the CH_2 protons with which they would couple are split.

Exchange of protons between different environments also is observed. In pure ethanol most of the protons are involved in hydrogen bonds to neighboring-molecule oxygen atoms, and presumably the liquid contains long polymeric chains of hydrogen-bonded molecules. Thus the chemical shift of the OH protons in pure ethanol is characteristic of the proton

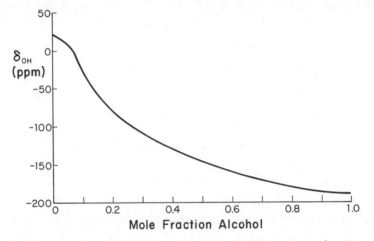

Fig. 11–32. Chemical shift of the OH peak of *t*-butanol as a function of the concentration of the alcohol in CCl_4. Shifts are measured relative to the CH_3 resonance peak.

environment in such a hydrogen bond. If, however, the ethanol is dissolved in a non-interacting solvent such as CCl_4 or cyclohexane, the OH resonance is observed to move to higher and higher applied fields. As the solution of ethanol in solvent approaches infinite dilution, the OH resonance has actually moved to a higher applied field than the CH_3 resonance. A plot of this behavior is illustrated in Fig. 11–32. Toward infinite dilution the chemical shift of the OH protons appears to approach a limiting value.

The explanation for this behavior is again easily comprehended. In pure ethanol essentially all the OH protons are experiencing the environment of a hydrogen bond, while at infinite dilution in an inert solvent none of the OH protons are involved in hydrogen bonds. At any intermediate concentration both kinds of protons will exist in the solution, but we do not observe separate resonances for the monomeric and hydrogen-bonded protons because the rate at which the hydrogen bonds are made and broken again is so rapid that a given proton can respond only to an average environment intermediate between the two extremes. Thus, a peak is observed somewhere between the two extreme chemical shifts for OH. It would be expected that the position of this peak depends on the relative amounts of the two kinds of protons, and this dependence has been used to calculate equilibrium constants for the hydrogen-bonding interaction in alcohols and similar systems.

The exchange process between different magnetic environments can be described in terms of the rate of exchange from one situation to

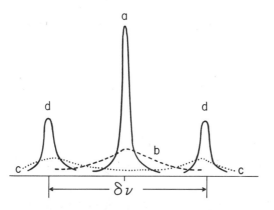

Fig. 11–33. Theoretical magnetic resonance line shapes in a chemically exchanging two-species system with equal lifetimes and equal atomic fractions, computed for different chemical lifetimes τ: (a) $2\delta\nu\tau = 10^{-2}$; (b) $2\delta\nu\tau = 1$; (c) $2\delta\nu\tau = 10$; (d) $2\delta\nu\tau = 100$. (After Gutowsky, McCall, and Slichter, J. Chem. Phys., 21, 279 (1953).)

another, or alternatively by assuming that the exchange process is instantaneous and describing the time during which the nucleus resides in a given environment before it is again removed by the exchange process. This time is often called the *correlation time* and given the symbol τ (not to be confused with one of the symbols for chemical shift). Mathematical analysis of the effects of exchange can be summarized in the statement that, if in the absence of exchange the resonances of the two environments are separated by an amount $\delta\nu$, then, when exchange occurs, both resonances will be observed so long as the correlation time is appreciably greater than $1/\delta\nu$. If this lifetime shortens, however, and becomes comparable to $1/\delta\nu$, then the two resonance peaks will be broadened; and they will give rise to a single peak between the two original peaks when the correlation time becomes smaller than $1/\delta\nu$. These effects are illustrated schematically in Fig. 11–33.

Thus, from a study of the coalescence of lines as a function of concentration and temperature, it is possible to deduce rate constants and energies of activation, while from shifts of the coalesced line it is possible to deduce equilibrium constants and heats of interaction. The word "exchange" is used here in the broadest possible sense and does not imply necessarily a physical transfer of a nucleus from one molecule to another. A hydrogen bond may be formed and broken, for example, without a movement of the proton involved from one molecule to the next. In the process, however, the environment of the proton has changed, and it is this change in environment to which we refer. Such an environmental change might also take place in a single molecule without any interactions with neighboring molecules.

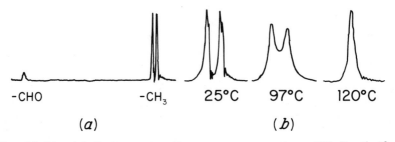

Fig. 11–34. (a) Proton magnetic resonance spectrum NN-dimethylformamide. (b) Effect of temperature on the two methyl-group resonance peaks.

This latter possibility can occur in such phenomena as *cis-trans* isomerization, changes in ring conformation, internal rotation, and similar molecular motions. A simple example is afforded by NN-dimethylformamide, the spectrum of which is shown in Fig. 11–34.

The absence of splitting in the lower peak indicates immediately that the two peaks observed at higher field are not caused by spin-spin splitting, but must arise from different magnetic environments for the two methyl groups. Such differences might be expected if the molecule were planar, in which case one of the methyl groups would be closer to the carbonyl oxygen than the other, and the anisotropic shieldings of the carbonyl group would have more effect on one than on the other. Such a planar structure is not unexpected, as resonance structures can be drawn giving the C—N bond partial double-bond character. Hindrance to rotation would not be expected to be as severe as in the case of a normal double bond, however.

The spectrum of NN-dimethylformamide has been studied as a function of temperature, and it is found that at higher temperatures the two methyl peaks coalesce into a single resonance. These changes are shown in Fig. 11–34. A mathematical analysis of the line shapes as a function of temperature allows evaluation of the rates of interconversion and the barrier to rotation, which for NN-dimethylformamide has been estimated at 7 kcal. Numerous similar cases have been studied by NMR.

The range of problems that have been attacked by nuclear magnetic resonance techniques is far too extensive to survey here. Studies of the solid state have elucidated crystal structures and the mechanism of different kinds of motion in solids. Large chemical shifts have been observed also for metals in solids, and these have been used to gain information about electron density and mobility in solid elements and compounds. Studies in the liquid state have been more familiar to chemists and, as we have seen, provide a means for obtaining a variety of information about molecular systems. Not only can chemical shifts be used to identify structural types of nuclei, but, perhaps more importantly, they can lead to further understanding of electron distributions, hybridization, electronegativity, anisotropy effects, association, and similar electronic phenomena which shape the chemical and physical properties of molecules. In the same way the electron-coupled spin-spin splittings are useful for structural identification as well as for information about specific interactions in the molecule. Considerable gains are being made theoretically to explain observed chemical shifts and splittings on a firm basis.

The use of nuclear magnetic resonance methods to study both interactions and rates of processes is undoubtedly unique among the various spectroscopic techniques. The absence or presence of resonance peaks gives definite information about the rates of various motional processes in a system, and detailed studies of line shapes determine not only rates but energy barriers. Thus, NMR has been utilized to examine processes whose rates are not convenient for measurement by other methods. Internal motions and exchange in solution are the most characteristic of such interesting explorations. The measurement of relaxation times also plays an important role in understanding rate processes.

Further information about the kinds of problems that have been examined by NMR is found in the references cited at the end of the chapter.

11.10   ELECTRON MAGNETIC RESONANCE

Although the basic phenomena giving rise to nuclear resonance absorption and electron resonance absorption are the same, there are a number of features that lead to different experimental and theoretical problems. Not the least of these is the much larger value of the Bohr magneton, which requires in an applied magnetic field of several thousand gauss the use of techniques of the microwave-frequency region of the electromagnetic spectrum.   A simple spectrometer which might be used to observe electron resonance is pictured in Fig. 11–35.

The source of radiation is a klystron tube, and the radiation is directed down a wave guide to a resonant cavity which is designed to enhance strongly the oscillating magnetic field component of the microwave

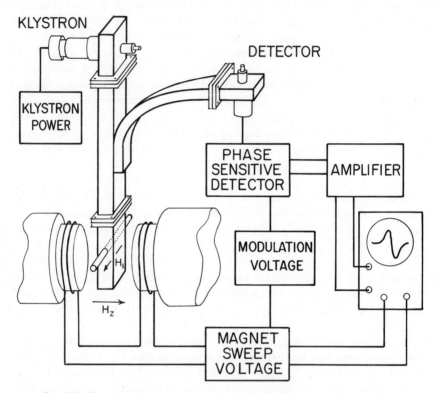

Fig. 11–35.   A simple electron magnetic resonance spectrometer.

radiation along the direction of the enclosed sample (Fig. 11–36) while at the same time minimizing the electric component of the radiation so that dielectric losses will not be serious.   Part of the radiation energy is reflected from the cavity and detected.   When the magnetic field is such that the Larmor frequency condition is satisfied, then transitions will occur between spin levels, energy will be absorbed in the cavity from the oscillating magnetic field, and less microwave energy will be detected. As usual, the level at the detector after amplification can be displayed on an oscilloscope or recorded.   To enhance the sensitivity of the spectrometer, the magnetic field is usually modulated by sweep coils, and a phase-sensitive detector is used to detect and display the first harmonic of the absorption signal. The result is a display of the derivative of the absorption curve, as in the case of the NMR of solids. A variety of arrangements of microwave components have been used successfully to measure resonance absorption and dispersion.

The electron magnetic resonance phenomenon can be described in the same terms as NMR. Thus, we must be concerned with relaxation times, saturation, and similar effects. The Bloch equations can be

H ——　　　　E----

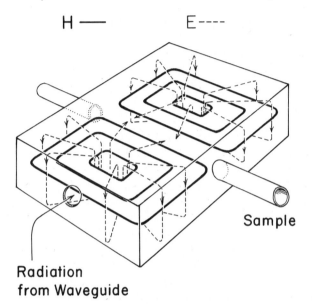

Sample

Radiation
from Waveguide

Fig. 11–36. Electric and magnetic fields in a resonant cavity. The cavity is designed to enhance the magnetic field at the sample.

applied, using the bulk magnetization of the sample as in the case of NMR. Obviously the magnetization (paramagnetic) is considerably larger in this case than in the case of nuclear polarization. In the literature, electron magnetic resonance (EMR) is variously termed electron spin resonance (ESR) and electron paramagnetic resonance (EPR). It might be remarked here that electron magnetic resonance has perhaps received less attention from chemists because most stable molecules are diamagnetic and have no unpaired electrons. On the other hand, many interesting species such as transition metal ions and their complexes, intermediate free radical species, and many organic ions do contain unpaired electrons. These techniques are then extremely fruitful in dealing with such entities.

Just as the NMR experiment is interesting because we deal with nuclei in a molecular environment rather than free and undisturbed, so also the importance of electron magnetic resonance lies in the fact that interactions between the electron spin and orbital motions, with nuclei and with electric fields, cause very pronounced perturbations of the simple energy-level system and transitions of Eq. (11–15). It is these perturbations and their effects on the absorption spectrum that give rise to information about the electron and its environment.

We have discussed a number of electron interactions that are of importance in atomic and molecular systems. One of these was the spin-orbit interaction by which electron spin and orbital angular momenta in atoms couple to form a resultant total angular momentum. When such coupling occurs, then the paramagnetism of the sample is no longer due only to electron spin, but depends on both **S** and **L** and their orientation. The Landé splitting factor discussed in Sec. 11.3 is the proportionality constant which must be used in Eq. (11–15) when spin and orbital angular momenta are both present. Thus, in a real system g may differ quite markedly from the free-electron value of 2.0023, and measurement of g can thus lead to information concerning the electronic environment.

The direct interaction of nuclear and electron spins, which depends on the electron density at the position of the nucleus, has also been mentioned. This interaction has an effect on the energy states of the electron and hence on the resonance absorption. In solids the direct dipole interaction between nuclear and electron moments is of importance, and in addition the strong electric fields in solids often interact with the orbital angular momenta to "quench" orbital changes. These various interactions will be discussed briefly.

A complete quantum-mechanical description of a system of nuclear and electronic spins in a static magnetic field should include in the Hamiltonian operator terms for the interaction of all spins with the field and terms for all other possible interactions in the system. This complete Hamiltonian would then be solved to obtain all the possible energy levels of the system. With the application of an oscillating $\mathbf{H}_1$ field, we would then add a perturbation term as in Sec. 11.4 and use time-dependent perturbation theory to calculate the possible transitions that would occur.

In a static magnetic field the Hamiltonian operator can be written

$$\mathcal{H} = \mathcal{H}_{\text{electrostatic}} + \mathcal{H}_{\text{magnetic}},$$

in which

$$\mathcal{H}_{\text{electrostatic}} = \mathcal{H}_{\text{Stark}} + \mathcal{H}_{\text{exchange}} + \mathcal{H}_{\text{nuclear electrostatic}}$$

and

$$\mathcal{H}_{\text{magnetic}} = \mathcal{H}_{\text{electron magnetic}} + \mathcal{H}_{\text{nuclear magnetic}}.$$

The electrostatic terms include the splitting of the atomic levels by electric fields as in a complex ion or crystal, the effect of asymmetric electric fields on the quadrupole moment of the nucleus, and exchange. The nuclear magnetic term is simply Eq. (11–28), which gives the effect of the magnetic field on the energy of the nuclear spins. The electron magnetic term can be further broken up into

$$\mathcal{3C}_{\text{electron magnetic}} = g\mu_B(\hat{\mathbf{L}} + 2\hat{\mathbf{S}}) \cdot \mathbf{H} + \mathcal{3C}_{\text{spin-orbit}} + \mathcal{3C}_{\text{spin-spin}},$$

where the first term is simply the Zeeman splitting of the energy due to the magnetic field acting on the combined spin and orbital electronic moments, the second term is the interaction of the spin and orbital moments, as discussed in Chapter 6, and is of the form $\mathbf{L} \cdot \mathbf{S}$, and the last term is an electronic spin-spin interaction, which is often negligible.

A perturbation treatment of these interactions, all of which are generally small compared to the electrostatic splitting of the atomic states, gives a simple form for the "spin" Hamiltonian, which includes the most important effects on the state of lowest energy upon application of a magnetic field. This more usable expression is

$$\mathcal{3C} = g\mu_B(\hat{\mathbf{L}} + 2\hat{\mathbf{S}}) \cdot \mathbf{H} + \lambda\hat{\mathbf{L}} \cdot \hat{\mathbf{S}} + A\hat{\mathbf{I}} \cdot \hat{\mathbf{S}}. \qquad (11\text{–}30)$$

The first term here is the Zeeman splitting, the fundamental interaction giving rise to electron magnetic resonance. The second term is the spin-orbit interaction, which affects the Zeeman levels to some extent, and the last term is the so-called hyperfine interaction, which is the nuclear-electron spin coupling described earlier.

11.11   HYPERFINE STRUCTURE AND THE SPECTRA OF FREE RADICALS

Although the magnitude of the electron-nuclear spin interaction is not as great as electric field splittings and spin-orbit couplings, it is possibly the simplest to understand. This is the same interaction that is involved in the indirect nuclear spin-spin splitting in nuclear magnetic resonance, and the effect of different nuclear spin orientations via the last term in Eq. (11–30) is qualitatively similar to the effect of nuclear spin orientations on a nearby nucleus. That is, the different nuclear spin orientations each produce a slightly different magnetic field at the interacting electron, and hence each result in a slightly different energy for the electron.

Consider, for example, an electron with $S = \frac{1}{2}$ interacting with a nucleus with $I = \frac{1}{2}$. In a magnetic field there will be two energy levels for the electron in the absence of the nuclear-electron coupling. These separate as the applied magnetic field is increased, as in Fig. 11–37a. The nuclear spin, however, can exist in two orientations also, and each of these orientations will alter the energy of the electron slightly, as in

Fig. 11–37b. If a fixed frequency of H_1 radiation is used, then as the magnetic field is increased, there will be two occasions when a transition can occur with a change in the electron spin orientation, and two resonance peaks will occur, as shown in Fig. 11–37b. A study of this situation and of the Hamiltonian operator will verify that for a nucleus of spin I the electron magnetic resonance will be split into $2I + 1$ lines with intensities as predicted in the NMR case when several nuclei are involved.

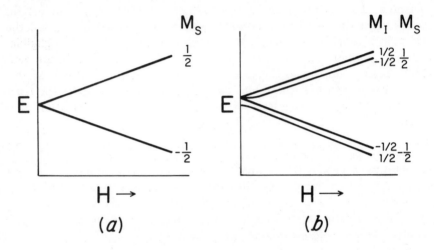

Fig. 11–37. (a) Variation of electronic energy levels in a magnetic field. (b) Variation of electronic energy levels in a magnetic field with a nuclear-electron coupling interaction present. $I = \frac{1}{2}$.

A simple free radical species that has been studied in some detail is the peroxylamine disulfonate ion, $ON(SO_3)_2^=$, which at a microwave frequency of 9500 Mcps and a magnetic field of about 3400 gauss shows three equally spaced resonance peaks of equal intensity (Fig. 11–38). The splitting of the resonance is 13 gauss (36 Mcps). Since the only nuclear species with a magnetic moment that is incorporated in the structure of this ion is N^{14}, it is a simple matter to explain the three-line spectrum as caused by the nuclear-electron spin-spin coupling with the N^{14} nucleus. The spin of the nitrogen nucleus is 1 so that we expect $2I + 1 = 3$ resonance lines of equal intensity.

An important free radical species is the stable crystalline radical 1,1-diphenyl-2-picryl hydrazyl (DPPH), which has frequently been used for the calibration of spectrometers because of the intense and narrow absorption peaks. A five-line spectrum is observed for this compound, as shown in Fig. 11–39, and is interpreted easily as arising from the coupling of the unpaired electron equally with the two N^{14} nuclei. We

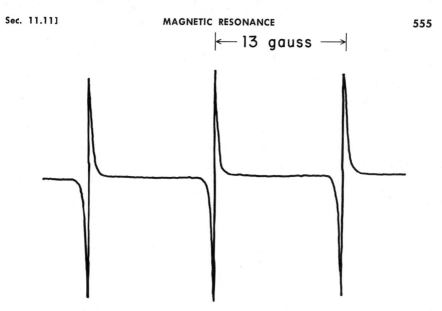

Fig. 11–38. Electron magnetic resonance spectrum of $ON(SO_3)_2^=$ at 9500 Mcps and 3400 gauss.

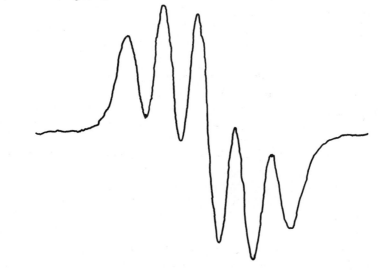

Fig. 11–39. Electron magnetic resonance spectrum of DPPH in benzene solution.

might also note that, from the center of the spectrum and the values of the field and frequency used, the splitting factor g is calculated to be 2.0036, very close to the free-electron value. This behavior is characteristic of many free radicals, whereas in transition metal ions g may be considerably larger than 2. From these results we infer that in most free radicals of the molecular type there is no significant orbital contribution. The splitting of the lines in DPPH is about 23 gauss.

In the discussion of the nuclear-electron coupling it was observed that the significant contribution to the interaction is via the so-called Fermi contact interaction, which depends on the electron density at the nucleus. This means that it should be possible to deduce information about the electron density of the unpaired electron in a free radical at a given nucleus from the magnitude of the observed spin-spin splitting.

An interesting case in point is diphenyl-dinitro-sulfophenyl hydrazyl, which is identical with DPPH except for the replacement of one of the NO_2 groups of the picryl ring by an SO_3 group. This compound has a nine-line spectrum, which indicates that, although the unpaired electron is interacting with both nitrogen nuclei, the interaction is not the same in the two cases. Thus, the coupling with one N^{14} nucleus results in a triplet of a spacing different from that resulting from coupling with the second nucleus. From the line spacings the two different couplings are found to be 12 gauss (33 Mcps) and 8 gauss (23 Mcps) respectively. These hyperfine splittings are extremely valuable, not only for qualitative estimates of electron distribution, but also for quantitative adjustment of molecular orbital calculations on molecular species.

Some of the most extensive studies that have been made by electron magnetic resonance have involved aromatic ions of various kinds. In these species it is observed again that the value of g calculated from the spectra usually is close to the free-electron value. One of the more interesting features of these spectra, however, is that hyperfine interaction is observed between the unpaired electrons (generally believed to be in π orbitals in aromatic systems) and ring protons, which are usually described only in terms of σ bonds between the hydrogen and carbon atoms. Because the unpaired electron in such a system is in a π orbital, we would expect no interaction of this electron with a nucleus at all, since the electron density is significant at a nucleus only in the case of σ orbitals. Nonetheless, splittings are observed with C^{13} nuclei in the ring, protons on the ring, and protons on alkyl groups attached to the ring.

These nuclear-electron interactions are not really so unexpected if we consider for a moment what we actually mean when we describe an electron as being in a π molecular orbital, or when we say that a hydrogen atom is involved with a carbon atom only via a σ bond. In Chapters 7 and 10 it was emphasized that in principle the only way to obtain the correct energy levels and wave functions for a molecular system is to solve the complete Schrödinger equation directly. Since this is impossible, we take recourse to constructing approximate wave functions from simpler wave functions which we already have available. In complex atoms we perturb hydrogen-like functions and hybridize them, if necessary, to obtain electron distributions that have the geometry we require for later use in constructing molecular wave functions. These atomic wave functions are generally rather poor, except in those cases in which very detailed and extensive calculations can be carried out. When using these approximate atomic functions to construct molecular wave functions, we obviously will obtain even less satisfactory results, since not only are the wave functions that we begin with not exact, but the methods used (valence-bond, LCAO molecular orbital, etc.) are in turn only approximations. Even in the case of a simple molecule like benzene, comparison with experimental data makes it clear that locating electrons in σ bonds, π orbitals, and the like is a very crude way of describing the molecule. We use these conventions because they are the only practical way of reaching any solution of the Schrödinger equation and can be used conveniently to relate the electronic distribution to chemical and physical behavior.

Once we have described a molecule in conventional terms, it is necessary to introduce new "interactions" such as resonance, configuration interaction, and hyperconjugation in order to adjust our wave functions to something more closely approximating the actual state of affairs. The tests of how good our wave functions have become lie in examining the energy levels via spectra and other techniques that can be related to the electron distribution. We would not have to resort to fictitious phenomena such as hyperconjugation if we could have written the correct wave function to begin with.

In aromatic systems we have seen that we can dispense with the idea of resonance, which arises in a valence-bond calculation, if we can construct the proper molecular orbitals. Even so, these orbitals are still only approximate. In particular, the σ and π orbitals which we populate with electrons still are not exactly correct in describing the electron distribution. The electrons that we have described as π electrons, for example, do have a finite probability of existing at the positions of the carbon nuclei as well as at other nuclei in the molecule. In order to construct our wave functions better, then, we write new wave functions by combining ground-state and excited-state wave functions in such proportion that our experimental measurements are more exactly predicted. This is the meaning of configuration interaction.

Detailed calculation of the sort of interaction to be expected on this basis between an unpaired electron and a proton attached in the plane of the aromatic ring gives an expected splitting of about 28 gauss, and numerous aromatic negative ions are observed to have such splittings ranging from about 23 to 30 gauss. In the benzene negative ion the electron magnetic resonance spectrum consists of seven lines with a splitting of 22.5 gauss. The symmetry and intensities (1:6:15:20: 15:6:1) of the peaks indicate equal coupling of the unpaired π electron with each of the six protons in the ring.

Unequal coupling is found in the naphthalene negative ion because the spin density of the unpaired electron is less at the β carbon atoms

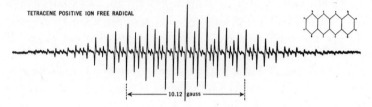

Fig. 11–40. Electron magnetic resonance spectrum of the tetracene positive radical ion. (Courtesy of Varian Associates.)

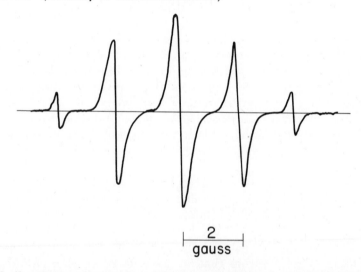

Fig. 11–41. Electron magnetic resonance spectrum of p-benzosemiquinone.

than at the α atoms. Thus the electron couples with the four β protons most strongly, giving a five-line spectrum with the intensities 1:4:6:4:1. Each of these is in turn split into five lines with the same relative intensities, but the coupling with the β protons is about one-third that with the α protons, so that with poor resolution the resulting lines overlap somewhat, giving a 16-line spectrum with relative intensities 1:1:1:2: 2:1:2:2:1:2:2:1:2:2:1:1:1. Under higher resolution all 25 lines are seen. A similar case is that of the tetracene positive ion radical illustrated in Fig. 11–40.

Measurement of the coupling constants in spectra of species such as these has proved highly informative in interpreting electron densities in molecules. Indirect nuclear-nuclear spin-spin coupling constants have been studied for the same reason.

Another interesting group of ions that has been studied extensively is the semiquinones. The simplest of these, p-benzosemiquinone has the spectrum shown in Fig. 11–41, where the quintet indicates immediately coupling of the odd electron with the four equivalent ring protons. The splitting in this case is 9.48 gauss, indicating significantly less configuration interaction than in the simpler aromatic ions.

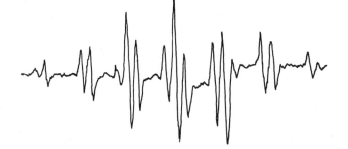

Fig. 11–42. Electron magnetic resonance spectrum of 2,5-dimethyl-benzo-semiquinone which is formed from the condensation of diacetyl.

An interesting phenomenon appears in the spectrum of 2,5-dimethyl-benzosemiquinone, which is an intermediate in the condensation of diacetyl to form 2,5-dimethyl-benzoquinone. In Fig. 11–42 we observe a pattern of seven lines, each of which is a triplet, 21 lines in all. These splittings correspond to coupling of the electron with the six methyl protons (the stronger interaction), with a weaker coupling to the two ring protons. The interaction of the electron with the methyl protons is explained on the basis of hyperconjugation. That is, the methyl proton electron clouds can overlap directly with the π cloud of the ring. Again it should be remembered that this explanation is simply a description of how the simple electron clouds we use to describe these molecules are only an approximation.

A large variety of stable and unstable free radicals, both organic and inorganic, have been studied by resonance methods. Such species can be produced chemically, electrolytically, photochemically, and by irradiation with high-energy particles. Ingenious techniques have been devised to measure spectra for highly unstable radicals, using flow techniques, low temperature, or continuous irradiation. Electron magnetic resonance is especially suited to identifying and studying in detail these transient molecules. Studies have been made in such widely divergent areas as the irradiation of polymers, catalysis, surface chemistry, and biological reactions. The biological field has benefited tremendously from magnetic resonance information about intermediate radical and ionic species in photochemical processes and enzymatic reactions. Many examples are cited in the references at the end of this chapter.

Although we have not explored the matter here, it should be apparent that at these frequencies various exchange and motional processes will have a pronounced effect on line widths and on the observed splittings in electron magnetic resonance spectra. In solids, for example, direct dipole-dipole interactions may be important. Also, the splitting factor g is often found to be anisotropic. The exchange of nuclei or electrons at sufficient rate will have an effect on the lifetimes of various spin states, and hence on the spectra. In DPPH or the naphthalene negative ion, for example, the hyperfine structure is seen only at low concentrations of the radicals. As the concentration is raised, the wave functions of the different radicals can overlap, and the nuclear-electron coupling is washed out because exchange of the odd electrons limits the lifetimes of the states. As in nuclear magnetic resonance studies the measurement of relaxation times is important in understanding various inter- and intramolecular processes that may be occurring.

11.12   THE STUDY OF IONS AND SOLIDS

The transition metal ions have been among the most thoroughly studied elements in the periodic system because of the numerous physical and chemical methods that may be used to elucidate their structure. We have already mentioned visible-UV absorption spectra that arise because of the splitting of degenerate d levels by the strong asymmetric electric fields in complexes and solids. We have discussed also the use of magnetic susceptibility measurements, which substantiate the theoretical and spectral arguments. These are discussed extensively in inorganic chemistry texts. Because many of these ions are paramagnetic and have unpaired electron spins, they have been subjected to thorough electron magnetic resonance investigation as well. Unfortunately, the multitude of interactions and exchange phenomena that may occur in these ions often complicate the spectra greatly, but we will examine a few simple examples in order to obtain an appreciation for the nature of the spectra and their interpretation.

In a free ion with a single unpaired electron with no orbital angular momentum, the electron magnetic resonance conditions could be predicted readily from Eq. (11–15) since there are no electrostatic or spin-orbit effects. If the electronic state also has orbital angular momenta which couple to form a total angular momentum, then a spin-orbit contribution might be important, and g could be calculated from the Landé equation.   Ions are seldom found free, however, but may be coordinated by solvent or other molecular species giving rise to strong electric fields at the atom of interest.   In crystalline solids electrostatic forces are obviously also very large.

In our discussion of the atomic spectra of transition metals, it was observed that the effect of these electric fields is to break the degeneracy of the d levels.   If the interaction with the electric field is small compared to the spin-orbit coupling, then the only degeneracy that will be removed is the separation of the $2J + 1$ degenerate levels with the same value of J.   This is often observed, for example, in the rare earths, where the f electrons are well shielded from external forces.

In the transition metal ions, however, the magnitude of the electric fields is generally sufficient to interact strongly with the orbital angular momenta directly, and the d levels are hence split into groups depending on the symmetry of the electric field.   Unless the fields are extremely large, as is the case in strong ligand binding, the spin-orbit interaction is not completely overcome, and the resulting levels may be shifted or split by spin-orbit coupling.   Finally, application of a magnetic field splits the spin-degenerate levels, and it is the transition between these levels that can be observed in the microwave region, provided the proper magnetic separation can be produced and other effects do not cause adverse relaxation times and broadening.

A simple case, which we have considered previously, is the Cu^{+2} ion, in which there are nine d electrons.   It will be recalled that the electronic system can be treated as a single positive charge because of the symmetry involved.   The ground state is ^2D.   In a cubic electric field the degenerate d orbitals are split into a pair and a triplet, and in the less symmetrical tetragonal field, more common in real systems, some of this degeneracy is further removed.   These effects are shown in Fig. 11–43.   Because these splittings are large, all the d electrons in an atom of Cu^{+2} will occupy only the lowest state, E_1.   For this reason we say that the orbital moment has been "quenched."   It is transitions between these orbitally split levels that we observed give rise to the color of the ions.

The lower two states in the tetragonal field are widely separated, and the spin-orbit interaction is small.   In the upper state this coupling removes the last of the orbital degeneracy.   If we now apply a magnetic field, these energy levels will be further split, but the magnitude of this splitting is considerably smaller than the previous effects.   In Fig. 11–43 only the lowest state is illustrated for the magnetic field effect.   Finally, if we consider the nuclear-electron spin-spin coupling, we see the further splitting of the magnetic levels and the resulting four-line spectrum $(I_{Cu} = \frac{3}{2})$ of Cu^{+2} in the microwave region.   It should be pointed out that the g value used to calculate the magnetic splitting is no longer the Landé value, since the spin and orbital angular momenta are largely uncoupled. Equations can be derived which give g in terms of the orbital energy levels, and as the orbital splittings become greater, g approaches the spin-only value of 2. The splitting factor is also found to be asymmetric.

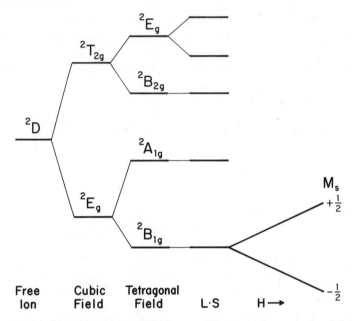

Fig. 11–43. Energy levels of Cu^{+2} in electric and magnetic fields. The magnetic splittings have been greatly exaggerated.

All transition metal ion spectra are not so simple. In Mn^{+2}, for example, the $3d$ shell is half-full, and the free ion is in an S state. An electric field thus will not separate orbitally degenerate levels. It is found, however, that the electrostatic distortion of the spherically symmetric cloud of the free ion is sufficient to split the d levels slightly into three levels. Each of these is subsequently split by a magnetic field, as shown in Fig. 11–44, and the coupling with the nuclear spin ($I_{Mn^{55}} = \frac{5}{2}$) splits each of these into six levels. Transitions are possible between adjacent levels with $\Delta M_S = 1$ and $\Delta M_I = 0$. The resulting spectrum is five sets of six lines each.

Electron magnetic resonance spectra of the transition metal ions, and of similar elements, have provided some of the most detailed information about the splitting of atomic levels and spin-orbit interaction. In turn, once these levels are understood, it is possible to use variations in these

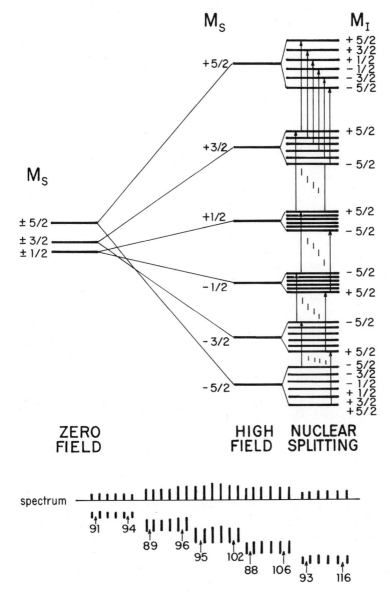

Fig. 11–44. Energy levels and electron magnetic resonance transitions of Mn^{+2}. Magnitudes of the splittings are indicated between components of the spectrum.

splittings. The magnitude of the orbital splitting depends very much on the nature of the complexing ligand or crystalline field, and the spin-orbit coupling in turn depends on the separation of the split-orbital levels. Hence, changes in the environment of the ion may have very definite effects on the magnetic resonance absorption and it is possible to estimate the nature of the complexing ligands interactions and crystalline field symmetries.

Ions of this type have been studied both in solution and in the solid state. In the former, exchange phenomena with respect to solvation can have important effects on line widths and splittings. Relaxation-time measurements have been useful in determining rates of exchange and the extent of coordination. In solids, electron magnetic resonance absorption is affected by electric field asymmetry, lattice vibrations, and similar forces. In line with current interest in the solid state, magnetic resonance methods have been employed to explore many phenomena of interest. The electrons trapped in color centers of irradiated ionic crystals give measurable absorption, as do the unpaired electrons that result when impurities are introduced into semiconductor lattices. Observations have been made also of conduction electrons in metals, and considerable work is being performed on the radicals which are trapped in solids upon irradiation by electrons, UV, or high-energy nuclei. In all these fields, application of magnetic resonance has opened up a large new area of information and ideas.

11.13 NUCLEAR QUADRUPOLE SPECTRA AND ELECTRONIC ENVIRONMENT

In Chapter 8 it was seen that molecular rotational spectra are affected when the nuclei in the molecule have a spin angular momentum with I greater than $\frac{1}{2}$. These effects were described as arising from the interaction of the nuclear electric quadrupole moment with the asymmetric electric field in the molecule, resulting in a coupling of the rotational and nuclear angular momenta. The nuclear quadrupole moment is important also in nuclear and electron magnetic resonance.

In NMR, for example, nuclei with a quadrupole moment can interact with the electric field in the atom or molecule and undergo a transition from one magnetic state to another without the prerequisite oscillating magnetic field of the proper frequency. As a result the lifetimes of nuclear spin states are shortened considerably, with the result that spin-spin splittings may be averaged out, or it may even be impossible to observe resonance. In solids, the shifting of levels because of the quadrupole interaction can also lead to new splittings of the NMR absorption.

In electron magnetic resonance the quadrupole moment of a nucleus can interact with the electron of interest and shift the energy levels, resulting in shifts of the resonance absorption, usually observed as unsymmetrical line splittings. Relaxation effects may be important here, also.

Measurement of shifts and splittings in microwave and radiofrequency spectroscopy lead to information about nuclear quadrupole moments and electric field asymmetries, but it is also possible to observe more directly transitions between states arising from the interaction of the nuclear electric quadrupole with the internal electric field in a molecule.

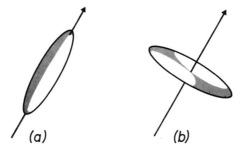

Fig. 11–45. Charge distribution of (a) positive (prolate) and (b) negative (oblate) nuclear quadrupoles. (Highly exaggerated.)

Because of the close similarity with magnetic resonance techniques, we will discuss briefly the nature of pure quadrupole resonance spectroscopy and its use.

Nuclei with a spin greater than $\frac{1}{2}$ have an asymmetric electric charge distribution that can be described in terms of an electric quadrupole moment, which is defined classically by the integral

$$eQ = e \int r^2(3 \cos^3 \theta - 1)\rho_n \, d\tau,$$

in which e is the proton charge, r and θ are polar coordinates from the center of the nucleus and ρ_n is the density of nuclear charge at a given point in the nucleus. From the definition it can be seen that the quadrupole moment eQ has the dimensions of *charge* $\times$ *area* and is positive when the positive charge of the nucleus is greater along the direction of the z axis (taken to be the axis of the nuclear spin) and negative when the charge is greater in the x-y plane. Whether the actual physical shapes of nuclei are elongated and flattened, or whether it is only the charge density that is asymmetric, it is nonetheless convenient to visualize the nucleus that has a positive quadrupole moment to be elongated in the direction of the spin axis, and to imagine that, when eQ is negative, the nucleus is flattened in the plane perpendicular to the axis (Fig. 11–45). In either case there is cylindrical symmetry about the spin axis.

In a uniform electric field, all orientations of the nuclear quadrupole have equal energy. In an inhomogeneous electric field, however, a torque will be exerted on the nucleus, and the energy of the system will depend on the orientation of the quadrupole moment with respect to the electric field gradients. The simplest case is that in which the electric field also has cylindrical symmetry and the variation of the electric field is given by

$$\frac{\partial^2 V}{\partial z^2} = 2\,\frac{\partial^2 V}{\partial x^2} = 2\,\frac{\partial^2 V}{\partial y^2}.$$

Since two of the field gradients are determined by the third, the interaction between the quadrupole and the field gradient can be written as

$$E = eQq_{zz}f(\theta), \tag{11–31}$$

where $q_{zz} = \partial^2 V/\partial z^2$.

The Hamiltonian operator for the quadrupole-field interaction is

$$\mathcal{3C} = \tfrac{1}{8}eQ^*q_{zz}\,\frac{3\hat{I}_z{}^2 - \hat{I}^2}{\hat{I}^2}, \tag{11–32}$$

in which $Q^* = 2Q(I + 1)/(2I - 1)$.

Since the square of the spin angular momentum of the nucleus is a constant of motion, we do not need the wave functions to obtain the energy eigenvalues from (11–32). The resulting energy-level expression will be

$$E_m = eQq_{zz}\,\frac{3m_I{}^2 - I(I + 1)}{4I(2I - 1)}. \tag{11–33}$$

This same expression can be obtained from the classical expression of Eq. (11–31) if we observe that the usual quantum-mechanical restriction on angular momentum is that its component in the z direction is limited to the values $m_I\hbar$. This restriction, using trigonometric relations, will result in

$$f(\theta) = \frac{3m_I{}^2 - I(I + 1)}{4I(2I - 1)},$$

which, when substituted in (11–31), gives (11–33).

Classically, the torque produced on the nucleus by the electric field is similar to the torque exerted on the nuclear magnetic dipole by a magnetic field. In both cases the presence of the intrinsic angular momentum of the nucleus results in a precessional motion about the direction of the field. In this case, however, it should be noted that it was not necessary to apply an electric field externally, as was the case with the magnetic field in NMR and electron resonance. Here the electric field is that already existing in the molecule. Hence, the energy levels that result exist without any external conditions being required. Also, the precessional frequency of the spin angular momentum about the direction of the electric field is dependent on the angle between the spin and the field in this case. Thus we would not expect the energy levels corresponding to different orientations of the spin to be equally spaced, and this is verified in (11–33). The energy levels for nuclei with integral and half-integral spins are shown in Fig. 11–46.

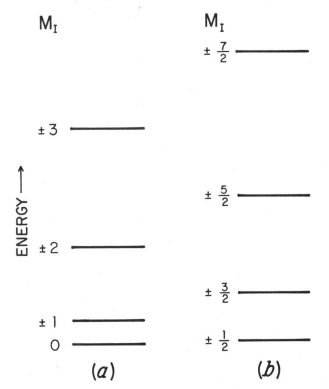

Fig. 11–46. Energy levels arising from the interaction of a quadrupole nucleus with an axially symmetric electric field and with the quadrupole moment positive: (a) I = integer; (b) I = half-integer.

If the electric field is not axially symmetric, then an asymmetry parameter

$$\epsilon = \left| \frac{q_{xx} - q_{yy}}{q_{zz}} \right|$$

may be defined and treated as a perturbation. The result of asymmetry is a small shifting of the levels and a splitting of the degenerate $m_I = \pm 1$ level.

The question now arises as to how one may induce transitions between these levels. Application of an electric field would alter the levels, and large fields would be required to overcome the internal interaction. But any nucleus with a quadrupole moment will also have a magnetic dipole moment, and hence an oscillating magnetic field of the correct frequency should interact with the nuclear magnetic dipole and cause transitions from one level to another.

From Eq. (11–33) it can be seen that the order of the energy levels depends on the sign of eQq_{zz}, but that, regardless of sign, the difference between levels is

$$\Delta E = \tfrac{1}{2}|eQq_{zz}|,$$

and hence the frequency required for the oscillating H_1 field is

$$\nu = \frac{|eQq_{zz}|}{h}.$$

The quantity eQq_{zz} is called the nuclear quadrupole coupling constant and is usually expressed in units of Mcps.

We have, then, essentially a nuclear magnetic resonance experiment without application of a static magnetic field. This is possible because the nuclear energy levels are split by the electrical interaction between the electric quadrupole moment and the internal electric fields. The nuclear magnetic moment is the property that is used to cause interaction with radiation (the oscillating H_1 field), and hence transitions occur with the same selection rules as in NMR spectroscopy. We are not looking at transitions between magnetic levels, however, but at transitions between electrical levels.

The item of information immediately forthcoming from the measurement of a line in a nuclear quadrupole resonance spectrum is the quadrupole coupling constant, and if the quadrupole moment of the nucleus is known, then the electric field gradient can be determined. The latter is an important indication of the charge distribution in the molecule. Known electric quadrupole moments are listed in Table 11–4 along with the other nuclear properties. NQR spectroscopy is limited practically to the solid state because rapid motions in fluid states average out the orientation of electric field and quadrupole moment. Fortunately the $1/r^3$ dependence of the electric field interaction reduces the effect of crystalline fields somewhat, so that the internal fields are predominant in the solid state.

Since the first pure quadrupole resonance was measured for Cl^{35} and Cl^{37} in 1950, numerous studies have been made of halogen compounds and molecules containing other nuclei with quadrupoles. In single crystals NQR splittings have been used to determine the relative numbers of certain nuclei with the same electric environment symmetry. Magnetic fields can be used to produce a Zeeman splitting of the levels that are degenerate in nuclear spin. The effect of weak bonding in crystal structures on the internal electric field in a molecule can also be observed, for example, in the halogens. Perhaps most interesting to chemists have been measurements made of the quadrupole coupling constants for Cl^{35} in various compounds. Some of the values obtained are listed in Table 11–7. These results are both from pure NQR and from rotational spectra.

TABLE 11–7. Cl^{35} Quadrupole Coupling Constants*

Substance	State	Structures	$-eQq$ (Mcps)	% Ionic Character	
				eQq	Pauling
Cl(atom)			109.7		
KCl	Gas	K^+Cl^-	<0.04	100	70
NaCl	Gas	Na^+Cl^-	<1	>99	66
TlCl	Gas	Tl^+Cl^-, Tl—Cl	15.8	86	
SiH_3Cl	Gas	$SiH_3^+Cl^-$, SiH_3—Cl	40.0	64	30
HCl	Solid	H^+Cl^-, H—Cl	53.4	51	19
$ClCH_3$	Solid	CH_3—Cl, $CH_3^+Cl^-$	68.1	38	
$ClCH_3$	Gas	CH_3—Cl, $CH_3^+Cl^-$	75.3	31	5
CCl_4	Solid	CCl_4, CCl_3^+ Cl^-	81.9	30	
ICl	Gas	I—Cl, I^+Cl^-	82.5	25	5
BrCl	Gas	Br—Cl, Br^+Cl^-	103.6	5	1
Cl_2	Solid	Cl—Cl	109.0	<1	0
FCl	Gas	F—Cl, F^-Cl^+	146.0		

* From Brand and Speakman, *Molecular Structure*, Edward Arnold, 1960, p. 124.

It is fairly obvious that for the ionic compounds in which the Cl nucleus is in a spherically symmetric electron cloud the quadrupole coupling constant is small, while in covalently bonded environments it is large. It has been suggested that the quantity $(1 - q_{zz})/q_{zz}$ (atomic) be used as an index of fractional ionic character of a bond, but there is some dispute as to the exact significance of the coupling constant in terms of the concepts that have arisen in calculations of wave functions for molecules.

In conjunction with other techniques such as NMR and electron resonance and electron and x-ray diffraction, the information gained from nuclear quadrupole resonance spectroscopy promises to allow us to probe further into the interesting areas inside crystals and molecules.

SUPPLEMENTARY REFERENCES

Magnetic Susceptibility

STONER, E. C., *Magnetism*, Methuen & Co., Ltd., London, 1948.
BATES, L. F., *Modern Magnetism*, 4th ed., Cambridge University Press, London, 1961.

SELWOOD, P. W., *Magnetochemistry*, 2nd ed., Interscience Publishers, New York, 1956.

VAN VLECK, J. N., *Electric and Magnetic Susceptibilities*, Oxford University Press, London, 1932. Advanced.

Nuclear Magnetic Resonance

ROBERTS, J. D., *Nuclear Magnetic Resonance*, McGraw-Hill Book Co., New York, 1959.

JACKMAN, L. N., *Applications of Nuclear Magnetic Resonance to Organic Chemistry*, Pergamon Press, London, 1959.
These are both readable, qualitative introductions to NMR and its chemical applications.

POPLE, J. A., W. G. SCHNEIDER, and H. J. BERNSTEIN, *High Resolution Nuclear Magnetic Resonance*, McGraw-Hill Book Co., New York, 1959. This text deals with NMR in more mathematical detail and with summaries of experimental work up to the time of publication. A handbook for NMR spectroscopists.

ANDREW, E. R., *Nuclear Magnetic Resonance*, Cambridge University Press, London, 1956. A concise summary of basic theory and experimental work. Includes much physical experimentation, including the solid state.

SLICHTER, C. P., *Principles of Magnetic Resonance*, Harper & Row, New York, 1963. A more sophisticated but very readable presentation of theoretical foundations with some experimental examples. Includes a chapter on electron magnetic resonance.

ABRAGAM, A., *Principles of Nuclear Magnetism*, Oxford University Press, London, 1961. An advanced and thorough treatment.

FLUCK, E., *Die Kernmagnetische Resonanz und Ihre Anwendung in der Anorganischen Chemie*, Springer-Verlag, Berlin, 1963. A useful survey of experimental work, particularly elements other than H^1.

Electron Magnetic Resonance

PAKE, G. E., *Paramagnetic Resonance*, W. F. Benjamin, Inc., New York, 1962. A readable review of theory and some applications.

INGRAM, D. J. E., *Spectroscopy at Radio and Microwave Frequencies*, Butterworths Scientific Publications, London, 1955. Contains information on experimental techniques and a summary of applications, particularly transition metal ions.

INGRAM, D. J. E., *Free Radicals*, Butterworths Scientific Publications, London, 1958. Emphasis on radicals and their EPR spectra.

PROBLEMS

11-1. From Eqs. (11-1) and (11-2) derive an expression for the magnetic induction **B** in a sample as a function of the field strength **H** and the volume susceptibility of the sample.

11-2. Calculate the molar diamagnetic susceptibility of atomic hydrogen using the ground-state wave function for hydrogen. Compare with Eq. (11-6).

11-3. Calculate the apparent change in weight of a 0.1 M solution of CoF_6^{-3} ions, which have four unpaired electrons, in a 1-cm-diameter test tube, which is suspended in a Guoy balance, when a magnetic field of 5000 gauss is applied.

11-4. Using the Slater screening constants discussed in Chapter 7, calculate the molar susceptibility of atomic helium.

11–5. Calculate the diamagnetic susceptibilities of benzene, pyridine, methyl chloride, cyclohexane, propane, cyclopropane, chlorobenzene, and ethyl alcohol, using the method of Pascal's constants. Compare with experimental values reported in the literature whenever possible.

11–6. Atomic hydrogen has an unpaired electron spin, so that it should actually be paramagnetic. Considering both the diamagnetic susceptibility and paramagnetic susceptibility contributions, what is the molar susceptibility of atomic hydrogen?

11–7. Using the appropriate values of the nuclear magnetic moments, verify the resonance frequencies of several nuclear species in a field of 10,000 gauss.

11–8. At what frequency would protons resonate in a field of 5000 gauss? What field would be required if the oscillator frequency were 30 Mcps? 100 Mcps?

11–9. Calculate the nuclear paramagnetism of atomic hydrogen at room temperature, and compare it with the electronic magnetization. Also compare the two at 1°K. Molecular hydrogen is diamagnetic. How would the nuclear paramagnetism of hydrogen compare with the electronic diamagnetism at room temperature and at 1°K?

11–10. What is the maximum dipolar splitting that can be observed for a pair of protons located in a solid 1.3 Å apart? At what orientation of the proton pair with respect to the magnetic field does this maximum splitting occur? What would be the dipolar splitting for a pair of fluorine atoms at this separation?

11–11. What is the second moment of the absorption line for the preceding case? Assume that no other magnetic nuclei are present. What would be the effect of placing a second pair of nuclei 5 Å from the first?

11–12. Show that the chemical shift δ, defined as the difference in shielding constants for the resonance of interest and the resonance of a reference compound, is given by the approximate forms in Eq. (11–25). Show that the error in assuming that the denominator should be H_0, H_c, or H_r is negligible.

11–13. From the definition of δ, confirm Eq. (11–26) and again show that small variations in the denominator are negligible.

11–14. In acetic acid the sideband method of measuring chemical shifts locates the methyl resonance 126 cps to lower applied field than the peak from dissolved tetramethylsilane. The carboxyl proton peak is 682 cps to lower field than TMS. The spectrum was observed at 60 Mcps. Calculate the chemical shifts of the two acetic acid peaks in τ units.

11–15. The chemical shifts (in ppm from a benzene reference) are given below for several ethyl halides. Using electronegativities from the literature, derive an expression for the electronegativity of the substituent atom in terms of the difference in the CH_2 and CH_3 chemical shifts.

	CH_2	CH_3
CH_3CH_2I	4.33	5.73
CH_3CH_2Br	4.08	5.83
CH_3CH_2Cl	3.80	5.93
CH_3CH_2F	2.87	6.07

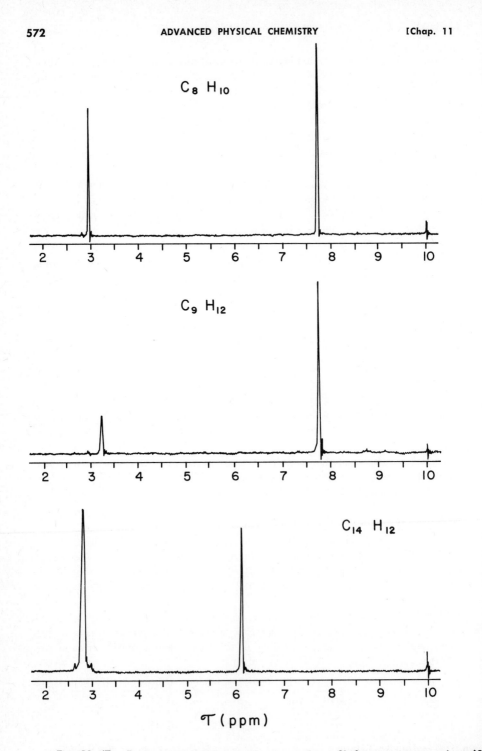

Fig. 11–47. Proton magnetic resonance spectra. Shifts are measured at 60

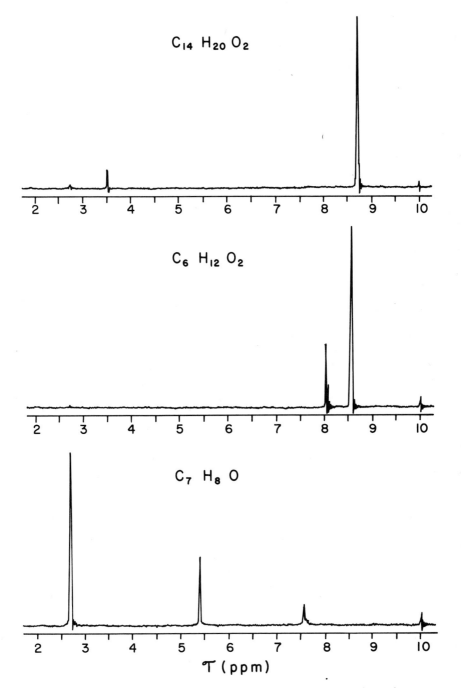

$C_{14} H_{20} O_2$

$C_6 H_{12} O_2$

$C_7 H_8 O$

τ (ppm)

Mcps from tetramethylsilane as zero. Increasing magnetic field is to the right.

11–16. From the shifts given in the preceding problem and the shifts in Table 11–5, what general conclusion can you reach about the effect of the electronegativity of substituents on chemical shifts? Give a qualitative picture of why this effect might be observed.

11–17. From the table of chemical shifts and the examples given in the figures of Sec. 11.7, determine the structure of the compounds in Fig. 11–47 from their NMR spectra. Shifts are given in cps measured from TMS at 60 Mcps and in ppm, with increasing field to the right.

11–18. On the basis of the π-electron current effects on the resonance of protons on and around the benzene ring, discuss what sort of chemical shift would be expected for each type of proton in a compound of the structure

where the methylene protons are in a position above the plane of the benzene ring.

11–19. On the basis of the π-electron current effects in benzene, discuss the probable reason for the different chemical shifts observed for the olefinic protons in *cis* and *trans* stilbene (Table 11–5). What effects might be expected on the phenyl protons?

11–20. Borazole is a cyclic boron-nitrogen ring compound which is isoelectronic with benzene. On the basis of the chemical shift observed for boron in this compound, do the boron atoms appear to have six electrons around them, as would be the case of single bonds between boron and the surrounding nitrogen and hydrogen atoms, or does it appear that possible back-coordination from a nitrogen atom gives boron the opportunity to share eight electrons?

11–21. In Figs. 11–25 and 11–26 the chemical shifts in cps from TMS are measured at 60 Mcps. Calculate the positions in cps from TMS that would be observed at 30 Mcps for each separate line in the spectrum, and sketch the appearance of the spectrum as contrasted with the 60-Mcps spectrum.

11–22. Show that all the spin functions used in the coupled two-spin problem are orthogonal.

11–23. From the equations for the energy levels of the two-spin coupled system and the resulting expressions for the frequencies of the observed lines, derive expressions for the true coupling constant and chemical shift between the two spins in terms of the observed line frequencies.

11–24. On the basis of the boron-proton coupling constants in Table 11–6, does it appear that the boron in borazole has a trigonal or tetrahedral configuration? How does this support the conclusions of Problem 11–20?

11–25. Using both the chemical shifts and spin-spin splittings, deduce the structures of the compounds in Fig. 11–48.

11–26. The splitting observed in the OH resonance of pure, dry ethanol is 4 cps. Addition of a trace of HCl to the alcohol produces a single sharp OH peak.

What can be said about the lifetime of an OH proton in a particular spin state in the acidified alcohol?

11–27. If a small amount of water is added to pure ethanol, a peak is observed at 373 cps below a TMS standard (measured at 60 Mc). As water is added, this peak grows, but when the concentration of water becomes greater than 30 per cent, this peak and the ethanol OH peak disappear, and a peak appears at 355 cps below TMS. What is the minimum rate of exchange of a proton between water and ethanol molecules in this solution?

11–28. The EPR spectrum of sodium trimesityl boron

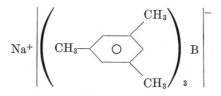

consists of four peaks of equal intensity split by 14 gauss. Where is the unpaired electron located in the trimesityl boron negative ion?

11–29. Draw the EPR spectrum that would be expected for diphenyl-dinitro-sulfophenyl hydrazyl, showing the effect of the coupling constants given on page 556.

11–30. The EPR spectrum of 1,4-naphthosemiquinone consists of three lines, each of which is split into a quintuplet of lines. Interpret this spectrum in terms of the structure of the molecule.

11–31. In the EPR spectrum of the benzyl negative ion ($C_6H_5CH_2^-$) it has been observed that the absorption is split into three lines of intensity 1:2:1. What does this indicate about the environment of the excess electron in the ion?

11–32. One of the features of the EPR spectrum of solid methanol, CH_3OH, which has been irradiated with UV light is a quartet of lines of intensity 1:3:3:1 symmetrically spaced about $g = 2$. A sample of CD_3OH produces, however, a seven-line pattern on UV irradiation. What is the nature of the free radical produced by the UV in each case?

11–33. What connection could there be between the ability to observe phosphorescent radiation from a substance and the ability to observe an EPR signal?

11–34. What are the relative populations of two-electron spin levels at room temperature in a magnetic field of 10,000 gauss? How does this compare with the case of nuclear spins? What does this indicate about the possible use of non-resonance methods for the detection of electron paramagnetism as opposed to nuclear paramagnetism?

11–35. The anthracene negative ion has a 21-line spectrum. Explain.

11–36. The EPR spectra of chlorinated p-benzosemiquinones are illustrated in Fig. 11–49. What can one conclude from these spectra about the magnitude of the coupling between the unpaired electron and the chlorine nuclei? What is the reason for this?

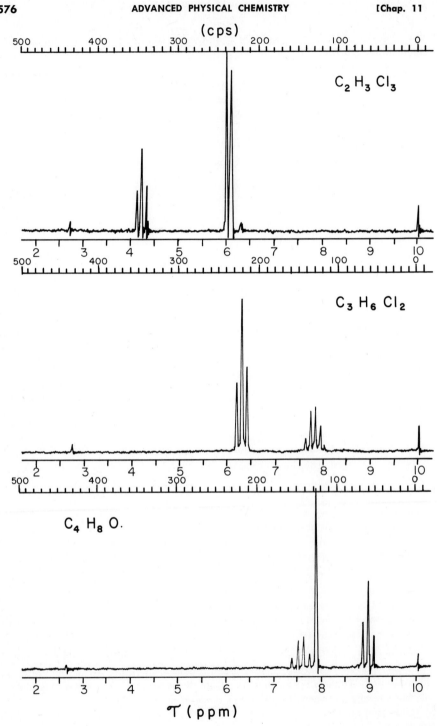

Fig. 11–48. Proton magnetic resonance

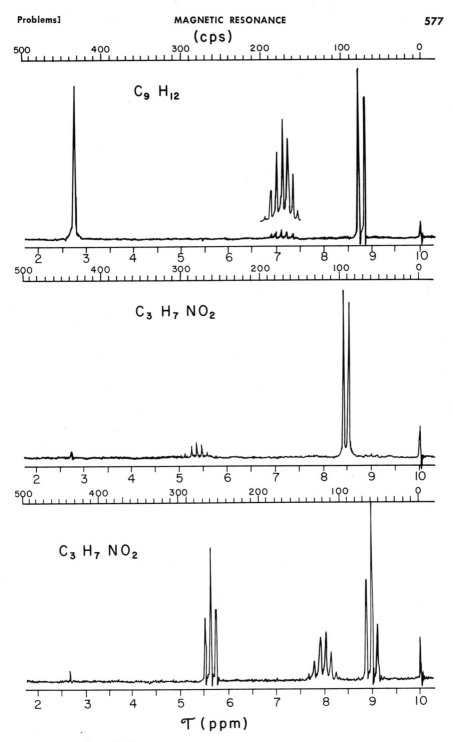

spectra measured at 60 Mcps.

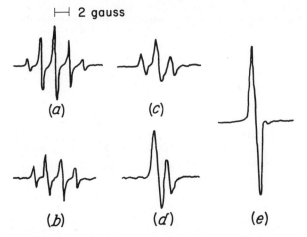

Fig. 11–49.   Electron magnetic resonance spectra of (a) benzosemiquinone, (b) monochlorobenzosemiquinone, (c) 2,3-dichlorobenzosemiquinone, (d) trichlorobenzosemiquinone, and (e) tetrachlorobenzosemiquinone.

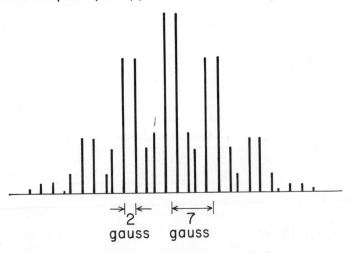

Fig. 11–50.   Lines observed in the electron magnetic resonance spectrum of perinaphthene.

11–37. When perinaphthene in CCl_4 is allowed to stand for several hours, it becomes yellow in color, and an EPR spectrum can be obtained, which is shown in Fig. 11–50. What could be the cause of this spectrum?   Explain.

11–38. When alkali metals are dissolved in liquid ammonia, the resulting solutions show an EPR absorption.   It is believed that the metal atoms are ionized, and the free electron resides in the region of the ammonia molecules.   However, no hyperfine structure is observed, and the resonance line is very narrow.   What phenomenon might cause this?

12
Structure, Theory, and Reality

On surveying the vast areas of nature explored by chemical science, it is amazing to consider how much of our chemical knowledge does not require a detailed knowledge of atoms and molecules, or hardly a belief in their existence. Although the very earliest of chemical laws, the laws of conservation of mass and of definite and multiple proportions, very strongly suggest an ultimately discrete subdivision of matter, these findings were for many years regarded largely in their most direct connection as a basis for chemical stoichiometry. The preparation and purification of compounds and the study of their properties and reactions have been carried out for decades in countless laboratories without regard for the atoms and molecules believed to constitute these substances. One of the most fundamental and powerful of theoretical structures, thermodynamics, takes little cognizance of whether sulfur is S or S_8 or whether a benzene molecule is round, flat, long, or square. From straightforward thermal, mechanical, and electrical measurements we can predict equilibrium constants, heats of reaction, and countless other relations.

Nevertheless man's curiosity has led him to explore further than required by utility, and his theories have ultimately proved to be of great utility as well. The successful application of the laws of physics in the kinetic theory of gases, coupled with the basic chemical laws, gradually led to the acceptance of the concept of atoms and molecules, and belief in their reality inevitably led to questions about their internal structure. The late nineteenth and early twentieth centuries saw this inquiry lead into exciting new realms of fact and fancy. While the physicist searched for the significance of electrical and optical phenomena, chemists began to explore the molecular concept from the standpoint of chemical properties and the ability to predict these properties. It was during this period that the brilliant intuitive conceptions of such men as Kekule, van't Hoff, and Werner set the stage for our present ideas of molecular geometry and chemical bonding. One is awed by the agreement between the structures found by modern physical methods and these early chemical pictures.

Our emphasis in this text has been on but one area of the theoretical and experimental approaches to understanding molecular structure. We have attempted to lay the basic foundations of quantum mechanics and statistics and have employed these methods several times in the exploration of particular molecular characteristics. We have restricted our study to those properties most conveniently deduced from spectroscopic measurements and have seen how the theory has been strengthened by many threads of experience that meet in agreement.

Because of our somewhat restricted view, we have not explored numerous non-spectroscopic methods that are equally valuable in the chemists' search for information. The powerful techniques of x-ray, neutron, and electron diffraction, for example, not only have verified our ideas about molecular geometry, but have substantiated many of our pictures of electron distributions and molecular motions. Very often they are able to provide a detailed picture of molecular structure. Also, we have not discussed other interactions of electromagnetic radiation with matter, many of which can be explained reasonably well in classical rather than quantum-mechanical terms. The importance of dielectric constants and dielectric dispersion, optical rotation and optical rotary dispersion, conductor and semiconductor properties, macromolecular films, the behavior of gases, liquids, and solids, nuclear phenomena, rates of reaction, and numerous other physical phenomena is well known to the research and academic chemist alike.

It is perhaps worthwhile to inquire whether the bits and pieces of information obtained by different methods form a consistent picture of molecular structure. The fact that we have chosen to discuss them in such detail would indicate an answer in the affirmative. Bond lengths and bond angles, atomic and molecular masses, and other parameters are generally consistent. It is not at all surprising, of course, that the agreement may not be perfect, for each method represents a different way of looking at the molecule. We can calculate a bond distance, for example, from various kinds of spectra, or we might determine a molecular size from the non-ideal behavior of the compound as a gas, or finally from x-ray scattering in a crystal. In each case we have chosen a different interaction with our molecule, and the response will not always lead to exactly the same interpretation. We have even seen the effects that approximations and lack of precision can have on such estimates. All in all, however, our general picture is well supported and consistent.

The success of any theory leads naturally to widespread use of the terminology and symbolism and particularly the models and concepts inherent in the development of the theory.   It was exactly this tendency that led Maxwell to postulate the "aether," which was supposed to support the transmission of electromagnetic radiation through space, and which sent scores of physicists on attempts to detect the presence of this medium.   It is also this tendency that results in a chemist's description of a molecule as existing in one of several resonance forms and as oscillating rapidly from one form to another.   The success of the electron-pair bond concept was so great that it took years for electron-deficient structures such as those of the boron hydrides to be considered acceptable.   Each theory views the universe through different-colored glasses, and the skeptic is likely to view the theories in turn through a jaundiced eye.   Do not all theories, after all, die off, to be replaced by more consistent theories?   Are our original views of the intimate structure of matter really satisfactory, for example, now that there are over 30 elementary particles in the books?   What, then, is the correct picture of atoms and molecules; what truly represents reality?

A philosophic question such as this is not answered with finality, but there are at least some cautions that are in order.   Unless we take the view, with Bishop Berkeley, that we never come into contact with reality but view the universe only in the deceptive framework of our senses, we are prone to feel that at least our closest approach to reality is afforded by what we can perceive directly through sight, touch, and our other senses, or at least a common denominator perceived by many persons in order to eliminate individual difficulties such as color blindness or other peculiarities.   Although philosophies and religions can be built on factors that depend on unseen and unproved truths, such systems must invariably fail to have any significance in our existence unless they come at least in contact with the world we perceive and are generally consistent with it.

The primary difficulty we face in chemistry and physics at present is that we have gone into a realm in which we cannot view the basic assumptions of our theories directly.   The circumstantial evidence is overwhelming, and certainly such techniques as electron microscopy and field-emission microscopy so closely parallel ordinary optics that we feel rather certain that the existence of molecules is unquestionable.   We are faced, then, with a number of different models and descriptions of molecules, and we judge these models on the basis of their success in correlating and predicting phenomena that are directly observable.   The failure to observe subatomic particles in molecules directly means, of course, that we can make no final absolute choice from these descriptions. Of quantum mechanics we can say that it is the most successful theoretical approach that can provide quantitative agreement with experimentally measured quantities.   The quantum-mechanical model assumes

a probability description of matter, and hence we are led to talk of electron clouds or probability distributions rather than simple planetary
orbits. We find quantization of energy and angular momentum and
other quantities, and we can relate these findings to spectral lines,
energies of dissociation, rates of reactions, and thermodynamic functions.

Quantum mechanics is, and will continue to be, under revision as our
knowledge accumulates. At present, it represents our best contact with
the invisible atomic world. We have seen also that one of the greatest
barriers to more extensive calculations is the mathematical difficulty
of solving complex equations, and unfortunately many of our models and
descriptions of molecular behavior are based primarily on the mathematical approximations we use and not on the theory itself. We are
led to resonance structures and resonance stabilization when we start
with approximate electron-pair bond wave functions. The use of simple
hydrogen-like atomic functions and H_2^+ molecular orbital functions for
the description of more complicated systems leads to electron correlation,
configuration interaction, and other "interactions," which are used to
reach a more satisfactory result. Such factors are useful and play an
important role in describing and correlating properties, but it must be
remembered that they cannot be taken too literally as "real" effects.
The argument that a molecule is in such and such a molecular orbital
state and not in such and such a valence-bond state is meaningless,
except insofar as it indicates which approximation, considering how far
the approximation is carried, yields the most satisfactory answers. The
δ's and arrows and charges that are drawn so freely in describing reaction
mechanisms must always be considered as partly mnemonic devices that
are likely to yield useful predictions. The reality of the configurations
and intermediates involved may well escape us for a long time to come.

Hopefully, quantum mechanics and allied theoretical approaches will
some day allow us to make predictions and correlations even more
directly and systematically than is now possible. Until that time, there
is no doubt that the theoretical methods and experimental techniques
at our disposal will play an intimate role in our search for knowledge.

Appendix A

Vector Relations

Many physical quantities are completely defined by a numerical magnitude according to some conveniently defined scale. Familiar examples of these so-called *scalar* quantities are mass, length, temperature, area, and volume. Scalar quantities obey the familiar laws of algebra.

Magnitude alone is insufficient to designate adequately many other physical quantities such as velocity, force, and electric field strength. These quantities are not completely described unless direction is specified as well as magnitude. Such quantities, called *vector* quantities, obey a somewhat different algebra, which will be outlined briefly here.

A vector quantity can be defined as one that obeys the relations of vector algebra, and although a number of different mathematical descriptions are possible (and are used), the simplest and most generally useful formulation is based on the representation of a vector quantity by a line segment which is oriented in the direction of the vector and whose length is equal to the magnitude of the vector quantity. Thus **A** and **B** in Fig. A–1a represent two vectors which differ in both direction and magnitude.

The sum of two vectors can be defined as a vector that is represented by a line extending from the beginning of the first vector to the terminus of the second when the second is placed so that it begins at the end of the first, as in Fig. A–1b. It is seen that the vector

$$C = A + B$$

is the diagonal of a parallelogram of which **A** and **B** are the sides. Similarly the difference of two vectors **A** − **B** can be obtained as the sum of **A** and a vector equal in magnitude to **B** but in the opposite direction, as in Fig. A–1c, i.e.,

$$C = A - B = A + (-B).$$

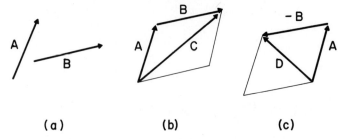

Fig. A–1. (a) Representation of vector quantities by directed line segments. (b) Vector addition. (c) Vector subtraction.

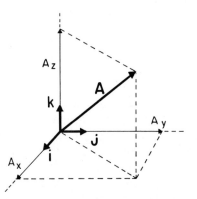

Fig. A–2. Resolution of a vector into its component vectors along the x, y, and z axes.

A vector can be represented also by its projections along the x, y, and z axes, where the vectors $\mathbf{i}$, $\mathbf{j}$, and $\mathbf{k}$ are unit vectors along these axes (Fig. A–2):

$$\mathbf{A} = A_x\mathbf{i} + A_y\mathbf{j} + A_z\mathbf{k}.$$

Hence,

$$\mathbf{A} + \mathbf{B} = (A_x + B_x)\mathbf{i} + (A_y + B_y)\mathbf{j} + (A_z + B_z)\mathbf{k}.$$

The *scalar product* of two vectors, $\mathbf{A} \cdot \mathbf{B}$, is a scalar quantity equal in magnitude to the magnitude of one vector multiplied by the component of the second parallel to the first (Fig. A–3). If the angle between $\mathbf{A}$ and $\mathbf{B}$ is θ, then

$$\mathbf{A} \cdot \mathbf{B} = \mathbf{B} \cdot \mathbf{A} = AB \cos \theta.$$

It is seen that

$$\mathbf{i} \cdot \mathbf{i} = \mathbf{j} \cdot \mathbf{j} = \mathbf{k} \cdot \mathbf{k} = 1$$

and

$$\mathbf{i} \cdot \mathbf{j} = \mathbf{j} \cdot \mathbf{k} = \mathbf{k} \cdot \mathbf{i} = 0,$$

so that

$$\mathbf{A} \cdot \mathbf{B} = A_x B_x + A_y B_y + A_z B_z.$$

Also,

$$\mathbf{A} \cdot (\mathbf{B} + \mathbf{C} + \cdots) = \mathbf{A} \cdot \mathbf{B} + \mathbf{A} \cdot \mathbf{C} + \cdots.$$

An important example of a scalar product is the work dW, done when a force $\mathbf{F}$ moves a body an increment of distance $\mathbf{ds}$. The work is defined as the product of the distance moved and the component of the force along the direction of motion:

$$dW = \mathbf{F} \cdot \mathbf{ds}.$$

The *vector product* of two vectors, $\mathbf{A} \times \mathbf{B}$, is defined as a vector perpendicular to both $\mathbf{A}$ and $\mathbf{B}$ of magnitude $AB \sin \theta$, where θ is the angle

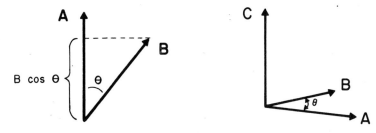

Fig. A–3. The scalar product of vectors A and B.   **Fig. A–4. The vector product of vectors A and B.**

between $\mathbf{A}$ and $\mathbf{B}$. The direction of the cross vector is that in which a right-hand screw would move if $\mathbf{A}$ is rotated into $\mathbf{B}$ through an angle less than 180° (Fig. A–4).

From the definition of $\mathbf{C} = \mathbf{A} \times \mathbf{B}$,

$$C = AB \sin \theta,$$

and if $\mathbf{A}$ and $\mathbf{B}$ are parallel, the vector product is zero. Also from the definition,

$$\mathbf{A} \times \mathbf{B} = -(\mathbf{B} \times \mathbf{A}).$$

For the unit vectors,

$$\mathbf{i} \times \mathbf{i} = \mathbf{j} \times \mathbf{j} = \mathbf{k} \times \mathbf{k} = 0$$

and

$$\mathbf{i} \times \mathbf{j} = \mathbf{k} = -\mathbf{j} \times \mathbf{i},$$
$$\mathbf{j} \times \mathbf{k} = \mathbf{i} = -\mathbf{k} \times \mathbf{j},$$
$$\mathbf{k} \times \mathbf{i} = \mathbf{j} = -\mathbf{i} \times \mathbf{k}.$$

Thus,

$$\mathbf{A \times B} = (A_y B_z - A_z B_y)\mathbf{i} + (A_z B_x - A_x B_z)\mathbf{j} + (A_x B_y - A_y B_x)\mathbf{k}$$

$$= \begin{vmatrix} \mathbf{i} & \mathbf{j} & \mathbf{k} \\ A_x & A_y & A_z \\ B_x & B_y & B_z \end{vmatrix}.$$

Also

$$\mathbf{A \times (B + C + \cdots)} = (\mathbf{A \times B}) + (\mathbf{A \times C}) + \cdots.$$

Angular momentum is an important vector quantity which is the vector product of the vector distance $\mathbf{r}$ from a point to a moving mass m with velocity $\mathbf{v}$:

$$\mathbf{M} = \mathbf{r} \times m\mathbf{v} = m(\mathbf{r \times v}).$$

Products of three or more vectors are possible, such as

$$\mathbf{A \cdot (B \times C)} = (\mathbf{A \times B}) \cdot \mathbf{C} = \mathbf{ABC}.$$

This is a scalar quantity known as the *scalar triple product* and investigation shows

$$\mathbf{ABC} = \mathbf{BCA} = \mathbf{CAB} = -\mathbf{ACB} = -\mathbf{BAC} = -\mathbf{CBA}.$$

The magnitude of this quantity is given by

$$\mathbf{ABC} = \begin{vmatrix} A_x & A_y & A_z \\ B_x & B_y & B_z \\ C_x & C_y & C_z \end{vmatrix}.$$

The *vector triple product* is a vector defined as

$$\mathbf{A \times (B \times C)} = \mathbf{B(A \cdot C)} - \mathbf{C(A \cdot B)}.$$

Vectors can be differentiated with respect to variables that affect the magnitude and direction of the vectors. If $\mathbf{s}$ is a vector in cartesian coordinates, the increment $\mathbf{ds}$ is

$$\mathbf{ds} = \mathbf{i}\,dx + \mathbf{j}\,dy + \mathbf{k}\,dz.$$

If ϕ is some function that depends on x, y, and z, so that

$$d\phi = \frac{\partial \phi}{\partial x}\,dx + \frac{\partial \phi}{\partial y}\,dy + \frac{\partial \phi}{\partial z}\,dz,$$

then the dependence of ϕ on $\mathbf{ds}$ is given by

$$d\phi = (\text{grad } \phi) \cdot \mathbf{ds} = \nabla\phi \cdot \mathbf{ds},$$

where the *gradient* of ϕ is a vector

$$\nabla\phi = \mathbf{i}\frac{\partial \phi}{\partial x} + \mathbf{j}\frac{\partial \phi}{\partial y} + \mathbf{k}\frac{\partial \phi}{\partial z}.$$

The vector ∇ (*del*) is a vector operator defined as

$$\nabla = \mathbf{i}\frac{\partial}{\partial x} + \mathbf{j}\frac{\partial}{\partial y} + \mathbf{k}\frac{\partial}{\partial z}.$$

The scalar product of ∇ and a vector is called the *divergence* of that vector:

$$\text{div } \mathbf{A} = \nabla \cdot \mathbf{A} = \left(\mathbf{i}\frac{\partial}{\partial x} + \mathbf{j}\frac{\partial}{\partial y} + \mathbf{k}\frac{\partial}{\partial z}\right)(A_x\mathbf{i} + A_y\mathbf{i} + A_z\mathbf{k})$$

$$= \frac{\partial A_x}{\partial x} + \frac{\partial A_y}{\partial y} + \frac{\partial A_z}{\partial z},$$

which obviously is a scalar quantity.

The vector product of ∇ and a vector is known as the *curl* of that vector:

$$\text{curl } \mathbf{A} = \nabla \times \mathbf{A} = \begin{vmatrix} \mathbf{i} & \mathbf{j} & \mathbf{k} \\ \dfrac{\partial}{\partial x} & \dfrac{\partial}{\partial y} & \dfrac{\partial}{\partial z} \\ A_x & A_y & A_z \end{vmatrix},$$

which is a vector quantity.

The product *del-squared*,

$$\nabla \cdot \nabla = \nabla^2 = \frac{\partial^2}{\partial x^2} + \frac{\partial^2}{\partial y^2} + \frac{\partial^2}{\partial x^2},$$

is called the *Laplacian operator*. Expressions for this operator in other coordinate systems are given in Appendix B.

Appendix B

Coordinate Systems

1. Cartesian (axes mutually perpendicular):

$$\nabla^2 = \frac{\partial^2}{\partial x^2} + \frac{\partial^2}{\partial y^2} + \frac{\partial^2}{\partial z^2};$$

$$d\tau = dx\,dy\,dz;$$

$$-\infty \leqslant x \leqslant \infty, \quad -\infty \leqslant y \leqslant \infty, \quad -\infty \leqslant z \leqslant \infty.$$

2. Cylindrical polar (Fig. 2–2):

$$x = r\cos\theta, \quad y = r\sin\theta, \quad z = z;$$

$$d\tau = r\,dr\,d\theta\,dz;$$

$$\nabla^2 = \frac{1}{r}\frac{\partial}{\partial r}\left(r\frac{\partial}{\partial r}\right) + \frac{1}{r^2}\frac{\partial^2}{\partial\theta^2} + \frac{\partial^2}{\partial z^2};$$

$$0 \leqslant r \leqslant \infty, \quad 0 \leqslant \theta \leqslant 2\pi, \quad -\infty \leqslant z \leqslant \infty.$$

3. Spherical polar (Fig. 6–2):

$$x = r\sin\theta\cos\phi, \quad y = r\sin\theta\sin\phi, \quad z = r\cos\theta;$$

$$d\tau = r^2\sin\theta\,dr\,d\theta\,d\phi;$$

$$\nabla^2 = \frac{1}{r^2}\frac{\partial}{\partial r}\left(r^2\frac{\partial}{\partial r}\right) + \frac{1}{r^2\sin\theta}\frac{\partial}{\partial\theta}\left(\sin\theta\frac{\partial}{\partial\theta}\right) + \frac{1}{r^2\sin^2\theta}\frac{\partial^2}{\partial\phi^2};$$

$$0 \leqslant r \leqslant \infty, \quad 0 \leqslant \theta \leqslant \pi, \quad 0 \leqslant \phi \leqslant 2\pi.$$

4. Confocal elliptical (Fig. 10–1 with z along the internuclear axis, ϕ measured from the x-z plane, and the origin of the cartesian coordinates midway between the foci):

$$x = \frac{r_{AB}}{2}\sqrt{(\xi^2 - 1)(1 - \eta^2)}\,\cos\phi, \quad \xi = \frac{r_A + r_B}{r_{AB}},$$

$$y = \frac{r_{AB}}{2}\sqrt{(\xi^2 - 1)(1 - \eta^2)}\,\sin\phi, \quad \eta = \frac{r_A - r_B}{r_{AB}},$$

$$z = r_{AB}\xi\eta;$$

$$d\tau = \frac{r_{AB}^3}{8}(\xi^2 - \eta^2)\,d\xi\,d\eta\,d\phi;$$

588

$$\nabla^2 = \frac{4}{r_{AB}(\xi^2 - \eta^2)} \left[\frac{\partial}{\partial \xi} \left\{ (\xi^2 - 1) \frac{\partial}{\partial \xi} \right\} + \frac{\partial}{\partial \eta} \left\{ (1 - \eta^2) \frac{\partial}{\partial \eta} \right\} \right. $$
$$ \left. + \frac{\xi^2 - \eta^2}{(\xi^2 - 1)(1 - \eta^2)} \frac{\partial^2}{\partial \phi^2} \right], $$

$$1 \leqslant \xi \leqslant \infty, \quad -1 \leqslant \eta \leqslant 1, \quad 0 \leqslant \phi \leqslant 2\pi.$$

SUPPLEMENTARY REFERENCES

Similar expressions for other coordinate systems are found, for example, in MAR-GENAU and MURPHY, *The Mathematics of Physical Chemistry*, D. Van Nostrand Co., Princeton, N.J., 1943.

Appendix C

Probability

The theory of probability is one that is based on human experience, and its general features are well known to most persons in connection with games of chance. A mathematical formulation of these experiences provides us with equations that can be used in specific problems.

The following definition of mathematical probability has been given:

Definition. *If, consistent with conditions S, there are n exhaustive, mutually exclusive, and equally likely cases, and m of them are favorable to an event A, then the mathematical probability of A is defined as the ratio m/n.*[1]

Examination of this definition shows that experience is the basis for the definition. That is, if we perform some defined repetitive operation and find that a number of different results, A, B, C, . . . , are obtained, then after a large number of repetitions (n) the probability of A is defined as the number of times A is observed (m) divided by n. After 1000 tosses of a coin, for example, if we find that heads lands up 500 times, the probability for obtaining heads is $\frac{500}{1000} = \frac{1}{2}$. In most instances the actual measurements must be made, but if we know ahead of time that neither heads nor tails is preferred over the other, then we can predict the probability of heads as $\frac{1}{2}$ without the actual measurements. The latter conclusion usually follows, however, after many experiments have already been performed.

The probability that at least some one of all the possible events results from an operation is complete certainty and is equal to unity. In the case of a tossed coin, for example, the probability of heads is $\frac{1}{2}$ and that of tails is $\frac{1}{2}$. The maximum probability is that one or the other will appear and is $\frac{1}{2} + \frac{1}{2} = 1$.

[1] Uspensky, *Introduction to Mathematical Probability*, McGraw-Hill Book Co., New York, 1937, p. 6.

Theorem. *The total probability of an event A is the sum of the probabilities of its mutually exclusive forms.*[2]

Consider, for example, the probability that one head will appear when three coins are simultaneously tossed. There are three mutually exclusive ways in which this can occur:

	Desired (one head)			Undesired				
Coin 1	H	T	T	H	H	H	T	T
Coin 2	T	H	T	H	T	H	H	T
Coin 3	T	T	H	H	H	T	H	T

The probability that the first arrangement above will be obtained is $\frac{1}{8}$ because there is only one way in which heads on coin 1, tails on coin 2, and tails on coin 3 can be obtained. But there are a total of eight ways in which both heads and tails can be obtained on all three coins, i.e., eight mutually exclusive ways in which the three coins will come to rest after a toss. Hence the probability of each of the desired arrangements is $\frac{1}{8}$, so the total probability of obtaining one head and two tails is $\frac{1}{8} + \frac{1}{8} + \frac{1}{8} = \frac{3}{8}$. This can be verified easily from the table.

Theorem. *The probability of the simultaneous occurrence of A and B is given by the product of the unconditional probability of the event A by the probability of B, supposing that A actually occurred.*[3]

In the example above, the probability that a head will be obtained if coin 1 is tossed is $\frac{1}{2}$. After it has been obtained, the probability that coin 2 will land heads is also $\frac{1}{2}$. In this case coin 1 has no effect on what coin 2 will do. Similarly, the probability that coin 3 will be heads is $\frac{1}{2}$. Therefore the compound probability that all three coins will simultaneously land heads up is $(\frac{1}{2})(\frac{1}{2})(\frac{1}{2}) = \frac{1}{8}$. This again, can be verified from the table. There are situations, however, in which one event may control another, in which case the probability of succeeding events B, C, etc. might be altered.

In scientific measurements we often are able to measure some variable x and from its behavior construct some function $f(x)$ which depends on x. It may be likely also that in a given measurement we cannot predict exactly what value of x will be measured. The probability density function $P(x)$ is defined so that the probability of observing x to have a value between x and $x + dx$ is $P(x)\, dx$, and since the probability that some value of x will be measured must be complete certainty, then,

$$\int_{-\infty}^{\infty} P(x)\, dx = 1.$$

[2] *Ibid.*, p. 28.
[3] *Ibid.*, p. 31.

Out of a series of measurements of x, a number of different values will be observed, and hence a number of different values of $f(x)$ calculated. From a large number of measurements, the mean, or average value, of $f(x)$ is defined to be

$$\overline{f(x)} \equiv \int_{-\infty}^{\infty} f(x)P(x)\ dx.$$

This corresponds to multiplying $f(x)$ for a given value of x by the probability that that particular value of x will be measured, and then summing over all values of x to obtain the average value of $f(x)$.

The average value of $[f(x)]^2$ is

$$\overline{[f(x)]^2} \equiv \int_{-\infty}^{\infty} [f(x)]^2 P(x)\ dx.$$

The uncertainty or spread in the predicted values for $f(x)$ is measured by the standard deviation σ, which is defined by

$$\sigma^2 = \overline{[f(x) - \overline{f(x)}]^2} = \overline{[f(x)]^2} - [\overline{f(x)}]^2.$$

Some problems to illustrate these equations are given at the end of Chapter 3. It is evident from examination of the postulates and definitions in Chapter 3 that the formulation of the quantum-mechanical wave function is closely related to these probability functions.

Appendix D
Special Differential Equations

The equation

$$\frac{dy}{dx} + 2xy = 0 \tag{D–1}$$

is an example of a differential equation, i.e., an ordinary algebraic equation that contains derivatives of various parameters or functions. The solution of a differential equation is the process of finding the particular set of variables or functions that will satisfy the equation. In this example the equation can be rearranged to

$$\frac{dy}{y} = -2x \, dx.$$

Integrating both sides gives

$$\int \frac{dy}{y} = - \int 2x \, dx,$$

or

$$\int d \, (\ln y) = - \int 2x \, dx,$$

so that

$$\ln y = -x^2 + \text{constant of integration},$$

or

$$y = ce^{-x^2}. \tag{D–2}$$

That this is a solution can be verified by placing the expression in the original equation. From Eq. (D–2), we have

$$\frac{dy}{dx} = -2xce^{-x^2}$$

and

$$2xy = 2xce^{-x^2},$$

which, by addition gives the original differential equation (D–1),

$$\frac{dy}{dx} + 2xy = 0.$$

In some cases solution of a differential equation is relatively straightforward. In the preceding example the variables x and y could be separated with their respective differentials dx and dy and the resulting expressions integrated separately. Constants of integration can be evaluated by placing requirements (boundary conditions) on the relationship as required by the model or experimental conditions. More commonly more complicated manipulation is required for solution.

The Schrödinger equation is an example of a second-order differential equation (second derivatives are the highest order of differentiation found in the equation). Not only are these equations frequently difficult to solve, but in quantum mechanics we require that the solutions be well-behaved functions. This often limits the possible solutions even further. Some general procedures have been found for solution of second-order equations. If the equation can be put in the form

$$P(x) \frac{d^2y}{dx^2} + Q(x) \frac{dy}{dx} + R(x)y = 0, \tag{D–3}$$

where $P(x)$, $Q(x)$, and $R(x)$ are polynomials in x, solution is reasonably simple; for y can be expanded as a power series in x:

$$y = a_0 + a_1x + \cdots + a_nx^n + \cdots, \tag{D–4}$$

from which

$$\frac{dy}{dx} = a_1 + 2a_2x + \cdots + (n+1)a_{n+1}x^n + \cdots$$

and

$$\frac{d^2y}{dx^2} = 2a_2 + 6a_3x + \cdots + (n+2)(n+1)a_{n+2}x^n + \cdots.$$

These are substituted into the differential equation (D–3). It is then necessary, if (D–3) be true, that the coefficient of each power of x separately go to zero. From the terms in x^n, for example, we find

$$a_n = c_1a_{n-1} + c_2a_{n-2} + \cdots + c_ja_{n-j}, \tag{D–5}$$

where the c's are constants that depend on the particular form of $P(x)$, $Q(x)$, and $R(x)$. Equation (D–5) is known as a recursion formula, and from it the whole series (D–4) can be found if the first few terms are known.

A power series expansion can be made around $x = 0$ only if $P(x)$ and $Q(x)$ do not become infinite at this point. In addition, all solutions of an equation may not be well-behaved. Thus, in many cases an attempt is made first to find the general nature of the equation and its solutions at $x = \infty$, to assure that the functions remain finite, and then to form a function that is the product of a power series and the asymptotic solution. This method, illustrated in Chapter 4 for the harmonic oscillator, is a common approach to equations of this form. The solutions of the Θ and R equations in Chapter 6 follow a similar procedure, except that in the case of the Θ equation there are two singular points, i.e. points at which the polynomials in x go to infinity, so that the solution is in turn more difficult.

Although power series are useful for some mathematical manipulations, they are difficult to interpret, and so it is useful to find other definitions for the functions that correspond to the series and use these forms instead.

HERMITE POLYNOMIALS

If (D–1) is differentiated $n + 1$ times, we obtain

$$\frac{d^2z}{dx^2} + 2x\frac{dz}{dx} + 2(n + 1)z = 0, \tag{D–6}$$

where

$$z = \frac{d^ny}{dx^n} = c\frac{d^n}{dx^n}\left(e^{-x^2}\right) = \mu(x)e^{-x^2}$$

and $\mu(x)$ is a polynomial of degree n. By substituting into (D–6) it is found that $\mu(x)$ satisfies the equation

$$\frac{d^2\mu}{dx^2} - 2x\frac{d\mu}{dx} + 2n\mu = 0, \tag{D–7}$$

which is known as Hermite's equation. If $c = (-1)^n$ the solution is known as the Hermite polynomial of degree n, $H_n(x)$. That is,

$$H_n(x) = (-1)^n e^{x^2}\frac{d^n}{dx^n}\left(e^{-x^2}\right),$$

which can be shown to be equivalent to the series

$$H_n(x) = (2x)^n - \frac{n(n - 1)(2x)^{n-2}}{1!}$$
$$+ \frac{n(n - 1)(n - 2)(n - 3)(2x)^{n-4}}{2!} + \cdots.$$

If this series is differentiated term by term, and the resulting expressions of the first and second derivatives put back into (D–7), a useful recursion formula is obtained:

$$xH_n = nH_{n-1} + \tfrac{1}{2}H_{n+1}. \tag{D–8}$$

This recursion formula can be used to evaluate particular polynomials from when others are known, or it can be used in integrals to facilitate evaluation of matrix elements. The functions

$$\frac{1}{(2^n n! \sqrt{\pi})^{1/2}} H_n(x) e^{-x^2/2}$$

can be shown to form an orthonormal set. These are the harmonic-oscillator functions, except for constant terms involving mass and the force constant.

ASSOCIATED LEGENDRE POLYNOMIALS

The solution of the equation

$$(1 - x^2) \frac{dy}{dx} + 2lxy = 0 \tag{D-9}$$

is found by separation of variables to be

$$y = c(1 - x^2)^l.$$

If (D-9) is differentiated $l + 1$ times, the resulting equation is

$$(1 - x^2) \frac{d^{l+2}y}{dx^{l+2}} - 2x \frac{d^{l+1}y}{dx^{l+1}} + l(l + 1) \frac{d^l y}{dx^l} = 0,$$

or

$$(1 - x^2) \frac{d^2 z}{dx^2} - 2x \frac{dz}{dx} + l(l + 1)z = 0, \tag{D-10}$$

which is known as Legendre's equation, where

$$z = \frac{d^l y}{dx^l} = c \frac{d^l}{dx^l} (1 - x^2)^l.$$

The solution

$$z = P_l(x) = \frac{1}{2^l l!} \frac{d^l}{dx^l} (x^2 - 1)^l \tag{D-11}$$

is known as the Legendre polynomial of degree l, where $P_0(x) = 1$. These functions are orthogonal in the interval $-1 \leqslant x \leqslant +1$.

If (D-9) is differentiated $m + l + 1$ times, the resulting equation is

$$(1 - x^2) \frac{d^{m+l+2}y}{dx^{m+l+2}} - 2(m + 1)x \frac{d^{m+l+1}y}{dx^{m+l+1}} + (m + l + 1)(l - m) \frac{d^{m+l}y}{dx^{m+l}} = 0,$$

which, if

$$z = \frac{d^{m+l}y}{dx^{m+l}} = \frac{d^m P_l(x)}{dx^m} = c \frac{d^{m+l}}{dx^{m+l}} (1 - x^2)^l,$$

can be written

$$(1 - x^2) \frac{d^2z}{dx^2} - 2(m + 1)x \frac{dz}{dx} + (m + l + 1)(l - m)z = 0.$$

If we write z as $z = \mu(1 - x^2)^{-m/2}$ and differentiate, to obtain dz/dx and d^2z/dx^2, this becomes

$$(1 - x^2) \frac{d^2\mu}{dx^2} - 2x \frac{d\mu}{dx} + \left[l(l + 1) - \frac{m^2}{1 - x^2} \right] \mu = 0, \quad \text{(D–12)}$$

which is known as the associated Legendre equation. The function $\mu = P_l^m(x)$ is the associated Legendre polynomial of degree n and order m. From the definitions of μ and z it follows that

$$P_l^m(x) = (1 - x^2)^{m/2}z = (1 - x^2)^{m/2} \frac{d^m}{dx^m} P_l(x). \quad \text{(D–13)}$$

It is seen that $P_l^0(x) = P_l(x)$, and that, since $P_l(x)$ is a polynomial of degree l, $P_l^m(x) = 0$ if $m > l$.

The associated Legendre polynomials are orthogonal, and the normalized functions over the interval $-1 \leqslant x \leqslant 1$ are

$$\sqrt{\frac{2l + 1}{2} \frac{(l - m)!}{(l + m)!}} P_l^m(x). \quad \text{(D–14)}$$

The identification of the Θ equation (6–11) with the associated Legendre equation is straightforward. The equation to be solved is

$$\frac{1}{\sin \theta} \frac{d}{d\theta} \left(\sin \theta \frac{d\Theta}{d\theta} \right) - \frac{m^2\Theta}{\sin^2 \theta} + \beta\Theta = 0,$$

or, by taking the indicated derivative,

$$\frac{d^2\Theta}{d\theta^2} + \frac{\cos \theta}{\sin \theta} \frac{d\Theta}{d\theta} + \left(\beta - \frac{m^2}{\sin^2 \theta} \right) \Theta = 0. \quad \text{(D–15)}$$

The resulting Θ must be well-behaved in the interval $0 \leqslant \theta \leqslant \pi$. If we make the change of variable $x = \cos \theta$, this corresponds to $-1 \leqslant \cos \theta \leqslant 1$, or $-1 \leqslant x \leqslant 1$. From the laws of calculus,

$$\frac{d}{d\theta} = -\sin \theta \frac{d}{dx}, \quad \frac{d^2}{d\theta^2} = \sin^2 \theta \frac{d^2}{dx^2} - \cos \theta \frac{d}{dx},$$

and substituting in (D–15), we obtain

$$\sin^2 \theta \frac{d^2\Theta}{dx^2} - 2 \cos \theta \frac{d\Theta}{dx} + \left(\beta - \frac{m^2}{\sin^2 \theta} \right) \Theta = 0.$$

Since $x = \cos \theta$ and $\sin^2 \theta + \cos^2 \theta = 1$, this becomes

$$(1 - x^2) \frac{d^2\Theta}{dx^2} - 2x \frac{d\Theta}{dx} + \left(\beta - \frac{m^2}{\sin^2 \theta}\right)\Theta = 0. \qquad (D\text{--}16)$$

This is seen to correspond exactly to (D–12) if $\beta = l(l + 1)$. Therefore $\Theta = \mu = P_l^m$. Since m enters (D–16) only as m^2, it follows that $\Theta_{l,m} = \Theta_{l,-m}$ so that (D–14) is written

$$\Theta_{l,m}(\theta) = \sqrt{\frac{2l + 1}{2} \frac{(l - |m|)!}{(l + |m|)!}}\, P_l^{|m|} (\cos \theta).$$

In addition, since m is an integer, and since the solution to the associated Legendre equation is acceptable only if $l - m$ is an integer, it is necessary that l be an integer and that $l \geqslant |m|$. These functions can be written explicitly as

$$\Theta_{l,m}(\theta) = \frac{(-1)^l}{2^l l!} \sqrt{\frac{2l + 1}{2} \frac{(l - |m|)!}{(l + |m|)!}}\, \sin^{|m|} \theta \, \frac{d^{l+|m|} (\sin^{2l} \theta)}{[d (\cos \theta)]^{l+|m|}}.$$

A number of these are given in Table 6–1.

A useful recursion formula for P_l^m is

$$(2l + 1)(1 - x^2)^{1/2}P_l^m = P_{l+1}^{m+1} - P_{l-1}^{m+1}, \qquad (D\text{--}17)$$

or, in terms of $\cos \theta$,

$$(2l + 1)(\cos^2 \theta)^{1/2}P_l^{|m|} = P_{l+1}^{|m|+1} - P_{l-1}^{|m|+1},$$

which can be differentiated and rearranged several times to yield two relations convenient to use in evaluating matrix elements:

$$\cos \theta \, P_l^{|m|} = \frac{1}{2l + 1} \{l - |m| + 1\} P_{l+1}^{|m|} + (l + |m|)P_{l-1}^{|m|},$$

$$\sin \theta \, P_l^{|m|} = \frac{1}{2l + 1} \{P_{l+1}^{|m|+1} - P_{l-1}^{|m|+1}\}$$

$$= \frac{1}{2l + 1} \{(l + |m|)(l + |m| - 1)P_{l-1}^{|m|-1}$$

$$- (l - |m| + 1)(l - |m| + 2)P_{l+1}^{|m|-1}\}.$$

ASSOCIATED LAGUERRE FUNCTIONS

The polynomials

$$L_n(x) = e^x \frac{d^n}{dx^n} (x^n e^{-x})$$

are called Laguerre polynomials. The βth derivatives of these polynomials are known as the associated Laguerre polynomials and are

$$L_n^\beta(x) = \frac{d^\beta}{dx^\beta} L_n(x) \qquad (\beta \leqslant n)$$

$$= (-1)^n \frac{n!}{(n-\beta)!} \left\{ x^{n-\beta} - \frac{n(n-\beta)}{1!} x^{n-\beta-1} \right.$$

$$\left. + \frac{n(n-1)(n-\beta)(n-\beta-1)}{2!} x^{n-\beta-2} + \cdots \right\}. \qquad \text{(D–18)}$$

They are the solutions, μ, of Laguerre's associated equation,

$$x\frac{d^2\mu}{dx^2} + (\beta + 1 - x)\frac{d\mu}{dx} + (n - \beta)\mu = 0.$$

Although the Laguerre polynomials do not form an orthogonal set, it can be shown that the associated Laguerre functions defined as

$$G_n^\beta(x) = e^{-x/2} x^{(\beta-1)/2} L_n^\beta(x) \qquad \text{(D–19)}$$

are orthogonal, and it is noted that $G_n^\beta(x) \to 0$ as $x \to \infty$. These functions are the solutions, μ, of

$$x^2\frac{d^2\mu}{dx^2} + 2x\frac{d\mu}{dx} + \{[n - \tfrac{1}{2}(\beta - 1)]x - \tfrac{1}{4}x^2 - \tfrac{1}{4}(\beta^2 - 1)\}\mu = 0. \qquad \text{(D–20)}$$

That the solution of the radial equation for the hydrogen atom involves the associated Laguerre polynomials can be seen from Eq. (6–16), if this equation is differentiated as indicated and multiplied by ρ^2, to yield

$$\rho^2\frac{d^2R}{d\rho^2} + 2\rho\frac{dR}{d\rho} + \left[-\frac{\rho^2}{4} - l(l+1) + \lambda\rho\right]R = 0.$$

This can be seen to correspond exactly to (D–20) if

$$\tfrac{1}{4}(\beta^2 - 1) = l(l+1)$$

and

$$n - \tfrac{1}{2}(\beta - 1) = \lambda.$$

From the first of these we have

$$\beta^2 - 1 = 4l(l+1) = (2l+1)^2 - 1,$$

or

$$\beta = 2l + 1.$$

Substituting this into the second gives

$$\lambda = n - \tfrac{1}{2}(2l + 1 - 1) = n - l.$$

The solutions are thus

$$R(\rho) = G_n^\beta(\rho) = e^{-\rho/2}\rho^{(\beta-1)/2}L_n^\beta(\rho)$$
$$= e^{-\rho/2}\rho^l L_{n+l}^{2l+1}(\rho).$$

Normalization in the range $0 \leqslant \rho \leqslant \infty$ yields the normalizing factors

$$\left(\frac{2n[(n+l)!]^3}{(n-l-1)!}\right)^{-1/2}$$

A number of these functions are listed in Table 6–3.

SUPPLEMENTARY REFERENCES

For additional properties of the functions and equations discussed in this Appendix the reader is referred to EYRING, WALTER, and KIMBALL, *Quantum Chemistry*, John Wiley & Sons, Inc., New York, 1944. A general discussion can be found in any standard text on differential equations, and a more detailed treatment in JOHNSON and JOHNSON, *Mathematical Methods in Engineering and Physics—Special Functions and Boundary-Value Problems*, The Ronald Press Co., New York, 1965. Useful tables for solving equations of various forms are found in *Handbook of Mathematical Tables*, 2nd ed., Chemical Rubber Publishing Co., Cleveland, 1964.

Appendix E

Evaluation of Matrix Elements

$$\left\langle 1s_A(1)1s_A(2) \left| \frac{e^2}{r_{12}} \right| 1s_A(1)1s_A(2) \right\rangle$$

The first-order perturbation correction to the energy of the helium atom is found (Sec. 7.3) to be

$$E' = \left\langle 100,100 \left| \frac{e^2}{r_{12}} \right| 100,100 \right\rangle$$

$$= \iint \frac{Z^3}{\pi a_0^3} e^{-\rho_1/2} e^{-\rho_2/2} \frac{e^2}{r_{12}} \frac{Z^3}{\pi a_0^3} e^{-\rho_1/2} e^{-\rho_2/2} \, d\tau_1 \, d\tau_2,$$

where $\rho = 2Zr/a_0$ and $a_0 = \hbar^2/me^2$, and the integration is carried out over all coordinates ρ_1, θ_1, ϕ_1, ρ_2, θ_2, ϕ_2. It represents the mutual electrostatic interaction energy of two spherically symmetrical distributions of electrical charge with density $(Z^3/\pi a_0^3)e^{-2Zr/a_0}$ and can be evaluated by calculating the potential due to the first distribution (integration over $d\tau_1$) and then evaluating the energy of the second distribution in the field of the first.

Expanding the integral and substituting for ρ gives

$$E' = e^2 \int_0^{2\pi} \int_0^{\pi} \int_0^{\infty} \int_0^{2\pi} \int_0^{\pi} \int_0^{\infty} \left(\frac{Z^3}{\pi a_0^3} \right)^2 e^{-2Zr_1/a_0} \left(\frac{1}{r_{12}} \right) e^{-2Zr_2/a_0} \, r_1^2 \, dr_1$$
$$\sin \theta_1 \, d\phi_1 \, d\theta_1 \, r_2^2 \, dr_2 \sin \theta_2 \, d\theta_2 \, d\phi_2. \quad \text{(E–1)}$$

Since the functions have no angular dependence, the charge distributions are spherically symmetric, and integration over angles is straightforward.

Evaluation is aided by the known properties of electrical distributions. In particular, it is a property of spherical charge distributions that the potential is constant inside a spherical shell of charge, and outside such a shell the potential is the same as if the entire charge of the shell were at the center of the sphere. For a shell of radius r_1 and thickness dr_1

the charge contained is

$$\frac{4Z^3}{a_0{}^3} e^{-2Zr_1/a_0} r_1{}^2 \, dr_1,$$

and the constant potential inside this shell is therefore

$$\frac{4Z^3}{a_0{}^3} e^{-2Zr_1/a_0} r_1 \, dr_1 \quad \text{for} \quad r_2 \leqslant r_1.$$

Outside the shell the potential is

$$\frac{1}{r_2} \frac{4Z^3}{a_0{}^3} e^{-2Zr_1/a_0} r_1{}^2 \, dr_1 \quad \text{for} \quad r_2 \geqslant r_1.$$

Therefore the potential energy at a point r_2 due to the first charge cloud is obtained by integrating over all such spherical shells ($r_1 = 0$ to $r_1 = \infty$) and is

$$V(r_2) = \frac{4Z^3}{a_0{}^3} \frac{1}{r_2} \int_0^{r_2} e^{-2Zr_1/a_0} r_1{}^2 \, dr_1 + \frac{4Z^3}{a_0{}^3} \int_{r_2}^{\infty} e^{-2Zr_1/a_0} r_1 \, dr_1. \quad \text{(E–2)}$$

These are integrals that involve only exponentials and simple powers of r_1 and can be evaluated with the aid of integral tables. Putting in the limits, we find

$$V(r_2) = \frac{1}{2r_2} \left[2 - e^{-2Zr_2/a_0} \left(\frac{2Zr_2}{a_0} + 2 \right) \right].$$

E' is then the integral of the second charge over all space in the presence of this potential:

$$E' = e^2 \frac{4Z^3}{a_0{}^3} \int_0^{\infty} V(r_2) e^{-2Zr_2/a_0} r_2{}^2 \, dr_2, \quad \text{(E–3)}$$

which again can be broken down into several integrals involving exponentials and powers of r_2. The result is

$$E' = \frac{5Ze^2}{8a_0}.$$

Since $E_{\mathrm{H}} = -e^2/2a_0$, it follows that

$$E' = -\tfrac{5}{4}ZE_{\mathrm{H}}.$$

A more general approach is possible that does not require a knowledge of electrostatics. It can be shown that if r_i and r_j are measured from the same origin, then $1/r_{ij}$ can be expanded in terms of the associated Legendre polynomials in one of the equivalent forms,

$$\frac{1}{r_{ij}} = \sum_{l=0}^{\infty} \sum_{m=-l}^{l} \frac{(l - |m|)!}{(l + |m|)!} \frac{r_<^l}{r_>^{l+1}} P_l^{|m|}(\cos \theta_i) P_l^{|m|}(\cos \theta_j) e^{im(\phi_i - \phi_j)}$$

$$\frac{1}{r_{ij}} = \sum_{l=0}^{\infty} \sum_{m=-l}^{l} \frac{2}{2l + 1} \frac{r_<^l}{r_>^l} \Theta_l^{|m|}(\theta_i) \Theta_l^{|m|}(\theta_j) e^{im(\phi_i - \phi_j)}$$

$$\frac{1}{r_{ij}} = \sum_{l=0}^{\infty} \sum_{m=-l}^{l} \frac{4\pi}{2l+1} \frac{r_<^l}{r_>^{l+1}} Y_l^m(\theta_i, \phi_i) Y_l^{m*}(\theta_j, \phi_j)$$

where $r_<$ is the smaller and $r_>$ is the larger of the quantities r_i and r_j.

In the general case of integrals such as (E–1), the wave functions may include Legendre polynomials. Insertion of the above expression for $1/r_{ij}$ will cause many terms in the summation to vanish because of the orthogonality of the polynomials. The evaluation of the integral is then completed with the remaining terms. In the specific case of (E–1) the functions do not involve angles explicitly, i.e., only the constant functions $P_0^0(\cos\theta_1)$ and $P_0^0(\cos\theta_2)$ are involved. Thus, all the terms in the expansion of $1/r_{ij}$ will vanish except those for $l = 0$, $m = 0$; and since $P_0^0(\cos\theta) = 1$,

$$\frac{1}{r_{ij}} = \frac{1}{r_>}$$

is the integral, leaving only the exponential terms to integrate. The result is identical with (E–3).

$$\left\langle 1s_A \left| -\frac{e^2}{r_B} \right| 1s_A \right\rangle$$

The coulomb integral arising from the one-electron H_2^+ calculation can be evaluated in confocal elliptical coordinates. That is, substituting the $1s$ functions (Table 6–4) and then the equivalent coordinates from Appendix B gives

$$\left\langle 1s_A \left| -\frac{e^2}{r_B} \right| 1s_A \right\rangle = -\frac{e^2}{\pi a_0^3} \int \frac{e^{-2r_A/a_0}}{r_B} d\tau$$

$$= -\frac{e^2}{\pi a_0^3} \iiint \frac{2e^{-r_{AB}(\xi+\eta)/a_0}}{r_{AB}(\xi-\eta)} \frac{r_{AB}^3}{8}(\xi^2-\eta^2)\, d\xi\, d\eta\, d\phi.$$

The integral over $d\phi$ from 0 to 2π gives 2π, and since $\xi^2 - \eta^2 = (\xi+\eta)(\xi-\eta)$, this becomes

$$-\frac{e^2 r_{AB}^2}{2a_0^3} \iint e^{-r_{AB}(\xi+\eta)/a_0}(\xi+\eta)\, d\xi\, d\eta$$

$$= -\frac{e^2 r_{AB}^2}{2a_0^3} \left[\iint e^{-r_{AB}(\xi+\eta)/a_0}\, d\xi\, d\eta \iint \eta e^{-r_{AB}(\xi+\eta)/a_0}\, d\xi\, d\eta\right]$$

$$= -\frac{e^2 r_{AB}^2}{2a_0^3} \left[\int_1^\infty e^{-r_{AB}\xi/a_0}\, d\xi \int_{-1}^1 e^{-r_{AB}\eta/a_0}\, d\eta + \int_1^\infty e^{-r_{AB}\xi/a_0}\, d\xi \int_{-1}^1 \eta e^{-r_{AB}\eta/a_0}\, d\eta\right].$$

The result is again a series of integrals of the form $\int x^n e^{-ax}\, dx$, this time with limits different from the 0 to ∞ limits of spherical polar coordinates. These integrals are listed at the end of this Appendix. When evaluated, the total integral becomes

$$\left\langle 1s_A \left| -\frac{e^2}{r_B} \right| 1s_A \right\rangle = -\frac{e^2}{r_{AB}} \left\{ 1 - e^{-2r_{AB}/a_0} \left(1 + \frac{r_{AB}}{a_0} \right) \right\}$$

$$= e^{-2r_{AB}/a_0} \left(\frac{e^2}{a_0} + \frac{e^2}{r_{AB}} \right) - \frac{e^2}{r_{AB}}.$$

This integral could have been evaluated by electrostatic considerations as in the previous case for He. It represents the coulomb interaction of nucleus B with the electron in $1s_A$.

$$\left\langle 1s_A \left| -\frac{e^2}{r_A} \right| 1s_B \right\rangle$$

This exchange integral is a two-center integral; that is, it involves charge distributions measured from two different nuclei. Putting in the $1s$ functions, converting to confocal elliptical coordinates, and integrating over ϕ, we obtain

$$\left\langle 1s_A \left| -\frac{e^2}{r_A} \right| 1s_B \right\rangle = -\frac{e^2}{\pi a_0{}^3} \int \frac{e^{-r_A/a_0}e^{-r_B/a_0}}{r_A} \, d\tau = -\frac{e^2}{\pi a_0{}^3} \int \frac{e^{-(r_A+r_B)/a_0}}{r_A} \, d\tau$$

$$= \frac{e^2 r_{AB}{}^2}{2a_0{}^3} \iint e^{-\xi r_{AB}/a_0}(\xi - \eta) \, d\xi \, d\eta$$

$$= -\frac{e^2 r_{AB}{}^2}{2a_0{}^3} \left[\iint e^{-\xi r_{AB}/a_0}\xi \, d\xi \, d\eta - \iint e^{-\xi r_{AB}/a_0}\eta \, d\xi \, d\eta \right]$$

$$= -\frac{e^2 r_{AB}{}^2}{2a_0{}^3} \left[\int_{-1}^{1} \frac{a_0{}^2}{r_{AB}{}^2} e^{-r_{AB}/a_0} \left(1 + \frac{r_{AB}}{a_0} \right) d\eta \right.$$

$$\left. - \int_{-1}^{1} \frac{a_0}{r_{AB}} e^{-r_{AB}/a_0} \, \eta \, d\eta \right]$$

$$= -\frac{e^2 r_{AB}{}^2}{2a_0{}^3} \left[\frac{2a_0{}^2}{r_{AB}{}^2} e^{-r_{AB}/a_0} \left(1 + \frac{r_{AB}}{a_0} \right) \right]$$

$$= -\frac{e^2}{a_0} e^{-r_{AB}/a_0} \left(1 + \frac{r_{AB}}{a_0} \right).$$

Use was made again of the standard exponential integrals.

$$\langle 1s_A | 1s_B \rangle$$

The non-orthogonality overlap integral is evaluated in the same way:

$$\left\langle 1s_A \left| 1s_B \right. \right\rangle = \frac{1}{\pi a_0{}^3} \int e^{-r_A/a_0}e^{-r_B/a_0} \, d\tau = \frac{1}{\pi a_0{}^3} \int e^{-(r_A+r_B)/a_0} \, d\tau$$

$$= \frac{r_{AB}{}^3}{4a_0{}^3} \iint e^{-\xi r_{AB}/a_0}(\xi^2 - \eta^2) \, d\xi \, d\eta$$

$$= \frac{r_{AB}{}^3}{4a_0{}^3} \left[\iint e^{-\xi r_{AB}/a_0}\xi^2 \, d\xi \, d\eta - \iint e^{-\xi r_{AB}/a_0}\eta^2 \, d\xi \, d\eta \right]$$

$$= \frac{r_{AB}{}^3}{4a_0{}^3} \left[\int_{-1}^{1} \frac{2a_0{}^3}{r_{AB}{}^3} e^{-r_{AB}/a_0} \left(1 + \frac{r_{AB}}{a_0} + \frac{r_{AB}{}^2}{2a_0{}^2} \right) d\eta \right.$$

$$\left. - \int_{-1}^{1} \frac{a_0}{r_{AB}} e^{-r_{AB}/a_0} \eta^2 \, d\eta \right]$$

$$= \frac{r_{AB}{}^3}{4a_0{}^3} \left[\frac{4a_0{}^3}{r_{AB}{}^3} e^{-r_{AB}/a_0} \left(1 + \frac{r_{AB}}{2a_0{}^2} \right) - \frac{2a_0}{3r_{AB}} e^{-r_{AB}/a_0} \right]$$

$$= e^{-r_{AB}/a_0} \left(1 + \frac{r_{AB}}{a_0} + \frac{r_{AB}{}^2}{2a_0{}^2} - \frac{r_{AB}{}^2}{6a_0{}^2} \right)$$

$$= e^{-r_{AB}/a_0} \left(1 + \frac{r_{AB}}{a_0} + \frac{r_{AB}{}^2}{3a_0{}^2} \right)$$

SUPPLEMENTARY REFERENCES

The evaluation of integrals such as these is the primary difficulty around which atomic and molecular calculations revolve. The integrals considered here are far simpler than many complex integrals encountered in more exact solutions. Many useful compilations have been made of such integrals, and the development of high-speed computing systems has aided in quantum-mechanical calculations. A useful summary of compilations of this sort is given in DAUDEL, LEFEBURE, and MOSER, *Quantum Chemistry—Methods and Applications*, Interscience Publishers, New York, 1959. The mathematical problem of integral evaluation is discussed in SLATER, *Quantum Theory of Atomic Structure* and *Quantum Theory of Molecules and Solids*, McGraw-Hill Book Co., New York, 1960 and 1963. Values of some of the more important exponential definite integrals are given in the accompanying table. Other indefinite and definite integrals can be found in standard compilations.

Exponential Integrals

$$\int_0^\infty x^n e^{-ax} \, dx = \frac{n!}{a^{n+1}} \quad (n > -1, \, a > 0)$$

$$\int_0^\infty e^{-ax^2} \, dx = \frac{1}{2}\sqrt{\frac{\pi}{a}}$$

$$\int_0^\infty x e^{-ax^2} \, dx = \frac{1}{2a}$$

$$\int_0^\infty x^2 e^{-ax^2} \, dx = \frac{1}{4}\sqrt{\frac{\pi}{a^3}}$$

$$\int_0^\infty x^{2n} e^{-ax^2} \, dx$$

$$\int_0^\infty x^{2n+1} e^{-ax^2} \, dx = \frac{n!}{2a^{n+1}}$$

$$= \frac{1 \cdot 3 \cdots (2n-1)}{2^{n+1}} \sqrt{\frac{\pi}{a^{2n+1}}}$$

$$\int_0^\infty \frac{x^3}{(e^x - 1)} \, dx = \frac{\pi^4}{15}$$

$$\int_1^\infty e^{-ax} \, dx = \frac{e^{-a}}{a}$$

$$\int_1^\infty x e^{-ax} \, dx = \frac{e^{-a}}{a^2} (1 + a)$$

$$\int_1^\infty x^2 e^{-ax} \, dx = \frac{2e^{-a}}{a^3} \left(1 + a + \frac{a^2}{2} \right)$$

$$\int_1^\infty x^n e^{-ax} \, dx = \frac{n! e^{-a}}{a^{n+1}} \sum_{k=0}^{n} \frac{a^k}{k!}$$

$$\int_{-1}^{+1} e^{-ax} \, dx = \frac{1}{a} (e^a - e^{-a})$$

$$\int_{-1}^{+1} x e^{-ax} \, dx = \frac{1}{a^2} \{ e^a - e^{-a} - a(e^a + e^{-a}) \}$$

$$\int_{-1}^{+1} x^n e^{-ax} \, dx = (-1)^{n+1} \frac{n! e^a}{-a^{n+1}} \sum_{k=0}^{n} \frac{-a^k}{k!} - \frac{n! e^{-a}}{a^{n+1}} \sum_{k=0}^{n} \frac{a^k}{k!}$$

Appendix F

Electromagnetic Field Relations

The description of electric and magnetic phenomena is most familiarly in terms of such quantities as the electric field strength **E** and the magnetic field strength **H**.

In electrostatics, for example, the magnitude of an electric field at a given point is measured by the force acting on a unit positive change at that point, and the direction of the electric field vector is the direction of the force; e.g., according to Coulomb's law

$$\mathbf{E}(\mathbf{r}) = \frac{e}{r^3}\,\mathbf{r}, \qquad \mathbf{E}(r) = \frac{e}{r^2}$$

where e is the charge giving rise to the field and **r** is the direction vector from the charge to the point in question. One can also describe the electrical potential at that point, which in a conservative system is related to the force by

$$\mathbf{F}(\mathbf{r}) = -\boldsymbol{\nabla} V = -\frac{\partial V}{\partial x}\,\mathbf{i} - \frac{\partial V}{\partial y}\,\mathbf{j} - \frac{\partial V}{\partial z}\,\mathbf{k}.$$

Thus

$$\mathbf{E}(\mathbf{r}) = -\boldsymbol{\nabla} V.$$

For the field arising from the charge e, this equation and the preceding are satisfied by

$$V(\mathbf{r}) = \frac{e}{r}.$$

A distribution of electric charge in space can be described by a charge density $\rho(\mathbf{r})$, which in general will depend on the position **r**. At any point in space

$$\boldsymbol{\nabla} \cdot \mathbf{E} = 4\pi\rho(\mathbf{r}),$$

and since $\mathbf{E} = -\boldsymbol{\nabla} V$, we obtain Poisson's equation,

$$\nabla^2 V = -4\pi\rho(\mathbf{r}),$$

and Laplace's equation, which applies at all points in space where $\rho = 0$,

$$\nabla^2 V = 0.$$

A flow of electric charge can be described by a current density vector $\mathbf{j}^*$, which is also a vector point function and defined so that the total current I flowing across a surface S is given by

$$I = \int_S \mathbf{j}^* \cdot \mathbf{dS} \text{ per second}$$

and

$$\mathbf{j}^* = \sigma\mathbf{E}$$

where σ is the conductivity. If charge is flowing out of a surface which completely encloses a volume of charge density ρ, then it can be shown that

$$\nabla \cdot \mathbf{j}^* + \frac{\partial \rho}{\partial t} = 0.$$

Magnetic fields arise from the motion of charge. For current I flowing through a small closed loop that encloses a surface area dS, it can be shown that a magnetic field is produced corresponding to a magnetic dipole:

$$\mathbf{y}_m = I \, \mathbf{dS},$$

which is perpendicular to the plane of the coil. It can be shown also that

$$\nabla \times \mathbf{H} = 4\pi\mathbf{j}^*.$$

The magnetic field strength can be related also to the force exerted on a current-carrying wire in a manner analogous to the relation between force on a charge and electric field strength.

In an isotropic medium other than free space, the electrical nature of the medium alters the interactions of the fields. The electric displacement vector is defined as

$$\mathbf{D} = \epsilon_e\mathbf{E},$$

where ϵ_e is the dielectric constant (permittivity) of the medium. In the presence of an electric field, the orientation of permanent electric dipoles and the displacement of charges by the field to produce induced dipoles results in a polarization vector $\mathbf{P}$ such that

$$\mathbf{D} = \mathbf{E} + 4\pi\mathbf{P}$$

and

$$\nabla \cdot \mathbf{D} = 4\pi\rho,$$

so that $\mathbf{D}$ replaces $\mathbf{E}$ as the field of importance in the medium. When the medium is isotropic and uniform, it is often true that $\mathbf{P} = \chi_e\mathbf{E}$, so that $\mathbf{D} = \mathbf{E} + 4\pi\chi_e\mathbf{D} = (1 + 4\pi\chi_e)\mathbf{E}$, giving $\epsilon_e = (1 + 4\pi\chi_e)$. χ_e is known as the electric susceptibility.

The magnetic induction vector is defined as

$$B = \mu H,$$

where μ is the permeability of the medium (*not* dipole moment here). The presence of a magnetic field induces motion of charges in a medium and a resulting magnetization M such that

$$B = H + 4\pi M$$

and

$$\nabla \cdot B = 0$$

in the absence of any other currents. If $M = \chi_m H$, then $\mu = 1 + 4\pi\chi_m$, where χ_m is the magnetic susceptibility.

Maxwell's equations provide a unifying set of relations between the various vector point functions we have mentioned. They are

$$\nabla \cdot D = 4\pi\rho,$$
$$\nabla \cdot B = 0,$$
$$\nabla \times H = 4\pi j^* + \frac{1}{c}\frac{\partial D}{\partial t},$$
$$\nabla \times E = -\frac{1}{c}\frac{\partial B}{\partial t}.$$

From these it can be shown that in a non-conducting medium ($\sigma = 0$)

$$\nabla^2 H = \frac{\epsilon\mu}{c^2}\frac{\partial^2 H}{\partial t^2}$$

and

$$\nabla^2 E = \frac{\epsilon\mu}{c^2}\frac{\partial^2 E}{\partial t^2},$$

which are the standard equations of wave motion with velocity $c/\sqrt{\epsilon\mu}$. In free space $\epsilon = \mu = 1$, so the velocity of propagation is c, the velocity of light. This, then, is the basis for the electromagnetic description of radiation. Phenomena such as the diffraction of light beams by dielectric media and other optical properties can be predicted from Maxwell's equations and have been verified experimentally.

For mathematical generality it is found useful to define a magnetic vector potential A defined by

$$B = \nabla \times A.$$

In free space $B = H$, so that this becomes

$$H = \nabla \times A.$$

These equations do not completely define A, and an extra condition often added is

$$\mathbf{\nabla} \cdot \mathbf{A} + \frac{\epsilon\mu}{c} \frac{\partial\phi}{\partial t} = 0.$$

The scalar potential, ϕ, is defined by

$$\mathbf{E} = -\mathbf{\nabla}\phi - \frac{1}{c} \frac{\partial\mathbf{A}}{\partial t}.$$

When there is no change of magnetic field, $\partial\mathbf{A}/\partial t = 0$, so that $\mathbf{E} = -\mathbf{\nabla}\phi$, which shows that ϕ is the usual electrostatic potential V mentioned earlier.

From Maxwell's equations and the definition of $\mathbf{A}$, it is found that in non-conducting, uncharged media

$$\nabla^2\mathbf{A} = \frac{\epsilon\mu}{c^2} \frac{\partial^2\mathbf{A}}{\partial t^2},$$

which is similar to the wave equations for $\mathbf{E}$ and $\mathbf{H}$.

The force acting on a charge e moving in an electromagnetic field is given by

$$\mathbf{F} = m\ddot{\mathbf{r}} = e\left[\mathbf{E} + \frac{1}{c}(\mathbf{v} \times \mathbf{H})\right].$$

Substitution of the equations for $\mathbf{E}$ and $\mathbf{H}$ in terms of ϕ and $\mathbf{A}$ results in expressions for kinetic and potential energy of the charge, and these can then be used to calculate the Hamiltonian operator for this situation:[1]

$$\mathcal{H} = \frac{1}{2m}\left(-\hbar^2\nabla^2 + i\hbar\frac{e}{c}\mathbf{\nabla}\cdot\mathbf{A} + 2i\hbar\frac{e}{c}\mathbf{A}\cdot\mathbf{\nabla} + \frac{e^2}{c^2}|\mathbf{A}|^2\right) + e\phi.$$

Considerable confusion arises in connection with the units employed in electromagnetic calculations. All the equations here are in *Gaussian* units; i.e., e, $\mathbf{E}$, $\mathbf{D}$, ϕ, and related electrical quantities are in esu; while $\mathbf{j}^*$, $\mathbf{H}$, $\mathbf{B}$, $\mathbf{A}$, etc. are in emu. Both the esu and the emu systems are self-consistent, and the units in each system are based on *cgs* measurements of force, distance, etc. The velocity of light is the proportionality between the two systems that appears in many of the equations. Absolute cgs, mks, and rationalized systems are also in use. Relations between these systems can be found in standard texts on electricity and magnetism.

[1] The details of this procedure are found in EYRING, WALTER, and KIMBALL, *Quantum Chemistry*, John Wiley & Sons, Inc., New York, 1944, pp. 108–109.

Appendix G

Simplification of the Dipole Moment Matrix Element

The matrix element

$$\left\langle k \left| \frac{\partial}{\partial x_i} \right| n \right\rangle$$

can be put into a more useful form for calculation purposes. Assume for the moment that ψ_k^{0*} and ψ_n^0 are functions of only one coordinate x, in which case they satisfy the equations

$$\frac{d^2\psi_k^{0*}}{dx^2} + \frac{2m}{\hbar^2}[E_k - V(x)]\psi_k^{0*} = 0$$

and

$$\frac{d^2\psi_n^0}{dx^2} + \frac{2m}{\hbar^2}[E_n - V(x)]\psi_n^0 = 0.$$

Multiplying the first by $x\psi_n^0$ and the second by $x\psi_k^{0*}$ and subtracting, we obtain

$$x\psi_n^0 \frac{d^2\psi_k^{0*}}{dx^2} - x\psi_k^{0*} \frac{d^2\psi_n^0}{dx^2} = \frac{2m}{\hbar^2}(E_n - E_k)\psi_k^{0*}x\psi_n^0,$$

since $V(x)$ is the same for the two equations. Integrating over all values of x, we obtain

$$\int_{-\infty}^{\infty}\left[x\psi_n^0 \frac{d^2\psi_k^{0*}}{dx^2} - x\psi_k^{0*} \frac{d^2\psi_n^0}{dx^2}\right]dx = \frac{2m}{\hbar^2}(E_n - E_k)\int_{-\infty}^{\infty}\psi_k^{0*}\,x\psi_n^0\,dx.$$

$$(G-1)$$

The integrand on the left can be integrated by parts. For example, in the first term, with $u = x\psi_n^0$ and $dv = (d^2\psi_k^{0*}/dx^2)\,dx$, integration by parts is

$$\int u\, dv = uv - \int v\, du$$

or

$$\int_{-\infty}^{\infty} x\psi_n^0 \frac{d^2\psi_k^{0*}}{dx^2}\, dx = x\psi_n^0 \frac{d\psi_k^{0*}}{dx} \Big|_{-\infty}^{\infty} - \int_{-\infty}^{\infty} \frac{d\psi_k^{0*}}{dx} \frac{d}{dx}(x\psi_n^0)\, dx.$$

The uv term goes to zero since the wave function and its derivative are zero at infinity. Taking the derivative of $x\psi_n^0$ in the integral gives

$$-\int_{-\infty}^{\infty} \frac{d\psi_k^{0*}}{dx} \frac{d}{dx}(x\psi_n^0)\, dx = -\int_{-\infty}^{\infty} \frac{d\psi_k^{0*}}{dx} x \frac{d\psi_n^0}{dx}\, dx - \int_{-\infty}^{\infty} \frac{d\psi_k^{0*}}{dx} \psi_n^0\, dx.$$

$$\text{(G-2)}$$

A similar integration by parts of the second term in the integral of (G–1) yields

$$-\int_{-\infty}^{\infty} x\psi_k^{0*} \frac{d^2\psi_n^0}{dx^2}\, dx = \int_{-\infty}^{\infty} \frac{d\psi_n^0}{dx} \frac{d}{dx}(x\psi_k^{0*})\, dx$$

$$= \int_{-\infty}^{\infty} \frac{d\psi_n^0}{dx} x \frac{d\psi_k^{0*}}{dx}\, dx + \int_{-\infty}^{\infty} \frac{d\psi_n^0}{dx} \psi_k^{0*}\, dx. \quad \text{(G-3)}$$

The first integrals in (G–2) and (G–3) are identical, and hence reconstructing the original integral of (G–1) by the addition of (G–2) and (G–3) yields

$$\int_{-\infty}^{\infty} \left[x\psi_n^0 \frac{d^2\psi_k^{0*}}{dx^2} - x\psi_k^{0*} \frac{d^2\psi_n^0}{dx^2} \right] dx = -\int_{-\infty}^{\infty} \left(\psi_n^0 \frac{d\psi_k^{0*}}{dx} - \psi_k^{0*} \frac{d\psi_n^0}{dx} \right) dx,$$

or

$$\int_{-\infty}^{\infty} \left(\psi_n^0 \frac{d\psi_k^{0*}}{dx} - \psi_k^{0*} \frac{d\psi_n^0}{dx} \right) dx = \frac{2m}{\hbar^2}(E_k - E_n) \int_{-\infty}^{\infty} \psi_k^{0*} x\psi_n^0\, dx. \quad \text{(G-4)}$$

Let us now integrate the first term of the left integral by parts:

$$\int_{-\infty}^{\infty} \psi_n^0 \frac{d\psi_k^{0*}}{dx}\, dx = \psi_n^0 \psi_k^{0*} \Big|_{-\infty}^{\infty} - \int_{-\infty}^{\infty} \psi_k^{0*} \frac{d\psi_n^0}{dx}\, dx.$$

Again, the uv term vanishes with infinite limits. It can be seen, then, that the first term in the integral of (G–4) is equal to the second term, so that (G–4) can be written

$$-2 \int_{-\infty}^{\infty} \psi_k^{0*} \frac{d\psi_n^0}{dx}\, dx = \frac{2m}{\hbar^2}(E_k - E_n) \int_{-\infty}^{\infty} \psi_k^{0*} x\psi_n^0\, dx,$$

or more compactly,

$$\left\langle k \left| \frac{\partial}{\partial x} \right| n \right\rangle = -\frac{m}{\hbar^2}(E_k - E_n)\langle k|x|n \rangle.$$

Appendix H

The Born-Oppenheimer Approximation

The actual mathematical procedure used by Born and Oppenheimer to verify the approximate separation of nuclear and electronic energies employed in Chapter 8 is long and involved. It is possible, however, to explore in a simple way the significance of this separation and to examine its validity.

The total Hamiltonian operator for a molecular system can be written

$$\mathcal{H} = - \sum_j \frac{\hbar^2}{2m_j} \nabla_j{}^2 - \sum_i \frac{\hbar^2}{2m_i} \nabla_i{}^2 + V_{nn} + V_{ne} + V_{ee}$$

where i indexes electrons, j nuclei, and the potential-energy terms have been simply labeled to indicate the coulombic nuclear-nuclear repulsions, nuclear-electron attractions, and electron-electron repulsions.

If the nuclei were fixed in position, then there would be no kinetic-energy terms for the nuclei, and the V_{nn} terms would be a constant. In this situation the electrons would then be described by the Hamiltonian operator

$$\mathcal{H}_e = - \frac{\hbar^2}{2m_i} \sum_i \nabla_i{}^2 + V_{ee} + V_{ne},$$

and the electronic energies and wave functions would satisfy

$$\mathcal{H}_e \psi_e = E_e \psi_e.$$

These functions and energies will depend on the various r_j since these will affect the terms in V_{ne}. We will denote all the remaining terms in $\mathcal{H}$

as $\mathcal{K}_n$

$$\mathcal{K}_n = -\sum_j \frac{\hbar^2}{2m_j} \nabla_j^2 + V_{nn},$$

so that

$$\mathcal{K} = \mathcal{K}_e + \mathcal{K}_n.$$

Several levels of approximation are possible. In the case of many polyatomic molecules, for example, the separation of electronic, vibrational, and rotational energies is not very exact. Nevertheless, the most commonly used approximation is the zero-order approximation, in which it is assumed that an approximate total wave function can be written as

$$\psi = \psi_e \psi_n$$

where ψ_e is the eigenfunction of $\mathcal{K}_e$ and ψ_n depends only on the r_j. This approximation can be tested by investigating whether it satisfies the equation

$$\mathcal{K}\psi = (\mathcal{K}_e + \mathcal{K}_n)\psi_e\psi_n = E\psi_e\psi_n,$$

or

$$-\left\{ \sum_j \frac{\hbar^2}{2m_j} \nabla_j^2 \psi_e\psi_n + \sum_i \frac{\hbar^2}{2m_i} \nabla_i^2 \psi_e\psi_n \right\} + (V_{ee} + V_{ne} + V_{nn})\psi_e\psi_n$$
$$= E\psi_e\psi_n.$$

ψ_n is independent of r_i, so that

$$\nabla_i^2 \psi_e\psi_n = \psi_n \nabla_i^2 \psi_e,$$

but ψ_e depends indirectly on the r_j, so that

$$\nabla_j^2 \psi_e\psi_n = \nabla_j(\nabla_j \psi_e\psi_n) = \nabla_j(\psi_e\nabla_j\psi_n + \psi_n\nabla_j\psi_e)$$
$$= \psi_e\nabla_j^2\psi_n + \nabla_j\psi_e\nabla_j\psi_n + \psi_n\nabla_j^2\psi_e + \nabla_j\psi_n\nabla_j\psi_e$$
$$= \psi_e\nabla_j^2\psi_n + 2\nabla_j\psi_e\nabla_j\psi_n + \psi_n\nabla_j^2\psi e.$$

Therefore,

$$(\mathcal{K}_e + \mathcal{K}_n)\psi_e\psi_n = -\left\{ \sum_j \frac{\hbar^2}{2m_j} \nabla_j\psi_e\nabla_j\psi_n + \sum_j \frac{\hbar^2}{2m_j} \psi_n\nabla_j^2\psi_e \right\}$$

$$- \psi_e \sum_j \frac{\hbar^2}{2m_j} \nabla_j^2\psi_n - \psi_n \sum_i \frac{\hbar^2}{2m_i} \nabla_i^2\psi_e + (V_{nn} + V_{ne} + V_{ee})\psi_e\psi_n$$

$$= -\{ \quad \} + \psi_n\mathcal{K}_e\psi_e + \psi_e\mathcal{K}_n\psi_n$$
$$= -\{ \quad \} + E_e(j)\psi_e\psi_n + \psi_e\mathcal{K}_n\psi_n.$$

If the terms $\{ \quad \}$ can be neglected, we have

$$E_e(r_j)\psi_e\psi_n + \psi_e\mathcal{K}_n\psi_n = E\psi_e\psi_n,$$

or on factoring out ψ_e, which is not operated upon,

$$[\mathcal{3C}_n + E_e(j)]\psi_n = E\psi_n.$$

This is the Schrödinger equation solved in Chapter 8 for the nuclear motions. If the first-order approximation is valid, it says that the nuclei move in a potential made up of the electronic energy and the internuclear repulsions. This seems reasonable since the light electrons can move much more rapidly than the nuclei, and hence for a given internuclear separation the electronic motions give rise to an effective electronic energy.

To test the validity of the approximation, we must consider the term { }, which was neglected. This term can be viewed as a perturbation $\mathcal{3C}'$. If $\mathcal{3C}'$ is significant in magnitude, it will add first-order correction terms to $\psi_e\psi_n$ such as $\psi'_e\psi'_n$. Since $E' = \Sigma\,[\langle n|\mathcal{3C}'|m\rangle/(E_n - E_m)]$, if matrix elements of $\mathcal{3C}'$ are small compared to the energy difference between the various states, the approximation will be good.

The smallest energy difference will be from nuclear kinetic energy and will be of the order of $\int \psi_n \nabla_j^2 \psi_n$. The perturbation matrix elements will be of the order of $\int \psi_e \nabla_j \psi_e \int \psi_n \nabla_j \psi_n + \int \psi_e \nabla_j^2 \psi_e$. The electronic functions ψ_e extend over the entire molecule and change only slowly if the r_j are changed. On the other hand ψ_n is localized within the amplitude of the zero-point motion of the nuclei and varies rapidly with internuclear separation. Thus $\int \psi_e \nabla_j \psi_e \ll \int \psi_n \nabla_j \psi_n$. The ratio of the amplitude of vibrational motion to the internuclear distance is usually only a few per cent, in which case the approximation is reasonable. Corrections to the approximation can be conveniently handled as additional "coupling" terms in the energy-level equations.

Appendix I

Physical Constants, Units, and Conversions

The fundamental constants given below are those recommended by the Committee on Fundamental Constants of the National Academy of Science–National Research Council and adopted by the National Bureau of Standards.[1] The student should note that the accuracy

Defined Values and Equivalents

Unit	Abbreviation	Definition
Meter	m	1,650,763.73 wavelengths *in vacuo* of the unperturbed transition $2p_{10} - 5d_5$ in ^{86}Kr
Kilogram	kg	Mass of the international kilogram at Sevres, France
Second	sec	1/21,556,925.9747 of the tropical year at 12^{h}ET, 0 January 1900
Degrees Kelvin	°K	Defined in the thermodynamic scale by assigning 273.16°K to the triple point of water (freezing point, H_2O, 273.15°K = 0°C)
Unified atomic mass unit	amu	$\frac{1}{12}$ the mass of an atom of the C^{12} nuclide
Mole	mole	Amount of substance containing the same number of atoms as 12 g of pure C^{12}
Standard acceleration of free fall	g	980.665 cm sec^{-2}
Normal atmospheric pressure	atm	1,013,250 dyne cm^{-2}
Thermochemical calorie	cal	4.1840×10^7 erg
Liter	l	1,000.028 cm^3
Inch	in	2.54 cm
Pound	lb	453.59237 g

required or even permitted by the available data for most problems does not require as many significant figures as given here.

[1] See *J. Opt. Soc. Am.*, **54**, 281 (1964).

Adjusted Values of Constants

Quantity	Abbreviation	Value	Maximum Error in Last Digit
Speed of light *in vacuo*	c	2.997925×10^{10} cm sec^{-1}	3
Elementary charge	e	4.80298×10^{-10} cm$^{3/2}$ g$^{1/2}$ sec^{-1} (esu)	20
		1.60210×10^{-20} cm$^{1/2}$ g$^{1/2}$ (emu)	7
Avogadro constant	N_A	6.02252×10^{23} mole^{-1}	28
Electron rest mass	m_e	9.1091×10^{-28} g	4
		5.48597×10^{-4} amu	9
Proton rest mass	m_p	1.67252×10^{-24} g	8
		1.00727663 amu	24
Neutron rest mass	m_n	1.67482×10^{-24} g	8
		1.0086654 amu	13
Planck constant	h	6.6256×10^{-27} erg sec	5
	$\hbar$	1.05450×10^{-27} erg sec	7
Rydberg constant	R_{H}	1.0967760×10^5 cm^{-1}	3
	R_∞	1.0973731×10^5 cm^{-1}	3
Fine structure constant	$e^2/\hbar c$	7.29720×10^{-3}	10
Boltzmann constant	k	1.38054×10^{-16} erg °K^{-1}	18
First radiation constant	$2\pi hc^2$	3.7405×10^{-5} erg cm^2 sec^{-1}	3
Second radiation constant	hc/k	1.43879 cm °K	19
Wien displacement constant	b	2.8978×10^{-1} cm °K	4
Stefan-Boltzmann constant	σ	5.6697×10^{-5} erg cm^{-2} sec^{-1} °K^{-4}	29
Gravitational constant	G	6.670×10^{-8} dyne cm^2 g^{-2}	15
Zeeman splitting constant	μ_B/hc	4.66858×10^{-5} cm^{-1} gauss^{-1}	4
Bohr magneton	μ_B	9.2732×10^{-21} erg gauss^{-1}	6
Nuclear magneton	μ_n	5.0505×10^{-24} erg gauss^{-1}	4
Proton moment	μ_p	1.41049×10^{-23} erg gauss^{-1}	13
Gas constant	R	8.3143×10^7 erg °K^{-1} mole^{-1}	12
		1.9872 cal deg^{-1} mole^{-1}	2
Bohr radius (proton mass)	a_0	5.2960×10^{-9} cm	1
(infinite mass)	a_∞	5.29167×10^{-9} cm	7
Energy of hydrogen atom	E_{H}	13.605 ev	

The system of units used in this text is the cgs system. Thus the unit of force ($F = ma$) is g cm sec^{-2} = dyne, and the unit of energy or work ($F_x\, dx$) is g cm^2 sec^{-2} = dyne cm = erg. These can be converted readily to other units when necessary. The electrical and magnetic quantities defined in terms of dynes and ergs are the *esu* and *emu* systems. For example, the *esu* unit of charge is that quantity of electricity upon which there is exerted a force of 1 dyne when it is placed 1 cm from a second unit charge. Unfortunately, the resulting units for charge, electric potential, etc., are inconveniently small in terms of ordinary laboratory measurements, and hence the practical *cgs* and rationalized *mks* systems have been defined in terms of the more familiar electrical quantities such as coulombs, amperes, volts, etc. Although there are many advantages to the rationalized *mks* system, the literature in atomic and molecular phenomena still abounds with *cgs* formulas. In this text little use is made of practical electrical quantities, and hence equations are derived on the basis of the *cgs-esu-emu* system of units. When necessary, conversion to practical units can be made.

Energy Conversion Factors

	erg	ev	cm^{-1}	joule mole^{-1}	cal mole^{-1}
1 erg =	1	6.24210×10^{11}	5.0348×10^{15}	6.024×10^{16}	1.43956×10^{16}
1 ev =	1.6021×10^{-12}	1	8065.98	96,493	23,061
1 cm^{-1} =	1.9863×10^{-16}	1.23964×10^{-4}	1	11.9617	2.8589
1 joule mole^{-1} =	1.6601×10^{-17}	1.0363×10^{-5}	8.3591×10^{-2}	1	.239006
1 cal mole^{-1} =	6.946×10^{-17}	4.3361×10^{-5}	.34975	4.1840	1

Wavelength, Frequency, and Energy Relations in the Electromagnetic Spectrum

Region	λ (cm)	λ (other)	ν (sec^{-1})	ν (other)	Energy (cm^{-1})	Energy (ev)	Energy (kcal/mole)
Radio	10^6	10 km	3×10^4	30 kcps	10^{-6}	1.2×10^{-10}	2.9×10^{-9}
frequency	10^5	1 km	3×10^5	300 kcps	10^{-5}	1.2×10^{-9}	2.9×10^{-8}
	10^4	100 m	3×10^6	3 Mcps	10^{-4}	1.2×10^{-8}	2.9×10^{-7}
	10^3	10 m	3×10^7	30 Mcps	10^{-3}	1.2×10^{-7}	2.9×10^{-6}
	10^2	1 m	3×10^8	300 Mcps	10^{-2}	1.2×10^{-6}	2.9×10^{-5}
Microwave	10	100 mm	3×10^9	3 kMcps	.1	1.2×10^{-5}	2.9×10^{-4}
	1	10 mm	3×10^{10}	30 kMcps	1	1.2×10^{-4}	2.9×10^{-3}
Infrared	10^{-1}	1 mm	3×10^{11}	300 kMcps	10	1.2×10^{-3}	2.9×10^{-2}
	10^{-2}	100 μ	3×10^{12}		100	1.2×10^{-2}	.29
	10^{-3}	10 μ	3×10^{13}		1000	.12	2.9
	10^{-4}	1 μ	3×10^{14}		10,000	1.2	29
Red	7.5×10^{-5}	7500 Å	4×10^{14}		13,000	1.6	38
Orange	6.5×10^{-5}	6500 Å	4.6×10^{14}		15,400	1.9	44
Yellow	5.9×10^{-5}	5900 Å	5.1×10^{14}		17,000	2.1	49
Green	5.3×10^{-5}	5300 Å	5.7×10^{14}		18,900	2.3	54
Blue	4.9×10^{-5}	4900 Å	6.1×10^{14}		20,400	2.5	58.3
Violet	4.2×10^{-5}	4200 Å	7.1×10^{14}		23,800	3.0	68
Ultraviolet	4×10^{-5}	4000 Å	7.5×10^{14}		25,000	3.1	72
Vacuum UV	2×10^{-5}	2000 Å	1.5×10^{15}		50,000	6.2	143
	10^{-5}	1000 Å	3×10^{15}		10^5	12.4	290
	10^{-6}	100 Å	3×10^{16}		10^6	124	2.9×10^3
	10^{-7}	10 Å	3×10^{17}		10^7	1.2×10^3	2.9×10^4
X-ray	10^{-8}	1 Å	3×10^{18}		10^8	1.2×10^4	2.9×10^5

Index